The
Christian
Legal Advisor

A dual professional, **John Eidsmoe** earned his law degree from the University of Iowa, the M.A. from Dallas Theological Seminary, and M.Div. from Lutheran Brethren Seminary. He is presently Visiting Professor of Law at Oral Roberts University's O.W. Coburn School of Law, where students voted him the 1983-84 Professor of the Year honor, and Adjunct Professor of Theology at Tulsa Seminary of Biblical Languages. He is an ordained minister and the author of *God and Caesar: Biblical Faith and Political Action.*

The Christian Legal Advisor

John Eidsmoe

MOTT MEDIA

THE CHRISTIAN LEGAL ADVISOR

Copyright © 1984 by Mott Media, Inc., Publishers

First Edition

Edited by Leonard George Goss
Copyedited by Leonard George Goss and Ruth Schenk
Typeset by Joyce Bohn, Suzanne DePodesta and Karen White

Manufactured in the United States of America

ISBN 0-88062-118-4 pb
ISBN 0-88062-119-2 hb

To my wife, Marlene,
who has taught me her love and reverence
for God and His Word,
and
to my brother, Attorney Robert Eidsmoe,
who inspired me to enter the legal profession.

I would like to make the following acknowledgements:

To Leonard George Goss, Executive Editor of Mott Media Publishers, and the rest of the Mott staff, for their encouragement and careful editing.

To those attorneys and law professors who have examined portions of this manuscript and offered their most helpful suggestions, among them professors Herb Titus, Ed Youngs and Richard Edwards, and attorneys William Donovan III, John Whitehead and Wendell Bird.

To the secretaries at the O.W. Coburn School of Law and at the Oral Roberts University Word Processing Center for their faithful typing and copying, particularly Betty Patterson, Cheryl Veich and Rowena Mills.

To my research assistants, law students at O.W. Coburn School of Law, who have painstakingly proofread this manuscript and checked footnotes and case citations: Mike Schmidt, Jeff Dixon and Alan Meyer—all of whom will, I trust, by the time this book is in your hands, be lawyers.

And finally, to my students in Christian Ministry and Law class, who have put up with much of this manuscript in typewritten and photocopied form, and whose interaction with me in class has made this a better book.

Table of Contents

Part 3: The Christian and Man's Law

Foreword

There has been a great lack of Christian scholarship in terms of the law and its application to our lives and society. In recent years, however, some notable works have come forth. This volume is one such work.

The *Christian Legal Advisor* is no little undertaking. It is a voluminous work that is important reading for pastors, laymen and lawyers.

Churches and pastors should be concerned about the topics discussed in this book (especially with the ever-present threat of government involvement in Christian ministries).

John Eidsmoe's discussion of the background and meaning of the First Amendment is a valuable contribution. It is particularly relevant in light of the church-state issues that are presently besieging the Christian community.

Christians, in order to stand in the days to come, must be educated on not only how to think but why they think the way they do about the key issues of the day. This book goes a long way in solving this problem.

I know John Eidsmoe as a very capable attorney. I am glad that I can also say that John is also a capable writer and scholar.

JOHN W. WHITEHEAD
Manassas, Virginia
June 1984

Introduction

It is early evening. Several families have gathered at your home for a Bible study. You have just begun, when there is a knock on the door. A uniformed policeman politely but firmly informs you that your home Bible study constitutes church activity and therefore violates local zoning ordinances. He orders you to cease, desist, and disperse immediately or face arrest.

I am not talking about Soviet Russia. This is happening in cities across America! If it happens to you, what do you do? Does the First Amendment protect you? Or the Fourth, Fifth, Ninth or Fourteenth? See chapter 21.

Or perhaps your children attend a Christian school. State officials have threatened to close the school and force your children to attend a public school, because the Christian school does not use certified teachers. Can they legally do that? What are your rights in this case? See chapter 17.

Maybe you are concerned about the rise of pornography in your community but don't know what to do about it. See chapter 19.

Or possibly you are on the church board and need to know how to incorporate and get tax-exempt status, or how to plan the pastor's housing and book allowances to obtain maximum tax advantages. This book will show you how. See chapters 25 and 27.

Perhaps you wish to donate your farm to the church now, but still need an income and a home for the rest of your life. Can you have both? See chapter 26.

Or let us suppose you are a pastor. A woman has come to your office for marital counseling, claiming her husband has beaten her and the children. While you oppose divorce, you advise her and the children to move out of the house temporarily for their own safety. Shortly thereafter, you receive an angry call from her husband's lawyer, demanding to know what you told his client's wife. When you refuse, he threatens to sue you for alienation of affection, saying, "I can make you talk in court." Are you in trouble? Do you have to talk to him? Do you need a lawyer? How do you find one? See chapters 22, 23 and 24.

This book is written to help you with these and thousands of other legal problems. But it is more than that. It is a comprehensive statement of the Christian view of law.

Part 1, *The Christian and God's Law*, is an introduction to biblical principles of law and their application to modern society, and an explanation of the anti-Christian philosophy of legal positivism which now reigns in legal circles and threatens to subvert and destroy the American legal system.

Part 2, *The Christian and the Constitution*, explains the background and meaning of the First Amendment and other constitutional protections of particular interest to Christians. Subsequent chapters apply constitutional principles to such issues as humanism, the creation-evolution controversy, what a Christian can and cannot do in the public schools, private schools, cults, the media, libel and slander, pornography, home Bible studies, employment, and abortion laws.

Part 3, *The Christian and Man's Law*, deals with practical legal problems such as church incorporation and tax-exemption, estate planning and charitable giving, choosing and working with a lawyer, conducting yourself in court, tax planning for ministers (these tax tips alone could save you many times the price of this book), church property problems, privileged communications, clergy malpractice, and similiar problems.

I have called this book *The **Christian** Legal Advisor* because it does not purport to be a general legal handbook of everyday legal problems such as landlord-tenant relations and traffic tickets. There are other excellent books which do that. This book concentrates on problems which especially affect Christians.

It is called *The Christian **Legal** Advisor* because it deals with legal problems. There is much Scripture, theology, and philosophy in this book, particularly in Parts 1 and 2—and much of it could make excellent sermon material! But it is presented in a context which relates to law.

And I have called it *The Christian Legal **Advisor*** because it does exactly that—it advises. It is a handy reference manual for lawyers, pastors, school officials, teachers, and laymen alike. For this reason, I have avoided confusing legal terminology wherever possible (some lawyers may appreciate this, too!) and when legal terminology is used, it is explained clearly and simply. Since the book will be of value to lawyers, case citations are included—and for laymen who wonder what all the numerical mumbo jumbo after each case means, it is explained in chapter 22.

But this book is only an advisor. If you absorb the information about the First Amendment in Part 2 and about church law in Part 3, you will know more about these specialized areas than many lawyers. But that will not make you a lawyer, and it will not enable you to handle complex legal problems by yourself. It will help you to spot and avoid legal problems, to know when you need a lawyer, and to work with your lawyer more effectively.

The advice given in this book should be qualified in three ways: (1) While God's law is eternal and unchanging, human law changes often. Some of the laws and court decisions cited may have been amended or superseded even by the time you read this book. (2) Law varies from state to state. Unique laws in your particular jurisdiction may affect the legal principles set forth in this book. (3) The art of "lawyering" consists of applying legal principles to unique factual situations, no two of which are exactly alike. Certain unique facts of your situation may require a different legal conclusion. To be safe, it is always best to obtain competent legal counsel.

Lawyers have created a mystique about the law. They have made themselves the law's high priests and have erected a veil to hide the law's mysteries from the uninitiated. In this book I hope to remove some of that veil and explain in common terms the mysteries of the law.

Now you may prepare to enter the inner sanctum of the temple known as "The Law." Read on!

Part 1

The Christian
and
God's Law

Chapter 1

God's Law and Man's Law

The law!

God reveals it, the preacher proclaims it. Legislators enact it, judges interpret it, policemen enforce it, lawyers practice it. Men tremble before it, and parents lay it down to their children.

But what is law? When the preacher and the policeman talk about law, do they mean the same thing?

As our society deteriorates into anarchy and permissivism, more and more Christians call for a return to the law of God. But how does a nation return to God's law? Do we simply ask the legislature to codify the Old Testament? To be scripturally consistent, if we follow God's law in some respects, must we also stone to death sabbath-breakers and homosexuals? Does the law of God have any relevance at all for those of us who are "not under the law, but under grace" (Romans 6:14)? Throughout Part 1 of this book, this chapter and the six which follow, we shall explore the relationship between the law of God and the law of man.

The term *law* is found about 200 times in the Bible, but several different terms are used. The most common Hebrew term is *torah*, which comes from the root *yarah* meaning "to point out" or "to direct and lead." Barry states that *torah* represents the law's "moral authority as teaching truth and guiding in the right way."[1] The term *dabhar* normally means "word," but it is used for the Decalogue in Deuteronomy 4:13 where the Ten Commandments are called the "ten words." This shows the revelational character of law as well as the authority behind law; law is revealed by God and derives its authority from God.[2] A related term, *mishpat*, refers to judgment.

1. Rev. Alfred Barry, *Smith's Dictionary of the Bible*, Volume 2, "Law" (Grand Rapids, Michigan: Baker Book House, 1869, 1971), p. 1600.
2. R. A. Cole, *Zondervan Pictorial Encyclopedia of the Bible*, Volume 3, "Law and the Old Testament" (Grand Rapids, Michigan: Zondervan, 1975), p. 884.

In the New Testament, the Greek term *nomos* is commonly used for law, and it comes from *nemo*, meaning "to assign or appoint." It emphasizes the constraining power of law, as imposed and enforced by a recognized authority. As with *torah*, it is "a commandment proceeding from without, and distinguished from the free action of its subjects, although not necessarily opposed thereto."[3]

Even when the same Greek or Hebrew word is used, "law" has different contexts and different meanings. Sometimes it refers to the Decalogue, sometimes to the first five books of the Old Testament, sometimes to the entire Old Testament (John 10:34; John 15:25; I Corinthians 14:21). Lewis Sperry Chafer, founder and first president of Dallas Theological Seminary, has identified several meanings of "law":

(1) Natural, inherent, or intrinsic. That which God requires of every creature because of His own character, as it is written: "be ye holy; for I am holy" (Leviticus 11:44; I Peter 1:16). This law was binding upon all, from Adam to Moses (compare Genesis 26:5; Romans 2:14-15; 5:12-14).

(2) Prescribed by man (Genesis 9:6; Matthew 20:15; Luke 20:22; Acts 19:38; I Timothy 1:8-10; II Timothy 2:5). That which human government requires of its subjects.

(3) Of Moses. A rule divinely given through Moses to govern Israel in the land of promise. It was commended to them because they were a covenant people. Thus it defined the matter of their daily life. It was itself a covenant of works (Exodus 19:5-6). They soon broke this covenant. It will yet be superseded by the new covenant (Jeremiah 31:31-34; Hebrews 8:8-13). This agreement will include the former law of Moses (Deuteronomy 30:8).

The law of Moses is recorded in three parts:

(a) Commandments. Embrace the moral government of Israel (Exodus 20:1-17). They are condensed and summarized in Matthew 22:36-40; fulfilled by love (Romans 13:10; Galatians 5:14; James 2:8); proved to be law in character (Romans 7:7-14).

(b) Judgments. Embrace the social requirements (Exodus 21:1 - 23:33).

(c) Ordinances. Regulate the worship (Exodus 25:1 - 31:18).

These three forms of law satisfied all of Israel's requirements before God. But the entire system including the commandments as a rule of life, ceased with the death of Christ (John 1:17; Romans 10:4). The law of Moses, to be sure, was an ad interim dealing in effect until Christ should come. For the time being, it gave to sin the character of transgression (Romans 5:13; Galatians 3:19). It was preceded (Exodus 19:4) and followed (John 1:17) by grace.

(4) Revealed will of God in any form. That which has been disclosed in addition to law codes. Observe the definite article with law in Romans 7:15-25 because thus Paul may refer to something besides the law of

3. Barry, Ibid.

Moses. The law as the will of God includes all his revealed orders for any people at any time. The word law in Romans, then, is used nine times without the article and many more times with the article (compare Romans 8:4), and not always referring to Moses.

(5) Messianic rule of life for the kingdom. That which governs the millenium (Matthew 5:1 - 7:29). Proof that the messianic rule is pure law may be gained in the following tests: (1) any action is legal which aims to secure merit (Matthew 6:14-15); (2) any action is legal which has been wrought in reliance upon the flesh (Romans 6:14).

(6) Of Christ. That which now governs the Christian (I Corinthians 9:20-21; Galatians 6:2). Observe the term "my commandments" which was used by Christ only in the upper room (John 14:15, etc.). This form of life direction includes all of the teachings of grace addressed to the Christian, who is not himself under law since grace has provided all the merit that ever could be required (John 1:16; Romans 5:1; 8:1; Colossians 2:10). The saved one is "inlawed to Christ" (I Corinthians 9:20-21, literally rendering). The believer is not without law to govern his conduct when "inlawed" to Christ.[4]

Law, then, includes but is not limited to the Ten Commandments. God's law reflects His will and His character; it is, we are told in Romans 7:12, "holy, and just, and good." Its moral force did not begin with Mt. Sinai. It was originally imprinted upon man's conscience, and it was reduced to writing at Mt. Sinai because man's conscience was becoming increasingly perverted by the spreading cancer of sin.

The first five books of the Bible are called the Torah, or the Law; but law is found throughout the Old and New Testaments. To fully understand the significance of law, it is necessary to distinguish law from Gospel. Here is Luther's distinction:

> The difference, then, between the Law and the Gospel is this: the Law makes demands of things that we are to do; it insists on works that we are to perform in the service of God and our fellow men. In the Gospel, however, we are summoned to a distribution of rich alms which we are to receive and take: the loving kindness of God and eternal salvation. Here is an easy way of illustrating the difference between the two: in offering us help and salvation as a gift and donation of God, the Gospel bids us hold the sack open and have something given us. The Law, however, gives nothing, but only takes and demands things from us. Now, these two, giving and taking, are surely far apart. For when something is given me, I am not doing anything towards that: I only receive and take; I have something given me. Again, when in my profession I carry out commands, likewise when I advise and assist my fellow men, I receive nothing, but give to another whom I am serving. Thus the Law and the Gospel are distinguished as to their formal statements (in causa formali): the one promises, the other

4. Lewis Sperry Chafer, *Systematic Theology*, Volume 7 (Dallas, Texas: Dallas Seminary Press, 1948, 1962), pp. 225-26.

> commands. The Gospel gives and bids us take; the Law demands and says, this you are to do.[5]

Law then, is what man does for God. Gospel is what God does for man. Both are found throughout the Bible; there is much law in the New Testament and much Gospel in the Old Testament. Law and Gospel both play a major role in every age of human history, though the exact nature of that role may differ from age to age.

So God's law is the revealed will of God for our lives. But what is man's law? Consider the definition found in *Black's Law Dictionary*:

> That which is laid down, ordained, or established. . . . That which must be obeyed and followed by citizens, subject to sanctions or legal consequences, is a "law" . . . general rule of human action, taking cognizance only of external acts, enforced by a determinate authority, which authority is human, and among human authorities is that which is paramount in a political society.[6]

Black's definition of law boils down to this: a rule of conduct backed by governmental force. Law differs from custom in that custom is not backed by governmental force; if you eat ice cream with your fingers or wear your overcoat backwards, you may be ridiculed or ostracized, but you won't be put in jail— at least not in America. To be law, the rule of conduct must be backed by governmental force.

And yet—is that really all there is to human law? Is it nothing more than a code of conduct imposed by the government? Are there no higher criteria by which human laws are to be evaluated? Is there no higher law by which governmental action can be judged?

People used to think so. Sir William Blackstone, whose *Commentaries on the Laws of England* were widely read in colonial America and shaped the colonists' understanding of law, believed that all human law depends upon the law of nature and the law of revelation, both of which have their source in God Himself.[7] He therefore defined law, not simply as a rule of conduct backed by governmental force, but as a human attempt to reflect the will of God in terms of right and wrong:

> " . . . *municipal law is a rule of civil conduct prescribed by the supreme power in a state.*" I proceed now to the latter branch of it; that it is a rule so prescribed, "*commanding what is right, and prohibiting what is wrong.*"[8] (emphasis original)

---

5. Martin Luther, *Sermon on the Distinction Between Law and the Gospel*, St. Louis Edition, Volume 9, p. 802f; quoted by Dr. C. F. W. Walther, *The Proper Distinction Between Law and Gospel* (St Louis, Missouri: Concordia Publishing House, 1884), p. 19.

6. *Black's Law Dictionary*, 4th Ed., p. 1028.

7. Sir William Blackstone, *Commentaries on the Laws of England* (New York: Augustus M. Kelley, 1765, 1803, 1969), orig. pp. 40-43; reprinted as pp. 39-42.

8. Ibid., orig. p. 53; reprinted as pp. 52-53.

Who is right?—Black or Blackstone? Is man's law really nothing but a rule of conduct backed by governmental force? Or is it something more, a reflection of God's law? Is God really interested in the affairs of human government? Has He said anything about civil government in His Word?

We will explore these questions in the next six chapters.

Chapter 2

God's Law Gives Authority
to Man's Law

The laws of God and the laws of civil government need not always be in conflict. In fact, civil government derives its authority from God.

On the sixth day of creation, when God created man, he gave man authority over the world. "And God said unto them, 'Be fruitful, and multiply, and fill the earth, and subdue it; and have dominion over the fish of the sea, and over the fowl of the air, and over every living thing that moveth upon the earth.' " (Genesis 1:28). This is commonly called the "creation mandate," by which God gave man authority or dominion over the earth.

The ten generations between Adam and Noah were a period of great longevity, and undoubtedly during this time the world's population increased. In fact, *The Living Bible* begins Genesis 6 by saying, "Now a population explosion took place upon the earth. . . ." No sooner did the population explosion begin, than someone probably started saying, "Let's get organized around here!" We read of the first city in Genesis 4:17: "And Cain knew his wife; and she conceived, and bore Enoch; and he builded a city, and he called the name of the city, after the name of his son, Enoch." The existence of a city must have required some type of civil government.

However, we do not find civil government instituted at God's authorization until Genesis 9. Here, in what is commonly called the "Noachic Covenant,"[1]

---

1. The common Old Testament term for covenant, used here in Genesis 9 as elsewhere, is *berith*. Both *berith* and its New Testament Greek counterpart, *diatheke*, can convey either the idea of a covenant, or of a testament, or both. Many have thought that the Old Testament covenants between God and man have parallels in the Hittite suzeranty treaties between kings and their vassals. Accordingly, the Noachic covenant may be regarded as both a sovereign delegation of authority and responsibility, and as a covenant between God and man. Good discussions of the covenant idea may be found in *Theological Dictionary of the Old Testament*, G. Johannes Botterweck and Helmer Ringgren, trans. John T. Willis (Eerdmans: Grand Rapids, Michigan, 1975), Vol. II "Berith" p. 253; *Zondervan's Pictorial Encyclopedia of the Bible*, (Zondervan: Grand Rapids, Michigan, 1975), Vol. I, "Covenant (In the Old Testament)," p. 1000, J. Barton Payne (Payne claims the Noachic Covenant is testamentary in character.); Meredith G. Kline, *Treaty of the Great King — The Covenant Structure of Deuteronomy: Studies and Commentary* (Eerdmans: Grand Rapids, Michigan, 1963).

God reaffirms the creation mandate of dominion (verse 1). He also gives man an important tool for self-government—the authority to execute justice and protect human life and safety by means of capital punishment if necessary: "Whoso sheddeth man's blood, by man shall his blood be shed; for in the image of God made He man." (Genesis 9:6). This authority is clearly not limited to Israel, for Israel was not yet a nation; nor is it limited to believers. Rather, the Noachic Covenant was established between God and "every living creature of all flesh that is upon the earth" (Genesis 9:16,17), and its duration is perpetual, "between me and you, and every living creature that is with you, for perpetual generations (Genesis 9:12)." That means it still applies today!

Dr. Robert Duncan Culver, professor and Chairman of the Division of Biblical and Systematic Theology at Trinity Evangelical Divinity School, makes some interesting observations concerning the Noachic Covenant:

> First, civil government is for "the protection, conservation, fostering, and improvement of human life." God made man for Himself and longs to see human life blossom, even under the curse of sin. Government has a general welfare design here at its inception.
>
> Second, government does not have its origin in some primeval social contract among our ancestors, as Hobbes, Locke, Rousseau, and their secular democratic followers would have it; neither does it arrive out of some immanent force in the world culminating in the state, as supposed Hegel and certain other later nineteenth-century German philosophers. It has its origin in God's sovereignty. He alone is sovereign, but has delegated the power of civil government to magistrates—the manner of their placement not being specified.
>
> Third, "the humane civil organization of men must have a moral basis," that is, it is acknowledged that in an important sense every man is brother to every other man. "At the hand of every man's brother will I require the life of man" (Genesis 9:5). The Hebrew idiom may be rendered, "from the hand of mankind [the man], that is to say, from the hand of each man's brother I will require life from man." This has a negative requirement in forbidding the killing of man by any individual. It has a positive side in making man owe a debt of life to his neighbor (Romans 13:8-9).
>
> This is closely connected, in the fourth place, with the religious foundation of civil government, "for in the image of God made he man" (Genesis 9:6). This is a fact of divine relation and is not only a matter of religious faith but a veritable reality. It is precisely this fact which gives the individual man his value.
>
> Take away this religious relation of man, and all the evils of totalitarian exploitation and oppression of men come in—man has no value, no unalienable rights except the ones the state says he has. Obviously the only adequate religious foundation is true biblical religion. Liberty has never flourished long in any other setting.
>
> . . . In the fifth place, the institution of government with coercive power ("by man shall his blood be shed") shows that fallen humanity, even among a pious remnant such as the eight who survived the deluge, has

"unmeasured potentialities for evil which must be curbed." That the biblical sentence quoted describes formal collective action by man is indicated by the Hebrew idiom, which employs the generic term for mankind rather than the individual person, and by the fact that it is followed immediately by "for in the image of God made he him." . . .

In the sixth place, it must be emphasized that the death penalty for murder, the ultimate crime against one's neighbor, is not personal revenge by the dead man's family against the murderer, but divine vengeance, the just retribution upon the offender for wrong done against the God in whose image every man has been made.

This leads to the seventh point, that we have here the basis of all penalty or punishment—not reformation primarily (in the case of murderers certainly out of the question if they are executed), not protection of society (though society is protected), but the purpose of God to vindicate Himself as Governor of the universe. . . .

Eighth and finally, the moral justification for the institution of human government and for the capital punishment of murder is the sacredness of human life—man's dignity as a responsible being. "In the image of God made he man." . . . Take a murderer promptly to court, convict and punish him just as promptly, and you treat him as a responsible man. Treat him as a mere victim of his environment and history, attempt merely to rehabilitate him from his murdering tendencies, and you treat him as a thing or commodity to be manipulated.[2]

The precise details by which the government of Israel was established may be found in the Mosaic Covenant, and in the law which forms a part thereof and which was given by God through Moses in Exodus 20-23 as well as in other portions of the Pentateuch. The way the Mosaic Law should be applied to civil government in this age will be discussed in chapter 5.

Probably the most precise and systematic statement of the biblical view of civil government is set forth in Romans 13:1-7:

(1) Let every soul be subject unto the higher powers. For there is no power but of God; the powers that be are ordained of God. (2) Whosoever, therefore, resisteth the power, resisteth the ordinance of God; and they that resist shall receive to themselves judgment. (3) For rulers are not a terror to good works, but to the evil. Wilt thou, then, not be afraid of the power? Do that which is good, and thou shalt have praise of the same; (4) For he is the minister of God to thee for good. But if thou do that which is evil, be afraid; for he beareth not the sword in vain; for he is the minister of God, an avenger to execute wrath upon him that doeth evil. (5) Wherefore, ye must also needs be subject, not only for wrath but also for conscience sake. (6) For, for this cause pay ye tribute also; for they

---

2. Robert Duncan Culver, *Toward a Biblical View of Civil Government* (Chicago: Moody Press, 1974), pp. 74-80. As to Dr. Culver's reference to Locke and the social contract, it should be noted that Locke identified the social contract with the Noachic Covenant; see Locke, *Of Civil Government*, paragraph 200.

are God's ministers, attending continually upon this very thing. (7) Render, therefore, to all their dues: tribute to whom tribute is due; custom to whom custom; fear to whom fear; honor to whom honor.

Paul wrote the book of Romans probably about A.D. 56 to the Christian community at Rome.[3] Nero, the ungodly emperor, would soon begin a vicious persecution of Christians, even burning some as torches to light his garden parties. Still Paul advised the Roman Christians that "there is no power but of God; the powers that be are ordained by God." (Rom. 13:1). In other words, even an ungodly emperor like Nero is "of God," has been "ordained of God," and is "the minister of God to thee for good" (Rom. 13:14). Paul therefore exhorted these Roman Christians to (1) obey the laws of Rome; (2) try to please the Roman rulers by doing good works (by being good citizens); (3) pay taxes to Rome; (4) be obedient not only to avoid punishment but also because of conscience; and (5) give due honor and respect to the Roman rulers in accordance with the custom of the time.

We cannot grasp the full significance of Romans 13:1-7 unless we view it in the context of the preceding chapter. In chapter 12, Paul directs the Roman Christians (and all Christians by application) to live a life of love toward others. He says in Roman 12:17, "Recompense to no man evil for evil. Provide things honest in the sight of all men." And in verse 19, "Avenge not yourselves, but, rather, give place unto wrath; for it is written, Vengeance is mine; I will repay, saith the Lord." Individual Christians, then, are to forgive their enemies, not take vengeance upon them. In chapter 13, however, Paul makes it clear that this is not true of the civil ruler. Unlike the private citizen, the civil ruler is "the minister of God, an avenger to execute wrath upon him that doeth evil" (13:4). In other words, God has delegated to the civil ruler the power to execute God's retribution upon those who transgress the civil law. And the purpose is not only to effect retribution, but also to deter potential offenders: "Rulers are not a terror to good works, but to the evil" (Rom. 13:3).[4] The private citizen has no such authority.

Similarly, I Peter 2:13-17 states:

(13) Submit yourselves to every ordinance of man for the Lord's sake, whether it be to the king, as supreme, (14) Or unto governors, as unto them that are sent by him for the punishment of evildoers, and for the praise of them that do well. (15) For so is the will of God, that with well-doing

---

3. Everett F. Harrison, *Introduction to the New Testament* (Grand Rapids, Michigan: Eerdmans, 1977), pp. 229-307.

4. Culver (p.80) and many others have noted that the primary purpose of punishment by civil rulers, as found in Scripture, is not to deter evil or protect society, but to vindicate God as ruler of the universe, and to execute divine vengeance, the just retribution upon the offender for the wrong he has done against God. While I do not totally disagree with this position, I maintain that there is a scriptural basis for regarding punishment as deterrence. At least three times in Scripture we see a punishment upon a wrongdoer administered "so that all Israel will hear, and fear" (Deuteronomy 13:11; 17:33; 21:21).

ye may put to silence the ignorance of foolish men; (16) As free, and not using your liberty for a cloak of maliciousness, but as the servants of God. (17) Honor all men. Love the brotherhood. Fear God. Honor the king.

Peter, the author of this epistle (1:1), wrote from Babylon (1 Peter 5:13; the question of which Babylon is referred to need not be determined here) to believers in the Roman provinces of Asia Minor sometime around A.D. 64. Nero was still on the throne at this time, although the great persecution probably had not yet started. Despite the character of the Roman government and its ruler, Peter, writing under divine inspiration, exhorted his readers to (1) obey every law of Rome "for the Lord's sake," whether it was an edict of the emperor himself or only that of a local governor; (2) recognize that the function of government is to punish evildoers (and thereby deter potential evildoers); (3) be law-abiding citizens in order to stifle false rumors about lawlessness and licentiousness among Christians; (4) win the approval of the Roman rulers by means of good works, including obedience to the law of Rome; and (5) show honor to the Roman ruler. Anyone who takes the Scriptures seriously, then, cannot escape the conclusion that God has delegated authority to civil government. As Daniel states while in the captivity of a pagan king, "he (God) removeth kings, and setteth up kings" (Daniel 2:21).

Augustine (A.D. 354-430) took the position that civil government is rooted in man's sinful nature. As Hallowell summarizes Augustine's position:

> Because man has fallen away from that state of innocence in which he was created, external coercion is necessary as a partial remedy for the consequences of sin. Because men apart from the grace of God do not and will not love one another as brothers it is necessary to establish by coercion just relations among them, that they may not harm one another and may live orderly, if not entirely peaceful, lives. Were men motivated solely by love there would be no need for law and the state, but since men will not love God and cannot, therefore, love each other, law and the state are necessary in order to bring about that condition of earthly justice which is an approximation of God's love for man.[5]

Thomas Aquinas (A.D. 1225-1274), took a somewhat different view. Aquinas placed less emphasis on man's sin nature than did Augustine, and believed more strongly than Augustine in man's ability to come to God and the truth by means of human reason. Accordingly, Aquinas explained the origin of the state "in terms of man's innate social structure and needs and ascribed to the state functions that were primarily positive—promotion of the common good, in contrast to Augustine's essentially negative view that the role of the state is to restrain evil."[6] Like Luther and Calvin, I am inclined to agree with Augustine.

---

5. John H. Hallowell, *Main Currents in Modern Political Thought* (New York: Holt, Rinehart & Winston, 1950, 1960), p. 23.

6. Ibid., pp. 27-28.

Chapter 3

God's Law Limits The Authority of Man's Law

In the biblical view, then, civil law occupies a very special place. Law is God-given, and those who enforce and administer the law are God's servants— from the king or president, all the way down to the local policeman.

But pagan civilizations often believed the same. It was very common—in fact, practically universal—for pagan societies to worship the state as a god, or the king as a descendent of the gods.

Biblical law is unique because, while God has given divine authority to government, He has also placed well-defined limits on that authority. Let us examine those limits.

The Creation Mandate—
A Command For Wise Stewardship

In chapter 2 we discussed the Creation Mandate of Genesis 1:28 by which God gave man authority to subdue the earth and use it for his benefit: "And God blessed them, and God said to them, Be fruitful and multiply, and fill the earth, and subdue it; and have dominion over fish of the sea, and over fowl of the air, and over every living thing that moveth upon the earth."

God has given man authority to subdue the earth and all that is therein. But He has also given man the responsibility to rule wisely over His creation. We read in Genesis 2:15, "And the Lord God took the man, and put him into the garden of Eden to till it and to keep it." God gave man dominion, but He also requires man to use good husbandry, good stewardship, good conservation practices, in the way he makes use of God's creation.

"Render Unto Caesar"—A Jurisdictional Limit

The most dramatic and far-reaching limit on civil government is found in

Luke 20:22-25, where Jesus was asked whether the Jews should pay taxes to Caesar. Jesus examined a denarius, noted the image of Caesar and thereby implied that material possessions are under the jurisdiction of the civil government. He then declared, "Render, therefore, unto Caesar the things which are Caesar's, and unto God the things which are God's." He affirmed that Caesar (civil government) has authority over certain aspects of human life, but He also declared that there are other aspects of human life beyond Caesar's jurisdiction. As Lord Acton has noted,

> . . . when Christ said "Render unto Caesar the things that are Caesar's and unto God the things that are God's, He gave to the State a legitimacy it had never before enjoyed, and set bounds to it that had never yet been acknowledged. And He not only delivered the precept but he also forged the instrument to execute it. To limit the power of the State ceased to be the hope of patient, ineffectual philosophers and become the perpetual charge of a universal Church.[1]

Christ's words constituted a jurisdictional limit upon the state. He did not say there are things that Caesar would be wise or honorable or generous to leave alone. Rather, He said that some things do not belong to Caesar, but to God. Since things do not belong to Caesar, he has no jurisdiction whatsoever over them. This probably refers, at least in part, to the emperor's demand that all citizens worship him as though he were a god. No Caesar has the right to make any such demand, and if a Caesar does make such a demand, he is to be resisted even unto death (see Exodus 1:17-21; Daniel 2; Daniel 6; Acts 4:13-21; Acts 5:29).

Limitations Based on Man's Nature

We saw in the last chaper that the primary reason for the institution of civil government is the need to curb the sinful actions of men, which arise out of man's sin nature. The same sin nature which gives rise to the need for civil government, also gives rise to the need for limitations upon civil government. For the Bible tells us that "all have sinned and come short of the glory of God" (Romans 3:23; cf 5:12), and "There is none righteous, no, not one" (Romans 3:10). Paul didn't say all *except rulers* have sinned. He didn't say there is none righteous *except* policemen and judges. He said *all* have sinned! That means those who run the government are sinners too!

There is danger when sinners exercise power, because the more power one has, the greater his potential to do evil. And power is intoxicating; it leads to pride, greed, and monstrous results. As Lord Acton noted, "Power corrupts; absolute power corrupts absolutely."

The founders of our country were mostly Calvinists. They believed strongly

---

1. Lord Acton, quoted by Gertrude Himmelfarb (London, 1955), p. 45; in E. L. Hebden Taylor, *The Christian Philosophy of Law, Politics, and the State* (Nutley, New Jersey: Craig Press, 1966), pp. 445-446.

in the total depravity of man. Even those who were not orthodox Christians were, for the most part, strongly influenced by the biblical view of the world and of the nature of man. They were not utopians who believed in human perfectability; they were realists who recognized the fact of human sin. They knew the danger of placing too much power in the hands of sinful men, and they strongly believed that government must be limited. As the Puritan preacher John Cotton declared:

> It's necessary, therefore, that all power that is on earth be limited, church-power or other. . . . it's counted a matter of danger to the state to limit prerogatives; but it is a further danger not to have them limited; they will be like a tempest if they be not limited. . . . It is therefore fit for every man to be studious of the bounds which the Lord hath set; and for the people, in whom fundamentally all power lies, to give as much power as God and His Word gives to men. . . . All intrenchment upon the bounds which God hath not given, they are not enlargements, but burdens and snares.[2]

R. J. Rushdoony writes:

> When Americans were more keenly aware of the sinful character of human nature, they were more properly suspicious of the exercise of power. . . . The Constitution was a triumph for the Puritan idea of limitation of man's power. The federal structure, checks and balances, separation of powers, the ninth and tenth amendments, and other provisions reflected Cotton's belief that, "If you tether a beast at night, he knows the length of his tether before morning." In the last half century, many of the Puritan-inspired checks on human power have been avoided, and we have seen a pronounced abuse of governmental power.[3]

While their theology was probably less orthodox, Madison and Jefferson took a similar view of human nature, and incorporated it into their view of government. They recognized that government must be based upon a realistic view of human nature, and that view includes human sin. Consider the words of James Madison, who, probably more than any other one person, took a leading role in the formulation of the U.S. Constitution:

> It may be a reflection of human nature that such devices (i.e., the division of powers) should be necessary to control the abuses of government. But what is government itself, but the greatest of all reflections on human nature? If men were angels, no government would be necessary. If angels were to govern men, neither external nor internal controls on government would be necessary. In framing a government which is to be administered by men over men, the great difficulty lies in this: You must first enable

---

2. John Cotton, quoted by R. J. Rushdoony, "Human Nature and the Abuse of Power," *The Chalcedon Report*, No. 187 (March 1981), p. 1.

3. Rushdoony. Ibid.

the government to control the governed; and in the next place oblige it to control itself.[4]

Some years later in his first inaugural address, Jefferson echoed a similar theme:

> Sometimes it is said that man cannot be trusted with the government of himself. Can he, then, be trusted with the government of others? Or have we found angels in the forms of kings to govern him? Let history answer this question.[5]

Madison and Jefferson were democratic-republicans who feared excessive government power. George Washington was more aligned with the Federalists who favored a stronger central government, but he too recognized the danger of too much power in government:

> Government is not reason; it is not eloquence; it is force. Like fire, it is a dangerous servant, and a fearful master.[6]

Lord Acton commented that the authors of the U.S. Constitution, with amazing ease, had solved one of the thorniest problems of mankind: how to effect a central government strong enough to control the sinful nature of men, yet limited enough so it would not become tyrannical and destroy human freedom.[7] They did so by dividing the powers and functions vertically between the federal, state, and local governments, by separating these powers horizontally between the legislative, executive, and judicial branches of government, by providing checks and balances between these branches, and by making special provision for the rights of the citizens which no unit of government, even with overwhelming popular support, could take away.

The principle of decentralized government has its roots in Scripture. In Exodus 18:13-26 we read that Moses' father-in-law Jethro noted his exhaustion from holding court from dawn to dusk in an effort to settle all the people's disputes. As a result Jethro suggested a system of decentralized government whereby persons were selected to be judges over various units: first a judge/ruler over ten families, then a higher judge/ruler over fifty families, then over a hundred families, then a thousand families, and finally Moses himself as Chief Justice of the Supreme Court. While it appears from verse 25 that Moses himself chose the first judges, Deuteronomy 16:18 indicates that the Israelites in some way consented to the selection of their rulers. Starting in Deuteronomy 5:1, God spoke through Moses to "all Israel," and continuing through Deuteronomy

---

4. James Madison, *The Federalist Papers*, No. 51.

5. Thomas Jefferson, First Inaugural Address, March 4, 1801; reprinted in Samuel K. Padover, *The Complete Jefferson*, Containing His Major Writings, Published and Unpublished, Except His Letters (New York: Duell, Sloan & Pearce, Inc., 1943), p. 385.

6. George Washington, quoted by G. Edward Griffin, *The Fearful Master*, (Los Angeles: Western Islands, 1964, 1965), p. ii.

7. Perkins, *Criminal Law* 40 (1957), quoted by Inbau, Thompson, & Moenssens, *Criminal Law Cases and Comments*, 2nd ed., (Foundation Press), p. 442.

16:18 we read that he directed the Israelites as follows: "Judges and officers shalt thou [all Israel] make thee [all Israel] in all they gates, which the Lord thy God giveth thee, throughout thy tribes, and they shall judge the people with just judgment." This indicates that the Israelites selected or at least acknowledged their leaders.

Whether or not it was God's perfect or direct will that Israel should have a king is a hotly debated theological question, open to serious doubt in light of I Samuel 8. But Moses prophesied that the day would come when Israel would demand a king. God therefore imposed certain limits upon that king:

> (17) Neither shall he multiply wives to himself, that his heart turn not away; neither shall he greatly multiply to himself silver and gold. (18) And it shall be, when he sitteth upon the throne of his kingdom, that he shall write him a copy of this law in a book out of that which is before the priests, and Levites. (19) And it shall be with him, and he shall read therein all the days of his life, that he may learn to fear the Lord his God, to keep all the words of this law and these statutes, to do them. (20) That his heart be not lifted up among his brethren, and that he turn not aside from the commandment, to the right hand, or to the left; to the end that he may prolong his days in his kingdom, he, and his children, in the midst of Israel. (Deuteronomy 17:14-20)

The limits God placed upon the king include the following: (1) He was not to take unto himself excessive wealth or wives. This means, at the very least, that he was not to enrich himself at the expense of his subjects. (2) The king must know and follow the law of Scripture. The king was beneath the law, not above it. (3) The king must not become "lifted up above his brethren." Here again is a distinctly biblical concept. Can you imagine Moses telling Pharaoh of Egypt that his heart must not be lifted up above his brethren, or that he must not become too wealthy, or proud, or that he was subject to the law of God? Those rulers thought they *were* gods! In contrast, the king of Israel was to be one of the people!

Scriptural Limitations Upon Criminal Justice
Intentional vs. Unintentional Acts

The biblical limitations upon the power of the state are probably nowhere more clear than in criminal justice. For example, for centuries the common law provided that no one could be punished for his actions unless those actions were accompanied by a criminal intent, or, in legal terminology, a *mens rea* or "guilty mind."

The Mosaic Law made a sharp distinction between an intentional crime and an accident. The Jews were commanded to establish three separate cities of refuge to which one could flee if he had killed another by accident. There he would be safe from retribution until the courts determined whether the killing was accidental or an act of murder (Numbers 35:9-28; Deuteronomy 4:41-43; 19:1-10). However, an act of extreme recklessness, amounting to what Perkins called an "unjustified, unexcusable, and unmitigated man-endangering state of mind.[7] . . . constituted murder." Exodus 21:28-29 distinguishes these situations, the one involving either unavoidable accident or simple negligence, and the other involving a grossly negligent, man-endangering state of mind:

> (28) If an ox gore a man or a woman, that they die; then the ox shall be surely stoned, and his flesh shall not be eaten; but the owner of the ox shall be clear. (29) But if the ox were accustomed to push with his horn in time past, and it hath been testified to his owner, and he hath not kept him in, but that he hath killed a man or a woman; the ox shall be stoned, and his owner also shall be put to death.

Why stone the ox? Obviously not to punish it, but rather to preserve society from a creature that has been shown to be dangerous, and perhaps for a ritual cleansing as well. In verse 28 the owner was not aware that his animal was dangerous, and while he may have been slightly negligent in allowing his ox to run loose, he was not considered a criminal. But in verse 29, the owner was told that his ox has dangerous tendencies but has done nothing to restrain it. He showed such contempt and indifference for human life, that he was to be treated as a murderer.

The biblical law, then, makes a distinction between an accidental act, and one which is malicious or shows wanton disregard for the rights and safety of others. That distinction has been carefully preserved in the common law and in *Blackstone's Commentaries*, but unfortunately has been eroded in recent years by the development of strict liability offenses.

Presumption of Innocence

Bibical law contains many safeguards to make sure no innocent person is wrongly convicted. For example, the court could convict no one except on the testimony of a least two witnesses (Numbers 35:30; Deuteronomy 17:6-7). The obvious reason for this requirement is to prevent an unjust conviction; two witnesses are less likely to lie or be mistaken than one witness. But even with two witnesses perjury is possible, and therefore the Bible places a severe penalty upon perjury: the accusing witness who perjures himself must suffer the same penalty that the defendant would have suffered had he been found guilty (Deuteronomy 19:16-21). Later Jewish law developed many other protections for the accused, including the right to counsel in many circumstances, requirements of a quorum for the court, the hours the court had to meet, a unanimous verdict in capital cases, a second deliberation in capital cases to see whether any juror may have changed his mind, and many others. We could learn a lot from the Jewish law!

Limits on Punishment

Even when a person was justly convicted, there were restrictions on punishment. Deuteronomy 24:16 directs that only the convicted defendant, not his family, can be punished for his crime (with very few exceptions[8]): "The fathers shall not be put to death for the children, neither shall the children be put to death for the fathers; every man shall be put to death for his own sin." This is in marked contrast to the practice of many pagan societies of the time in which the entire family of a convicted criminal was put to death (see Daniel 6:24).

The types of punishment were also limited. The Bible provides specific punishments for some crimes. In this way government is authorized to impose these punishments, but in the same way government is prohibited from imposing more severe punishments. These passages of Scripture serve both as a grant of authority and as a limitation upon that authority.

For most offenses, the punishment was determined by a general rule known as the *lex talionis* or law of retributive justice: " . . . life shall go for life, eye for eye, tooth for tooth, hand for hand, foot for foot" (Deuteronomy 19:21; cf Leviticus 24:20; Exodus 21:18-25). The principle is simply this: Let the punishment fit the crime! Not only does it mean criminals must not be coddled; it also means one may not be punished with undue severity for a minor offense. (It is true that the Old Testatment law punished offenses like blasphemy with death (Leviticus 24:16). But this does not mean God's law allows the death penalty for minor offenses; rather, it means God considers blasphemy against His name and character to be much more serious than we regard it today.)

Frequently the *lex talionis* is misconstrued to require mutilation: If I put out your eye, you can put out my eye. More likely, however, the *lex talionis* refers to restitution. If I put out your eye, I have to pay you the value of your eye (as determined by the court), and if I don't have the money to pay, I might be made a bondservant until the next Year of Jubilee. In a few instances where ritual uncleanness was involved, the punishment might be carried out literally (Deuteronomy 25:11, for example), but generally the *lex talionis* refers to restitution.

Furthermore, certain punishments are specifically limited or prohibited as barbaric or contrary to human dignity. Whipping was expressly permitted, but only within a certain limit: "Forty stripes he may give him, and not exceed; lest, if he should exceed, and beat him above these with many stripes, then thy brother should seem vile unto thee"[9] (Deuteronomy 25:3). To exceed that

---

8. The obvious exception is Achan (Joshua 7). But this involved a ritual cleansing outside the normal criminal law. Also, since the family lived in a tent without much individual privacy, it seems likely the rest of the family knew of Achan's act and were accomplices thereto.

9. Corporal punishment has been entirely abolished in American criminal justice and in that of most "civilized" countries. Instead, we make extensive use of a prison system. Only the Soviet Union and South Africa have a larger proportion of their population in prison than does the United States. But prisons are unknown in the Jewish law and not used in Israel until introduced by the Romans in the first century B.C. In the Old Testament the only examples of imprisonment were Jews in foreign lands such as Joseph. Jeremiah had to be sequestered in an abandoned cistern,

limit could cause the person imposing punishment to feel contempt for his victim and could also cause the defendant to be bitter against the criminal justice system.

God Demands Honest Government

God's law also prohibits civil government from perverting justice. In Deuteronomy 1:16-18, God spoke to Israel through Moses:

> (16) And I charged your judges at that time, saying, Hear the causes between your brethren, and judge righteously between every man and his brother, and the sojourner who is with him. (17) Ye shall not respect persons in judgment, but ye shall hear the small as well as the great; ye shall not be afraid of the face of man, for the judgment is God's; and the cause that is too hard for you, bring it unto me, and I will hear it. (18) And I commanded you at that time all the things which ye should do.

This command may be compared to Exodus 23:1-3 and Leviticus 19:15; Psalms 73:1-4, 82:2-4; Proverbs 18:5; and Zechariah 7:9-10. The words of the prophets are replete with condemnations of Israel's rulers for ignoring these commands and perverting justice. Isaiah declares, ''Thy princes are rebellious, and companions of thieves: everyone loveth bribes, and followeth after rewards: they judge not the fatherless, neither doth the cause of the widow come unto them.'' (Isaiah 1:23; compare Micah 3:11; Amos 8:4-6).

The command not to pervert justice is a limitation upon civil government. Furthermore, it implies that there is an absolute standard—God's standard—to which man must adhere, and from which man is not permitted to deviate.

The King is Below The Law

An interesting limitation upon government is found in Daniel, chapter 6. Darius, the Medo-Persian ruler over Babylon, had been tricked by his administrators (satraps) into signing a decree which stated that no one was to ask anything of any god or man for thirty days, except of Darius the king, or he would be thrown into a den of lions. Daniel refused to obey this decree, and openly prayed to God.

But here is an important principle of Medo-Persian law: The king was below the law! Once the king had issued the decree, even he could not change it; it became part of the ''law of the Medes and the Persians, which changeth not'' (Daniel 6:8, 12, 15, 17 and Deuteronomy 17:18-19). Law is supreme over kings and other government officials. That is an important principle in combating tyranny.

---

apparently because there were no prisons. Today we think of corporal punishment as barbaric and inhuman. But is moderate corporal punishment really more inhumane than our prison system, which demoralizes and dehumanizes, reduces people to bitterness, idleness, and sexual perversion, works as great a hardship upon the prisoner's family as upon the prisoner himself, and results in a high rate of recidivism? Is it not possible that the Author of Scripture, like our Puritan forefathers, knew some things about human nature and criminal justice that we have forgotten?

Civil Disobedience

Daniel 6 also establishes another limit on government—that in some circumstances the individual has the right to deny or disobey. Daniel is an excellent example of a faithful, godly believer in a pagan society. He took a high position in the government of Babylon and later of Persia, performed his duties faithfully, won the respect of his superiors, and was always respectful toward his superiors. Note his language in Daniel 1:12-13; 4:19; 27; 6:21-22. But when Darius commanded him not to pray to God, Daniel faced the death penalty rather than obey.

Other passages can be cited. In Exodus 1 we read that the Hebrew midwives refused to obey Pharoah's command to kill the Hebrew babies, and that God blessed them as a result (vv. 19-22). As previously noted, Peter wrote that Christians are to submit to every ordinance of man (I Peter 2:13-17), but when the authorities forbade him to preach, he answered, "We ought to obey God rather than men" (Acts 5:29). Paul's command to obey the authorities is indeed far-reaching, but as Paul's own imprisonment demonstrates, it is not without limits.

Government Must Repect Freedom of Worship

Christ's words in Luke 20:25, "Render unto Caesar the things that are Caesar's, and unto God the things that are God's," is a declaration that some things are beyond Caesar's jurisdiction. Foremost of these is the worship and service of God. The state may not interfere with the legitimate affairs of the church.

Old Testament Israel was a theocracy. But theocracy does not mean that the church rules the state, or that the church and the state are merged into one. Rather, theocracy comes from two Greek words, *theos* meaning "God" and *kratos* meaning "ruler." It means the rule of God.

Because of Israel's special place in God's plan for the world, Israel was a theocracy. But even in Old Testament Israel the civil and ecclesiastical authorities exercised separate sources of jurisdiction. The civil rulers of Israel generally came from the tribe of Judah (see Genesis 49:10), while the priests always came from the tribe of Levi. Even before the monarchy, the priests were Levites while the judges were usually from other tribes. In a few instances priests also served as judges; Moses and Samuel, for example. But the offices were distinct even though held by the same person. The situation might be comparable to a present-day minister of a church also serving on the city council.

Civil rulers were prohibited from interfering with the work of the priests. Those who went beyond their jurisdiction and usurped the priestly functions were judged very severely. In I Samuel 13 we read that King Saul, preparing for battle against the Philistines, waited for Samuel to come and offer a burnt offering to God. When Samuel hadn't arrived after seven days, Saul made the offering himself (vv. 8-9). As a result, God cut off Saul's descendants from the throne of Israel (vv. 13-14) and gave the throne to David and his descendants.

Centuries later, King Uzziah usurped the role of the priests and burned incense to God in the sanctuary. Because of this, God smote him with leprosy, and he remained a leper the rest of his life (II Chronicles 26:16-21).

In later chapters we shall examine the relationship of the church to the state. For now, suffice it to say that I view religious liberty in general, and the First Amendment in particular, as primarily *jurisdictional* in nature. The church is to be free, because the state has no jurisdiction over the church. God's message to Caesar concerning the church is simply this: Hands off!

Governmental authority, then, is limited. The consequences of ignoring the limits which God has placed upon governmental authority can be disastrous, as we shall see in chapter 6.

CHAPTER 4

God's Law is Revealed to Men

Since we cannot attend law school in heaven, how can man discover God's law? How does the civil authority know the will or law of God—whether he be a judge, legislator, president, king, or policeman?

The most basic and simple answer is—he doesn't. The Scriptures teach that, due to man's fallen nature, his reason is somewhat clouded, and he is unable, through his own efforts, to discover the will and law of God. "Such knowledge is too wonderful for me; it is high, I cannot attain unto it." (Psalm 139:6).

Accordingly, if man is to know God's will and God's law, it can only be because God has chosen to reveal His will and His law to man—though God may also utilize man's reason in enabling men to apprehend God's law. God has revealed his law to men in two ways: (1) His special revelation, the Holy Scriptures; and (2) His general revelation, through creation and through man's conscience. We shall discuss each of these separately.

Special Revelation

Much of God's law is contained in the Holy Scriptures, which I believe to be the inspired and inerrant Word of God.

As we have seen, the Scriptures contain much that may be called law, particularly in the Pentateuch, but actually throughout the entire Bible. The civil ruler can read God's Word and meditate upon it to gain wisdom and insight in making the decisions. The legislator may read God's Word and derive principles which may instruct him as to how he should vote on a particular bill. The same may be said of the judge who has to decide a difficult case, or of the administrator faced with policy decisions. History affords many examples of rulers who applied biblical law to the government of their kingdoms.

Charlemagne: A Ruler Who Applied Biblical Law

Charlemagne, the great king of the Franks, is a fascinating historical figure.

A devout Christian, he committed great portions of the Old Testament to memory and was conversant in Latin and Greek. But he had one great mental block—though he often tried, he was unable to learn to read! Though basically illiterate, Charlemagne (742-814 A.D.) understood biblical law, and applied it to his kingdom:

> Charles saw the state as more than the king's private property. He was strongly influenced by the ideas of St. Augustine and the Old Testament, and felt a responsibility to create an ordered, harmonious society in which all men could work together toward eternal salvation. To achieve Christian concord, he labored to discover the causes of disorder and injustice. He issued a flood of laws, called capitularies, to correct abuses and prevent their reoccurrence. He imposed on his local agents, the courts, the responsibility to enact these laws and to do justice to all who had complaints. Repeatedly he sent his loyal agents to the *missi dominici* across his realm to check on the state of local affairs and correct abuses. This activity did much to bring order and justice out of the political chaos that had plagued the Frankish state at an earlier age.[1]

A Dictionary of Christian Biography notes of Charlemagne, "The maxims of government which he adopted were drawn much more from the theocracy of the Old Testament than from the despotism of the Roman Empire."[2]

The Biblical Basis of English Common Law

Many legal scholars today claim that the English common law is based on Roman rather than biblical law. This suggestion is utterly wrong. Many factors influenced English common law, but of these biblical law was by far the most important. In fact, most of the others were in turn based upon biblical law.

Anglo-Saxon Law

First, there was the law of the Anglo-Saxons prior to the Norman conquest of 1066 A.D. These early Anglo-Saxons maintained a legal and political system very much similar to that of Old Testament Israel. They had a system of decentralized government in which the head of ten families was called a tithing man, the head of fifty families was called a vil-man, the head of a hundred families was called a hundred-man, and the head of a thousand families was called an eolderman, later shortened to earl (perhaps related to the Scandinavian term "jarl"). The earl governed a territory called a shire, and his assistant was called a "shire reef," later shortened to sheriff.[3]

1. *New Catholic Encyclopedia* (St. Louis: McGraw-Hill, 1967), "Charlemagne," by G. De Berrier de Sauvigny, 3:498.

2. William Smith and Henry Wale, *A Dictionary of Christian Biography* (AMS Press: New York, 1967) 1:460.

3. W. Cleon Skousen, *Miracle of American Study Guide* (Salt Lake City, Utah: Freemen Institute, 1981), p. 20.

The Code of Alfred the Great

Much like Charlemagne, Alfred the Great codified biblical law in his kingdom:

> The Laws of Alfred (about A.D. 890) start with a recitation of the Ten Commandments and excerpts from the Mosaic Law; and in restating and revising the native Anglo-Saxon laws. Alfred includes such great principles as: "doom (i.e. judge) very evenly; doom not one doom to the rich, another to the poor; nor doom one to your friend, another to your foe." (Cf. Exodus 23:1-3; Deut. 1:16-18)[4]

Ecclesiastical Law

Another important influence upon English common law was the ecclesiastical law, or law of the church. The church had its own court system in early England, and the law of these courts was, of course, based on the Bible.

Jewish Law

Still another source of influence was Jewish law, not only in England but also on the continent. Throughout much of the Middle Ages, the church prohibited money lending, based upon its interpretation of various passages of Scripture. But the Jews were not bound by the interpretation of the church, and they interpreted these passages differently. Consequently, throughout much of the Middle Ages the Jews were almost the only source from which one could borrow money. Outstanding Jewish scholars such as the Rabbi Moses Ben Maimon, (known better as Maimonides), codified the Jewish law, and this formed much of the basis for the commercial law of England and much of the rest of Europe. This, of course, was based largely upon the Old Testament as the Jews interpreted it.[5]

Viking Law

Another influence, often ignored, is the viking law of Scandinavia. In the ninth century the Danes and Norwegians held considerable portions of England, Scotland, and Ireland. There was a boundary in England, the north of which was called the "Danelaw" where viking law held sway. Thamar E. Dufwa has traced the effect of viking law upon the Magna Carta, comparing the wording of portions of the viking law to portions of the Magna Carta and demonstrating that the noblemen who forced King John to sign the Magna Carta in 1215 A.D. came mostly from the area north of the Danelaw where the vikings had ruled several centuries earlier.[6] The highly individualistic

---

4. Harold J. Berman, *The Interaction of Law and Religion* (Nashville, Tennessee: Parthenon Press, 1974), p. 55.

5. R. J. Rushdoony, *The Institutes of Biblical Law*, pp. 788-789.

6. Thamar E. Dufwa, *The Viking Laws and the Magna Carta: A Study of the Northmen's Cultural Influence on England and France* (New York: Exposition Press, 1963), pp. 32-92.

character of viking law is reflected in the Magna Carta and in English and American institutions today.

Roman Law

This is not to suggest that Roman law had no influence on English common law. Certainly it did. But two points must be noted: (1) Roman law was not the only influence or even the primary influence; and (2) Roman law itself was largely biblical law.

Even classical Roman law was in many ways compatible with biblical law, but after the Empire adopted Christianity, Roman law was revised to further reflect biblical principles. In the latter period of the Empire, Roman law went through three major revisions: the Constantinian Code of the fourth cerntury, the Theodosian Code of the fifth century, and the Justinian Code of the sixth century. The purpose of each revision was to bring Roman law more in line with biblical principles. In the eleventh century, when Roman law was rediscovered and reapplied in England, it was not the classical Roman law but the much-revised Justinian Code.

The Magna Carta

Signed by the unwilling King John in 1215 A.D., the Magna Carta is often called the "fountainhead of Anglo-American liberty." Helen Silving, Professor of Law at the University of Puerto Rico, has traced in exhaustive and precise detail the biblical roots of the Magna Carta:

> Some scholars have noted a similarity between the English and the Spanish charter, and inferred from this feature that the latter charter must have served as a pattern for the former. While there is no reason to exclude altogether the possibility of such a direct relationship between the two charters, it seems to be equally, or even more likely, that this similarity is referable to the charters' common origin in the Bible. Such a probability is supported by the fact that the draftsmen of both charters were undoubtedly Churchmen, learned in the Bible and Canon law.[7]

Among the parallels Silving notes between the Bible and the Magna Carta are the "self-curse" found in both documents, the fear of monarchy and requirement that the king adhere to the law found in the Magna Carta and in Deuteronomy 17, the power of excommunication or being "cut off from the people," the land as a sanctioning agent under an oath, the requirement that law be clearly written (Deut. 27:8) and clearly explained (Deut. 1:5), limitations upon punishment (Deut. 25:1-3), like punishment for perjury in criminal cases (Deut. 13:15; 19:17-21; *Magna Carta Leonesa*, articles 12-13), and the covenant as the ultimate source of authority.[8]

Silving continues that many other old legal documents of the Western world

7. Helen Silving, *Sources of Law* (Buffalo, New York: William S. Hein & Co., 1968) p. 243.
8. Ibid., pp. 243-248.

may well have their origins in the Bible. Her closing comment is thought-provoking:

> It is remarkable, indeed, and has an interesting bearing on the nature of our reactions to the Bible, that this has passed unnoticed, while efforts have been made to connect our constitutional documents with Greek and Roman ideas.[9]

We may conclude, then, that the English common law reflects the biblical heritage of the Western world. Eugen Rosenstock-Huessy states flatly, "Common law was Christian law."[10] And Keeton adds, "The judges of earlier times spoke with a certainty which was derived from their conviction that the common law was an expression of Christian doctrine, which none challenged."[11]

Biblical Sources of American Law

American law, of course, has many sources, but the most significant is the English common law. This English common law, as we have seen, was based largely upon biblical principles. Sir William Blackstone, whose *Commentaries* were the basic compilation of the English common law, was widely read in America; nearly 2,500 copies of Blackstone's *Commentaries* were sold in the ten years prior to the War of Independence. The other great English common law scholar, Coke, was more widely read and respected in America than in England.[12]

Nevertheless, many of the colonists wanted to "biblicize" their legal system even further. As Peter Marshall and David Manuel have well demonstrated and documented in their outstanding work, *The Light and the Glory*,[13] the early colonists saw themselves as a new Israel, whom God had planted in a new promised land. As the Pilgrim pastor John Robinson said,

> Now as the people of God in old time were called out of Babylon civil, the place of their bodily bondage, and were to come to Jerusalem, and there to build the Lord's temple, or tabernacle . . . so are the people of God now to go out of Babylon spiritual to Jerusalem . . . and to build themselves as lively stones into a spiritual house, or temple, for the Lord to dwell in.[14]

Similar themes were echoed by the Puritans, who began the settlement of Massachusetts in 1630. As they approached New England, their leader, John

---

9. Ibid., p. 248.

10. Eugen Rosenstock-Huessy, *Out of Revolution, Autobiography of Western Men*, p. 270; quoted by Rushdoony, *The Institutes of Biblical Law*, p. 789.

11. George W. Keeton, *The Norman Conquest and the Common Law* (London: Ernest Bend, 1966), p. 221; quoted by Rushdoony, *The Institutes of Biblical Law*, ibid.

12. R. J. Rushdoony, *This Independent Republic* (Fairfax, Virginia: Obern Press, 1978), p. 32.

13. Peter Marshall and David Manuel, *The Light and the Glory* (Old Tappan, New Jersey: Fleming H. Revell Co., 1977).

14. John Robinson, quoted in ibid., p. 110.

Winthrop, declared (using language later to be reiterated by President Ronald Reagan):

> We shall find that the God of Israel is among us, when ten of us shall be able to resist a thousand of our enemies, when He shall make us a praise and glory, that men of succeeding plantations shall say, "the Lord made it like that of New England." For we must consider that we shall be as a City upon a Hill . . .[15]

As they left England, Pastor John Cotton preached a farewell sermon on II Samuel 7:10, of which Samuel Eliot Morison says, "Cotton's sermon was of the nature to inspire these new children of Israel with the belief that they were the Lord's chosen people; destined, if they keep the covenant with Him, to people and fructify this new Canaan in the Western wilderness."[16]

This vision gradually expanded to encompass a much broader area than just the few small colonies. In 1768, attorney William Livingston declared,

> Courage, Americans . . . the finger of God points out a mighty empire to your sons . . . the land we possess is a gift of heaven to our fathers, and Divine Providence seems to have decreed it to our latest posterity . . .[17]

As the American War for Independence[18] drew near, the men of the town of Marlborough asked God to "make bare His arm in the defense of His Church and people, and let Israel go."[19] During the war, while George Washington and his soldiers struggled at Valley Forge, many sermons were preached likening him to Moses.[20]

The early Americans believed they were a people chosen of God, in many respects similar to Israel. Accordingly, many laws in the colonies were enacted to reflect the law of the Bible, particularly that of the Old Testament. An outstanding example is the Massachusetts Body of Liberties, December 10, 1641, Article 94, which reads:

MASSACHUSETTS BODY OF LIBERTIES	PARALLEL SCRIPTURE
1) If any man after legal conviction shall have or worship any other god, but the lord god, he shall be put to death.	*For thou shalt worship no other god; for the Lord, whose name is Jealous, is a jealous god.* Exodus 34:14; also Deuteronomy 30:17-18, 8:19, and 11:16.

---

15. John Winthrop, *Winthrop Papers II*, quoted in ibid., p. 162.

16. Samuel Eliot Morison, quoted in ibid., p. 157.

17. William Livingston, quoted in ibid., p. 266.

18. I refer to this war as the War for Independence, not the American Revolution, because I do not consider it to be a revolution. For explanation, see Eidsmoe, *The Bible Speaks to American Voters*.

19. Marshall and Manuel, p. 267.

20. Ibid., p. 324.

(2) If any man or women be a witch, (that is hath or consulteth with a familiar spirit) They shall be put to death.

Thou shalt not suffer a witch to live.
Exodus 22:18

A man also or woman who hath a familiar spirit, or who is a wizard, shall surely be put to death . . . Leviticus 20:27; also Leviticus 19:31; 20:6; Deuteronomy 18:10-11.

(3) If any man shall Blaspheme the name of god, the father, Sonne or Holie ghost, with direct, expresse, presumptuous or high handed blasphemie, or shall curse god in the like manner, he shall be put to death.[21]

And he who blasphemeth the name of the Lord, he shall surely be put to death . . .
Leviticus 24:16.

Another interesting attempt to conform the civil law to the biblical code is found in the New Haven Colony Laws:

This Court thus frames, shall first with due care and diligence from time to time provide for the maintenance of the purity of Religion, and suppresse the contrary, according to their best Light, and directions from the word of God. [Note the similarities to Psalm 2:10, 11:12; I Timothy 2:2.]

Secondly, though they humbly acknowledge, that the Supreme power of making Lawes, and of repealing them, belongs to God onely, and that by Him this power is given to Jesus Christ as mediator, Matthew 28:19. John 5:22., And that the Lawes for holiness, and Righteousnesse, are already made, and given us in the scriptures, which in matters morall, or of morall equity, may not be altered by a humane power, or authority, Moses onely shewed Israel the Lawes, and Statutes of God, and the Sanhedrim the highest Court, among the Jewes, must attend those lawes. Yet Civill Rulers, and Courts, and this Generall Court in particular (being intrusted by the freemen as before) are the Ministers of God for the good of the people; And have power to declare, publish, and establish, for the plantations within their Jurisdictions, the Lawes he hath made, and to make, and repeale Orders for smaller matters, not particularly determined in Scripture, according to the more Generall Rules of Righteousnesse, and while they stand in force, to require due execution of them.[22] [Note the similarity to Isaiah 33:22; Deuteronomy 5:8; 17:11; Romans 13:4.]

21. *Massachusetts Body of Liberties*, December 10, 1641, quoted by Charles E. Rice, *The Supreme Court and Public Prayer: The Need for Restraint* (New York: Fordham University Press, 1964), p. 162.

22. "New-Haven's Settling in New-England, and Some Lawes for Government" (London, 1656), in Charles Hoadly, ed., *Records of the Jurisdiction of New Haven from May 1653 to the Union* (Hartford: Case, Lockwood, and Company, 1858), p. 569; quoted by R. J. Rushdoony, *The Institutes of Biblical Law*, p. 791.

Biblical Law Reaches Pagan Rulers

The influence of the Bible upon American law, and Western law in general, is thus obvious. But what about the civil ruler who refuses to read the Bible, or who does not have a Bible? How is he to receive God's special revelation?

The effects of biblical law have extended far beyond those who have actually read the Bible. Many who are unfamiliar with Scripture unconsciously carry scriptural principles into effect because they are permeated with the Scripture-oriented culture in which they live. Many nations which show little interest in Christianity have nevertheless patterned their constitutions after the American Constitution. Possibly without knowing it, they too have been in-direct recipients of God's revelation.

As Christ said in Matthew 5:14: "Ye are the light of the world. A city that is set on a hill cannot be hid." Just as the Christian by his testimony both by word and by life-style serves as an example to others, so a nation can be an example to others. Perhaps this is what John Cotton (and President Reagan) meant when they referred to America as "a city on a hill."

But there are other ways in which the law of God is communicated to men besides through the Bible, God's special revelation. We will discuss these under the next section, General Revelation.

General Revelation

God's general revelation may be divided into two categories: (1) God's revelation through nature; "The Starry Heavens Above" and (2) God's revelation through reason or conscience; "The Still Small Voice Within."

The Starry Heavens Above

In Psalm 19:1-4 we read:

> (1)The heavens declare the glory of God, and the firmament showeth his handiwork. (2) Day unto day uttereth speech, and night unto night showeth knowledge. (3) There is no speech nor language, where their voice is not heard. (4) Their line is gone out through all the earth, and their words to the end of the world. . . .

Verse 1 tells us that the heavens preach a perpetual sermon about the glory of God, and that the firmament (the earth) gives visual evidence of the work of God. Verse 2 tells us that this revelation of God through nature is perpetual, day unto day, night unto night. It extends to all generations. Verses 3 and 4 tell us that this reaches all the earth, even to the end of the world, and reaches people of all languages.[23]

God's revelation through nature gives man adequate notice of God's creative activity, of his majesty and power, of his beauty and love for beauty, and of

---

23. A fascinating explanation of the full nature of this revelation may be found in E. W. Bullinger, *The Witness of the Stars* (Grand Rapids, Michigan: Kregel, 1893, 1970).

His love for order and design. By comparison we may see our own frailness and inadequacy, and our own disordered state of affairs. General revelation through nature can show us God and our need, but in and of itself it cannot show us the way of salvation through the Lord Jesus Christ. Rather, general revelation brings us to the realization that we need special revelation—which is then supplied by God (Hebrews 11:6). Nor can God's revelation through natural creation impart a very thorough understanding of God's law. It can show us that God is a god of law and it can show us His physical laws, but to apprehend His moral laws, we need further revelation.

The Still Small Voice Within

Conservative legal scholars have traditionally believed that there are certain eternal, unchanging, absolute principles of right, law, and justice, which are established by God and which God has made known to men or has enabled men to know through their God-given powers of human reason. These principles are commonly referred to as the "law of nature."

At the outset, the law of nature must be distinguished from various other systems. First, it must be distinguished from the school of legal positivism which could perhaps best be described as the belief, commonly held by legal scholars today, that law consists of nothing more than the dictates of legislatures, courts, and other human authorities and is utterly devoid of any absolute principles of "higher law."

Also, the law of nature must be distinguished from the historical school, which holds that law is a product of evolution and of public consciousness, and from the school of conventionalism, which holds that a fundamental distinction must be drawn between nature and convention, and that right and justice are conventional and have no basis in nature.

And the law of nature as here defined must be distinguished from natural law as occasionally used elsewhere. My view of natural law does not include the idea of some that natural law is that which has become "natural" as a result of time-honored customs which are deeply ingrained in society. How long must a custom exist before it becomes "natural"—one hundred years? One thousand years? Is this not merely a drawn-out form of conventionalism, historicism, or positivism?

Also, by natural law I do not mean what Thomas Hobbes meant by natural law. To him, natural law was that which accords with nature. Hobbes' natural law was based upon the natural instincts of men, and upon what people do naturally.[24] For example, it is natural for persons to preserve themselves, and therefore the right of self-preservation is a natural law. I will not dispute the fact that any successful and effective system of law must be based upon a realistic view of human nature—specifically, that view of human nature which is

24. Leo Strauss, *Natural Right and History* (Chicago: University of Chicago Press, 1953, 1963), pp. 166-202.

expressed in the Bible. But this is not the same as saying that human nature is an absolute principle of right and wrong. The fact that something is "natural" does not make it right. A survey of history and a perusal of the daily newspaper could easily convince one that it is "natural" for men to murder, steal, conquer, and enslave each other; but this certainly does not make these acts right. Natural law in the sense of a "higher law" must be something more than what is natural.

The law of nature must also be distinguished from the view of Jacques Ellul. Ellul is a scholar whose works are abstract and at times difficult to understand. But he appears to say that natural law as an abstract, independent, objective or ideal concept is nonexistent or irrelevant. To Ellul, natural law as an event— that is, the fact that people throughout history have believed in natural law and have acted and effected policies based upon that belief—is a significant factor in history.[25] By natural law I mean a "higher law" or set of God-given principles which are eternally valid regardless of whether men acknowledge or follow them.

By natural law I refer to a body of eternal principles of right and wrong which are established by God and which man is able to know by observing nature, or through his reason, or through his conscience.

Closely related to the concept of natural law is that of natural rights. Natural rights are simply human rights which have their root in natural law. Since I view natural law as of divine origin, I therefore view natural rights as being equally of divine origin.

Scriptural Support for the Law of Nature

The primary scriptural support for the concept of natural law is found in Romans 2:14-15:

> (14) For when the Gentiles, who have not the law, do by nature the things contained in the law, these, having not the law, are a law unto themselves;
> (15) Who show the work of the law written in their hearts, their conscience also bearing witness, and their thoughts the meanwhile accusing or else excusing one another.

Walther, the eminent Lutheran theologian, stated concerning this verse:

> Here we have the apostle's testimony that even the blind pagans bear the Moral Law with them in their heart and conscience. No supernatural revelation was needed to inform them concerning the Moral Law. The Ten Commandments were published only for the purpose of bringing out in bold outline the del script of the original Law written in men's hearts.[26]

25. Jacques Ellul, *The Theological Foundation of Law*, pp. 9, 13-14, 70-74.
26. C. F. W. Walther, *The Proper Distinction Between Law and Gospel* (St. Louis, Missouri: Concordia Publishing House; from lectures delivered 1884-1885, published in German, 1897, translated by W. H. T. Dau, 1928), p. 8.

Ellul has objected that the text of Romans 2:15 does not say that the *law* is written in men's hearts; rather, it speaks of the *"work* of the law written in their hearts."[27] Technically Ellul is correct: the Greek phraseology is *ergon tou nomou grapton* ("work of the law written"), and the accusative form of the adjective *grapton* ("written") corresponds with the accusative form of *ergon* ("work"), rather than the genitive *nomou* ("law"), thus indicating that "written" modifies "work" rather than "law"—though it could modify the entire phrase "work of the law".

But even if Ellul is correct, the verse still establishes that the Gentile or unregenerate man who has not had the benefit of God's special revelation, the Scriptures, still has a knowledge of God's law. Adam Clarke says concerning this verse,

> In acting according to justice, mercy, temperance, and truth, they show that the great object of the law, which was to bring them from injustice, cruelty, intemperance, and falsity, is accomplished so far in them . . . from the correct sense which they have of natural justice in their debates, either in their course of law, or in their treatises on morality. All these are ample proof that God has not left them without light; and that, seeing they have such correct notions of right and wrong, they are accountable to God for their conduct in reference to these notions and principles.[28]

Likewise, William M. Greathouse explains that the phrase "work of the law" means, "the effect of the law." He says, "The law has, as it were, left its stamp upon their minds; this stamp is their conscience."[29] But Lange probably gives the best explanation: "Not the Law itself . . . for the Ten Commandments are not formally written in their heart, but the essential meaning of their requirement."[30] The work of the law, then, is the essential meaning of the law. Paul does not say that the Gentiles have the Decalogue, or the Torah, or the Old Testament itself written on their heart, but they have its essential meaning, and are therefore able to carry it out to a large extent.

Many parallels to this text exist in classical Greek literature, parallels with which Paul was probably familiar and upon which, under the inspiration of the Holy Spirit, he probably drew in his choice of words in Romans 2:14-15. John Owen quotes a passage from a lost work of Cicero, retained by Lactantius (an early church father), which remarkably coincides with the language of Paul in Romans 2:14-15.[31] The Greek poet Sophocles spoke of the "unwritten and

27. Ellul, p. 89.

28. Adam Clarke, *Clarke's Commentaries* (Nashville, Tennessee: Abingdon Press), vol. 6, p. 49.

29. William M. Greathouse, *Beacon Bible Commentary* (Kansas City, Missouri: Beacon Hill Press, 1968), 8:68.

30. John Peter Lange, *Lange's Commentary on the Holy Scriptures*, trans. Phillip Schaff (Grand Rapids, Michigan: Zondervan, 1960), 10:101.

31. John Owen, editorial note in *Calvin's Commentaries, Romans*, by John Calvin, trans. John Owen (Grand Rapids, Michigan: Eerdmans, 1959), p. 97.

indelible laws of the gods'' in the hearts of men, and the Platonic philosopher Plutarch referred to "a law which is not outwardly written in books, but implanted in the heart of man."

To understand Paul's full meaning, this passage must be compared with Romans 1 and the other portions of chapter 2. In Romans 1 Paul demonstrates the Gentiles' decline into degeneracy (1:18-32). He shows that they are accountable for what they have done, because they have this basic knowledge of right and wrong, yet they have rejected their knowledge and have degenerated into extreme depravity. Furthermore, the previous verse (2:14) states that the Gentiles "do *by nature* the things contained in the law." This again indicates some natural knowledge of right and wrong or good and evil.

Others have found a basis for the law of nature in Proverbs 30:24-28:

> (24) There are four things which are little upon the earth, but they are exceedingly wise: (25) The ants are a people not strong, yet they prepare their food in the summer; (26) the badgers are but a feeble folk, yet make they their houses in the rocks; (27) The locusts have no king, yet go they forth all of them by bands; (28) The spider taketh hold with her hands, and is in kings' palaces.

This passage may demonstrate an innate love for order and an instinctive sense of order that applies to animals and therefore, *a fortiori*, also applies to man.

Historical Belief in Law of Nature

Many question whether the Bible teaches natural rights. I believe a biblical doctrine of natural rights can best be developed by positive use of negative commands; for example, when God gave the negative command "Thou shalt not kill," he conferred upon the innocent person the right to life. When He said, "Thou shalt not steal," he conferred the right to private property.

While belief in natural law predates Christianity, Christian theologians have generally believed in natural law:

> Augustine (A.D. 354-430) introduced the pre-Christian concept "law of nature" into Christian theology; but to him the eternal law (*lex aeterna*) is the expression—not of impersonal fate, as in stoicism, but—of the will of a personal God who commands mankind to preserve the natural order and forbids us to destroy it. This eternal law of God—as it were, the original order of God's creation—assumes concrete forms in the natural law (*lex naturalis*) and in the temporal law (*lex temporalis*), the former residing in man's conscience, the latter in the positive law.[32]

Thomas Aquinas (A.D. 1225-1274) was a firm believer in the law of nature and made it an integral part of his systematic theology. Believing that the ultimate source of all law is God, the law as it exists in the mind of God must be *eternal law*. The portion of that *eternal law* which God has revealed in

---

32. *Encyclopedia of the Lutheran Church* (Minneapolis: Augsburg Press, 1965), vol. 3, "Natural Law".

Scripture is the *divine law*, of which the Ten Commandments is the best illustration. That portion of the *eternal law* which man as a rational creature discovers by his participation in the eternal reason that governs the universe is *natural law*. The statutes, precedents, etc., by which these principles are applied to concrete situations are *human law*, which is always fallible and relative to changing human situations and needs.[33]

Martin Luther placed considerably less emphasis upon the role of reason than did Aquinas. And Luther saw the role of the state more in the Augustinian sense of sin rather than in the Aquinas sense of social organization. But like Augustine and Aquinas, Luther was a strong believer in the law of nature:

> . . . Luther showed himself to be still a medieval man in his attitude to natural law. The authority behind his appeal to the landed nobility is not only Scripture, but the law of nature, written on the very heart of man at the creation, and having a divine sanction. According to Luther, the divine sanction of law extends beyond the Decalogue; it covers all the permanent forms and structures of human society—marriage, family, the principle of paternal authority as well as the principle of the "godly" prince. For a princely rule corresponds in civil society to the position of a father in a family. According to Luther the sanctions of natural law give the same honor and obedience to the territorial prince as it gives to parents on the basis of the Fourth Commandment. In the name of natural law the German nobility and princes can rightly demand from their subjects reverence, honor, taxes and various other feudal services. On this basis alone can the prince take police action at home and wage war outside his territory.[34]

Calvin also believed in the law of nature, but faced a difficult problem: How could he reconcile his strong belief in total depravity with his belief that man has a natural ability to know right and wrong? His answer was the doctrine of common grace.[35] A leading Calvinist theologian, Charles Hodge, defines common grace as "that influence of the Spirit, which in a greater or less measure, is granted to all who hear the truth."[36] Hodge identifies the effects of common grace as:

> To the general influence of the Spirit (or to common grace), we own,—
>   1. All the decorum, order, refinement, and virtue existing among men. Mere fear of future punishment, the natural sense of right, and the restraints of human laws, would provide feeble barriers to evil, were it not for the repressing power of the Spirit, which, like the pressure of the atmosphere, is universal and powerful, although unfelt.
>   2. To the same divine agent is due specially that general fear of God, and that religious feeling which prevail among men, and which secure for

33. Hallowell, p. 28.
34. Taylor, p. 483.
35. Ibid., pp. 484-486.
36. Charles Hodge, *Systematic Theology* (New York: Charles Scribner's Sons, 1895), 2: 654.

the rites and services of religion in all its forms, the decorous or more serious attention which they receive.

3. The Scriptures refer to this general influence of the Spirit though as religious experiences, varied in character and degree, which so often occur where genuine conversion, or regeneration does not attend or follow. To this reference has already been made in a general way as a proof of the doctrine of common grace.[37]

Lutherans speak of "natural grace" or *gratia naturalis*, which the *Lutheran Cyclopedia* defines as "Grace which comes to man from creation. This is distinguished from *gratia supernaturalis* (supernatural grace) which comes to man in a supernatural way through the redemption."[38] So far as the law of nature is concerned, natural grace would have a practical meaning similar to common grace.

Theologians, particularly those of the Calvinist and Lutheran traditions, have pondered the meaning of the "image of God" (Genesis 1:27). The original languages give little assistance in identifying exactly what the image of God is. Theologians have at various times considered the image of God to be innocence, righteousness, dominion over nature, and rationality or the ability to reason. Theologians have also differed over the question of what was lost of the image of God in man's Fall.[39] Whatever else may have been lost in the Fall, it seems likely that man's rationality, his ability to know right from wrong, was not totally lost, though it must have been somewhat dulled. Furthermore, in Romans 2:15 the use of the term *grapton* ("written") instead of the participle *gegrammenon* implies greater permanency,[40] again indicating that the knowledge of natural law persists in man's mind even after the Fall.

John Locke (1632-1704) is often called the father of the law of nature, though the preceding discussion makes it clear that belief in the law of nature preceded Locke by thousands of years. Taylor calls Locke a humanist,[41] but this is an overstatement. It is true that Locke's idea of an original "state of nature" is difficult to reconcile with the biblical account of creation (though Locke did believe in special creation), and his idea that children begin life with a "blank slate" is difficult to reconcile with the view of original sin that is found in Psalm 51:2 and 58:3. Also, Locke may have placed too much faith in man's power of reason, although he did recognize that reason is a gift of God[42] and stressed

---

37. Ibid., p. 617.

38. *Lutheran Cyclopedia* (St. Louis: Concordia Press, 1954, 1975), p. 348.

39. For an excellent discussion of this subject, see Hodge, pp. 96-116.

40. Lange, p. 101.

41. Taylor, p. 199.

42. John Locke, *Of Civil Government, Book II*, reprinted in *The Christian History of the Constitution of the United States of America*, Verna M. Hall (San Francisco: Foundation for American Christian Education, 1966, 1978), p. 58: "The State of Nature has the Law of Nature to govern it, which obliges everyone: And Reason, which is that Law, teaches all Mankind who will but consult it, that being all equal and independent, no one ought to harm another in his Life, Health, Liberty

that reason demonstrates the veracity of God's perfect revelation, the New Testament.[43]

It is well established, however, that Locke was a dedicated Christian and a student of the Bible. He was raised in a strong Puritan family, and his Christian faith is described as follows:

> In 1695 Mr. Locke published his treatise of "The Reasonableness of Christianity," in which he has proved that the Christian Religion, as delivered in the scriptures, and free from all corrupt mixtures, is the most reasonable institution in the world . . . the last fourteen or fifteen years of his life Mr. Locke spent chiefly at Oates, seldom coming to town; and, during this agreeable retirement, he applied himself to the study of the scriptures . . . the admired the wisdom and goodness of God in the method found out for the salvation of mankind: and when he thought about it, he could not forbear crying out, "Oh the depths of the riches of the goodness and knowledge of God." He was persuaded that men would be convinced of this, by reading the scriptures without prejudice; and he frequently exhorted those with whom he conversed to a serious study of these sacred writings. His own application to this study had given him a more noble and elevated idea of the Christian religion.[44]

Locke clearly recognized that the "law of nature" had its origin and authority in God:

> Thus the Law of Nature stands as an Eternal Rule to all Men, Legislators as well as others. The Rules that they make for other Men's Actions, be conformable to the Law of Nature, i.e., to the Will of God, of which that is a Declaration, and the fundamental Law of Nature being preservation of Mankind, no Human Sanction can be good, or valid against it.[45]

Locke at times identified Scripture with the natural law and at times distinguished between Scripture and natural law, although at all times he emphasized their compatibility:

or Possessions. For Men being all the Workmanship of one Omnipotent, and infinitely wise Maker: All the Servants of one Sovereign Master, sent into the World by his Order, and about his Business, they are his Property, whole Workmanship they are, made to last during his, not one another's pleasure: And being *furnished with like Faculties* sharing all in one Community of Nature, there cannot be supposed any such Subordination among us that may authorize us to destroy one another, as if we were made for one another's Uses, as the inferior ranks of Creatures are for ours." [emphasis supplied]; p. 71: "Adam was created, a perfect Man, his Body and Mind in full possession of their Strength and Reason, and so was capable, from the first Instant of his Being, to provide for his own Support and Preservation and govern his Actions according to the Dictates of the Law of Reason which God had implanted in him."; p. 64: "God, who has given the World to Men in common hath also given them reason to make use of it to the best Advantage of Life, and Convenience."

43. Strauss, p. 204.

44. John Locke, *An Essay Concerning Human Understanding*, 2nd American ed. (Brattleboro, Vermont, 1806); reprinted in Hall, p. 56.

45. Locke, *Of Civil Government*, op. cit, p. 94.

Human Laws are measures in respect of Men whose Actions they must direct, albeit such measures they are as have also their higher Rules to be measured by, which Rules are two, the Law of God, and the Law of Nature; so that Laws Human must be made according to the general Laws of Nature, and without contradiction to any positive Law of Scripture, otherwise they are ill made.'' (At this point Locke indicates the Reverend Thomas Hooker, *Ecclesiastical Policy Law, Part III, Section 9*, as his authority for this proposition.)

At another point, however, Locke identified the law of nature with Scripture: ''And upon this is grounded the great Law of Nature, whoso sheddeth Man's Blood by Man shall his Blood be shed.'' The ''Law of Nature'' he cites is quoted directly from Genesis 9:6.[46]

Even in Locke's concept of the social contract, he recognized divine origin and divine authority. As authority for this social contract, he cited a speech made to Parliament by King James I in 1609, in which James I recognized the origin of the contract in the Noachic covenant:

And again, in his speech to the parliament 1609, he hath these Words, The King binds himself by a double Oath, to the Observation of the fundamental Laws of his Kingdom. Tacitly, as by being a King, and so bound to protect as well the People, as the Laws of the Kingdom, and expressly by his Oath at his Coronation; so as every just King, in a settled Kingdom, is bound to observe the Paction made to his People, by his Laws in framing his Government agreeable Thereunto, *according to that Paction which God made with Noah after the Deluge*. Hereafter, seed Time and Harvest, and Cold and Heat, and Summer and Winter, and Day and Night, shall not cease which the Earth remaineth. And therefore a King governing in a settled Kingdom, leaves to be a King, and degenerates into a Tyrant, as soon as he leaves off to rule according to his Laws[47] (emphasis supplied).

Locke, then, understood natural rights and social contract within a biblical context. His methods of arriving at truth may not have been orthodox, but his conclusions generally were.

Sir William Blackstone, the English jurist whose *Commentaries* served more than the works of any other man to reduce the English common law to writing, was also an orthodox Christian and firm believer in natural law. Blackstone believed that all law had its origin in God, and identified various types of law: law as order in the universe, that is, scientific laws; law as rule of human action, that is, rules of action dictated by superior beings; law of nations, that is, international law based on compacts, treaties, leagues, and agreements; municipal law, or the enacted laws of local governments. Two other types of law are particularly significant to note. One is the revealed law:

46. Ibid., p. 60.
47. ''King James I Speaks to Parliament 1609,'' quoted by Locke, in Hall, p. 112.

Revealed law.—This has been given manifold occasion for the benign interposition of divine providence; which, in compassion to the frailty, the imperfection, and the blindness of human reason, hath been pleased, at sundry times and in diverse manners, to discover and enforce its laws by an immediate and direct revelation. The doctrines just delivered we call the revealed or divine law, and they are to be found only in the Holy Scriptures. These precepts, when revealed, are found upon comparison to be really a part of the original law of nature, as they tend in all their consequences to man's felicity. But we are not from thence to conclude that the knowledge of these truths was attainable by reason, in its present corrupted state; since we find that, until they were revealed, they were hid from the wisdom of the ages. As then the moral precepts of this law are indeed of the same original with those of the law of nature, so their intrinsic obligation is of equal strength and perpetuity. Yet undoubtedly the revealed system is of infinitely more authenticity than that moral system, which is framed by ethical writers, and denominated the natural law. Because one is the law of nature, expressly declared so to be by God Himself, the other is only what, by the assistance of human reason, we imagine to be that law. If we could be as certain of the latter as we are of the former, both would have an equal authority; but, till then, they can never be put in any competition together.[48]

Blackstone recognized that our ability to apprehend the law of nature is limited due to man's corrupted state of reason due to the Fall. But he nevertheless believed very strongly that there is a law of nature and that said law of nature is the will of God and therefore binding upon man:

Law of nature.—This will of his Maker is called the law of nature. For as God, when He created matter, and endued it with the principle of mobility, established certain rules for the perpetual direction of that motion; so, when He created man, and endued him with free will to conduct himself in all parts of life, He laid down certain immutable laws of human nature, whereby that free will is in some degree regulated and restrained, and gave him also the faculty of reason to discover the purport of those laws.

Considering the Creator: only a Being of infinite power, He was able unquestionably to have prescribed whatever laws He pleased to His creature, man, however unjust or severe. But as he is also a Being of infinite wisdom, He has laid down only such laws as were found in those relations of justice, that existed in the nature of things antecedent to any positive precept. These are the eternal, immutable laws of good and evil, to which the Creator Himself in all his Dispensations conforms; and which He has enabled human reason to discover, so far as are necessary for the conduct of human actions. Such, among others, are these principles: that we should live honestly, should hurt nobody, and should render to everyone his due; to which three general precepts Justinian has reduced the whole doctrine of law. . . .

48. William Blackstone, *Commentaries*, 1765, Jones ed., 1915 (reprinted in Hall), pp. 142-143.

This law of nature, being coeval with mankind as dictated by God Himself, is of course superior in obligation to any other. It is binding over all the globe and all countries, and at all times; no human laws are of any validity, in contrary to this; and such of them as are valid derive all their force and all their authority, mediately or immediately, from this original. But in order to apply this to the particular exigencies of each individual, it is still necessary to have recourse to human reason; whose office it is to discover, as was before observed, what the law of nature directs in every circumstance of life; by considering, what method will tend most effectually to our own substantial happiness. And if our reason were always, as in our first ancestor before his transgression, clear and imperfect, unruffled by passions, unclouded by prejudice, unimpaired by disease or intemperance, the task would be pleasant and easy; we should need no other guide but this. But every man now finds the contrary in his own experience; that his reason is corrupt, and his understanding full of ignorance and error.[49]

The influence of Blackstone upon American colonial thinking has already been noted. He and John Locke are recognized as the men who probably influenced American legal thinking more than any other individuals. These men, along with such other firm believers in the law of nature as Algernon Sidney, Baron Montesquieu, John Calvin and other Calvinist theologians such as John Milton, Thomas Hooker, John Cotton, and Jonathan Edwards, brought about an almost universal acceptance of the natural rights philosophy among the American colonists.[50]

The natural rights philosophy clearly found its way into the American Declaration of Independence. Thomas Jefferson was not an orthodox Christian, but he was strongly influenced by the biblical view of man. He was a noted student of the Scriptures, and at one time even wrote his own version of the Bible—eliminating many of the miracles! But Jefferson firmly believed in the law of nature, as evidenced by his statements in the Declaration. In its opening paragraph the Declaration speaks of people assuming among the powers of the earth "the separate and equal station to which the *Laws of Nature and of Nature's God* entitle them." In the next paragraph the Declaration speaks of human rights and ascribes their origin to God: "We hold these Truths to be self evident, that all Men are *created* [note that he did not say "evolved"] equal, that they are *endowed by their Creator with certain unalienable rights*, that among these are Life, Liberty, and the Pursuit of Happiness. . . ." The Declaration closes by "appealing to the Supreme Judge of the World for the Rectitude of our Intentions" and expressing a "firm Reliance on the Protection of divine Providence. . . ." The recognition of God as the author of natural law and unalienable rights is, in Jefferson's words, "self-evident." This does not mean

49. Locke, *An Essay Concerning Human Understanding*, p. 51.

50. Merle Curti, *The Growth of American Thought* (Evanston, Illinois: Harper & Row, 1943, 1964), pp. 111-114.

that Jefferson and the other founding fathers wanted to establish a "Christian state." Rather, they wanted to establish a state that was based upon sound principles in accordance with the law of God—as revealed in Scripture, in conscience, and in nature.

The belief in natural rights continued after independence. Merle Curti, professor of history at the University of Wisconsin, writes:

> Many trained lawyers figured in the accommodation of English common law to American but two figures, Joseph Story of Massachusetts and James Kent of New York, stood head and shoulders above the other. Both shaped much law by their notable court decisions. Story in his *Commentaries on the Constitution* and Kent in his *Commentaries on American Law* supplemented and systematized their court decisions, thus further *contributing to the acceptance of English law. This they did by identifying it with the generally accepted law of nature*, supplementing it through comparative law, and translating many of the social and political ideas and practices of the new world into legal concepts in harmony with common law tradition.[51] (emphasis added)

Curti continues by noting that, while the reform movement of the 1800s may have disagreed with many social conditions that prevailed under the natural rights philosophy, they nevertheless appealed to natural rights in support of their proposed movements:

> No reform movement failed to support its program by appeals to the inherent and inalienable rights of man to life, liberty, and the pursuit of happiness. Advocates of the abolition of capital punishment pointed out that the gallows destroyed the most basic of all the natural rights; temperance enthusiasts declared that unless society restricted the right of inebriates to frequent the dram shop their offspring would be deprived of their natural right; labor reformers decried moneyed monopolies and corporations on the score that they violated all the natural rights of men; and the abolitionists, in the use they made of the doctrine of "the higher law," were merely putting to work the venerable eighteenth century concept of natural rights and natural laws.[52]

Men such as Ralph Waldo Emerson, Henry David Thoreau, and William Lloyd Garrison firmly emphasized natural law, or higher law, to declare that a single individual in the right is more worthy of allegiance than an overwhelming majority in the wrong. Garrison argued that "That which is not just is not law, and that which is not law should not be enforced."[53] Abraham Lincoln considered the Declaration of Independence to be part of the fundamental law of the United States. He believed in the existence of an absolute, unchangeable moral law, though he also criticized appeals to "higher law" as a basis for

---

51. Ibid., p. 229.
52. Ibid., p. 360.
53. William Lloyd Garrison, quoted in Edward McNall Burns, *The American Idea of Mission: Concepts of National Purpose and Destiny* (New Brunswick, New Jersey: Rutgers University Press, 1957), p. 114.

civil disobedience and rebellion because he believed the American system was founded upon justice and right. Theodore Parker, who provided Lincoln with some of his slogans, declared that government must be ''according to the natural law of God, by the eternal justice to which you and I and all of us owe reverence,'' and that ''democracy can exist only on condition that this human substance is equally respected in the greatest and the least. Each man's natural rights are to be sacred against the wrongdoing of any other man, or of the whole nation of men.''[54]

It seems readily apparent, then, that much of the Western legal tradition has been shaped by a belief in the law of nature and natural rights, and a belief that these rights are in some way to be identified with the will of God. I believe in the law of nature, and I consider the law of nature, properly applied, to be part of God's law. Furthermore, I believe both Scripture and the law of nature are made known to man by God's revelation—the former through the revelation of Scripture, and the latter through the revelation of nature, the revelation of God-given human reason, and the revelation of God-given conscience.

Divine Guidance

In addition to God's special revelation through Scripture and His general revelation through nature and reason or conscience, God may at times give special guidance to a ruler or judge. In Proverbs 16:10 we read, ''A divine sentence is in the lips of the king; his mouth transgresseth not in judgment.'' Similarly, in Proverbs 21:1, ''The king's heart is in the hand of the Lord, like the rivers of water; he turneth it whithersoever he will.'' And in I Kings 3:28 we see an example of God's guidance: ''And all Israel heard of the judgment which the king had judged, and they feared the king; for they saw that the wisdom of God was in him, to do justice'' (cf. Isaiah 56:1).

Divine Judgment

Also, God leads nations to the acceptance of His laws by either causing or allowing disastrous consequences to fall upon them as a result of their violations of his laws. Repeatedly in Scripture, we see God's judgments upon Israel. R. B. Thieme, Jr., a retired Air Force lieutenant colonel and Dallas Theological Seminary graduate who has a widespread Bible teaching ministry, has analyzed Leviticus 26:14-40 in terms of five cycles of divine discipline upon the nation which turns away from God:

> *First cycle of discipline*: loss of health, decline of agricultural prosperity, terror, fear and death in combat, loss of personal freedoms due to negative volition toward Bible doctrine (Lev. 26:14-46).

54. Theodore Parker, *Writings*, Centenary Edition, XII:436, XIV:169-170, ed. S. B. Stewart, *Sins and Safeguards of Society* (Boston: American Unitarian Association, n.d.), pp. 6-7; cited by Burns, *The American Idea of Mission*, p. 115.

Second cycle of discipline: economic recession and depression, increased personal and individual discipline for continued negative attitude in spite of the first warning (Lev. 26:18-20).

Third cycle of discipline: violence and breakdown of law and order; cities broken up (Lev. 26:21,22).

Fourth cycle of discipline: military conquest and/or foreign occupation, scarcity of food (reduced to one-tenth of the normal supply), the breaking up of families (Lev. 26:23-26).

Fifth cycle of discipline: destruction of a nation due to maximum rejection of biblical principles (Lev. 26:27-39).

See also Deuteronomy 28:15-48 for the five cycles, where their listing is not progressive, but is specified as part of the same curse. Verse 49 begins the description of the fifth cycle.[55]

Other scriptural examples of divine discipline may be found in 2 Chronicles 16:9; Isaiah 13:17; 10:5-7, 12-15; Hebrews 12:5-8.

Modern examples also exist. The Communist rulers of the Soviet Union, shortly after the 1917 revolution, tried to abolish marriage and family life, as these "reactionary" institutions are inconsistent with the Marxist ideal of community of women. The result was hordes of wild, homeless children, widespread pregnancy and abortion, and much mental illness. The social chaos forced the Communists to reluctantly return to the institutions of marriage and the family as being essential, at least temporarily, to the maintenance of an orderly society.[56] Similarly, here in the United States the breakdown of traditional morals, the traditional family, the work ethic, and respect for authority has led to an epidemic of promiscuity, illegitimacy, venereal disease, welfarism, a breakdown of law and order resulting in fear of violence, and many other social evils. As a result, in recent years there have been signs that, even among unregenerate men, there is a return to traditional values—an example of God either causing or allowing natural disaster to result from the folly of man's actions, and thereby calling men back to His divine laws of establishment.

So God has revealed His law to men and nations. Some men and nations learn His law by reading the Scriptures. Others apprehend His law through His natural revelation—nature, reason and conscience. Still others follow His law, perhaps unwittingly, by copying the example of others. In some cases God may give more direct guidance. And some—those who refuse to learn any other way—are brought back to the law of God by the tragic consequences of their departures from His law.

God does not leave Himself without a witness! He reveals His law to all who desire to know it—and sometimes even to those who do not!

---

55. R. B. Thieme, Jr., *Daniel Chapter 6* (Houston, Texas: Berachah Tapes and Publications, 1975).

56. Omar Gjerness, *Knowing Good From Evil* (To Be Published: Fergus Falls, Minnesota), pp. 196-197.

CHAPTER 5

Principles for Applying
God's Law to Man's Law

John Warwick Montgomery tells of a Kansas legislature that, apparently for the sake of convenience, changed the meaning of π —the ratio of a circle's circumference to its diameter—from 3.1416 to an even 3.[1]

But did this change the circumference of circles in Kansas? Can men, by a mere act of the legislature, alter the physical or mathematical laws of God?

Just imagine the possibilities available to a legislature capable of performing such wonders. They could pass a law providing that, henceforth, $2-3=0$. Then they could collect two billion in taxes, spend three billion, and still have a balanced budget!

The absurdity of such a proposal is obvious. God's physical and mathematical laws are fixed and unchanging—or at least, man cannot change them. Is there any reason to believe God's law as revealed in Scripture, or as revealed in the law of nature, is any more changeable than his other natural laws?

If we agree that God's law exists and that it applies today, there remains a further question—how do we apply it?

And what portions of God's law do we apply? If we cite Exodus 21:12 to justify imposing capital punishment upon murderers, must we also favor stoning people to death for blasphemy (Leviticus 24:14, 16, 23), Sabbath breaking (Exodus 31:14; 35:2), idolatry (Leviticus 20:2; Deuteronomy 13:6; 17:2-7), or homosexuality (Leviticus 20:13)? All too often, Christians apply only those portions of the Bible they happen to like, and disregard those they dislike or find inconvenient. An accurate biblical hermeneutic is needed for the careful and consistent application of God's revealed law.

And what do we do with God's general revelation through reason and

---

1. John Warwick Montgomery, *The Law Above the Law* (Minneapolis: Bethany Fellowship, 1975), p. 29.

conscience, the law of nature? In the absence of biblical revelation, how do we know that what one person proclaims as the law of nature is not merely his own idea?

These are difficult and important questions. I must admit I am still struggling with these issues, but I offer the following as guidelines that I hope will be of help.

Applying the Law of Nature

I suggest four basic guidelines for the apprehension and application of the law of nature. I present them as four basic questions one should ask:

First, is this alleged law of nature consistent with, or at least not inconsistent with, the Holy Scriptures properly interpreted? Both John Locke[2] and Sir William Blackstone[3] recognized that the natural law cannot conflict with Scripture.

Second, is the alleged law of nature consistent with the character of God as His character is revealed in Scripture? Laws that are manifestly contrary to God's character of justice, mercy, righteousness, veracity, love, etc., are therefore suspect.

Third, is the alleged law of nature consistent with God-given principles of human reason? Human reason, of course, is fallible; but it is God-given and to some extent is an indicator of right and wrong.

Fourth, is this proposed law of nature universally accepted, or nearly so? Berman emphasizes that such universally accepted principles do exist:

> . . . Anthropologists are able to show by empirical observation that no society
> tolerates indiscriminate lying, stealing, or violence within the in-group,
> and indeed, the last six of the Ten Commandments, which require respect
> for parents and prohibit killing, adultery, stealing, perjury, and fraud, have
> some counterpart in every known culture.[4]

Common consent, to be sure, is not an absolute or ironclad requirement, especially in a fallen and depraved world. As Strauss states:

> ". . . 'consent of all mankind' is by no means a necessary condition of
> the existence of natural right. Some of the greatest natural right teachers
> have argued that, precisely if natural right is rational, its discovery presup-
> poses the cultivation of reason, and therefore natural right will not be known

2. Locke, *An Essay Concerning Human Understanding*, cited by Hall, p. 94: "So that Laws Human must be made according to the general Laws of Nature, and without contradiction to any positive Law of Scripture, otherwise they are ill made."

3. Blackstone, *The Commentaries on the Laws of England*, cited by Hall, p. 143: "Because one is the law of nature, expressly declared so to be by God Himself; the other is only what, by the assistance of human reason, we imagine to be that law. If we could be as certain of the latter as we are of the former, both would have an equal authority; but, till then, they can never be put in any competition together."

4. Harold J. Berman, *The Interaction of Law & Religion* (Nashville, Tenn.: Parthenon Press, 1974), p. 37.

universally: one not even to expect any real knowledge of natural right among savages. In other words, by proving that there is no principle of justice that has not been denied somewhere or at some time, one has not yet proved that any given denial is justified or reasonable.[5]

Nevertheless, if there is widespread disagreement as to whether or not a particular principle of natural law is in fact natural law, it should be held suspect, as it may be man's law rather than God's law.

Applying Biblical Law

I assume for purposes of this book that the Bible is God's inspired and inerrant Word, and that my readers will, for the most part, share this assumption. The reliability of God's Word has been the subject of great scholarship over the centuries, and a full discussion of the subject is not possible here. Those who question the reliability of God's Word are therefore referred to a number of scholarly works on the subject, among the best of which are the following: *The New Testament Documents: Are They Reliable?*, by F. F. Bruce (Grand Rapids, Mich., Eerdmans, 1960; *Many Infallible Proofs*, by Dr. Henry Morris (Creation-Life Publishers, San Diego, Calif., 1974; and *Evidence That Demands a Verdict*, and *More Evidence That Demands a Verdict*, by Josh McDowell (Campus Crusade, San Bernadino, Calif., 1972, 1975).

But assuming God's word is true, how do we apply the Scriptures to modern society? Let me suggest several basic principles:

Interpret the Bible According to Sound Principles of Hermeneutics

Before we can apply the Bible to contemporary situations, we must first interpret it correctly. This is not the place for a complete course on hermeneutics (the science of Bible interpretation), but let me suggest several practical and useful principles of biblical interpretation: (1) A literal meaning is to be preferred unless the context clearly indicates otherwise. There are several sensible reasons for such an approach. It causes us to take the text seriously, making its words the basis of our interpretation. It gives us an objective standard to follow, the plain printed word, instead of departing into the subjectivity of imagination that can so often characterize nonliteral interpretations. And it is rooted in reality, since most people mean exactly what they say most of the time. This does not mean that everything in the Bible is to be taken literally. There is a difference between literalism and "letteralism." Even the most extreme fundamentalist does not believe the beast of Revelation 13 is a literal monster with seven literal heads and ten literal horns, or that when Jesus called Herod a fox he meant a four-legged animal with a reddish-brown coat and bushy tail. But it means we presume a literal interpretation unless the context clearly calls for a non-literal interpretation. It has been aptly said of biblical interpretation, "When the plain sense of Scripture makes common sense, seek

5. Leo Strauss, *Natural Right & History* (Chicago: Univ. of Chicago Press, 1953, 1963), p. 9.

no other sense."[6] If the average "man on the street" of biblical times would have understood a passage of Scripture in a literal sense, that is probably the way we should understand it today.

(2) If the language used in a Bible passage is not clear by itself, consider the intent of the human author. Insofar as possible we should try to put ourselves into the minds of the authors of Scripture, to understand what they meant by their words. To do so we need to look at the historical setting, the context, the purpose of the writing, the audience, and the author's other writings.

(3) Look at the context. It is improper to take a verse out of context, and doing so produces bizarre results. Psalm 14:1, "There is no God," can be a prooftext for atheism, until it is taken in context: "The fool hath said in his heart, 'There is no God.' "

(4) Every verse, phrase, and word should be presumed to have been written for a purpose and to have meaning. There are places where repetition is used for poetic or other effect, but generally every word has special meaning.

(5) Apparent conflicts in the Bible should be harmonized wherever possible. That is, if two problem passages could be interpreted in one way by which they contradict each other, and in another way by which they agree, the latter interpretation should be preferred.

(6) Apparent conflicts should be resolved by letting the latter passage control the earlier passage. If there are any conflicts between the Old Testament and the New Testament, the New Testament should be regarded as the more applicable expression of the mind of God.

(7) Apparent conflicts should be resolved by letting the more specific passage control the more general passage. This does not mean the more general passage is wrong. Rather, the Hebrew mind often did not think in terms of Western precision and may well have stated general principles without noting specific exceptions.

(8) Harmonize obscure passages in accordance with clear ones. If one passage is clear, and another is ambiguous but possibly in conflict, let the clear passage control the interpretation of the ambiguous one.

(9) Let God the Holy Spirit guide you, both through prayer and through the application of your God-given power of reason, as you seek to learn His meaning.

Distinguish Law From Gospel

Law is not limited to the Old Testament, and gospel is not limited to the New Testament. There is much law and much gospel in each. The law is what God demands of us; the gospel is what God offers to us. The law says, "This is what you must do for God." The gospel says, "This is what God has done for you."

---

6. David L. Cooper, *The God of Israel* (Los Angeles: The Biblical Research Society, 1945), p. iii.; quoted by J. Dwight Pentecost, *Things to Come* (Grand Rapids: Zondervan, 1958, 1978), p. 42.

Distinguish Uses and Categories of the Law

Luther and Calvin both distinguished three uses of the law:

(1) The first use of the law is called the social or political use: to constrain people to do good, by punishing those who do evil. This is primarily the role of civil government, a task given to government by God.

(2) The second use is pedagogical. "Pedagogue" means schoolmaster, and in Galations 3:24 we are told that "the law was our schoolmaster to bring us into Christ"; that is, the law convicts us of our sins by showing us the perfect and holy standards of God, and thereby shows us that we need forgiveness for our sins through faith in Christ's finished work on the cross.

(3) The third is the didactic use. This refers primarily to believers and describes the process by which God uses the law to teach believers to conform their lives to the will of God—not as a means of salvation but as a means of growing to spiritual maturity.

Of these three uses, the first clearly is the province of civil government. The latter two are more the responsibility of the individual and the church.

The law may also be divided into various categories. There are many ways of categorizing the law, but the most useful for our purposes is that of Patrick Fairbairn, who distinguishes between the "symbolic or ritual things of the Old Covenant" and its "strictly moral precepts."[7] These ceremonial aspects of the law were a foreshadowing of the finished work of Christ on the cross, have their fulfillment in the Cross, and are therefore not applicable today. Believers look back upon the Cross today with baptism and communion. The ceremonial law may have application today for teaching purposes, but it has no saving power today except to point to Christ, and it has no application for the state.

The moral law, on the other hand, still applies today, for it reflects the holiness, justice, and righteousness of God (Romans 7:12). We are told in Romans 6:14-15 that we are not under law, but under grace. I believe Paul is speaking there about the ceremonial law, which is now abrogated. He may also refer to the tendency of many Jews in his day to slavishly keep the law as a means of salvation, though that was never the true purpose of the law. There may be a further sense in which the believer of this age is not "under" the law in the same sense Israel was under it. But this does not mean that the moral law has no application today. The moral law of God is an eternal reflection of God's absolute standards of holiness, justice, and righteousness, and it stands today as a means by which we may know how God would have us live. We may still look to the moral law for guidance in the ordering of modern society.

Apply God's Law Differently in Different Periods of History

Jesus Christ is the same yesterday, today, and forever (Hebrews 13:8). He

---

7. Patrick Fairbairn, *The Revelation of Law and Scripture* (P. and T. Clark, 1869, reprint ed., Winona Lake, Indiana: Alpha Publications, 1979), p. 216.

does not change, His character does not change, and His law does not change. But His law may apply differently in one period of history than in another, and it may apply differently to different peoples.

God, you will recall, made a covenant with Noah that applies to all people of perpetual generations (Genesis 9:12, 13, 16, 17,). That covenant covers us as much as it covered Shem and his descendents. But God also made a covenant with Abraham that applies primarily to Abraham and his descendents (Gen.17:7), and covenants with Moses and David that apply primarily to the Jews. One basic element of the Abrahamic covenant is the promise of land to Abraham and his descendents, a promise which was fulfilled when the Israelites under Joshua took the Promised Land and which may be in the process of final fulfillment as Israel is regathered to its land today.

Because of this, land plays a unique role in the Mosaic economy. God designed special rules to prevent the land from falling into non-Jewish hands because He had promised it to the Jews in perpetuity. God therefore placed restraints on alienation into the Jewish law, provisions by which the land could not be sold to foreigners on a permanent basis. The land was not owned by private individuals, nor was it owned by the state; it was apportioned among the twelve tribes, and then subdivided among the various families or clans within each tribe. Land was owned ultimately by God but in an earthly sense by families, and an individual could not permanently deprive his family of the land. In Leviticus 25:23-28 we read:

> (23) The land shall not be sold forever: for the land is mine; for ye are strangers and sojourners with me.
> (24) And in all the land of your possession ye shall grant a redemption for the land.
> (25) If thy brother hath become poor, and hath sold away some of his possession, and if any of his kin come to redeem it, then shall he redeem that which his brother sold.
> (26) And if the man have none to redeem it, and he himself be able to redeem it,
> (27) Then let him count the years of the sale thereof, and restore the overpayment unto the man to whom he sold it, that he may return unto his possession.
> (28) But if he be not able to restore it to him, then that which is sold shall remain in the hand of him that hath bought it until the year of jubilee; and in the jubilee it shall go out, and he shall return unto his possesion.

The Year of Jubilee took place after every seventh sabbath year, that is, every fiftieth year. No outsider could buy a fee simple title to land in Israel; he could only lease the land until the next Year of Jubilee. If the last Year of Jubilee was fifteen years ago, the outsider could obtain the land for a maximum of thirty-five years, at which time the land would revert to the family.

In most other respects Israel practiced a system of private ownership of property—cattle, coins, etc. The Tenth Commandment would certainly imply private ownership of property, for it states, "Thou shalt not covet thy neighbor's house, thou shalt not covet thy neighbor's wife, nor his manservant, nor his maidservant, nor his ox, nor his ass, nor any thing that is thy neighbor's" (Exodus 20:17). Many of Christ's parables, such as the pearl of great price, the prodigal son, the just and unjust steward, the virgins and their lamps, and the vineyard parables, speak of private ownership, sale, or possession of property. There is reason to believe that private ownership of property will continue even in the millennial rule of Christ, for Micah declares that in that day every man shall sit under his vine and under his fig tree (Exodus 4:4), and Isaiah adds that everyone will have his own house and reap the fruit of his own labor (Exodus 65:21-23). Even the Commandment, "Thou shalt not steal," implies respect for property rights. (One could possibly say it means thou shalt not steal from the commune, but the Israelites of that day did not have communal property.)

And the biblical principle of private ownership of property applies in other lands as well. Job is described as a man of great property (Job 1:42); and Jeremiah exhorted the Israelite captives in Babylon to build houses and plant gardens and conduct themselves generally as good citizens of Babylon (so long as this is consistent with godly living), because the Babylonian captivity will be lengthy and "in the peace (welfare) thereof shall ye have peace" (Jeremiah 29:4-7, 28).

The general biblical principles concerning private possession and use and transfer of property can be considered as normative of the will of God and applicable today. But the unique provisions concerning the Year of Jubilee, family ownership of real estate in Palestine, and the restrictions on alienation are based on the special relationship of the Israelites to their land in light of God's promises to Israel. Those principles need not be applied literally to American secular society today, since America is not Israel and the Abrahamic and Mosaic covenants concerning land are of limited application to America.

Other aspects of Mosaic Law pertain solely to Israel, such as the rite of circumcision. While there appear to be valid hygienic reasons for circumcision, it should not be consider a religious requirement for Christians or a civil requirement for Americans. This is a different dispensation and a different people.

Also, many of the Old Testament rituals concerning the tabernacle, sacrifices, the priesthood, etc., were ceremonial. They were to serve as a "shadow Christology," as "object lessons" for Jewish-age believers concerning the future sacrifice of Jesus Christ on the cross. As he saw the lamb being sacrificed on the altar, the Old Testament Jew was to recognize the grace principle of substitutionary atonement, whereby, just as that lamb died for sin, so in the fullness of time Jesus Christ would die on the cross for the sins of men.

Now Christ's sacrifice for sin has been completed, there is no reason to continue the ceremonial law anymore. For instead of anticipating, we are to remember—by means of the Lord's Supper.

Still other portions of the Bible may have secondary but not primary applications today. As a premillennialist, I view the Sermon on the Mount as having its primary application and complete fulfillment during the Millennium when Christ shall rule the earth. This does not mean the Sermon on the Mount has no application today. It does, but it is a secondary application. Today the Sermon must be applied with discernment because conditions are different from what they will be in the Millennium. At that time, Satan will be bound, sin will be greatly restrained, and most people will know and practice the Word of God. One will be able to give to those who ask without having to worry about "chislers" taking advantage of him. Conditions today force us to distinguish between the deserving poor, those who are genuinely in need due to circumstances beyond their control, and the undeserving poor who are lazy or dishonest. The former deserve our help; the latter do not. During the Millennium, the latter will be virtually nonexistent.

Apply Scripture Differently to Government Than to Private Individuals

Some say the Bible has no application to government. I emphatically reject this view. The Old Testament prophets preached to their rulers, and sometimes they emphatically condemned them for violations of God's law.

However, God's law applies differently to government than to private individuals, because the civil ruler has privileges and responsibilities that the private citizen does not have.

Romans 12 and 13 are a good illustration. Remember that these chapter divisions are not in the original, and that Paul proceeds logically from the thoughts of the last part of chapter 12 into the beginning of chapter 13. In the last five verses of chapter 12 he admonishes individual Christians not to recompense evil for evil (v. 17), that they should live peaceably with all men inasmuch as possible (v. 18), that they should not avenge themselves (v. 19), but rather forgive their enemies (v. 20), and that they should overcome evil with good (v. 21).

But in Romans 13:1-7 he draws a sharp contrast between the individual believer and the civil ruler. Unlike the individual believer of chapter 12, the ruler is a terror to evil works (13:3); he bears not the sword in vain, for he is the minister of God, an avenger to execute wrath upon evildoers (13:4). The reason is that he is ordained of God (13:1) for this very purpose. God has delegated to this civil ruler the authority to punish evildoers and avenge crimes; He has not delegated this power to the private citizen. The ruler therefore has responsibilities both to God and to his subjects; he must execute God's justice and protect his subjects from criminals. There is a Latin maxim that expresses it well: *Minatur innocentibus qui parcit nocentibus* (He threatens the innocent who spares the guilty). This does not mean mercy has no place in the criminal justice system, but that it must be exercised with due concern for the rights and safety of innocent citizens.

God's Law Must Be Applied In Accordance With
The Church Age Principle Of Separation Of Church And State.

As we have previously noted, Old Testament Israel was a theocracy. But even then, the roots of separation of church and state existed, in that the civil rulers were prohibited from interfering with the legitimate functions of the priesthood, and the civil rulers came from the tribe of Judah whereas the priests came from the tribe of Levi.

In the New Testament, and the church age which followed, there is no divinely established theocracy. The church and the state have almost always had separate rulers, though they have frequently interacted with each other and occasionally wrongly interfered with each other. Separation of church and state has probably been better realized in America than any other nation of the world.

Separation of church and state does not mean separation of the state from God. Rather, God has established two kingdoms, or two institutions, to rule society: the church, to rule over believers, and the state, to rule over both believers and unbelievers. Both are the establishment of God (compare Matthew 16:18 with Romans 13:1-7). God has given authority to each: Some authority is given to the state, and other authority is given to the church.

In the Old Testament, the theocratic authorities only had to ask, did this individual violate God's law? Today, however, the state must ask the following: (1) Did the individual violate God's law? (2) Is that portion of God's law applicable today? (3) Has God given the state the authority to punish this violation of God's law?

Some things, such as blasphemy, are clear violations of God's law, but they are outside the jurisdiction of the state. God has relegated this matter to the church, not to the state. The church is to handle these matters—seldom if ever by force, but rather by preaching the law and the gospel.

How do we determine which areas of human conduct are the province of the state and which are the province of the church? That is a difficult question, one which church leaders and civil rulers have wrestled with and often quarreled about for centuries.[8]

It is difficult to give a precise answer. However, I would suggest the following guidelines:

(1) Does the offense involve actions or words, or does it involve thoughts only? Actions and to a somewhat lesser extent words can be within the province of the state; thoughts are beyond the state's jurisdiction. To be sure, one's thoughts can violate the law of God. Christ declared that anyone who looks upon a woman with lust has already committed adultery in his heart

---

8. An interesting dicussion of this issue in light of the British Wolfendon report, Justice Patrick Devlin's argument against it, and the debate between Justice Devlin and Professor H. L. A. Hart, appears in Basil Mitchell, *Law, Morality and Religion in a Secular Society* (New York: Oxford University Press, 1967, 1978).

(Matthew 5:28). But no one in the Bible was ever stoned to death for lust, nor did Christ recommend this. John declares that whosoever hateth his brother is a murderer (I John 3:15). Exodus 21:12 provides that a murderer shall be put to death; yet no one was ever put to death for hatred. Proverbs 6:16-19 lists seven sins that are abominations before God. Two of these are sins of the mind: a proud look, and a heart that deviseth wicked imaginations. Yet no one in the Bible is punished by the civil authorities for pride or for the thoughts of his heart.

Why? Because even in the Old Testament theocracy, the civil rulers had only limited authority. Human thoughts were beyond their jurisdiction. That is even more true today.

(2) Man's responsibilities under the moral law in the Scriptures may be roughly divided into two categories: his horizontal responsibilities, that is, his responsibilities toward other men (though these are also to God); and his vertical responsibilities, that is, his responsibilities directly to God. For example, the commandment, "Thou shalt have no other gods before me," is a vertical responsibility: it involves man's responsibility to God. On the other hand, "Thou shalt not kill," is a horizontal responsibility: it involves man's responsibility not to kill his fellow man. It has been said that the first four commandments are vertical, and the last six are horizontal.

Horizontal requirements—those involving man's duty to his fellow man, such as not stealing, not murdering, etc.—are the responsibility of the state. Vertical requirements—those involving man's responsibility to God, such as worship, refraining from idolatry, refraining from blasphemy, etc.—are outside the jurisdiction of the state and are the responsibility of the individual and the church. But the last of the Ten Commandments—"Thou shalt not covet"—is horizontal but outside the jurisdiction of the state since it involves only thoughts rather than words or action.[9]

(3) Does the conduct in question relate to all people, believers and unbelievers alike, or does it relate only to believers, such as church attendance, prayer, etc.? That which relates to believers and unbelievers alike may fall within the jurisdiction of the state; that which relates to believers only most likely does not.

---

9. The classification of conduct into vertical and horizontal is at times difficult, as involving such areas as drunkenness, sexual perversion, etc. In some sense of the word, drunkenness may be a private matter, but when an intoxicated person drives a motor vehicle and endangers the lives and property of his fellow citizens, it takes on horizontal dimensions. The use of drugs may affect only a private individual and be a "victimless crime," but when persons who use drugs are compelled to resort to stealing and prostitution to support their habit, or when persons under the influence of drugs commit violent crimes, drug abuse takes on horizontal dimensions and comes within the responsibility of the state. Homosexuality is an especially difficult question. Studies showing the effect of homosexuality upon community life in general, including but not limited to the propensity of homosexuals to commit violent crimes, would be most relevant here. There is absolutely no question that the Scriptures strongly condemn homosexuality as a violation of God's law (Leviticus 20:13; Romans 1:26-27); but whether God has delegated to the civil authority the responsibility to control homosexuality between consenting adults is a more difficult question.

(4) A final guideline concerns the individual's duty. Law textbooks often pose the following question: Suppose a stranger, lying on a beach, sees a child foundering in the water and screaming for help. If he refuses to help the child, and the child drowns, can the stranger be prosecuted for his refusal? There is no question that such a person is morally depraved and in violation of the law of God. But has God delegated to the civil government the authority to punish him? Probably not, unless he has some duty to act.

Some may argue that he had a moral duty to act. Certainly that is true. But upon what was that moral duty based? Upon some claimable right that the child had to assistance, or solely upon the man's moral duty as a creature of God?

A distinction must be drawn between duties based on claimable rights which vest in others, and duties based solely upon responsibility to God. The former would be based upon some type of claimable right. In the instance of the drowning child, if the stranger had previously promised to help the child, thereby inducing the child to enter the water, he would have a responsibility to act based upon contractual reliance, and his failure to act would be ground for civil suit as well as criminal charges. If he had contracted with the city to serve as a lifeguard, or if he had represented himself as a lifeguard by sitting in the lifeguard chair or wearing a shirt saying "Lifeguard," again there would be a moral duty to act. If he had a direct responsibility to the child, such as being the child's father, again there would be a duty to act based upon special relationship. This duty to act could be enforced by the state by appropriate criminal charges and/or civil remedies. However, duties based solely on God's requirements of man are for the most part outside the jurisdiction of the state. God may judge and punish the transgressor under these circumstances; the state cannot.

I emphasize that these guidelines are only that; guidelines. They are not to be regarded as ironclad, infallible laws, as many exceptions can probably be imagined. But the basic principle in this: God has given only limited authority to the state, and that authority is even more limited in the church age than in the age of the Israelite theocracy. Everything that is sinful is not necessarily illegal. One may transgress God's moral law without transgressing the civil law.

God's Word Must Often Be Applied As Principle Rather Than As Law

Again we are considering application. I retain my preference for literal interpretation, but often literal interpretation requires a nonliteral application.

As I examine the Scriptures I find no precise verse that tells me exactly what the speed limit ought to be on Lewis Avenue, or how long the moose hunting season should be in North Dakota, or whether the investment credit should be continued or repealed. But as we search the Scriptures we find many principles that can apply to such situations.

One of the most basic, frequent, and convincing arguments of those who reject God's law or who believe it is either nonexistent or irrelevant to modern society, is that law varies greatly from one jurisdiction to the other. Charles Herman Kinnane, professor of law of De Paul University, states:

> Aside from the field of legislation, however, many people have, or have had, the idea that there is some universally valid body of ever-existing law upon which the courts, God-inspired or otherwise, need only draw as occasion demands. We assume often that law exists and need only be applied by the courts, but we do not often inquire as to how this law came to exist. Justice Stone, however, has inquired in a famous passage about the exactly opposite rules in New York and in Massachusetts, regarding whether or not a letter accepting an offer made by mail must be received by the person who made the offer, that being the rule in Massachusetts, or whether the contract is complete and binding when the letter of acceptance is mailed, that being the rule in New York. In light of such a situtation, Justice Stone then went on to inquire, in effect, which rule is "the law," if it is true that there is some ever-existing body of ideal law which the courts need only "apply." Need it be pointed out that the law of New York differs from that of Massachusetts, and that the case is not one where the courts of one state or the other are mistaken as to what the law is? There is no THE law. There is only law of this time and of that time, and of this place and of that place. Would a perfect God give a perfect rule to some and a different—and so an imperfect rule—to others? It looks more like the work of man.[10]

Professor Kinnane's question is important, and it deserves an honest answer. Let me suggest three possible answers.

First, it is possible that New York, or Massachusetts, or both, *have* misunderstood or misinterpreted the Divine Will. As Blackstone noted, our apprehension of God's natural law is limited and subject to error.

A second possible answer is that God's law does not cover every aspect of human conduct. Rather, God has left a certain "area of freedom" in which man can make his own decisions. John Calvin believed in such an area of freedom. Taylor writes:

> While Calvin never developed a doctrine of sphere sovereignty as such, it was implicit in his recognition of the independence of the sphere of the adiaphora, the things indifferent. He recognized alongside of church and state a third realm, an area of life having a separate existence and jurisdiction. In this realm where conscience reigns supreme, no pope or king may hold sway. This area of free conscience Calvin did not restrict to a few mere details such as personal taste in clothing and food, but it includes music, agriculture, science, technical learning, and social festivities. Henry Van Til points out:
>
> > Calvin proclaims freedom from both church and state for this

---

10. Charles H. Kinnane, *A First Book on Anglo-American Law* (Indianapolis: Bobbs-Merrill Co., Inc., 1932, 1952), p. 45.

whole large area of life in his doctrine of Christian liberty, making man responsible and accountable to God alone and his conscience. This doctrine of Christian liberty is therefore one of the foundation stones of Calvin's cultural philosophy (Inst. III, 19).

> For Calvin the kingdom of God is not completely contained within the two magnitudes of church and state as medieval catholic philosophy had supposed in its doctrine of nature and grace. Neither church nor state for Calvin occupy a place above all other societal relationships.[11]

But Calvin does not say that this "area of freedom" is an area in which God has no will. Rather, he says this is outside the authority of the church or the state, and Scripture does not directly address the issue. The person is therefore answerable in this area directly to God, by means of his reason and his conscience. He does not mean to say that God does not have a will in such matters. If New York has a 45 m.p.h. speed limit and Wyoming has a 65 m.p.h. speed limit, do we conclude that God is not interested in speed limits? I believe otherwise. I believe the God who has numbered the hairs on our head and notices even the fall of the sparrow, is also concerned with such details as speed limits and even parking regulations.

A third, and in my opinion the best answer, is to regard God's law as a statement of principles. These principles might be applied differently in different situations. As Calvin said in his *Institutes,*

> For the statement of some, that the law of God given through Moses is dishonored when it is abrogated and new laws preferred to it, is utterly vain. For others are not preferred to it when they are more approved, not by a simple comparison, but with regard to the condition of the times, place, and nation; or when that law is abrogated which was never enacted for us. For the Lord through the hand of Moses did not give that law to be proclaimed among all nations and to be in force everywhere; but when he had taken the Jewish nation into his safekeeping, defense, and protection, he also willed to be a lawgiver especially to it; and—as he became a wise lawgiver—he had special concern for it in making its laws.[12]

Let us look at hunting laws. The state of North Dakota has only a few bighorn sheep. They are out in the western badlands country of the state, but in recent years their number has been increasing. Likewise, North Dakota has only a small number of moose, located mostly in the northeast part of the state, and their number has recently also been increasing. Until a few years ago, North Dakota did not allow bighorn sheep hunting or moose hunting at all, although North Dakota's Canadian neighbors to the north and Minnesota to the east have allowed moose hunting, and Montana to the west has allowed the hunting

---

11. Taylor, p. 495.
12. John Calvin, *Institutes of the Christian Religion, Book IV* (Philadelphia: Westminster Press, reprinted 1960, 1973), IV:XX:16; Vol. 2, p. 1505.

of bighorn sheep. In recent years, however, North Dakota has allowed a season in certain western counties for bighorn sheep, and a season in certain northeastern counties for moose, although these seasons are far more limited than in North Dakota's neighbors.

How do we explain this change in the law? Why is the North Dakota law different from that of Minnesota? Was North Dakota right and its neighbors wrong? Or was North Dakota right a few years ago, and wrong now, or vice-versa?

Not necessarily. North Dakota and her neighbors may all have been right at all times.

How can this be? Do principles change? Not at all! God's law, like God Himself, is eternal and immutable. But circumstances do change, and an absolute unchanging principle must be applied to different circumstances in different ways.

Remember the creation mandate: God gave man dominion over the earth (Genesis 1:28). This includes the right to hunt animals for food, at least after the Flood (Genesis 9:3). But He also requires man to exercise this dominion in ways consistent with good stewardship. Man must not waste and destroy his environment, for he is responsible to preserve it for God (Genesis 2:15). From these principles we may derive a general principle concerning hunting laws: Man should be given maximum freedom to hunt for food, consistent with good conservation practices.

Ten years ago, the number of moose and bighorn sheep in North Dakota was so small that good conservation practices dictated that there should be no hunting of those animals at all. But the circumstances have changed. The bighorn sheep and moose in North Dakota have increased. Today a limited hunting season is consistent with good conservation practices. The day may come when the good conservation practices require an expanded season, so the moose don't become overpopulated and destroy the food supply and bring about mass starvation of moose and perhaps deer as well.

The principle doesn't change, but the circumstances do. And when the same principle is applied to different circumstances, the results will vary.

The same is true of speeding laws. If the speed limit on Broadway in New York City is 25 m.p.h., but on Interstate 94 in Montana it is 55 m.p.h., that doesn't necessarily mean tht Montana or New York City has misunderstood God's will concerning speed limits. It may be that different circumstances require different applications.

Knowing that God desires maximum freedom and efficiency, but knowing also that God is concerned for our safety and welfare, we could state a general principle as follows: It is God's will that men be free to drive at maximum speeds consistent with human safety. Obviously, in traffic-ridden New York City that maximum speed has to be much lower than in the wide open spaces of Montana. To allow people to drive 55 m.p.h. on Broadway in New York would be disastrous, and to require people to drive 25 m.p.h. on the freeways of Montana would be a tedious waste of time. Same principle, different circumstances, different results.

This, then, is the job of the Christian lawmaker: the application of God's principles to man's circumstances. The result is what man's law should be.

Chapter 6

The Dangers of
Rejecting God's Law:
Evolution and Positivism,
Anarchy and Tyranny

The Impact of Evolution on the American Legal System

On July 4, 1982, TV host Phil Donahue featured a discussion of the current controversy over the teaching of creation or evolution in the public schools. At one point he remarked that the whole argument is over "a couple of lines in a biology text."

That statement probably represents a substantial number of Americans who feel the question of origins is a relatively minor academic or historical exercise which has little effect on our lives today. However, this is far from the truth. Evolution has had a far greater impact upon modern thought than most of us realize. Few people understand the extent to which the philosophy of evolution has permeated almost every aspect of human thought and human life. As Richard Hofstadter says in the introductory paragraph of his book, *Social Darwinism in American Thought*:

> In 1959, one hundred years after the publication of Darwin's *The Origin of Species*, mankind has lived so long under the brilliant light of evolutionary science that we tend to take its insights for granted. It is hard for us fully to realize the immense thrill of enlightenment experienced by Darwin's own generation; it is harder still to appreciate the terrors experienced by the religiously orthodox among them. But John Fiske, the American evolutionist, put it well when he said that to have lived to see the old myths dissolved was "a rare privilege in the centuries."

Many scientific discoveries affect ways of living more profoundly than evolution did; but none have had a greater impact on ways of thinking and believing. In this respect, the space age does not promise even remotely to match it.[1]

Huntington Cairns similarly comments, "Nineteenth-century social thought, after the formulation of the theory of biological evolution, was dominated by a theory of cultural evolution."[2]

Darwin's theory of evolution cannot be considered in a vacuum, apart from other ideas which affected American thought at or around that time. It seems likely that Darwin's theory of evolution was so readily accepted, not because of any overwhelming logical argument or scientific evidence on its behalf (both of which were at the time and are today largely lacking), but rather because it came at a time when the American intellectual environment was ready to accept it. As Hallowell says,

> The popularity of Darwin's theory is to be accounted for, at least in part, by the fact that it suited the times in which it was formulated, it confirmed many individuals in believing what they already wanted to believe.[3]

Many intellectual forces combined to create this climate. For one thing, the theory of evolution itself did not originate with Darwin; Darwin only systematized and popularized it. Others, such as his grandfather Erasmus Darwin (1739-1802), had also formulated theories of evolution, as had the French naturalist Jean Lamarck (1744-1829). Actually, the theory of evolution antedates even these men by thousands of years. Forms of evolutionary thought may be traced to such early Greek thinkers as Anaximander, Thales, and Empedocles, as well as Roman, Babylonian, and other ancient thinkers. The great reformers Martin Luther and John Calvin were well aware of the existence of evolutionary thought and took great pains to refute it.[4]

Jean Jacques Rousseau (1712-1778) is often called the father of modern democracy. Rousseau argued that man is by nature good, and has only been corrupted by his social and political institutions. This contradicts the Christian view of original sin. The salvation of mankind, for Rousseau, is not the saving grace of the Lord Jesus Christ, but a return to nature.

Closely related was the "great chain of being" idea, the belief that man and all animals are all part of one family of nature,[5] which is contrary to the biblical view of man in a place of dominance over nature.

1. Richard Hofstadter, *Social Darwinism in American Thought* (New York; George Braziller, Inc., 1944, 1955), p. 3.

2. Huntington Cairns, *Law and the Social Sciences* (New York: Augustus M. Kelly, 1935, 1969), p. 161.

3. Hallowell, p. 303.

4. Paul A. Bartz, "Luther on Evolution" (Master's thesis, Concordia Theological Seminary, Fort Wayne, Indiana, 1977), p. 13-22, 48-55, *Calvin's Commentaries*, *Genesis*, chapters 1 and 2.

5. Hallowell, p. 300.

In the early nineteenth century the philosopher Georg Wilhelm Friedrich Hegel (1770-1831) became influential. Hegel's primary contribution to human thought was the dialectic, by which truth is conceived not as a God-given absolute, but as utilitarian. Truth does not exist as an absolute, according to Hegel; rather, it develops by dialectics: a thesis is created; it is challenged by an antithesis; and in the resulting conflict a synthesis develops, which becomes a new thesis which in turn is challenged by another antithesis, ad infinitum. Instead of being static, truth changes and develops as time goes on. This developmental concept of truth is compatible with the upward progress of the theory of evolution.

This concept of upward motion also found fertile ground in America, due to the tendency of Americans in the nineteenth and twentieth centuries to almost worship a god called "progress." Perhaps fueled in part by the postmillennial tradition of New England,[6] this led to the belief that America was developing into the "Kingdom of God," and that America would one day become a utopian nation whose "alabaster cities gleam, undimmed by human tears." In the nineteenth century, America's expansion as a nation toward its "Manifest Destiny," its remarkable technological achievements, scientific discoveries, and other advances, led most Americans to think of "progress" as the normal direction in which history and human life moves. As the early socialist Albert Brisbane stated,

> Nature—not trusting the fulfillment of her plans to human science or to the efforts of individuals—has implanted in man an instinct of social progress, which, it is true, will lead him through a series of transformations, to the attainment of his Destiny; but she has also reserved for his intelligence the noble prerogative of hastening this progress, and of anticipating results, which, if left to the gradual movement of society, would require centuries to effect.[7]

The Darwinian theory of evolution, holding that all life evolves upward from simple to complex, from weaker to stronger, getting better and better all the time, was most compatible with this American mind-set which was already conditioned to look upon life as "progress."

6. In no sense should this be construed as a criticism of postmillennial thought. The early New England postmillennialists were godly men, and our nation's legal system owes a great debt to them. Likewise, in the forefront of the modern resurgence of postmillennialism are some of the most zealous and articulate defenders of creation and critics of evolution. But postmillennialism eventually developed into two camps, the conservative postmillennialists who based their views upon the Scripture and the power of God, and the liberal or evolutionary postmillennialists whose faith really consisted of a confidence in man to achieve progress through natural means. As Walvoord notes in *Bibliotheca Sacra* 106:154 (April 1949), the one common theme of liberal and conservative postmillennialism was: "the idea of ultimate progress and solution of present difficulties."

7. Albert Brisbane, *A Concise Exposition of the Doctrine of Association*, 7th ed. (New York, 1844), p. 331; quoted in L. L. Bernard and Jessie Bernard, *Origins of American Sociology* (New York: Russell & Russell, Inc., 1943, 1965), p. 81.

Still another influence that must be mentioned is environmental determinism. Orthodox Christians had held that God at the time of creation placed man in authority over his environment, and equipped him with volition, that is the capacity to make decisions as to how he controlled his environment. God held man responsible for use of the environment, as well as for the way he responded to other persons. Environmental determinists, such as Helvetius, La Mettrie, and Rousseau, held that man, instead of controlling his environment, was controlled and shaped by his environment. Again we find this view compatible with evolution, which treats man as a product of nature rather than as a master of nature.

Finally let us consider Auguste Comte (1798-1857), often referred to as the founder of sociology or the founder of positivism. Positivism denies the existence of absolute, fixed, God-given truth. According to this philosophy, truth exists only in what *is*—what can be empirically observed and verified. Comte spoke of "the law of the three stages" showing the way man has devoloped. Early man, according to Comte, thought in "theological" terms—that is, he attempted to explain everything in terms of supernatural causes. Gradually, the "theological" stage was replaced by the "metaphysical" stage in which God, or gods, were replaced by abstract ideas, such as "natural rights." The ultimate state, however, is the "positive" stage, which Comte calls "the age of Science." In the positive stage man discards all abstractions about God and metaphysical concepts and confines himself to the empirical observation of objects and events and inductively reasons out natural or scientific principles as a result.[8]

These, then, are some of the predecessors of Darwin who shaped the intellectual environment of nineteenth century America and created an intellectual climate which was receptive to Darwin's theory of evolution. The impact of evolution upon law cannot be understood apart from that of these other thinkers.

Nor can Darwin's impact upon law be considered apart from its impact upon other areas of human thought. For Darwin's ideas had a tremendous impact upon nearly every area of human thought, including sociology, political science, economics, psychology, history, and religion—all of which interact with law on a much deeper and more complex level than most of us realize.

Darwin systematized and popularized the theory of evolution as it pertained to the physical development of plants, animals, and human beings. But the application of Darwin's thought to the various disciplines mentioned above was due in large part to the work of Herbert Spencer (1820-1903). Hofstadter describes Spencer's influence as follows:

> The generation that acclaimed Grant as its hero took Spencer as its thinker.
> "Probably no other philosopher," wrote Henry Holt in later years, . . .

8. Hallowell, pp. 291-296.

. . . ever had such a vogue as Spencer had from about 1870
to 1890. Most preceding philosophers had presumably been
mainly restricted to readers habitually given to the study of
philosophy, but not only was Spencer considerably read and
generally talked about by the whole intelligent world in
England and America, but that world was wider than any that
preceded it.

Spencer's impact upon the common man in the United States is impossible
to gauge, although its effects are dimly perceptible. That he was widely
read by persons who were partly or largely self-educated, by those who
were laboriously plodding their way out of theological orthodoxy in a thousand towns and hamlets, is suggested by casual references to him in the
lives of men who later achieved some fame. Theodore Dreiser, Jack London,
Clarence Darrow, and Hamlin Garland have given intimations of Spencer's
influence on their formative years. . . .[9]

What, then, was the philosophy of Herbert Spencer? Cairns gives the following explanation:

Herbert Spencer, in his autobiography, has related how, in the last days
of 1857, at about the age of 37, when he was collecting, revising and
publishing a number of essays, he was impressed with the kinship and con-
nections between the ideas of his various articles. Suddenly there came to
him the thought that the concrete sciences at large—astronomy, geology,
biology, psychology and sociology—should have their various classes of
facts presented in subordination to the universal principle of evolution.
Clearly, it seemed to him, these sciences form a connected and unified
aggregate of phenomena; and clearly, therefore, they should be arranged
into a coherent body of doctrine. Thereafter, he set himself to the formidable
task of composing the volumes which would relate all departments of
knowledge, which he believed were separated only by conventions, to the
theory of evolution. . . . For the next forty-odd years Spencer carried out
his plan of demonstrating the universal application of this formula.[10]

Hallowell corroborates Cairns by saying, ". . . Spencer believed he had found
the formula that would bring about the complete unification of the various
sciences, and that was the doctrine of evolution."[11]

The versatility of Spencer and the numerous disciplines to which he directed
his writing and thinking, can best be illustrated by the titles of some of his
books: "*Social Statics* (1850), *Man vs. the State* (1884), *First Principles* (1882), *Principles of Psychology* (1855), *Date of Ethics* (1879), *Justice* (1892), *Principles of Sociology*
(1897), *Synthetic Philosophy* (1864). As Hofstadter says, "In the three decades

9. Hofstadter, p. 34.
10. Cairns, pp. 136-137.
11. Hallowell, p. 305.

after the Civil War it was impossible to be active in any field of intellectual work without mastering Spencer."[12]

We feel Spencer's influence today even though many Americans have never heard his name, because his ideas have been carried on by men who were influenced by him. Today, Spencer is best known for his economic theories, which are commonly referred to as "Social Darwinism." Social Darwinism is basically a restatement of laissez-faire economics in evolutionary terms. Life consists of a struggle for existence in which the fittest survive, and the principle of natural selection dictates that the most fit will reproduce themselves and pass on superior genetic traits to succeeding generations, thereby improving the race. In the economic sphere, this struggle for survival is best allowed to function when capitalism and free competition are given full rein. In this way, the most fit succeed and become wealthy, marry the prettiest wives and reproduce themselves, while the least fit fail and perish through disease, starvation, or rejection. Government should not aid the poor, because to do so impedes this process of natural selection, hinders the survival of the fittest, and slows the evolutionary development of the human race.

In the decades following the American Civil War, in which America was thinking in terms of big business, these words fell upon receptive ears. Industrialist Andrew Carnegie had been disturbed over what he thought had been the collapse of Christian theology, until he read Darwin and Spencer:

> I remember that light came as in a flood and all was clear. Not only had I got rid of theology and the supernatural, but I had found the truth of evolution. "All is well since all grows better," became my motto, my true source of comfort. Man was not created with an instinct for his own degradation, but from the lower he had risen to the higher forms. Nor is there any conceivable end to his march to perfection. His face is turned to the light; he stands in the sun and looks upward.[13]

It's interesting to note that Carnegie devoted much of his wealth to the development of public libraries—a fact which may help to explain the widespread dissemination of evolutionary writings.

Railroad magnate James J. Hill, echoing social Darwinism, declared that "the fortunes of railroad companies are determined by the law of the survival of the fittest."[14] And John D. Rockefeller declared in a Sunday school address:

> The growth of a large business is merely a survival of the fittest. . . . The American Beauty rose can be produced in the splendor and fragrance which bring cheer to its beholder only by sacrificing the early buds which grow up around it. This is not an evil tendency in business. It is merely the

12. Hofstadter, p. 33.

13. *Autobiography of Andrew Carnegie* (Boston, 1920), p. 339; quoted in Hofstadter, p. 45.

14. James J. Hill, *Highways of Progress* (New York, 1910), p. 126; quoted in Hofstadter, ibid.

working out of the law of nature and the law of God.[15] [Note the Hobbesian view—natural law is that which comes naturally!]

Spencer's economic views, further developed and popularized in America by William Graham Sumner and others, influenced American economic thought for many years. But Spencer's view of the state probably had more lasting impact. In classical political thought, the state was viewed as a divinely ordained institution for fixed and limited purposes. Orthodox theologians saw the beginning of the state and the authority of the state in the Noachic Covenant of Genesis 9. Even the social contract theory of the 1700s and 1800s did not materially alter the fixed and limited nature of the state; in fact, John Locke at least partially identified the social contract with the Noachic Covenant.[16]

But Spencer saw the state as an organism. According to Spencer there arises in the state as a social organism "a life of the whole quite unlike the lives of the units, though it is a life produced by them."[17] Society, he said, is like a biological organism. Social and biological organisms are similar in the following ways: (1) They both grow; they begin small and gradually increase in size. (2) As they grow, both exhibit differentiation of structures and functions, becoming more complex as they grow. (3) Both are composed of individuals. (4) The more they grow the more interdependent the cells or individuals within the organism become. (5) Both have a special sustaining system for taking in food and other necessities—a mouth and stomach or similar system for biological organisms, and agriculture and industry for society. (6) Both have a special distributive system—a circulatory system for biological organisms, and shipping, rails, etc., for society. (7) Both have a special regulatory system—the nervous system for biological organisms, and the government for society. Spencer also noted differences, but felt the similarities sufficiently strong to apply the biological principle of evolution to society as well.[18]

Just as biological organisms evolve from small to large, from simple to complex so the social organism evolves as well. Society, and through it the state, likewise grows from simple to complex, and government by nature must grow from small to large.

Though he probably did not realize it, Spencer's organic theory of the state sounded the death knell to his laissez-faire economics. Others used the organic theory to justify government intervention in the economy, social leveling, government ownership of the means of production, redistribution of income, etc. Other sociologists—and it must be remembered that sociology as an academic discipline was just beginning in the late 1800s when Darwin and Spencer made their influence felt—expanded upon Spencer's organic view of society to justify social intervention. Lester Frank Ward, the first president

---

15. Quoted in William J. Ghent, *Our Benevolent Feudalism*, p. 29; quoted in Hofstadter, ibid.
16. Locke, *Of Civil Government*, section 200; reprinted in Verna M. Hall, p. 112.
17. Hebert Spencer, *The Principles of Sociology*, 3rd. ed., 1:457; quoted by Hofstadter, p. 221.
18. Hallowell, pp. 306-307.

of the American Sociological Society, believed that the purpose of sociology was to "accelerate social evolution,"[19] and believed that government should intervene in society to advance those goals.

Darwin's theory of evolution also affected socioeconomic thought in a very different quarter—that of Karl Marx. Marx saw in Darwin's theory of evolution a natural explanation for the origin of man (thereby justifying his atheism and materialism), and a biological basis for the class struggle. Having read *The Origin of Species* in 1860, Marx stated to Friedrich Engels, and later to Ferdinand Lassalle, that "Darwin's book is very important and serves me as a basis in natural science for the class struggle in history.[20] He even offered to dedicate the English edition of *Das Kapital* to Darwin, who refused the "honor."[21] It is most significant that Marx would be so impressed by Darwin's work even though Darwin was strongly opposed to Marx's socioeconomic and political views. It may seem strange that laissez-faire capitalists, social reformers, and Marxists alike look to Darwin as a pillar of support. But in debates between the social Darwinists, liberals, and Marxists, evolution is not questioned; it is accepted by all. As Hofstadter states,

> Darwinism had from the first this dual potentiality; intrinsically it was a neutral instrument, capable of supporting opposite ideologies. How, then, can one account for the ascendency, until the 1890s, of the rugged individualists' interpretation of Darwinism?
>
> The tooth-and-claw version of natural selection, and its dominant groups were therefore able to dramatize this version of competition as a thing good in itself. . . . Darwinian individualism has persisted as a part of political folklore, even though its rhetoric is seldom heard in formal discussion; the folklore of politics can embrace contradictions that are less admissible in self-conscious social theory. But with these allowances, it is safe to say that Darwinian individualism is no longer congenial to the mood of the nation.[22]

Darwin's influence may also be seen in psychology. Sigmund Freud based much of his psychological theory upon the "primal horde," the early "caveman" who lived with his brothers and sisters and parents in one horde, resented but also revered his primal father who denied him the power and women that he wanted. Eventually, he united with his brothers and killed and ate the father, thus satisfying the id, but then the superego reasserted itself and he and his brothers began to worship the memory of the father, and also feel guilt over what they had done. Thus, in an oversimplified manner, we may summarize Freud's theories of ego, id and superego, sin and guilt.

19. William F. Fine, *Progressive Evolution and American Sociology, 1890-1920* (UMI Research Press, 1976, 1979), p. 183.

20. *The Correspondence of Marx and Engels* (New York, 1935), pp. 125-126; quoted in Hofstadter, p. 115.

21. *Encyclopedia Brittanica: Macropaedia Knowledge in Depth*, 15th ed., s.v. "Darwin, Charles," by Sir Gavin DeBeer, 5:495.

22. Hofstadter, pp. 201, 203.

Although Freud was actually a follower of Lamarck's theory of evolution rather than Darwin's, it still played a fundamental role in his own theory. Evolutionary thought also provided a basis for Freud to regard the mind as a mere physical organ, a product of evolution from less complex minds of other animals, and the result of environmental determinism.[23]

Perhaps nowhere has the effect of evolution been more pronounced, or more controversial, than in theology. Though Darwin himself appears to have been an agnostic, it would certainly be a mistake to suggest that all evolutionists are atheists or agnostics. Many of the more liberal theologians of the late 1800s and early 1900s attempted to reconcile evolution with theology.

The liberal or modernist view of the origin of Scripture and the development of theology was greatly influenced by evolutionary thought. Modernists generally hold that the first five books of the Bible were not written by Moses but by several authors at substantially later dates. They also generally believe that early men were polytheistic and became monotheistic only at a late date in history. Herbert F. Hahn, while not rejecting the views of the liberal critics of Scripture, makes some interesting observations in his work, *The Old Testament in Modern Research*:

> The transfer of the "Mosaic law" from the beginning to the end of the history did away with all theories based on the supposition that the religious institutions of the Levitical legislation were characteristic of the age of Moses. [Hahn refers here to the belief of liberal critics that the Mosaic law was not received by Moses on Mt. Sinai around 1400 BC but rather was developed by the Hebrews at a much later time.] With these elaborate institutions shifted to the end, the history of Israel's religion no longer appeared as a continual struggle to maintain an ideal system established at the beginning; instead, it took on the character of *gradual growth from the simple to the complex*, with the Levitical institutions as the climax of the whole development. . . . The *evolutionary conception proved of great value* in ordering and explaining various phenomena of this sort which had puzzled earlier scholars. Now the characteristic ideas and institutions of each age could be understood as parts of the continuous process of development through which Israel's religion had gone. (p. 8) . . .
>
> The conception of historical development was the chief contribution of the liberal critics to the exegesis of the Old Testament. It is true, of course, that this conception did not grow merely from an objective reading of the sources. In a larger sense, it was *a reflection of the intellectual temper of the times. The genetic conception of Old Testament history fitted in with the evolutionary principle of interpretation prevailing in contemporary science and philosophy.* In the natural sciences, the influence of Darwin had made the theory of evolution the predominant hypothesis affecting research. In the historical sciences and in the areas of religious and philosophical thought, the evolutionary concept had begun to exercise a powerful influence after Hegel had substituted

23. R.J. Rushdoony, *Freud* (Nutley, New Jersey: Presbyterian and Reformed Publishing Company, 1977), pp. 21-27.

the notion of "becoming" for the idea of "being." . . . *In every department of historical investigation the conception of development was being used to explain the history of man's thought, his institutions, and even his religious faiths. It was not strange that the same principle should be applied to the explanation of Old Testament history.* (pp. 9-10)

Behind this methodology was not only the *hypothesis that religion, like other aspects of human culture, had evolved from elementary forms of belief and practice to higher and more complex forms*, but also the assumption that cultural evolution was a uniform process that went through the same stages everywhere. This assumption, of course, was not peculiar to the anthropologists. But, for more than a generation after *Herbert Spencer had popularized the notion that biological evolution had an analogue in the cultural history of mankind*, the ideas of unilinear evolution and parallel development dominated anthropological research. (pp. 46-47)

The theory that Hebrew religious conceptions were derived in fully developed form from a highly mature intellectual background at the very beginning of Old Testament history ran counter to the evolutionary interpretation of religious history popularized by both the critical and the anthropological schools of Old Testament study. (p. 91)[24] (emphasis added)

Hahn says concerning Julius Wellhausen, one of the principle architects of the Graf-Wellhausen theory that the Pentateuch was the work of four authors rather than Moses:

> He consciously based his exposition on the evolutionary view of history. . . . From the evolutionary point of view, which assumed that development invariably took place from lower to higher forms, it was inconceivable that the nomadic ancestors of the Israelites could have held the lofty, monotheistic conceptions ascribed to Abraham. . . .[25]

It is easy to see, then, that the creation/evolution issue greatly affects one's theology. The creationist sees the first man as created with a mind and body just as intelligent and advanced as man's mind and body today—perhaps more so, because modern man suffers the degenerative effects of sin—and he was from the first the recipient of direct divine revelation. Though from the first he knew the true God, after the Fall he degenerated into polytheism and idolatry. The evolutionist sees early man as evolving from lower forms of life, and as he develops the capacity to reason, he gradually gropes with the concept of supernatural powers, starting first with polytheism and gradually growing toward monotheism.

By no means do I wish to suggest that evolutionists are all atheists or agnostics. Certainly some are, but many are deeply committed to a more liberalized form of Christianity. Nevertheless, the theory of evolution did provide a framework for atheism or agnosticism, and for a continuing de-emphasis

24. Herbert F. Hahn, *The Old Testament in Modern Research* (Philadelphia: Fortress Press, 1954, 1966), pp. 8, 9-10, 46-47, 91.

25. Ibid., p. 12

upon the supernatural. First, Darwinism, if accepted as true, refutes one of the most basic arguments classical theologians have used for the existence of God: the teleological or design argument. It had been argued that the complexities of nature evidence the handiwork of God, but the theory of evolution provided an alternative explanation for their development.

Second, evolution provided a partial answer to the argument from causation. Defenders of the existence of God had traditionally argued that there must have been a first cause, an "unmoved Mover," to cause the worlds and living things to come into being. After all, it was asked, if God didn't create the world, how did it begin? While evolution has never provided a satisfactory answer to the question of ultimate causation, and while there may be other flaws in evolutionary theory of development, defenders of evolution saw in their theory at least a partial answer to the question of origins.

Evolution further advanced atheism and agnosticism through its conflict with the Scriptures. A literal interpretation of the Scriptures with a six-day creation, is totally inconsistent with the evolutionary view of life evolving over millions or billions of years. If one accepts evolution, he must either reject the biblical account or give it a more liberal interpretation.

Fourth, evolution provided an alternative explanation of sin. Instead of sin coming into the world at the instigation of Satan when Eve was tempted in the Garden of Eden, sin is merely a continuation of the animal instincts of man.

Evolution also provided a different direction to history. The biblical view is that man was created by God in an ideal state, but that he fell through sin and has degenerated ever since, his only hope for salvation being the saving grace of God as provided for man on the cross, and his only hope for a paradise on earth being Christ's millennial rule. But Darwin's theory of evolution sees man as having evolved continually upward from some lower form of life down in the primeval mists, toward a better person and a better society. If the evolutionary principle may be applied to other areas of life besides biology, it is a philosophical basis for believing that through the process of evolution and the help of the organic state, man may ultimately build a paradise on earth for himself. A leading liberal theologian of that period, Walter Rauschenbusch, wrote:

> Translate the evolutionary theories into religious faith, and you have the doctrine of Kingdom of God. This combination with scientific evolutionary thought has freed the kingdom ideal of its catastrophic setting and its background of demonism, and so applied it to the climate of the modern world.[26]

Lastly, if the principle of biological evolution is in fact universal, then it can apply to God himself. Instead of being the same yesterday, today, and forever (Hebrew 13:8), God is continually evolving and improving as time goes on. Thus we have the basis for what today is called "process theology."

26. Walter Rauschenbusch, *Christianizing the Social Order*, p. 90; quoted in Hofstadter, p. 108.

We have seen that Darwin's theory of evolution, as applied by Spencer and others, is more than a mere academic question of origins. It is a total philosophy of life and history which profoundly affects American thinking. It permeates nearly every academic discipline, including that of law, where it is closely related to the philosophy of legal positivism which dominates contemporary American jurisprudence. Sociologists, psychologists, political scientists, economists, historians and jurists debate the applications of evolution, but they seldom question the truth of the theory itself. Rather, evolution is taken as an article of faith, despite its many fallacies and the weakness of evidence to support it.

The Marxists and socialists were willing to accept Darwinism, not because of inherent truth or the evidence on its behalf, but because it served their social theories. As Hofstadter states,

> Only when biology seemed to agree with their social preconceptions were they ready to build a sociology upon it. They were willing to use the struggle for existence to validate the class struggle, but not individualistic competition. They objected to Darwinism as a conservative rationale, but they saw nothing wrong with the conception of a biologically centered social theory if it could be fastened to their own system.[27]

In fact, a recent controversy has developed among evolutionists as to which model of evolution to believe—the traditional uniformitarian model which holds that evolution has proceeded very gradually over time, or the punctuated model which holds that evolution proceeds by leaps and jumps. It is interesting that Soviet scientists have favored the latter theory—not primarily because it is supported by the evidence, but because it is more consistent with the Marxist idea of the class struggle and violent revolution.

Hallowell's comment is most appropriate:

> The popularity of Darwin's theory is to be accounted for, at least in part, by the fact that it suited the times in which it was formulated, it confirmed many individuals in believing what they already wanted to believe. As Jacques Barzun declares, it "captivated a generation of thinkers whose greatest desire was to get rid of vitalism, will, purpose, or design as explanations of life, and to substitute for them an automatic material cause."[28]

The Rise of Legal Positivism

The American legal community accepted Darwinism as quickly as every other element of society. As a result, many intellectual leaders in the late nineteenth and early twentieth century legal circles no longer felt comfortable with the biblical or Blackstonian view that the civil law should reflect the law of God. As they rejected the biblical view of law, a new legal philosophy was needed

---

27. Hofstadter, p. 117.
28. Jacques Barzun, *Darwin, Marx, Wagner* (Boston, 1941), p.69; quoted in Hallowell, p. 303.

to fill the vacuum. That which arose is called legal positivism.

Legal positivism, of course, is but one aspect of the total philosophy of positivism. It is said to have begun with Auguste Comte (1798-1857), who denied the existence of absolute, fixed, God-given truth. It could be said that Comte absolutely denied the existence of absolutes! Truth, he said, consists only in that which can be seen or heard or smelled or touched or felt—that which can be empirically verified by the scientific method. As society advances toward maturity, it casts off theological and metaphysical concepts and confines its interest to scientifically observable phenomena.

The early pioneers of legal positivism were many: C. C. Langdell and Roscoe Pound, both deans of the Harvard Law School; Jerome Frank; Thomas Franck of New York University, and others. However, probably none were as influential as Oliver Wendell Holmes, Jr., philosopher, writer and Associate Justice of the United States Supreme Court.

Burns offers the following description of Justice Holmes' philosophy:

> In few respects was Holmes either a democrat or a liberal. Though he sometimes wrote as if he had faith in the wisdom and virtue of the masses, such was not really the case. His philosophy was deeply imbued with the cynicism of the Social Darwinists. The law of the universe was competition and conflict, a struggle for existence and survival of the fittest. Ideas and projects for social welfare were subject to this iron law. Those which emerged victorious in the struggle were the ones that would be best for a particular time and condition. The others would suffer elimination as ruthless as the destruction of summer insects by an autumn frost. Holmes' paramount concern was to make sure that the struggle went on unimpeded. For this reason the court should not interfere with the activity of legislatures in experimenting or with the tendency of individuals to express unorthodox ideas. But he had almost no sympathy with reform and none at all with panaceas or nostrums. He scoffed at proposals for tinkering with the economic system, and doubted that the condition of the lower classes could be much improved except by "taking life in hand" and building a better race.[29]

What really is legal positivism? Basically, it has five characteristics:

(1) Denial of divine absolutes.

In the biblical and Blackstonian viewpoint, civil law should reflect the Law of God, commmanding that which is right and forbidding that which is wrong.

This view is obviously unacceptable to the legal positivist. To him, God and His law, even if they exist, are irrelevant to legal philosophy, and there are no fixed standards of right and wrong. As Professor Thomas Franck of New York University has written, in contrast to religion, law has "become undisguisedly a pragmatic human process. It is made by men, and it lays no claim to divine origin or eternal validity." Law, he says, is now characterized by

29. Burns, pp. 118-119.

"existential relativism," and it is now generally recognized "that no judicial decision is ever 'final', that the law both follows the event (is not eternal or certain) and is made by man (is not divine or true).[30]

Justice Holmes, too, would divorce law from morality:

> For my own part I often doubt whether it would not be a gain if every word of moral significance could be banished from the law altogether, and other words adopted which should convey legal ideas uncoloured by anything outside the law. We should lose the fossil records of a good deal of history and the majesty got from ethical associations, but by ridding ourselves of unnecessary confusion we should gain very much in the clearness of our thought.[31]

If civil law does not reflect God-given laws or moral standards, then of what does civil law consist? The legal positivist would answer,

(2) Law is what the lawmaker says it is—nothing more, nothing less.

The school of legal positivism holds that law is law, not because it is "natural" or because it reflects the will of God or is of divine origin, but simply because a court, legislative body, or other governmental authority has decreed it to be law and has the power to enforce it as such. Justice Holmes expressed this view:

> What contitutes the law? You will find some text writers telling you that it is something different than what is decided by the courts of Massachusetts or England, that it is a system of reason, that it is a deduction from principles of ethics or admitted axioms or what-not, which may or may not coincide with the decisions. But if we take the view of our friend the bad man we shall find that he does not care two straws for the axioms or deductions, but that he does want to know what the Massachusetts or English courts are likely to do in fact. *I am much of this mind. The prophecies of what the court will do in fact and nothing more pretentious, are what I mean by the law.*[32] (emphasis supplied)

Another influential legal scholar, Jerome Frank, considers the "myth" that there exist absolute, fixed, God-given standards of law, to be the infantile wish of the child who unrealistically craves a "father-substitute" through the legal system. The most pressing need of the American legal system, according to Frank, is to throw off this "myth":

> Modern civilization demands a mind free of father-governance. To remain father-governed in adult years is particularly the modern sin. The modern mind is a mind free of childish emotional drags, a mature mind. And law,

---

30. Thomas M. Franck, *The Structure of Impartiality: Examining the Riddle of One Law in a Fragmented World* (New York, 1968), pp.62, 68-69; quoted by Berman, pp. 27-28.

31. Lerner, pp. 78-79.

32. Max Lerner, ed., "The Path of the Law" in *The Mind and Faith of Justice Holmes* (Boston: Little, Brown & Company, 1943), p. 75; cited by Hallowell, p. 363.

if it is to meet the needs of modern civilization, must adapt itself to the modern mind. It must cease to embody a philosophy opposed to change. It must become validly pragmatic. . . . until we become thoroughly cognizant of, and cease to be controlled by, the image of the father hidden away in the authority of the law, we shall not reach that first step in the civilized administration of justice, the recognition that man is not made for the law, but that the law is made by and for men.[33]

Interestingly, chapter 2 of Frank's book is titled: "Mr. Justice Oliver Wendell Holmes, the Completely Adult Jurist!"[34]

(3) Law is constantly changing or evolving.

Holmes wholeheartedly accepted the evolutionary views of Darwin and Spencer. Of Spencer he declared that it is doubtful that "any writer of English except Darwin has done so much to affect our whole way of thinking about the universe.[35]

Darwin and Spencer taught that animals and men are continually evolving. Spencer taught the organic view of the state, that the state is an organism and therefore evolves like other organisms. Now, if man and animals are evolving, if the state is an evolving organism, and if laws are made by men acting through the state, then what must the positivist conclude about law? Obviously, he concludes that law evolves, too! Since the positivist has already established that laws are not God-given absolutes, there is nothing to prevent that conclusion.

It is common in legal circles to speak of the "evolution" of a particular legal doctrine. There is a legitimate sense in which this may be done, to illustrate how our perception of a particular doctrine has changed over the years. But the legal positivists mean something different. They mean that law is evolving, not in the way men perceive the law, but that the legal system itself is gradually changing, and, it is hoped, in an upward direction.

Holmes shared Spencer's organic view of the state. He once declared, "The glory of lawyers, like that of men of science, is more corporate than individual. Our labor is an endless organic process. The organism whose being is recorded and protected by the law is the undying body of society."[36]

Likewise Harvard Law School Dean Roscoe Pound held to an "evolutionary theory of law."[37] He identified five stages of legal development: (1) primitive law which achieved merely the peaceable ordering of society; (2) strict law which achieved security, certainty and uniformity; (3) equitable or natural law which stressed ethical conduct and conformity to good morals and resulted in good faith and moral conduct attained by reason through the enforcement of legal duties; (4) mature law which stressed the maintenance of individual rights,

33. Jerome Frank, *Law and the Modern Mind* (New York: Coward-McAnn, Inc., 1935), p. 252.

34. Ibid., p. 253.

35. M. De Wolf Howe, ed., *Holmes-Pollock Letters* (Cambridge, 1941), 1:57-58; cited by Hofstadter, p.32.

36. Oliver Wendell Holmes, Jr., quoted in Seagle, p. 41.

37. Alan Hunt, *The Sociological Movement in Law* (London: Macmillan Press, 1978), p. 29.

equality of opportunity, and security of acquisitions; and (5) socialized law which stressed the maximum satisfaction of wants by recognition of interests and overcoming of individualism. In *Jurisprudence*, Pound suggested a possible sixth stage, "the law of the world."[38]

Oliver Wendell Holmes' biographer, Max Weber, divides the evolution of law into four stages, in the last of which the legal system is administered by law school graduates.[39] Emile Durkheim saw the evolution of law in anthropological terms.[40] But they disagree only on stages and method of analysis. All of these men agree that there are no fixed legal principles; law changes or evolves.

The evolutionary view of law has affected the interpretation of statutes and particularly the Constitution. Seeking "progressive" legislation which some thought violated strict construction of the Constitution, President Woodrow Wilson declared,

> One of the chief benefits I derived from being President of the University was that I had the pleasure of entertaining thoughtful men from all over the world. I cannot tell you how much has dropped into my granary by their presence. I have been casting around in my mind for something by which to draw several parts of my political thoughts together but it was my good fortune to entertain a very interesting Scotsman who had been devoting himself to the philosophical thought of the 17th Century. His talk was so engaging that it was delightful to hear him speak of anything, and presently there came out of the unexpected region of his thought the thing I had been waiting for. He called my attention to the fact that in every generation all sorts of speculation and thinking tend to fall under the formula of the dominant thought of the age. For example, after the Newtonian Theory of the Universe had been developed, almost all thinking tended to express itself in the analogies of the Newtonian Theory and since the Darwinian Theory has reigned amongst us, everybody is likely to express whatever he wishes to expound in terms of development and accomodation to environment.
>
> Now, it came to me, as this interesting man talked, that the Constitution of the United States had been made under the dominion of the Newtonian Theory. You have only to read the papers of *The Federalist* to see that fact written on every page. They speak of the "checks and balances" of the Constitution, and use to express their idea the simile of the organization of the universe, and particularly of the solar system, how by the attraction of gravitation the various parts are held in their orbits; and then they proceed to represent Congress, the Judiciary, and the President as a sort of imitation of the solar system.
>
> They were only following the English Whigs, who gave Great Britain its modern Constitution. Not that those Englishmen analyzed the matter,

38. Ibid., pp. 29-30.
39. Ibid., p. 107.
40. Ibid., pp. 60-92.

or had any theory about it; Englishmen care little for theories. It was a Frenchman, Montesquieu, who pointed out to them how faithfully they had copied Newton's description of the mechanism of the heavens.

The makers of our Federal Constitution read Montesquieu with true scientific enthusiasm. They were scientists in their way—the best way of their age—those fathers of the nation. Jefferson wrote "the laws of Nature"—and then by way of after thought—"and of Nature's God." And they constructed a government as they would have constructed an orrery—to display the laws of Nature. Politics in their thought was a variety of mechanics. The Constitution was founded on the law of gravitation. The government was to exist and move by virtue of the efficacy of "checks and balances."

The trouble with the theory is that government is not a machine, but a living thing. It falls, not under the theory of the universe, but under the theory of organic life. It is accountable to Darwin, not to Newton. It is modified by its environment, necessitated by its tasks, shaped to its functions by the sheer pressure of life. No living thing can have its organs offset against each other, as checks, and live. On the contrary, its life is dependent upon their quick co-operation, their ready response to the commands of instinct or intelligence, their ammicable community of purpose. Government is not a body of blind forces; it is a body of men, with highly differentiated functions, no doubt, in our modern day, of specialization, with a common task and purpose. Their co-operation is indispensable, their warfare fatal. There can be no successful government without the intimate, instinctive co-ordination of the organs of life and action. This is not theory, but fact, and displays its force as fact, whatever theories may be thrown across its track. Living political constitutions must be Darwinian in structure and in practice. Society is a living organism and must obey the laws of Life, not of mechanics; it must develop.

All that progressives ask or desire is permission—in an era when "development," "evolution," is the scientific word—to interpret the Constitution according to the Darwinian principle; all they ask is recognition to the fact that a nation is a living thing and not a machine.[41]

And the courts soon began applying evolutionary concepts to the Constitution. In *Trop v. Dulles*, 356 U.S. 86, Chief Justice Earl Warren issued an opinion concerning the forfeiture of citizenship as a result of court-martial conviction for wartime desertion. Trop had contended that forfeiture of citizenship constituted cruel and unusual punishment in violation of the Eighth Amendment to the Constitution. Agreeing with *Trop*, Warren declared in his opinion "that the words of the Amendment are not precise, and that their scope is not static. The Amendment must draw its meaning from the *evolving standards of decency that mark the progress of a maturing society*."[42] (emphasis added) Such seemingly

---

41. Woodrow Wilson, *The New Freedom* (New York, 1914), pp. 44-48; quoted in Hofstadter, pp. 230-231.

42. *Trop v. Dulles*, 356 U.S. 86.

innocent words are significant indeed, for they signal a departure from previously held theories of constitutional law.

Traditionally, it was believed that the Constitution should be interpreted according to what the words actually mean. And if the words themselves are ambiguous, then the court should look to the intent of the framers of the Constitution. Jefferson put it well:

> The Constitution on which our Union rests, shall be administered by me according to the safe and honest meaning contemplated by the plain understanding of the people of the United States, at the time of its adoption.[43]

George Washington made a similar declaration:

> If, in the opinion of the people, the distribution or modification of the Constitutional powers be at any particular wrong, let it be corrected by an amendment in the way the Constitution designates. But let there be no change by usurpation; though this may in one instance be the instrument of good, it is the customary weapon by which we governments are destroyed.[44]

James Madison, the chief architect of the Constitution, expressed a similar view:

> (If) the sense in which the Constitution was accepted and ratified by the Nation . . . be not the guide in expounding it, there can be no security for a faithful exercise of its powers.[45]

This was practically the universal view of constitutional interpretation in the eighteenth and most of the nineteenth centuries. For example, Justice Thomas Cooley wrote,

> The meaning of the Constitution is fixed when adopted, it is not different at any subsequent time. The object of construction, as applied to a written Constitution, is to give effect to the intent of the people adopting it.[46]

43. Thomas Jefferson, *Writings of Thomas Jefferson*, 9 vols. (1853-54), Henry A. Washington, Editor; vol. 4, p. 158, quoted in American Classic Series: Thomas Jefferson, Salt Lake City, Utah: Freemen Institute, 1981), p. 65.

44. George Washington, *American Historical Documents*, New York: Barnes and Noble, Inc., 1960, p. 144.

45. James Madison, *The Writings of James Madison* (G. Hunt ed. 1099-1910), p. 191; quoted by Raoul Berger, *Government by Judiciary*, (Harvard University Press, 1977), p. 364; quoted by William D. Graves, Brief of Defendants, Joann Bell and McCord; The Little Axe Independence School District No. 70 of Cleveland County, in the U.S. District Court for the Western District of Oklahoma, filed May 13, 1982, p. 17.

46. Thomas Cooley, "Constitutional Limitations, pgs. 68-69, quoted by W. Cleon Skousen, *Miracle of America Study Guide*, (Salt Lake City, Utah: Freemen Institute, 1981), p. 144.

This does not mean they worshipped the Constitution. They recognized that it was an imperfect document, and the changing times might require changes. But they believed the Constitution should be changed by the amendment process, not by simply reinterpreting it to mean whatever we want it to mean at the time.

But Chief Justice Warren and his supporters rejected that viewpoint. They agreed with Governor (later Chief Justice) Charles Evans Hughes, when he said, "We are under a Constitution, but the Constitution is what the judges say it is. . . . "[47] Like Justice Hughes, Justice Warren believed the intent of the authors was not controlling; the words of the Constitution take on new meaning as society progresses and matures. In other words, just as men and animals evolve, and the state as an organism evolves, so the Constitution also evolves, and its meaning changes with succeeding generations.

Similar words may be found in Justice Brennan's concurring opinion in the famous death penalty case, *Furman v. Georgia*. It will be recalled that there was no single majority opinion in *Furman*; rather, five separate justices wrote concurring opinions concluding that the death penalty as administered is unconstitutional, but for different reasons. Justice Brennan declared, "The evolution of this punishment evidences, not that it is an inevitable part of the American scene, but that it has proved progressively more troublesome to the national conscience."[48] Four years later, in *Gregg v. Georgia*, the effect of *Furman* was limited. Justice Stewart, writing for the majority, commented:

> Four years ago, the petitioners in *Furman* and its companion cases predicated their argument primarily upon the asserted proposition that standards of decency had evolved to the point where capital punishment could no longer be tolerated. The petitioners in those cases said, in effect, that the evolutionary process had come to an end, and that standards of decency required that the Eighth Amendment be construed finally as prohibiting capital punishment for any crime regardless of its depravity and impact on society. This view was accepted by two Justices. Three other Justices were unwilling to go so far; focusing on the procedures by which convicted defendants were selected for the death penalty rather than on actual punishment inflicted, they joined in the conclusion that the statutes before the Court were constitutionally valid.[49]

Stewart and the majority disagreed with the holding in *Furman*, and contended that capital punishment does not *invariably* violate the Constitution. However, Stewart and his fellow justices did not reject the evolutionary theory of constitutional interpretation; they only rejected the contention that the Constitution had evolved that far at the time. Both the majority and minority fully

---

47. Hughes, quoted by Craig R. Ducat and Harold W. Chase, *Constitutional Interpretation*, third edition, St. Paul, Minnesota, West Publishing Co., 1983, p. 3.

48. *Furman v. Georgia*, 408 U.S. 238 at 299, U.S. 2726 (1972).

49. *Gregg v. Georgia* 428 U.S. 153, 96 Sup. Ct. 2909 (1976).

accepted the evolutionary view of law; they disagreed only on how far law had evolved at that time!

Innocent though it may sound, this evolutionary approach to constitutional rights actually leaves freedom on very shaky ground. For if a constitution can evolve one way, it can evolve the other way as well. If this "evolving standard of decency" can change so as to make society more humane, can it not also evolve so as to make society more barbaric?

What if the Court were to say the following?

> The Defendant claims that his sentence—being slowly boiled in oil until dead—is cruel and unusual in violation of the Eighth Amendment. We recognize that being boiled in oil would have seemed cruel and unusual to the framers of the Eighth Amendment. But our inquiry must not stop there, for those framers lived in the delicate era of the Eighteenth Century. Now, nearly 200 years later, our society has matured. Abortion and euthanasia have become accepted practices. Our soaring crime rates have made violence commonplace, and our movie and television fare show that our society has acquired a taste and even love for violence. The Eighth Amendment must take its meaning from an evolving standard of decency, and given today's standards we can no longer say that being boiled in oil is cruel and unusual punishment.

As the above fictitious "ruling" demonstrates, under an evolving standard of constitutional interpretation, no one's rights are really secure.

So we see two schools of constitutional interpretation: that which views the meaning of the Constitution as fixed by the intent of the framers, and that which assumes the framers' intent as no longer controlling. Speaking for the former view, Justice Frankfurter said, "The ultimate touch-stone of constitutionality is the Constitution itself and not what we have said about it."[50] And speaking for the latter (evolutionary positivist view, New York Governor and later Chief Justice of the U.S. Supreme Court Charles Evans Hughes said, "We are under a Constitution, but the Constitution is what the judges say it is."[51]

One wonders if Justice Hughes, Warren, and the other legal positivists learned their views of jurisprudence from Lewis Carroll's *Through the Looking Glass*:

> "I don't know what you mean by 'glory,' " Alice said.
>
> Humpty Dumpty smiled contemptuously. "Of course you don't—till I tell you. I meant 'there's a nice knock-down argument for you!' "
>
> "But 'glory' doesn't mean 'a nice knock-down argument,' " Alice objected.
>
> "When *I* use a word," Humpty Dumpty said in rather a scornful tone, "it means just what I choose it to mean—neither more nor less."

---

50. *Graves v. O'Keefe*, 306 U.S. 466, 491-492 (1939).

51. Charles Evans Hughes, quoted by Craig R. Ducat and Harold W. Chase, *Constitutional Interpretation*, Third Edition. (St. Paul: West Publishing Co., 1983), p. 3.

"The question is," said Alice, "whether you *can* make words mean different things."

"The question is" said Humpty Dumpty, "which is to be master—that's all."[52]

How about Humpty Dumpty for Chief Justice?

The dangers of subjectivism in such an approach to constitutional law are obvious.

(4) Law is judge-made.

The legal positivist has established (actually, he has only assumed) that law is not God-made.

So who made it? The positivist answers: Men.

But if we may be so bold as to ask, What men? Carpenters? Mechanics? Lawyers? Politicians? The people as a whole?

The positivist answers: To the largest extent, judges.

Jerome Frank summarized it well:

> There is no rule by which you can force a judge to follow an old rule or by which you can predict when he will verbalize his conclusion in the form of a new rule, or by which be can determine when to consider a case an exception to an old rule, or by which he can make up his mind whether to select one or another old rule to explain or guide his judgment. His decision is primary, the rules he may happen to refer to are incidental.
>
> The law, therefore, consists of *decision*, not of rules. If so, then *whenever a judge decides a case he is making law.*[53] (emphasis original)

There is some truth in Professor Frank's statement. The positivists have made it true. By creating a legal climate in which lawyers and judges regard law as man-made rather than God-man, relative rather than absolute, and changing rather than static, the positivists have opened the floodgates to judicial subjectivism, and judges are free to conduct themselves precisely as Professor Frank has described.

(5) The case law method of legal education.

Let's stop for a moment and put all of this together. Positivism is concerned, not with metaphysical realities, but with empirically verifiable truth—hard, testable facts, the "scientific method." Law, we are told, does not exist as abstract metaphysical reality, but only in what is actually pronounced and enforced as the law of the state. And the actual law of the state does not consist of textbooks, legal encyclopedias, or even constitutions and statutes; it consists largely of the decision of the judges.

Now, positivism stresses the scientific method and empirical verification of hard physical data. So, if the hard physical data in the field of law is the decisions of judges, how should one study law? According to Christopher Columbus

---

52. Lewis Carroll, *Through The Looking Glass; The Best of Lewis Carroll* (Secaucus, New Jersey: Castle, n.d.), p. 238.

53. Frank, p. 128.

Langdell, Dean of the Harvard Law School around 1870, and those who followed him, one studies law by studying the decisions of the judges.

One hundred fifty years ago, if one wanted to become a lawyer, he probably would not have gone to law school. Though some law schools existed, most aspiring lawyers "read for the law" by apprenticing themselves to a practicing attorney. Many of the greatest legal minds in history—Sir William Blackstone, Chief Justice John Marshall, Justice Joseph Story, Clarence Darrow and President Abraham Lincoln—became lawyers in this way. Those who did attend law school spent their time studying treatises, commentaries, the Constitution, statutes, works of jurisprudence, etc.

But the "Langdell revolution" has swept the country. In nearly all law schools the primary means of study is the "casebook" method, by which students read the leading decisions by judges in a particular field of law to learn how the legal doctrine has "evolved." Students at many law schools study almost nothing but cases—and graduate almost unaware that other sources of law exist! The introduction and spread of the case-study method, largely through the inspiration of Dean Langdell, has been well-documented by Professor Herbert Titus (a Harvard Law School graduate) in "God, Evolution, Legal Education, and Law," *Journal of Christian Jurisprudence*, 1980, pp. 11-48.

This evolutionary/positivist view of the law has dramatically affected the American legal system in many ways. Let us consider several.

Denial of Human Rights.

The Christian view of human rights has already been documented. The negative commands of Scripture, such as "Thou shalt not kill" and "thou shalt not steal," constitute divine recognition of human rights such as life and property. This is also the view of human rights upon which the American legal system was founded. Thomas Jefferson, who once again, was one of the least orthodox believers among the Founding Fathers, proclaimed in the Declaration of Independence: "We hold these truths to be self-evident"—that is, so commonly accepted among men that a full explanation and defense of them is unnecessary—"that all Men are *created* equal, that they are endowed by their *Creator* with certain unalienable *Rights*, that among these are Life, Liberty, and the Pursuit of Happiness—That to secure these Rights, Governments are instituted among Men. . . . " (emphasis supplied). Jefferson clearly recognized God as the Creator, and that human rights have their source in God and are unalienable—that is, they cannot be taken away.

The creationist, then, has a firm basis for believing in human rights. He believes they are a gift from God, who has created man. But what basis has the evolutionist for believing in human rights? One who believes some form of theistic evolution, might maintain that God has guided the process of evolution and taken man under His special care in some way. But at what point in man's ascent from the primeval mists did he suddenly acquire human rights? Do fish have rights? Do amphibians or reptiles have rights? Do monkeys have rights? How about Java man, Zinjanthropus man, Ramapithecus, Neander-thal, or Cro-Magnon? If human rights exist at all, do they appear full-blown all at once? Or, in accordance with the rest of the theory of evolution, do human rights evolve as man evolves? To maintain some consistency, those who reject natural or God-given law must also reject natural or God-given rights.

The legal positivist viewpoint has the same problem with human rights. Believing that law is man-made and that there is no such thing as God-given or natural law, the positivist likewise has no basis for believing in God-given or natural human rights. In the positivist view, man has no rights; he has only such "privileges" as those in power choose to allow him.

Hallowell says concerning Justice Holmes:

> In the tradition of Hobbes, Bentham and Austin, Justice Holmes conceived of the law as the command of the dominant social group. He rejected the doctrine of natural law and of natural rights and he argued that "no society has ever admitted that it could not sacrifice individual welfare to its own existence." Such thought is more congenial to despotism than it is to the preservation of individual freedom and the rights of man. It did not seem dangerous at the time it was expounded because it was linked to a faith in democratic procedure which could not envisage the use of that procedure to do things which are essentially undemocratic. It was expounded, moreover, by a man whose personal character was beyond reproach. But the recognition that Holmes was a gentleman and an ardent champion of freedom of speech and of press must not obscure the recognition that his underlying philosophy was potentially dangerous to the foundations of the democracy he thought he was defending.[54]

The danger of the evolutionary and positivist approaches—especially when the state is regarded as an evolving organism—is that the state becomes the source of human rights. Notice that Jefferson in the Declaration of Independence did not say that governments give us these rights; God has already given us rights, and the purpose of government is merely to secure them. But if one regards the government as the source of his rights, then freedom is on dangerous ground. For if government can grant rights, it can also take them away. And if one holds, with Spencer, that the state is an evolving organism which becomes increasingly large and complex, then that is the inevitable direction in which government will move.

Denial of Human Responsibility

The creationist has a firm basis for believing in human responsibility. He accepts the Genesis 1 and 2 account of creation which informs us that God gave man dominion over the earth; that is, God placed man over nature. In so doing, God gave him a certain measure of volition in order to exercise control. God gave man freedom and responsibility, and man is accountable to

54. Hallowell, pp. 362-363.

God and to his government for the use he makes of that freedom and responsibility.

But the evolutionist sees man, not as created by God and placed in dominion over nature, but rather as a product of nature and controlled by nature. When evolutionary theory is united, as it generally has been, with environmental determinism, it becomes a basis for believing that man has no real freedom of choice but is merely a product of his heredity and his environment. And if man has no control over what he does, then it follows that he cannot legally or morally be held responsible for what he does. The result is that man, while seeking to free himself from the dominion of God, makes himself a slave of nature, and leaves himself at the mercy of that evolving social organism, the state. Rushdoony's portrayal of the logical conclusion of evolutionary humanism is graphic.

> When man makes himself and his reason god over creation, he thereupon destroys all meaning in creation and leaves himself a chained and jibbering baboon, sitting in terror on a wired electric chair in the midst of a vast universe of nothingness.[55]

(1) Criminal Punishment

We have all heard of the psychologist or sociologist who insists that man has no control over his actions and that society, not the individual, is to blame for crime. Clarence Darrow, who acknowledge the influence of Spencer on his life,[56] used this argument in 1924 when he defended Richard Loeb and Nathan Leopold in what was called "the crime of the century," the wanton murder of a fourteen-year-old boy. In a brilliant closing argument which lasted two days and which succeeded in getting life imprisonment instead of the death penalty for his clients, Darrow insisted that social and intellectual influences had deprived Loeb and Leopold of their ability to make responsible decisions, and therefore they were not fully responsible for their actions. Darrow declared:

> I know that they cannot feel what you and I feel; that they cannot feel the moral shocks which come to men that are educated and who have not been deprived of an emotional system or emotional feelings. I know it, and every person who has honestly studied this subject knows it well. Is Ricky Loeb to blame because out of the infinite forces that conspired to form him, the infinite forces that were at work producing him ages before he was born, that because out of these infinite combinations he was born without it? If he is, then there should be a new definition for justice. . . .
>
> Is there any blame attached because somebody took Neitzsche's philosophy seriously and fashioned his life in it? [The defense contended that Leopold had been corrupted by reading Neitzsche's philosophy of moral nihilism at the University of Chicago.] And there is no question in this

---

55. R. J. Rushdoony, *The Biblical Philosophy of History* (Phillipsburg, New Jersey: Presbyterian and Reformed Publishing Company, 1979), p. 15.

56. Hofstadter, p. 34.

case that it is true. Then who is to blame? The university would be more to blame than he is. The publishers of the book—and Nietzsche's books are published by one of the biggest publishers in the world—are more to blame than he. Your Honor, it is hardly fair to hang a nineteen-year-old boy for the philosophy that was taught him at the university.

Why did they kill little Bobby Franks? Not for money, not for spite, not for hate. They killed him as they might kill a spider or a fly, for the experience. They killed him because they were made that way. Because somewhere in the infinite processes that go to the making up of the boy or the man something slipped, and those unfortunate lads sit here hated, despised, outcasts, with the community shouting for their blood.[57]

This was not merely a sophistic argument that Darrow contrived on behalf of his client. It was basic to Darrow's philosophy. Twenty-two years earlier, he had delivered a speech to the prisoners in the Cook County jail, declaring:

There is no such thing as crime as the word is generally understood. I do not believe there is any sort of distinction between the real moral conditions of the people in and out of jail. One is just as good as the other. The people here can no more help being here than the people outside can avoid being outside. I do not believe that people are in jail because they desire to be. They are in jail simply because they cannot avoid it on account of circumstances which are entirely beyond their control and for which they are in no way responsible.[58]

It is interesting to note that shortly after the Leopold-Loeb trial, Darrow faced Judge Alfred J. Talley of New York's Court of General Sessions in a debate on the issue of capital punishment. Judge Talley had previously criticized Darrow's view, saying: "It is not the criminals, actual or potential, that need a neuropathic hospital. It is the people who slobber over them in an effort to find excuses for their crimes. There are lots of sick people who concern themselves with crime, but the criminals are not numbered among them."[59]

(2) Juvenile Law

This tendency to deny responsibility for crime is especially apparent in juvenile court. The juvenile court movement began in the late 1800s, the same time frame in which the evolutionary views of Darwin and Spencer became prevalent. The pioneers of the juvenile court movement generally believed that, contrary to Christian theology (see Psalms 51:2, 58:3), children are not born in a state of original sin. Rather, as Supreme Court Justice Fortas said concerning the founders of juvenile court:

They believed that society's role was not to ascertain the child was "guilty" or "innocent," but "What is he, how has he become what he is, and what

---

57. Clarence Darrow, quoted in Arthur Weinberg, ed., *Attorney for the Damned* (New York: Simon & Schuster, 1957) p. 35; quoted in Titus, pp. 43-44.

58. Ibid, pp. 3-4.

59. Tierney, pp. 346, 350-351.

had best be done in his interest and in the interest of the state to save him from a downward career.'' The child—essentially good, as they saw it— was to be made ''to feel that he is the object of [the State's] care and solicitude,'' not that he was under arrest or on trial.[60]

These principles are almost universally applied in juvenile court today. The court avoids terms like guilt or innocence, and seeks only to determine whether or not a child is or is not in need of treatment by the juvenile court. In the event the court determines that the child has in fact committed delinquent acts (i.e., crimes in most instances), the court determines, not how should he be punished to pay for his crime, but how can he best be reformed or reintegrated into society. Again we see a denial of human responsibility.

But along with this denial of human responsibility came a denial of human rights and freedoms. As Fortas continued in his opinion: ''The rules of criminal procedure were therefore altogether inapplicable. The apparent rigidities, technicalities, and harshness which they observed in both substantive and procedural criminal law were therefore to be discarded.''[61] Since the court was acting *in loco parentis*, or in place of the parents, the court was to respond to the child's offense or condition as a parent. And since a parent does not read his child the Miranda warnings, provide him with counsel, the right to subpoena witnesses, etc., before disciplining his child, neither did the court. Rather, the court worked in the child's ''best interest,'' and in the process denied the child his liberty and his personhood. The *Gault* decision and several subsequent decisions, while not abandoning the ''best interest of the child'' concept, did nevertheless require that some but not all of the safeguards and rights of adult criminal proceedings be applied to juvenile court as well.

(3) Mental Commitments

The same tendency to de-emphasize human responsibility may be seen in the frequency of commitments to mental hospitals. I am not suggesting that such commitments are never necessary, or that the insanity defense should be entirely eliminated. But I do suggest that mental illness can at times be a deliberate retreat from responsibility, and that commitment in such circumstances can do more harm than good.[62]

Furthermore, the denial of human freedom which accompanies the denial of responsibility can often work to the disadvantage of the wrongdoer. As C. S. Lewis wrote in 1950,

> The concept of desert is the only connecting link between punishment and justice . . . thus we cease to consider what the criminal deserves and consider only what will cure him . . . we have tacitly removed him from the

60. *In re Gault*, 387 U.S. 1, 87 Sup. Ct. 1428, lawyer's edition, 2nd, 527 (1967).

61. Ibid.

62. For a good discussion on this subject see Jay Adams, *Competent to Counsel.* (Grand Rapids, Mich: Baker Book House, 1970).

sphere of justice altogether; instead of a person, a subject of rights, we now have a mere object, a patient, "a case."[63]

There is much truth in what Lewis has to say. While in recent years courts have begun to recognize that mental patients do have certain rights, it is in many instances easier for a county attorney to have a wrongdoer committed than to have him jailed. To have him committed as insane, the prosecutor does not need to prove beyond a reasonable doubt that he is guilty of a crime, only that he is dangerous to himself or others (the exact statutory requirements vary from state to state), and that usually by a lesser burden of proof.

(4) No-Fault Divorce

This denial of responsibility is not limited to criminal justice. In the last ten to fifteen years about one-third of the states have enacted "no-fault" divorce laws, and most others have such grounds as "irreconcilable differences" or "cruel and inhuman treatment" which are often interpreted by the courts to mean essentially the same thing as no-fault divorce. This constitutes a deliberate departure from the traditional view of marriage and divorce. Marriage had traditionally been regarded as a lifelong contract which can be terminated only if one party or the other has breached the contract. The ways in which he could breach the contract varied from state to state, but commonly included cruel and inhuman treatment, desertion, nonsupport, alcoholism, lengthy imprisonment, adultery, etc. In order to obtain a divorce, then, the party seeking the divorce had to prove to the satisfaction of the court that the other party was "at fault," that is, that the other party had breached the contract by committing one of those acts listed above as a ground for divorce.

But no-fault divorce means that neither party has to prove that the other has broken the marriage contract in any way. He need only prove, to use the approximate language of most statutes, that the legitimate objects of matrimony have broken down and there is no reasonable likelihood that they can be restored. In the "modern" view marriage failure is nobody's fault; it is the circumstances; the parties are "incompatible."

In effect, this means that anyone who wants a divorce can get one, regardless of how good his spouse has been or how bad he has been. Even the term "divorce" is often changed to the more innocuous "dissolution of marriage." There may be some practical advantages to the no-fault divorce system (although I personally believe they are greatly overrated and outweighed by disadvantages), but it cannot be denied that no-fault divorce represents a departure from the concept of human responsibility.

(5) No-Fault Insurance

A final area which I will mention concerns "no-fault" insurance. This applies principally to automobile accidents. The traditional view of tort law has been that the party who negligently causes injury or damage to another party must

---

63. C. S. Lewis, *God in the Dock* (Eerdmans: Grand Rapids, Mich.), p. 288; quoted in Titus, p. 45.

pay damages to that person to compensate for the injury or damage. If he had insurance, his insurance company would pay the damages for him, and if the matter involved a lawsuit, his insurance company would generally defend him in court.

No-fault insurance works differently in different states, but essentially it means that if two vehicles have an accident, each party submits a claim to his own insurance company and is paid by his own company, regardless of which party was at fault. Sometimes the insurance company of the innocent party has a right of subrogation (a right to claim against the insurance company of the party who was at fault), sometimes not. There were practical problems with the old system of insurance, though in my opinion those problems could have been worked out by better means than no-fault insurance. But once again, in no-fault insurance we see a departure from human responsibility.

Anarchy

The positivist/evolutionist view of law threatens to lead our nation into anarchy. So long as people regard law as an expression of the divine will, or at least as the expression of definite fixed principles of right and wrong, they are likely to respect and obey it.

But if they regard law as nothing more than the will of those in power, respect for law diminishes and lawlessness increases. There ceases to be any moral compunction to obey the law; rather, law is reduced to a "weighted alternative" whereby one simply weighs the anticipated benefits of breaking the law against the probability and disadvantage of being caught. The jewel thief, for example, might weigh a $5,000 diamond ring against his chances of getting caught, and decide it is worth the risk.

I believe the solution to the rampaging crime in this country today lies not so much in stiffer punishments (although in some cases that, too, is a good idea) but in building respect for law. We might begin by stressing its biblical origins.

Tyranny

But a second and greater danger is tyranny. In fact, the very word *tyranny* comes from the Greek *tyrannos*, which refers to one who rules without the sanction of divine law.[64]

One who rules without God's authority also rules without God's limitations on authority, and he thereby becomes despotic. He intrudes into areas in which he has no jurisdiction, and rides roughshod over the rights of his subjects because he believes they have no rights.

This is the logical consequence of evolution and legal positivism. If there

64. R. J. Rushdoony, *The Nature of the American System* (Thoburn Press, Fairfax, Virginia, 1978) p. 45.

is no higher law, God-given or natural, if law is nothing more or less than what the courts and legislatures say it is, then there can be no such thing as a bad or unjust law, because there is no higher law or authority by which to judge it. The law is right and just because the lawmaker said it is right and just. Man has only such "rights" as the government says he has, and those rights are lost when the government decides to take them away. Rights are limitations upon the power of the state. If there are no God-given or natural rights, there are no limits to the state's jurisdiction other than those which the state sets for itself. Given the tendency of the state to expand its influence, it soon works its way into every aspect of human existence, and the result is totalitarianism. As Hallowell says,

> It is a short step from the conception of law as the product of the will of the state, whether the state be conceived as an instrument for the satisfaction of human desires (utilitarianism) or whether conceived as the personification of the good life (idealism) to the notion that law is the command of the stronger. . . . Since the will of the state has no reality apart from the will of individuals who act in the name of the state the identification of the law with the will of the state amounts in practice to the identification of the law with the will of those who act in the name of the state. . . .
>
> From this point of view every decision is a correct one. There can be no such thing as an incorrect decision nor an unjust one. It is not the content of a decision that makes it law but the source from which it emanates. . . . Ultimately the basis of law is fear and force rather than consent and justice. . . .
>
> As an augury of things to come realistic jurisprudence certainly suggests that tyranny is an inevitability. For the only way out of the intellectual and moral anarchy underlying the realist's conception of the law is tyranny. If force alone, as Justice Holmes believed, is the only possible arbiter of our "deep-seated preferences," if moral judgments are nothing more than expressions of individual taste or preference, and if law, as Jerome Frank declares, is simply what men arbitrarily declare it to be, then we have no choice but to submit our differences to the arena of force. . . . In that arena it is not the best reason that will prevail but the mightiest fist.[65]

It has happened before. As Herbert Schlossberg notes,

> It is no wonder that for the seventy-five years prior to Hitler's rise in power the positivist philosophy of law achieved a standing in Germany that it had attained nowhere else. The German scholars considered it scientific, and thought that, in contrast, Anglo-Saxon law was a mess.[66]

And tyranny generally leads to emperor worship. The failure of humanism

---

65. Hallowell, op. cit., pp. 343, 363-64, 367.

66. Lon L. Fuller, "Positivism and Fidelity to Law—A Reply to Professor Hart," *Harvard Law Review*, Vol. 71, No. 4, February 1958, pp. 630-672; cited by Herbert Schlossberg, *Idols for Destruction* (Nashville: Thomas Nelson, 1983), p. 207.

is that man can worship himself for only so long, before he senses the emptiness of such worship and turns to idolatry instead (Note the progression from self worship to idol worship in Romans 1:21-25). And when government becomes the source of all law and all benefits, men make a "god" out of the state. The tendency toward state worship and emperor worship in pagan tyrannies is very common.[67] As Rushdoony says in *Law and Liberty*,

> Behind every system of law there is a god. To find the god in any system, locate the source of law in that system. If the source of law is the individual, then the individual is the god of that system. If the source of law is the people, or the dictatorship of the proletariat, then these things are the gods of those systems. If our source of law is a court, then the court is our god. If there is no higher law beyond man, then man is his own god, or else his creatures, the institutions he has made, have become his gods. When you choose your authority, you choose your god, and where you look for your law, there is your god.[68]

Is it strange to speak of anarchy and tyranny in the same breath? Not at all. It was the anarchy of the French Revolution that led to Napoleon. In today's America we see both tendencies. Government has retreated from those areas in which it has a right and duty to rule, and the result is anarchy: lack of support for law enforcement, soaring crime, unsafe streets, riots, weakening military defenses, etc. Where government has intruded into those areas where it has no right to be involved, the result is tyranny: Christian parents jailed for sending their children to "unaccredited" schools, farmers and businessmen prosecuted over oppressive government regulations, ad infinitum.

The choice America faces is this: man's anarchy and man's tyranny, or God's liberty and God's law. Christian people must once again become the "salt of the earth" (Matthew 5:13), for if they lose their savor, they are of no value. Salt has two functions: it gives flavor, and it preserves. The role of the believer is to give a Christian flavor to society, and thereby preserve it from destruction.

It is unfortunate that the evangelical church has retreated from this responsibility. Too often, evangelicals have stressed only the salvation of the individual soul (and make no mistake about it, that is the heart of the gospel and the mark of a Christian), and have ignored the implications of God's Word for society and its institutions. As a result, they have largely surrendered the institutions of society to the secular humanists and to Satan himself. But the world is God's world, and it must be reclaimed for Him.

Many born-again Christian lawyers and lawmakers know virtually nothing about the law of God as revealed in His Word and its implications for our society. As a result, except for an occasional testimony, their influence is nil. They are like salt that has lost its savor.

Christian lawyers and lawmakers, as well as Christian voters, need to be

---

67. Henry Parkes, *Gods and Men: The Origins of Western Culture* (New York: Knopf, 1964).
68. R. J. Rushdoony, *Law and Liberty* (Thoburn Press, Fairfax, Virginia, 1971) p. 33.

instructed in the principles of God's law. The church should provide that instruction through its various ministries: the pulpit, the Sunday school classroom, the Christian school and college, the church periodicals, the radio broadcasts and so on. The individual Christian should then carry the principles of God's law into society and put them into effect in society's institutions.

Secular humanists have decried efforts to return to God's law. They denounce those who approach truth by means of God's special revelation as "authoritarian." They attack reliance upon God's law as "authoritarianism."

But the question is, really, which authority do you prefer?—the authority of God, or the authority of men? By rejecting the authority of God, the secular humanists would wittingly or unwittingly impose upon us (and upon themselves) a worse form of authoritarianism than even they have ever dreamed.

We would all do well to remember the admonition of William Penn: "Men must choose to be governed by God or condemn themselves to be governed by tyrants."[69]

---

69. William Penn, quoted by Jeremiah A. Denton, *When Hell Was In Session* (Clover, South Carolina: Commission Press, Riverhills Plantation, 1976), p. 239.

Part 2

The Christian
and
The Constitution

Chapter 7

The Genius of the
American Constitution

God did not speak to the framers of the American Constitution in the same way that He spoke to the authors of Scripture. Unlike Scripture, which is divinely inspired and infallible, the United States Constitution is a human document, the product of fallible men.

But it is nevertheless a work of genius.

President Reagan, speaking in 1979 to an American Farm Bureau Federation Convention in Miami, Florida, cited Lord Acton as saying that the framers of the American Constitution had solved with amazing ease the most perplexing problem of political philosophers throughout the ages: how to endow a government with enough power to preserve public order and govern effectively, yet at the same time restrain that government from unduly infringing upon the liberties of its citizens.[1] And Lord Acton was right—the basic theme of the Constitution is the distribution and limitation of powers and liberties.

The reason power and liberty have been such problems throughout man's history, is the fact of sin. Since people have sin natures, rulers need strong authority to preserve public order. But rulers are also human, and just as sinful as anyone else. Consequently, if given unrestrained power, rulers will tend to tyrannize their subjects. Again Lord Acton put it well: "Power corrupts; absolute power corrupts absolutely."[2]

The founders of this country were well aware of man's true nature. Most of them were Calvinists or at least held a Calvinistic world view, and therefore believed in the total and universal depravity of man. As Dr. Loraine Boettner writes:

---

1. Ronald Reagan, "The Problems We Face in America," speech given at the American Farm Bureau Federation Convention, Miami, Florida, 1979; cassette tape (Salt Lake City, Utah: The Freeman Institute, 1981).

2. Ibid.

It is estimated that of the 3,000,000 Americans at the time of the American Revolution, 900,000 were of Scotch or Scotch-Irish origin, 600,000 were Puritan English, and 400,000 were German or Dutch Reformed. In addition to this the Episcopalians had a Calvinistic confession in their Thirty-nine Articles; and many French Huguenots also had come to this western world. Thus we see that about two-thirds of the colonial population had been trained in the school of Calvin.[3]

Among the remainder of the population were Lutherans and Baptists who would, for the most part, share the Calvinistic emphasis on sin. Others such as Methodists and Catholics, while not going so far as Calvin to emphasize total depravity, nevertheless recognized man's sinful nature. Boettner continues,

"When the fathers of our Republic sat down to frame a system of representative and popular government," says Dr. E. W. Smith, "their task was not so difficult as some have imagined. They had a model to work by.

"If the average American citizen were asked, who was the founder of America, the true author of our great Republic, he might be puzzled to answer. We can imagine his amazement at hearing the answer given to this question by the famous German historian, Ranke, one of the profoundest scholars of modern times. Says Ranke, 'John Calvin was the virtual founder of America.' "

D'Aubigne, whose history of the Reformation is a classic, writes: "Calvin was the founder of the greatest of republics. The Pilgrims who left their country in the reign of James I, and landing on the barren soil of New England, founded populous and mighty colonies, were his sons, his direct and legitimate sons; and that American nation which we have seen growing so rapidly boasts as its father the humble Reformer on the shore of Lake Leman."

Dr. E. W. Smith says, "These revolutionary principles of republican liberty and self-government, taught and embodied in the system of Calvin, were brought to America, and in this new land where they have borne so mighty a harvest were planted, by whose hands?—the hands of the Calvinists. The vital relation of Calvin and Calvinism to the founding of the free institutions of America, however strange in some ears the statement of Ranke may have sounded, is recognized and affirmed by historians of all lands and creeds."

All this has been thoroughly understood and candidly acknowledged by such penetrating and philosophic historians as Bancroft, who far though he was from being Calvinistic in his own personal convictions, simply calls Calvin "the father of America," and adds: "He who will not honor the memory and respect the influence of Calvin knows but little of the origin of American liberty.[4]

3. Loraine Boettner, *The Reformed Doctrine of Predestination* (Philadelphia: Presbyterian & Reformed, 1972), p. 382.

4. Boettner, pp. 389-90.

Even the Roman Catholic scholar Emilio Castelar, Professor of Philosophy at the University of Madrid and later President of the Republic of Spain in 1873, acknowledged:

> It was necessary for the republican movement that there should come a morality more austere than Luther's, the morality of Calvin, and a Church more democratic than the German, the Church of Geneva. The Anglo-Saxon democracy has for its lineage a book of a primitive society—the Bible. It is the product of a severe theology learned by the few Christian fugitives in the gloomy cities of Holland and Switzerland, where the morose shade of Calvin still wanders . . . And it remains serenely in its grandeur, forming the most dignified, most moral and most enlightened portion of the human race.[5]

This does not mean that all those who took a hand in the founding of America were Calvinists, or even orthodox Christians. The majority were, but some were not. Some were Unitarians, though Unitarianism in that day was much closer to orthodox Christianity than it is today. Some were Deists (*not* including Jefferson, Franklin, or Washington,[6] contrary to the suggestion of some), though the influence of Deism has been greatly exaggerated.

---

5. Emilio Castelar, *Harper's Monthly*, June and July 1872; quoted by Boettner, p. 384. For a good discussion of the influence of Calvinism upon America generally, see Boettner, pp. 382-399. Lest this sound unduly biased, I hasten to add that my own theology is more Lutheran than Calvinist.

6. Deism could best be described as the belief that God created the world, established natural laws for its operation, does not intervene in its operation or in human affairs, and has revealed Himself not through Scripture but through nature and human reason. It is often claimed that Thomas Jefferson, Benjamin Franklin, and George Washington were Deists, but this is demonstrably false. Jefferson was not an orthodox Christian, but he also was not a Deist as demonstrated by his many public pronouncements about the role of God in the life of the nation: "I sincerely supplicate that overruling Providence which governs the destinies of men and nations, to dispense His choicest blessings on yourselves and our beloved country." (Henry A. Washington, ed., *The Writings of Thomas Jefferson*, viii:161; quoted in *American Classics: Thomas Jefferson*, Freemen Institute, Salt Lake City, Utah, 1981, p. 110.

Benjamin Franklin says in his *Autobiography* that while a youth he became a "thorough deist" (p. 114). But by 1728, at the age of 22, he began to have doubts: "I began to suspect that this doctrine, though it might be true, was not very useful." (pp. 114-115). And by the time of the Constitutional Convention, at age 82, his views had changed a great deal. During the difficult times of that convention, Franklin moved for daily prayer, saying,

> In the beginning of the contest with Britain, when we were sensible of danger, we had daily prayers in this room for the divine protection. Our prayers, Sir, were heard—and they were graciously answered. . . .
>
> I have lived, Sir, a long time; and the longer I live, the more convincing proofs I see of this truth, that *God governs in the affairs of men*. And if a sparrow cannot fall to the ground without his notice, is it probable that an empire can rise without his aid? We have been assured, Sir, in the sacred writings that 'except the Lord build the house, they labor in vain that build it.' I firmly believe this; and I also believe that, without his concurring aid, we shall succeed in this political building no better than the builders of Babel . . . (*American Classics: The Real Benjamin Franklin*. [Salt Lake City; Freemen Institute, 1982], pp. 40-41, 258-259).

What is important for our purposes today, is not whether the founders were personally regenerate or unregenerate men. What really matters is that their view of the world and of the nature of man was shaped by the Bible. Perhaps not all of them read the Bible regularly, though it was read much more then than it is today. Some of them, as John Warwick Montgomery says, may have "lived precariously off inherited capital"[5]—that is, they inherited a world view that was based on the Bible, even though they themselves did not obtain that world view directly from the Bible but rather from other, more indirect sources. But it was a biblical world view nevertheless, and they shared the biblical view of human sin.

Nor did our founders wish to establish a Christian state. Certainly many of the early colonists did, particularly those in New England. But by the time of the Constitutional Convention it was generally agreed that government—at least, the Federal government—should not be involved with religion to any great extent.

What the founders of our country wanted was not a Christian state, but a government founded upon a biblical world view and a biblical view of human nature. And they recognized that the biblical view of human nature includes human sin.

True to their Calvinistic tradition, the founders recognized that human depravity is total and universal. It applies to everyone, ruler and peasant alike. Common people are sinful, and therefore government is needed to check their sinful tendencies—otherwise they will murder, rape, kidnap and rob each other, and the life, liberty and property of no man will be secure. But government officials are also sinful, and unless their power is held in check, they will become tyrannical and oppressive. James Madison saw the problem clearly:

> But what is government itself but the greatest of all reflections on human nature? If men were angels, no government would be necessary. If angels were to govern men, neither external nor internal controls on government would be necessary. In framing a government which is to be administered by men over men, the great difficulty lies in this: You must first enable the government to control the governed; and in the next place, oblige it to control itself.[8]

Jefferson echoed a similar theme in his First Inaugural address:

Franklin probably never became an orthodox Christian, but clearly he had moved a long way from Deism! Unlike Jefferson and Franklin, George Washington was basically an orthodox Christian. The charges of Deism are thoroughly refuted by his church participation, his person piety, his prayer and reading of Scripture, and his public and private pronouncements. See William J. Johnson, *George Washington the Christian* (Milford, Michigan: Mott Media, 1976).

7. John Warwick Montgomery, *The Shaping of America* (Minneapolis: Bethany House, 1976, 1981), pp. 47-68. Montgomery's book is a worthwhile contribution on the thought of the Founding Fathers, though I believe he overemphasizes Deism and under-emphasizes Christianity.

8. James Madison, *The Federalist No. 51* in *The Federalist Papers* (New York: Mentor, 1961), p. 322.

Sometimes it is said that man cannot be trusted with the government of himself. Can he, then, be trusted with the government of others? Or have we found angles in the forms of kings to govern him? Let history answer this question.[9]

As a result, the founders not only feared anarchy; they also feared excessive government power. As John Adams said, "Power in every form . . . when directed only by human Wisdom and Benevolence is dangerous."[10]

Once gratified, the lust for power fed upon itself and increased. Throughout his life, Adams uttered his warning. It applied to the American as well as to others. As much as he trusted the wisdom of Americans, he recognized that even among them popular powers must be regulated. This could be accomplished, he emphasized, only by balanced governments.

Under every form of government, liberty was constantly threatened by men's love of power. It was, therefore, essential to any stable political system that no man or group of men be permitted to gather a preponderance of power into its own hands. Care must be taken to check and control this tendency. The only maxim of a free government, Adams cautioned, ought to be to trust no man living with power to endanger the public liberty.[11]

The framers of the American Constitution solved the power/liberty dilemma by making sure there was enough power to regulate society, but not too much power concentrated in any one individual or group. Alexander Hamilton stated the view of many:

If government is in the hands of the few, they will tyrannize over the many; if in the hands of the many, they will tyrannize over the few. It ought to be in the hands of both, and they should be separated. This separation must be permanent. Representation alone will not do; demagogues will generally prevail; and, if separated, they will need a mutual check.[12]

The check Hamilton recommended was a limited, constitutional monarchy. But Hamilton's view did not prevail. Instead, the authors of the Constitution chose a system with separation of powers, in which the powers of the federal government are divided between the legislative branch, which makes the laws, the executive branch, which carries out the laws, and the judicial branch, which interprets the laws. The legislative branch was divided into two bodies, the House of Representatives and the Senate. Knowing that governmental bodies

9. Thomas Jefferson, First Inaugural Address, March 4, 1801; reprinted in Saul K. Padover, *The Complete Jefferson: Containing His Major Writings, Published and Unpublished, Except His Letters* (New York: Duell, Sloan & Pearce, Inc., 1943), p. 385.

10. John Adams, "Sui Juris," *Boston Gazette*, 23 May 1768; quoted in *New England Quarterly*, XXXI (1958), p. 97; quoted in John R. Howe, Jr., *The Changing Political Thought of John Adams* (Princeton, New Jersey: Princeton University Press, 1966), p. 90.

11. Howe, p. 90.

12. *Hamilton's Works*, 2:440; quoted in Lord Acton [John Emerich Edward Dalberg Acton], *Essays on Freedom and Power* (London: Meridian, Thames & Hudson, 1956), p. 176.

tend to aggrandize more power for themselves, and to jealously guard their accumulated power against others, the founders wisely placed checks and balances in the Constitution, by which each branch would check the others to prevent one from becoming too powerful. For example, while Congress must pass legislation, the President can veto acts of Congress, subject to being over-ridden by a two-thirds vote of both houses. The President has wide powers, but he is dependent upon legislative appropriations for funding to carry out the duties of his office. The Supreme Court has the power to declare acts of Congress and actions of the President unconstitutional; but Supreme Court justices are appointed by the President, subject to confirmation by the Senate. The founders wisely anticipated that congressmen would be concerned about the dangers of an "imperial presidency"; that the president and his officers would be concerned that Congress was interfering with the president's ability to govern; and both would be concerned about "judicial tyranny" by the Supreme Court. As each branch jealously guards its own power, it prevents the others from becoming too powerful.

But this represents only a horizontal separation of powers within the federal government. In addition, the founders established a vertical division of powers, in which certain powers were delegated to the federal government (legislative, executive and judicial), and other powers reserved for the states and local communities. As we shall see later, the Tenth Amendment makes unmistakably clear (to all except those who are determined not to see it) that ours is a system of delegated powers, and that the federal government has only those powers which have been delegated to it by and through the Constitution. Any powers not delegated by the Constitution to the federal government are reserved by the Constitution for the states, or for the people.

The founders also established a system of representative government. Ultimately, all public officials are responsible to the people, directly or indirectly. Supreme Court justices, of course, are not directly elected, but appointed by the president who was chosen by electors from each state. Yet the Constitution does not place absolute power in the hands of a majority of the people.

It is a mistake, technically speaking, to say that the United States of America is a democracy. At least, that was not the intention from the beginning. Democracy can be defined in many ways. The first definition listed by *Webster's Third New International Dictionary* is "government by the people: rule of the majority."[13] Other definitions are also listed, because of the loose way the term has been used; but the true idea of democracy is absolute majority rule. It comes from the Greek terms *demos*, meaning people, and *kratos*, meaning ruler. Democracy, then, means rule of the people, or the people as rulers. But it was never the intention of the framers of the Constitution to give all power to the people, any more than to give all power to the government or a branch of government.

13. *Webster's Third New International Dictionary*, 1976 ed., s.v. Democracy.

It would be more accurate to say that the founders intended to establish a constitutional republic, not a democracy. Justice Story, whose commentaries on the Constitution played an important role in shaping American constitutional thought in the nineteenth century, wrote:

> I would say in a republican government the fundamental truth, that the minority have indisputable and inalienable rights; that the majority are not everything, and the minority nothing; that the people may not do what they please.''[14]

The American constitutional republic is different from a democracy in several respects. First, as we have noted, it does not place all power in any branch of government, level of government, or even in the people.

Second, while it provides for representative government, the right to vote is limited to those who are qualified to vote. In most of the colonies, the right to vote was limited to those who were male, of voting age (normally 21 at that time), property owners, and of the white race. In addition, poll taxes and literacy tests were occasionally imposed. The trend of the past two centuries has been toward expanding the right to vote in almost every category listed above. In some respects this is justified, but in others it could lead to an irresponsible electorate.

Also, many public officials are elected indirectly. United States senators, for example, were not elected directly by the voters of their respective states until 1915, when the Seventeenth Amendment was ratified. Previously, senators had been appointed by the state governments. And the president is still not directly elected. Rather, the voters vote for electors, who meet in the electoral college and cast their votes for the president and vice-president. There is presently a move to establish direct popular elections for the office of the presidency. That was not the intention of the framers of the Constitution.

But more significantly, even those who have the right to vote do not have absolute power. The minority has certain constitutional rights that even an absolute majority cannot abrogate, even if they gain control of all branches and levels of government. The framers of the Constitution were very concerned that minority rights be fully protected. They were afraid that a democracy could become a ''mobocracy'' which would result in a ''tyranny of the majority.'' As Hamilton said:

> Gentlemen say that we need to be rescued from the democracy. But by what means proposed? A democratic Assembly is to be checked by a democratic Senate, and both these by a democratic chief magistrate.[15]

Hamilton's point was well taken. Even if the powers of government were separated among different levels and different branches, if an intolerant majority

---

14. Justice Story; quoted in Acton, p. 184.
15. *Hamilton's Works*, 2:415; quoted in Acton, p. 185.

were to gain control of all branches and all levels of government, it could use the powers of government to suppress the rights of the minority. The minority needed specific protection of its constitutional rights.

Madison did not always agree with Hamilton, but on this point he did agree:

> The regulation of these various and interfering interests forms the prin-
> cipal task of modern legislation, and involves the spirit of party and faction
> in the necessary and ordinary operations of the government. . . . When
> a majority is included in a faction, the form of popular government enables
> it to sacrifice to its ruling passion or interest both the public good and the
> rights of other citizens. . . . It is of great importance in a republic not only
> to guard the society against the oppression of its rulers, but to guard one
> part of the society against the injustice of the other part. Different interests
> necessarily exist in different classes of citizens. If a majority be united by
> common interests, the rights of the minority will be insecure.[16]

But the means the founders chose to safeguard the rights of the minority and to limit the powers of government were different from those proposed by either Madison or Hamilton. They were, first, a careful system of delegated powers; that is, the principle was firmly established that the federal government had *only* such powers as were delegated to it by the Constitution, and those powers not delegated were reserved to the states. Second, certain limitations were expressly written in the Constitution, such as the prohibitions against a bill of attainder, suspension of the right of habeas corpus, ex post facto laws, letters of marque and reprisal, and other prohibitions which limit the power of government. Still other limitations were enumerated in the Bill of Rights. As we shall see, many of the founders took the position that the Bill of Rights was unnecessary because the federal government had no powers other than those delegated to it by the Constitution, and there was no point in prohibiting the government from doing that which it had no power to do. But others were concerned that this principle could be overlooked, and consequently the Bill of Rights was added to the Constitution in 1791. Among other things, the Bill of Rights limits the government's power to interfere with freedom of religion, free speech, free press, freedom of assembly, the right to bear arms, the right to be secure in one's home, the privilege against self-incrimination, the right to due process of law, the right to a speedy and public trial by jury with confrontation and cross-examination of witnesses and compulsory process for attaining witnesses in his favor and assistance of counsel, the right to be free from excessive bail or cruel or unusual punishment, and other rights retained by the people at common law.

These are rights all American citizens possess. They are rights which even an overwhelming majority of the population cannot deny to a small and despised minority. Let us suppose that a Christian majority wanted to outlaw the Jehovah's Witnesses, and successfully pressured Congress into doing so. Such

---

16. *James Madison*, quoted in Acton, p. 183.

law would be struck down by the Supreme Court as a violation of the First Amendment, which protects the free exercise of religion. The same would be true of laws which attempt to deny Republicans the right to trial by jury, Lutherans the right to free speech, or anarchists the right to be secure in their homes and persons. The majority rules in the United States of America, in the sense that public officials are directly or indirectly chosen by the people. But the majority cannot infringe upon the constitutional rights of the minority.

Over the past two centuries, America has moved at an ever-accelerating pace, from the constitutional republican framework upon which our country was founded, toward a pure democracy. Constitutional restraints are frequently declared relative, rather than absolute, and then more increasingly relative, until finally rendered nullities. Limitations on the franchise have gradually disappeared and are now practically nonexistent, except for age, and even that has been chipped away. As this happens, government grows ever stronger, ever larger, and because as its limitations are erased, its power ever grows. One of the most important works on the American system of government was written by Alexis de Tocqueville. A French scholar and political scientist, de Tocqueville traveled throughout America in 1831 and 1832 to study the American people and their institutions. He returned to France, highly impressed with what he had seen, and wrote at length about America. But one of the gravest dangers he foresaw was that America would someday lose its freedom, not through dictatorship, but through the tyranny of a totalitarian majority. De Tocqueville's words are worth quoting:

> I seek to trace the novel features under which despotism may appear in the world. The first thing that strikes the observation is an innumerable multitude of men all equal and alike, incessantly endeavouring to procure the petty and paltry pleasures with which they glut their lives. . . .
>
> Above this race of men stands an immense and tutelary power, which takes upon itself alone to secure their gratifications, and to watch over their fate. That power is absolute, minute, regular, provident, and mild. It would be like the authority of a parent, if, like that authority, its object was to prepare men for manhood; but it seeks on the contrary to keep them in perpetual childhood: it is well content that the people should rejoice, provided they think of nothing but rejoicing. For their happiness such a government willingly labours, but it chooses to be the sole agent and only arbiter of that happiness: it provides for their security, foresees and supplies their necessities, facilitates their pleasures, manages their principal concerns, directs their industry, regulates the descent of property, and subdivides their inheritances—what remains, but to spare them all the care of thinking and all the trouble of living?
>
> Thus it every day renders the exercise of the free agency of man less useful and less frequent; it circumscribes the will within a narrower range, and gradually robs a man of all the uses of himself. The principle of equality has prepared men for these things: it has predisposed men to endure them, and oftentimes to look on them as benefits.

After having thus successively taken each member of the community in its powerful grasp, and fashioned them at will, the supreme power then extends its arm over the whole community. It covers the surface of society with a network of small complicated rules, minute and uniform, through which the most original minds and the most energetic characters cannot penetrate, to rise above the crowd. The will of man is not shattered, but softened, bent, and guided: men are seldom forced by it to act, but they are constantly restrained from acting: such a power does not destroy, but it prevents existence; it does not tyrannize, but it compresses, enervates, extinguishes, and stupefies a people, till each nation is reduced to nothing better than a flock of timid and industrious animals, of which government is the shepherd.

I have always thought that servitude of the regular, quiet, and gentle kind which I have just described, might be combined more easily than is commonly believed with some of the outward forms of freedom; and that it might even establish itself under the wing of the sovereignty of the people.

Our contemporaries are constantly excited by two conflicting passions; they want to be led, and they wish to remain free: as they cannot destroy either one or the other of these contrary propensities, they strive to satisfy them both at once. They devise a sole, tutelary, and all-powerful form of government, but elected by the people. They combine the principle of centralization and that of popular sovereignty; this gives them a respite: they console themselves for being in tutelage by the reflection that they have chosen their own guardians. Every man allows himself to be put in leading-strings, because he sees that it is not a person or a class of persons, but the people at large that holds the end of his chain.[17]

Let us stop and reflect for a moment. In previous chapters we have examined the rise of legal positivism. Modern jurisprudence proclaims that there are no absolute, fixed principles of higher law; the only law there is is that which is made by men, and that mostly by judges. We see the courts rendering the Ninth and Tenth Amendments as constitutional nullities, and allowing government to intervene in areas the framers of our Constitution believed were beyond the government's jurisdiction. Increasingly we hear the cry, "All power to the people!", a slogan which sounds like freedom but really means tyranny. The legal positivists and the radical democrats have one thing in common: they both make man the supreme authority, the supreme power, and the supreme source of law.

How, then, can we preserve freedom in an orderly society? The legal positivists answer, "All power to the rulers!" The radical democrats answer, "All power to the people!" They both say in common, "All power to man!"

But over and above their cries stand the timeless words of President John

---

17. Alexis de Tocqueville, *On Democracy, Revolution, and Society: Selected Writings*, ed. John Stone and Stephen Mennell (Chicago: University of Chicago Press, 1980), pp. 375-376.

Adams: "The very definition of a republic is 'an empire of laws, and not of men.' "[18]

If we are to remain free, we must recognize and reassert that the United States was not intended to become and should not become a democracy; rather it was designed as a constitutional republic. Furthermore we must recognize and reassert that the ultimate authority of the American system does not rest in the majority, or even in the people as a whole, but in law—the law of God as revealed to man through His special and general revelation, and as applied by God's ministers in civil government (Romans 13:1-7) through the Constitution and laws of the United States.

To remain free, we must reassert the primacy of law.

18. Adams, "Thoughts on Government," *Works*, 4:106, 194; quoted in Howe, p. 91.

Chapter 8

The Background
of the First Amendment

Hegel once noted that the spread of freedom in the world has largely coincided with the spread of Christianity.[1] The reason is that in pagan societies the state generally recognizes no limit whatsoever on its power. Its rulers often deify the state or themselves and become the object of worship. In the Hammurabi code of laws of ancient Babylon, the pantheon of the gods is listed along with the various civil laws, and in ancient Greece and Rome, as in most other pagan societies, the chief civil figure and chief religious figure were generally the same.[2]

Today, many of the most strident advocates for separation of church and state are strongly anti-Christian. They often fail to realize that separation of church and state, and the entire concept of limited government, is a uniquely Judeo-Christian idea. Even though many civil libertarians have left the traditional faith, their views on church-state relations have developed from the very Judeo-Christian culture they now reject.

In most pagan cultures, church and state were one. The king was not only head of the state but also head of the church, with no distinction between these offices. The unity of the state was founded on a common religion, and the king was frequently considered to be either a demigod, a descendent of a god, or a god himself. Emperor worship and state worship were the order of the day.

This was particularly true of ancient Rome. As Waring notes,

> In the history of Rome there was a time when the word of Caesar was the
> law and the worship of Caesar was the religion of the world. As Pontifex
> Maximus he was the high priest of the national religion. He held control

1. Omar Gjerness, *Knowing Good from Evil* (to be published), p. 99.
2. Leo Pfeffer, *Church, State and Freedom* (Boston: Beacon Press, 1953), pp. 3-4.

of both church and state in his own person. Indeed, in a large sense, he was the state, and he was the church.[3]

Other religions received a considerable measure of toleration. People could generally worship whatever additional gods they wished, so long as they worshiped the emperor and gave their supreme allegiance to the state. If Christians could have proclaimed Christ as just another god, they would have had little opposition from Rome. The anger of the authorities was aroused by the exclusiveness of their claim: "Thou shalt have no other gods before me." (Exodus 20:3).

In a world accustomed to Caesar worship, the Christian view sounded very strange indeed: a kingdom that is not of this world, a God who had ordained Caesar but given him only limited authority, a suffering Servant who died on a cross but who will come again in glory as King of Kings and Lord of Lords to rule all nations with a rod of iron. But Christianity spread coterminous with freedom. Let us examine its biblical and historical basis.

The Biblical Background

Old Testament Israel was a theocracy.

That term is commonly used today in reference to a society in which the church rules the state, but that is not its true meaning. The word actually comes from two Greek words, *theos* meaning God, and *kratos* meaning ruler. Theocracy, then, is a society ruled by God.

Old Testament Israel did not practice separation of church and state as we practice it today. But the concepts of separation and limited government have their roots even in the Old Testament.

Before the time of King Saul, Israel was governed by judges. The office of judge was distinct from the offices of prophet and priest. The priests, it will be recalled, came only from the tribe of Levi, but nearly all of the judges—Joshua, Othniel, Ehud, Shamgar, Deborah, Barak, Gideon, Abimelech, Tolah, Jair, Jephthah, Ibzan, Elon, Abdon and Samson—came from various other tribes including Ephraim, Judah, Benjamin, Naphtali, Manasseh, Zebulon, and Dan. On rare occasions the same person held both offices and possessed the office of prophet or gift of prophecy as well. But these were exceptions rather than the rule (Moses and Samuel are the only two), and it seems to have occurred only in times of dire need in Israel.

After the establishment of the monarchy, the distinction became even clearer. The kings always came from the tribe of Judah, while the priests continued to come from the tribe of Levi. A king could not be a priest, and a priest could not be a king. On at least two occasions Israel's king tried to usurp the functions of the priesthood—and was severely punished by God! In battle with the

---

3. Luther Hess Waring, *The Political Theories of Martin Luther* (Port Washington, New York: Kennikat Press, Inc., 1910, 1968), p. 2.

Philistines, King Saul waited seven days for Samuel to reach Gilgal to the peace offering. When Samuel didn't appear, Saul went ahead and offered it himself. As a result, God cut Saul's line off from the kingship of Israel (I Samuel 13). Later, King Uzziah became proud and tried to burn incense upon the altar. In punishment, God smote him with leprosy, and he remained diseased the rest of his life (II Chronicles 26:16-21). In these passages God's clear message to civil rulers is to keep their hands off the church!

Jesus shed further light on the "two kingdoms" concept when He answered the Pharisees' question about paying tribute to Caesar. Even their question, "Is it lawful for us to give tribute unto Caesar, or not?" (Luke 20:22) seems to imply a higher standard of "lawfulness"—God's law—by which Caesar's demands are to be judged. And while Jesus confirmed that the requirement of tribute was within Caesar's jurisdiction, He implied that some things are beyond Caesar's control: "Render, therefore, unto Caesar the things which are Caesar's, and unto God the things which are God's" (Luke 20:25). Lord Acton has recognized in this charge a clear declaration of the authority of the state but also of its limits.

> When Christ said "Render unto Caesar the things that are Caesar's and unto God the things that are God's," He gave to the State a legitimacy it had never before enjoyed, and set bounds to it that had never yet been acknowledged. And He not only delivered the precept but He also forged the instrument to execute it. To limit the power of the State ceased to be the hope of patient, ineffectual philosophers and became the perpetual charge of a universal church.[4]

The "Two Kingdoms" Concept In Church History

The relationship of church and state has received much attention throughout history. There have been many different perspectives on the subject, but let us identify four basic positions.

The Catholic View

Catholic theologians have generally recognized the two kingdoms and the distinct role played by each. But they have usually considered the church to be the greater kingdom and the state to be the lesser kingdom, because the church is eternal while the state is only temporary (Augustine's explanation), and because the church must answer to God for the conduct of the state. As Pope Gelasius I declared to the Roman Emperor in 496 A.D.:

> There are two things, most august emperor, by which this world is chiefly ruled: the sacred authority of the priesthood and the royal power. Of these two the priests carry the greater weight, because they will have to render

---

4. Lord Acton, quoted by Gertrude Himmelfarb (London, 1955), p. 45; in E. L. Hebden Taylor, *The Christian Philosophy of Law, Politics, and the State* (Nutley, New Jersey: Craig Press, 1966), pp. 445-446.

account in the divine judgement even for the kings of men.[5]

Some argued that the power of the keys given to Peter in Matthew 16:19 gave the church the authority to control the state. Many medieval theologians saw the church's authority in the two swords of Luke 22:38. One of these swords is the sword of the church, to be wielded by the church, and the other is the sword of the state, to be given by the church to the state. As Pope Boniface VIII decreed in his papal bull, *Unam Sanctum*, in 1302 A.D.:

> We are told by the word of the gospel that in this His fold there are two swords,—a spiritual, namely, and a temporal. For when the apostles said "Behold here are two swords"—when, namely, the apostles were speaking in the church—the Lord did not reply that this was too much, but enough. Surely he who denies that the temporal sword is in the power of Peter wrongly interprets the word of the Lord when He says: "Put up thy sword in its scabbard." Both swords, the spiritual and the material, therefore, are in the power of the church; the one, indeed, to be wielded for the church, the other by the church; the one by the hand of the priest, the other by the hand of kings and knights, but at the will and sufferance of the priest. One sword, moreover, ought to be under the other, and the temporal authority to be subjected to the spiritual. For when the apostle says "there is no power but of God, and the powers that are of God are ordained," they would not be ordained unless sword were under sword and the lesser one, as it were, were led by the other to great deeds.[6]

Still others looked to a medieval document known as the Donation of Constantine, by which the Roman Emperor Constantine I supposedly gave the Western Roman Empire into the hands of Pope Sylvester I. For centuries popes and other officials relied upon this document, but today even Catholics generally regard it as a forgery.[7]

In this view, the relationship of church to state and to believers and unbelievers could be conceptualized by the following diagram:

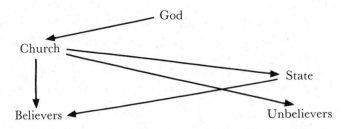

5. Gelasius I, cited by M. Searle Bates, *Religious Liberty: An Inquiry* (New York: International Missionary Council, 1945), p. 134; quoted in Pfeffer, p. 13.

6. Pope Boniface VIII, *Unam Sanctum*, 1304 A.D., printed in Ernest F. Henderson, *Select Historical Documents of the Middle Ages* (New York: Biblo & Tannen, 1965), pp. 435-37.

7. W. Ullman, "Donation of Constantine," *New Catholic Encyclopedia* (New York: McGraw-Hill, 1967), 4:1000-1001.

The Anabaptist View

We must be careful to distinguish the Anabaptists of the Reformation, led by men such as Menno Simmons, from today's Baptists. The former are in many ways the spiritual ancestors of today's Baptists, but like many families, they have undergone many changes over the generations. In their views of church-state relations, most Baptists in America today would find themselves closer to Luther and Calvin than to the early Anabaptists, though there are many strains of opinion among Baptists and Anabaptists then and now.

Many of the early Anabaptists believed that the state was part of the evil world system from which believers were to separate. They regarded the state as worldly and satanic; if Satan was not actually the founder of the state, he had at least taken control of it. Consequently, believers were to separate themselves from the state as much as possible; they were not to vote, hold public office, serve in the armed forces, or involve themselves with government in any other way. As a matter of public testimony they were to obey the state except where inconsistent with God's Word; but the state had no real authority over believers, nor did the church have any authority over unbelievers. In the extreme Anabaptist model, the lines of authority could be conceptualized as follows:

As indicated earlier, most modern Baptists would not accept the Anabaptist model, but it does have varying degrees of adherence among some "peace" churches and "brethren" groups.

The Calvinist View

Unlike some of the Anabaptists, Calvin recognized that the authority of the state comes from God. Unlike many Catholic theologians, Calvin believed that authority came directly from God to the state rather than through the church. The believer was a citizen of both kingdoms and under the authority of both the state and the church. However, the state's authority over the believer was limited to that which God had given to the state; if the state stepped beyond that authority, it acted without legitimacy, and believers were to resist.

Furthermore, the mission of the church was to renovate the world, including the state, according to Christian concepts. And the state was to assist the church in Christianizing the world. Consequently, Calvin served as a political leader as well as a church leader in Geneva, and he saw no problem in using the machinery of the state to further his version of Christianity by punishing heretics, etc. Here is the Calvinist model:

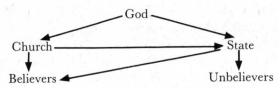

The Lutheran View

Of the three views just discussed, Luther's view was closest to that of Calvin. Since Luther had been an Augustinian monk, he was greatly influenced by Augustine's view that the purpose of the state was to restrain man's sin nature. Like Calvin, he recognized that the church and the state are each ordained by God. Also in agreement with Calvin, he recognized that believers belonged to both kingdoms, the church and the state, and had responsibilities to each. But unlike Calvin, he hesitated to impose Christian precepts upon an unbelieving world. Luther distinguished between faith and reason, and believed that Christians relate to the first kingdom (the church) primarily by means of faith in divine revelation, and to the second kingdom (the state) primarily by means of reason. In theology he emphasized reason less strongly than Calvin, but in politics he emphasized reason more strongly than Calvin. Luther even went so far as to say that if he were faced with the choice between a ruler who was prudent and bad and another who was good but imprudent, he would choose the prudent and bad, because the good by his imprudence would throw everything into disorder, whereas the prudent, however bad, would have enough sense to restrain evil.[8]

Luther's primary difference with Calvin, then, would be that he did not believe Christians had the right to use the state to promote Christianity and to Christianize the world. Christians in government could invoke Christian principles in the affairs of state, only to the extent that those Christian principles could be defended and justified by natural reason. The Lutheran model would look like this:

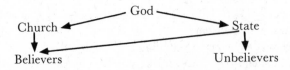

My own view is somewhere between those of Luther and Calvin. Luther possibly drew too sharp a distinction between faith and reason, for the two need not be incompatible. Faith may transcend reason, but faith need not contradict reason.

8. Martin Luther, *Weimarer Ausgabe* I, p. 535, cited by Roland Bainton, *Christian Attitudes Toward War and Peace: A Historical Study and Critical Re-evaluation* (Nashville: Abington, 1950, pp. 137-138).

Since God has revealed Himself and His will through the Scriptures, I would not hesitate to use the authority of Scripture in the political arena. Knowing, however, that in the political arena I will be dealing to a large extent with unregenerate men, I would also be prepared to defend my position with sound reasoning and empirical evidence. And while I would be hesitant to use the power of the state to advance the goals of the church, I would strongly resist efforts by the state to combat the church or to promote non-Christian religions. One of the greatest dangers in America today is the establishment of the religion of secular humanism, particularly in the public schools. Unfortunately, our courts and legislatures have often mistaken secularism for neutrality.

The Reformation

The Reformation did not immediately bring toleration; rather, at first it brought wars of religion. As a result of one such war, it was agreed at the Peace of Augsburg (1555) that the various "mini-states" of Germany would each follow the religion chosen by its prince. Most of the northern princes chose Lutheranism for their states, and most of the southern princes chose Catholicism for their kingdoms. After the Thirty Years War, the Peace of Westphalia (1648) reached a similar agreement that included a wider area and included Calvinists as well as Lutherans and Catholics. For the most part, neither the Catholics, Lutherans, nor Calvinists were much interested in granting toleration to the Anabaptists and other such groups.

England remained Catholic until 1534, when King Henry VIII called the members of Parliament together and ordered them to declare that the king was the supreme head of the Church of England. Henry VIII's dispute with the Catholic Church was not over doctrine. He was thoroughly Catholic in his beliefs, and the pope had given him the title "defender of the faith" for writing a book defending the sacraments and opposing Martin Luther. Henry VIII left the Catholic Church because he wanted to marry Anne Boleyn, and the pope refused to annul his marriage to Katherine of Aragon. At first, the Church of England was doctrinally in accord with the Catholic Church on nearly every issue, and even today is probably closer to Catholicism than any other Protestant body. But it gradually became more Calvinistic under the influence of Presbyterians and Puritans.

Elizabeth, who reigned from 1558 to 1603, held the title, "Supreme Governor of this Realm as well as in all Spiritual or Ecclesiastical things or causes as temporal." Seeking to make the Church of England more acceptable to the Calvinists, she issued the Articles of Religion, Article 31, which declared the Mass to be a "blasphemous fable and dangerous deceit." Nevertheless, within limits Elizabeth tried to create an environment in which the various religious factions of England could all function and believe within the framework of the Anglican Church, though at times she ruthlessly suppressed those who insisted on remaining outside the Church of England.

This policy continued under James I who ruled from 1603 to 1625, and

Charles I who succeeded him until 1649. The Cromwells governed England from 1649 to 1659, on behalf of a coalition of various groups within a Puritan framework. Cromwell extended a policy of toleration to all except Catholics and "extremist" Protestant groups who refused to work within his Puritan framework.[9]

When the Stuarts were restored to the throne in 1660, Charles II declared:

> We do declare a liberty to tender consciences; and that no man shall be disquieted or called in question, for differences of opinion in matters of religion which do not disturb the peace of the kingdom . . . [10]

Parliament, however, was concerned that Charles was pro-Catholic and would lead a return to Catholicism. Between 1660 and 1672 Parliament passed acts ejecting dissenting clergymen from their posts in the Church of England, forbidding those of other religions to serve as municipal officials or in the national, civil, military, or parliamentary service; prohibiting meetings of dissenting churches; and even preventing Separatist clergymen from approaching towns in which they had once preached. Charles II on several occasions asked Parliament to show toleration, but in 1681 Parliament passed a Toleration Bill and Charles rejected it.[11]

The uneasy peace between Charles and the Protestants ended abruptly in 1685 when James II, an avowed Roman Catholic, succeeded him to the throne. James tried to appease the Protestants by issuing the Declaration of Indulgence in 1687, but in the Glorious Revolution the Protestants dethroned him and invited William and Mary of Holland to take the throne.

William and Mary were champions of Calvinism, but also sincere believers in religious toleration. As a result, a Toleration Act was passed in 1689 which, except for a brief interval under Queen Anne (1702-1714), resulted in a continuing policy of toleration through the American War for Independence and even up to the present time. It is interesting to note that, among the many grievances against England listed by the colonists in the Declaration of Independence, religious intolerance is not mentioned.

There is, however, a major difference between religious tolerance and religious liberty. For one thing, the Church of England remained the established church, supported by public taxation. Those who did not want to belong to the Church of England were allowed to go elsewhere at their own expense.

But second and more important, tolerance does not mean that the state has no jurisdiction over religion; it means only that the state for some reason has decided not to exercise its right to control religion at the present time, reserving, of course, the privilege of doing so in the future.

9. Ralph Barton Perry, *Puritanism and Democracy* (New York: Vanguard Press, 1944), pp. 344-347.

11. Charles II, quoted in William Penn, *England's Present Interest Discover'd* (London, 1675), pp. 49-50; quoted in Perry, p. 348.

11. Loren P. Beth, *The American Theory of Church and State* (Gainesville, Florida: University of Florida Press, 1958), pp. 22-23.

Religious liberty, on the other hand, is a very different concept. Religious liberty goes hand-in-hand with limited government, for it means that government has no jurisdiction to regulate religion. Under religious liberty I am free to worship God according to the dictates of my conscience, not because the government has decided to tolerate my doing so, but because government has no right to interfere with my worship of God even if it wanted to. As Beth says, "Toleration is a concept of expedience, liberty is a concept of rights."[12]

Religious Liberty in the American Colonies

Americans are fond of saying that our forefathers came to this country to find religious liberty.

But this is not entirely accurate. True, most of them came to America because of persecution in England. They came because they wanted the right to worship God as they believed He should be worshiped. But most of them were not particularly eager to grant that freedom to others.

This was particularly true in Puritan New England. The Pilgrims and Puritans are often identified with each other, and after 1691, when Plymouth merged with the rest of Massachusetts, the differences between them gradually disappeared. But at first, substantial differences existed.

The Pilgrims were Separatists. They believed the Church of England was so lax, so corrupt, and so permeated with false doctrine, they had no choice but to separate from it. For this they were persecuted in England, so they migrated to Holland and, later, to Plymouth, Massachusetts in 1620.

The Puritans shared the Pilgrims' Calvinist theology, and agreed with their complaints about the Church of England. But while the Pilgrims believed they should leave the Church of England, the Puritans believed they should remain in the church and work to "purify" it; hence their title.

Why did they come to America? To prove that a theocracy could be run according to strict Puritan standards. Many did not intend to stay long; many intended to return to England at some future time and continue the battle to "purify" the church.[13]

It is important to understand that the Puritans did not come to America because the Church of England was too intolerant or too strict. They came because the Church of England was too tolerant and too lax. They left England not because England was a theocracy, but because England's theocracy was too corrupt and worldly. They came to America to show England and the world how to establish and run a true theocracy.

The early colonists lived in the shadow of the Reformation. The Mayflower sailed in 1620, only 103 years after Luther posted the *Ninety-Five Theses* on the door of Wittenberg Castle, and only 63 years after the death of John Calvin.

---

12. Beth, p. 27.

13. Dr. J. Steven O'Malley, Lectures, "Theology and Jonathan Edwards," Oral Roberts University, Autumn 1982.

And Calvin had stressed that the state should aid the church in promoting the Kingdom of God.

Calvin was an amillennialist, that is, he did not believe there would be a literal thousand year reign of Christ on earth. But among the New England Calvinists the postmillennial view gradually became prevalent, and the Puritans believed they were establishing God's kingdom on earth, here in this American wilderness, the new promised land. They saw a holy purpose to this colony. They were to be the community of the redeemed, the city upon a hill, the example to other nations of what a truly Christian commonwealth could be, and in many ways similar to Israel itself.

The Pilgrims' pastor, John Robinson, drew this comparison between Old Testament Israel and their new colony:

> Now as the people of God in old time were called out of Babylon civil, the place of their bodily bondage, and were to come to Jerusalem, and there to build the Lord's temple, or tabernacle . . . so are the people of God now to go out of Babylon spiritual to Jerusalem . . . and to build themselves as lively stones into a spiritual house, or temple, for the Lord to dwell in.[14]

Similar themes were echoed by the Puritans, who began the settlement of Massachusetts in 1630. As they approached New England, their leader, John Winthrop, declared,

> We shall find that the God of Israel is among us, when ten of us shall be able to resist a thousand of our enemies, when He shall make us a praise and glory, that men of succeeding plantations shall say, ''The Lord made it like that of New England.'' For we must consider that we shall be as a City upon a Hill. . . .[15]

As they left England, pastor John Cotton preached a farewell sermon on II Samuel 7:10. The renowned historian Samuel Eliot Morison says,

> Cotton's sermon was of a nature to inspire these new children of Israel with the belief that they were the Lord's chosen people; destined, if they kept the covenant with Him, to people and fructify this new Canaan in the western wilderness.[16]

One can easily see how this theology affected their view of church and state.

However, other elements in Puritan theology laid the groundwork for liberty and republican government in America. The Calvinistic doctrine of the total

14. John Robinson, quoted by Peter Marshall, Jr., and David Manuel, Jr., *The Light and the Glory* (Old Tappan, New Jersey: Revelle, 1977), p. 110.

15. John Winthrop, *Winthrop Papers II* quoted by Marshall and Manuel, p. 162.

16. Samuel Eliot Morison, quoted by Marshall and Manuel, p. 157. The reader should not infer from the above quotations that I endorse British-Israelism. I use these quotations only to demonstrate the mindset of the early colonists and to show how this mindset influenced the First Amendment.

depravity of man is a great leveler, for it means that rulers as well as the common people are unable to please God by their own merits and are in need of God's grace. Because of their belief in original sin and total depravity, the Puritans distrusted concentration of power in the hands of any ruler or body of rulers, and this formed the basis for our system of limited government and separation of powers. Their congregational system of church government, though not always fully practiced in Massachusetts, provided a model for representative and republican government. The Reformation concept of the priesthood of all believers, which holds that each man can come directly to God through the mediation of the Lord Jesus Christ and does not stand in need of a priest and that each man can read and understand Scripture for himself, again provides a basis for equality. The Calvinist emphasis on the Scriptures as the means of learning God's law and conforming one's life to His will, led to a strong stress on education. And finally Calvin and the Puritans taught and firmly believed that government was legitimate only if it governed in accordance with the will of God, and that government which acted contrary to the will of God was not legitimate at all and not to be obeyed.

Let us examine the status of religious liberty on a colony-by-colony basis, starting with the stern Puritanism of New England, then work our way down through the Mid-Atlantic and southern colonies.

Massachusetts, Connecticut, New Hampshire

The early Puritans and Pilgrims believed with Calvin that unrighteousness affects all of society, and that it is therefore the responsibility of government as well as the church to fight unrighteousness. They therefore hoped to create a community of believers in Massachusetts, their stronghold against the corruption of the outside world.

The theocratic nature of the Puritan establishment in Massachusetts is clear from the Massachusetts Body of Liberties dated December 10, 1641:

> The free fruition of such liberties, Immunities and Priveledges as humanitie, Civilitie, and Christianitie call for as due to every man in his place and proportion without impeachment and Infringement hath ever bene and ever will be the tranquillitie and Stabilitie of Churches and Commonwealths. And the deniall or deprivall thereof, the disturbance if not the ruine of both.
> 58. Civill Authoritie hath power and libertie to see the peace, ordinances and Rules of Christ observed in every church according to his word. So it be done in a civill and not in an Ecclesiastical way.
> 59. Civill Authoritie hath power and libertie to deale with any Church member in a way of Civill Justice, notwithstanding any Church relation, office or interest.
> 60. No church censure shall degrad or depose any man from any Civill dignitie, office, or Authoritie he shall have in commonwealth.
> 94.
>> 1. If any man after legall conviction shall have or worship any other god, but the lord god, he shall be put to death.

2. If any men or women be a witch, (that is hath or consulteth with a familiar spirit,) They shall be put to death.

3. If any man shall Blaspheme the name of god, the father, Sonne or Holie ghost, with direct, expresse, presumptous or high handed blasphemie, or shall curse god in the like manner he shall be put to death.

95.

1. All the people of god within this Jurisdiction who are not in the church way, and the orthodox Judgment, and not scandalous in life, shall have full libertie to gather themselves into a Church Estaite. Provided they doe it in a Christian way, with due observation of the rules of Christ revealed in his word . . .

10. Wee allow private meetings for edification in religion amongst Christians of all Sortes of people. So be it without just offence for number, time, place, and other cercumstances.[17]

Armed with the authority of the state, the Puritan ministers of Massachusetts regulated persons' names, their clothing, and most ordinary social customs.[18]

In 1646, the general court adopted the Act against Heresy, which imposed banishment on any person denying the immortality of the soul, or the resurrection, or sin in the believer, or the need of repentance, or the baptism of infants. Contemptuous conduct toward preachers was punishable by making the offender stand on a block four feet high and have on his breast a placard with the words "An Open and Obstinate Contemner of God's Holy Ordinances."

A group of the king's commissioners sent from London to investigate conditions in the colonies reported in 1661:

Puritans have put many Quakers to death, of other provinces. First they banished them as Quakers upon pain of death, and then executed them for returning. They have beaten some to jelly, and been exceedingly cruel to others.[19]

In 1647 the general court decreed:

No Jesuit or spiritual or ecclesiastical person ordained by the pope of Rome shall henceforth come into Massachusetts. Any person not freeing himself of suspicion shall be jailed, then banished. If taken a second time he shall be put to death.[20]

---

17. *Massachusetts Body of Liberties*, quoted in Rice, pp. 162-163.

18. Beth, p. 41.

19. Gustavus Meyers, *History of Bigotry in the United States* (New York: Random House, 1943), p. 5; quoted in Pfeffer, pp. 67-68. Pfeffer adds, however, that actually only four Quakers were executed. We might also remember that the Church of England was at odds with the Puritans, and consequently the report may be biased.

20. Pfeffer, p. 68. Pfeffer adds that "tempering justice with mercy and commercial considerations, exceptions were made for shipwrecked Jesuits and priests transiently in the colony business."

When a tiny group of Anabaptists came to Charlestown, Massachusetts, in 1681, they appealed for religious toleration. But Samuel Willard, minister of the Third Church in Boston, answered them:

> I perceive they are mistaken in the design of our first Planters, whose business was not Toleration; but were professed enemies of it, and could leave the World professing they died *no Libertines.* Their business was to settle, and (as much as in them lay) secure Religion to Posterity, according to that way which they believed was of God.[21]

New Hampshire and Connecticut were also Puritan Congregationalist establishments. New Haven, which had been independent for a quarter-century before merging with Massachusetts, was "possibly more extreme in its theocracy than Massachusetts."[22]

While Massachusetts gradually became more liberal in the 1700s, Connecticut remained much more conservative. Puritan preachers in Connecticut were fond of lambasting the liberalism and Unitarianism of their Massachusetts contemporaries. Yale Divinity School was founded by conservatives as a reaction against the liberal tendencies of Harvard, and Yale held fast to the conservative position for several generations. But the fervor of the early years, when God led his people to establish a "city upon a hill," was starting to fade.

In the late 1600s and early 1700s, Unitarianism arose in New England, a more potent force than most modern Americans realize. That, coupled with the defection of many Congregational Churches to liberalism during that period, did much to weaken the Puritan theocracy. The theocracies continued for several generations, but gradually became less strict.

The fervor of the first generation continued for a time. But eventually, new generations arose which retained the form of godliness but lacked the power thereof. These new generations of the early 1700s were more worldly minded than their forefathers had been, but still respected the church as an institution and saw they could personally benefit from church membership.

In the 1700s the Congregational Church in New England faced the difficult question, what should we do with those who were raised in the covenant and brought up in the church, who have not rejected the church or its doctrine but do not show outward signs of regeneration?

A substantial number of Congregational Churches adopted a new policy called the "half-way covenant." Under this covenant, such persons were allowed to attend church, vote on church matters, and receive the sacraments, even though their eternal destiny was uncertain. This was especially important to many citizens because without church membership one often could not

---

21. NeSutor Ultra Crepidam (Boston 1681), p. 4; quotes by William H. Marnell, The First Amendment: *The History of Religious Freedom in America* (Garden City, New York, Doubleday, 1964) p. 57 (Emphasis original)

22. Pfeffer, p. 68.

vote in civil elections, hold public office, own property, or enjoy other privileges of citizenship.

Around 1750 New England's leading intellectual, Rev. Jonathan Edwards, challenged the half-way covenant. He argued that there could be no such thing as a half-way covenant with God, that those who are unregenerate should not be led into a fake sense of security, and that the unregenerate should not have a voice in the growth of the church. Edwards, however, was willing to give these people their rights as citizens of civil society.

Edwards' congregation in Southampton, Connecticut split over this issue, and he was forced to resign as pastor, but his influence continued. He became a missionary to the Indians, and this endeavor gave him more time to write. In late 1757 he accepted the presidency of Princeton, but died of a smallpox inoculation after only a few weeks in office.

Edwards was essentially a conservative, calling his fellow New Englanders back to the stern Puritanism of the glorious early days. But the full significance of Edwards' opposition is often overlooked—his willingness to allow unregenerate people the rights of citizenship while refusing them the right of church membership and participation. By separating church membership from civic privileges, Edwards conceded that the Puritan ideal of society as the community of the redeemed, a society composed entirely of believers, was no longer realizable, if it ever was. Edwards saw the choices as between (1) a church-run society in which the "church" was little more than a social club; or (2) a non-theocratic society with a strong and faithful church within it. Edwards chose the latter, and his thinking was significant for Americans of the next generation who were concerned with such issues as independence and religious freedom.[23]

Virginia

Virginia, from its inception in 1624, was by the terms of its charter part of the domain of the Church of England.[24] But the establishment was less rigid in Virginia than in New England, largely because the Anglican Church of Virginia was weaker and less zealous than the Puritan churches of New England. In Virginia the Presbyterians, Baptists, and Methodists were strong enough to challenge the Anglican establishment, and in 1776 the Anglican Church was officially disestablished. The Act of 1776 still allowed the state to collect taxes for the support of the Anglican Church and its ministers, but it allowed those who did not belong to the Anglican Church to be exempt from the tax. A subsequent bill in 1779 also ended the requirement that members of the Anglican Church contribute to its support. In 1784, however, Patrick Henry, whose "Give me liberty or give me death!" speech before the Virginia House of Commons in 1775 had been replete with biblical allusions, proposed

23. O'Malley, ibid.
24. Marnell, p. 64.

a "Bill Establishing a Provision for Teachers of the Christian Religion." This bill required all those of the Christian religion to pay a moderate tax annually for the support of the Christian religion, because "the general diffusion of Christian knowledge hath a natural tendency to correct the morals of men, restrain their vices, and preserve the peace of society . . . "[25] In committee the term "Christian" was deleted and "religious" substituted in its place, but on the floor of the assembly "Christian" was reinserted.

In order to become law, the bill had to pass three times. It passed its first and second readings by narrow votes, the second being 44 to 42, despite the vigorous opposition of James Madison. Madison was able to postpone the third reading until the next session of the legislature, in 1785, and in the meantime Patrick Henry was elected governor of Virginia. With Henry out of the legislature, Madison was able to marshall the necessary support to defeat the bill on its third reading, winning much support through his famous "Memorial and Remonstrance against Religious Assessments."

Rhode Island

Rhode Island has been described as the first colony ever to achieve complete separation of church and state.[26] This was due to the influence of Roger Williams, a firm believer in religious liberty. Williams had been banished from Massachusetts in the winter of 1635-36 because of "divers new and dangerous opinions," among them the doctrine of the two tables, i.e., that the second table of the Ten Commandments which concerned man's dealings with his fellow men was the business of the civil magistrate, but the first table which governs man's relations with God was outside the proper sphere of the state.[27] All religious groups were allowed to practice their faiths in Rhode Island, and the first Hebrew congregation in North America was founded in Rhode Island in 1658. Ironically, Catholics were officially disenfranchised for a substantial portion of Rhode Island's history, although there is reason to question whether that law had ever been legally enacted and whether it was generally enforced.[28]

Maryland

Maryland was founded about 1649 by William Calvert (Lord Baltimore). Lord Baltimore was Catholic, but his colony's charter at its inception established the Church of England as the state church of Maryland. Lord Baltimore therefore worked for toleration in the colony, and was to a large measure successful. The 1649 Act of Toleration is said to be the first act of toleration ever passed by an assembly in an American colony. It provided toleration for the various sects of Christendom, but it did not extend to atheists, Jews, or

---

25. Pfeffer, pp. 97-98.
26. Beth, p. 53.
27. Pfeffer, p. 75.
28. Beth, pp. 54-55; compare Pfeffer, pp. 75-76.

Unitarians, and did not allow any speech disrespectful of the Virgin Mary or any act inappropriate to Sunday as a day of worship. In 1689 the Protestants gained control of Maryland and again established the Church of England by taxation in 1692. In 1704 Catholics were forbidden to hold Mass, to support Catholic teachers, or to vote, and many of them migrated to Philadelphia. It seems that, unlike the other colonies who gradually became more tolerant, Maryland began as a pioneer of tolerance and regressed thereafter.[29]

Pennsylvania

Pennsylvania was among the most tolerant of the colonies, largely because of the influence of William Penn, its founder. Penn had been imprisoned for his beliefs in England, and firmly championed tolerance in America. In 1682 he granted refuge to the Mennonites, so that they could settle in Pennsylvania. However, Penn was also convinced that God was the author of religious liberty, and therefore religious liberty depended upon Him. Profanity was prohibited in Pennsylvania and Sunday rest was required. The Frame of Government of Pennsylvania, dated April 25, 1682, made specific reference to Romans 13 as the source of governmental power. The Pennsylvania Charter of Privileges (October 28, 1701) declared that "No People can be truly happy, though under the Greatest enjoyment as to their Religious Profession and Worship. . . . " The charter went on to declare that "No Person or Persons, inhabiting this Province or Territory, who shall confess and acknowledge One Almighty God, the Creator, Upholder and Ruler of the World; and profess him or themselves obliged to live quietly under the Civil Government, shall be in any case molested or prejudiced, in his or their Person or Estate. . . . " The charter further provided that "All Persons who also profess to believe in Jesus Christ, the Saviour of the World, shall be allowed to hold offices in government."[30] At one point the Test Act disenfranchised Catholics, and at the insistence of England the act was enforced.

New York

Early in New York's history, the Dutch Reformed Church was established under Peter Stuyvesant. Swedish Lutherans in 1653 petitioned for liberty of worship and for permission to have a Lutheran minister, but were denied. Baptists were subject to arrest, fine, whipping and banishment. Quakers were subject to arrest and expulsion if they entered "New Netherlands," and the ship that brought them was subject to confiscation. Shortly after the Dutch colony fell to the English in 1664, the Reformed Church was disestablished, and the Duke of York prescribed that:

29. Beth, pp. 51-52.

30. *Frame of Government of Pennsylvania*, April 25, 1682; *Pennsylvania Charter of Privileges*, October 28, 1701; quoted in Rice, pp. 163-164.

In all the territories of his Royal Highness liberty of conscience is allowed, provided such liberty is not converted to licentiousness or the disturbance of others in the exercise of the protestant religion. Every township is obliged to pay their minister, according to such agreement as they make with him, and no man shall refuse his proportion; the minister being elected by the major part of the householders, inhabitants of the town.[31]

The meaning of this act appears to be that, like the Peace of Westphalia in Europe only sixteen years earlier, each local township could establish its own religion. Note, however, that the edict limits this freedom to those of the Protestant religion.

In 1683, the New York assembly adopted the "Charter of Liberties" which provided that "all churches presently in New York should have full religious liberty, and that all other 'Christian Churches' that shall hereafter come to New York shall have the same privileges."[32] Despite these restrictions, New York was among the freest of the colonies in granting religious liberty.

Delaware and New Jersey

There appears to have been no establishment of religion in New Jersey, and none in Delaware, although Delaware did have occasional official days of prayer.

North Carolina

In the southern colonies, the Church of England was dominant. It was the established church in North Carolina, although it was relatively weak there, and freedom was provided for dissenters. The Church of England was officially disestablished when North Carolina adopted its new constitution in 1776.[33]

South Carolina

In South Carolina the Church of England was well-organized and strong. It was established as the state church and supported by taxation, but freedom was provided for dissenters. In 1778 South Carolina adopted a new constitution which provided that "The Christian Protestant religion shall be deemed and is hereby constituted and declared to be the established religion of this State," and assured equal privileges to all Protestant denominations. Churches could be incorporated with fifteen or more adult males, but they had to have articles of faith which included belief in one eternal God and a future state of rewards and punishments, public worship of God, that the Christian religion is true religion, that the Holy Scriptures are of divine inspiration and the rule of faith in practice, and that it is the duty of every man to bear witness to the truth.[34]

31. Pfeffer, p. 70.
32. Ibid., p. 71.
33. Ibid., p. 105.
34. Ibid., p. 105.

Georgia

Georgia's original charter of 1732 tolerated all "except papists," but this was voided in 1752 when the Church of England became the established church of Georgia.

Rising Sentiment for Religious Liberty

U.S. Supreme Court Justice Hugo Black has noted that

> As late in time as the Revolutionary War, there were established churches in at least 8 of the 13 former colonies and established religions in at least 4 of the other 5.[35]

While Black is probably applying an extreme definition of "establishment," it is clear that separation of church and state as we talk about it today was virtually unknown of in colonial America.

These established churches continued after the War for Independence and even into the 1800s—after the adoption of the Constitution and the First Amendment. Their presence and activity help us to understand why the framers wrote the First Amendment and what they meant by it.

Nevertheless, between 1620 and 1789 American thought definitely moved in the direction of religious liberty. The stern New England Puritanism relaxed a great deal, though it certainly did not disappear. As succeeding generations became more worldly and less interested in the Puritan vision, it became increasingly difficult for Puritan leaders to enforce their vision by means of the state.

The growth of rationalism was certainly a factor. The eloquent arguments for religious liberty by men like Jefferson and Madison stirred the hearts and minds of many, both inside and outside Virginia.

But the evangelistic fervor of the First Great Awakening in the mid-1700s was equally a factor. Great preachers like George Whitefield and Jonathan Edwards led many to convert from the established churches to other churches. Citizens then objected to paying taxes to maintain the established church, losing certain civic privileges, etc. This happened throughout the colonies, and it became more difficult for the established churches to maintain their privileged positions. The battle for religious liberty thus produced interesting allies, such as the rationalist Thomas Jefferson and Baptist leader John Leland.

Still another factor was the rivalry among the colony/states under the shadow of national union. A state church in Connecticut was one thing; but what about a national church for the United States? Colonies and churches alike worried about this. Many feared that the New England Puritans would establish the Congregational Church as the federal church. The Puritans feared the Church of England, already established in Virginia and the South. Many feared that, since Philadelphia was the first capital, the pacifist Pennsylvania Quakers would

---

35. *Engel v. Vitale*, 370 U.S. 421, 427-28 (1962).

exert an undue influence on the nation's defense policies. The Rhode Island Baptists feared everyone and everyone feared the Catholics. This led many to believe that, at the federal level at least, it might be a good idea not to have any established church at all.

Chapter 9

The Framing
of the First Amendment

By the time of the Constitutional Convention in 1787, there was a general consensus in America that the federal government should not interfere in matters of religion.

It might therefore seem strange that the new Constitution did not contain a provision protecting religious freedom, except for a brief phrase forbidding religious tests for public office. One reason is that many were afraid that the naming of certain rights would prejudice other rights not named. There is a well-known legal principle, *Expressio unius, exclusio alterius* ("The Expression of one thing is the exclusion of others"). As Alexander Hamilton wrote in the *Federalist*:

> . . . Bills of Rights in the sense and to the extent in which they are contended for, are not only unnecessary in the proposed constitution, but would even be dangerous. They would contain various exceptions to powers not granted; and, on this very account, would afford a colorable pretext to claim more than was granted. For why declare that things shall not be done which there is no power to do?[1]

James Madison further argued that a Bill of Rights was not necessary because the multiplicity of sects in the United States and the jealousy between them would prevent any one sect from establishing itself at the expense of the others.

But many were very concerned about the lack of such a provision—so concerned, in fact, that the ratification of the new Constitution was in jeopardy. Thomas Jefferson had been in France during the Constitutional Convention, but after reviewing the proposed Constitution he wrote to Madison:

> I will now add what I do not like. First, the omission of the Bill of Rights providing clearly and without the aid of sophisms for freedom of religion, freedom of the press, protection against standing armies, restriction against

---

1. Alexander Hamilton, "The Federalist," No. 84, Sec. 11, in Jacob E. Cooke, ed., *The Federalist* (Middletown, Connecticut: Wesleyan University Press, 1961), p. 579.

monopolies, the eternal and unremitting force of the habeas corpus laws, and trials by juries.[2]

In order to satisfy those who objected to the proposed Constitution, the others agreed that promptly after the Constitution was ratified, it would be amended by adding the Bill of Rights. The Constitution was then ratified by the required number of states upon that guarantee.

After ratification, the new Congress adopted ten amendments, commonly known as the Bill of Rights. They were ratified and became effective on December 15, 1791. The First Amendment reads in part: "Congress shall make no law respecting an establishment of religion, or prohibiting the free exercise thereof. . . . "

That's what the First Amendment says. But what does it mean? Several words are somewhat ambiguous. What does *establishment* mean? What is *religion?* What is *free exercise?*

To answer these questions, we need to look at the intent of the framers of the First Amendment.[3]

In determining the intent of the framers, we are somewhat limited. The congressional committees at that time generally did not make formal reports, except for the actual wording of their proposed legislation. There was no *Congressional Record* to record the speeches made on the floor. Some of the deliberations were even secret. We thus have to rely in many cases upon the notes of other legislators concerning what was said and done in Congress. Nevertheless, certain facts are known. Let us look at the process by which Congress adopted the First Amendment.[4]

Several states, when they ratified the Constitution, made specific proposals for amendments concerning religious freedom. James Madison took these proposals and condensed them into two amendments, which he offered on the floor of the House of Representatives on June 7, 1789. These two amendments were worded as follows:

> The Civil Rights of none shall be abridged on account of religious belief or worship, nor shall any national religion be established, nor shall the full and equal rights of conscience be in any matter, nor on any pretext infringed.

2. Thomas Jefferson, cited by Pfeffer, p. 112.
3. Earlier we noted the effect of the theory of evolution upon constitutional interpretation, through such cases as *Trop v. Dulles*, 356 U.S. 86, and others. Such cases hold that the Constitution must be interpreted by an evolving standard, and cannot mean today what it meant when written. If the evolutionary theory of constitutional interpretation is accepted and carried to its logical conclusion, the intent of the framers is largely irrelevant. Fortunately, most courts have not carried the evolutionary theory to its logical conclusion—yet.
4. A more detailed account of this process may be found in Pfeffer, pp. 103-159; Michael J. Malbin, *Religion and Politics: The Intentions of the Authors of the First Amendment* (Washington, D.C.: American Enterprise Institute for Public Policy Research, 1978), pp. 1-40. Rather than footnoting each individual fact, I refer the reader to these general sources.

> No state shall violate the equal right of conscience or the freedom of the press, or the trial by jury in criminal cases.

Since both houses of Congress had to agree on an amendment, Madison's proposed amendments were referred to the Committee of the Whole House, who in turn referred it to a specially formed Select Committee which included Madison. On July 28, the committee reported to Congress that its members had agreed upon the following wording:

> No religion shall be established by law, nor shall the equal rights of conscience be infringed.

Debate in the House took place on August 15, 1789. Congressman Peter Sylvester of New York objected that the language used "might be thought to have tendency to abolish religion altogether." Perhaps as a result of his objection, Massachusetts' Congressman Eldridge Berry proposed to reword the amendment to read "no religious doctrine shall be established by law." After further debate, Samuel Livermore of New Hampshire proposed the following language:

> Congress shall make no laws touching religion, or infringing the rights of conscience.

This amendment carried, 31 to 20. Five days later, on August 20, Congressman Fisher Ames of Massachusetts offered a further change:

> Congress shall make no law establishing religion, or to prevent the free exercise thereof, or to infringe the rights of conscience.

This proposal carried the House and was sent to the Senate.

Senate floor debates during the early congresses were not recorded, so we do not know exactly what was said. The *Senate Journal* tells us only whether a given motion passed or was defeated. We do know that three amendments were offered to the Senate of September 3, and all three were defeated. They were as follows:

> Congress shall make no law establishing one religious sect or society in preference to others, or to infringe on the rights of conscience. *Defeated.*
> Congress shall not make any law infringing the rights of conscience, or establishing any religious sect or society. *Defeated.*
> Congress shall make no law establishing any particular denomination of religion in preference to another, or prohibiting the free exercise thereof, nor shall the rights of conscience be infringed. *Defeated.*

The phrase "or to infringe on the rights of conscience" was dropped, but other than that the Ames version survived the September 3 Senate debate intact.

But on September 9, Senator Oliver Ellsworth of Connecticut proposed an amendment which narrowed the provision considerably:

> Congress shall make no law establishing articles of faith or a mode of worship, or prohibiting the free exercise of religion.

Ellsworth's amendment carried, and that version was sent back to the House.

On September 21, 1789, the House rejected the Senate's proposal, and a conference committee was established. The committee consisted of representatives James Madison (Virginia), Roger Sherman (Connecticut), John Vining (Delaware), Oliver Ellsworth (Connecticut), Charles Carroll (Maryland), and William Patterson (New Jersey). The committee proposed the wording we have today, and the First Amendment as it exists today passed the House on September 24, 1789, and the Senate on September 25.

It may be significant that on the same day the Senate passed the final version of the First Amendment, New Jersey Congressman Elias Boudinot (who also chaired the Committee of the Whole which first considered the First Amendment), requested the President to recommend a day of "public thanksgiving and prayer, to be observed by acknowledging . . . the many signal favors of Almighty God," because "he could not think of letting the session pass over without offering an opportunity to all the citizens of the United States of Joining . . . in returning to Almighty God their sincere thanks for many blessings he had poured down upon them." Apparently there was some opposition, but another committee member, Connecticut's Roger Sherman, spoke in favor of the proposal, and it passed. The next day the Senate affirmed the House's resolution.[5]

---

5. *Journal of the House* (1789), p. 914; *Senate Journal* (1789), pp. 914-915, 155, 154; cited by Chester James Antieau, Arthur T. Downey, and Edward C. Roberts, *Freedom from Federal Establishment: Formation and Early History of the First Amendment Religion Clauses* (Milwaukee: Bruce, 1964), p. 131.

Chapter 10

The Meaning
of the First Amendment

We have seen the background of the First Amendment, its adoption, and its present wording: "Congress shall make no law respecting an establishment of religion or prohibiting the free exercise thereof. . . . " Now let us consider what this amendment means.

Those portions of the First Amendment which relate to religious freedom can be divided into two sections. The first, *Congress shall make no law respecting an establishment of religion* . . . , is called the establishment clause. The other portion, *or prohibiting the free exercise thereof*, is called the free exercise clause. Let us look at them in order.

The Establishment Clause

"Congress shall make no law respecting an establishment of religion. . . . " So far so good. But what is religion? What is an establishment of religion? And why does the clause speak only of Congress?

"Congress Shall Make No Law Respecting"

We will note in the outset that the First Amendment only prohibits *Congress* from establishing a religion. The courts have never directly addressed the question but apparently assume that the entire federal government is intended.[1] It may be helpful to recall that when James Madison introduced the original

---

1. *Watson v. Jones*, 80 U.S. (13 Wall) 679 (1871); *Presbyterian Church v. Mary Elizabeth Blue Hull Presbyterian Church*, 393 U.S. 440 (1969); *Serbian Eastern Orthodox Diocese v. Milivojevich*, 426 U.S. 696 (1976); *Kedroff v. St. Nicholas Cathedral*, 344 U.S. 94 (1952). As Justice Black said in *Everson v. Board of Education*, 330 U.S. 15 (1947): " 'Establishment of religion' clause . . . means at least this: Neither a state nor the Federal Government can set up a church."

draft of the First Amendment to Congress on June 7, 1789, the establishment clause read, "nor shall any national religion be established." When, in the course of debate, the clause was ultimately changed into active voice, it may be that the framers of the First Amendment simply spoke of "Congress" because the possibility of the president or the federal judiciary trying to establish a religion was beyond their imagination, in view of the limited powers they intended those branches of government to hold.

Again, the First Amendment says only that Congress may not establish a religion; it does not say the states cannot do so.

The First Amendment was not applied to state and local governments until after the adoption of the Fourteenth Amendment July 9, 1868. This amendment reads in part:

> No state shall make or enforce any law which shall abridge the privileges or immunities of citizens of the United States; nor shall any State deprive any person of life, liberty, or property, without due process of law; nor deny to any person within its jurisdiction the equal protection of the laws.[2]

Prior to the adoption of the Fourteenth Amendment, everyone agreed that the First Amendment did not apply to the states. They were free to establish their own religions. The U.S. Supreme Court had specifically so held in *Permioli v. First Municipality*, 44 U.S. (3 Howard) 589 (1845).

This seems consistent with the intent of the framers. After Madison presented his proposed amendment, Representative Elbridge Berry of Massachusetts objected to the term "national religion"—not because he wanted the term to apply to the states, but because of a dispute over the nature of the federal system of government. *National* referred to a government in which the states had largely lost their powers; in contrast, a *confederation* was a government in which the states were the basic units with very little power ceded to the federal government. The *federal* system ultimately adopted was a middle ground between a *national* government and a confederation. Berry simply didn't like the term *national*.

For quite some time after the enactment of the First Amendment, many states continued their religious establishments. For example, in Connecticut, pastors

---

2. Whitehead, John W., *The Separation Illusion: A Lawyer Examines the First Amendment* (Milford, Michigan: Mott Media, 1977), pp. 70-83, presents strong arguments to the effect that the Fourteenth Amendment was never legally ratified and that, even if properly ratified, its authors did not intend it to apply the Bill of Rights to the states. However, the Supreme Court held otherwise in *Cantwell v. Connecticut*, 310 U.S. 296 (1940) and consistently thereafter. This view was virtually unchallenged until Federal District Judge W. Brevard Hand of Alabama ruled on January 14, 1983, that the Supreme Court had misinterpreted the authors' intent and that the Constitution itself, not what the courts have said about it, is what ultimately governs. His decision in *Jaffree v. Mobile County* was reversed by the Circuit Court and the case is currently on its way to the U.S. Supreme Court. While the Supreme Court seldom changes direction so dramatically as this case would require, Judge Hand's scholarly opinion raises valid arguments that deserve serious consideration.

were called by vote of an entire town, and paid out of the town treasury. All who could not prove that they had contributed to other churches were taxed for the support of the Congregational State Church.[3]

In Massachusetts, in 1801, Father Cheverus, who later became the first bishop of Boston, was tried in Wiscasset for officiating at a marriage, even though the couple had also been before the local justice of the peace.[4] Another Catholic, Edward Kavanagh, sued for relief from taxes to support the Congregational Church. The Supreme Court of Massachusetts turned him down, declaring:

> The Constitution obliges everyone to contribute to the support of Protestant ministers and them alone. Papists are only tolerated, and as long as their ministers behave well, we shall not disturb them. But let them expect no more than that.[5]

Pennsylvania prohibited blasphemy against the Trinity at least through 1824,[6] and Virginia prohibited Sabbath breaking.[7] As Roberts summarizes the situation:

> . . . under all the foregoing state constitutions it was legally proper for the state to aid religion and religious education in the period immediately following ratification of the Bill of Rights. Indeed, there is ample evidence that the states aided religious institutions after 1789, as they had previously, by continuing:
> 1. To aid churches and church-related schools by the grant of lands;
> 2. To aid religion and religious education by providing public funds;
> 3. To empower churches and church-related schools to conduct lotteries;
> 4. To grant tax exemption to churches and religiously oriented schools;
> 5. To grant legal status and powers to churches by incorporation; 6. To employ and compensate chaplains, and give public prayer; 7. To proclaim days of prayer, fast, and thanksgiving; 8. To enact and enforce laws making it a crime to blaspheme or to engage in non-religious activities on Sunday.

There was widespread agreement that the new federal government should not interfere with the states concerning religion. In particular, the Congregationalists of New England were concerned. Not only did they not want the Anglicans of Virginia (or other bodies) to establish themselves as the official state religion of the new nation; just as strongly they did not want the federal government to interfere with their own religious establishments of Congregationalism. This is probably the reason the earlier wording, "Congress shall make no laws *touching* religion," was finally changed to "*respecting an establishment*

---

3. Roberts, p. 69.

4. Joseph F. Thorning, *Religious Liberty and Transition* (New York, 1931), p. 52, note 87; cited by Roberts, p. 170.

5. Thorning, p. 52; cited by Roberts, p. 170.

6. Roberts, p. 79.

7. Ibid., p. 81.

of religion.'' Many of the New Englanders, such as Roger Sherman of Connecticut, thought the First Amendment unnecessary. Others, like Elbridge Berry of Massachusetts and Samuel Livermore of New Hampshire, wanted to protect their own state establishments. Consequently, the neutral word ''respecting'' was used. The impact of this neutral word is twofold: (1) Congress may not establish a religion at the federal level; and (2) Congress may not interfere with the religious establishments of the state and local governments.

This seems consistent with Jefferson's view of the First Amendment, for he wrote in 1808:

> I consider the government of the United States as interdicted by the Constitution from intermeddling with religious institutions, their doctrines, discipline, or exercises. This results not only from the provision that no law shall be made respecting the establishment or free exercise of religion, but from that which reserves to the States the powers not delegated to the United States. Certainly, no power to prescribe any religious exercise, or to assume authority in religious discipline, has been delegated to the General Government. It must then rest with the States, as far as it can be in any human authority.[8]

But the Fourteenth Amendment changed all of that. Whether or not that was its authors' intent, over a period of time the courts held that various rights and privileges found in the Bill of Rights applied to the states by virtue of the Fourteenth Amendment's ''due process clause,'' which provides, ''nor shall any law. . . . '' That means the states may not deny anyone the right to life, liberty or property without due process. And what does ''liberty'' include? In *Cantwell v. Connecticut*, 310 U.S. 296 (1940), the Court declared:

> The fundamental concept of liberty embodied in the Fourteenth Amendment embraces the liberties guaranteed by the First Amendment. The First Amendment declares that Congress shall make no law respecting an establishment of religion or prohibiting the free exercise thereof. The Fourteenth Amendment has rendered the legislatures of the states as incompetent as Congress to enact such laws.[9]

Like it or not, then, that is the way the courts interpret the First and Fourteenth Amendments today. The First Amendment now applies to the states just as it applies to the federal government. And it applies not only to states, but to subdivisions of state government as well: counties, townships, cities, school boards, etc.

Establishment

What is an establishment of religion? The *Encyclopaedia Britannica* offers the following explanation:

---

8. Thomas Jefferson, letter to Presbyterian clergyman, 1808; cited by *Jefferson's Writings*, Monticello ed., 1905, 11:428-430; cited by Pfeffer, p. 224.

9. *Cantwell v. Connecticut*, 310 U.S. 296, 303 (1940).

Establishment, a word applied to certain religious bodies and their relation to the State. Perhaps the best definition which can be given and which will cover all cases, is that establishment implies the existence of some definite and distinctive relation between the State and a religious society (or conceivably more than one) other than that which is shared by other societies of the same general character. Any special connection with the State or privileges and responsibilities before the law, possessed by one religious society to the exclusion of others; in a word, establishment is of the nature of a monopoly.[10]

But what did the framers of the First Amendment mean by the term? Let us see how various people used the term "establishment of religion" around the time the Constitution was written. That will give insight as to what the authors of the First Amendment had in mind.

James Madison, during the August 15, 1789 debate on the First Amendment, gave the following explanation according to Floyd's summary:

Mr. Madison said, he apprehended the meaning of the words to be, that Congress should not establish *a* religion and enforce the legal observation of it by law, nor compel men to worship God in any manner contrary to their conscience. Whether the words are necessary or not, he did not mean to say, but they had been required by some of the State Conventions, who seemed to entertain an opinion that under the clause of the constitution, which gave power to Congress to make all laws necessary and proper to carry into execution the constitution, and the laws under it, enabled them to make laws of such nature as might infringe the rights of conscience and establish a National Religion.[11]

Alexander Hamilton, in 1775, offered the following:

In order to do this more satisfactorily, I beg leave to adopt the definition given of an established religion, by a certain writer who has taken great pains to evince the contrary. "An established religion," says he, "is a religion which the civil authority engages, not only to protect, but to support."[12]

Others tied "establishment" in with the religious tests which were prohibited by the Constitution. At the 1788 ratifying convention in Massachusetts, Major Thomas Lusk of West Stockridge objected to the prohibition of religious tests, saying that "he shuddered at the idea, that Roman Catholics, Papists and Pagans might be introduced into office; and the Popery and the Inquisition may be established in America."[13] A Baptist delegate to the same convention

10. *Encyclopaedia Britannica*; cited by Pfeffer, p. 139.

11. *I Annals*, p. 730; quoted in Malbin, p. 8.

12. John C. Hamilton, "Remarks on the Quebec Bill," *The Works of Alexander Hamilton*, 2 vol. (New York, 1850-1851), 2:131; cited by Roberts, p. 134.

13. *Debates and Proceedings of the Massachusetts Convention Held in the Year 1788* (Boston, 1856), p. 251; cited by Roberts, p. 133.

from Plymouth Colony, Reverend Isaac Backus argued that there could be no establishment of religion without a religious test for public office.

In the House debate, Representative Huntington of Connecticut compared the proposed constitutional amendment to the Charter of Rhode Island, which also prohibited an establishment of religion and thereby prevented the state from requiring persons to conform to the public exercise of religion, follow the liturgy in forms and ceremonies of the Church of England, or take oaths to the Church of England, or be punished for differing from the Church of England. Huntington equated an establishment of religion with compulsory worship of an alien faith or with a loss of civic privileges for following a different faith.[14]

In 1777, during a debate over the disestablishment of the state church of South Carolina, a Presbyterian minister named William Tennant spoke against an establishment of religion using the following language:

> My first, and most capital reason, against all establishments is, that they are an infringement to Religious Liberty.
>
> Religious establishments, as far as they operate, do interfere with the rights of private judgment and conscience: In effect, they amount to nothing less, than the legislatures taking the conscience of men into their own hands, and taxing them at discretion. . . .
>
> Its chief characteristics are, that it makes a legal distinction between people of different denominations; equally offensive, it taxes all denominations for the support of the religion of one; it only tolerates those that dissent from it, while it deprives them of sundry privileges which the people of the establishment enjoy.[15]

Tennant also at first objected to the idea of establishing all religions and supporting all through taxation, as this would destroy the very purpose of an establishment and reduce things to the same state as before: "The establishment of all religions would be no establishment at all." Later, however, he appears to have mellowed in his objection to this multiple establishment.[16]

In Virginia a vigorous battle had been waged in the 1770s and 1780s as Baptists, Presbyterians, Methodists, Lutherans and others fought to disestablish the Church of England. The main argument dealt with the payment of taxes to support the state church. The Presbytery of Hanover referred to such a practice as an establishment of religion and argued against it:

> There is no argument in favor of establishing the Christian religion of what

14. U.S., Congress, House, *The Federal and State Constitutions and Colonies Now or Heretofore Forming the United States of America*, 7 vol., by Frances M. Thorpe, 59th Cong., 2nd sess., 1909, 4:3212-3213; cited by Roberts, p. 135.

15. Reverend William Tennant, "Address of the Reverend William Tennant to the House of Assembly, November 11, 1777," (Charleston, 1778) in *American* State Record Series (Library of Congress); quoted in Roberts, p. 39.

16. Thorpe, 6:3255; cited by Roberts, pp. 53-54.

may be pleaded with equal propriety for establishing the tenants of Mahomet.[17]

James Madison, in his "Memorial and Remonstrance Against Religious Assessments," argued:

> Who does not see that the same authority which would establish Christianity, in exclusion of all other Religions, may establish with the same ease any particular sect of Christians, in exclusion of all other Sects? That the same authority which can force a citizen to contribute three pence only on his property for the support of any one establishment, may force him to conform to any other establishment in all cases whatsoever.[18]

Many states, such as New York, proposed constitutional amendments dealing with religious freedom. Many of these used language similar to that of New York: "No religious sect or society ought to be favored or established by law in preference to others."[19] Amendments by other states, such as New Jersey, Pennsylvania, and Georgia, indicate that they probably considered the First Amendment in a similar light: The establishment of one sect of Christianity over another.[20]

We may gain more insight into the intention of the framers by observing what Congress thought acceptable and proper before the adoption of the First Amendment. Repeatedly, the Continental Congress had invoked on the nation's behalf, "God," "Almighty God," "Nature's God," "God of Armies," "Lord of Hosts," "His Goodness," "God's Superintending Providence," "Providence of God," "Providence," "Supreme and Universal Providence," "Overruling Providence of God," "Creator of All," "Indulgent Creator," "Great Governor of the World," "The Divinity," "Supreme Disposer of All Events," "Holy Ghost," "Jesus Christ," "Christian Religion," "Free Protestant Colonies," and other expressions of Christianity and/or Protestantism.[21]

In 1778 Congress urged the states to encourage religion and suppress vice. Shortly thereafter it officially endorsed an American edition of the Bible and recommended it to the people as a careful and accurate work.[22] The 1783 peace treaty with England was heralded "In the name of the Most Holy and Undivided Trinity."[23]

But one of the most significant and revealing actions of the early Congress was the Northwest Ordinance of 1787. This ordinance provided for the

17. Presbytery of Hanover, cited by Pfeffer, p. 96.
18. Madison, cited by Arthur Frommer, *The Bible in the Public Public Schools* (New York: Liberal Press, 1963), p. 10.
19. Roberts, p. 121.
20. Roberts, pp. 148, 149, 151-152.
21. Pfeffer, p. 107.
22. Pfeffer, p. 108.
23. Ibid.

organization and disposition of Western lands, and directed that one section of each township be set aside for the use of schools. This included church-supported schools and was not limited to public schools until 1845.[24] Most interesting, though, is the preamble of the ordinance, which declares in part:

> Religion, morality and knowledge, being necessary to good government and the happiness of mankind, schools and the means of education shall forever be encouraged.[25]

Note that the purpose of schools was to advance "religion, morality and knowledge," these in turn being necessary to "good government and the happiness of mankind." Americans at this time perceived a close relationship between religion and good government, and they believed a major purpose of education was to advance religion. The close relationship between education and religion will be discussed further in subsequent chapters.

It is also helpful to know how early American jurists interpreted the First Amendment. Probably the best known and most respected constitutional scholar of the nineteenth century was Joseph Story, a justice of the U.S. Supreme Court. In his classic work, *Commentaries on the Constitution* (1833), Justice Story wrote,

> Probably at the time of the adoption of the Constitution, and of the amendment to it now under consideration, the general, if not the universal sentiment was, that Christianity ought to receive encouragement from the state, so far as was not incompatible with the private rights of conscience and the freedom of religious worship. An attempt to level all religions, and to make it a matter of state policy to hold all in utter indifference, would have created universal disapprobation, if not universal indignation.[26]

Many claim that James Madison and Thomas Jefferson gave the First Amendment a more separatist interpretation than most of the Founding Fathers. Madison was clearly more separatist than many others, as his "Memorial and Remonstrance Against Religious Assessments" demonstrates. But even he would not approve the absolute separatist position commonly espoused today. The "Remonstrance" can be interpreted as opposing the establishment of Christianity in particular rather than opposition to aid to religion in general. In 1789, the same year Congress approved the First Amendment, Madison served on the Congressional Committee that recommended the establishment of chaplains. On four occasions—July 9, 1812; July 23, 1813; November 16, 1814; and March 4, 1815—President Madison proclaimed days of thanksgiving. His Thanksgiving Day Proclamation of March 4, 1815, read as follows:

---

24. Roberts, p. 163.

25. Northwest Ordinance; cited by Pfeffer, p. 108.

26. Joseph Story, *Commentaries on the Constitution of the United States* (Boston, 1833); vol. 2, sec 1874, p. 593; quoted by Robert L. Cord, *Separation of Church and State: Historical Fact and Current Fiction* (New York: Lambeth Press, 1982), p. 13.

By the President of the United States of America.

A Proclamation.

The Senate and House of Representatives of the United States have by a joint resolution signified their desire that a day may be recommended to be observed by the people of the United States with religious solemnity as a day of thanksgiving and of devout acknowledgements of Almighty God for His great goodness manifested in restoring to them the blessing of peace.

No people ought to feel greater obligations to celebrate the goodness of the Great Disposer of Events and of the Destiny of Nations than the people of the United States. His kind providence originally conducted them to one of the best portions of the dwelling place alloted for the great family of the human race. He protected and cherished them under all the difficulties and trials to which they were exposed in their early days. Under His fostering care their habits, their sentiments, and their pursuits prepared them for a transition in due time to a state of independence and self-government. In the arduous struggle by which it was attained they were distinguished by multiplied tokens of His benign interposition. During the interval which succeeded He reared them into the strength and endowed them with the resources which have enabled them to assert their national rights and to enhance their national character in another arduous conflict, which is now so happily terminated by a peace and reconciliation with those who have been our enemies. And to the same Divine Author of Every Good and Perfect Gift we are endebted for all those privileges and advantages, religious as well as civil, which are so richly enjoyed in this favored land.

It is for blessings such as these, and more especially for the restoration of the blessing of peace, that I now recommend that the second Thursday in April next be set apart as a day on which the people of every religious denomination may in their solemn assemblies unite their hearts and their voices in a freewill offering to their Heavenly Benefactor of their homage of thanksgiving and of their songs of praise.

Given at the city of Washington on the 4th day of March, A.D. 1815, and of the Independence of the United States the thirty-ninth.

James Madison

In the "Detached Memoranda," a document apparently written by Madison after he left the presidency, Madison indicated that he had changed his views on national days of thanksgiving and congressional chaplains, and that he had decided such practices violated the establishment clause. However, his intent at the time the First Amendment was written is what is relevant to the Amendment's proper interpretation, not the fact that he changed his mind later. At the time he wrote the First Amendment in its original form, Madison's only concern seems to have been the establishment of one denomination in preference to another, not aid to religion in general. Madison's veto of an attempt to incorporate the Episcopal Church, and later his veto of a gift of land to the Baptist Church, would be consistent with this principle.[27]

27. All of the above information concerning James Madison is taken from Robert Cord, pp. 20-36.

Thomas Jefferson was not an orthodox Christian, but he was not so much a freethinker or Deist as some have imagined. As noted in chapter 7, his many statements about God actively guiding and blessing our nation clearly place him outside the Deist camp. His statement that "The God who gave us life, gave us liberty at the same time"[28] shows that he continued to recognize God as the source of liberty, even as he had years earlier when he penned the Declaration of Independence and wrote that all men "are endowed by their Creator with certain unalienable rights" and referred to "the laws of nature and of nature's God."

As President, Jefferson objected to nationally-sponsored days of prayer. But he supported state-sponsored days of prayer when he was governor of Virginia, because he did not believe the First Amendment applied to the states. Most interesting of all, in 1803 President Jefferson recommended to Congress the passage of a treaty with the Kaskaskia Indians which provided, among other things, a stipend of $100 annually for seven years from the Federal treasury for the support of a Catholic priest to minister to the Kaskaskia Indians. This and two similar treaties were enacted during Jefferson's Administration—one with the Wyandot Indians and other tribes in 1806, and one with the Cherokees in 1807. Still another act of Congress, in 1787, ordained special lands "for the sole use of Christian Indians" and reserved land for the Moravian Brethren "for civilizing the Indians and promoting Christianity." This was, in effect, renewed in 1796 with a new law entitled "An Act regulating the grants of land appropriated for Military services and for the Society of the United Brethren, for propagating the Gospel among the Heathen." No less than three times during President Jefferson's Administration, Congress extended this act and each time, Jefferson signed the extension into law. Professor Robert Cord, citing these facts in detail concludes,

> These historical facts indicate that Jefferson . . . did not see the First Amendment and the Establishment Clause requiring "complete independence of religion and government."[29]

Even Jefferson and Madison, then, did not advocate absolute separation of church and state. And they were the most separatist of all the Founding Fathers! What, then, did the Founders mean by an establishment of religion?

Thomas Jefferson's most widely quoted statement concerning religious freedom is found in his address to the Danbury Baptists (1802) in which he declared,

> . . . I contemplate with sovereign reverence that act of the whole American

---

28. Thomas Jefferson; *The Writings of Thomas Jefferson* (1892, 1899), comp. Paul Leicester Ford, Vol. 1, p. 447; cited by *Freemen Digest: Thomas Jefferson* (Freeman Institute, Salt Lake City, Utah, 1981), p. 92.

29. Robert L. Cord, *Separation of Church and State: Historical Fact and Current Fiction* (New York: Lambeth Press, 1982), pp. 36–47; quote on p. 45.

people which declared that their legislature should "make no law respecting an establishment of religion, or prohibiting the free exercise thereof," thus building a *wall of separation between Church and State*.[30] (emphasis supplied)

This was more than a hastily conceived remark. Before delivering his address to the Danbury Baptists, he sent a copy to his attorney general, Levi Lincoln, for comments and suggestions. He wrote to Lincoln, "I know it will give great offense to the New England clergy; but the advocate of religious freedom is to expect neither peace nor forgiveness from them."[31] Very possibly he derived the phraseology from the Baptist leader and advocate of religious liberty of the previous century, Roger Williams of Rhode Island. Williams had written,

> . . . when they have opened a gap in the hedge or wall of separation between
> the garden of the church and the wilderness of the world, God hath ever
> broke down the wall itself, removed the candlestick, and made His garden
> a wilderness, as at this day. And that therefore if He will eer please to restore
> His garden and paradise again, it must of necessity be walled in peculiarly
> unto Himself from the world. . . . [32]

Like Jefferson, Williams spoke of a "wall of separation" between church and state. But to Williams, the "wall" existed to protect the church from the state, not to protect the state from the church. Speaking to a Baptist audience, it seems likely that Jefferson intended the same meaning.

But where was the wall to be placed? What did Jefferson really mean by "state"? It seems likely that he used the term in its generic sense to refer to government in general and the federal government in particular, not to the state governments. For Jefferson recognized that the state governments could regulate religion. In his second inaugural address he said,

> In matters of religion I have considered that its free exercise is placed by
> the Constitution independent of the powers of the General Government.
> I have therefore undertaken on no occasion to prescribe the religious exer-
> cises suited to them, but have left them, as the Constitution found them,
> under the direction and discipline of the church or state authorities
> acknowledged by the several religious societies.[33]

Based on this and similar statements, Whitehead suggests that Jefferson understood the "wall" to separate the federal government from the states and churches, not to separate the federal and state governments from the churches.[34]

And yet, this phrase "wall of separation" has been repeatedly quoted by

---

30. Thomas Jefferson, "Address to the Danbury Baptists, 1802," quoted by Frommer, p. 19.

31. Thomas Jefferson to Levi Lincoln, 1 January 1802; quoted by Frommer, p. 20.

32. Roger Williams, quoted by Lynn R. Buzzard and Samuel Ericsson, *The Battle for Religious Liberty* (Elgin, Illinois: David C. Cook, 1982), p. 51.

33. Thomas Jefferson, "Second Inaugural Address," quoted in Whitehead, *The Separation Illusion*, p. 89.

34. Whitehead, Ibid.

the courts as the definitive statement of the meaning of the First Amendment. Justice Black declared in *Everson v. Board of Education*, 330 U.S. 1, 15-16 (1947), that "in the words of Jefferson, the clause against establishment of religion by law was intended to erect 'a wall of separation between church and State.' "

While the courts have used the "wall of separation" metaphor, they have occasionally recognized the problems it creates. Chief Justice Burger declared that "The line of separation, far from being a 'wall,' is a blurred, indistinct, and variable barrier depending on all the circumstances of a particular relationship." *Lemon v. Kurtzman*, 403 U.S. 602, 614 (1971). Noting that some court decisions have allowed government school buses for parochial school children but other courts have struck down school prayer, former Brigham Young University president and Utah Supreme Court Justice Dallin Oakes wryly commented,

> Certainly there is something anomalous about a wall that will admit a school bus without the "slightest breech," but is impermeable to a prayer. . .
> The metaphor is not an aid to thought and it can be a positive barrier to communication.[35]

The phrase has received far more attention than it rightfully deserves. The words "separation", "church", and "state" do not even appear in the First Amendment. Jefferson penned the phrase in 1802, thirteen years after the First Amendment was ratified. He was not even in the country at the time the Constitution was written; he was abroad serving as ambassador to France. He had written to Madison about the need for an amendment to preserve religious liberty, but he did not write the First Amendment. He was not a member of the Congress that passed the First Amendment, nor of any state legislature that ratified it.

It is therefore surprising that modern judges and scholars should seize upon Jefferson's metaphor and use it as the definitive statement of the First Amendment's meaning. A strange phenomena of modern history is that constitutional scholars seem obsessed with Jefferson but ignore Washington. Yet Washington was president of the Constitutional Convention and President of the United States when the First Amendment was passed and ratified. He would therefore be more in tune with the spirit of the Constitution and the First Amendment than Jefferson, who was out of the country at the time.

Washington would not have endorsed the radical separationism of today. As general of the Continental Army he strictly forbade gambling, profanity, and intemperance.[36] At times he ordered his troops to fast.[37] He procured military chaplains, directed them to conduct worship services, and even ordered his soldiers to attend services.[38] One such order is dated July 20, 1775:

35. Dallin Oakes; quoted by Joel F. Hansen, *Brigham Young University Law Review*, 1978, p. 647.
36. William J. Johnson, *George Washington the Christian*. (Milford, Michigan: Mott Media, 1976) pp. 44, 72, 76, 136-7.
37. Ibid., pp. 77, 81.
38. Ibid., pp. 45, 70, 99-100, 122, 134.

The General orders this day to be religiously observed by the Forces under his Command, exactly in (the) manner directed by the Continental Congress. It is therefore strictly enjoined on all Officers and Soldiers to attend Divine Service; and it is expected that all those who go to worship do take their Arms, Ammunition, and Accoutrements, & are prepared for immediate action if called upon.[39]

As President, Washington proclaimed days of thanksgiving.[40] At state dinners he led in grace himself if no chaplain was present.[41] He frequently spoke in churches,[42] and regularly invoked the Name of God in his public pronouncements. His Farewell Address of September 17, 1796, is most noteworthy:

> Of all the dispositions and habits, which lead to political prosperity, religion and morality are indispensable supports. In vain would that man claim the tribute of patriotism, who should labor to subvert these great pillars of human happiness, these firmest props of the duties of men and citizens. The mere politician, equally with the pious man, ought to respect and cherish them. A volume could not trace all their connexions with private and public felicity. Let it simply be asked, where is the security for property, for reputation, for life, if the sense of religious obligation desert the oaths, which are the instruments of investigation in courts of justice? And let us with caution indulge the supposition, that morality can be maintained without religion. Whatever may be conceded to the influence of refined education on the minds of peculiar structure, reason and experience both forbid us to expect, that national morality can prevail in exclusion of religious principle.
>
> It is substantially true, that virtue or morality is a necessary spring of popular government. The Rule, indeed, extends with more or less force to every species of free government. Who, that is a sincere friend to it, can look with indifference upon attempts to shake the foundation of the fabric?[43]

And yet, modern scholars and judges ignore Washington. Instead, they narrowly focus upon Jefferson's "wall of separation" metaphor. Why? Probably because it fits their preconceived notions.

It is important to understand that these men never envisioned a society in which government would permeate the lives of its citizens to the extent it does today. They knew that religion permeated the lives of the American people. But they envisioned a government that would, for the most part, leave its citizens alone. Consequently they expected that government would, for the most part, leave religion alone also.

39. Ibid., p. 70.
40. Ibid., pp. 172, 215.
41. Ibid., pp. 162-63, 198-99.
42. Ibid., pp. 163, 167, 168, 169.
43. George Washington, Farewell Address, September 17, 1796; quoted by Rousas J. Rushdoony, *The Nature of the American System* (Fairfax, Virginia: Thoburn Press, 1978), pp. 46-47.

But today government is involved in the lives of the American people far more than anyone in 1789 dreamed possible. Whereas, when Washington became president there were a total of only 350 civilian federal employees, today there are over three million—each one regulating some aspect of our lives.[44] State and local government employees have increased as well. That being the case, government and religion are certain to come in contact and conflict far more often than the Founders expected.

So what should government do when it comes into contact with religion? Must it be hostile toward religion, or must it, as Justice Story said, "hold all [religions] in utter indifference"? Certainly that was not the authors' intent, for as Justice Story went on to say, any such proposal at the time the First Amendment was adopted "would have created universal disapprobation, if not universal indignation." Justice Clark recognized this in *Abington Township v. Schempp*, 374 U.S. 203, 294 (1963), when he said,

> . . . we agree of course that the State may not establish a "religion of secularism" in the sense of affirmatively opposing or showing hostility to religion. . . .

To delineate the difference between showing hostility toward religion and simply prohibiting the establishment of religion, the courts have sometimes used the term "accommodation of religion." Accommodaton is permissible; establishment is not. As the U.S. Supreme Court said in *Zorach v. Clausen*, 72 S.Ct. 679, 684 (1952),

> When the state encourages religious instruction or cooperation with religious authorities by adjusting the schedule of public events to sectarian needs, it follows the best of our traditions. For it then respects the religious nature of our people and accommodates the public service to their spiritual needs. To hold that it may not would be to find in the Constitution a requirement that the government show a callous indifference to religious groups that would be preferring those who believe in no religion over those who do believe.

The *Zorach* case involved a "released time" statute which allowed public school children to be released from their classes at certain times for religious instruction. In a case only five years earlier, *McCollum v. Board of Education*, 333 U.S. 203 (1948), the Supreme Court had struck down as unconstitutional a different released time statute, claiming it was an establishment of religion. The Court distinguished between the statute in *McCollum* and the one in *Zorach*, since in

---

44. W. Cleon Skousen, *"Miracle of America" Study Guide* (Salt Lake City, Utah: Freemen Institute, 1981), p. 103.

McCollum the religious instruction took place in public school classrooms whereas in *Zorach* the children left the school to attend religious instruction in their respective churches. When the instruction took place in the public school classrooms, it appeared as though the state was sponsoring that religious instruction; but when it took place away from the school, the appearance of state sponsorship was much less. Hence the *McCollum* statute was struck down as an establishment of religion; the *Zorach* statute was upheld as an accommodation of religion.

The courts have had difficulty delineating the fine line between establishment and accommodation. Probably their best attempt to do so is found in *Lemon v. Kurtzman*, 403 U.S. 602 (1971), in which the Supreme Court developed a three-part test for judging the constitutionality of any government action that affects religion:

(1) The statute must have a secular purpose.

(2) The statute's primary effect must not be to either advance or inhibit religion.

(3) The statute or government action must not foster "an excessive government entanglement with religion."

While this rule leaves many unanswered questions, it is the rule followed by the courts today in deciding establishment clause cases. And yet, I doubt the Founding Fathers would have been satisfied with this rule. Recalling the way Tennant, Hamilton, Madison and others used the term establishment, they seemed to think it included the following:

(1) Compelling people to attend worship services or other religious activites (One wonders what they would have thought of laws which in effect require attendance at public, secular humanist schools);

(2) Using government money to support a particular church or denomination in a way that prefers that church or denomination above others; or

(3) Subjecting those who do not support the "established" religion to civil disability, such as depriving them of the right to vote or hold public office.

Hopefully, as the personnel on the Court change, they will re-examine the establishment clause in light of its historical meaning and devise a new test that more accurately reflects the framers' intent.

Religion

We have examined what the framers meant by "establishment." But what did they mean by "religion"? Did they mean only specific denominations within Christendom? Did they equate religion with Christianity? Did they mean to include atheism as a religion?

Justice Story gives the following answer:

The real object of the First Amendment was not to countenance, much less to advance, Mohammedanism, or Judaism, or infidelity, by prostrating Christianity; but to exclude all rivalry among Christian sects, and to prevent any national ecclesiastical establishment which should give to a hierarchy the exclusive patronage of the national government. It thus cut off the means of religious persecution (the vice and pest of former ages), and of the subversion of the rights of conscience in matters of religion which had been trampled upon almost from the days of the Apostles to the present age. . . .[45]

John W. Whitehead and John Conlan, joint authors of a law review article, come to the same conclusion as Justice Story. They state:

The concern of Madison and the founding fathers was that one Christian denomination would prevail over the others. Thus the First Amendment was not meant to prevent the "establishment" of Christianity as a religion, but to prevent one Christian denomination from dominating the others.[46]

Whitehead, Conlan, and Story seem to have accurately captured the mind and intent of a majority of those who ratified the First Amendment. When the First Amendment was proposed in Congress, Congressman Benjamin Huntington took the floor to say he hoped the amendment would be made

. . . in such a way as to secure the rights of conscience, and a free exercise of the rights of religion, but not to patronize those who profess no religion at all.

Huntington clearly opposed any construction that would give legitimacy to atheists or agnostics. No member of Congress expressed disagreement with his viewpoint.[47]

This clearly is the view the courts took of the First Amendment through the end of the nineteenth century. In *Church of the Holy Trinity v. United States*, 143 U.S. 457 (1892), the U.S. Supreme Court considered whether a federal statute prohibiting U.S. citizens from contracting labor with foreigners could be used to prohibit a church from hiring a foreign minister. Ruling that the statute could not be so used, the Court explained at great length the Christian influence upon the history of our nation. Beginning with Christopher Columbus whose commission to sail declared that he sailed "by God's assistance", the Court narrated the colonial grant to Sir Walter Raleigh, the Charter of Virginia, the Mayflower Compact, the fundamental orders of Connecticut, William Penn's Charter of Privileges for Pennsylvania, the Declaration of Independence, the various state constitutions, and the Northwest Ordinance. The Court then cited

---

45. Joseph Story, Op. Cit., Vol.II, Sec. 1877, p. 594; quoted by Cord, op. cit., p. 13.

46. John W. Whitehead and John Conlan, "The Establishment of the Religion of Secular Humanism and its First Amendment Implications," *Texas Tech Law Review*, Vol. 10, No. 1 (Winter 1978), p. 3.

47. Annals of Congress, I, pp. 730-731; cited by William D. Graves, Little Axe Brief, p. 19.

other court decisions establishing that the United States is a Christian nation:

> While because of a general recognition of this truth the question has seldom been presented to the courts, yet we find that in *Updegraph v. The Commonwealth*, 11 S.&R. 394, 400, it was decided that "Christianity, general Christianity, is, and always has been a part of the common law of Pennsylvania; . . . not Christianity with an established church and tithes, and spiritual courts; but Christianity with liberty of conscience to all men." And in *The People v. Ruggles*, 8 Johns. 290, 294, 295, Chancellor Kent, the great commentator on American law, speaking as Chief Justice of the Supreme Court of New York, said: "The people of this State, in common with the people of this country, profess the general doctrines of Christianity, as the rule of their faith and practice; and to scandalize the author of these doctrines is not only, in a religious point of view, extremely impious, but, even in respect to the obligations due to society, is a gross violation of decency and good order. . . . The free, equal and undisturbed enjoyment of religious opinion, whatever it may be, and free and decent discussions on any religious subject, is granted and secured; but to revile, with malicious and blasphemous contempt, the religion professed by almost the whole community, is an abuse of that right. Nor are we bound, by any expressions in the Constitution as some have strangely supposed, either not to punish at all, or to punish indiscriminately, the like attacks upon the religion of Mahomet or of the Grand Lama; and for this plain reason, that the case assumes that we are a Christian people, and the morality of the country is deeply ingrafted upon Christianity, and not upon the doctrines or worship of those impostors." And in the famous case of *Vidal v. Girard's Executors*, 2 How. 127, 198, this court, while sustaining the will of Mr. Girard, with its provision for the creation of a college into which no minister should be permitted to enter, observed: "It is also said, and truly, that the Christian religion is a part of the common law of Pennsylvania."
>
> If we pass beyond these matters to a view of American life as expressed by its laws, its business, its customs and its society, we find everywhere a clear recognition of the same truth. Among other matters note the following: The form of oath universally prevailing, concluding with an appeal to the Almighty; the custom of opening sessions of all deliberative bodies and most conventions with prayer; the prefatory words of all wills, "In the name of God, amen;" the laws respecting the observance of the Sabbath, with the general cessation of all secular business, and the closing of courts, legislatures, and other similar public assemblies on that day; the churches and church organizations which abound in every city, town and hamlet; the multitude of charitable organizations existing everywhere under Christian auspices; the gigantic missionary associations, with general support, and aiming to establish Christian missions in every quarter of the globe. These, and many other matters which might be noticed, add a volume of unofficial declarations to the mass of organic utterances that this is a Christian nation.

An official declaration by the Supreme Court: "This is a Christian nation."

In related cases, the Supreme Court held that the Mormon practice of polygamy was not protected by the First Amendment because "It is contrary to the spirit of Christianity and of the civilization which Christianity has produced in the Western world." (*Late Corporation of the Church of Jesus Christ of Latter Day Saints v. United States*, 136 U.S. 1 (1890). And a year earlier, in *Davis v. Beason*, 133 U.S. 333, 341-342 (1890), the Court declared that "Bigamy and polygamy are crimes by the laws of all civilized and Christian countries. . . . To call their advocacy a tenet of religion is to offend the common sense of mankind." Clearly at this time the Court understood the First Amendment to protect only Christians, and they defined Christianity so narrowly as not to include Mormons.

But at the time the First Amendment was adopted there was a minority view, held mostly by an interesting alliance of devout Baptists (who had always held a more separatist view of church/state relations), and unorthodox thinkers. In persuading his fellow Baptists to support ratification of the First Amendment, Virginia Baptist leader John Leland explained that the amendment permitted "every man [to] speak freely without fear, maintaining the principle he believes, [and to] worship according to his own faith either *one God, three Gods or no God or twenty Gods*, and let government protect him in doing so."[48] [emphasis supplied] And Thomas Jefferson understood "religion" to include "all believers or unbelievers of the Bible . . . ."[49]

In words which seem to contradict the Supreme Court's language in the *Holy Trinity* case mentioned above, the United States negotiated a treaty with the government of Moslem Tripoli in 1796. Article XI of the treaty declared that

> The government of the United States of America is not in any sense founded on the Christian religion; . . . it has in itself no character of enmity against the laws, religion, or tranquility of Mussel men.[50]

However, Professor Leo Pfeffer notes that this treaty was incorporated into a more extensive treaty with Tripoli eight years later, and in the new treaty the phrase, "is not, in any sense, founded on the Christian religion" was omitted.[51] Many Americans must have found the phrase objectionable.[51]

It seems clear that at the time the First Amendment was adopted, most Americans considered this to be a Christian nation. But that is not the view the courts have taken in the twentieth century. In this century we find a stark absence of court references to America as a Christian nation. Justice Douglas probably came closest when he said in *Zorach v. Clausen*, supra., in 1951, "We are a religious people whose institutions presuppose a Supreme Being." A

---

48. Mecklin, *The Story of American Dissent* (New York, 1934), p. 323; cited by Beth, p.71.

49. Thomas Jefferson quoted in Tim LaHaye, *The Battle for the Mind* (Old Tappan, New Jersey: Revell, 1980), p. 130.

50. U.S. Department of State, *Treaties and International Acts of the United States of America*, 2:362-366, 1931; cited by Beth, p. 74.

51. Pfeffer, p. 211.

religious people, yes; but religious is not the same as Christian.

The Court did not stop there. In *Torcaso v. Watkins*, 367 U.S. 488 (1961), Roy Torcaso wanted to become a notary but the Montgomery County (Maryland) clerk would not swear him in because he refused to affirm a belief in God. Torcaso sued, claiming this violated the First Amendment. The State responded that merely requiring a person to profess a belief in God is not establishing a religion, for all religions believe in God.

But the Supreme Court agreed with Torcaso. First, the Court said, no government can constitutionally force any person "to profess a belief or disbelief in any religion." Neither the federal nor a state government "can constitutionally pass a law or impose requirements which aid all religions as against nonbelievers, and neither can aid those religions based on a belief in the existence of God as against those religions founded on different beliefs." The Court went on to say in a footnote that some religions do not believe in God, and specifically named secular humanism as one of them.

The Court took still another step in *U.S. v. Seeger*, 380 U.S. 163 (1965). Seeger claimed exemption from military service as a conscientious objector. But the Selective Service refused to exempt him because the law required that his conscientious objection to war be based on "religious training and belief", as "an individual's belief in relation to a Supreme Being involving duties superior to those arising from any human relation, but [not including] essentially political, sociological, or philosophical views or merely personal moral code." Seeger's beliefs were not based upon God in any traditional sense. He apparently "held skepticism or disbelief in the existence of God," and supported his views with references to Plato, Aristotle, and Spinoza for support of his ethical beliefs "without belief in God, except in the remotest sense." The Court held, however, that Seeger's beliefs were religious:

> We believe that under this construction, the test of belief "in relation to a Supreme Being" in whether a given belief that is sincere and meaningful occupies a place in the life of its possessor parallel to that filled by the orthodox belief in God of one who clearly qualifies for the exemption.[52]

That's quite a shift from the days of Justice Story! Consider the progression (or regression) of the Court's thinking:

1899, *Holy Trinity*: ". . . this is a Christian nation."

1951, *Zorach*: "We are a religious people whose institutions presuppose a Supreme Being."

1961, *Torcaso*: ". . . neither can aid those religions based on a belief in the existence of God as against those religions founded on different beliefs."

---

52. *Seeger* involves a definition of the term "religious training and belief" as it is used in a federal statute rather than as the term "religion" is used in the First Amendment. Nevertheless, it gives some indication of the Court's current thinking about religion.

1965, *Seeger*: ". . . whether a given belief that is sincere and meaningful occupies a place in the life of its possessor parallel
to that filled by the orthodox belief in God. . . ."

The Court has thus moved from Christian, to religions presupposing a Supreme
Being, to religions whether or not they believe in God, to whatever is meaningful to the individual. Most of the Founding Fathers would only shake their
heads in disbelief.

The Free Exercise Clause

There is a second important section to the religion clauses of the First Amendment: ". . . or prohibiting the free exercise thereof. . . ." Sometimes the courts
seem to downplay the free exercise clause and treat it as subordinate to the
establishment clause. Yet at least two leading constitutional scholars, Professor
Leo Pfeffer and Professor Lawrence Tribe of Harvard, agree that the free
exercise clause should be the more dominant of the two. Pfeffer has called the
free exercise clause, the "favored child" of the First Amendment.[53] Tribe says
bluntly, ". . . the free exercise principle should be dominant in any conflict
with the anti-establishment principle."[54] He reasons that the First Amendment
embodies two basic principles: separatism (the establishment clause) and volun-
tarism (the free exercise clause). "Of the two principles," he says, "volun-
tarism may be the more fundamental."[55]

Conflict does develop between the two clauses occasionally. The use of
military chaplains is one such issue. Those opposed to military chaplains argue
that a chaplain wearing a Christian cross on a military uniform, paid by the
government, commissioned by the government, and using military chapels on
government property, violates the establishment clause. Supporters of the
chaplaincy counter that without chaplains many military personnel would be
denied their right to free exercise of religion, especially those stationed in remote
areas. So far the courts have resolved this question in favor of allowing chaplains
(*Cruz v. Beto*, 405 U.S. 319, 1972), but the issue is currently being litigated
again. Another establishment/free exercise conflict currently being litigated involves the rights of religious student groups to use public school facilities for
their meetings.

Still another such conflict concerns government aid to private schools. Supporters argue that such aid is necessary to preserve the right of Christian parents
to send their children to schools of their faith, especially since they are already
forced to subsidize the public schools with taxes. But opponents argue that
government aid to private schools furthers the religious purpose of those schools
and thus violates the establishment clause. Courts have decided this issue both

53. Leo Pfeffer, p. 74.
54. Lawrence H. Tribe, *American Constitutional Law* (Mineola, New York: Foundation Press,
1978),§14-7, p. 833.
55. Ibid., §14-3, p. 818.

ways, as we will see in chapter 16. But in a recent case in which the Supreme Court struck down certain types of aid as violating the establishment clause, two dissenting judges accentuated the establishment/free exercise conflict. Justice Rehnquist wrote,

> The Court apparently believes that the Establishment Clause of the First Amendment not only mandates religious neutrality on the part of government but also requires that this Court go further and throw its weight on the side of those who believe that our society as a whole should be a purely secular one.

And Chief Justice Burger wrote an additional dissenting opinion, saying,

> One can only hope that at some future date the Court will come to a more enlightened and tolerant view of the First Amendment's guarantee of free exercise of religion, thus eliminating the denial of equal protection to children in church-sponsored schools, and take a more realistic view that carefully limited aid to children is not a step toward establishing a state religion—at least while this court sits. (*Meek v. Pittenger*, 421 U.S. 349 (1975)

Let us now examine the free exercise clause, phrase by phrase.

Thereof

"Congress shall make no law respecting an establishment of religion, or prohibiting the free exercise *thereof*. . . ." Clearly the word "thereof" refers back to the word "religion" in the establishment clause.

But does religion have the same meaning in both clauses? Tribe says that it doesn't. He suggests that religion should be defined more broadly in the free exercise clause than in the establishment clause:

> For the free exercise clause, a dichotomy can usefully be drawn between things "arguably religious" and things not even arguably having a religious character; all that is "arguably religious" should be considered religious in a free exercise analysis. For the establishment clause, an analagous dichotomy distinguishes all that is "arguably non-religious" from all that is clearly religious; anything "arguably non-religious" should not be considered religious in applying the establishment clause.[56]

Professor Tribe argues convincingly, but he ignores the basic principle of statutory construction that when a term is used more than once in a statute, it is presumed to have the same meaning in both instances unless clearly differentiated. In this particular case, framers did not even use the word "religion" in the free exercise clause. Instead, they simply said "thereof", clearly showing they intended the word to have the same meaning in both clauses. And while certain advantages could result from Tribe's interpretation, dangers exist as well. Secular humanism could be considered "arguably religious" and

56. Tribe, §14-6, p. 828.

thereby protected under the free exercise clause yet at the same time "arguably non-religious" and thereby exempted from the establishment clause.

But another question arises. Did the framers mean religion in an institutional or denominational sense, or in an individual way? Whom does the First Amendment protect—churches, or individuals, or both? I believe it protects both, but primarily individuals. Some courts have recently taken the view that a belief not based upon the teachings of a particular church or denomination is a "personal belief" rather than a "religious belief."

But no such dichotomy existed in the minds of the framers. Three of our first four Presidents—Adams, Jefferson and Madison—were apparently not formal members of churches[57], at least while they served in the presidency. Certainly they were devoutly religious men, and considered themselves Christians as they understood the term (Washington was undoubtedly more orthodox in his faith than were the others).[58] And certainly formal church membership is not the *sine qua non* of a Christian. But it seems inconceivable that these men could have intended to limit the protection of the First Amendment to institutions and those belonging to them. Jefferson declared that "religion is a matter which lies solely between man and his God."[59]

In 1981 the Supreme Court moved much closer to the individualist interpretation of the First Amendment in *Thomas v. Review Board of the Indiana Employment Security Division*, 450 U.S. 707. Thomas was a Jehovah's Witness who worked for a foundry and machine company. All was well until he was transferred to the company's munitions department to work on turrets for military tanks. A pacifist, he refused the work, claiming it violated his religious beliefs. When he was fired, he applied for unemployment compensation. The Indiana Supreme Court denied benefits, claiming that his decision was a "personal-philosophical choice rather than a religious choice." The Indiana court pointed out that while the doctrine of the Jehovah's Witnesses prohibits serving in war, it does not specifically prohibit working on military equipment. The court further noted that another Jehovah's Witness testified that he was willing to work on tank turrets and didn't consider such work a violation of his beliefs or of Jehovah's Witness teachings.

But the U.S. Supreme Court reversed and held for Thomas! Ruling that "the guarantee of free exercise is not limited to beliefs which are shared by all of the members of a religious sect", the Court said,

> Intrafaith differences of that kind are not uncommon among followers of a particular creed, and the judicial process is singularly ill equipped to resolve such differences in relation to the Religion Clauses. One can, of

57. Beth, p. 73. Beth also claims that President Washington was not a church member, but this claim is thoroughly refuted by William J. Johnson, *George Washington the Christian* (Milford, Michigan: Mott Media, 1976), pp. 159-202.

58. Johnson, Ibid.

59. Thomas Jefferson, quoted in *Braunfeld v. Brown*, 366 U.S. 599, 604 (1961).

course, imagine an asserted claim so bizarre, so clearly nonreligious in motivation, as not to be entitled to protection under the Free Exercise Clause; but that is not the case here, and the guarantee of free exercise is not limited to beliefs which are shared by all the members of a religious sect. Particularly in this sensitive area, it is not within the judicial function and judicial competence to inquire whether the petitioner or his fellow worker more correctly perceived the commands of their common faith. Courts are not arbiters of scriptural interpretation.

The Court also said in *Thomas*,

The determination of what is a ''religious belief or practice'' is more often than not a difficult and delicate task, as the division in the Indiana Supreme Court attests. However, the resolution of that question is not to turn upon a judicial perception of the particular belief or practice in question; religious beliefs need not be acceptable, logical, consistent, or comprehensible to others in order to merit First Amendment protection. . . .

The Indiana Supreme Court had found that Thomas' beliefs were inconsistent in that he was willing to work for U.S. Steel producing the raw product necessary for the production of tanks, but would not work on the production of the actual tanks themselves. But the U.S. Supreme Court said the Indiana Supreme Court's comments were ill-founded:

The [Indiana Supreme] court found this position inconsistent with Thomas' stated opposition to participation in the production of armaments. But, Thomas' statements reveal no more than that he found work in the roll foundry sufficiently insulated from producing weapons for war. We see, therefore, that Thomas drew a line, and it is not for us to say that the line he drew was an unreasonable one. Courts should not undertake to dissect religious beliefs because the believer admits that he is ''struggling'' with his position or because his beliefs are not articulated with the clarity and precision that a more sophisticated person might enjoy.

Most of the Founding Fathers would have abhorred Thomas' beliefs. But once they figured out what tank turrets were and what unemployment compensation was, I think they would have applauded the Court's decision.

While religious beliefs need not be institutionalized, they must be sincere and deeply held as upheld in *Wisconsin v. Yoder*, 406 U.S. 205 (1972). And the courts are more likely to protect a citizen's right to free exercise of religion if the issue concerns a doctrine or practice that is ''central'' to his religion, than if it is merely a peripheral or insignificant minor detail. In examining centrality, the court considers how important the religious belief or practice is to the person or church, and how severely the conflicting governmental action will affect the religion. For example, in *People v. Woody*, 394 P.2d 813 (1964), the California Supreme Court held that the sacramental use of peyote in Navaho religious ceremonies was such a cornerstone of the Navaho religion, that they ruled California anti-drug laws inapplicable to such practices.

Obviously, the centrality test raises problems. It requires the government to examine religious beliefs and make often subjective judgements as to the importance of those beliefs. Consider Communion, for example. A court might consider Communion less "central" to a Baptist who regards Communion as a symbolic ordinance than to a Catholic or Lutheran who regards Communion as a sacrament in which God's grace is imparted to the believer. When government starts making determinations such as this, it runs the risk of "excessive entanglement" in violation of the three-prong establishment clause set forth in *Lemon v. Kurtzman.*

Free Exercise

In *Reynolds v. United States*, 98 U.S. 145 (1878), another Mormon polygamy case, the Supreme Court said of the free exercise clause:

> Congress was deprived of all legislative power over mere opinion, but was left free to reach actions which were in violation of social duties or subversive of good order.

In so ruling, the Court set forth the famous "belief-action dichotomy"—the First Amendment protects religious beliefs, but not religious actions. Of all the theories the courts have ever come up with concerning religious freedom, this is among the most dangerous and ill-founded.

If religious freedom protects belief only, it is meaningless and ineffective. Freedom of belief exists in every nation of the world and at all times in history. Even in the most dictatorial, tyrannical, and totalitarian nation of the world, you are free to believe whatever you want so long as you keep your mouth shut and don't do anything about it. If religious liberty means only freedom of belief, perfect religious liberty exists in Cambodia and Russia! It will always be so until technology develops a device to read and control the thoughts of man.

Only when beliefs manifest themselves in words and actions does religion become a threat to totalitarian government. It is actions, not beliefs, that stand in need of constitutional protection.

The framers of the First Amendment recognized that. When Congress considered the First Amendment, its earlier proposed forms prohibited Congress from making any law "to infringe on the rights of conscience" or "infringing the rights of conscience." But Congress changed the wording to read, "prohibiting the free *exercise* thereof." Exercise clearly relates to the practice of religion, not just belief. It is an action word!

More recently the courts have retreated somewhat from the "belief-action dichotomy" of *Reynolds.* They now generally hold that while both beliefs and actions are protected, they are protected in different degrees: beliefs are absolutely protected, but actions may be restricted in some very limited circumstances. Justice Roberts explained in *Cantwell v. Connecticut*, 310 U.S. 296 (1940):

. . . the amendment raises two concepts—freedom to believe and freedom to act. The first is absolute, but, in the nature of things, the second cannot be. Conduct remains subject to regulation for the protection of society. The freedom to act must have appropriate definition to preserve the enforcement of that protection. In every case the power to regulate must be so exercised as not, in attaining a permissible end, unduly to infringe the protected freedom.

So when may the state restrict religious actions? Let us consider that question under the term "prohibiting."

Prohibiting

If a state passed a statute forbidding anyone to worship at a Baptist Church, that would clearly violate the free exercise clause. By so doing, the government would be prohibiting the free exercise of religion.

But the prohibition need not be that explicit or direct. What if a state passed a law forbidding worship at Baptist churches at any time except between the hours of 2:00 and 3:00 AM Wednesday mornings? Or what if a state were to impose a $100 tax on everyone, but an additional $400 tax on all Baptists? While the state has not made it totally impossible for Baptists to exercise their faith, such laws substantially burden the Baptist faith and would undoubtedly be struck down as unconstitutional violations of the free exercise clause.

However, not every action that affects religion is unconstitutional. The mere fact that a state regulation makes it somewhat more difficult to practice religion does not necessarily make that regulation unconstitutional. What prohibitions will be upheld by the courts, and what prohibitions will be struck down?

The courts used to distinguish between "direct" and "indirect" burdens upon free exercise of religion. For example, in *Braunfeld v. Brown,* 366 U.S. 599 (1961), a Jewish businessman objected to a Sunday closing law, saying it infringed upon his right to freely exercise his religion. In obedience to his Jewish faith, his business was closed on Saturday. Since the law required him to also close on Sunday, he was open only five days a week. This gave his non-Jewish competitors an advantage since they were open six days a week. But the Supreme Court upheld the constitutionality of Sunday closing laws, and held that the burden this law imposed upon Braunfeld was only indirect and thus permissable. Braunfeld's religion did not require that he be open on Sunday, and the law did not require that he close on Saturday. The law only said he had to close on Sunday. If Braunfeld's religion had required him to be open on Sunday, that would be a direct burden and probably unconstitutional. If the law had required Braunfeld to be open on Saturday, that again would be a direct burden. But the law did not require Braunfeld to do anything contrary to his faith; it only made it more inconvenient or expensive for him to follow his religion. Thus the "direct/indirect" test was born.

However, the *Braunfeld* case did not go so far as to say that any burden upon religion would be upheld so long as it is only indirect. Some indirect burdens may be unconstitutional, too:

> Of course, to hold unassailable all legislation regulating conduct which imposes solely an indirect burden on the observance of religion would be a gross simplification.

The direct/indirect test seems to have been modified further by *Sherbert v. Verner*, 374 U.S. 398 (1963), and by *Thomas v. Review Board*, 450 U.S. 707 (1981). In *Thomas* the Court said:

> Where the state conditions receipt of an important benefit upon conduct proscribed by religious faith, or where it denies such a benefit because of conduct mandated by religious belief, thereby putting substantial pressure on an adherent to modify his behavior and to violate his beliefs, a burden upon religion exists. While the compulsion may be indirect, the infringement upon free exercise is nonetheless substantial.

This seems to be the test the Supreme Court now follows in determining whether legislation unduly infringes upon free exercise—not whether the infringement is direct or indirect, but whether the infringement is 'substantial.''

In free speech and equal protection cases the courts sometimes employ the term ''chilling effect''—is the government action cited likely to cause people to refrain from exercising their right to free speech? The principle seems applicable to freedom cases as well.

Of course, the fact that a state statute imposes a substantial burden upon the free exercise of religion does not automatically mean the statute will be held unconstitutional. Sometimes the public interest is so great, so compelling, that the courts conclude the burden on religion must be allowed to stand.

Suppose a religious cult practices human sacrifice. Let us concede they deeply and sincerely believe their god requires human sacrifice, and that human sacrifice is ''central'' to their religion. May they practice human sacrifice and evade laws against homicide on the ground of free exercise of religion?

Certainly not! The court would undoubtedly hold that the state has a ''compelling interest'' in protecting human life, and laws against human sacrifice would be upheld even though they did substantially burden the free exercise of religion in this case.

That's the test the courts impose in free exercise cases—compelling state interest. Earlier cases used a balancing test, balancing the interest of the state in enforcing its statute against the interest of the individual in pursuing his religion. But more recent cases, such as *Sherbert v. Verner*, 374 U.S. 398 (1963), have held that the free exercise of religion is such a preferred or fundamental right that a mere balancing test is not enough. Rather, the state must show that its interest is of the very highest order, that its interest is ''compelling''.

But the state's burden does not stop there. Not only must the state show that its interest is compelling; it must also show that that interest cannot be achieved by less restrictive means. In other words, if a means exists whereby the state can fulfill its compelling interest without burdening the individual's free exercise of religion, the state must use that less restrictive means.

Wisconsin v. Yoder, 406 U.S. 205 (1972), illustrates this principle. Jonas Yoder, an Amishman, refused to send his children to public school beyond the eighth grade. Instead, he sent them for two years to an informal private school taught by Amish teachers who were not certified and had less than a high school education. The state therefore prosecuted him for violating Wisconsin's compulsory school attendance law.

The U.S. Supreme Court examined the case carefully. The Court noted that Yoder's refusal was based on deeply and sincerely held religious convictions, and that the compulsory attendance law imposed a substantial burden upon his religious convictions.

The Court then noted that the state of Wisconsin had a legitimate interest in making sure the Amish children receive an education. Without an education, they might not be good citizens, and might not be able to support themselves and thus end up public charges.

But the Court then employed the "less restrictive means" test: must the state require him to send his children to "school" in order for the state to fulfill its interest? The Court found that the Amish children were learning basic skills, good work habits, and good citizenship in their informal school setting, and that the state's interest in education was thereby adequately fulfilled. Since the state's interest could be fulfilled without requiring Yoder and other Amishmen to send their children to formal schools, the Court exempted the Amish from the compulsory attendance law using the doctrine of "less restrictive means."[60]

Other cases have held that the "less restrictive means" test must be employed where fundamental constitutional rights are at stake, even though to do so might involve greater expense or administrative inconvenience. See *Stanley v. Illinois*, 405 U.S. 645 (1972); and *Cleveland Board of Education v. LaFleur*, 414 U.S. 632 (1974).

In cases like *Yoder* the courts do not always strike down a statute in its entirety.

---

60. Some commentators have suggested that the *Yoder* case signaled a court shift away from the "compelling state interest" doctrine and a retreat to the "balancing of interests" test employed in earlier decades. I disagree. The Court said that only interests of an "overriding magnitude" and "of the highest order" could justify an intrusion on religious liberty. These terms seem to have the same meaning as "compelling state interest." The reason the Court did not specifically designate the state's interest in education as "compelling" was that it had no reason to do so. Having already determined that the state's interest in education was adequately fulfilled through the informal Amish schools, the Court had no reason to determine whether the state's interest was compelling or not. Subsequent cases have labeled the government's interest as "very high"(*United States v. Lee,* 102 S. Ct. 1051, 1982); "pressing"(*Heffron v. International Society for Krishna Consciousness,* Inc., 452 U.S. 640, 1981); and not "of the highest order" (*McDaniel v. Paty, 435 U.S. 618, 1978*). See Leonard F. Manning, *The Law of Church-State Relations in a Nutshell* (St. Paul: West, 1981), pp. 277-280.

Increasingly they have practiced "constitutional exemption." That is, the court holds the statute constitutional on its face but unconstitutional as applied to the particular defendant who objects to it on religious grounds. In effect, the court grants the particular defendant—and those who object for similar reasons—an exemption from the requirements of the statute.

For example, in *Yoder* the Court did not strike down Wisconsin's compulsory attendance law and say that school attendance is no longer compulsory. Rather, the Court said that everybody else has to obey the law, but the Amish are exempt because (1) they object on religious grounds and (2) they can fulfill the state's interest in a less restrictive way.[61] This practice of exemption, like the practice of accommodation under the establishment clause, is the Court's way of trying to reconcile the legitimate interests of the state with the legitimate free exercise rights of the individual.

A Question of Jurisdiction

We have spoken of the belief-action dichotomy, the compelling state interest test, the centrality test, the less restrictive means test, and the like. All of these have value, and we must understand them to know what the courts are thinking and saying. But the terminology largely avoids the real issue.

In reality, the First Amendment is a matter of *jurisdiction*.

Two concepts influenced the Founding Fathers. One was the Christian view of government, which holds that God has given the state only certain limited powers, and government can exercise only such powers as are given by God. The source of these powers, it is often held, is God's covenant with Noah found in Genesis 9.

The other concept is the theory of social contract. John Locke promoted this view, influencing Jefferson and others. Under this view, at some time in history (whether literally or figuratively), men entered into a social contract among themselves to establish a government. They agreed to surrender certain powers to that government so that the government would have enough power to function effectively. Government has only those powers delegated to it by men under the social contract, and no more.

These two concepts are not incompatible. As noted earlier, Locke identified the social contract with the Noachic Covenant.[62] Both concepts lead to the same

---

61. It is often difficult to know how broadly or how narrowly to construe a constitutional exemption. In Christian school cases a debate is currently raging in the courts as to whether *Yoder* applies only to the Amish or whether it includes other Christians who object to public schools on religious grounds. I will consider this question more fully in Chapter 16. Suffice it to say for now that I believe all who object to public schools on religious grounds are covered by *Yoder*. To apply the *Yoder* decision narrowly to the Amish would be to "establish" the Amish religion by giving the Amish preferential treatment over others, and also it would deny other faiths the equal protection of the law to which they are entitled under the Fourteenth Amendment.

62. John Locke, quoting King James I, reprinted in Hall, p. 112: ". . . every just King, in a settled Kingdom, is bound to observe the Paction made to his Poeple, by his Laws in framing his Government agreeable Thereunto, according to that Paction which God made with Noah after the Deluge."

conclusion: government power is strictly limited to those spheres over which it has been granted jurisdiction.

Relying on social contract theory, Jefferson argued that the regulation of religious opinions was beyond the government's jurisdiction, because it was not included in the social contract:

> Our rulers can have no authority over such natural rights, only as we have submitted to them. The rights of conscience we have never submitted, we could not submit. We are answerable for them to our God.[63]

Many of the American colonists recognized the jurisdictional nature of religious liberty. Roger Williams was one such person. Vernon Parrington writes concerning Roger Williams:

> It was not toleration in the narrow sense of benevolent non-interference by an authority that refrained from exercising its reserved right, that Roger Williams was interested in; it was rather religious liberty as a fundamental human right, that had never been surrendered to the civil power, that lay *beyond its jurisdiction* and was in no way answerable to it. [64](emphasis supplied)

Similarly, J. B. Bury says: "To Roger Williams belongs the glory of having founded the first modern state which was really tolerant and based on the principle of *taking the control of religious matters entirely out of the hands of civil government.*"[65] (emphasis supplied)

In his second inaugural address, Jefferson declared: "In matters of religion, I have considered that its free exercise is placed by the Constitution *independent of the powers of the general government.*"[66] (emphasis supplied) Jefferson expressed the same theme when he wrote to a clergyman in 1808:

> I consider the government of the United States as interdicted by the Constitution from intermeddling with religious institutions, their doctrines, discipline, or exercises. This results not only from the provision that no law shall be made respecting the establishment or free exercise of religion, but from that also which reserves to the states the powers not delegated to the United States. Clearly, no power to prescribe any religious exercise, or to assume authority in religious discipline, has been delegated to the general government.[67]

63. Thomas Jefferson, "Notes on Virginia, Query XVII: The Different Religions Received Into That State," *Complete Jefferson*, p. 675; quoted by Michael J. Malbin, *Religion and Politics: The Intentions of the Authors of the First Amendment* (Washington, D.C.: American Enterprise Institute for Public Policy Research, 1978), p. 34.

64. Vernon Parrington, *Main Currents in American Thought* (New York: Harcourt, 1930), 1:71; cited by Taylor, p. 519.

65. J. B. Bury, *A History of Freedom of Thought* (Oxford University Press, 1947), p. 97; quoted in Taylor,, p. 542.

66. *Writings of Thomas Jefferson*, Ford ed., 8:344; quoted in Roberts, p. 200.

67. *Jefferson's Writings*, Monticello ed., 1905, 9:428-430; cited by Roberts, p. 200.

James Madison, in his famous "Memorial and Remonstrance Against Religious Assessments", stated in part:

> We maintain, therefore, that in matters of religion no man's right is abridged by the institution of civil society; and that religion is wholly exempt from its cognizance. . . . If religion be exempt from the authority of the society at large, still less can it be subject to that of the legislative body. The latter are but the creatures and vice-regents of the Former. Their jurisdiction is both derivative and limited. It is limited with regard to the coordinate department; more necessarily is it limited with regard to the constituents. . . .[68]

Some years later, Madison argued that the Constitution was not to create "a shadow of right in the general government to intermeddle with religion."[69] Likewise Edmund Randolf pointed out to the Virginia ratification convention that "no power is expressly given to Congress over religion."[70] A Congregational minister who was a delegate to the Massachusetts ratifying convention argued that "God alone is the God of conscience, and, consequently, attempts to erect human tribunals for the conscience of men, are impious encroachments upon the prerogatives of God."[71]

Isaac Backus, the agent for the Baptists in their relations with the State of Massachusetts, argued against state interference with religion on jurisdictional grounds. He declared,

> The free exercises of private judgement, and the unalienable rights of conscience, are of too high a rank and dignity to be submitted to the decrees of councils, or the imperfect laws of fallible legislator . . . religion is a concern between God and the soul with which no human authority can intermeddle. . . .[72]

Samuel Stillman, pastor of the First Baptist Church in Boston, in his election sermon of 1779, proclaimed that the "jurisdiction of the magistrate neither can nor ought in any manner to be extended to the salvation of souls."[73] And John Leland, Baptist leader in Virginia, argued that "Government has no more to do with the religious opinions of men than it has with the principles of mathematics."[74]

This jurisdictional view of religious liberty is embodied in the First Amendment but does not depend upon the First Amendment for its validity. It is

---

68. James Madison, "Memorial and Remonstrance Against Religious Assessments" (1784); quoted by Frommer, pp. 9-14.

69. *Madison*, 5:176; quoted in Pfeffer, p. 110.

70. Pfeffer, ibid.

71. Elliott, *Debates*, 2:118-120, 148-149; quoted in Pfeffer, p. 116.

72. Isaac Backus, quoted by Pfeffer, p. 89.

73. Samuel Stillman, quoted in Humphrey, p. 333; quoted in Pfeffer, p. 89.

74. John Leland, "Rights of Conscience and therefore Religious Opinions not cognizable by law," quoted by Humphrey, p. 466; quoted by Pfeffer, p. 89.

inherent in the Constitution itself, which delegates certain powers to government and impliedly reserves all other powers from the general government. Were there any question about this, the Tenth Amendment would settle it: "The powers not delegated to the United States by the Constitution, nor prohibited by it to the States, are reserved to the States respectively, or to the people." As the historian George Bancroft has noted, "Congress therefore from the beginning was as much without the power to make a law respecting the establishment of religion as it is now after the amendment has been passed."[75] And the historian Charles Beard says, "The Constitution does not confer upon the Federal government any power whatever to deal with religion in any form or manner. . . . the First Amendment merely confirms the intention of the framers."[76]

It is interesting to note that the founding fathers recognized this jurisdictional limit even before the Constitution was enacted. In 1783 a Catholic official in Paris wrote to Benjamin Franklin suggesting that a Catholic bishopric be established in one of the American cities. Franklin forwarded the request to Congress. Congress directed Franklin to reply

> that the subject of his application to Dr. Franklin, being purely spiritual,
> it is *without the jurisdiction and powers of Congress*, who have *no authority* to permit or refuse it; these powers being reserved to the several States individually.[77] (emphasis supplied)

The advantage of the jurisdictional approach to religious freedom is that it is a more objective test than either the "reasonable relationship" or the "compelling interest" test. Both of those tests depend upon the subjective view of a judge as to whether a relationship is reasonable or a state interest is compelling. But once it is established that religious freedom is outside the jurisdiction of government, then all that is necessary to establish that the activity in question is religious in nature. Then it doesn't matter whether the relationship is reasonable or the state interest is compelling; the court is utterly without jurisdiction to grant the state the relief it requests, because neither the court nor the state has any jurisdiction over religion.

This jurisdictional view of the First Amendment, while it is not a new one, is nevertheless likely to strike many lawyers and judges as unique. For it is not the usual basis upon which courts decide First Amendment cases today. However, the jurisdictional objection could and should be asserted along with other more common grounds in the defense of First Amendment cases. Proposed government interference with the free exercise of religion is invalid, first, because the Constitution confers upon the government no jurisdiction over

---

75. George Bancroft, quoted in Schaff, *Church and State in the United States* (Papers of the American Historical Society, 1888), p. 137; quoted in Pfeffer, p. 115.

76. Charles Beard, *The Republic* (New York: Viking Press, 1944), pp. 166, 170; quoted in Pfeffer, ibid.

77. Pfeffer, p. 108.

religious matters; and second, because even if it does, the state has no compelling interest in enforcing this regulation. Substantiating either point could bring victory.

Chapter 11

Other Constitutional Rights
of Special Significance
for Christians

As important as the religion clauses of the First Amendment are in defending Christian liberty, they are not the only weapons in the Christian's arsenal. Here are several others, starting with the remainder of the First Amendment itself.

Or Abridging The Freedom of Speech

The First Amendment contains more than the religion clauses. It reads in its entirety:

> Congress shall make no law respecting an establishment of religion, or prohibiting the free exercise thereof; or abridging the freedom of speech, or of the press; or of the right of the people peaceably to assemble, and to petition the Government for a redress of grievances.

The average person would probably define freedom of speech as the right to say whatever one wants to say. This definition is essentially correct. However, freedom of speech also includes means of expression besides the spoken word, such as gestures, symbols like armbands, modes of dress, etc. For this reason the various forms of free speech are often lumped under one general title: freedom of expression.

It is sometimes said that freedom of speech, like other freedoms, is relative rather than absolute; that is, it must be balanced against rights of other persons and against the interest of the state.

However, a better view in my opinion is that freedom of speech is absolute, but that certain types of speech are not included in the First Amendment. In other words, every type of speech protected by the First Amendment is an absolute right, but some types of speech do not come within the scope of the First Amendment and are not protected at all. As the Supreme Court stated in *Chaplinsky v. New Hampshire*, 315 U.S. 568 (1942):

> There are certain well-defined and narrowly limited classes of speech, the prevention and punishment of which have never been thought to raise any Constitutional problem. These include the lewd and obscene, the profane, the libelous, and the insulting or "fighting" words—those which by their very utterance inflict injury or tend to incite an immediate breach of the peace. It has been well observed that such utterances are no essential part of any exposition of ideas, and are of such slight social value as a step to truth that any benefit that may be derived from them is clearly outweighed by the social interest in order and morality.

Let me suggest nine categories of speech which are not covered by the First Amendment and which the government may regulate or prohibit:

(1) *Defamatory or slanderous speech*; that is, speech which untruly and maliciously maligns another person.

(2) *Obscenity*. Obscenity is difficult to define; such dictionary definitions as "offensive to accepted standards of decency or modesty"[1] do little to clarify its meaning for us. That which is truly obscene, however, is not protected by the First Amendment. The meaning and status of obscenity will be discussed more fully in chapter 19.

(3) *Commercial speech*, such as the distribution of advertising leaflets, etc. The courts have not been entirely clear on the extent to which commercial speech is entitled to First Amendment constitutional protection, but in general the courts have held that commercial speech is entitled to at least some protection but may be regulated more than religious or political speech. Comparing *Valentine v. Chrestensen*, 316 U.S. 52 (1942) to *Martin v. Struthers*, 319 U.S. 141 (1943), it would appear that speech for religious purposes is a "fundamental" or "preferred" right whereas mere commercial speech is not, and consequently commercial speech is subject to reasonable regulation by the state whereas religious speech cannot be regulated without the showing of a compelling state interest.

(4) *Speech in a restricted environment*, such as a prison or a military reservation. With the increasing tendency of the courts to recognize that military personnel are entitled to exercise their constitutional rights, and the growing emphasis on the rights of prisoners, it will be interesting to see whether the courts continue to view this type of speech in the same way.

(5) *Speech outside a "First Amendment forum"*. A "First Amendment forum" is a place in which public discussion is reasonably to be expected, such as public buildings, public streets, schools and classrooms, public meeting places, etc. Normally such forum is a public place, but at times courts have recognized

---

1. *The American Heritage Dictionary of the English Language*, 1976 ed., s.v. "Obscenity."

privately owned facilities such as parking lots, shopping centers, etc., as First Amendment forums as well. If a place or facility is a First Amendment forum, then the First Amendment right of free speech applies and may not be regulated without a compelling state interest. If it is not a First Amendment forum, then the right does not apply and speech is a privilege which may be regulated according to reasonable purposes of the state. The Supreme Court has recognized that the public schools are, at least part of the time, a First Amendment forum (*Tinker v. Des Moines School District*, 393 U.S. 503 [1969]), but that a city-owned bus service is not a First Amendment forum and therefore advertising space on the bus to a candidate for public office could be denied (*Lehman v. Shaker Heights*, 418 U.S. 298 [1974]).

(6) *Speech that creates a clear and present danger to public order*, the 'fighting words'' referred to earlier. Included in this category would be communicating threats to another person.

(7) *Speech that creates a clear and present danger to national security*, such as advocating the violent overthrow of the United States government with a reasonable possibility of success, or divulging military secrets.

(8) *Speech that creates a clear and present danger to public safety*, such as shouting "fire" in a crowded theater.

(9) *Speech that advocates violating the law*. One who encourages another to rob a bank cannot rely upon the First Amendment for his defense.

The First Amendment protection of free speech is of special interest to Christians because our expression and proclamation of the Christian faith is just as much "speech" as any other kind of speech. Therefore the Christian lawyer, when he defends a case involving the liberty of Christian people to express themselves (such as witnessing on a college campus or in a public shopping mall, broadcasting over the airwaves, etc.) might very well wish to frame his defense on both the "free exercise" clause and the "free speech" clause. There are three advantages in doing so:

(1) As we discussed in the last chapter, the courts sometimes weigh the significance of a religious belief in terms of its "centrality" or importance to the person or religious group involved. No such centrality test is used in free speech cases.

(2) In free exercise of religious cases, the courts frequently try to determine whether the beliefs asserted are truly religious as against philosophical or ideological, and whether they are sincere and deeply held. Sometimes the courts raise this question in terms of whether the beliefs are "convictions" or mere "preferences." No such test is employed in free speech cases.

(3) Still a third reason is that some judges regard the protection of religious liberty as being less important in this day and age than the protection of free speech. Some judges aren't particularly concerned about religion themselves and therefore don't see why others should be. By phrasing a constitutional

defense in terms of free speech as well as free exercise of religion, the Christian may have a greater chance of winning in court.

One of the greatest victories Christians have won before the Supreme Court in recent years is the case of *Widmar v. Vincent*, 454 U.S. 263 (1981), involving the right of a Christian student group called Cornerstone to meet on the campus of the University of Missouri-Kansas City. When the university denied Cornerstone the right to meet on campus, members of Cornerstone sued. Not only did they claim that they were being denied their right to the free exercise of religion; they also claimed they were being denied their right to freedom of speech and freedom of association. They further claimed they were denied equal protection under the law in violation of the Fourteenth Amendment, since nonreligious groups were allowed to meet on campus. The Supreme Court decided in favor of Cornerstone by an 8-1 margin, but they did so on the basis of the free speech clause rather than the other rights mentioned above. The decision was a landmark because it established that religious speech is entitled to the same protection under the free speech clause as any other type of speech.

Or of the Press

In the popular mind, freedom of speech and freedom of the press are closely linked together. They should be. But do they mean the same thing? How are they different?

Former Supreme Court Justice Potter Stewart says the purpose of the free press guarantee is "to create a fourth institution outside the government as an additional check on the three official branches."[2] Justice Stewart believes the free press clause gives the press special protection:

> Most of the provisions of the Bill of Rights protect specific liberties or specific rights of individuals: freedom of speech, freedom of worship, the right to counsel, the privilege against compulsory self-incrimination, to name a few. In contrast, the free press clause extends protection to an institution. The publishing business is, in short, the only organized private business that is given explicit constitutional protection.
>
> . . . it is tempting to suggest that freedom of the press means only that newspaper publishers are guaranteed freedom of expression. They are guaranteed that freedom, to be sure, but so are we all because of the free speech clause. If the free press guarantee meant no more than the freedom of expression, it would be a constitutional redundancy. . . . By including both guarantees in the First Amendment, the Founders quite clearly recognized the distinction between the two.[3]

Justice Stewart continues:

> For centuries before our Revolution, the press in England had been licensed,

2. U.S. Supreme Court Justice Potter Stewart, "Or of the Press," *Hastings Law Journal* 26:631 (1975), p. 634.
3. Ibid.

censored, and bedeviled by prosecutions for sedition and libel. The British Crown knew that a free press was not just a neutral vehicle for the balanced discussion of diverse ideas. Instead, the free press meant organized, expert scrutiny of government. The press was a conspiracy of the intellectuals, with the courage of numbers. This formidable check on official power was what the British Crown had feared—and what the American Founders decided to risk.[4]

Some constitutional scholars do not accept Justice Stewart's assertion that the free press clause gives the press special protection not afforded the general masses. Writing in *First National Bank of Boston v. Bellotti*, 435 U.S. 765 (1978), Chief Justice Burger says,

> . . . although certainty on this point is not possible, the history of the clause does not suggest that the authors contemplated a "special" or "institutional" privilege. . . .
>
> Indeed most pre-First Amendment commentators "who employed the term 'freedom of speech' with great frequency, used it synonomously with freedom of the press." L. Levy, *Legacy of Supression: Freedom of Speech and Press in Early American History*, 174 (1963)
>
> Those interpreting the press clause as extending protection only to, or creating a special role for, the "institutional press" must either (a) assert such an intention on the part of the Framers for which no supporting evidence is available, . . . (b) argue that events after 1791 somehow operated to "constitutionalize this interpretation", . . . or (c) candidly acknowledging the absence of historical support, suggest that the intent of the Framers is not important today. . . .
>
> To conclude that the Framers did not intend to limit the freedom of the press to one select group is not necessarily to suggest that the press clause is redundant. The speech clause standing alone may be viewed as a protection of the liberty to express ideas and beliefs, while the press clause focuses specifically on the liberty to disseminate expression broadly and "comprehends every sort of publication which affords a vehicle of information and opinion." *Lovell v Griffin*, 303 U.S. 444, 452, 58 S. Ct. 666, 669 (1938). Yet there is no fundamental distinction between expression and dissemination. The liberty encompassed by the press clause, although complimentary to and a natural extension of speech clause liberty, merited special mention simply because it had been more often the object of official restraints.

I lean toward Chief Justice Burger's interpretation. I think the Framers intended the free speech clause to protect oral communication and the free press clause to protect written, especially printed communication. One modern development which may affect the way these clauses are applied today is the development of the electronic media. In 1791, one could reach more people

4. Ibid.

by a written or printed communication than by a verbal one. Today, with national network radio and television, the reverse may be true.

Christian writers and publishers—whether of major books or merely of church newsletters—might well consider using the free press guarantee as well as the free exercise of religion guarantee in the defense of First Amendment cases.

Freedom of Assembly and Association

Freedom of assembly and association are not synonymous, but both are thought to be related to freedom of expression. They include the right to associate for economic and noneconomic purposes alike, *NAACP v. Alabama*, 357 U.S. 449 (1958). The state probably has a compelling interest to assert reasonable regulations on an assembly and association for purposes of traffic control, etc., such as requiring permits to march on public streets, etc., *Cox v. New Hampshire*, 312 U.S. 569 (1941). But an arbitrary denial of this right would be unconstitutional, *Fowler v. Rhode Island*, 345 U.S. 67 (1953).

The Ninth Amendment

"The enumeration in the Constitution, of certain rights, shall not be construed to deny or disparage others retained by the people."

In his well-written book, *The Forgotten Ninth Amendment*, Bennet Patterson explains its purpose: "The Ninth Amendment to the Constitution is a basic statement of the inherent natural rights of the individual"[5]

The Ninth and Tenth Amendments, far from being "dead letters" as is commonly assumed by modern jurists, are pivotal to a proper understanding of government as being limited in nature and derivative in its powers. (In fact, that is precisely why these amendments are being ignored!) When the Bill of Rights was adopted in 1789, some objected that by enumerating certain rights, they might prejudice other rights that were not mentioned. James Madison explained that the purpose of the Ninth Amendment was to overcome that problem and establish once and for all that men possess certain natural and inherent rights which exist whether or not they are mentioned in the Constitution. As Madison said,

> It has been objected also against the bill of rights, that, by enumerating particular exceptions to the grant of power, it would disparage those rights which were not placed in that enumeration; and it might follow by implication, that those rights which were not singled out, were intended to be assigned into the hands of the General Government, and were consequently insecure. This is one of the most plausible arguments I have ever heard against the adoption of the bill of rights into this system; but, I conceive that it may be guarded against. I have attempted it, as gentlemen may see by turning to the last clause of the fourth resolution [the Ninth Amendment].[6]

5. Bennett B. Patterson, *The Forgotten Ninth Amendment* (Indianapolis: Bobbs-Merrill, 1955), p. 19.
6. James Madison, *I Annals of Congress* 439 (1789).

Justice Goldberg, arguing that the Ninth Amendment is a constitutional guarantee of the individual's right of privacy, stated in *Griswold v. Connecticut*, 381 U.S. 479 (1965), "The Ninth Amendment to the Constitution may be regarded by some as a recent discovery and may be forgotten by others, but since 1791 it has been a basic part of the Constitution which we are sworn to uphold." Justice Goldberg went on to say that for the court to deny that the individual has a right to privacy merely because that right to privacy is not specifically spelled out in the Constitution, violates the meaning and spirit of the Ninth Amendment. Christians possess many fundamental rights in common with all other Americans, even though they are not expressly stated in the Constitution. Among these are the right to privacy, the right to travel, the right to freedom of choice in regard to marriage, procreation, contraception, education and upbringing of children, the freedom to care for their own health and person, the freedom from bodily restaint and compulsion, freedom of movement, freedom of action, and freedom to participate in government.

The Tenth Amendment

"The powers not delegated to the United States by the Constitution, nor prohibited by it to the States, are reserved to the States respectively, or to the people."

Like the Ninth Amendment, the Tenth Amendment has been largely ignored in recent years. Pritchet in *The American Constitution* dismisses the significance of the Tenth Amendment by saying, "Actually it adds nothing new to the Constitution, being simply declaratory of the relation between the national government and the states."[7] And Grimes says,

> Only three amendments—the Tenth, Eleventh, and Twenty-fifth,—would appear to be indifferent or irrelevent to democratic principles. The Tenth Amendment simply declares the federal principle that the powers not delegated to the national government are reserved to the states or to the people.[8]

But far from being "indifferent or irrelevant to democratic principles," the Tenth Amendment safeguards the basic principle upon which limited government rests. The Tenth Amendment establishes the proposition, lest any question should exist concerning it, that the federal government has only those powers delegated to it by the Constitution. If the Constitution doesn't delegate a power to the federal government, that power belongs to the states, or to the people. In other words, the burden does not rest upon the private citizen to show that the Constitution prohibits the government from taking that contemplated action. Rather, it is up to the government to show that the

---

7. C. Herman Pritchet, *The American Constitution* (St. Louis: McGraw-Hill, 1959,1977), p. 48.

8. Allen P. Grimes, *Democracy and the Amendments to the Constitution* (Lexington, Massachusetts: Lexington Books, 1978), p. 166.

Constitution has delegated that power to the government. If the government cannot show that it has that constitutional power, then by virtue of the Tenth Amendment it does not have that power.

In a further effort to dismiss the significance of the Tenth Amendment, Pritchet points out that the anti-federalists in Congress tried to insert the word "expressly" between "not" and "delegated", but they were defeated.[9] He is correct; the proposal was defeated 32 to 17, largely because Madison correctly pointed out that if the word "expressly" was included, the Constitution would have to specify every single power of the federal government in minute detail. Justice Marshall, in *McCulloch v. Maryland*, 4 L.Ed. 579 (1819), 4 Wheat. 316, noted that the framers of the First Amendment had experienced problems resulting from the use of the word "expressly" in the Articles of Confederation and probably omitted it to avoid those problems. Marshall therefore declared that certain "enumerated" powers are expressly granted to the federal government, but there are other "implied" powers which the federal government is implied to have by virtue of its responsibilities. However, Marshall strongly believed that the Federal government had no powers other than those expressly or impliedly delegated to it. The determination as to whether or not a particular power has been delegated to the federal government depends on "a fair construction of the whole instrument [the Constitution]."

In the first few decades of the twentieth century, the Tenth Amendment was cited by the U. S. Supreme Court many times in striking down, as unconstitutional, legislation and acts of Congress that the president designed to regulate various aspects of the nation's commercial life. But between 1937 and 1941 President Franklin D. Roosevelt replaced seven retiring conservative Supreme Court justices with liberals—Justices Black, Reed, Frankfurter, Douglas, Murphy, Byrnes, and Jackson. With the balance on the court changed, this type of government regulation has been regularly sustained as constitutional. Had the Tenth Amendment been given the vigorous interpretation it deserves, much of America's decline into socialism might have been averted.

The Fourteenth Amendment

Section 1 of the Fourteenth Amendment reads in part as follows:

> No State shall make or enforce any law which shall abridge the privileges or immunities of the citizens of the United States; nor shall any State deprive any person of life, liberty, or property, without due process of law; nor deny to any person within its jurisdiction the equal protection of the laws.

Let us analyze three separate clauses of the Fourteenth Amendment.

First, the "privileges and immunities" clause. Stated in very general terms, this clause means that rights you and I have as citizens of the United States— the right to inform U. S. authorities of violations of its laws, the right to vote

9. Pritchet, p. 51.

in national elections, the right to travel from state to state, the right to enter public lands, the right to petition Congress, etc.—may not be abridged by any state.

Second, and more significant, is the "due process" clause. It states simply, "nor shall any state deprive any person of life, liberty, or property, without due process of law." Here we see a constitutional protection of "life, liberty, or property" comparable to that found in the Fifth Amendment. The Fifth Amendment protection applies to the federal government; the Fourteenth Amendment applies to the states.

Obviously, however, some people are deprived of their property; they have to pay fines when convicted of criminal offenses. Some are deprived of their liberty by being sent to jail. On rare occasions someone is even deprived of his life. Note that the amendment says that no one may be deprived of these rights "without due process of law."

What is due process of law? Lawyers speak of due process as two-fold: (1) *Procedural due process*, which requires that the defendant be afforded notice of his trial and a reasonable opportunity to defend himself at the trial, including the right to counsel, to confront and cross-examine witnesses, to subpoena witnesses in his defense, etc.; and (2) *Substantive due process*, which means that governmental power must not be used against him arbitrarily or unreasonably to deny basic constitutional freedoms.

Some court decisions have interpreted the word *liberty* in the Fifth and Fourteenth Amendments ("life, liberty, or property"), as the right to privacy and other fundamental rights not spelled out in the Constitution. Intriguing though this view may be, I lean toward the opinion that deprivation of life, liberty or property refers to criminal penalties in the system of criminal justice, and that the right to privacy and other fundamental rights is better secured by the Ninth Amendment.

Third is the "equal protection" clause: "nor deny to any person within its jurisdiction the equal protection of the laws." "Equal protection" means that persons similarly situated are to receive equal treatment. This doesn't mean that everyone has to be treated exactly the same. Only persons who are similarly situated.

Let us suppose that A, having completed his undergraduate work with a D- average and a score of 127 on his LSAT (Law School Admission Test), sought admission to a state law school, as did B with a 4.0 average and an LSAT of 750. If B were admitted to law school and A was rejected, A would not have a basis for complaining that he had been denied the "equal protection of the laws." Why not? Because there was a rational reason for choosing B and rejecting A: his superior grade point, and his superior aptitude scores.

In other words, the equal protection clause does not prohibit all discrimination. It prohibits only discrimination that lacks a rational basis. Had A been rejected because of his race, he would have a basis for complaint, because race is not a valid basis for discrimination. Had A been rejected because of his religion, A again would have a valid basis for claiming denial of equal protection by a state institution. But A could not claim denial of equal protection of the laws if there was a valid or rational basis for choosing B and not choosing A.

In recent years, government agencies have at times applied a double standard, subjecting Christians to more legal disabilities than other persons. College campuses, for example, which often readily give or rent the use of their facilities to radical, atheist, or homosexual groups, often prohibit Christian groups from using those same facilities. Such action constitutes a denial of equal protection under the Fourteenth Amendment, as well as denial of freedom of speech and free exercise of religion under the First Amendment.

The Right to Privacy

Among the many rights not specifically declared in the Constitution, but nevertheless recognized as fundamental by the courts, is the right to privacy. The U. S. Supreme Court has at various times held that the right to privacy includes two basic aspects: (1) control over knowledge about oneself, that is, the right to access to information about oneself and the right not to give access to that information to others; and (2) self-direction, or the right to control one's destiny at least so far as the government is concerned. The courts have disagreed as to exactly where that right is found in the Constitution. Some have found at least the roots of it in the First Amendment (*Stanley v. Georgia*, 394 U.S. 557 [1969]). Others have seen it in the Third and Fourth Amendments which protect against quartering soldiers and against unreasonable search and seizures and thereby imply a right of privacy (*Terry v. Ohio*, 392 U.S. 1 [1968]; *Katz v United States*, 389 U.S. 347 [1967]; *Olmstead v. United States*, 277 U.S. 438 [1928], see Brandeis dissent); or in the word "liberty" in the Fifth or Fourteenth Amendment (*Meyer v. Nebraska*, 262 U.S. 390 [1923]).

My own view is that since it is expressly mentioned nowhere in the Constitution, it is best secured by reference to the Ninth Amendment (*Griswold v. Connecticut*, 381 U.S. 479 [1965], concurring opinion by Goldberg). However, the Fourteenth Amendment may be asserted as well.

Specific areas of personal life covered by the right to privacy include marriage (*Loving v. Virginia*, 388 U.S. 1 [1967]); procreation (*Skinner v. Oklahoma*, 316 U.S. 535 [1942]); contraception (*Eisenstadt v. Baird*, 405 U.S. 438 [1972]); abortion (*Roe v. Wade*, 410 U.S. 113 [1973]); family relationships (*Prince v. Massachusetts*, 321 U.S. 158 [1944]); and child rearing and education (*Pierce v. Society of Sisters*, 268 U.S. 510 [1925]; *Wisconsin v. Yoder*, 406 U.S. 205.

Fundamental Rights

In the past several decades, the courts have termed certain rights as "fundamental" or "preferred". Among the rights which are considered fundamental are freedom of religion (*Martin v. Struthers*, 319 U.S. 141 [1943]); free speech and press, right to trial by jury and other aspects of due process of law such as right to privacy (*Roe v. Wade*, and others).

Rights that are recognized as "fundamental" cannot be infringed by government unless it can show a "compelling state interest" for doing so (*Kramer v. Union Free School District*, 395 U.S. 621 [1969]; *Shapiro v. Thompson*, 394 U.S. 618 [1969]; *Sherbert v. Verner*, 374 U.S. 398 [1963]). Furthermore, legislative enactments must be narrowly drawn so as to infringe these fundamental rights as little as possible in securing this compelling state interest (*Griswold v. Connecticut*; *Aptheker v. Secretary of State*, 378 U.S. 500 [1964]; *Cantwell v. Connecticut*, 310 U.S. 296 [1940]). This is referred to as the doctrine of "least restrictive means" or "less drastic means."

State Constitutions

The Christian should know what state constitutional protections may be available. Most state constitutions contain express guarantees of religious liberty, although the wording differs greatly from one state to another.

At least in state court, provisions of the state constitution as well as the U.S. Constitution should be cited. Historical precedent may reveal that a particular state constitution has been given a broader interpretation than the federal courts have given to the First Amendment, even though the wording of each may be virtually identical.

In many areas there are few cases that shed light on the interpretation of state constitutional provisions. The Christian lawyer or layman might gain some insight from studying his state's "enabling act." The U.S. Constitution guarantees to every state a "republican form of government." Consequently, before admitting new states to the Union, Congress passed enabling acts which required those states to hold constitutional conventions and pass constitutions which contained certain protections for religious liberty. For example, Congress, on February 22, 1889, passed the Enabling Act for North and South Dakota, Chapter 180, 25 Statutes at Large 676. Section Four authorized the people of North Dakota and South Dakota to hold constitutional conventions, required that their constitutions be republican in form, and also required "that perfect toleration of religious sentiment shall be secured, and that no inhabitant of said states shall ever be molested in person or property on account of his or her mode of religious worship."

"Perfect toleration" and "no inhabitant . . . shall ever be molested" are pretty broad guarantees. And one could argue that Congress' acceptance of North and South Dakota into the Union was a legal determination by Congress that their respective constitutions provided those broad guarantees of religious liberty required by the enabling act. Though this argument is not without problems, and to my knowledge has never been presented to a court before, it is certainly worth further study.[10]

---

10. The possibility of arguing from the enabling acts was brought to my attention by the Reverend Jon Wall of Community Bible Church, Grand Forks, North Dakota.

The Civil Rights Act of 1871

Another nonconstitutional remedy is available to Christians, and it is a powerful weapon. The Civil Rights Act of 1871, 42 U.S.C. §1983, provides in part:

> Every person who, under color of any statute, ordinance, regulation, custom, or usage, of any State or Territory, subjects, or causes to be subjected, any citizen of the United States or other person within the jurisdiction thereof to the deprivation of any rights, privileges or immunities secured by the Constitution and laws, shall be liable to the party injured in an action at law, suit in equity, or other proper proceeding for redress.

The practical meaning of this statute is that when one's civil rights are violated, be the violation racial, religious, political, or otherwise, by someone acting under cover of state law (such as a school board member, zoning official, etc.), the injured person has the right to sue in federal court. This is helpful because the federal courts may be more respectful of constitutional rights than some state and local governments. This includes the right to sue the offending officials for monetary damages, both in their official capacities and in their own persons, and at times can include attorney fees. The courts have held that the plaintiff in such a suit need not have exhausted his state and local judicial remedies, but he must have exhausted his state and local administrative remedies. That is, before suing in federal court, he must go through whatever administrative hearings the local officials provide; but he need not sue in state court before suing in federal court.

A Two-edged Sword

The system of constitutional protections which we have discussed in this and the past several chapters, is a two-edged sword. These rights have been used as a shield for those who would undermine our country and our Christian faith; but they can also be used by Christians to secure the right to spread the Gospel and practice the Christian faith. The same right to privacy that was used in *Roe v. Wade* to justify legalized abortion, has also been used in *Wisconsin v. Yoder* to protect Christian schools. The same First Amendment that has been used in *Torcaso v. Watkins*, 367 U.S. 488 (1961) to permit a man to take office even though he refused to take an oath expressing a belief in God, can also be used to prevent the establishment of humanism as a state religion. The same free speech clause that was used in *Tinker v. Des Moines* to permit antiwar armbands in the public schools, established that the public schools are a "First Amendment forum" and may be relied upon by Christians asserting their rights in the public schools.

A double standard is applied today. The Left seem to believe that they have a monopoly on the Bill of Rights. If liberals wish to present their views in the public school classrooms, that is called free speech and free inquiry. If Christians wish to present their views, that is called an establishment of religion. If liberals protest a public speech by the president, that is called dissent and protest. If conservatives protest an obscene movie, that is called censorship.

Let us never forget that the First Amendment is not the sole property of the Left. The intent of its framers was to protect Christians as much as others. Paul asserted his rights as a citizen of Rome (Acts 22:24-30). Christians today must reassert their rights as American citizens, lest these rights be lost through disuse.

Chapter 12

Humanism as an Establishment of Religion

Have you ever wondered about the largest word in the dictionary?

Until recently, it was "antidisestablishmentarianism."

Let's analyze the term. *Establishment*, as we have seen in previous chapters, refers to one religion set up in preference to others as the official religion of the state. At the time the First Amendment was adopted, an establishment of religion was generally thought to encompass one or more of the following: public taxation to support a particular religion; compulsory attendance at the services or activities of a religious body; or punishments or legal disabilities as a result of refusal to adhere to or cooperate with the established religion.

Disestablishment, then, is seeking to deprive the established religion of its preferred status. When Jefferson, Madison and others fought for the Virginia Bill of Rights in 1784, they were trying to "disestablish" the Church of England.

What, then, is "antidisestablishmentarianism"?—opposition to disestablishment! Those who opposed Madison's and Jefferson's efforts to disestablish the Church of England, were antidisestablishmentarian.

Historically, America has been called a Christian nation. Today it may sound radical and strange to hear a Christian speak in favor of "disestablishment." However, that is exactly what I am advocating. In this and the following chapters, we will see that there is an established state religion in the United States of America today.

But it is not the Christian religion.

It is the religion of humanism.

It needs to be disestablished.

What is Humanism?

The term *humanism* has become a household word in the last several years. Unfortunately, while it is often used from the pulpits and in the media, it is seldom defined. Many Christians who use the term to attack doctrines or textbooks which they regard (correctly, in many cases) as un-Christian, would be hard pressed to give a precise definition. One public high school principal told me that at his graduate education workshops he and his fellow educators had been told the term simply meant putting the individual ahead of the system. That application seems rather noble. But what really does humanism mean and why is it so dangerous?

The *American Heritage Dictionary* offers the following definition: "a philosophy or attitude that is concerned with human beings, their achievements and interests, rather than with the abstract beings and problems of theology."[1] This definition captures the heart of humanism: a preoccupation with man as the supreme value in the universe and as the sole solver of the problems of the universe.

Humanism, then, is in direct conflict with traditional Christianity. For traditional Christianity holds God, not man, to be the supreme value in the universe. Man derives his significance from his creation in the image of God. Laws and morals have their force and value because they are ordained by God. And while Christianity recognizes human responsibility, the ultimate solution to the problems of the universe will come through the gracious intervention of the Lord Jesus Christ.

Not all humanists agree with one another on every single point, any more than all Christians agree on everything. There are many varieties of humanism, but nearly all humanists agree on the following five principles:

(1) God is either nonexistent or irrelevant to modern man.

Humanist thinking can be best documented by studying the Humanist Manifestos. A manifesto is a declaration of principles or intentions. In 1933 a group of American humanists prepared a declaration of the philosophical and religious principles that were fundamental to humanism, and they called it the Humanist Manifesto. Thirty-four leading humanists signed the document, among the most influential of whom were educator John Dewey and Fellowship of Religious Humanists president R. Lester Mondale (brother of former Vice-President Walter Mondale).

Forty years later, humanists decided that changes in American society required a restatement of these principles. Thus, Humanist Manifesto II was

---

1. *The American Heritage Dictionary of the English Language*, s.v. "Humanism." I have chosen the second definition listed, as it is most appropriate to a particular philosophy. The first definition, "the condition or quality of being human", and the third definition, "the study of the humanities; polite or cultured learning" clearly do not apply to the philosophy in question. The final definition relates to the particular brand of humanism that arose during the Renaissance and consequently is too narrow to apply to humanism today.

drafted and signed at first by 114 leading humanists and subsequently by many others.

Concerning a belief in God, Humanist Manifesto I stated as its sixth tenet: "We are convinced that the time has passed for theism, deism, modernism, and the several varieties of 'new thought.' "[2] Since "theism" simply refers to any belief in God, the declaration can be read as a rejection of all things supernatural.

Humanist Manifesto II states in its preface:

> As in 1933, humanists still believe that traditional theism, especially faith in the prayer-hearing God, assumed to love and care for persons, to hear and understand their prayers, and to be able to do something about them, is an unproved and outmoded faith. Salvationism, based on mere affirmation, still appears as harmful, diverting people with false hopes of heaven hereafter. Reasonable minds look to other means for survival.[3]

Tenet 1 of Humanist Manifesto II states:

> We find insufficient evidence for belief in the existence of a supernatural; it is either meaningless or irrelevant to the question of the survival and fulfillment of the human race. As non-theists, we begin with humans, not God, nature not deity. Nature may indeed be broader and deeper than we now know; any new discoveries, however, will but enlarge our knowledge of the natural.

Dr. Corliss Lamont, one of the signers of Humanist Manifesto II, sets forth the atheistic nature of humanism in his book *The Philosophy of Humanism*:

> First, humanism believes in a naturalistic metaphysics or attitude toward the universe that considers all forms of the supernatural as myth; and that regards nature as the totality of being and as a constantly changing system of matter and energy which exists independently of any mind or consciousness. . . .
>
> Humanism believes that Nature itself constitutes the sum total of reality, that matter-energy and not mind is the foundation stuff of the universe, and that supernatural entities simply do not exist. This nonreality of the supernatural means, on the human level, that men do not possess supernatural and immortal souls; and on the level of the universe as a whole, that our cosmos does not possess a supernatural and eternal God.[4]

While God is rejected as nonexistent or irrelevant, this does not mean that all humanists totally divorce themselves from organized religion. As the first tenet of Humanist Manifesto II notes,

---

2. *Humanist Manifesto I*, 1933; reprinted in *Humanist Manifestos I and II* (Buffalo, New York: Prometheus Books, 1973, 1978), p. 8.

3. *Humanist Manifesto II*, p. 13.

4. Corliss Lamont, *The Philosophy of Humanism* (New York: Frederick Unger Publishing Company, 1977), pp. 12-13, 116.

Some humanists believe we should reinterpret traditional religions and reinvest them with meanings appropriate to the current situation. Such redefinitions, however, often perpetuate old dependencies and escapisms; they easily become obscurantist, impeding the free use of the intellect. We need, instead, radically new human purposes and goals."[5]

There are many shades of humanism. It might be said that humanism is a relative term, and that one can be a humanist to greater or lesser degrees. Sincere Christian people may even promote humanistic ideas without realizing that these are inconsistent with Christian principles. Labels and terminology are unreliable in determining whether or not an idea or proposal is humanistic. Strychnine is poisonous with or without its label—and potentially more dangerous when not labeled at all.

(2) *Man is the supreme value in the universe.*

Protagoras, who has been called the father of humanism, declared that "Man is the measure of all things, of things that are that they are, and of things that are not that they are not."[6]

Having rejected the existence or relevance of God, the humanist has paved the way for man to worship himself.

As stated in Humanist Manifesto I, tenet 13: "Religious humanism maintains that all associations and institutions exist for the fulfillment of human life."[7] And Humanist Manifesto II declares in tenet 1, "As non-theists, we begin with humans, not God; nature not deity." As Lamont says,

> . . . Humanism, having its ultimate faith in man, believes that human beings possess the power or potentiality of solving their own problems, through reliance primarily upon reason and scientific method applied with courage and vision.[8]

(3) *Evolution is the unifying principle of all life.*

To the humanist, man is not a creature of God in need of divine grace. He was not created in an ideal state from which he fell and from which he continually degenerates. Rather, man's history is an upward progress of evolution from lower forms of life to his present state.

Quoting Humanist Manifesto I:

> First: Religious humanists regard the universe as self-existing and not created.
> Second: Humanism believes that man is a part of nature and that he has emerged as the result of a continuous process. . . .
> Third: Humanism recognizes that man's religious culture and civilization,

---

5. *Humanist Manifesto II*, p.16.

6. Protagoras; quoted in Robert L. Johnson, *Humanism and Beyond* (Philadelphia: United Church Press, 1973), p. 22.

7. *Humanist Manifesto II*; p. 9.

8. Lamont, p. 13.

as clearly depicted by anthropology and history, are the product of a gradual development due to his interaction with his natural environment and with his social heritage. The individual born into a particular culture is largely molded to that culture.[9]

Humanist Manifesto II echoes a similar theme:

> Modern science discredits such historic concepts as the "ghost in the machine" and the "separable soul." Rather, science affirms that the human species is an emergence from natural evolutionary forces.[10]

Evolution is far more than a mere by-product or "sidekick" of humanism. It is a central tenet of humanism and the integrating factor of all life. As Julian Huxley says in *The Humanist Frame*:

> This new idea-system, whose birth we of the mid-twentieth century are witnessing, I shall simply call *Humanism*, because it can only be based on our understanding of man and his relations with the rest of his environment. It must be focused on man as an organism, though one with unique properties. It must be organized round the facts and ideas of evolution, taking account of the discovery that man is part of a comprehensive evolutionary process, and cannot avoid playing a decisive role in it.[11] (emphasis original)

Huxley continues:

> Our prehuman ape ancestors were never particularly successful or abundant. For their transformation into man a series of steps was needed. Descent from the trees; erect posture; some enlargement of brain; more carnivorous habits; the use and then the making of tools; further enlargement of brain; the discovery of fire; true speech and language; elaboration of tools and rituals. These steps took the better part of half a million years; it was not until less than a hundred thousand years ago that man could begin to deserve the title of dominant type, and not less than 10,000 years ago that he became fully dominant.
>
> After man's emergence as truly man, this same sort of thing continued to happen but with an important difference. Man's evolution is not biological but psychosocial: it operates by the mechanism of cultural tradition, which involves the cumulative self-reproduction and self-variation of mental activities and their products. Accordingly, major steps in the human phase of evolution are achieved by breakthroughs to new dominant patterns of mental organization, of knowledge, ideas and beliefs—ideological instead of physiological or biological organization.
>
> There is thus a succession of successful idea-systems instead of a succession of successful bodily organizations. Each new successful idea-system spreads and dominates some important sector of the world, until it is

9. *Humanist Manifesto I*, p. 8.
10. *Humanist Manifesto II*, pp. 16-17.
11. Julian Huxley, *The Humanist Frame* (New York: Harper & Brothers, 1961), p. 14.

superseded by a rival system, or itself gives birth to its successor by a breakthrough to a new organized system of thought and belief. We need only think of the magic pattern of tribal thought, the God-centered medieval thought pattern organized round the concept of divine authority and revelation, and the rise in the last three centuries of the science-centred pattern organized round the concept of human progress, but progress somehow under the control of supernatural authority. In 1859 Darwin opened the door to a new pattern of ideological organization—the evolution-centered organization of thought and belief.[12]

(4) *Man is purely a physical or biological creature.*

Man, according to the humanist, possesses no soul or spirit. Rather, he is nothing but a highly complex animal, and even his brain is merely a physical organism which operates on electrical impulses and in accordance with scientific principles, like a highly complex computer. Humanist Manifesto I states: "Third: holding an organic view of life, humanists find that the traditional dualism of mind and body must be rejected."[13] Humanist Manifesto II enlarges upon this concept: "As far as we know, the total personality is a function of the biological organism transacting in a social and cultural context. There is no credible evidence that life survives the death of the body. We continue to exist in our progeny and in the way that our lives have influenced others in our culture."[14] As Lamont says:

> . . . humanism, drawing especially upon the laws and facts of science, believes that man is an evolutionary product of the Nature of which he is part; that his mind is indivisibly conjoined with the functioning of his brain; and that as an inseparable unity of body and personality he can have no conscious survival after death.[15]

Taking a wholly materialistic or physical view of man, the humanist necessarily believes that man, like all other physical things, is subject to the physical laws of cause and effect. Consequently he becomes an environmental determinist, while at the same time he calls for political freedom. Though he professes to believe in freedom, he destroys the theological and philosophical basis of freedom for he reduces man to a predetermined animal, a programmed machine. As Whittaker Chambers has written in defense of freedom,

> Freedom is a need of the soul, and nothing else. It is in striving toward God that the soul strives continually after a condition of freedom. God alone is the inciter and guarantor of freedom. He is the only guarantor. External

---

12. Ibid., pp. 16-17. Huxley appears to be saying that man's psychosocial evolution includes an evolution of ideas, in which new idea-systems replace old idea-systems. If we accept his premises and carry them to their logical conclusions, could it be that Huxley's own idea system of evolutionary humanism is about to be replaced by something better?

13. *Humanist Manifesto I*, p. 8.

14. *Humanist Manifesto II*, p. 17.

15. Lamont, p. 13.

freedom is only an aspect of interior freedom. Political freedom, as the Western world has known it, is only a political reading of the Bible. Religion and freedom are indivisible. Without freedom the soul dies. Without the soul there is no justification for freedom.[16]

(5) *No absolute morals or values exist.*

The existence of an absolute moral value must depend upon the authority behind that value, just as the validity of a law depends upon the authority behind that law. Since the humanist denies the possibility of God as a source of ultimate moral values, he turns to man as a source. The only possible basis for declaring a particular value as good or bad, then, must be based on whether or not it operates to the benefit of human beings. Again let us look at the manifestos. Humanist Manifesto I:

> Fifth: Humanism asserts that the nature of the universe depicted by modern science makes unacceptable any supernatural or cosmic guarantees of human values. Obviously humanism does not deny the possibility of realities as yet undiscovered, but it does insist that the way to determine the existence and value of any and all realities is by means of intelligent inquiry and by the assessment of their relation to human needs. Religion must formulate its hopes and plans in the light of the scientific spirit and method.[17]

Quoting Humanist Manifesto II:

> Third: We affirm that moral values derive their source from human experience. Ethics is *autonomous* and *situational*, meaning no theological or ideological sanction. Ethics stem from human need and interest. To deny this distorts the whole basis of life. Human life has meaning because we create and develop our futures. Happiness and the creative realization of human needs and desires, individually and in shared enjoyment, are continuous themes of humanism. We strive for the good life, here and now. The goal is to pursue life's enrichment despite debasing forces of vulgarization, commercialization, bureaucratization, and dehumanization. . . .
> Sixth: In the area of sexuality, we believe that intolerant attitudes, often cultivated by orthodox religions and puritanical cultures, unduly repress sexual conduct. The right to birth control, abortion, and divorce should be recognized.[18]

Lamont explains, "Humanism believes in an ethics or morality that grounds all human values in this-earthly experiences and relationships and that holds as its highest goal the this-wordly happiness, freedom and progress—economic, cultural, and ethical—of all mankind, irrespective of nation, race, or religion."[19]

The only absolute for the humanist, then, is man. John Dewey recognized

---

16. Whittaker Chambers, *Witness* (New York: Random House, 1952), p. 16.
17. Ibid.
18. *Humanist Manifesto II*, pp. 17, 18.
19. Lamont, p. 13.

no highest good or supreme test of value except one: social growth.[20] To the humanist, who recognizes no higher value than man, this makes sense.

But there is a higher value than man: God.

(6) *Man, through the use of his scientific reason will solve his own problems.*

Traditional Christians believe that God has given man responsibility, and also that through the indwelling power of the Holy Spirit God works through Christians to accomplish His will on earth. Ultimately, however, man is powerless to save himself. He is saved by grace through faith in the finished work of the Lord Jesus Christ on Calvary's cross. By virtue of Christ's first coming man is saved from the guilt and power of sin, and he will be saved from the very presence of sin at Christ's second coming, when Christ will return to establish His millennial kingdom on earth.

But the humanist sees a different future for man. As Humanist Manifesto I concludes, "Man is at last becoming aware that he alone is responsible for the realization of the world of his dreams, and that he has within himself the power for its achievement. He must set intelligence and will to the task."[21] Humanist Manifesto II repeats that theme: ". . . we can discover no divine purpose or providence for the human species. While there is much that we do not know, humans are responsible for what we are or will become. No deity will save us; we must save ourselves."[22]

And how is man to save himself? Listen to the answer of Humanist Manifesto II:

> Reason and intelligence are the most effective instruments that humankind possesses. There is no substitute: neither faith nor passion suffices in itself. The controlled use of scientific methods, which have transformed the natural and social sciences since the Renaissance, must be extended further in the solution of human problems.

Also:

> We need to extend the uses of the scientific method, not renounce them to fuse reason with compassion in order to build constructive social and moral values.[23]

Applying the "scientific method" to society is to result in a radical restructuring of the American social system:

> The humanists are firmly convinced that existing acquisitive and profit-motivated society has shown itself to be inadequate and that a radical change in methods, controls, and motives must be instituted. Socialized and cooperative economic order must be established to the end that the equitable distribution of the means of life be possible. The goal of humanism is a

20. Johnson, p. 53.
21. *Humanist Manifesto I*, p. 10.
22. *Humanist Manifesto II*, p. 16.
23. Ibid., p. 24.

free and universal society in which people voluntarily and intelligently cooperate for the common good. Humanists demand a shared life in a shared world.[24]

Humanist Manifesto II is less dogmatic than Humanist Manifesto I in calling for a socialist economy, but more explicit in its call for world government, world citizenship, and disarmament.

The Humanist (September/October 1980) suggests that it may already be time for Humanist Manifesto III.[25] Apparently the relativistic principles of 1973 have become outmoded even faster than did those of 1933.

Humanism is not new. It is history's second oldest faith. It began long ago when the serpent whispered in the garden, "Ye shall be as gods." For humanism dreams of man replacing God as the supreme intelligence, supreme value, and supreme force. Instead of kneeling before the throne of God, the humanist contemplates with monkey-like amazement the superiority of his own brain.[26]

But the irony of humanism is that, while purporting to give man ultimate dignity and ultimate value, it in fact robs man of that which alone can give him dignity and value: his immortal soul, which was created in the image of God. And while claiming to give man freedom, humanism robs man of his only basis for freedom, the human soul. For humanism reduces man to a physical organism, environmentally determined and subject to physical laws of cause and effect. To the humanist, man is nothing more than a naked ape.

Is Humanism a Religion?

I maintain that humanism is a religion. A close examination of the facts will demonstrate this is correct.

(1) *Humanism has the characteristics of a religion.*

Humanism involves faith assumptions. Despite his claimed monopoly on the scientific method and in the power of human reason, the humanist assumes many things he cannot prove. The humanist has not proven that God does not exist or that He does not intervene in human affairs. He simple assumes that to be the case, and builds a philosophy and plan of action based upon that faith assumption. The humanist believes by faith that man has no spiritual nature; he has not proven that. The humanist holds evolution as a tenet of faith, even though (as we will demonstrate in chapter 14) that also is an unprovable faith assumption. The humanist assumes by faith the absence of absolute morals. He has not proven they do not exist; he has only assumed

---

24. *Humanist Manifesto I*, p. 10.

25. Lloyd L. Morain, *The Humanist*, September/October 1980, p. 4.

26. Several of these figures of speech are adapted out of context from Whittaker Chambers' monumental book, *Witness* (New York, Random House), the introduction to which is the most profound and moving exposition of the conflict between Christianity and Marxist humanism I have ever read. I recommend it very highly.

it. The very supremacy of the scientific method is in and of itself a faith assumption.

Humanism has the creeds of a religious faith. Humanist Manifesto I and Humanist Manifesto II are just as much religious creeds as the Apostles' Creed or the Augsburg Confession.

Humanism develops out of a religious tradition. We could trace the development of humanism through the ancient Greeks or the Renaissance humanists, or even in more recent times through the works of men like Comte, Darwin, Dewey, and others. Especially in the case of Renaissance humanism and modern humanism, one can trace the gradual break from traditional Christianity toward a more liberalized Christianity and ultimately toward humanism.

Humanism evinces missionary zeal. Far from being detached and "scientific" in the way they present their causes, humanists frequently advocate their beliefs with passionate zeal and at times outright intolerance. Humanist Manifesto I explains it as follows: "Religious humanism considers the complete realization of human personality to be the end of man's life and seeks its development and fulfillment in the here and now. This is the explanation of the humanists' social passion."[27] According to R. J. Rushdoony,

> . . . humanism has proved itself to be one of history's most savage and intolerant faiths. The history of humanism is one of terror, slavery, and persecution, but, in its rewriting of history, it accuses all others of these things. From the French Revolution to the present, this humanistic totalitarianism has been spreading its infection in all the world.[28]

Finally, humanism attempts to answer the most basic and ultimate questions that every religion attempts to answer.

Ultimate Life Questions	Humanists' Answer:
Who am I?	A biological organism, a naked ape.
Where did I come from?	A lower form of life, via evolution.
Why am I here?	To serve my own ends, or at best those of mankind in general.
Where am I going?	Not to any afterlife, but only to a better world in this life, the here and now.
How can I get there?	Solely by human effort, with emphasis on reason and the scientific method applied to the reorganization of society.

27. *Humanist Manifesto I*, p. 9.
28. R.J. Rushdoony, *Law and Liberty*, pp. 52-53.

(2) *Humanism claims to be a religion.*

The authors of Humanist Manifesto I state, as their purpose, "in order that religious humanism may be better understood. . . ."[29] The Manifesto describes religion by saying that "Religions have always been means for realizing the highest values of life."[30] It then states:

> Today man's larger understanding of the universe, his scientific achievements, and his deeper appreciation of brotherhood, have created a situation which requires a new statement of the means and purposes of religion. Such a vital, fearless, and frank religion capable of furnishing adequate social goals and personal satisfactions may appear to many people as a complete break with the past. While this age does owe a vast debt to traditional religions, it is nonetheless obvious that any religion that can hope to be a synthesizing and dynamic force for today must be shaped for the needs of this age. To establish such a religion is a major necessity of the present. It is a responsibility which rests upon this generation. We therefore affirm the following: [the Manifesto follows].[31]

In the Manifesto which follows, the term "religious humanists" or "religious humanism" is found in tenets 1, 8, 12, and 13, with many religious references in between. Then comes the conclusion: "So stand the theses of religious humanism."[32]

This is not new. As early as 1872, Octavius B. Frothingham wrote *Religion of Humanity* in which he used the doctrine of evolution to establish a humanistic, naturalistic concept of religious and ethical values.[33]

Lloyd Morain, former president of the American Humanist Association, has said:

> Down through the ages men have been taking a universal religion or way of life. . . . humanism . . . shows promise of becoming a great world faith.
>
> Humanists are content with fixing their attention on this life and on this earth. Theirs is a religion without a God, divine revelation, or sacred scriptures.[34]

And Edwin H. Wilson, former director emeritus of the American Humanist Association and a signer of Humanist Manifesto II, has observed:

> Many well-known thinkers have given voice to the hope of Religious Humanism that a comprehensive world religion will develop through the creative processes of our times. Roy Wood Sellars in 1927 held humanism to be the next step in religion. John Dewey, in his book *A Common Faith*,

---

29. *Humanist Manifesto I*, p. 7.
30. Ibid.
31. Ibid., p. 8.
32. Ibid., p. 10.
33. Curti, p. 544.
34. Morain; quoted by Claire Chambers, *The SIECUS Circle* (Western Islands: Belmont, Massachusetts 1977), p. 87; cited by LaHaye, p. 126.

believed that we have all the materials available for such a faith. Sir Julian Huxley predicts that the next great religion of the world will be some form of humanism.[35]

The magazine *Religious Humanism* is replete with articles with such titles as "Liberal Religion and Humanism"[36], "Values for a Humanistic Society"[37], "Religion, Humanism and Popular Culture"[38], "Humanistic Eudaemonism"[39], "Evolution: the Way of Growth"[40] and others. One article by Sherwin Wine is entitled "If Humanism is a Religion."[41] Defining religion as "the way a community affirms and celebrates its connection to its past, present, and future"[42], Wine sets forth twelve activities upon which a humanistic religion must be based (community, human community, power, truth, loyalty, roots, symbols, heroes, holidays, ceremonies, futurism, and pioneering) and claims that religious humanism shares each of those activities.[43]

The high priests of humanism have spoken for themselves: they claim it to be a religion.

(3) The courts have recognized humanism as a religion.

On June 19, 1961, the United States Supreme Court decided a landmark case. Roy R. Torcaso wanted to become a notary, but had been refused by the clerk of court for Montgomery County, Maryland, because he would not declare his belief in the existence of God, which was required as a test for office by the Maryland Constitution. Torcaso sued, arguing that this provision of the Maryland Constitution violated the First and Fourteenth Amendments of the United States Constitution. The state argued that merely requiring a person to express a belief in God could not be considered an establishment of religion. (Obviously, all religions believe in God!)

But the U.S. Supreme Court agreed with Torcaso. The Court said:

> We repeat and again reaffirm that neither a State nor the Federal Government can constitutionally force a person "to profess a belief or disbelief in any religion." Neither can constitutionally pass a law or impose requirements which aid all religions as against nonbelievers, and neither can aid those religions based on a belief in the existence of God as against those religions founded on different beliefs.[11] [footnote in original text]

35. Edwin H. Wilson; quoted in Chambers, ibid.; quoted in LaHaye, ibid.

36. Donald Rowley, "Liberal Religion and Humanism," *Religious Humanism*, vol. 13 no. 4 (Autumn 1979), pp. 158-167.

37. Rodney Armour, "Values for a Humanistic Society," ibid., pp. 168-173.

38. Margaret J. King, "Religion, Humanism, and Popular Culture," ibid., vol. 13 no. 3 (Summer 1979), pp. 126-131.

39. Thomas Lewis, "Humanistic Eudaemonism," ibid., vol. 13 no. 2 (Spring 1979), pp. 64-73.

40. Robert Smudski, "Evolution: The Way of Growth," ibid., pp. 79-86.

41. Sherwin Wine, "If Humanism is a Religion," ibid., vol. 13 no. 3 (Summer 1979), pp. 107-114.

42. Ibid., p. 110.

43. Ibid., pp. 111-114.

But most interesting of all was the footnote referred to above. The footnote stated:

> 11. Among religions in this country which do not teach what would generally be considered a belief in the existence of God are Buddhism, Taoism, Ethical Culture, *Secular Humanism* and others. . . . [emphasis supplied]

Lower court cases could be cited, among them *Washington Ethical Society v. District of Columbia*, 101 U.S. Appellate D.C. 371, 249 F. 2d 127 (1957); *Fellowship of Humanity v. County of Alameda*, 153 Cal. App. 2d 673, 315 P. 2d 394 (1957).[44] But in *Torcaso* the U.S. Supreme Court itself listed humanism as a religion.

Humanism has the characteristics of a religion. Humanists call it a religion. The Supreme Court calls it a religion..

Is Humanism Established?

Throughout the history of both Christianity and Judaism, education and religion have gone hand in hand. The church has fostered education, and the primary purpose of education has been to promote religion and the fruits thereof. In early Judaism, the synagogue was the center of learning as well as of worship. In the early centuries of the church, as well as throughout the Middle Ages and thereafter, the cloisters and monasteries were the chief centers of learning. All knowledge was thought to have its source in God.

That has been true in America too. When the state undertook the promotion of education, it did so in large part to promote religion. You will remember from previous chapters that the First Amendment originally did not apply to the states, and consequently there were established churches in the states long after the adoption of the Constitution and the Bill of Rights. The "Old Deluder Satan Act" of colonial Massachusetts (1647) ordered that every township of fifty householders was to appoint a schoolteacher to educate the youth, "not only in good literature, but in sound doctrine" and the reason for this education was that it was "one chief project of Satan to keep them from the knowledge of the scripture. . . ."[45] The 1784 New Hampshire Constitution declared that "morality and piety, rightly grounded on evangelical principles, will give the best and greatest security to government, and '. . . is most likely to be propagated through a society by the institution of the public worship of the DEITY, and of public instruction in morality and religion. . . .' " For this reason the Constitution established a system of public instruction," for the support and

---

44. *Torcaso v. Watkins*, 367 U.S. 488 (1961).

45. Massachusetts, *"Old Deluder Satan" Act* (1647); cited by Herbert Titus, "Education, Caesar's or God's: A Constitutional Question of Jurisdiction," Journal of Christian Jurisprudence (1982), p. 101.

maintenance of "public protestant teachers of piety, religion and morality.
. . . "[46]

So religion and education were closely interrelated. Public support for education was closely related to public support for religion. When the Northwest Ordinance of 1787 was enacted, it also linked religion to education: "Religion, morality and knowledge, being necessary to good government and the happiness of mankind, schools and the means of education shall forever be encouraged." As a result of the Northwest Ordinance, newly opened lands were set aside for schools.[47]

The Fourteenth Amendment was passed in 1868. Over the next several decades everything changed through a series of decisions. It was gradually determined by the courts that the First Amendment applies to the states as well as to the federal government. Therefore the states could not have any established religion. That being the case, they had to either (1) divest themselves of their public school systems; or (2) divorce religion from the public schools. Supposedly they chose the latter course of action.

I maintain, however, that religion and education have never been divorced from each other and probably never could be. Rather, the religion of the public schools has changed. Formerly the religion of the public schools was Christianity. Today, the religion of the public schools is humanism.

This change came about gradually. Horace Mann, the nineteenth-century figure who is often called the father of the American public school system, believed that education should be used to modify the sentiments and opinions of the younger generation toward a more liberalized religion than the older Calvinistic theology. Mann himself was far from a thoroughgoing humanist. In his annual report for 1848 as secretary of the board of education of Massachusetts, Mann argued passionately that general Christian principles should be taught in the public schools, although he opposed teaching the "narrow" Calvinistic doctrines that some of his adversaries demanded.[48] But the problem was that:

> Mann was pious, and believed himself to be a true Christian; but by *interpreting Christianity as freedom, and education as salvation,* he undercut both Christianity and the republic. Since his day, Unitarianism has repudiated Christianity and become generally religious, seeing good in all religions; in terms of its basic convictions, this is an honest step. And in terms of man's presuppositions, what he envisioned was a new religion, with the state as its true church, and education as its Messiah. Mann's errors were to make this implicit faith explicit.
>
> It should be noted that Mann strongly insisted on the need for more

---

46. New Hampshire, *Constitution* (1784), art. 6.

47. U.S., *Northwest Ordinance*, Article 3 (1787); quoted in Pfeffer, p. 108.

48. Massachusetts, Board of Education, *Twelfth Annual Report* (1848), by Horace Mann, secretary; reprinted in Joseph L. Blau, ed., *Cornerstones of Religious Freedom in America* (Evanston, Illinois: Harper & Row, 1949), pp. 166-204.

Bible in the schools than existed in his day. He was ready to defend its value and *necessity* with documented testimonies of its effect on the lives of students. But it should be noted that Mann was not interested in the Bible as a means toward promoted *godliness* but rather *social efficiency*. Religion should be used because it is productive of civic virtue; social orientation was everything. Mann's basic principle was the pragmatic use of religion. The basic reference in religion is therefore not to God but to society. . . . [49]

Mann's 1972 biographer, Jonathan Messerli, described Mann's position as follows:

> What the church had become for medieval man, the public school must now become for democratic and rational man. God would be replaced by the concept of the Public good, sin and guilt by the more positive virtues of Victorian morality and conformity . . .   •
>
> All of this was now possible if only reasonable men and women would join together to create a well managed system of schooling, where educators could manipulate and control learning as effectively as the confident new breed of engineers managed the industrial processes at work in their burgeoning textile factories and iron and steel mills. For the first time in the history of western man, it seemed possible for an intellectual and moral elite to effect mass behavioral changes and bring about a new golden age of enlightened ethics, humanism, and affluence. [50]

With the possible exception of Horace Mann, probably no other single individual has influenced American education as much as has John Dewey. Dewey was a thoroughgoing humanist, one of the signers of Humanist Manifesto I. [51] One of Dewey's works was *The Influence of Darwin on Philosophy*, and in *The Making of the Modern Mind*, Randall says that Dewey "probably more than any other man, has caught the vision of what the scientific method and the idea of evolution really means. . . . "[52] Dewey believed that the public school had a higher mission than merely transmitting information or morality. The role of the public school was to condition the rising generation to live in a socialized society:

> Men will long dispute about material socialism, about socialism considered as a matter of distribution of the material resources of the community; but there is a socialism regarding which there can be no such dispute—socialism of the intelligence and of the spirit. To extend the range and the fullness of sharing in the intellectual and spiritual resources of the community is

---

49. R.J. Rushdoony, *The Messianic Character of American Education* (Nutley, New Jersey: Prague Press, 1963), pp. 31-32.

50. Jonathan Messerli; quoted in Titus, "Education, Caesar's or God's," pp. 140-141.

51. *Humanist Manifesto I*, p.11.

52. John Herman Randall, Jr., *The Making of the Modern Mind* (Chicago: Houghton Mifflin Company, 1940), pp. 491, 494.

the very meaning of the community. Because the older type of education is not fully adequate to this task under changed conditions, we feel its lack and demand that the school shall become a social center. The school as a social center means the active and organized promotion of this socialism of the intangible things of art, science, and other modes of social intercourse.[53]

Dewey declared that "education is the fundamental method of social progress and reform."[54] In an explanation of the role of the teacher, Dewey wrote:

I believe that
—the teacher is engaged, not simply in the training of individuals, but in the formation of the proper social life.
—every teacher should realize the dignity of his calling; that he is a social servant set apart for the maintenance of proper social order and the securing of the right social growth.
—in this way the teacher always is the prophet of the true God and the usherer in of the true kingdom of God.[55]

And listen to Dewey's explanation of the role of religion—his religion—in education:

. . . the American people are conscious that its schools serve best the cause of religion in serving the cause of social unification; and that under certain conditions schools are more religious in substance and in promise without any of the conventional badges and machinery of religious instruction than they could be in cultivating these forms at the expense of a state consciousness.[56]

Sidney Mead described the establishment of religion in the public schools in his book *The Lively Experiment*:

Of necessity the state in its public education system is and always has been teaching religion. . . . the public schools in the United States took over one of the basic responsibilities that traditionally was always assumed by an established church. In this sense the public school system of the United States *is* its established church.

In this context one can understand why it is that the religion of many Americans is democracy—why their real faith is the "democratic faith"— the religion of the public schools.[57]

The establishment of humanism in the public schools is probably nowhere

53. John Dewey, "The School as Social Center," *NEA Journal*, 1902, p. 382f; quoted in R.J. Rushdoony, *The Messianic Character*, pp. 150-151.

54. Dewey, quoted in ibid., p. 155.

55. Dewey, *My Pedagogic Creed* (Washington, D.C.: The Progressive Education Association, 1897,1929), p. 17; cited by Rushdoony, *The Messianic Character*, p. 155.

56. Dewey, *Characters and Events* (New York: Holt, 1929), 2:515; quoted in R.J. Rushdoony, ibid.

57. Sidney Mead, *The Lively Experiment, the Shaping of Christianity in America* (New York: Harper & Row, 1963), p. 68; quoted in DeJong, p. 158.

more apparent than in the teaching of evolution. This will be discussed in greater detail in the next chapter. But it is well-known that in most public schools in the nation, evolution is taught, not as theory but as fact. Evolution as we have seen is a fundamental tenet of the religion of humanism.

Another area of humanistic teaching is that of values clarification. Barbara Morris, in *Change Agents in the Schools* (Upland, California, 1979), has detailed the dangers of values clarification and it would be duplication to repeat that discussion here. Briefly, values clarification is a means by which students are taught to formulate values for themselves. On the surface this does not sound anti-Christian. The likely defense will be, ''We're not trying to inculcate humanist values! All we're trying to do is get the students to think for themselves and formulate their own values. If they should choose Christian values, that's great!''

But the problem is that the criteria which are given for forming values are humanistic criteria: experimentation, the scientific method, consideration of utilitarian consequences, etc. The student is taught, or at least led to believe, that he must think out his values for himself, instead of relying upon God's revelation, the Bible.

Dr. Sidney B. Simon, probably more than any other individual, has prepared and promoted values clarification programs for our nation's public schools. In his book, *Values Clarification: a handbook of practical strategies for teachers and students*, Dr. Simon argues against teaching moral values by ''moralizing'', which he defines as ''the direct, although sometimes subtle, inculcation of the adult's values upon the young.'' Simon prefers the values clarification approach whereby children are taught to ''build their own value system.''[58]

But in telling children to form their own values based on experimentation, science and utilitarianism, the student is taught something even deeper than values: he is taught the means by which values are achieved. And the means he is taught are at variance with the position of traditional Christianity, which has historically taught that reason is a valuable and God-given tool, but that it should never take the place of God's revealed work.

Sex education, of course, is another area of controversy. Evangelical Christians generally do not object to their children being taught about sex. But they insist that it is wrong to teach about sex without also teaching morality, and that morality cannot be taught without Christianity. All too often, the public school either teaches no morality at all in sex education, or teaches a relative and humanistic type of morality which leads the student to believe that premarital sex is not wrong after all—at least not all of the time. The use of values clarification from a humanist standpoint was recently articulated in *The Humanist*.[59]

58. Sidney B. Simon, Leland W. Howe, and Howard Kirschenbaum, *Values Clarification: a handbook of practical strategies for teachers and students*, New York: Hart Publishing Co. Inc., 1972, pgs. 15-19.
59. Howard Kirschenbaum, ''New Goals For Moral Education,'' *The Humanist*, November-December 1978, pp. 17-19. See other articles on same subject in same issue.

We see the humanistic emphasis elsewhere. The health text, *Your Health and Your Future*, states on page 62, "Perhaps the most important trait that separates man from other animals is the human brain."[60] Does that statement sound okay? Wait a minute; for the Christian, the most important trait that separates man from animals is his soul or spirit, his creation in the image of God, and his special responsibility in the Creation Mandate. The statement quoted above is pure humanism, for humanism teaches that man is a complex animal, distinguished from the other animals by his intelligence.

Example after example could be cited. But Paul Blanshard well summarized the role of the public school in guiding children from Christianity toward humanism, when he said:

> I think that the most important factor moving us toward a secular society has been the educational factor. Our schools may not teach Johnny to read properly, but the fact that Johnny is in school until he is sixteen tends to lead toward the elimination of religious superstition. The average American child now acquires a high school education, and this militates against Adam and Eve and all the other myths of alleged history.[61]

And perhaps the most revealing statement of all appeared in another issue of *The Humanist*, by a professor of English education. In an article entitled "Adolescent Literature: Humanism is Alive and Thriving in the Secondary School," Professor Schwartz wrote:

> Something wonderful, free, unheralded, and of significance to all humanists is happening in the secondary schools. It is the adolescent-literature movement . . . they may burn *Slaughterhouse Five* in North Dakota and ban a number of innocuous books in Kanawha County but thank God [sic] *the crazies don't do all that much reading. If they did they'd find that they have already been defeated.* . . . nothing that is part of contemporary life is taboo in this genre and any valid piece of writing that helps make the world more knowable to young people serves an important humanistic function. . . . none of the books are didactic, but all of them espouse the humanistic ideals to which young people would be exposed.[62] (emphasis supplied)

Earlier we saw that when the First Amendment was adopted, the most general consensus would probably have been that the word "establishment" referred to three things: the use of public taxation to support the beliefs or practices of a particular religion; compulsory attendance at the services or activities of

60. John T. Fodor etal., *Your Health and Your Future* (River Forest, Illinois: Laidlaw Brothers, 1974), p. 62.

61. Paul Blanshard, "Three Cheers for Our Secular State," *The Humanist*, March/April 1976, p. 17; quoted in Homer Duncan, *Secular Humanism* (Lubbock, Texas: Missionary Crusader, 1979), p. 18.

62. Sheila Schwartz, "Adolescent Literature: Humanism is Alive and Thriving in the Secondary School," *The Humanist*, January/February 1976, cited by Timothy D. Crater, "The Unproclaimed Priests of Public Education," *Christianity Today*, 10 April 1981, p. 46.

a particular religion; or public penalties or disabilities for those who did not accept the established religion. In this sense of the word, is humanism an established religion?

First, it is clear that tax money is being used to support it. The public school system takes billions upon billions of dollars, federal, state and local, nationwide.

Second, people are compelled to attend it. All states in the union, except for Mississippi, have compulsory education statutes, by which parents are required to send their children to school from certain ages, generally from about age seven to about age sixteen. This can be either a public school which is free (not really free; already paid for by tax dollars), or a private school at considerable extra expense. Many parents cannot afford private schools; others do not live where private schools are available. For them, attendance at public school is a virtual requirement. For others, it is a requirement that may be avoided only at substantial expense.

And there are persons who have suffered penalties for refusing to accept humanism. In 1980, a high school teacher from Lemmon, South Dakota, was terminated from his teaching position in the public schools because he refused to teach evolution and insisted on teaching creation instead. His case is still being considered in the courts.[63] Another case currently pending in the courts involves a state university professor who was denied tenure because he wrote a scientific treatise supporting creation and opposing evolution. Numerous other such instances of discrimination could almost certainly be found. Usually, however, they are much more carefully disguised. These blatant examples are the exception.

Consider the penalty paid by the Christian child who attends a secular humanist public school. As John Whitehead notes, the child becomes schizophrenic. He is forced to compartmentalize his life. In one area of his life (that of his public school education) he is forced to give God no place at all, whereas in the other part of life (his home and his church) he is urged to make Christ the center of his life. The result is that he becomes schizoid.[64] For by saying nothing about God, public schools are in fact saying a great deal about God: they are saying that God is either nonexistent or irrelevant, not important enough to be mentioned—exactly the humanist view of God.

On all three counts, then, the religion of humanism counts as an "establishment of religion."

Is the Establishment of Humanism Unconstitutional?

Humanism is a religion. Humanism is established. The two together constitute an "establishment of religion."

Once again, the First Amendment reads in part, "Congress shall make no law respecting an establishment of religion. . . ." Nothing in the amendment

---

63. *Bible-Science Newsletter*, vol. 19 no. 4 (April 1981), pp. 1-4, 8.
64. Whitehead, *The Separation Illusion*, p. 131.

which would exempt humanism or dictate that humanism should be treated different from other religions.

The U.S. Supreme Court declared in *Abington v. Schempp*, 374 U.S. 203 (1963), that ". . . the State may not establish the 'religion of secularism' in the sense of affirmatively opposing or showing hostility to religion, thus 'preferring those who believe in no religion over those who do believe.' " And the Ohio Supreme Court in *Ohio v. Whisner*, 351 NE2d 750 (1976) noted that state educational standards "may be interpreted as promoting 'secular humanism.' "

But that is precisely what has been established: a religion of secular humanism. We need to get to work to "disestablish" secular humanism now! Proving secular humanism is a difficult task but by no means insurmountable. It involves exhaustive discovery, going through the public school textbooks in painstaking detail to document statements that contradict Christian doctrine.

You will recall that according to the three-prong test that the U.S. Supreme Court cited in *Lemon v. Kurtzman*, government involvement with religion is an establishment of religion, unless the following three conditions are met: (1) the involvement has a primary secular purpose; (2) the primary purpose of the involvement is neither to help nor to hinder religion; and (3) the involvement does not constitute excessive entanglement of the state with religion. If government involvement with humanism fails on any one of these three counts, it is an establishment of religion. Of these, the most frequently litigated condition is "excessive entanglement." If the state is in the business of writing or selecting and purchasing texts, and teaching out of those texts to the students, and those texts contain humanistic doctrine, then clearly the state is entangled with humanistic religion. The state is even choosing which form of humanism to teach! Bear in mind that school boards, administrators, and even individual teachers are in some sense state officials. The laws of most states establish that fact for pension and dismissal and other purposes. Their actions, then, constitute "state action." And their involvement with the religion of secular humanism may well constitute "excessive entanglement."

Christians should take a stand against humanism based upon the free exercise clause as well as the establishment clause. Free exercise of religion includes the right to teach one's religious beliefs to his children, and no one should have to compete with the government for the allegiance of his own children. To establish a violation of the free exercise clause, one need not show excessive entanglement, but must show that the subject matter in question violates deepseated religious convictions. Objections must be Bible-based convictions and not mere opinions.

The case of *Davis v. Page*, 385 Fed. Supp. 395 (1974) involves some parents and students of the Apostolic Lutheran faith who objected to various practices of the local school system, including watching movies, watching television, viewing audiovisual projections, listening to the radio, engaging in playacting, singing or dancing to worldly music, studying evolution, and studying humanistic philosophy. The parents wanted their children exempted from these classes and practices. The court denied the exemption, finding that the practices did not violate the parents' free exercise of religion.

Taking the language of the case as a whole, it seems obvious that that particular judge was unsympathetic to the Apostolic Lutherans and did not give them fair consideration. He took their statements in the worst light possible. Though sincere objections to the practices in question were presented, these objections were not carefully researched and articulated. For example, the judge stated, "The Pastor of the church which the Davises attend was unable to specify what tenets of the Apostolic Lutheran faith the health course would violate." A thorough examination of the material used in the health course, when juxtaposed against Scripture, would probably have answered this question. As to their objection to worldly music, the court noted that "none of plaintiffs' witnesses could describe what constituted 'worldly' music. Instead, they transposed Justice Stewart's definition of obscenity and testified that "they knew it when they heard it." The court then said, "The Davis children are very young. It is difficult to argue or believe that they are presently aware of the distinction between worldly and spiritual music. If they can hear music with their parents, then they can hear music in the schools." Once again, it would appear that an unsympathetic judge looked for an excuse to rule against Christian parents. But a better formulation of the objection might have prevented an unfavorable outcome.

First Amendment objections to humanistic teaching have been successfully raised. But it isn't easy. After all, the "antidisestablishmentarians" don't give up easily!

Chapter 13

Scopes I:
Disestablishing the Creationists

At a recent Republican precinct caucus, when I offered a resolution calling for balanced treatment for creation and evolution, a doctor argued against my position, saying, "I thought that was all settled in the Scopes Trial!"

Though the resolution passed, the question still remains: What did the Scopes trial really decide?

Unfortunately, current perception of the Scopes trial is distorted. Partly this is a result of the extensive coverage of the trial by columnist H. L. Mencken, a vitriolic opponent of organized Christianity. Also in part it is due to the play by Jerome Lawrence and Robert E. Lee, *Inherit the Wind* (New York: Bantam, 1955, 1969). The motion picture version of the play has in recent years been shown on national television, and performed in high schools and theatres throughout the country. While the play's authors acknowledge that their drama is *not* a historical recounting of the Scopes trial, it is certainly accepted as such by the public. Herron states, the play's purpose is that of "exposing bigotry and taking a stand for personal integrity and the right to think. . . ."[1] Whose bigotry? Whose personal integrity? Whose right to think? Popular perception of the Scopes trial today is largely based on *Inherit the Wind*, and many people accept as fact the authors' departures from historical truth. Almost without exception, departures from the actual transcript of the trial are designed to make Darrow and the evolutionists appear open-minded and intelligent, and make Bryan and the creationists look ignorant and bigoted.

Let's take a careful look at the Scopes trial and see what really happened in comparison to events as portrayed in *Inherit the Wind*. The names in the play are changed, but to avoid confusion we will refer to all parties by their actual historical names.

1. Ima Honaker Herron, *The Small Town in American Drama* (Dallas: Southern Methodist University Press, 1969), p. 233.

The play opens with Bert Capes (John Scopes), a young schoolteacher, in jail, nervous and confused, for having violated Tennessee's law which prohibits the teaching of evolution. He is afraid of going to prison, and afraid also of the combined forces of the community prejudiced against him and hateful toward him, the only man in the community who dares to speak out for the truth.[2] But is this really the way it happened? Not exactly. Scopes was never in jail; the anti-evolution law only provided for a $100-$500 fine.[3] And far from being hated by the community, Scopes and some of his friends actually arranged the trial as a means of testing the law. Scopes voluntarily agreed to be the defendant. Here is how Scopes himself describes it in his memoirs:

> On a warm May afternoon, four days after the term was over, I was playing tennis on the old outdoor clay court at school with some of my students. Although the full blast of summer hadn't hit Dayton yet, it was already warm, and it didn't take much swinging and ball-swatting to work up a healthy sweat.
>
> In the middle of our game, a little boy walked up and watched us smack the ball back and forth. He was waiting for me and when we had finished a point, he called, "Mr. Scopes?"
>
> I nodded and trotted over to him.
>
> "Mr. Robinson says, if it's convenient, for you to come down to the drugstore," he said. The boy didn't work at the drugstore. He had been summoned off the street to fetch me.
>
> There was no urgency in the message. Fred E. Robinson, the owner of Robinson's Drugstore—"Doc," as we called him because of his profession as a pharmacist—also was chairman of the Rhea County School Board, and I assumed he wanted to talk to me about school business. We finished the game. I was wearing a shirt and trousers and the shirt was stained with sweat. It was about three-quarters of a mile downtown to the drugstore, and I walked there dressed as I was.
>
> Robinson's Drugstore was a social center for Dayton, where people would get together for a soda and stay to discuss any local issues or just to pass the time of day. Toward the back of the drugstore, near the fountain, there were wire-backed chairs arranged around wooden-topped tables. It was always a pleasant refuge from the outside heat.
>
> That afternoon there was plenty of heat inside. Past the screened double doors at the front was the fountain and at a nearby table were half a dozen men in the midst of a warm discussion. In addition to Doc Robinson, there was Mr. Brady, who ran the town's other drugstore; Sue Hicks, the town's leading lawyer, who had been arguing for the Butler Law [the anti-evolution law]; Wallace Haggard, another attorney, whose father owned the leading bank and was "Mr. Dayton"; a fellow who worked in the post office; and George Rappelyea.

2. Jerome Lawrence and Robert E. Lee, *Inherit the Wind* (New York: Bantam, 1955, 1969), pp. 6-8, 45-47, 96. Act one, Scenes 1 & 2; Act Three.

3. John T. Scopes and James Presley, *Center of the Storm, Memoirs of John T. Scopes* (Chicago: Holt, Rinehart & Winston, 1967), p. 52.

Robinson offered me a chair and the boy who worked as a soda jerk brought me a fountain drink.

"John, we've been arguing," said Rappelyea, "and I said that nobody could teach biology without teaching evolution."

"That's right," I said, not sure what he was leading up to.

A copy of George William Hunter's *Civic Biology* lay on a nearby shelf. Robinson's drugstore supplied Rhea County's textbooks. Hunter's was the text used in Tennessee for biology. It had been used since 1909. The state textbook commission had adopted it in 1919 and although the contract had expired in 1924, no other book had been adopted in the meantime. I got a copy of it and showed it to the men at the table.

"You have been teaching 'em this book?" Rappelyea said.

"Yes," I said. I explained that I had got the book out of stock and had used it for review purposes while filling in for the principal during his illness. He was the regular biology teacher. I opened the book and showed them the evolutionary chart and the explanation of evolution. "Rappelyea's right, that you can't teach biology without teaching evolution. This is the text and it explains evolution."

"Then you've been violating the law," Robinson said.

I didn't know, technically, whether I had violated the law or not. I knew of the Butler Act; I'd never worried about it. At the term I had substituted in the classes of the principal while he was ill; I assumed that if anyone had broken the law it was more likely to have been Mr. Ferguson.

"So has every other teacher then," I said. "There's our text, provided by the state. I don't see how a teacher can teach biology without teaching evolution."

Robinson [the school board president] handed me a newspaper. It was the Chattanooga *News*, the afternoon paper, and he pointed to an advertisement, placed by the American Civil Liberties Union, which offered to pay the expenses of anyone willing to test the constitutionality of the Butler law forbidding the teaching of evolution in any public school.

"John, would you be willing to stand for a test case?" Robinson said. "Would you be willing to let your name be used?"

I realized that the best time to scotch the snake is when it starts to wiggle. The snake already had been wiggling a good long time.

I said, "If you can prove that I've taught evolution, and that I can qualify as a defendant, then I'll be willing to stand trial."

"You filled in as a biology teacher, didn't you?" Robinson said.

"Yes." I nodded. "When Mr. Ferguson was sick."

"Well, you taught biology then. Didn't you cover evolution?"

"We reviewed for final exams, as best I remember." To tell the truth, I wasn't sure I had taught evolution.

Robinson and the others apparently weren't concerned about this technicality. I had expressed willingness to stand trial. That was enough.

Robinson didn't indicate that my acquiescence would lead to an ordeal, and I didn't suspect it. Nor did he suggest that trouble might come out of the trial in any way. Instead, he walked over to the telephone and called the city desk of the Chattanooga *News*.

"This is F. E. Robinson in Dayton," he said. "I'm chairman of the school board here. We've just arrested a man for teaching evolution."

I drank the fountain drink that had been handed me and I went back to the high school to finish playing tennis with the kids. I assume everyone else in the drugstore went about his normal business too.

Afterward, Rappelyea wired the American Civil Liberties Union and got a promise to assist in my defense.

Rappelyea had argued with the townspeople over the Butler law before that afternoon. He would sit in Robinson's Drugstore and expound his views on evolution and the law. He said he at first got the idea of holding a test case in Dayton as he read the Chattanooga *Times* before dinner on Monday, May 4—the day before our encounter. An article stated that Superintendent of Schools Ziegler in Chattanooga had refused to sponsor a test case there. If Chattanooga backed down, then why not have the trial in Dayton? So Rappelyea had reasoned. The following afternoon, he precipitated the incident in the drugstore.

Rappelyea already knew me as an independent thinker, and he knew that I had subbed as a biology teacher during that spring. He reasoned that, if Doc Robinson asked me, I would agree to become a defendant in a test case. Relying upon this analysis of my character, he convinced the businessmen of the town that the publicity of such a case would put Dayton on the map and benefit business. His was a convincing argument and the businessmen went along with it.[4]

Far from being the victim of a bigoted community, Scopes was a willing participant in a trial which had been eagerly sought by the American Civil Liberties Union and which was arranged over drugstore drinks among Scopes, the school board chairman, and other members of the community. Even the argument which led to a shooting incident later, and which the news media played up, was, according to Scopes, nothing but a stunt staged for publicity, using blank bullets.[5] The only reason Scopes had stayed in Dayton during the summer was that there was an attractive blonde in town that he wanted to date. But Lawrence and Lee, in *Inherit the Wind*, play this up into a major love affair, with the young lady being forced by the callous Bryan to testify against Scopes at the trial, and ultimately leaving the home of her father—a bigoted fundamentalist preacher whom she secretly feared.[6]

However, the trial probably achieved more publicity than even Rappelyea intended. Though there were several able lawyers on each side, the trial boiled down to a contest between two giants, William Jennings Bryan for the prosecution and Clarence Darrow for the defense.

To both men, this was more than just another case. Bryan, in addition to having been a three-time candidate for the presidency, was a national figure

4. Scopes and Presley, pp. 57-61.

5. Ibid., p. 76.

6. Lawrence and Lee, pp. 5-8, 28-31, 48-49, 59, 67-71, 110, 115. Act 1, Scene 1, 1:1, 1:2, 2:1, 2:2, 3:3.

in the Presbyterian Church, and had preached vigorously against the theory of evolution. Among Bryan's repertoire of speeches was one entitled "The Menace of Darwinism," and four years before the Scopes trial he had written: "Darwinism is not science at all; it is a string of guesses strung together. There is more science in the 24th verse of the first chapter of Genesis . . . than in all that Darwin wrote."[7]

And Darrow, who volunteered his services for the defense, was just as adamant in his belief in evolution. In his autobiography Darrow declared:

> . . . man was never made. He was evolved from the lowest form of life. His ancestor in the sea slowly threw its jelly-like structure around something that nourished it and absorbed it. Slowly through ages of continued development and change and mutations the present man was evolved, and with him the more perfect and adaptable and specialized structure, with which he sees and hears and takes his food, and digests it and assimilates it to his structure. . . .
>
> To discover that certain forms and formations are adjusted for certain action has nothing to do with design. None of these developments are perfect, or anywhere near so. All of them, including the eye, are botchwork that any good mechanic would be ashamed to make. All of them need constant readjustment, are always out of order, and are entirely too complicated for dependable work. They are not made for any purpose; they simply grew out of needs and adaptations; in other words, they happened. Just as God must have happened, if he exists at all.[8]

In fact, it was not an even match. Bryan was in failing health,[9] as evidenced by his death five days after the trial. And while Bryan was a superb orator and politician, unlike Darrow he was not an experienced trial lawyer.[10] Nevertheless, Bryan did his level best, and on July 10, 1925, the trial opened.

Though the trial was lively, it was far from the "kangaroo court" depicted in *Inherit the Wind*. The play pictures a patient but exasperated Darrow doggedly pleading with the court to allow him to introduce scientific experts to testify concerning the theory of evolution. Bryan smugly objects and the court promptly rules for Bryan on every objection. Bryan makes smug statements about "evil"-ution and "zoo"-ology, while Darrow does his best to maintain a fair and orderly trial.[11]

7. William Jennings Bryan, "The Menace of Darwinism," *The Commoner*, April 1921, pp. 5-8; quoted in Lawrence W. Levine, *Defender of the Faith: William Jennings Bryan: The Last Decade*, 1915-1925 (New York: Oxford University Press, 1965), pp. 265-266.

8. Clarence Darrow, *The Story of My Life* (New York: Charles Scribner's Sons, 1932); reprinted in Paul Edwards and Arthur Pap, *A Modern Introduction to Philosophy* (New York: Free Press of Glencoe, 1957, 1963), p. 511.

9. Kevin Tierney, p. 357.

10. Louis W. Koenig, *Bryan: A Political Biography of William Jennings Bryan* (New York, Putnam, 1971, p. 615, 652).

11. Lawrence and Lee, pp. 72-74 Act II, Scene 2.

In fact, Judge Raulston did not prohibit the testimony; he only refused to allow it to go before the jury. The experts read their testimony into the record, while the jury was excused. This was an entirely proper decision. For the issue to be determined was not whether evolution was good or bad or true or false, but whether or not Scopes had taught evolution in violation of the Butler Act. Such scientific testimony may well be relevant in determining the constitutionality of the statute, but the statute's constitutionality was for the judge and appellate courts to determine, not the jury. Any sensible judge would have ruled exactly as Judge Raulston.[12] It is interesting to note that Darrow's experts relied in part on Piltdown man. This supposed "missing link" turned out to be a fraud, the skull of a man attached to the jawbone of an ape with the teeth filed down.[13] Darrow also used "Nebraska man," later conceded to be an extinct pig.

In his autobiography, Darrow wrote: "My object, and my only object, was to focus the attention of the country on the program of Mr. Bryan and the other fundamentalists in America."[14] That being the case, he desperately wanted a confrontation with Bryan on the creation-evolution issue. So in a surprise move, he called Bryan to the stand. In an even more surprising move, Bryan agreed to be questioned, even though it was clearly out of order for an attorney to be both witness and counsel.

In the play, as in the media, Darrow is pictured as having devastated Bryan on the stand. But Darrow's biographer, Tierney, says:

> Owing largely to the writing of Henry Mencken, the impression was created that the exchanges between Darrow and Bryan were entirely one-sided; that Darrow outshone Bryan every step of the way. In fact this was far from the case. The sparring of the two men reflected some credit on Bryan as a tactician, though his position weakened as cross-examination continued.[15]

But the authors of *Inherit the Wind* go even further than the media in portraying Bryan as a pompous, self-righteous ignoramus who gets his just deserts on the stand. In their play, when Darrow asks Bryan if he is in fact an authority on the Bible, Bryan answers: "I believe it is not boastful to say that I have studied the Bible as much as any layman. And I have tried to live according to its precepts."[16]

But in fact, Bryan didn't answer that way at all. The question wasn't whether he was an authority on the Bible, but whether he had given it considerable study:

> Mr. Darrow—You have given considerable study to the Bible, haven't you, Mr. Bryan?

12. Levine, p. 347.
13. Tierney, p. 360.
14. Darrow, p. 249, quoted in Levine, pp. 332-333.
15. Ibid., p. 366.
16. Lawrence and Lee, p. 76. Act II Scene 2.

Mr. Bryan—Yes, sir, I have tried to. I have studied the Bible for about
fifty years, or some time more than that. I studied it more lately than in
my youth.[17]

The distortions continue. In the play, Darrow asks Bryan if he is familiar
with *Darwin's Origin of Species,* and the following exchange ensues:

Brady [Bryan]—I am not in the least interested in the pagan hypotheses
of that book.
Drummond [Darrow]—Never read it?
Brady [Bryan]—And I never will.[18]

That exchange is pure fabrication. No such questions were asked or answered.
In fact, in the arguments over the admissibility of scientific evidence, Bryan
quoted from Hunter's *Civic Biology* and Darwin's *Descent of Man*[19] and showed
familiarity with Huxley as well.

The questioning proceeded into various teachings of the Bible. They argued
about Jonah and the fish/whale with Bryan claiming the Bible says "fish" and
Darrow claiming it says "whale." (Actually, in the King James Version they
were both right. The Book of Jonah uses the term "fish" (Jonah 1:17; 2:1,
10) while Matthew 12:40 uses "whale." But both the Hebrew *da'g* and the
Greek *ketos* can be translated as sea creature or sea monster.) Then they dueled
over the long day of Joshua. Here is how the exchange appears in *Inherit the
Wind*:

Drummond [Darrow]—If they say that the sun stood still, they must have
a notion that the sun moves around the earth. Think that's the way of
things? Or don't you believe the earth moves around the sun?
Brady [Bryan]—I have faith in the Bible!
Drummond [Darrow]—You don't have much faith in the solar system.
Brady [Bryan] (doggedly)—The sun stopped.[20]

Sounds like good drama, but that's not what was said at all. In fact, Bryan
answered that the Bible used "phenomenal" language in that account describing
the event as it appeared to the Israelites:

Darrow—Do you think whoever inspired it believed that the sun went
around the earth?
Bryan—I believe it was inspired by the Almighty and He may have used
language that could be understood at the time, instead of using language
that could not be understood until Darrow was born. (Laughter and
applause.)[21]

---

17. Genevieve Forbes Herrick and John Origen Herrick, *The Life of William Jennings Bryan* (Boston,
1925), p. 364.
18. Lawrence and Lee, pp. 76-77. Act II Scene 2.
19. Levine, pp. 342-344.
20. Lawrence and Lee, pp. 76-77. Act II Scene 2.
21. Herrick and Herrick, p. 367.

The examination then turned to the age of the earth. The authors of *Inherit the Wind* have Bryan accepting literally the Usher chronology:

> Brady [Bryan]—It is not an opinion. It is literal fact, which the good Bishop arrived at through careful computation of the ages of the prophets as set down in the Old Testament. In fact, he determined that the Lord began the Creation on the 23rd of October in the year 4004 B.C. at—uh, at 9 a.m.!
> Drummond [Darrow]—That Eastern Standard Time? (Laughter) Or Rocky Mountain Time? (More laughter) It wasn't daylight Savings Time, was it? Because the Lord didn't make the sun until the fourth day.[22]

In fact, Bryan stated that he was not convinced of the accuracy of the Usher chronology,[23] and disappointed many of his fundamentalist followers by answering concerning the day of creation:

> I don't think it necessarily means a twenty-four hour day. I do not think it does. But I think it would be just as easy for the kind of God we believe in to make the earth in six days or in six years, or in six million years, or in six hundred million years. I do not think it important whether we believe one or the other.[24]

I personally would disagree with that answer; I believe the six days of creation were twenty-four hour periods, though I fully respect Bryan's right to believe as he did. But such a moderate answer was not "bigoted" enough for the authors of *Inherit the Wind*. Here's how they rewrote the testimony:

> Brady [Bryan]—The Bible says it was a day.
> Drummond [Darrow]—There wasn't any sun. How do you know how long it was?
> Brady [Bryan] (determined)—The Bible says it was a day.
> Drummond [Darrow]—A normal day, a literal day, a twenty-four-hour day? (Pause. Brady is unsure.)
> Brady [Bryan]—I do not know.
> Drummond [Darrow]—What do you think?
> Brady [Bryan] (floundering)—I do not think about these things . . . I do not think about!
> Drummond [Darrow]—Do you ever think about things that you do think about? [These last two sentences did take place, though much earlier in the examination and in a much different context]. . . . Isn't it possible that the first day was twenty-five hours long? There was no way to measure it, no way to tell! Could it have been twenty-five hours? (Pause. The entire courtroom seems to lean forward.)

---

22. Lawrence and Lee, p. 85. Act II, Scene 2.
23. Herrick and Herrick, p. 369.
24. Ibid., p. 374. If Bryan lost popularity as a result of the Scopes trial, it was not because Darrow had defeated him in court, but because he departed from the strict Fundamentalist viewpoint by testifying that the long day of Joshua involves phenomenal language and the six (6) days of Creation were probably not twenty-four hour days. See Koenig, 651-652; Levine, pp. 352-3.

Brady [Bryan] (hesitates—) It is . . . possible . . . .[25]

Darrow then quizzed Bryan as to how the serpent moved before he was condemned to crawl on the ground (a question that was not original with Darrow; among others, John Calvin writing nearly four hundred years earlier offered solutions to the problem in his commentary on Genesis 3). The questioning then came to a dramatic close. As Lawrence and Lee describe it in *Inherit the Wind*:

> Brady [Bryan]—It is the revealed word of the Almighty. God spoke to the men who wrote the Bible.
> Drummond [Darrow]—And how do you know that God didn't "spake" to Charles Darwin?
> Brady [Bryan]—I know, because God tells me to oppose the evil teachings of that man.
> Drummond [Darrow]—Oh. God speaks to you.
> Brady [Bryan]—Yes.
> Drummond [Darrow]—He tells you exactly what's right and what's wrong?
> Brady [Bryan] (doggedly)—Yes.
> Drummond [Darrow]—And you act accordingly?
> Brady [Bryan]—Yes.
> Drummond [Darrow]—So you, Matthew Harrison Brady, through oratory, legislation, or whatever, pass along God's orders to the rest of the world! (Laughter begins) Gentlemen, meet the "Prophet From Nebraska!". . .[26]

At that point Bryan begins to lose his mind, shouts that he believes the Bible, and begins mindlessly chanting the names of the books of the Bible, and the trial comes to a close. Good drama, but fiction. Let's look at the record:

> Darrow—Now, you refer to the bow that was in the Heaven, after the flood, the rainbow. Do you believe in that?
> Bryan—Read it.
> Darrow—All right, Mr. Bryan, I will read it for you.
> Bryan—Your Honor, I think I can shorten this testimony. The only purpose Mr. Darrow has is to slur at the Bible, that I will answer his question. I will answer it all at once, and I have no objection in the world. I want the world to know that this man, who does not believe in God, is trying to use the court and Tennessee—
> Darrow—I object to that.
> Bryan—To slur at it, and while it will require time, I am willing to take it.
> Darrow—I object to your statement. I am examining you on your fool ideas that no intelligent Christian on earth believes.
> Once more, tumult, at that bitter attack on the great commoner and his faith. The crowd was in a stir, adherents of Bryan, proponents of Darrow, adding their voices to the clamor on the platform. Darrow was shaking his finger in Bryan's face now, and Bryan was returning the gesture with

25. Lawrence and Lee, pp. 86. Act II Scene 2.
26. Ibid., p. 88. Act II Scene 2.

vehemence. No stenographer could catch all the quick words. Then the Judge cut in, and the gavel halted this day, one of the most eventful in American court history, as well as one of the most eventful in the life of Bryan.[27]

Bryan had done his best, but Darrow had the advantage of surprise. Darrow and his questions were carefully prepared, Bryan and his answers were not. Bryan badly wanted to place Darrow on the stand and question him the next day, but the other members of the prosecution had opposed Bryan taking the stand and would not agree to it.[28] Darrow did not put his client, Scopes, on the stand to testify. Darrow had him exercise his right to remain silent, not because he might say something that would incriminate himself—the defense wanted a verdict of guilty so they could make it a test case in the appellate courts—but because they questioned whether Scopes could effectively handle cross-examination on the truth of evolution.[29]

Bryan had prepared an eloquent closing argument. Among other things, he had intended to show the effect of worldly philosophies on peoples' minds by quoting Darrow's own words back to him, when, representing Leopold and Leob in Chicago, he had blamed their crimes on their having been taught Neitzsche's philosophy in college.[30] But Bryan never had the opportunity to give his closing argument. Aware of Bryan's oratorical powers, Darrow engineered a clever maneuver. Sensing that it was the right time to quit, Darrow waived closing argument, thereby depriving the prosecution of its opportunity to argue under Tennessee law.

The next scene of the play opens with Darrow and Scopes nervously and pessimistically awaiting the jury's decision. In fact, there was no question about the outcome. The facts were clear, and *the defense wanted a guilty verdict* so they would have a test case to appeal. After only eight minutes' deliberation, the guilty verdict was returned. The court then imposed upon Scopes the minimum fine required by law, $100.

To create a vindictive spirit in the fundamentalists, *Inherit the Wind* has the following exchange:

> Brady [Bryan]—Did your honor say $100?
> Judge—That is correct. (Trying to get it over with) This seems to conclude the business of the trial—
> Brady [Bryan] (thundering)—Your Honor, the prosecution takes exception! Where the issues are so titanic, the court must mete out more drastic punishment—[31]

27. Herrick and Herrick, p. 375.
28. Levine, p. 351.
29. Scopes and Presley, p. 184-186, 187-188.
30. Clarence Darrow, quoted in Arthur Weinberg, ed., *Attorney for the Damned* (New York: Simon & Schuster, 1957), p. 35ff.
31. Lawrence and Lee, p. 103. Act III.

Again, this is a complete fabrication. As Levine says,

> The one point about which Bryan was adamant from the beginning of his
> association with the prosecution was the question of punishment. ". . .
> I don't think we should insist on more (than) the minimum fine." he
> informed Sue Hicks, "and I will let the defendant have the money to pay
> if he needs it. It is a test case and will end all controversy."[32]

And so, the play and the trial came to a close. But as the play ends, Bryan
begins a dramatic oration after the court has recessed, in which it is obvious
that he is out of touch with reality. In his speech he wavers between biblical
allusions and an acceptance speech he had once prepared for the presidency,
and finally collapses, dead, on the courthouse floor.[33] In fact, Bryan briefly
thanked the court, declaring that "this case will stimulate investigation and
investigation will bring out information,"[34] and his death occurred five days
later.

With a concluding demonstration of Darrow's generous disposition,
[Drummond] Darrow praises [Brady] Bryan, and sharply criticizes Hornbeck
(the playwrights' version of columnist H. L. Mencken) for saying sarcastically
that Bryan "died of a busted belly"—a reference to Bryan's habit of
overeating.[35] In fact, Darrow's biographer Irving Stone attributes the "busted
belly" quote to none other than Darrow himself.[36]

The case was duly appealed, and the Supreme Court of Tennessee upheld
the constitutionality of the Butler Act. Two judges ruled it was constitutional;
one ruled it was unconstitutional; and the fourth ruled that it was constitutional but did not apply to the facts at hand. However, the sentence was reversed
because it should have been passed by the jury instead of the judge.

Legally, the results were not far-reaching. The case stimulated other states,
like Arkansas in 1928, to pass new anti-evolution laws, which were not struck
down until the *Epperson* case in 1968.[37]

From a legal and constitutional standpoint, the case must be regarded as
a moderate victory for creationism. But from a public relations standpoint,
the evolutionists scored a great victory. For today, when people think of the
Scopes trial, the picture that comes to their minds comes not from history,
but from *Inherit the Wind*. They envision not Bryan, but Brady; not Darrow,
but Drummond.[38]

But why did the authors of *Inherit the Wind* take such liberties with the facts?

---

32. Levine, p. 335.
33. Lawrence and Lee, pp. 104-113 Act III.
34. Levine, p. 352.
35. Lawrence and Lee, pp. 112-115. Act III.
36. Irving Stone, *Clarence Darrow for the Defense* (Garden City, New York: Doubleday & Co.
Inc., 1941), p. 464.
37. Tierney, pp. 371-373; *Epperson v. Arkansas* 393 U.S. 97 (1968).
38. Koenig, p. 656.

Was it mere poetic license? Was it necessary to make a good story? Was it necessary to sell copies?

Or was it a deliberate attempt to place creationists and evangelical Christians in an unfavorable light, making them appear to be narrow-minded, bigoted, hateful, ignoramuses, afraid of the advances of modern science?

I leave the readers to decide.[39]

---

39. For further information see an article by R.M. Cornelius entitled "Their Stage Drew All the World: A New Look at the Scopes Evolution Trial," *Tennessee Historical Quarterly*, XL:2, Summer 1981, and a master's thesis submitted by Warren Allem to the Graduate Council of the University of Tennessee entitled "Backgrounds of the Scopes Trial at Dayton, Tennessee." Both of these sources largely corroborate what I have said in this chapter, and add a wealth of interesting data. In particular, Allem's thesis is based largely on personal interviews with persons who were involved in the Scopes trial.

Chapter 14

Scopes II:
Disestablishing the Evolutionists

"It is bigotry for public schools to teach only one theory of origins."[1] Thus thundered Clarence Darrow, the attorney for John Scopes. Darrow's co-counsel, Dudley Malone, declared: "The truth does not need the forces of government."[2] These sound like noble libertarian sentiments. Yet, while disestablishing the creationists, the forces of evolution somehow managed to turn the tables and become the establishment!

The Establishment of Evolution

Have you ever stopped to consider to what extent your tax dollars are used to promote evolution?

If you enjoy backpacking, perhaps you have been to Glacier National Park. There you can backpack from Lake McDonald Lodge to Sperry Glacier, and listen to an employee of the United States Government, paid by tax dollars, explain the ages of the various rock formations in terms of millions of years in accordance with uniformitarian geology. Historical markers, (again, financed by your tax dollars) boldly proclaim that various geological formations have existed for millions or billions of years, or are the result of certain natural forces. In museums, the evolutionary hypothesis is set forth in explanation after explanation on exhibit after exhibit—generally at taxpayers' expense. Evolution is promoted by government-financed research, by public television shows, and by government publications.

But undoubtedly, the most significant establishment of evolution is found in our public schools. Most public school textbooks treat evolution, not as

1. R. O'Bannon, "Creation, Evolution, and Public Education," #5 Dayton Symposium on Tennessee's Evolution Laws, May 18, 1974; quoted by Wendell R. Bird, "Freedom of Religion and Science Instruction in Public Schools," *Yale Law Journal*, Vol. 87, No. 3 (January 1978), p. 561.

2. Dudley Malone, quoted by Scopes & Presley, p. 154.

theory, but as fact. Even though they may technically call it a theory, they seldom acknowledge that there are alternatives. Sometimes they even mention various possibilities within the evolutionary framework, but almost never mention creation as a viable alternative.

One such text is *Earth-Space Sciences: Investigating Man's Environment*.[3] In Minnesota, earth science is a required subject, and this textbook is therefore used in many Minnesota eighth-grade public school classrooms. Listen to what this text says about origins:

> The earliest writings of ancient man, dating back more than five thousand years to the ancient Egyptians, describe ideas about the origin of the earth and the universe. This ancient record and all the writings in subsequent years indicate that the problem has been important to man throughout the centuries of his existence. On the basis of modern scientific standards, we cannot accept these early descriptions. Nevertheless, many of them are quite picturesque and imaginative.[4]

Note that the text did not explicitly mention the Bible, but since few eighth-graders today are very concerned about the writings of the ancient Egyptians, the "earliest writings of ancient man" will undoubtedly connote the Bible to the average student and leave the impression in his mind that the Bible is on the same "picturesque and imaginative level" as legends of the ancient Egyptians and cannot be accepted by modern man.

At the close of the chapter a question is posed for discussion: "Why were ancient man's explanations for the origin of the solar system impractical?"[5] Note the clever wording of this question. It avoids the objective question of whether these explanations are true or false and concentrates instead on their "practicality." And the question is not, "Were ancient man's explanations for the origin of the solar system impractical?" That they were impractical is assumed. The question asked is, *Why* were they impractical?

Except for that one cleverly disparaging reference, the creation model is ignored. In chapter 7, the various possible theories of the origin of the universe are discussed: The big bang theory, the oscillating universe theory, the steady-state theory, etc. The creation model is not mentioned. In chapter 11, we find various theories: the two-star theory, the protoplanet theory, the vortex theory, and others. But, again, divine creation is excluded.

In chapter 16, the history of the North American continent is presented, showing the glaciers that allegedly formed the geography of much of the northern portion of the United States and most of Canada. The book does not even mention that some do not accept the glacial theory, and the alternative

3. Albert R. Hibbs and Albert F. Eiss, *Earth-Space Sciences: Investigating Man's Environment*, (River Forest, Illinois: Laidlaw Brothers, 1971).

4. Ibid., p. 197.

5. Ibid., p. 214.

of the Flood theory is ignored.[6] In chapter 21, the book discussed the history of the North American continent in terms of historical periods, the first billion years, the second billion years, the third billion years, the fourth billion years, and the most recent 600 million years. The fact that many scientists believe the earth is not billions, or even millions of years old, but rather that its age may be measured in terms of thousands of years, is once again not even mentioned.

After reading such a textbook, is it any wonder that young people emerge with a firm belief in evolution? Science teachers whom they respect as authority figures have told them that it is true, and most of them are not even aware that another viable possibility exists.

Let us also examine a biology text. Though *Modern Biology*[7] is probably more careful with its language than some, the evolutionary hypothesis is given free rein. On page 148 the student is told: "Scientists estimate that the earth is more than five billion years old." I appreciate the fact that they use the word "estimate" instead of "have proven," but the student is not advised that not all scientists agree with that estimate. And on page 149 the student is told: "Evidence indicates that life on the earth began more than three billion years ago. But how did life begin? We cannot be certain. Several hypotheses have been offered but none proved. However, there does seem to be growing support for one hypothesis." The book then presents the theory of Russian scientist A. I. Oparian concerning the production of organic molecules, but emphasizes that the beginning of life is still an open question. The possibility of a divine Creator is not even mentioned.

A table on page 152 shows the various ages of the earth. The student is given no indication that this geological timetable is questionable. On page 154 the

---

6. On page 371 is a map of the North American continent, showing the area that the ice age supposedly covered. It is alleged that the ice sheet gradually moved southward, covering the Great Lakes and much of the upper Midwest. A question comes to mind: What caused the ice cap to move? Nowhere in the world today do we see glaciers moving uphill; they always move downhill. Yet, the area of Northern Canada—the eastern part of the Northwest Territories, Northern Manitoba and Ontario, the Hudson Bay, Baffin and Ellesmere Island, etc.—is lowland country, most of it close to sea level. What could have caused that glacier to move uphill from that lowland country into the upper Midwest, which is higher than the area from which the glacier supposedly came? The answer given by uniformitarian geologists is that the Northern Canada region was once much higher in elevation, but sank under the weight of the ice cap. One problem with that theory besides the fact that it seems to fit facts to conclusions instead of the other way around: Greenland has been under the ice cap much longer than Northern Canada, and 80 percent of Greenland remains under an ice cap today, an ice cap that is two miles thick in places. Yet, as I personally observed on a backpacking trip to Greenland in 1976, it is a very mountainous country with mountains in eastern Greenland rising over 11,000 feet out of the sea. Why has Greenland remained a mountainous area while under the weight of the glacier? The answer the uniformitarians give is that Greenland also is sinking, and that at one time its mountains were much higher than they are today. After hearing that explanation, I will never accuse uniformitarian geologists of lacking faith!

7. James H. Otto and Albert Towle, *Modern Biology* (New York: Holt, Rinehart & Winston, 1963, 1977).

student is shown drawings of the various embryonic stages of a bird and a man, emphasizing the similarity of the two.

On pages 154 to 157, the various evolutionary theories of Darwin, Lamarck, and De Vries are presented. They are carefully labeled theories, but the creation model is not mentioned, and the possibility that there is any alternative other than some theory within the general framework of evolution never comes to the student's attention.

On page 490, Figure 38-3 shows the student the various bones of the supposed "ancestors" of the modern horse. The student is not told that tiny Eohippus had eighteen ribs, his "descendent" Mesohippus had fifteen ribs, followed by Merychippus with fifteen ribs. By the time Pliohippus "evolved," he had nineteen ribs, and when the horse reached its present stage of development, modern Equus is now back to eighteen ribs once again.

On page 513 drawings of the human pelvis are placed beside those of a gorilla pelvis; on page 514 the human skull is compared to the chimpanzee skull, and on page 515 we are shown the teeth of the chimpanzee, the human, and the baboon. Also on page 514 are two photographs: one showing a human holding a board and another showing the chimpanzee holding a tree. The similarities and differences of the human's hands and the ape's hands are brought to the student's attention. Radiocarbon dating is discussed on page 517, with none of its fallacies mentioned. Various "missing links" receive their due recognition on pages 518-521. The implication is that similarity indicates common ancestry.[8] The possibility that similarity may indicate common design by a common Designer is ignored. Throughout this textbook, not one word makes the student aware of another viewpoint of origins: the creation model.

Many other examples could be cited, not just in science texts, but also in social studies texts, health texts, and many others. *Inquiring About Communities*[9] contains pictures of ape-men, based on mere conjecture but reinforcing the evolutionary theory that men and apes had a common ancestor.[10]

The workbook *Ventures in Science* further reinforces this uniformitarian approach by presenting the story of the life of a star, a star that originated a few billion years ago and will end a few billion years from now.[11] And the workbook *All Sorts of Things* further reinforces the uniformitarian approach and debases the creationist view by directing the student to make up his own "myth" as to how the stars were formed. This leads him to conclude that his own myth is just as good as the biblical "myth."[12]

Space and time do not permit a thorough discussion of every textbook that covers evolution. But these texts are typical of public-school textbooks currently in use throughout the nation.

8. It is just as logical to believe that similarity indicates common design.
9. *Inquiring About Communities* (New York: Holt, 1976), pp. 98-99.
10. Ibid.
11. *Ventures in Science* (Chicago: Sadlier, 1974), pp. 112-114.
12. *All Sorts of Things* (Lexington, Massachusetts: Ginn, 1973).

We see the degree to which evolution has been established. Now let us examine whether evolution is a religion.

Evolution As A Religious Tenet

Rather than saying that evolution is a religion, as many have said, it would probably be more accurate to say that evolution is a religious tenet. There is, of course, no evolutionist church, any more than there is a creationist church, but evolution is a fundamental tenet of many religions, just as creation is a fundamental tenet of many religions.

For purposes of argument, let us concede that evolution is also a science—an inaccurate science, but a science nevertheless. But it is also a religion. As Dr. Donald Johanson, a leading evolutionary scientist, recently told the *Tulsa Tribune* (October 3, 1981), "I do not see religion and evolution as mutually exclusive." C. F. Weizsacker observed at a scientific gathering:

> Science today is the only thing in which men as a whole believe: it is the only universal religion of our time. . . . The scientist has thus got himself into an ambiguous position: he is a priest of this new religion, possessing its secrets and marvels; for what to others is puzzling, strange or secret is plain to him.[13]

Some, of course, will say with Clarence Darrow that religion is confined to matters of faith, and that faith begins where reason leaves off. But that is by no means an accurate or comprehensive definition of religion. Some religious people believe that—notably those of the mystic school and the existentialist school. But traditional Christianity has generally recognized the essential compatibility of reason and faith, and most conservative or evangelical Christians today hold strongly to that position. Faith may transcend reason, but faith is not incompatible with reason. And if religion is concerned with ultimate values, it includes both faith and reason.

What reason do we have, then, for concluding that evolution is a religion?
(1) *The Theory of Evolution Necessarily Includes Faith Assumptions*.

As I have said, religion is not limited to matters of faith. According to evolutionists, however, science cannot take matters on faith. If evolution includes faith assumptions, then by their own reasoning, it must be something more than a science.

One faith assumption of the evolutionist is that the universe is millions or probably billions of years old. But no evolutionist knows the exact date of the formation of the universe. The various means by which the evolutionist tries to prove the age of the earth, or the age of fossils, radiocarbon dating, and carbon-14 dating are themselves based upon faith assumptions: the assumption

---

13. C.F. Weizsacker: *Reports of Geigy Bicentenary Scientific Day*, (Basel, Switzerland, June 3, 1958), quoted in Evan Shute: *Flaws in the Theory of Evolution*, p. 228, (London, Canada: The Temside Press, 1961; Nutley, New Jersey: The Craig Press, 1966); quoted by R.J. Rushdoony, *The Mythology of Science*, (Nutley, New Jersey: The Craig Press, 1967), p. 53.

that rocks have lost their radiation at uniform rates throughout history, that they began with a certain radiocarbon level, etc. As will be demonstrated later, there is as much evidence for a young universe as for an old universe. Another faith assumption is that the formation of life has been a process, not a catastrophic creative act. If this is not based upon proof, it is faith. The evolutionist cannot prove that God did not create the earth. When Julian Huxley declared that "Modern science must rule out special creation or divine guidance,"[14] he did not demonstrate scientific evidence, he expressed faith.

The evolutionist must therefore assume by faith that life can begin spontaneously. Yet no scientist has yet proven that this can or did happen. It is a necessary faith assumption for the evolutionist. (Of course, if he wishes to be a theistic evolutionist, he could say that the first living cell was formed by God; but then he is back to the same "unverifiable hypothesis" as the creationists and for which he accuses them of being unscientific.)

Evolution also assumes an upward progress. It is not called *devolution*—that is, downward regression—but evolution, or upward progress. In defiance of the laws of thermodynamics and the law of entropy and the fact that mutations are almost always harmful, evolution teaches that life is moving from the simple to the complex, and constantly improving as time goes on. Again, a faith assumption, and there is more evidence to refute than support it.

The evolutionist must also assume that there are "missing links" to explain the transition in the evolution of one species into another. Yet, such "missing links" have not been found. Darwin himself acknowledged:

> In fact the belief in Natural Selection must at present be grounded entirely on general considerations. (1) On its being a vera causa, from the struggle for existence; and the certain geological fact that species do somehow change. (2) From the analogy of change under domestication by man's selection. (3) And chiefly from this view connecting under an intelligible point of view a host of facts. When we descend to details, we can prove that no one species has changed (i.e., we cannot prove that a single species has changed): nor can we prove that the supposed changes are beneficial, which is the groundwork of the theory. Nor can we explain why some species have changed and others have not. The latter case seems to me hardly more difficult to understand precisely in a detail than the former case of supposed change.[15]

Darwin said that in 1863. Nearly a century later, Dr. Austin H. Clarke, noted biologist of the Smithsonian Institution, revealed that the evolutionists have made little, if any, progress over the past century in their search for this "missing link":

14. Julian Huxley, *Evolution: The Modern Synthesis* (New York: Harper & Brothers, 1943), p. 457; quoted in Robert T. Clark and James D. Bales, *Why Scientists Accept Evolution* (Grand Rapids, Michigan: Baker Book House, 1966), p. 6.

15. Charles Darwin to G. Benthin, 22 May 1863; in Francis Darwin, ed., *The Life and Letters of Charles Darwin* (New York: D. Appleton & Co., 1898), 2:210; quoted in Clarke and Bales, p. 96.

There is no evidence which would show a man developing step by step from lower forms of life. There is nothing to show that man was in any way connected with monkeys . . . he appeared suddenly and in substantially the same form as he is today . . . there are no such things as missing links. . . . so far as concern the major groups of animals, the creationists appear to have the best of the argument. There is not the slightest evidence that any one of the major groups arose from any other. Each is a special animal complex, related more or less closely to all the rest, and appearing therefore as a special and distinct creation.[16]

In 1981, Dr. Colin Patterson of the British Museum of Natural History in London confirmed that the missing link is still missing:

Gradualism is a concept I believe in, not just because of Darwin's authority, but because my understanding of genetics seems to demand it. Yet Gould and the American Museum people are hard to contradict when they say that there are no transitional fossils. As a paleontologist myself, I am much occupied with the philosophical problems of identifying ancestral forms in the fossil record. You say that I should at least show a photo of the fossil from which each type of organism was derived. I will lay it on the line— there is not one such fossil for which one could make a watertight argument. The reason is that statements about ancestry and descent are not applicable in the fossil record. Is Archaeopteryx the ancestor of all birds? Perhaps yes, perhaps no; there is no way of answering the question. It is easy enough to make up stories of how one form gave rise to another, and to find reasons why the stages should be favoured by natural selection. But such stories are not part of science, for there is no way of putting them to the test.[17]

According to Albert Fleishman, Professor of Comparative Anatomy at Earlangen University:

The theory of evolution suffered some grave defects which are becoming more and more apparent as time advances. It can no longer square with practical scientific knowledge, nor does it suffice for our theoretical grasp of the facts. The Darwinian theory of Descent has not a single fact to confirm it in the realm of nature. It is not the result of scientific research, but purely the product of imagination.[18]

Canadian geologist Sir William Dawson said of evolution: "It is one of the strangest phenomena of humanity; it is utterly destitute of proof."[19]
Why, then, do evolutionists accept the theory? Dr. D. M. S. Watson writes:

---

16. Austin H. Clarke; quoted in Fred John Meldau, *Witness Against Evolution* (Denver: Christian Victory Publishing Co., 1953), pp. 73-74; quoted in Duncan, pp. 27-28.
17. Colin Patterson to creation advocate Luther Sunderland, 5 May 1981; quoted in *Bible-Science Newsletter*, Vol. 19, No. 8 (August 1981), p. 8.
18. Albert Fleishman, Victoria Institute, 65:194-195; quoted by Duncan, p. 29.
19. Sir William Dawson, *Story of Earth and Man*, p. 317; quoted by Duncan, p. 29.

"The theory of evolution itself [is] a theory universally accepted, not because it can be proved by logically coherent evidence to be true, but because the only alternative is special creation, which is clearly incredible."[20]

Dr. G. A. Kerkut, of the Department of Physiology and Biochemistry at the University of Southhampton, does not reject the evolutionary hypothesis, but he does feel evolutionists need to be circumspect in proclaiming their theories as fact instead of as theory:

> It seems at times as if many of our modern writers on evolution had had their views by some sort of revelation and they base their opinions on the evolution of life, from the simplest form to the complex, entirely on the nature of specific and intra-specific evolution. It is possible that this type of evolution can explain many of the present day phenomena, but it is possible and indeed probable that many as yet unknown systems remain to be discovered, and it is premature, not to say arrogant, on our part if we make any dogmatic assertion as to the mode of evolution of the major branches of the animal kingdom.[21]

Harold E. Wright has described the faith of the evolutionists in terms which sound similar to Hebrews, chapter 11:

> By faith, Thales saw everything coming out of water which he acclaimed to be the original substance.
>
> By faith, Anaximander proclaimed the original earth to be mud. By faith, he declared life arose out of this mud. By faith, he saw man produced by a shark.
>
> By faith, Anaximenes saw man and animals being spontaneously generated out of mud by air condensing and rarefacting its surroundings.
>
> By faith, Empedocles saw parts of animals being formed and coming together by chance. By faith, he saw some animals adapting while others died off because they were not fit to survive. And by his wonderful "observations" he became the father of evolution.
>
> By faith, Buffon denied creationists' "theory" and the idea of fixity of species. By faith, he acclaimed the earth to be much older than 6,000 years.
>
> By faith, Huxley proclaimed evolutionary change to be "an incontrovertible fact."
>
> By faith, Lamarck stated his findings on use and misuse.
>
> By faith, Stensen proclaimed fossils to be of an organic origin.
>
> By faith, Charles Darwin left the ministry and the faith of his fathers. He boarded the H.M.S. Beagle, not knowing where it would take him. He climbed mountains, risked his life in disease-ridden areas, and looked at life around the world to seek out the answer to the origin of life.
>
> They were often tempted to give up their faith. They wandered about in sheepskins and goatskins. Being destitute, afflicted and tormented, they wandered in deserts, and in mountains, and in dens and caves of the earth.

20. D.M.S. Watson, "Adaptation," *Nature*, 1929, 24:233; quoted by Duncan, pp. 29-30.
21. G.A. Kerkut, *Implications of Evolution* (London: Pergamon Press, 1960, 1965), p. 155.

They all died in the faith, looking for a better hope. Whose god was chance, whose hope was the "super race."[22]

(2) *Evolution Is a Comprehensive World View.*

Jacques Barzun noted the phenomenal sales of *Darwin's Origin of Species* and commented that Darwinism placed its opposition in an immediate minority and "superseded all other beliefs. Nor is it hard to understand why, for it fulfilled the basic requirement of any religion by subsuming all phenomena under one case."[23]

We have previously seen the impact of the theory of evolution upon law, sociology, economics, political science, criminology, psychology, and other fields. It is in fact a total philosophy. Furthermore, it is foundational to the religion of secular humanism. Dr. Herbert H. Ross, principal scientist of the Illinois Natural History Survey and Professor of Entomology at the University of Illinois, labels it the "unifying principle of the universe."[24]

Lloyd Dale, speaking at a meeting of the Twin-Cities Creation Science Association, well summarized the comprehensive theology of evolution:

> . . . evolution is the Jesus Christ of Humanism. According to the Bible, Jesus Christ is the Creator (Colossians 1:17). Jesus Christ is the Redeemer and He is the Judge. Finally, He will complete the work He has begun. These are the five things that Jesus does. Evolution, according to my analysis, attempts to fill those five positions.
>
> (1) Evolution is the Creator, beginning with spontaneous generation and a primordial soup, to what we have today.
> (2) Evolution is the Sustainer. Everything in life is sustained by the ongoing struggle for survival.
> (3) Evolution is the Redeemer. In this ongoing struggle for survival, everything is judged whether it is fit to survive or not. Everything fit is saved through propagation for continuation of the species. This is salvation and redemption by evolution.
> (4) There is also a Judgement. The only sin in evolution is failure to adapt. The resolution is death, but salvation is survival.
> (5) Evolution is the Completer. Man has come to the place where he can now control his evolution. Eventually, one organism carried to the extreme will arrive as God.[25]

(3) *Evolutionists Advance their Cause with Religious Zeal.*

In 1947, an eminently qualified scientist named Immanuel Velikovsky contracted with Macmillan Company to publish his book, *Worlds in Collision*. Velikovsky was far from being a creationist, but his book presented scientific

---

22. Howard E. Wright, "The Mythology of the Evolutionists," *Bible-Science Newsletter*, May 1981, 5:2.

23. Barzun, p. 73; quoted by R.J. Rushdoony, *The Mythology of Science*, p. 14.

24. Herbert H. Ross, *A Synthesis of Evolutionary Theory* (Englewood Cliffs, New Jersey: Prentice-Hall, Inc., 1962, 1964), p. vii.

25. Lloyd Dale, Talk presented to February 17, 1981, meeting of the Twin-Cities Creation Science Association, printed in *Bible-Science Newsletter* (April 1981), 19:8.

evidence which challenged the assumptions of uniformitarian geology and evolutionary science in general. He hoped the scientific community would read his work, evaluate its merits, and change their thinking if they concluded he was correct.

But the evolutionary establishment reacted to Dr. Velikovsky like the Inquisition would react to an Albigensian. Rather than refuting his theories, they tried to suppress him without a hearing. Macmillan received letters from a Harvard professor, urging the publisher not to venture into the "black arts" and implying that Macmillan's reputation in the academic community would suffer as a result. When Macmillan refused to back down, a number of professors at prestigious universities organized a boycott of the publisher. They refused to submit works to Macmillan for publication and refused to order works published by Macmillan for their classes. Dr. Gordon Atwater, Curator of the Hayden Planetarium and Chairman of the Department of Astronomy, supported Velikovsky to the extent of asking that his views be given fair consideration; for this he was fired from both positions and asked to vacate his office immediately. Velikovsky was abused in the press, not by scholarly rebuttals but by statements such as "This incredible book . . . is too ludicrous to merit serious rebuttal." Because of this pressure, Macmillan was forced to transfer its publishing rights to Doubleday even though *Worlds in Collision* was at the time number one on the *New York Times* nonfiction best-seller list. Concerning the transfer, the June 18, 1950, *New York Times* stated:

> The greatest bombshell dropped on Publishers' Row in many a year exploded the other day. . . . Dr. Velikovsky himself would not comment on the changeover. But a publishing official admitted, privately, that a flood of protests from educators and others had hit the company hard in its vulnerable underbelly—the textbook division. Following some stormy sessions by the board of directors, Macmillan reluctantly succumbed, and surrendered its rights to the biggest moneymaker on its list.

Velikovsky's books continued to sell, and over the past thirty years he has gained a sizable number of adherents although his views are still in the minority among scientists. But don't these antics seem strange, coming from professors who in almost any other context would prate self-righteously about academic freedom? Why the hostility? It certainly sounds like more than a scholarly debate among scientists. Did Dr. Velikovsky hit a raw nerve somewhere? Did he challenge the evolutionists at the very core of their belief?

One Harvard scientist, who acknowledged he had not read Velikovsky's book, simply stated, "If Dr. Velikovsky is right, the rest of us are crazy." A disturbing thought, but hardly an excuse for supression of a book.[26]

All of this indicates that many evolutionists feel much more strongly about

---

26. The incident is described in detail in Alfred deGrazia, *The Velikovsky Affair* (New Hyde Park, New York: University Books, 1966); and in Fred Warshofsky, "When the Sky Rained Fire: the Velikovsky Phenomenon," *Reader's Digest*, December 1975, pp. 220-240.

evolution and uniformitarianism than one might expect them to feel about any mere scientific theory. It might also help to explain why creationist materials are published mostly by Christian publishers instead of the large publishers of scientific textbooks.

In recent years a number of debates have taken place between creationists and evolutionists, and the creationists have generally done quite well. Frequently, however, the evolutionists refuse to debate. Stanley Weinberg, a leading evolutionist and author of numerous textbooks on biology, recently advised a convention in New York City:

> They [the creationists] love to debate evolutionists and they always win because they are [unintelligible] without facts . . . so my advice is: do not debate the creationists. There is nothing to be gained. You are not going to convince them. They are not going to convince you, especially without convincing the audience. All that you do is give them the floor. . . .[27]

Weinberg is far from alone in his refusal to debate creationists. A creationist leader, Dr. Henry M. Morris, reports:

> The gigantic American Association for the Advancement of Science, for example, most powerful of all scientific organizations, views creationism with great fear. "We are very concerned about creationism," states William Kary, executive officer of AAAS, "and it was the subject of long discussion at our recent board meeting" ("A Response to Creationism Evolves," *Science* V. 214. November 6, 1981, p. 638). Evolutionists are especially afraid of participating in scientific debates on evolution versus creation. "All but one voice at the NAS (National Academy of Sciences) gathering agreed that debating with creationists should be avoided" (Ibid, p. 635). Instead, AAAS has arranged for 100,000 free copies of a special anti-creationist diatribe in the December issue of its popular magazine *Science 81* to be given to the nation's science teachers. This particular tract closes with the following distress call: "What is at stake is how the people of the United States look at sciences in the next decades and what they teach their children."[28]

This is a strange science indeed. Evolutionists cannot agree on what their theory means; they can only agree that it is undeniably true. They won't debate the creationists; they won't give the creationists equal time. They try to suppress publications that challenge their opinions; and they regard their opponents as ignorant and unscientific. What kind of "science" is this?

Evolution is a philosophy of life that addresses the ultimate concerns that religions commonly address. In the final analysis, evolution is a religious tenet.

---

27. Stanley Weinberg, 6 December 1980, New York City; quoted by Luther D. Sunderland, "Evolution of Evolution and the Creation of New Tactics," *Bible — Science Newsletter*, Vol. 19, No. 8 (July 1981) p. 8.

28. Henry M. Morris, "Goliath Crieth" *Good News Broadcaster*, May 1982, p. 17.

(4) *The Theory of Evolution Profoundly Affects Other Religious Doctrines.*

We have noted many of these implications of evolution before. Evolution affects our view of history, for it views man in continual upward progression from a lower form of life instead of a creature of God, fallen from God's ideal state.

It affects our view of man, for instead of the traditional view of man as having a body and a soul or spirit, which leaves the body at death, and which survives death, it views man as a physical entity, with no supernatural soul or spirit. Theistic evolutionists may, of course, believe that God infused man with a soul at some point in his evolutionary development, but the theory of evolution removes the necessity for this and creates serious problems with ensoulment.

It affects our view of sin. Whereas traditional Christians have viewed man as having been created with moral responsibility, and through an act of his volition having fallen and thereby acquired original sin, evolution removes the concept of original sin. Some evolutionists regard man as a "noble savage" who is basically good and needs only to be freed from the evils of his environment to realize his full potential. Others would attribute the evil in man to the "primeval beast" within him or the "killer ape" of his ancestry. (But most apes, unlike man, are *not* killers!''

Evolution affects our view of nature. Christians believe God specially created man and placed him over nature. The evolutionists regard man as the product and captive of nature.

Evolution affects our view of God. Evangelical Christians believe that God created man through an act of His will; He spoke the word, and it was so. Some evolutionists reject God entirely; others view God's creative activity as, at best, a continuing process. "Process theology" holds that God as well as man is evolving and moving toward a perfect state.

Evolution affects our view of the future. Traditional Christians, especially those of the premillennial school of thought, believe the world is getting worse and worse, and will continue to get worse until the return of Jesus Christ. Evolution sees man as getting better and better, and the logical conclusion of evolution is that man will evolve into a better species or "super-race." Together with the organic theory of the state propounded by Spencer and others, evolution means that man will ultimately build a paradise here on earth. He does not need God to build his paradise for him, nor does he need heaven.[29]

Evolution affects our view of the Bible. It may affect our view of the Bible's reliability; at the very least it affects the way we interpret the Bible. Personally, I do not believe the Bible can be interpreted to allow for the "day-age theory" or for theistic evolution. Even if it can be reconciled, evolution still means that the Genesis account must be regarded as something less than literal. This affects

---

29. Charles Howard Hopkins, *The Rise of the Social Gospel in American Protestantism 1865-1915* (New Haven, Conn.: Yale U. Press) pp. 123-148.

a basic principle of biblical hermeneutics, which is that the literal interpretation is to be preferred unless the context clearly indicates otherwise.

In fact, as we noted in chapter 6, the nineteenth century school of biblical criticism was largely the result of evolutionary thinking. Traditional Christianity has taught that in the beginning man worshipped the one true God, but due to the cancer of sin he degenerated into polytheism and idolatry (Romans 1:21-25). But more liberal theologians hold that as man evolved from less intelligent beings, he gradually became conscious of the supernatural. At first he worshipped animals and idols, then many gods, and eventually came to the knowledge of the one true God. Since people as early as Moses could not have held the monotheistic views expressed in the first five books of the Bible, those books must have been written by someone much later than Moses. Thus the documentary hypothesis of Graf, Wellhausen and others developed, the view that the Pentateuch was actually the later work of four authors known as J,E,D & P.[30]

Some argue that it is possible to believe in evolution and traditional Christianity at the same time because they involve separate and unrelated spheres of knowledge. We learn evolution through the scientific method; we accept creation by faith. In 1982 I participated in a debate in which a science professor said that he becomes an evolutionist when he puts on his white coat at 9:00 every morning, and he becomes a creationist when he takes that white coat off at 5:00 every night.

That position leads to a compartmentalized view of truth. God's truth cannot contradict itself. The proposition that God created the world in six days, and the proposition that the world developed (with or without God's help) over millions or billions of years, are mutually exclusive. One or the other (or both) must be false. One cannot be true from 9:00 to 5:00 and the other true the rest of the time.

Furthermore, true science and true religion cannot contradict each other. God is the Author of both. He reveals one through the laws of science, and He reveals the other through Scripture. If God's revelations are true, and truth cannot contradict itself, then God's revelation through science and God's revelation through Scripture, cannot contradict. If they appear to do so, then we have misunderstood one or the other.

Still others argue that creationists have taken an overly literal reading of Genesis and ignored the symbolism and poetry in the Bible. Certainly much of the Bible is poetry and symbolism, but not Genesis. It has all the trappings of a historical account. The author takes great pains to tell us what happened each day of creation, when man was placed in the Garden of Eden, and where

---

30. Herbert F. Hahn, *The Old Testament in Modern Research* (Philadelphia: Fortress Press, 1954, 1966), pp. 8, 9-10, 12, 46-47, 91.

that garden was located.[31] At great length, he narrates how old each person was when his children were born, and how long he lived thereafter. He records with meticulous detail who became the father of what tribe of people—the Ammonites, the Amalekites, the Edomites, the Moabites, and others. Genesis is just what its title indicates—a true account of the origins of the universe, the earth, the human race, the Hebrew people and their neighbors. To read it otherwise is to force a meaning upon it that neither its author nor its intended audience ever dreamt.

(5) *The Theory of Evolution is Compatible With Some Religions But Incompatible With Others.*

In early 1981 the state of Arkansas enacted a law providing balanced treatment for creation and evolution. Opponents of the law promptly sued, successfully, to have the new law declared unconstitutional. But it is most interesting to observe that nearly all of the plaintiffs were churches, religious organizations, or employees thereof. They included a United Methodist bishop, an Episcopal bishop, a Catholic bishop, an African Methodist Episcopal bishop, a Southern Baptist minister, a Presbyterian state leader, five other ministers, the American Jewish Congress, the Union of American Hebrew Congregations, the American Jewish Committee, and the National Coalition for Public Education and Religious Liberty, as well as several secular organizations such as the Arkansas Education Association and the National Association of Biology Teachers. The primary concern of most of these individuals and groups involves religion. And yet, they were very concerned about the teaching of creation and evolution. It would seem that they felt it has religious implications.

Even Darwin himself was influenced by religious considerations. Although he was an agnostic for much of his later life, as a young man he believed the Bible to be the literal and true Word of God.[32] He had planned, partially at his father's insistence, to become a clergyman. Although he had studied medicine briefly, his only earned degree was a Bachelor of Arts in Theology, Euclid and the Classics from Christ's College, Cambridge, England in 1831.[33]

In 1979, when the *Scientific Origins Bill* was presented to the Minnesota House of Representatives by State Representative Paul Aasness (R-Wendell), the House Education Committee took testimony concerning the bill. Most of those who testified against it had strong ties with organized religion. They included a local official of the National Conference of Christians and Jews, a Catholic nun, a Catholic priest, and a Lutheran seminary professor. Many others who testified against the bill emphasized their own personal religious affiliations.

---

31. The location of the Garden of Eden is meticulously spelled out in Genesis 2:10-14. The reason it cannot be located today is that the earth's geography was radically transformed by the ravages of the Noachic Flood.

32. Francis Darwin, Editor, *The Autobiography of Charles Darwin and Selected Letters* (New York: Dover Publications, 1958) pp. 17-18, 66.

33. Julian Huxley and H.B.D. Kettlewell, *Darwin and His World* (New York: Viking Press, 1965), pp. 13-19.

They stressed that they had been teaching evolution for many years and saw no conflict between evolution and their religious beliefs.

What are we to make of this? Are evolution and religion compatible after all?

The answer is that evolution is very compatible with some religions, but utterly incompatible with others.

What about Christianity? The answer again has to be that there are many different kinds of Christians, and that these differences cut across denominational lines. With some versions of Christianity, evolution is quite compatible; it could perhaps even be an integral tenet. With others, it is utterly incompatible, and, if accepted, would destroy the very foundation of belief.

Despite all the variations, and acknowledging that it is an oversimplification, let me suggest that Christians could be roughly divided into two catagories: liberal Christians and conservative Christians. Liberal Christians, while acknowledging that man is not perfect, nevertheless would not hold to a strict doctrine of original sin. They sometimes regard Christ as a son of God, perhaps even as the Son of God, but often believe that every man has within himself a spark of divinity that can be developed to become more like Christ. Christ's death on the cross, while it was a wonderful expression of God's love for man, was not an atoning death in the traditional sense of the term. Man is saved by living the social gospel, working to bring about the kingdom of God on earth. The Bible is a wonderful book that contains much wisdom, but it is the work of men, not God, and reflects primitive man's early conceptions of God. Much of the Bible contains myth that cannot be accepted as historical or scientific fact. This is an overgeneralization, as there are many shades of liberal theology. One variation, "process theology," holds that even God is "evolving," and His creative activity continues through all time.

The conservative or evangelical Christian, on the other hand, believes the Bible to be the inspired and inerrant Word of God. He therefore believes, in accordance with Genesis 1-3, that God created man and placed him in an ideal state and then finished His creative activity (Genesis 2:2-3). Man fell from that state by succumbing to the temptation of Satan, and because of that was driven from the Garden of Eden. A curse was placed upon creation and the curse spread like a cancer leading to increased degeneracy both for man and for all of creation (Genesis 3:17; Romans 8:22). The history of man is one of continued and increasing degeneracy, except for man's one hope: the Lord Jesus Christ. Christ died on the cross to pay for man's sin, and man finds salvation by trusting in Him. Nevertheless, the world continues to be under the power of Satan, and will remain so until the Second Coming of Christ.[34]

For the liberal Christian, evolution is quite compatible with his faith. In fact, evolution may be a basic tenet of his faith.

---

34. In setting forth these two types of Christianity, I use the term "Christian" only in the sense that it is commonly used throughout Christendom today. I make no judgment as to whether any professing Christian is saved or unsaved, regenerate or unregenerate.

But for the evangelical Christian, evolution is utterly incompatible with his faith. Creation is a fundamental tenet of his faith.

The dispute, then is not between science and religion. Rather the dispute is between two scientific models, each of which has strong religious implications and each of which has adherents among both scientists and theologians.[35]

So when someone says that evolution does not conflict with his religion, I can only answer, "That doesn't tell me anything about evolution. That tells me more about your religion."

Now, the point of this section is not to prove that conservative Christians are right and liberal Christians are wrong. Throughout history evolution has sharply conflicted with the religious beliefs of conservative Christians. Martin Luther stated:

> Therefore, when Moses writes that God created heaven and earth and whatever is in them in six days, then let this remain six days, and do not venture to devise any comment that six days were one day. But if you cannot understand how this could have been done in six days, then grant the Holy Spirit the honor of being more learned than you are.[36]

Luther was not alone in his creationist stand. Christians of many denominations agree with him. Among those religions whose members, for the most part, adhere to the creationist position are the following:

Lutheran Church - Missouri Synod
Wisconsin Evangelical Lutheran Synod
Association of Free Lutheran Churches
Apostolic Lutherans
Evangelical Lutheran Synod

---

35. There is a marked similarity between this dispute and that of Galileo with the Catholic Church in the seventeenth century. That was not a dispute between science and religion. Galileo had been educated in a monastery and was a very religious man. The dispute was whether his scientific theory was correct and whether the Catholic church was correctly interpreting several Scripture passages which appeared to indicate that the sun rotated around the earth (which are subject to other exegesis). Galileo was charged in 1633 with teaching the Copernican system as absolute fact, rather than as an hypothesis, which would have been acceptable. He was also charged with disobeying an earlier promise not to defend the Copernican theory.

Galileo had no intention of contradicting Scripture. As he once stated, "As to the [physical] propositions which are stated but not rigorously demonstrated, anything contrary to the Bible involved in them must be considered undoubtedly false and should be proved so by every possible means." His disagreement was not with the Scriptures, but with the interpretations the early church fathers had given to the Scriptures. And the Catholic church at the time took the position that unless Galileo could absolutely prove the Copernican hypothesis to be true, the early church fathers' interpretation of Scripture was to stand. Most of the "scientific establishment" of the day, including many of the Jesuit astronomers, took the same viewpoint as the church. The issue, then, was not religion vs. science, but the religious/scientific establishment vs. an individual religious scientist. One wonders what Galileo would think of the creation/evolution controversy of today. (*New Catholic Encyclopedia*, Vol. 6, pp. 250-255, s.v. "Galilei, Galileo" by J.J. Langford.)

36. *Luther's Works*, Weimar Edition, 24:19f; quoted in *What Luther Says*, 1:93.

Church of the Lutheran Brethren of America
Seventh Day Adventists
Baptist Bible Fellowship
Southern Baptist Convention
American Baptist Association
General Association of Regular Baptist Churches
Independent Baptists
Conservative Baptists
Southwide Baptist Fellowship
Orthodox Baptist
New Testament Association of Independent Baptist Churches
World Baptist Fellowship
Free Methodists
Wesleyans
Assemblies of God
Church of God
Pentecostal Church of God
Church of God in Christ
Church of God of Prophecy
Presbyterian Church of America
Reformed Presbyterian Church, Evangelical Synod
Orthodox Presbyterian Church
Christian Reformed Church
Christian and Missionary Alliance
Mennonite General Conference
Plymouth Brethren
Grace Brethren
Evangelical Free Church
Church of God - Anderson
Church of Christ
Amish
Most Mormons
Islam
Jehovah's Witnesses
Orthodox Judaism[37]

Of course, not everyone affiliated with the above-mentioned denominations rejects evolution. But most of these denominations would reject evolution and adhere to creation.

On the other hand, there are many religions which accept and even actively promote the theory of evolution. Among those whose members would almost uniformly accept the theory of evolution:

Unitarianism
Reformed Judaism
Secular Humanism

37. Bird, pp. 519-520.

Buddhism

Atheism

Additionally, many clergy and laity of the more liberal Protestant denominations accept evolutionary thought. These include a large number of United Methodists, Presbyterians, and Lutherans of more liberal synods.[38]

(6) *The Dogmatic and Exclusive Teaching of Evolution Advances Some Religions and Inhibits Others.*

Let us imagine that your house is located between two churches. The doctrine of the church on your right is strongly creationist, while that of the church on your left is strongly evolutionist.

Now, let us further suppose that all your life you have been taught in the public schools that evolution is a fact and creation is an unscientific myth. As a good student who trusts his teachers, you have accepted their position as true.

Now, which church would you probably attend? The way your mindset has been shaped, aren't you more likely to feel comfortable in the evolutionist church than in the creationist church?

In chapter 10 we saw the three-prong test the Supreme Court developed in *Lemon v. Kurtzman* to determine whether state involvement with religion constitutes an establishment of religion. The second prong of that test, you will recall, is this: Does the state activity in question have a primary effect of advancing or inhibiting religion?

The dogmatic and exclusive teaching of the theory of evolution in public schools has a primary effect of advancing those religions which are compatible with evolution and inhibiting those religions which are incompatible with evolution. A case challenging the teaching of evolution as an establishment of religion could possibly be successful. However, it would require a great deal of preparation and expert testimony to "educate" the court.

A recent case failed, *Crowley v. Smithsonian Institution*, 636 Fed. 2d 738 (D.C. Cir. 1980). Plaintiff Crowley challenged certain exhibits of the Smithsonian Institution, claiming their evolutionary character constituted an establishment of the religion of secular humanism. The court ruled, however, that the mere presence of an exhibit that favored an evolutionary theory which happened to coincide with the religion of secular humanism did not by itself constitute an establishment of religion. The court noted that the Smithsonian had not shown any hostility toward Christianity or creationism, that the Smithsonian had not refused to display other exhibits supporting creationism, that there was a solid secular purpose in showing the exhibit (the dissemination of knowledge), and that visiting and viewing the exhibits at the Smithsonian was entirely voluntary.

One could distinguish between the Crowley case and the teaching of evolution

---

38. Lest anyone take offense, I hasten to add that not all or even the majority of those involved in these denominations accept evolution, only that a sizeable number do.

in the public schools. Crowley dealt with only one narrow aspect of the establishment of evolution. In contrast to a few exhibits in the Smithsonian, teaching evolution is part of the daily diet of public school children across the nation. And public school teachers have a captive audience which the Smithsonian does not.

The exclusive and dogmatic teaching of evolution has been challenged elsewhere. In March 1981, a trial in the Superior Court of California drew nationwide attention: *Segraves v. California* (No. 278978, Dept. 15; decision filed June 12, 1981). Kelly Segraves, director of the Creation-Science Research Center of San Diego, California, along with his children and several other plaintiffs, challenged the dogmatic teaching of evolution in the California public schools. Creationists and evolutionists both geared up for a replay of the Scopes trial.

But the case actually did not resolve as much as either side had hoped. Segraves dropped his demand that the state be required to teach the creation model alongside the evolution model, so that issue was not resolved. The plaintiffs testified that merely hearing evolution taught as theory did not violate their religious beliefs; their religious beliefs were violated only when evolution was taught as dogmatic fact. Accordingly, the court ruled that the teaching of evolution as theory did not violate their religious convictions. The court had no alternative but to make that ruling since the plaintiffs had testified to that fact. However, the court's ruling also indicated that if evolution is taught as fact, the plaintiffs' rights under the First and Fourteenth Amendments could be violated. Consequently, the court directed the California State Board of Education to fully disseminate to all schools and other appropriate personnel copies of the state's policy concerning the teaching of evolution. That policy specifically directs that evolution is to be taught only as a theory and not in a dogmatic manner.

The news media, which misunderstood the issues throughout the trial, initially hailed the decision as a victory for evolution. The *Tulsa World* captioned its March 7, 1981, article, "Judge Upholds Teaching of Evolution." However, a more careful examination of the decision of Judge Perluss reveals that the decision might be a limited victory for creationists. For it indicates that a child's First Amendment right to free exercise of religion does apply to public school classroom situations in which a child is taught evolution. Though the precedent established by the *Segraves* case is limited, it could be helpful in future litigation.

The State of California had intended to argue in *Segraves* that, even if their practices did constitute an establishment of religion, the state had no alternative but to teach evolution, because there is no other credible theory of origins. Let us therefore examine whether the creation model is in fact a credible theory of origins.

Creation as a Scientific Model

Let us concede to begin with that creation is also a religious tenet. Again, religion and science are not mutually exclusive. The following establishes that creation is also a science.

(1) *A Substantial Number of Qualified Scientists Accept the Creation Model.*

At present, creationists are a minority among scientists, although they are a rapidly growing minority. Truth has never been determined by taking a majority vote, especially in scientific matters. If it had, Galileo would have been badly outvoted by the scientists of his day, as would most other pioneers of science. But creationists do have a large number of adherents within the scientific community. The Creation Research Society divides its membership into scientists and nonscientists; scientist members have to have degrees in some field of science. The Society has over 700 scientist members and many more nonscientist members, and its ranks are growing.

Gavin de Beer, writing on "Evolution" in *Encyclopedia Britannica*, assures us that "evolution is accepted by all biologists and natural selection is recognized as its cause by English-speaking biologists and others, though not widely in western continental Europe."[39] The scientist/members of the Creation Research Society would be surprised to hear that. So would Dr. Duane Gish. Dr. Gish has his Ph.D. in biochemistry from the University of California at Berkeley. He spent eighteen years in biochemical and biomedical research at Cornell University College, the Virus Laboratory of the University of California at Berkeley, and the Upjohn Company. He has written, lectured, and debated widely in his field, and is currently Associate Director of the Institute for Creation Research and Professor of Natural Science at Christian Heritage College. Dr. Gish mentions other scientists who hold the creationist viewpoint:

> It is often stated that there are no reputable scientists who do not accept the theory of evolution. This is just one more false argument to win converts to the theory. While it is true that creationists among scientists definitely constitute a minority, there are *many* creation scientists, and their number is growing. Among these may be numbered such well-established scientists as Dr. A. E. Wilder-Smith, Professor of Pharmacology in Boggern, Switzerland, and author of more than 50 technical publications; Dr. W. R. Thompson, world-famous biologist and former Director of the Commonwealth Institute of Biological Control of Canada; Dr. Melvin A. Cook, winner of the 1968 E.G. Murphee Award in Industrial and Engineering Chemistry from the American Chemical Society and also winner of the Nobel Nitro Award, now President of the Ireco Chemical Company, Salt Lake City; Dr. Henry M. Morris, for thirteen years Professor of Hydraulic Engineering and Head of the Civil Engineering Department at Virginia Polytechnic Institute and University, one of the largest in the U.S., now Director of the Institute for Creation Research and Academic Vice-President of Christian Heritage College, San Diego; Dr. Walter

39. *Encyclopaedia Brittanica: Macropedia: Knowledge in Depth*, s.v. "Evolution" by Sir Gavin de Beer, 723.

Lammerts, geneticist and famous plant-breeder; Dr. Frank Marsh, Professor of Biology at Andrews University until his retirement; and the late Dr. J. J. Duyvene De Wit, Professor of Zoology at the University of the Orange Free State, South Africa, at the time of his death.[40]

(2) *A Substantial Body of Scientific Literature Supports Creation.*

As we have seen, the major textbook producers do not publish creationist materials because of pressure from the scientific establishment. Nevertheless, scientific works supporting the creationist viewpoint do find their way into print. Most can be ordered through the Bible-Science Association (P.O. Box 6163, 2911 E. 42nd St., Minneapolis, Minnesota 55406), through the Creation-Science Research Center (P.O. Box 23195, San Diego, California 92123), or through local Christian bookstores.

Since a complete listing of these books would take too much space and is available from these organizations, I will discuss only a representative sample. Of books written by creationists which attempt to present both sides of the creation/evolution controversy in a fair manner, one of the best is *Biology: A Search for Order in Complexity*, by John N. Moore and Harold S. Slusher (Grand Rapids: Zondervan, 1970, 1977). It is written in the style of a high school science textbook and is intended for use in high school classes. Richard Bliss has written a good work entitled *Origins: Two Models—Evolution and Creation* (San Diego: Creation-Life Publishers, 1976). Dr. Duane Thurman, Professor of Biology at Oral Roberts University, has written a brief and fairly objective book entitled *How to Think About Creation/Evolution and Other Bible Science Controversies* (Downers Grove, Illinois: Inter-Varsity Press, 1978), and the reader might also consider *The Creation/Evolution Controversy* by R. L. Wysong (Kalamazoo, Mich.: Inquiry Press, 1978, 1980). Still another is *The Creation Explanation* by Robert E. Kofahl and Kelly Segraves (Wheaton, Illinois: Harold Shaw Publishers, 1975).

We have previously discussed the work of Immanuel Velikovsky. Dr. Velikovsky does not write from a Christian standpoint and might not be comfortable in the creationist camp, but his works are of the highest scholarship and do cast doubt upon the assumptions of evolution and uniformitarian geology. They include *Worlds in Collision* (1950), *Ages in Chaos* (1952), and *Earth in Upheaval* (1955), all by Doubleday of New York City. Velikovsky's works provide a basis for concluding that many of the miracles described in the Bible, such as the long day of Joshua and others, did actually happen, although he attributes them to astronomical catastrophes rather than to direct divine intervention. Donald Wesley Patton, writing from a Christian perspective, comes to some similar conclusions in his work, *The Biblical Flood and the Ice Epoch* (Seattle: Pacific Meridian Publishing Co., 1966, 1973).

Evolutionists often assume that fossils prove evolution; but actually, the fossil record (or lack thereof) is an embarrassment to them. Books which discuss the

---

40. Duane Gish, *Evolution: The Fossils Say No!* (San Diego: Creation-Life Publishers, 1972, 1977), pp. 8-9.

fossil record from a creationist standpoint include *Evolution: The Fossils Say No!* by Dr. Gish, already mentioned; M. Bowden's *Ape-Men: Fact or Fallacy?* (Bromley, Kent, England: Sovereign Publications, 1977), *Man and Dinosaurs in History* by Fredrick Beierle (Prosser, Washington, By Author, 1977), and *The Mammoth in Ice and Snow* by Hans Krause (Germany, By Author, 1978). As to the accuracy of the various methods for dating fossils, George Howe provides some interesting insight in *Carbon-14 and Other Dating Methods* (Minneapolis: Bible-Science Association, 1969).

Dr. A. E. Wilder-Smith examines the question of origins in *The Creation of Life: A Cybernetic Approach to Evolution* (Wheaton, Illinois: Harold Shaw Publishers, 1974), and discusses the problem from a more philosophical standpoint in *Man's Origin, Man's Destiny* (Minneapolis: Bethany Fellowship, 1968, 1975). Other analyses may be found in *The Origin of Life* by Richard Bliss and Gary Parker (San Diego: Creation-Life Publishers, 1979), and Harold Coffin's *Creation: Accident or Design?* (Washington, D.C.: Review and Herald Publishing Co., 1969).

Closely tied to the creation/evolution controversy is the issue of the Flood of Noah's time. One who believes the biblical account of creation, is likely to also believe the biblical account of the Flood as well, and vice-versa. Creationists believe that a worldwide flood as described in the Bible offers a better and more scientific explanation for geological phenomena than those of evolution and uniformitarian geology. John C. Whitcomb and Henry Morris present an excellent scientific defense of the biblical account of the Flood in their book, *The Genesis Flood* (Philadelphia: Presbyterian & Reformed Publishing Company, 1961). Another excellent work is Dr. Alfred M. Rehwinkel's *The Flood in the Light of the Bible, Geology, and Archeology* (St. Louis: Concordia, 1951). For centuries, scientists, explorers, and adventurers have noted a large wooden structure encased in ice near the summit of Ararat in Turkey and have speculated that it may be the remains of Noah's Ark, which the Bible says came to rest "upon the mountains of Ararat" (Genesis 8:4). Several books have been published expressing this viewpoint; one of the best is *The Ark on Ararat* by Tim LaHaye and John Morris (Nashville: Thomas Nelson, Inc., Publishers, 1976).

Scientific journals which present the creation viewpoint include the *Creation Research Society Quarterly* by the Creation Research Soceity, and the *Bible-Science Newsletter* by the Bible-Science Association. Still another is the *Creation Social Sciences and Humanities Quarterly*, published by the Creation Social Sciences and Humanities Society (1429 N. Holyoke, Wichita, Kansas 67208), which examines the impact of creation and evolution upon the social sciences.

Scientific organizations which support the creationist position include the Bible-Science Association, 2911 E. 42nd St., Minneapolis, Minn. 55406; Creation Research Society, 2717 Cranbrook Road, Ann Arbor, Michigan 48105; Institute for Creation Research, 2716 Madison, San Diego, California 92006; Creation-Science Research Center, P.O. Box 23195, San Diego, California 92123; Bible-Science Library, 19 Gallery Centre, Taylors, South Carolina

29687; Creation/Health Foundation/Creation Medical Fellowship, 19 Gallery Centre, Taylors, South Carolina 29687; Lutheran Science Institute, 8830 W. Blue Mound, Milwaukee, Wisconsin 53223; Students for Origins Research, 815 W. Tedregossa, Santa Barbara, California; Life Origins Foundation; 2412 Foothill Blvd., Sp. 18, Calistoga, California 94515; Geoscience Research Institute, Loma Linda University, Loma Linda, California 92354; Creation Filmstrip Center, Miriam Mitchem, Rt. 1, Haviland, Kansas 67059; Fair Education Foundation, Rt. 2, Box 415, Murphy, South Carolina 28906; Association for Biblical Research, 517 E. Moreland Rd., Willow Grove, Pennsylvania 19090; Creation-Research Science Education Foundation, Inc., Star Route, Box 4, Millersburg, Ohio 44654; Evolution Protest Movement of North America, 1557 Arrow Road, Victoria, British Columbia, Canada. This list is not complete as many local organizations and groups from other countries could also be listed.

(3) *Creation Is, at Least to a Degree, Empirically Verifiable by Scientific Evidence.*

The scientists and scientific works discussed above present a great deal of scientific evidence, coupled with sound reasoning to support their position.

Creation scientists point to the laws of thermodynamics. The first law holds that neither matter nor energy is either created or destroyed. The second law of thermodynamics holds that whenever matter is transferred into energy or energy into matter, a certain amount of matter or energy is rendered useless—not destroyed, but rendered useless. The effect of these laws is that the universe is gradually wearing down. Similarly, the law of entropy holds that unless a creative intelligence is superimposed upon things, they tend to break down when left to themselves. Order breaks down into disorder, complex structures break down into simple structures, etc. These scientific laws are perfectly compatible with the creationist position that God created an ideal universe, that He ceased from creation after the sixth day (first law of thermodynamics; see Genesis 2:1-2; Ecclesiastes 1:9), but that because of the spreading cancer of sin, God's creation is gradually wearing down, the earth is becoming less productive, etc. (second law of thermodynamics and law of entropy; see Genesis 3:17-19; Romans 8:22). But these laws are incompatible with the theory of evolution which sees life beginning from spontaneous generation and evolving from simple to complex, weak to strong, less intelligent to more intelligent.

The Space Age has revealed much that supports creation and refutes evolution. Many discoveries from space travel have indicated that our solar system could not be millions or billions of years old as evolutionists have to maintain. Before the first moon landing, for example, scientists widely speculated that the moon must be encased in cosmic dust many feet thick, since it had been without an atmosphere for billions of years. Yet when the first landing took place, very little cosmic dust was found! The absence of cosmic dust indicates a young earth.

The travels of Voyager in 1981 revealed some interesting data about the moons of Jupiter and the rings of Saturn. One of Jupiter's moons, it was discovered, shows fresh volcanic activity. This volcanic activity means that moon must have a hot liquid center of molten lava. But as far as Jupiter is from the sun, if that moon is in fact billions of years old as evolutionists maintain, its center would have cooled long ago—further evidence of a young solar system, and therefore a young earth.

Numerous other examples of scientific evidence could be cited—the lack of missing links, apparent dinosaur footprints and human footprints in the same hardened Paluxy River bed in Texas, frozen mammoths found in the Arctic with tropical vegetation in their mouths and stomachs (evidence of either a worldwide catastrophe such as the Flood, a pre-Flood worldwide tropical climate, or both), symbiotic relationships that could not have evolved, and many others.

It is sometimes argued that creationism cannot be a science because it assumes an unverifiable hypothesis, the existence of the Creator, God. Is this a valid reason to disqualify creationism as a science?

It depends upon the definition of science. *Webster's Third New International Dictionary* offers several definitions. The first is: "possession of knowledge as distinguished from ignorance or misunderstanding."[41] By this definition creation would certainly be just as much a science as evolution. In fact, when one considers that the Bible tells us that "The fear of the Lord is the beginning of wisdom" (Psalm 111:10), and "The fool has said in his heart, there is no God" (Psalm 141), one might conclude from this definition that evolution is not a science!

Webster's second definition: "a branch or department of systematized knowledge that is or can be made a specific object of study."[42] Again, by this definition creation is just as much a branch or department of systematized knowledge as evolution. Each can be made a specific object of study.

Webster's third definition: "accumulated and accepted knowledge that has been systematized and formulated with reference to the discovery of general truths or in the operation of general laws."[43] Creation fully fits this definition.

Webster's fourth definition: "a branch of study that is concerned with observation and classification of facts and especially with the establishment or strictly with the quantitative formulation of verifiable general laws chiefly by induction and hypothesis."[44] Only by this definition could it be argued that creation is not entirely a science, since God cannot be quantitatively formulated.

Is God empirically verifiable? Not in the sense that He can be discovered by a microscope, or observed through a telescope, or analyzed in a chemistry lab. But the evidence from causation and design certainly points to God.

41. *Webster's Third New International Dictionary*, unabridged (1976), s.v. "Science."
42. Ibid.
43. Ibid.
44. Ibid.

The scientific creationist does not necessarily presuppose the existence of God. Rather, he believes God's creative activity—and, therefore, His existence—can be demonstrated by the design of the universe. Just as the discovery of a watch empirically suggests the existence and prior involvement of a watchmaker, the creation-scientist believes the existence of the universe points to a first cause, that first cause being God.

Two leading scientists, Sir Fred Hoyle and Dr. Chandra Wickramasinghe, formerly unbelievers, now argue that a Creator God does exist and that His existence can be proven from science and mathematics. Science, they say, demonstrates to a virtual mathematical certainty the utter impossibility of spontaneous generation of life. The only alternative, they say, is a Creator.[45] While Hoyle and Wickramasinghe have raised serious doubts about evolution, they have not as this point embraced the six-day creationist position.

Even if one concludes that creationism rests upon unverifiable hypotheses, the same is true of evolution. We have noted the faith assumptions of the evolutionists earlier: either that life is capable of spontaneous generation (which has never been proven, and must be taken on faith) or that life in its original one-celled form was established by God (which brings the evolutionists to the same "faith assumption" or "unverifiable hypothesis" as the creationist).

The evolutionist operates on many other unverifiable hypotheses. Let us suppose, for example, that the evolutionist observes a marking in stone that appears to be the track of a dinosaur. He concludes, "That track didn't just happen by chance; a dinosaur must have walked here." But no one ever saw a dinosaur walk there, and there was no camera to photograph the dinosaur. That that particular track was made by a dinosaur is an unverifiable conclusion based on circumstantial evidence rather than direct observation, similar to the creationists' conclusion that the design of the universe presupposes a Creator. Just as the discovery of a watch is scientific evidence for the existence of a watchmaker, so the observation of the wonders of creation is scientific evidence for the existence of a Creator.

Let us suppose, just for the sake of argument, that someone found the so-called missing link—a genuine skeleton of an ape-man! What would this prove? Only that ape-men once walked the earth. It would not prove that apes evolved into ape-men and that ape-men evolved into humans, or that apes, ape-men, and humans all have the same ancestor. One could just as easily conclude that apes, ape-men, and humans all have the same designer, God.

Evolution is simply a hypothesis which attempts to explain the origin of the phenomena that have been discovered. The phenomena do not verify the hypothesis; in fact, the evidence and lack of evidence tend to cast doubt upon the evolutionary hypothesis. The evolutionist rests his case upon faith assumptions and unverifiable hypotheses just as much as does the creationist, if not more so.

---

45. "Two Astrophysicists Insist Creator Can Be Proven Mathematically: Ex-Disbelievers make analogy concerning Rubik's cube," Martin Gardner, *Tulsa World*, April 4, 1982, p. J-1.

As Henry Morris has stated, "Creation is as scientific as evolution . . . evolution is as religious as creation."[46]

The Two-Model Approach

The reader will recall from our earlier discussion that the framers of the First Amendment probably meant three things by "establishment of religion": (1) supporting a religious doctrine by public tax funds; (2) compelling adherence to religious doctrines or attendance at religious function; and/or (3) attaching civil disabilities (such as denying the right to vote or to hold public office) to those who do not support the established religion.

We have seen that evolution is a religious tenet. On all three of those counts, therefore, the promotion of evolution by governmental bodies constitutes an unconstitutional establishment of religion: (1) Evolution is taught in the public schools at enormous public expense, not just in the science classes but permeating the entire curriculum, (2) Children are compelled to attend school, and in many areas and for many persons, that, in effect, compels them to attend public school; furthermore, since a science teacher is an authority figure respected by impressionable children, this may also constitute coercion to adhere to evolution,[47] (3) In a few instances that we know of (and probably many more), teachers have lost their positions because of their creationist beliefs.

The reader will also recall the U.S. Supreme Court's three-prong test in *Lemon v. Kurtzman* as to whether government involvement in religious activity violates the establishment clause: (1) The activity must have a secular purpose, (2) Its primary effect must be neither to advance nor to inhibit religion, (3) It must not constitute excessive entanglement of government with religion. On the first count, the teaching of evolution may arguably have a secular purpose, the advancement of knowledge, although this could be achieved just as well or better by teaching creation or teaching both viewpoints. On the second count, a strong argument could be made that the primary effect of the teaching of evolution is to advance the liberal religion of evolutionists and inhibit the conservative religion of creationists. Wendell Bird, writing in the *Yale Law Journal*, cites studies which indicate that children's belief in the Genesis account of creation declines sharply between ages twelve and eighteen, the years children are taught evolution in the public schools.[48]

The government's promotion of evolution certainly fails the third prong of the test: excessive entanglement. By erecting school buildings in which evolution is taught, hiring teachers to teach evolution, designing curricula for the teaching of evolution, purchasing textbooks and other teaching aids, subsidizing

---

46. Henry Morris, *Introducing Scientific Creationism into the Public Schools* (San Diego: Institute for Creation Research, 1975), pp. 1, 11; quoted by Wendell R. Bird, "Freedom of Religion and Science Instruction in Public Schools," *Yale Law Journal*, 87:3 (1978), pp. 515, 557.

47. Wendell Bird, pp. 527, 537.

48. Ibid.

research into evolution, subsidizing the publishing of evolutionary literature, placing evolutionary exhibits on public display, erecting signs and historical markers expressing evolutionary theory as fact—in these and a thousand other ways, government has entangled itself with the religion of evolution. It even chooses which of the myriad conflicting versions of evolution it should promote!

Remember that under the rule of *Lemon v. Kurtzman*, government involvement with religious activity must pass all three tests. If it fails any one, it is unconstitutional. Government promotion of evolution might barely pass the first test (secular purpose). But it fails the second test (primary effect), and it fails the third test (excessive entanglement). Thus government promotion of evolution, including but not limited to teaching evolution in the public schools, constitutes an unconstitutional establishment of religion.

We have also seen that the theory of evolution directly contradicts the religious beliefs of many conservative Christians. By requiring these conservative Christians to pay taxes to support the government's promotion of evolution, by in effect requiring them to send their children to public schools to be taught evolution, and by requiring Christian teachers to teach evolution or risk losing their jobs, government promotion of evolution violates the First Amendment right of these conservative Christians to the free exercise of their religion. Government promotion of evolution thus violates both the establishment clause and the free exercise clause of the First Amendment.

One might also argue that it violates the free speech clause of the First Amendment, the liberty clause of the Fifth and Fourteenth Amendments, and the equal protection clause of the Fourteenth Amendment as well.

Horace Mann, often called the father of the American public school system, recognized the injustice of this type of situation when he said:

> . . . if a man is taxed to support a school where religious doctrines are inculcated which he believes to be false, and which he believes that God condemns, then he is excluded from the school by divine law, at the same time that he is compelled to support it by the human law. This is a double wrong.[49]

Another interesting supporter of the two-model approach was Clarence Darrow. In the *Scopes* trial of 1925, he declared:

> . . . let the children have their minds kept open . . . close no doors to their knowledge . . . shut no door to them . . . let them have both evolution and creation . . . the truth will win out in the end.[50]

In the 1981 *Segraves* case, the California Attorney General's office announced that it intended to argue that even if the teaching of evolution violated

---

49. Joseph L. Blau., *Cornerstones of Religious Freedom in America* (Boston: Beacon Press, 1949), pp. 179-182; quoted by Pfeffer, p. 285.

50. Richard B. Bliss, "Evolutionary Indoctrination and Decision Making in the Schools," *Impact*, June 1983, p. 4.

Segraves' right to free exercise of religion, the violation was justified because the state had a "compelling interest" in teaching about origins, and except for evolution, there is not acceptable scientific theory of origins. But as we have seen in this chapter, creation is just as scientific a model as evolution. We must, therefore, conclude that the state has no compelling interest in teaching evolution exclusively, and that the state's violation of the establishment and free exercise clauses cannot be justified. We must look for an alternative.

One possibility would be to abolish the public schools and end all government involvement in education except perhaps for financial aid to parents who cannot afford tuition for their children. This would solve the constitutional problem, but it is not likely to be accepted by the general public at this time.

A second possibility is to teach nothing at all about origins. Again, this would probably solve the constitutional problem, but it would leave a substantial gap in the students' knowledge.

A third possibility would be to continue to teach evolution but exempt children from the objectionable classes, or possibly from the compulsory attendance laws as a whole. But this would involve a great deal of peer pressure and would also require those children and their parents to forego a substantial public benefit in order to freely exercise their religion. In its famous decision striking down state-sponsored school prayer, the Supreme Court noted that the prayer was voluntary, that anyone who chose could remain silent or leave the room. Yet, because of peer pressure and other subtle coercion, the Court still struck down voluntary prayer as unconstitutional. Adopting the same solution to the creation/evolution controversy would be unconstitutional for the same reason.

Just for illustration, let's look at another possible remedy: teach only creation in the public schools, and let the evolutionists remove their children from objectionable classes or send them to private schools at considerable expense. Once the shoe is on the other foot, they would readily see the unfairness of the situation!

The best solution to the problem, in my opinion, is the two-model approach. Under this approach, balanced treatment is given to the scientific evidence for both viewpoints. Both viewpoints are presented from a scientific standpoint, with the presentation limited to the scientific evidence for and against each viewpoint. The Bible would probably not even be used in such an approach. Statutes could provide that no student shall be penalized in any way for accepting or rejecting either theory.

The two-model approach has many advantages. It reflects the traditional American belief in fundamental fairness and equality, by giving balanced treatment to both sides. And it is most compatible with the American libertarian notion that truth will win out if all the facts and ideas are fully exposed to the light of public examination. Nevertheless, several objections are commonly raised against the two-model approach:

(1) "Separation of Church and State"

It is argued that the two-model approach violates separation of church and state, since it brings religion and the Bible into the classroom. We have already discussed the founders' understanding of education and religion and the First Amendment. Suffice it to say that the government is already involved in the promotion of religion in the classroom by the religious tenet of evolution. In its present role, it advances those religions which are compatible with evolution, and inhibits those which are incompatible with evolution. By presenting both viewpoints, the public schools would simply be practicing "accommodating neutrality" as defined in *Zorach*. As to excessive entanglement, there is no more entanglement than when only the evolution model is presented exclusively. Furthermore, the issue is not bringing the Bible into the classroom, but giving balanced treatment to the scientific evidence for creation—nothing more.

(1) "It's Unconstitutional!"

Some argue that past court rulings have indicated the two-model approach is unconstitutional, citing *Epperson v. Arkansas*, 393 U.S. 97 (1968), and *Daniel v. Waters*, 515 F. 2d 485 (1975). Again, this is incorrect. *Epperson* did not involve the two-model approach; it involved a statute which prohibited the teaching of evolution. This was held unconstitutional, and it could be argued that a school policy which prohibits the teaching of creation is also unconstitutional.

Daniel involved a "two-model approach" which clearly favored the biblical view of creation. The statute required that any textbook which presented a view of origins must contain a disclaimer that its view was only theory and not fact, and must give commensurate attention to other theories "including, but not limited to, the Genesis account in the Bible." The act further provided that the Bible did not have to contain any such disclaimer, thereby putting the Bible in a preferred position over other books, and expressly excluded teaching "occult or satanic beliefs of human origin." The court struck this statute down as unconstitutional because its purpose was "establishing the biblical version of the creation of man over the Darwinian theory of the evolution of man." The court's view of the purpose of the Tennessee statute was also affected by the statute's apparent similarity to the statute which prompted the Scopes trial of 1925.

The most publicized creation/evolution trial since *Scopes* took place in December of 1981; *McLean v. Arkansas*, 529 F. Supp. 1255 (D.C.E.D. Ark., 1982). In this case, Judge William R. Overton struck down as unconstitutional an Arkansas statute which required balanced treatment for creation and evolution. Judge Overton ruled that creation science is only religion masked as science, that the true purpose of the balanced treatment act was to teach biblical creationism under a scientific guise, and consequently, the act was an establishment of religion. His ruling also indicated that the act may violate academic freedom as well.

Judge Overton's thirty-eight page opinion is filled with contradictions and quotations taken out of context, snide comments about creationist witnesses and abject deference to evolutionist witnesses. But to most creationists, his ruling came as no surprise for they expected to lose that trial long before it began.

Before, during, and after the trial, many creationists criticized the Arkansas attorney general for his handling of the case. The creation science legal defense fund sought to intervene in the case and arranged for expert witnesses and the services of attorneys Wendell R. Bird and John W. Whitehead at their own expense. However, the attorney general resisted their intervention and the court refused to allow it. Among other charges, creationists claimed that the attorney general had purchased tickets for a fund raising dinner of his opponent in the trial, the American Civil Liberties Union; that he and his assistants were unprepared; that he and his assistants did not expend sufficient time and money to present an adequate case; that the attorney general failed to call qualified experts to testify on behalf of creation; that the attorney general had expressed personal qualms about the validity of the balanced treatment act; and that the attorney general and his staff lacked experience in constitutional cases and refused to employ attorneys who had such experience. The newsletter of the Students for Origins Research raised many of these criticisms several months before the trial began.[51] Louisiana State Senator, Bill Keith, raised these and other criticisms in his book which was published shortly after the trial.[52]

However, Dr. Norman L. Geisler of Dallas Theological Seminary served as a witness for the creationist side of the trial. His book is much more defensive of the attorney general's role.[53] Instead, Geisler attributed the defeat to prejudice on the part of Judge Overton. He points out that Judge Overton's mother is an evolutionist who teaches biology and who attended every session of the trial. Furthermore, Judge Overton is a United Methodist whose own United Methodist bishop was the first witness who testified on the behalf of the ACLU.[54] To decide for the creationists, Judge Overton would have to have rejected the testimony of his own bishop! For that reason alone, he should have disqualified himself from the trial.

Whatever the cause, *McLean v. Arkansas* was a defeat for creationists. But by no means was it a fatal blow. The attorney general decided not to appeal the decision—a wise decision, perhaps, since the record was far from perfect. Consequently the case remains only a Federal District Court decision and is therefore of limited effect as a precedent.

During the summer of 1981, while the ACLU was preparing its case against

51. "Lawsuit Prospects Dim in Arkansas, Brighten in Louisiana," Students for Origins Research Newsletter, Vol. 4:2, Fall 1981.

52. Bill Keith, *Scopes II: The Great Debate* (Shreveport, Louisiana: Huntington House, 1982), pp. 116-117 ff.

53. Norman L. Geisler, *The Creator in the Courtroom: "Scopes II"* (Milford, Michigan: Mott Media, 1982), pp. 21-22.

54. Ibid, pp. 24-25.

the Arkansas balanced treatment law, a similar though not identical law was passed in Louisiana. Needless to say, the American Civil Liberties Union challenged the Louisiana law in court as well. That case is still pending in the courts. While no one can predict the outcome with certainty, it is reassuring to know that the Louisiana attorney general is vigorously defending the law and has employed the assistance of leading creationist attorneys Wendell Bird and John Whitehead. At the very least, when the case goes to trial in Louisiana, the creationist position should receive a valid defense.

(3) "Academic Freedom"

Others object that a state-mandated two-model approach interferes with academic freedom by dictating to teachers what they have to teach. First, let us observe that the state has some right to control the education of those children whom the parents have chosen to send to state-sponsored schools. At the very least, the state has the right to determine the general subject matter that shall be covered in public school courses.

And second, let us remember that a public school teacher is to some extent a state official. He is hired by the state, provided a classroom by the state, and paid by the state. This gives the state some control over his teaching. While the case law indicates that he has some academic freedom, this academic freedom is not without limits. (The exact limitations will be discussed in the next chapter on public schools). For example, academic freedom does not allow a public school math teacher to devote his whole math course to a discussion of the ecology crisis, though an occasional reference to ecology would be permissible. Since the taxpayers hired him to teach math to their children, they have a right to expect that he will in fact teach math skills.

A public school science teacher once wrote to me and about a preacher in his town who objected to evolution. "Why should he complain about me?" the teacher asked. "I don't complain about him. He has his church; I have my classroom." But there is a major difference. This science teacher does not have to pay one thin dime for that pastor's salary or church building, unless he chooses to do so. The pastor and his parishioners, on the other hand, must pay taxes to provide the teacher with a paycheck, classroom, and books. Second, the teacher is not required to attend the pastor's church or send his children there unless he chooses to; but as we have seen, public school attendance is semicompulsory.

Because of the sensitivity of the issue, the state's need to practice accommodating neutrality, and the public benefit of exposing students to the various beliefs of the society in which they live, the state has a public interest in presenting both the creation model and the evolution model to the students. The state, therefore, can require that science courses cover both viewpoints fairly.

This, however, need not preclude the teacher from expressing personal preference for one viewpoint, so long as he has given fair coverage to both. Most creationists would not object to that; most two-model statutes would not prohibit that if properly construed: and to clarify matters the two-model statutes could expressly provide that teachers may state their personal preferences for one theory or the other, so long as both viewpoints have been given fair coverage.

Finally, isn't it strange that no one considers the academic freedom of the Christian teacher who is forced to teach evolution? Many would like to present both models but can't because state or school board policy prohibits it or because two-model texts are not available.

(4) "Bias!"

Still others object that the two-model approach does not prevent a teacher from teaching one side or the other unfairly. I won't deny that is possible. Just by tone of voice or facial expression, a teacher can put one viewpoint or the other in an unfavorable light. I do not contend that the two-model approach is utterly without problems—only that it is the best solution yet proposed to a very difficult situation. I believe most teachers will try to be fair. But even those who are not fair themselves will be using textbooks that give fair treatment to both sides, and the students will have the opportunity to read both sides and know that another viewpoint does exist. And a few articulate student proponents of the opposite viewpoint can do much to offset a teacher's unfairness.

(5) "A Hodgepodge of Alternatives"

A final argument is that there are other viewpoints besides creation and evolution, and if we open the door to the Genesis account of creation, we will have to allow the Babylonian view, the Buddhist view, the American Indian view, and a myriad of others. The result would be hopeless confusion.

How do we answer this objection? First, note the spirit in which it is raised. I have never heard any Buddhists or Babylonians raise this argument. The only ones I have heard are the evolutionists. They are not interested in fairness to Buddhists or Babylonians, any more than they are interested in fairness to Christians. They are just trying to confuse the issue.

Second, we are not talking about the biblical view of creation; we are talking about scientific creationism. This is the scientific evidence which indicates that, instead of life evolving over millions or billions of years, life and the universe came into being suddenly, as a creative act. Whether the author of that creative act was the God of the Bible, or some other god or gods, or some impersonal first cause, and whether the method of creation was that described in the Bible or another method, is not the subject of scientific creationism. Scientific creationism is compatible with the biblical view, but it is broader than the biblical view, and it may also be compatible with other views. Most, if not all, of these other viewpoints could probably fit roughly into the broad categories of evolution or scientific creation.

Third, the two-model approach does not mean that a third model could not be considered if there were demand for it in a particular classroom or particular school district. The Scientific Origins Bill of 1979, which was considered but not passed by the Minnesota legislature, expressly provided for the inclusion of alternative viewpoints where desired.

Lest I may have seemed too hard on the evolutionists, let me emphasize that many evolutionists are sincere, practicing Christians. For those who profess both Christianity and evolution, I do not question the sincerity of their faith. But I do question whether they have truly considered the logical conclusions of their beliefs. Thorough examination leads to the conclusion that the two faiths—Christianity and evolution—are incompatible.

But I recognize that some will disagree with me, and I respect their right to those beliefs. However, I do not respect their desire to press them upon children in the public schools to the exclusion of all other beliefs. That is an establishment of religion. It needs to be disestablished.

And a final word to my fellow creationists: let us remember that God's truth stands whether we succeed or fail: "Let God be true, but every man a liar." (Romans 3:4) I remember a very disappointing day for me, in 1979, when the Minnesota House Education Committee defeated a bill giving balanced treatment to creation. The bill's sponsor, Rep. Paul Aasness (R-Wendell), took the defeat much better than I. As Paul and I left the Capitol, we entered Paul's pickup truck. As Paul turned on the ignition switch, the radio began, and the very first words we heard were J. Vernon McGee reading, "In the beginning God created the heavens and the earth."

Thank God! He is still on the throne, and whatever the courts and legislatures decide, His truth will prevail!

Chapter 15

The Christian
and the Public Schools

First Amendment litigation is at an all time high, and the schoolhouse is the primary battleground. That is understandable for the First Amendment deals with government's involvement in religion, beliefs, values, morals and ideas; and that is what education is all about. Since the state is greatly involved in education today, it is inevitable that constitutional questions will arise.

Education also involves a classic confrontation between establishment clause and free exercise clause principles. Those who object to prayer in public schools, or the use of Christmas carols in school programs, or nativity scenes on school property, argue that such activities violate the establishment clause because schools are, after all, government property. On the other hand, those who demand the right to pray in school, the right to organize voluntary religious student groups on campus, and the right to sing Christmas carols, argue that their right to free exercise of religion is denied if they are prohibited from doing so. Even in private education, such issues as government aid to and regulation of private schools raise establishment and free exercise issues.

The purpose of this chapter is not to advocate public schools. We cannot be blind to the fact that humanistic and evolutionary thinking pervades the public schools. But neither can we forget that the public schools also contain many dedicated Christian students, teachers, and administrators. Many Christians view the public schools as a mission field. Many others would like to use the public schools as a mission field to share their faith, but do not know for sure how this can be done without infringing upon the constitutional rights of others. The purpose of this chapter is to explain the legal rights of a public school teacher or student to witness for the Christian faith.

In earlier chapters we discussed higher law, the law of God. But in this chapter we are primarily concerned with how the courts apply this law on a daily basis.

We will examine how the Constitution has been interpreted in various cases which pertain to religious expression in the public schools.

This is a difficult area to document, for in many controversies over religious liberty the Supreme Court has not yet stated its position, and lower-court precedents are often conflicting, indefinite, or nonexistent. Based upon the rulings courts have rendered in the past, we can only guess how a court might rule in the present. Under the principle of *stare decisis* ("let the decision stand"), courts normally follow previous precedents. This has been true since the English common-law days and even the Roman law before that. It is less true today because of the subjective and positivist thinking that prevails in many judicial circles.

The Christian Teacher or Administrator

Teachers often wonder how much freedom they actually have in the classroom.

So do the courts. The courts have not definitely decided this question. It seems clear that a teacher is a state official, paid by the state and therefore to some extent subject to the control of the state. It is also clear that the state has a right to insist that certain materials be taught, and the teacher has been hired by the school board to discharge that responsibility of teaching that material. For example, a teacher who has been hired by the school board to teach math cannot claim that his right of academic freedom has been infringed if he is fired for spending most of his time lecturing about religion or politics to the neglect of mathematics. The parents who hired that teacher through their local school board representatives obviously have the right to expect and insist that the basic objectives for which they hired the teacher be met.

However, the teacher is not a mere teaching machine, programmed to say whatever the state wants nothing more and nothing less. As the Supreme Court said in *Epperson*, "It is much too late to argue that the State may impose upon the teachers in its schools any conditions that it chooses, however restrictive they may be of constitutional guarantees."[1] A year later the Court also declared that neither "students nor teachers shed their constitutional rights to the freedom of speech or expression at the schoolhouse gate."[2]

But how much academic freedom does the teacher have? How is the right of the teacher to academic freedom to be balanced against the right of the parents to insist upon certain educational standards? The courts have not yet answered this question. We have only a few precedents to use in judging what future courts could decide. The courts have held that a high school teacher has broad discretion to choose study materials, even to choose materials which the school board has prohibited, so long as they are not legally obscene.[3] Other courts

---

1. *Epperson v. Arkansas*, 393 U.S. 97, 107 (1968).
2. *Tinker v. Des Moines Independent Community School District*, 393 U.S. 503, 511 (1969).
3. *Keefe v. Geanakos*, (1 Cir. 1969), 418 F. 2d. 359.

have held that teachers are entitled to express their views about things they believe in,[4] but they may not indoctrinate their students in a narrow-minded or intolerant manner.[5] Obviously, there is a fine line between indoctrination and mere expression of opinion, especially if the person speaking is an authority figure such as a teacher.

The exact measure of what may and may not be allowed depends upon several factors:

(1) *The local school board policy.* This policy is not an absolute guide, but the school board has considerable discretion to make decisions in this area. In addition to school board policy, the teacher should also consider policies of the local principal, the state board of education, and applicable state law. The teacher needs to consider whether the school board allows the type of activity in question. If the answer is negative, then the teacher needs to consider whether the school board's prohibition is constitutional.

(2) *The age of the pupils.* The more mature the pupils are, the more freedom is accorded the teacher to express opinions. This is based upon the assumption that younger children are more impressionable than older children and are thus more easily indoctrinated.

(3) *Whether the teacher has tenure.* Gatti and Gatti offer the following explanation of tenure:

> Tenure is a job security device. Tenure does not guarantee continual employment, but it does provide that a tenured teacher or administrator may not be removed from his or her position without specific or good cause. In addition, the school board is obligated to follow certain procedures in order to establish whether or not such cause exists.[6]

American Jurisprudence 2d. explains that the purpose of tenure is "to promote good order and the welfare of the state and school system by preventing the removal of capable and experienced teachers by political or personal whims."[7]

Some believe that a nontenured teacher can be dismissed for any cause whatsoever, including expression of opinions that are unacceptable to the school board. The Supreme Court of the United States, however, has ruled that even the nontenured teacher has the right to academic freedom and cannot be fired or refused rehiring simply because he has exercised academic freedom over the objection of the board.[8] But the Court has also ruled (in fact, on the same day) that a nontenured teacher is not entitled to "procedural due process" if he is not rehired. That is, the school board does not have to give him a hearing,

4. *James v. Board of Education* (2 Cir. 1972), 461 F. 2d. 566, 573.

5. Ibid., p. 573.

6. Richard D. Gatti and Daniel J. Gatti, ed., *Encyclopedic Dictionary of School of Law*, 1975 ed., p. 287.

7. *American Jurisprudence 2d*, vol. 68, "School," sec. 151, p. 484.

8. *Perry v. Sindermann*, 408 U.S. 593, 597-598 (1972).

state to him reasons for refusing to rehire him, or provide other protections such as would be the entitlement of a tenured teacher.[9] The effect of this ruling is that, while nontenured teachers do have academic freedom, it is very difficult for the nontenured teacher to prove that he lost his job because he exercised academic freedom. The school board need not state its reasons to him at the time, and if the board is sued later, they can always claim that there were other reasons for their refusal to rehire. After all, there is no such thing as a perfect teacher; every teacher has a few imperfections that a school board could use to justify its decision.

(4) *Attitudes of students and their parents.* This makes a tremendous difference insofar as what types of witnessing are and are not permissible. One has to gauge students' and their parents' attitudes, to determine what actions are and are not likely to cause complaint to the school board.

(5) *Relevance to the subject matter.* This is of vital importance, as there is less problem in bringing Christian witness to bear where it is relevant to the subject matter at hand. For example, the teacher of world history, while discussing the Roman Empire, has an excellent opportunity to bring in the life of Jesus Christ, His crucifixion and the extent to which the Roman authorities were involved, the spread of Christianity across the Roman Empire, and the effect of Christianity upon the Roman Empire. The Christian who teaches health classes would certainly find opportunities to introduce Scripture references relevant to diet and health. Social studies classes provide opportunities to discuss the effect of religion on persons' lives, and create an excellent opportunity to give a personal testimony. The English teacher, in studying passages of literature, might compare style and ideas to those of the Bible. The liberty of the Christian teacher to witness for his faith is greatly increased if he can demonstrate that it is relevant to the subject matter.

Let us now look at some specific areas of Christian witness in the public schools.

Prayer and Bible Reading

In the entire history of the U.S. Supreme Court, few if any decisions have aroused as much public hostility as *Engel v. Vitale*, 370 U.S. 421 (1962). This is the famed Supreme Court prayer decision, in which the Court used the establishment clause of the First Amendment to strike down as unconstitutional a formally organized school prayer exercise. Upon recommendation of the State Board of Regents, the Board of Education of Union Free School District number 9, New Hyde Park, New York, had directed that each class recite at the beginning of each school day the following prayer: "Almighty God, we acknowledge our dependence upon Thee, and we beg Thy blessings upon us, our parents, our teachers and our country." While the board required that the prayer be said in each classroom, individual students were not required to say the prayer.

---

9. *Board of Regents v. Roth*, 408 U.S. 564, 570 (1972).

Nevertheless, the Supreme Court held such a prayer to be an establishment of religion, declaring "it is not part of the business of government to compose official prayers for any group of the American people to recite as a part of a religious program carried on by government."

Despite attempts to limit the courts' jurisdiction, attempts to pass a constitutional amendment, attempts to evade the effect of the rulings, and at times outright defiance of the ruling, and despite polls which consistently show an overwhelming majority of Americans opposed to the decision, the courts have followed the *Engel v. Vitale* decision and it remains in effect today.

In this case the courts may have gone too far in applying the establishment clause. As we have previously seen, at the time the First Amendment was adopted, the establishment of religion was commonly thought to include public taxation for the support of religion, special privileges for one religious group over others, and/or penalties or civil disabilities for those who do not adhere to the established religion. The school prayer in question appears to involve none of these. In fact, Thomas Jefferson advocated prayer and worship at the state-sponsored universities of Virginia, and on the very day after Congress approved the First Amendment, that same Congress called upon the President to issue a public proclamation of prayer and thanksgiving.

In my opinion the Supreme Court was wrong in declaring state-sponsored school prayer unconstitutional. However, such state-sponsored prayer may not be a good idea. Christians have traditionally believed that prayer is to be addressed to the Father (John 16:23-24), in the name of the Son (John 16:23-24), and in the power of the Holy Spirit (Romans 8:26). The New York prayer does not meet that standard. Do Christians really want their children to pray under the guidance of a teacher who may or may not be a Christian, with other students who may or may not be Christians, to a God who may or may not be the God of the Bible? These are troubling questions, but the prospect of children going through a school day without prayer is also troubling.

Many have thought that the Supreme Court in *Engel v. Vitale* went further in outlawing prayer than it actually did. A high school student at the time of the decision, I still remember a joke that went around school: "Did you hear about the kid who got kicked out of school?—he was caught praying!" But in fact the Courts never said that an individual student cannot pray. The Court only said that the state may not compose official prayers to be recited by students in an organized form. Note that this did not involve the action of an individual teacher but the recommendation of a state board of regents and a decision by a local board of education. What would happen if an individual teacher, acting on his own volition and without any direction from the principal, board of education, or state board or state law, decided to select or compose a prayer to be said by his students? Would that be an establishment of religion? The Court would probably say so. What would happen if the teacher were to pray aloud himself, without asking the students to join in the prayer? Even that might be held to be an establishment of religion given the present attitude of the courts.

On January 14, 1983, the Honorable W. Brevard Hand, Chief Judge of the Southern Division of the United States District Court for the Southern District of Alabama, rendered a controversial decision which, if sustained, would have the effect of overruling *Engel v. Vitale.* The state of Alabama had enacted a law which provided that children in the public schools could set aside a certain period ot time for the verbatim reading of the opening prayers of the chaplains of the United States House or Senate. It also provided a prayer which could be recited in the public school classrooms. In a scholarly opinion consisting of sixty-six pages, Judge Hand determined that the framers of the First and Fourteenth Amendments to the United States Constitution had not intended those amendments to prohibit voluntary prayers of this type. Noting that in so ruling he was going against a mountain of precedents in which the courts have ruled otherwise, Judge Hand quoted Justice Frankfurter as saying, ''The ultimate touch-stone of constitutionality is the Constitution itself and not what we have said about it.'' (*Graves v. O'Keefe,* 306 U.S. 466, 491-92 [1939]). He acknowledged that his opinion might be ''no more than a voice crying in the wilderness'' and that possibly ''this attempt to right that which this Court is persuaded is a misreading of history will come to nothing more than blowing in the hurricane. . . .'' Nevertheless, Judge Hand went forward and issued this courageous ruling.

Predictably, the Circuit Court of Appeals reversed, issuing a rather brief opinion that merely recited the precedents and did not do justice to Judge Hand's arguments. It is likely that this case will go to the U.S. Supreme Court. Should the Supreme Court reverse the Circuit Court and uphold Judge Hand, we will enter a new era of constitution interpretation.[10]

Leaving *Jaffree* aside for the moment, what can be done to accommodate the students' need to pray in school? One solution might be to follow the policy of my junior high school when I was a student from 1957-60. In the cafeteria at lunch time, when the students were seated, chimes were sounded, at which time all students were silent for a space of perhaps half a minute. There followed another chime, and the period of silent meditation was over.

A period of silent meditation has distinct advantages. First, no one is forced to pray, either expressly or by peer pressure. He can pray, meditate, contemplate infinity, sleep, or do whatever he chooses in the privacy of his own mind. Second, no one is compelled to use a form of prayer with which he disagrees. He can pray in the name of Jesus Christ, use an informal prayer, recite a formal litany, or pray in whatever form he chooses, to whatever god he chooses, or not pray at all.

John Whitehead notes that about fifteen states have laws which provide for silent meditation.[11] The New Hampshire Supreme Court has unanimously ruled

---

10. *Jaffree v. Mobile Country et. al,* (554 F. Supp. 1104 [D.C.S.D. Ala. 1983]).

11. *National Observer,* 18 September 1976, p. 1; cited by John Whitehead, *The Christian Teacher and the Law,Supplement 1978* (Oak Park, Illinois: Christian Legal Society, 1978), p. 13.

that such a practice is constitutional. (*Opinion of the Justices*, 228A. 2d 161 [1967]). Yet, incredible though it may seem, within the past year three federal district court judges have ruled the practice of silent meditation unconstitutional as an establishment of religion![12] To date, these are only federal district court decisions. The U.S. Supreme Court has not yet spoken on the question of silent meditation.

The wording of the silent meditation statutes and their legislative history may have contributed to the defeat of those statutes in the Tennessee, New Mexico, and New Jersey cases. Those statutes expressly mentioned prayer, and in some instances opponents used the legislative history (previous attempts at legislation, previous court battles, and social pressures brought upon the legislature to obtain passage of the bill) to make it appear that "silent meditation" was nothing more than a subterfuge to circumvent *Engel v. Vitale* and introduce prayer in the public schools by an alternative means.

One year after the prayer decision, the Supreme Court issued an almost equally controversial decision concerning Bible reading: *Abingdon Township v. Schempp*, 374 U.S. 203 (1963). There the Court invalidated as an establishment of religion a Pennsylvania statute which required that at least ten verses from the Holy Bible be read without comment at the opening of each public school day. The statute also provided that children whose parents objected to the Bible reading could be excused from class. The Court held that the reading of the Bible in that manner constituted an act of worship and an entanglement of government with religion, and therefore struck the practice down as unconstitutional.

I personally believe, even more strongly than with *Engel v. Vitale*, that the Court went too far in this decision. Nevertheless, the decision remains in effect and is followed by today's courts.

At the time of the *Abington Township v. Schempp* decision, there were jokes about the Bible being banned as a "dirty book." But the Court did not prohibit the study of the Bible as literature, nor did the court prohibit the study of religion as an academic exercise rather than as worship.

But even permitted practices are not without problems. Evangelical Christians do not regard the Bible merely as another work of literature, but as the inspired and infallible Word of God. Many argue that treating the Bible merely as literature demeans it and leads to a loss of faith. Others counter that the Bible is God's Word and speaks with authority regardless of how men view it, and that we should rejoice at every opportunity for the Bible to be studied, because the Bible can stand on its own.

One textbook commonly used in literature in high schools in Minnesota and

12. One such case was *Beck v. McElrath*, No. 82-3577 (M. D. Tenn. Oct. 7, 1982). The second comes from New Mexico; the third involved a New Jersey statue which did not get a fair trial in the court because the New Jersey Attorney General announced publicly beforehand that he considered the practice of silent meditation to be unconstitutional, and that he would not defend the statute in court.

elsewhere in the nation is *Adventures in World Literature*.[13] This text contains a section entitled "Sumarian and Hebrew Literatures," comparing the two or placing the two side by side as though they were equals. After "The Epic of Gilgamesh" (the Sumerian flood narrative), the book contains the Genesis account of creation, part of which is titled "The Story of Eden," using the term "story" instead of "account" which could imply that it is merely a legend. The text used is from the Anchor Bible, a rather liberal translation. But the major objection is the editors' comment at the end:

> Genesis was not the work of an individual. From studying textual differences, Bible scholars have agreed that "Creation" [Genesis 1 and "The Story of Eden" [Genesis 2], for example, show the work of two different writers.[14]

Many parents would object to their children being taught that the Pentateuch is the work of more than one writer. The statement that "Bible scholars have agreed" that Genesis 1 and Genesis 2 were the work of two different writers implies that anyone who doesn't hold that viewpoint is not a "Bible scholar." It is true that some Bible scholars have taken that viewpoint (commonly called the Documentary Hypothesis, the Graf-Wellhausen Theory, or the JEDP Theory), although their numbers have been decreasing in recent years. But many leading Bible scholars emphatically reject this viewpoint. The faculty members of such leading seminaries as Dallas Theological Seminary, Talbot Theological Seminary, Trinity Evangelical Divinity School, Western Theological Seminary, Concordia at St. Louis, Bob Jones University, and many others would unanimously reject this viewpoint and hold that Genesis was entirely the work of Moses. Many if not most of the faculty members at Fuller Theological Seminary, Oral Roberts University, Bethel Seminary, and many others would also reject the Documentary Hypothesis. To say that the creation account is the work of two different writers is an opinion—an erroneous opinion in my judgment, but an opinion nevertheless. But to say that "Bible scholars have agreed" that Genesis 1 and 2 are the work of two different writers is an outright lie!

In the last chapter we discussed liberal and conservative Christian viewpoints in regard to evolution. They also differ in their approach to God's Word and salvation. Liberal Christians generally regard the Bible as written by men who were striving to know God. The authors of Scripture, according to this view, derived these ideas in part from the Babylonians, Sumerians, and other peoples. The Bible may reflect loftier concepts of God and of ethics than does the literature of other nations, but the difference is only one of degree. And while the authors of Scripture have pointed out one way to God, they believe there

---

13. James Applegate, et al., eds., *Adventures in World Literature* (New York: Harcourt Brace Jovanovich, 1970).

14. Ibid., p. 23.

are other ways to God as well.

Conservative Christians regard Christianity as an exclusive religion, the only way of salvation (Acts 4:12, John 3:16-18). Other religions are true only insofar as they are in accord with Christianity. And the Bible is not man's attempt to find God; it is God's special revelation to men (I Peter 1:20; II Timothy 3:16). The liberal says Christ is *a* way, and *a* truth, and *a* life; *one* way to come to the Father is by Him. But Jesus said, "I am *the* way, and *the* truth, and *the* life; *no* man cometh unto the Father but by me" (John 14:6, emphasis supplied).

The courts say it is all right to teach the Bible as literature, but wrong to teach the Bible as the Word of God. One can teach about Christianity as an historical phenomenon, but not as the way of salvation. These decisions have made it much easier to present liberal Christianity than conservative Christianity in public schools. This may violate the second test of *Lemon v. Kurtzman*, since it advances liberal Christianity and inhibits conservative Christianity.

Teaching the Bible as literature, then, involves serious problems, though it also provides some opportunities for witnessing. The Christian teacher does have opportunities to use the Bible in his classroom. Merely having a Bible on one's desk, a practice that has never been challenged in court, is by itself a witness and can lead to questions and opportunities for discussion about the Bible. Nothing is wrong with occasional references to the Bible when it is relevant to the subject matter of the classroom. As Justice Clark said in the *Schempp* case: "It certainly may be said that the Bible is worthy of study for its literary and historic qualities. Nothing we have said here indicates that such study of the Bible or religion, when presented objectively as part of a secular program of education, may not be effected consistently with the First Amendment."[15]

Witnessing

The Christian teacher has more freedom to witness for his faith than is commonly supposed. So long as his witnessing does not become coercive, does not identify his views with those of the state or school, does not interfere with the full and proper coverage of the subject matter he is required to teach, and is relevant to the subject matter at hand, his freedom to express the Christian viewpoint is considerable. (If the term "considerable" sounds vague, it is because the courts have not definitely answered the question yet.)

Again, a key factor is relevance. If the teacher is teaching about science and the textbook presents the evolutionary view, the teacher should have the right to present the creationist view and express his disagreement with the text, provided he covers the material in the text thoroughly and fairly. One can readily imagine situations in health, sex education, values clarification, history, literature, and other courses where the Christian viewpoint is relevant.

15. *Abingdon Township v. Schempp*, 374 U.S. 203, 225 (1963).

The Christian teacher has still greater freedom to witness if he is responding to student questions, than if he is merely volunteering an opinion. The capable teacher will know how to elicit such questions and perpetuate the discussion. This is legitimate so long as it is not overdone.

The teacher's freedom to express his faith is expanded still further if students come to see him after hours, and even further yet off-campus. There should be no reason why a teacher could not invite his students into his home, so long as the student's parents do not object. Freedom of association is a right of both teachers and students.

Symbols

Here again, the teacher has considerable freedom. According to *Tinker*, he may wear an armband, so he should also be able to wear a cross or other religious symbols. Religious symbols on his desk should also be permissible. If such symbols are placed on the wall or in other parts of the classroom there might be more objection, as that might tend to identify the symbol with the school and the state instead of with the teacher personally. Hall suggests that one of the best religious symbols might be an open Bible on the teacher's desk. Not only is it a testimony; it may also provoke questions and provide opportunities to witness, and serve as a ready reference to answer student questions.

Religious Music

The courts have taken the position that religious music is primarily a reflection of the American culture. Since it is valuable to familiarize students with American culture, much religious music is permissible in the public school. Patriotic songs such as ''God Bless America'' and ''America the Beautiful'' contain references to God, but are nonetheless permissible because the promotion of patriotism is a secular purpose. Recently, in *Florey v. Sioux Falls Schools District*, 619 F. 2d 1311 (8th Cir. 1980), cert. den. 449 U.S. 987 (1981), the Court held that a school Christmas program may include religious carols so long as they are presented ''in a prudent and objective manner and as a traditional part of the cultural and religious heritage of the particular holiday.'' (9th Circuit Ruling).

Observance of Religious Holidays

The extent to which public schools may recognize and celebrate religious holidays is not yet decided. It is probably safe to say that, like religious music, religious holidays can be observed if they are part of our cultural tradition and their observance does not take on too many of the characteristics of worship. Various radical separationist groups have loudly insisted to school boards that they must ban carols, manger scenes, and all mention of Christ in the public schools, but the courts have not taken that position—yet.

The drive to secularize Christmas and other religious holidays is bizarre. What if you were informed that a colossal birthday party, the event of the season, would be held in your honor? But there were three restrictions: (1) You may not attend; (2) Your name may not be mentioned; and (3) Your picture may not be displayed.

That's exactly how some of the radical separationists would have us celebrate Christmas, the birthday of Christ. They are asking for cultural censorship. They are asking that a major part of our Judeo-Christian culture be censored, so that students may not be exposed to it in our public schools.

Despite their pious protests against the establishment of Christianity, they seem to have no objection to the establishment of other religions. They object to Christ and the Manger, but not to Santa Claus even though he is offensive to many Christians, or to holly and mistletoe which were ancient pagan symbols. They object to Christ and His Cross at Easter, but not to Easter bunnies and Easter eggs which were pagan fertility symbols. They object to songs of thankfulness at Thanksgiving, but not to black cats and witches at Halloween even though these are occult symbols. Paganism is a religion, too. If the establishment of Christianity is wrong, so is the establishment of Paganism.[16]

The Christian Student

Tinker v. Des Moines Independent Community School District, 393 U.S. 503 (1969), was a landmark case in which the U.S. Supreme Court recognized that public school students do have constitutional rights and that these rights may be exercised in school. The Court declared that neither "students or teachers shed their constitutional rights to freedom of speech or expression at the schoolhouse gate."

Tinker involved the wearing of armbands to protest the Vietnam war. But like many other constitutional principles in court decisions, the *Tinker* decision is a two-edged sword; it can be used by Christians as well as non-Christians, because religious speech is just as much speech as any other kind of speech. And "speech" includes such nonverbal means of expression as gestures, wearing symbols, etc.

In many respects, such as the wearing of religious symbols, the student has the same freedom as the teacher. He is free to wear such symbols so long as they do not disrupt order and discipline in the classroom, and school officials would probably have a very difficult time proving that such symbols do disrupt order and discipline. If they do cause angry reactions from other students, the school officials would be obliged to restrain those students rather than restricting freedom of expression (*Near v. Minnesota*, 283 U.S. 697, 1931), if that is a feasible alternative.

The Court added in *Tinker* that, "in the absence of a specific showing of constitutionally valid reasons to regulate their speech, students are entitled to

16. *Man, Myth and Magic: An Illustrated Encyclopedia of the Supernatural* (New York: Marshall Cavendish Corporation, 1970); See Cat 3:417; Egg 6:781; Hares 9:1210; Holly 10:1329; Mistletoe 14:1860; Witch 22:3041.

freedom of expression of their views.'' But what constitutionally valid reasons could exist? Here is what the Court said:

> Any conduct . . . in the class or out of it, which for any reason—whether it stems from time, place or type of behavior—materially disrupts class work or involves substantial disorder or invasion of the rights of others is, of course, not immunized by the constitutional guarantee of freedom of speech. (*Tinker*)

In other words, the public school is a ''First Amendment forum'' in which student ideas may be expressed and exchanged. But it is also a place where learning is imparted to the young. Restrictions can be placed upon this exchange of ideas, where necessary, to further the legitimate function of education. The public school is a First Amendment forum at some times but not at other times, as when there is a lecture or other activity that would be disrupted by the free expression of ideas. The student who interrupts a teacher's regularly scheduled lecture on mathematics to witness to the teacher and other students is infringing upon the rights of others to an education and is disrupting the good order of the school. In that circumstance, his ''speech'' is not protected by the First Amendment.

While state-sponsored prayers have been prohibited, there is nothing to prevent the student from praying on his own so long as he can do so without disrupting the rest of the class. He is similarly free to witness to his fellow students between classes, during lunch breaks, or at whatever other times free discussion among the students is permitted. He may not do so when he would disrupt a class or otherwise interfere with the academic process.

Literature

A student should be allowed to distribute tracts to his fellow students. A registration requirement might be valid, so long as the terms are not unreasonable. The school may also establish specified times and places for the distribution of literature.

Use of the school paper for expression of Christian witness is probably even permissible. The First Amendment right of the press has been held to allow student editors to write on religious subjects over the objections of the school administrators.[17]

The distribution of Gideon Bibles has been the subject of court litigation in the past. In several instances such distribution has been declared unconstitutional.[18] If such distribution is to be permitted at all, it has to be done discretely, clearly not sponsored by the government, under circumstances free from peer pressure to accept or refuse the Bibles, and in which the use

---

17. *Panarella v. Birenbaum*, 343 N.Y.S. 2d. 333, 339 (Cr. Apr. 1973).

18. *Tudor v. Board of Education* (N.J. 1953), 100 A. 2d. 857; *Brown v. Orange County Board of Public Instruction*, 128 So. 2d. 181 (Fla. App. 1960), affirmed 155 So. 2d. 371 (Fla. 1963).

of state facilities is kept to a minimum. Courts are more likely to allow such distribution if done outside the school building. Recently the courts have indicated that students have a right to receive information or the "right to hear."[19] In this light a student might argue to a court that the refusal to permit distribution of Gideon Bibles violates his right to receive information.

Classroom Comment

The teacher has broad authority to control the classroom. He can, if he wishes, close off discussion in the interest of time and efficiency.

However, if he opens the class to general discussion, he cannot forbid the Christian viewpoint from being presented so long as it is relevant to the subject matter being discussed. A student is free to express his views on such subjects as sexual morality and evolution.

The possibility always exists that a teacher will punish a student for expressing an opposing viewpoint by giving him a lower grade than he justly deserves. If a student could prove that this was done, he would have a valid constitutional case, if he could show that the teacher's action was arbitrary and capricious, violated his right to equal protection of the law, and had a "chilling effect" upon his freedom of expression and free exercise of religion. However, the subjective nature of grading makes it difficult to prove it was done solely on the basis of religious views.

Student Organizations

This is another difficult problem. Several cases currently before the courts involve a classic clash between the establishment and free exercise clauses of the First Amendment. Those who oppose such student groups argue that to permit them to meet in state facilities constitutes an establishment of religion since it involves state action which promotes that religion and since it entangles the state with that religion. On the other hand, Christian students argue that to deny them the right to meet on campus is a denial of their right to the free exercise of their religion, as well as a denial of freedom of expression, freedom of assembly, freedom of association, liberty, and possibly equal protection of the laws. If secular groups may meet but Christian groups may not, this may also be an unconstitutional establishment of a religion of secularism.

At the college and university level, the issue appears to be settled. In a landmark decision, *Widmar v. Vincent*, 454 U.S. 263 (1981), the Supreme Court held by an 8-1 margin that the University of Missouri/Kansas City could not ban a Christian organization called Cornerstone from meeting on campus facilities for religious worship and discussion. When the university refused to let them meet on campus, Cornerstone argued that it was denied free exercise of religion, free speech, freedom of association, and equal protection under

---

19. *Martin v. Struthers* 319 U.S. 141 (1943); *Lamont v. Postmaster General* 381 U.S. 301 (1965); *Tinker*, at p. 506.

the law. The Court decided the issue on free speech grounds. It ruled that by allowing other student groups to meet on campus, university officials had made their campus a First Amendment forum. Consequently, they could not prohibit free speech on campus solely because of the "religious" content of that speech. Religious speech, the Court held, is entitled to the same protection under the free speech clause as any other form of speech. Of course, the university can make reasonable restrictions as to time and place of meetings, so long as it does so in a reasonable and nondiscriminatory manner. But the right of college students to organize religious groups and meet on campus for the purpose of religious discussion, worship, and even evangelism, now seems protected by the courts.

The issue is not as clear for high school and elementary school students. In *Widmar*, the Court indicated that merely allowing a student organization to meet on campus was not an establishment of religion because university students are mature enough to realize allowing an organization to meet on campus does not necessarily mean that the university is approving or promoting that organization. But lower courts have indicated that high school students are not as mature, and to them permission to meet on campus might appear the same as school promotion or sponsorship. In several lower court decisions, such as *Brandon v. Board of Education*, 635 F. 2d 971 (2d Cir. 1980), the circuit upheld a school board policy prohibiting religious student groups from meeting in public high school facilities. But the *Brandon* court said only that school boards could prohibit student groups from meeting. The court did not say that school boards could not allow them to meet. The ruling left the impression that the right of student groups to meet rested with the school board's discretion.

In 1982 another court went a step further. In *Lubbock Civil Liberties Union v. Lubbock Independent School District*, 669 F. 2d 1038 (5th Cir. 1982), the federal courts struck down as unconstitutional a school board policy which allowed religious groups to meet on campus. The Lubbock School District petitioned to the U.S. Supreme Court for a writ of certiorari, but the Supreme Court refused to hear the case.

An unfortunate legislative history may have contributed to this defeat. The Lubbock Public School District had not only allowed student groups to meet on campus; it also allowed Bible reading and student-recited prayers over the public address system, a period of silent prayer ended by "Amen" over the public address system, the distribution of Gideon Bibles, and evangelistic speakers at school assemblies. Although these practices were somewhat curtailed in 1979 and 1980, this background might have led the court to conclude that the present practices were still an attempt to establish the Christian religion.

The Supreme Court's refusal to hear this case does not necessarily mean it agreed with the lower court's decision. The Supreme Court usually gives no reason for its refusal to accept a writ of certiorari, and it gave no reason in this case. Sometimes the Supreme Court refuses to take a case because the case was not tried properly in the lower courts, because the facts are not right for a proper adjudication, or just because the Court has too heavy a case load. The fact that the district court judge in *Lubbock* affirmed the school board's policy and four of the circuit court judges dissented from the majority opinion certainly indicates that the final word on this question has not yet been spoken.

As with silent meditation, before a case of this nature goes before the Supreme Court, Christians need to make sure the factual background is right. Ideally, the school board policy should allow student groups to meet and should make no specific reference whatsoever to religious groups. So that the policy does not appear to favor one religion over others, in the ideal case a wide variety of religious or quasi-religious groups should exist and be free to meet on campus: Young Life, Youth for Christ, Jewish student groups, Jehovah's Witness groups, and yes, even Atheist clubs or Humanist clubs. Then, if the school board's recognition of a Christian group is challenged, the school board would be able to make a much stronger showing of neutrality. The policy might be more likely to be upheld if it allows student groups to meet before or after regular school hours rather than during regular school hours.

The Supreme Court will have another chance to look at this issue. In May 1983, Judge William Nealon of the U.S. District Court for the middle district of Pennsylvania ruled in *Bender v. Williamsport Area School District* that a student-initiated prayer club may meet during the activity period established by the school.[20] Assuming the school district appeals, it could be another landmark case.

The Christian Parent

What do you do when your child comes home with an anti-Christian concept that he learned at school? Or when he learns in values clarification classes that morals and values are relative and humanistic rather than absolute and God-centered? Or when his sex education textbook is too graphic and condones premarital sex and homosexuality? Or when his biology textbooks teach evolution as established fact or ridicule creation?

As we will discuss in the next chapter, parents have substantial rights to determine the upbringing and education of their children. While parents must make sure their children are educated, they may choose alternative forms of education, within some limits, if they so desire.

However, when a parent chooses to send his child to the public schools, he delegates to that public school the responsibility to educate the child and thereby forfeits at least some control. What the courts say in many cases is, "If you want to send your child to a private school, fine; but if you want the public school to educate your child, you're going to have to play by their rules."

Still, this does not mean all parental control is relinquished. The parent still retains some right to direct his child's education, even when that child is enrolled in the public schools.

20. "An Open Forum:' Federal Judge Upholds Voluntary Prayer Groups at High School," *Church and State*, June 1983, p. 3.

First, the Christian parent can protest the objectionable materials and ask to have them removed or changed. The matter should first be brought to the attention of the teacher who assigned the materials. Parents should politely explain their concern. Possibly the teacher may readily agree to the change. He or she may have selected the materials without thorough examination and may not have been aware that they were objectionable or that some parents might consider them so.

If the teacher will not cooperate, then the parent should go to the principal or school board. The exact authority of the school board to remove objectionable materials or require that different materials be used varies with state statute and local school board policy. As to the relative merits of the parents' constitutional right to control their child's education as against the teacher's First Amendment right to assign the materials he or she chooses, the courts have issued no further guidelines as of yet. In *Board of Education v. Island Trees Union Free School District No. 26 v. Pico*, 50 U.S.L.W. 4831 (1982), the U.S. Supreme Court in a 5-4 decision ruled that school boards do not have unlimited discretion to remove objectionable books from high school libraries. The Court held that students should have wide access to information and ideas. At the same time, school boards have some authority to review and select textbooks and library books, but not unfettered authority. They may not remove books simply because they dislike the ideas they contain. The Supreme Court therefore remanded the case to the lower courts to determine whether sufficient guidelines were used in that case for the school board to exercise its discretion responsibly. The case establishes that school boards have considerable but not unlimited authority in this area, but gives no specific answers beyond that.

There are various ways to resolve conflicts like this short of actually removing the objectionable materials. The school board could make the objectionable course elective rather than required. The teacher could make the objectionable text recommended reading rather than the basic course textbook. Or the teacher could agree to assign an alternative text to the student whose parent objected. The Christian parent need not assume that public school officials are the enemy. He should always try to work out a solution that will satisfy all parties.

The Christian parent who protests objectionable textbooks may be labeled an enemy of the First Amendment. He may hear cries of ''censorship!'', ''repression!'', etc. But censorship is not necessarily a bad word. It goes on everyday. A newspaper editor practices censorship when he determines what articles to include and what to exclude in each day's edition. A book publisher practices censorship when he decides which manuscripts to accept and which to reject. A public school teacher practices censorship when he evaluates textbooks and establishes a curriculum. A librarian practices censorship when he or she determines which library books to order for the coming year. Almost everyone who works with books practices censorship, and in so doing, inevitably utilizes his own tastes and value judgments.

So the question is not whether censorship takes place. It will take place. The question is, who will exercise the censorship? School officials alone, or school officials with input from concerned parents and taxpayers?

The double standard is apparent. Christians are not the only ones protesting textbooks and library books. Others protest that certain books are racist, sexist, militaristic, chauvinistic, or many other things. When liberals protest against books they find objectionable, the media calls it dissent and protest. When Christians and conservatives use the same tactics, the media often calls it repression and censorship. Strange indeed!

Let us put the issue in perspective. Recently in Pennsylvania, parents objected to a requirement that their children read certain books which offended their religious convictions. Thanks to the usual biased and incomplete media reporting, people wondered "who are these narrow-minded parents who want to ban books?" But closer analysis revealed that parents did not object to the course being offered. They didn't even object to it being mandatory. Nor did they specifically object to a general assignment of the books in question. All they asked was that their children be allowed to read a different book because the one in question violated their religious convictions.

Which side is guilty of authoritarian tactics? The teacher with a captive audience in a required course, who assigns a required textbook, then refuses to cooperate with an alternative, or the parents who ask only that a different assignment be given to their child. Which should be labeled enemies of the First Amendment?

In another incident, parents in Broken Arrow, Oklahoma, sought removal of Halloween decorations in public school classrooms on the basis that such decorations advocate witchcraft.[21] Some might say that this is ridiculously narrow. But what about those who object to Christ-centered Christmas decorations? Is it fair to prohibit Christian symbols but allow displays of the occult?

If, despite your protest, school officials refuse to change their policy, must your child endure objectionable teaching? Courts have answered that question both ways. In *State Ex Rel Andrew v. Webber*, 8 N.E. 708 (1886), the Supreme Court of Indiana ruled that Mr. Andrew could not keep his son out of public school music classes so long as he was enrolled in the public schools. But in *Kelly v. Ferguson*, 144 N.W. 1039 (1914), the Nebraska Supreme Court reached the opposite conclusion and allowed exemption. Thus, while the right to keep one's child out of objectionable classes is not as clear cut as the right to send one's child to a private school, it does have some basis. Today, with the advent of the incorporation theory, the fundamental rights of doctrine, the compelling state interest doctrine, and the least restrictive means doctrine, it is more likely that a court would rule in favor of exemption now than a generation or so ago.

All too often, Christians forget that the best way to combat error is with truth. Instead of demanding that evolutionary materials be thrown out, why

---

21. "Challenges to the Schools," *Tulsa Tribune*, April 14, 1982, p. 1-F.

not ask that creationist materials be included to present the other side—if necessary, at personal expense? Instead of protesting immoral or anti-Christian books in the library, why not suggest to the librarian a list of Christian books that could be included—or personally donate those books to the library? The Lutheran Gospel Hour reports that this has recently been done in California:

> Norco, Calif. (E.P.)—Fifty-four Christian books have been stocked in each of four junior and two senior high schools of the Corona—Norco unified school district in a united witnessing effort by local Christians.
>
> "We knew we would need a program on an optional basis to keep from offending the non-Christian," says Nancy Heaton, owner of the Living Word Bookstore. "We have the tools for this inoffensive outreach—Christian books."
>
> Miss Heaton selected 54 books which were approved by the superintendent. He instructed the librarians in each school to display the books separately as Christian books to prevent their becoming lost in the maze of other volumes already stocked.
>
> Christian friends donated nearly twice the money required to pay for the books, the store donating its profits.
>
> "The results to date have been gratifying," says Miss Heaton. "The books are constantly in demand with waiting lists. Parents and friends are reading these books when children bring them home, and are being converted as a result."
>
> She said that Christian English teachers are encouraging the students to use these books for reports.[22]

Granted, it seems unfair that Christians should have to pay for these materials themselves, when the other side purchases anti-Christian materials using public tax dollars. But it is certainly better than conceding to the humanists a monopoly on the minds of our children. Selecting and supplying such books can be a most effective ministry for the Christian parent or any Christian citizen.

A Word of Caution

Two things must be emphasized: the need for vigilance and the need for restraint.

Infringements upon religious liberties can grow with time. Minor violations can set precedents for major infringements.

Attorney David Gibbs gives an example of this danger. Suppose, he says, that a preacher were to preach for eight hours, and a parishioner were to have a heart attack and die as a result. The city council therefore decides to pass a law that "no preacher shall preach longer than eight hours." Would you object to such a law?

You certainly should, because the law assumes that government may regulate the length of preaching. And if government has the authority to prohibit

---

22. *The Lamplighter*, 27:3, March 1981, p. 3.

preaching for longer than eight hours, it can also prohibit preaching for longer than six hours, or three hours, or one hour, or fifteen minutes. And if government can regulate the *length* of preaching, why not the *content* of preaching as well? Once we accept that premise, we have conceded that our liberties are relative rather than absolute.

But one might also win a battle but lose the war. A Christian might demand and win the right to express his faith in the classroom. But in so doing he might so antagonize his fellow classmates or teachers, that he has actually damaged his Christian witness, driven people away from Christianity, and has thereby done the Gospel a disservice.

The question whether to stand for your rights or bow to the restraint is a most difficult one. It requires good thinking and common sense, coupled with divine guidance through Bible study and prayer.

On March 5, 1984, since this chapter was written, the U.S. Supreme Court rendered a landmark decision. Speaking for a 5-4 majority, Chief Justice Burger ruled that the city of Pawtucket, Rhode Island, may display a manger scene on city property. The ramifications of this decision could do much to strengthen the right of teachers and school officials to use religious symbols and observances in the public schools (*Lynch v. Donnelly*, _____ U.S. _____).

Chapter 16

The Christian and
Private Schools

"There's going to be an increase of Christian schools for children—at high school, college, and university levels—where God will be invited back in to take charge of the education of our children and grandchildren. A new wave is already out there, but that new wave is only the forerunner of the schools to come. There will be thousands and tens of thousands. We are not going to let the secular world have our children any longer."[1]

So declared Oral Roberts, voicing the sentiment of an increasing number of Christians. His prediction certainly coincides with current trends. Private schools suffered declining enrollments for several decades, but the pendulum has begun to swing. Now public school enrollments are declining, and by contrast a new Christian school opens on the average of one every seven hours.[2] A U.S. Office of Education official acknowledges that Christian schools are "the fastest growing segment in private education today."[3]

Many are alarmed at this trend. Some in the public school establishment feel threatened by this new movement, and others are philosophically opposed to it. Others regard private and parochial schools as subversive or un-American, especially those in the more conservative areas of the country where, until recently, the public schools were bastions of American Protestant values and are still to a large extent so regarded. Public schools, many seem to think, are the American way.

1. Oral Roberts, "Five Great Healings are Coming to the Body of Christ," *Abundant Life,* July 1983, p. 7.
2. Eric E. Wiggin, "Should Your Grade Schooler Receive Accelerated Christian Education?", *Christian Life,* August 1981, p. 41.
3. Ibid.

It was not always so. Private education is actually more in tune with the American tradition of free enterprise. Socialism, which means government ownership and control of this means of production, has never been the American way, yet public schools imply government ownership and control of education. In fact, Karl Marx, in point ten of his platform for advanced countries in *The Communist Manifesto*, called for "free education for all children in public schools."[4] I hasten to emphasize that I am *not* calling public educators Communists! I am saying only that private schools are equally as "American" as public schools.

Furthermore, private schools have been the rule rather than the exception throughout most of America's history. And most of these private schools have been associated with the church. As Justice Frankfurter observed in *McCollum v. Board of Education*, 68 S.Ct. 461, 333 U.S. 203 (1948):

> Traditionally, organized education in the Western world was Church education. It could hardly be otherwise when the education of children was primarily study of the Word and the ways of God. Even in the Protestant countries, where there was a less close identification of Church and State, the basis of education was largely the Bible, and its chief purpose inculcation of piety. To the extent that the State intervened, it used its authority to further aims of the Church.
>
> The immigrants who came to these shores brought this view of education with them. Colonial schools certainly started with a religious orientation. When the common problems of the early settlers of the Massachusetts Bay Colony revealed the need for common schools, the object was the defeat of "one chief project of the old deluder, Satan, to keep men from the knowledge of the Scriptures." The Laws and Liberties of Massachusetts, 1648 ed. (Cambridge, 1929). 47.

But many will ask, what is Christian education? Let us address this question.

What Is Christian Education?

Christian education is more than just education in a church building. Though Christian schools often meet in churches, merely meeting in a church does not make education Christian. Even public schools occasionally rent church facilities. Merely holding school in a church does not make the education Christian any more than merely attending church makes a person a Christian, or standing in a barn makes a person a cow!

Nor does having Christian teachers make a school Christian. Christian teachers are a vital prerequisite to Christian education, but Christian teachers alone do not make education Christian. A Christian teacher could unconsciously teach from a humanistic perspective.

Christian schools involve more than firm discipline, clean language, and clean

---

4. Karl Marx and Friedrich Engels, *The Communist Manifesto* (New York: Washington Square Press, 1965) (originally published in 1848), p. 94, paragraph 125-10.

living. Again, these are vital to Christian education, and Christian education could not function effectively without these standards. But even the world can impose high standards. Merely cleaning up one's language or adopting a disciplined way of life does not make one a Christian, nor does it make education Christian.

Nor is Christian education that which involves a weekly or even daily chapel service, or Bible verses on the wall, or occasional Scripture-oriented illustrations in the classroom. Again, these are good practices for Christian schools, but they are not what makes a school Christian.

What, then, is Christian education? Christian education is education in which the entire curriculum is permeated by the Christian world view.

The Catholic Church recognized this at least back to the days of Thomas Aquinas.[5] As Justice Jackson recognized in *Everson v. Board of Education of Ewing Township*, 330 U.S. 1 (1947):

> I should be surprised if any Catholic would deny that the parochial school is a vital, if not the most vital, part of the Roman Catholic Church. If put to the choice, that venerable institution, I should expect, would forego its whole service for mature persons before it would give up education of the young, and it would be a wise choice. Its growth and cohesion, discipline and loyalty, spring from its schools. Catholic education is the rock on which the whole structure rests, and to render tax aid to its Church school is indistinguishable to me from rendering the same aid to the Church itself.

Protestants have also recognized that the Scriptures should permeate all facets of education. Martin Luther declared, "Above all things, the principal and most general subject of study, both in the higher and lower schools, should be the Holy Scriptures."[6] Luther continued:

> *But where the Holy Scripture does not rule I certainly advise no one to send his child.* Everyone not unceasingly occupied with the Word of God must become corrupt; therefore we must see what people in the higher schools are and grow up to be. . . .*I greatly fear that schools for higher learning are wide gates to hell if they do not diligently teach the Holy Scriptures and impress them on the young folk.*[7] (Emphasis supplied.)

We have seen that the founders of this country firmly believed that a primary purpose of education was to promote religion. They fostered a Christian world view. Gouverneur Morris, who was primarily responsible for writing the final draft of the U.S. Constitution, stated:

5. Edward H. Rian, "The Need: A World View," *Toward a Christian Philosophy of Education,* comp. John Paul von Grueningen (Philadelphia: Westminster Press, 1957), pp. 16-17.

6. *Luther's Works,* Weimar ed., 6:461; Ewald M. Plass, comp., *What Luther Says, An Anthology,* 3 vols. (St Louis: Concordia, 1959), 1:449.

7. *Luther's Works,* ibid., p. 462; Plass, ibid.

> . . .the State should provide for public education. . . . Religion is the only solid basis of good morals; therefore education should teach the precepts of religion, and the duties of man towards God . . . provision should be made for maintaining divine worship as well as education. But each one has a right to entire liberty as to religious opinions, for religion is the relation between God and man; therefore it is not within the reach of human authority.[8] [Morris does not appear to have attempted to reconcile the apparent contradiction in saying that the state should provide public education, that education should teach the precepts of religion, but that one should have entire liberty as to religious opinions.]

Not all schools that claim to be Christian have thoroughly integrated the Christian world view with their curriculum. This is sometimes difficult to do, since frequently the Christian teachers have been educated in secular schools and do not know how to effectively integrate the Christian world view. Professor Gordon Clark of Butler University offers the following description of many Christian colleges:

> . . . giving out tracts . . . holding fervent prayer meetings, going out on gospel teams, opening classes with prayer [are the accepted practice] . . . Yet the actual instruction is no more Christian than a respectable secular school . . . The program is merely a pagan education with a chocolate covering of Christianity. And the pill, not the coating, works . . . the students are deceived into thinking that they have received a Christian education when as a matter of fact their training has been neither Christian nor an education . . . Christianity, far from being a Bible-department religion, has a right to control the instruction in all departments. The general principles of Scripture apply to all subjects, and in some subjects the Scriptures apply rather detailed principles, so that every course of instruction is altered by a conscious adoption of Christian principles.[9]

Christians need to integrate their faith into every academic discipline, and are increasingly doing so. As R. J. Rushdoony says:

> Man must exercise dominion in the name of God, and in knowledge, righteousness, and holiness. Education must be Christian, because all non-Christian education is committed to beliefs which are either implicitly or explicitly at war with the Christian faith. Christian education must also be philosophically informed and epistemologically self-conscious: it cannot be Christian unless it re-thinks every area of study in terms of a consistent and systematic Biblical faith.
>
> The world, moreover, cannot be surrendered to Satan. It is God's world and must be brought under God's law, politically, economically, and in every other way possible.
>
> The Enlightenment, by its savage and longstanding attack on Biblical

8. Gouverneur Morris; quoted in Jared Sparks, *The Life of Gouverneur Morris*, 3 vols. (Boston, 1832), 3:483; quoted in Chester James Antieau, Arthur T. Downey, and Edward C. Roberts, *Freedom from Federal Establishment: Formation and Early History of the First Amendment Religion Clauses* (Milwaukee: Bruce Publishing Company, 1964), pp. 201-202.

9. Gordon Clark, *A Christian Philosophy of Education* (Grand Rapids, Michigan), pp. 204-210; quoted in Frank E. Gaebelein, *The Pattern of God's Truth: Problems of Integration in Christian Education* (New York: Oxford University Press, 1954), p. 17.

faith, has brought about a long retreat of Christianity from a full-orbed faith to a kind of last-ditch battle centering around the doctrines of salvation and of the infallible Scripture. The time has come for a full-scale offensive, and it has indeed begun, to bring every area of thought into captivity to Christ, to establish the whole counsel of God and every implication of His infallible word.[10]

The Christian world view applies to every area of academic study. In history, for example, we have seen that the entire direction of history, as viewed by creationist Christians, differs from that of evolutionists. The humanistic historian sees man as continually developing from a savage and primitive culture to a more advanced and civilized culture, whereas the Christian regards history as the story of man's fall into perpetually increasing degeneracy as the cancer of sin spreads across all creation . History classes should also recognize that the Scriptures contain a great deal of history, and that "history" which conflicts with Scripture is false. It is fascinating to study the impact of Christianity upon world civilizations and world history, and to examine empires in the light of Scripture.

The study of psychology is intimately bound up with one's view of the nature of man—whether one regards man as essentially good, but plagued with primitive notions of sin and guilt, or as a fallen creature of God who stands in need of God's salvation.

Health courses take on a special meaning if the human body is the "temple of the Holy Spirit," a special creation of God, and our responsibility to care for properly. Literature should be regarded as the flowering of man's creative ability, and the ideas found in literature evaluated according to Scripture. Music and art are expressions of the beauty and majesty of God, and any study of music and art which ignores God is woefully deficient. Science not only involves the controversy between creation and evolution, but involves the discovery of God's laws for the operation of the universe and the world of nature. Through science we see God's infinite wisdom and intricate design.

And even as "sterile" a subject as mathematics must be viewed as a study of God's physical laws. In fact, probably no subject better reveals God's orderliness and faithfulness than the study of the laws of mathematics.

What about athletics? Frank E. Gaebelein, headmaster of The Stony Brook School, says, "From the point of view of Christian doctrine, a mile race is in itself a neutral thing. The way in which a young man runs it, however, is so far from neutral that St. Paul did not hesitate to use the Greek games as a powerful figure of the Christian life."[11]

True Christian education, then, is Christ-centered education which views God as the Author and Source of all knowledge and God's Word as the authoritative revelation of knowledge. An education that leaves God behind

10. R. J. Rushdoony, *The Biblical Philosophy of History*, p. 16.

11. Frank E. Gaebelein, *The Pattern of God's Truth: Problems of Integration and Christian Education* (New York: Oxford University Press, 1954), p. 89. Gaebelein's book is an excellent explanation of the integration of the Christian world view with the academic curriculum.

at the school doorstep gives the child only a humanistic basis for knowledge and values. And it creates intellectual schizophrenia in the Christian child, for he is taught at home and at church that Christ is the center of his life, but he finds that at school, the center of his intellectual life, Christ is somehow left out. The idea that education can be neutral about God is sheer mythology. By saying nothing about God, one is in fact saying a great deal—that God is either nonexistent or irrelevant to modern life.

The view that knowledge and education alone will solve men's problems is equally a myth. Knowledge does not assure goodness. The Nazis were among the best-educated people in history; it has been estimated that one-fourth of Hitler's concentration camp guards held doctoral degrees.[12] As Chambers said,

> . . . man without God is a beast, never more beastly than when he is most intelligent about his beastliness. "Er nennt's Vernunft," says the Devil in Goethe's *Faust*, "und braucht's allein, nur tierisher als jedes Tier ze sein"—Man calls it reason and uses it simply to be more beastly than any beast.[13]

To be worthy of the name, then, Christian education must be carefully integrated with Christianity and the Bible.

Christian Education as a Church Ministry

The courts have recognized the pervasively religious character of Christian schools. Consequently, they have generally struck down most government aid to private schools as an establishment of religion. The few exceptions have involved government aid which does not directly relate to the sectarian interests of the church, such as busing students to and from the school, providing textbooks or allowing private-school students to participate in certain public-school activities.[14]

We have previously seen that the term "religion" must have the same meaning in the free exercise clause as in the establishment clause, since the word "thereof" in the free exercise clause refers back to the word "religion" in the establishment clause. It logically follows, then, that to the extent government aid to Christian schools violates the establishment clause, to that same extent government control of Christian schools violates the free exercise clause.[15]

If Christian schools are too religious to be aided by government, they are also too religious to be regulated by government. If the Christian school is the

---

12. Tom Anderson, "Straight Talk" lecture at Bob Jones University, October 14, 1981, Greenville, South Carolina.

13. Whittaker Chambers, *Witness* (New York: Random House, 1952), p. 13.

14. *Van Hoose v. William* 496 F. Supp. 947 (E.D. Ky. 1980); *California Teacher Association v. Wilson Riles* 632 P.2d 953, 176 Cal. Rptr. 300, 29 C.3d 794 (1981).

15. Opinion, Attorney General, State of California, No. 79-524 (1980); cited in *The Advocate*, April 1980, p. A-7.

ministry of a church, then it should be entitled to the same protection under the free exercise clause to which the church itself is entitled. This has been recognized in several cases involving zoning restrictions. *City of Concord v. New Testament Baptist Church and Heritage Christian School* (118 N.H. 56, 382 A. 2d 377, January 23, 1978) involved a Concord, New Hampshire zoning ordinance which exempted facilities "usually connected with a church." The defendants claimed that they were exempted from the ordinance because the Heritage Christian School was an activity usually connected with a church. The court agreed, saying:

> . . . we first note that the parents and members of the congregation believe as a matter of religious conviction that their children should not be taught secular humanism in the public schools but receive a Christian education. As in Yoder, they object to (public) education generally, because the values (it) teaches are in marked variance with (their) values and . . . way of life." *Wisconsin v. Yoder, supra,* at 210-11. This concept is not new to Roman Catholics and other faiths who run their own value-oriented schools. See *Pierce v. Society of Sisters, supra.*
>
> Historically, "in New England some of the schools are private, some public, and some partly public and partly private." (O. Chitwood, *History of Colonial America,* 457, 3rd Ed. 1961). The schoolhouse was "generally near the church and was regarded as a sort of annex to it. Religion had a large place in the Puritan school" *Id.* Even public schools in the colonies were "closely associated with the established church" *Id* at 458. Public compulsory education as it is known today was a rarity in the early years of this republic. Rothvard, *Historical Origins,* in W. Rickenbacker, The Twelve-Year Sentence, Radical Views of Compulsory Schooling 12-16 (1974). For instance, the Quakers in Pennsylvania believed the schools to be an important extension of the church, and by the end of the 18th Century sixty or seventy schools had been so established. O. Chitwood, *supra* 460. Probably the oldest corporation in Pennsylvania is the present private William Penn Charter School, charted by Penn as a Quaker school in 1689. J. Gummere, Old Penn Charter I (1973). Thus a school may be considered as an integral and inseparable part of a church. 2 R. Anderson, American Law of Zoning, 2d. Sec. 12.25, at 459-60 (1976); see *Westbury Hebrew Congregation, Inc., v. Downer,* 59 Misc. 2d 387, 302 N.Y.S. 2d 923 (1969). While every church may not "usually" have a full-time school associated with it, we hold that the Heritage Christian School is a proper permitted use connected with, and is part of, the New Testament Baptist Church. [unanimous decision][16]

A Superior Court in the state of California entered a similar ruling in June,

---

16. *County of Yolo v. Christian Life Center of West Sacramento* (Superior Court, State of California, County of Yolo, No. 40751).

1980, while in Canada the Supreme Court of Ontario entered a contrary decision.[17]

Another issue involving the relation of Christian schools to their sponsoring churches is that of unemployment taxes. Before 1976, the Federal Unemployment Tax Act, 25 U.S.C. 3301-3311, exempted persons "in the employ of a school which is not an institution of higher education. . . ." But in 1976 Congress amended the act, omitting that subsection, but continuing to exempt ministers and employees of organizations "operated primarily for religious purposes."

In 1978, the Secretary of Labor declared that the 1976 amendment was "clearly intended to result in a state coverage of church-related schools." But the church-related schools claimed that they were still exempt, because they were "operated primarily for religious purposes." This resulted in litigation in many states, including South Dakota, Alabama, California, Illinois, New Hampshire, North Carolina, Oregon, and Pennsylvania, with varying results. In 1981, the case of *St. Martin Evangelical Lutheran Church and Northwestern Academy v. State of South Dakota* came before the United States Supreme Court for a landmark ruling. The Court noted:

> Both St. Martin and the Academy are members of the Wisconsin Evangelical Lutheran Synod and, as such, are organizations exempt from federal income tax under 26 USC 501(c)(3). St Martin's operates a Christian day school at Watertown that offers kindergarten through eighth-grade education. The school, which is not a separate legal entity from the church, is controlled by a Board of Education elected from the local congregation. The congregation entirely finances the school's operation. The Academy is a state-certified 4-year secondary school at Mobridge and is owned, supported, and controlled by the Synod. It, also, is not separately incorporated. Approximately half of its students go on to become ministers within the Church. According to the record, all courses given at St. Martin and at the Academy are taught from a religious point of view based on the Synod's Scriptural convictions. . . .
>
> Only teachers trained and certified by the Synod may teach at either school, and, again as the referee found, these teachers, both male and female, "receive a divine, life-long call" to the church. . . . Male teachers ("teaching ministers") have equal status in the church and an equal vote on Synod matters, including matters of doctrine, with preaching ministers. . . . Neither school has a separate legal existence. Thus, the employees working within these schools plainly are "in the employ of . . . a church or convention or association of churches . . ."[18]

17. *Between the Corporation of the Township of Innisfil and Leroy O. Pennell and Trustees of the Heritage Bapist Church* (in the Supreme Court of Ontario Court of Appeals, June 2, 1980); cited by *The Advocate*, July 1980; p. a6. (See also *Damascus Community Church v. Clackama County*, 45 Or. App. 1065, 610 P.2d 273 [1980]).

18. *St. Martin Evangelical Lutheran Church and Northwestern Lutheran Academy v. State of South Dakota*, 68 L.Ed. 2d 612, 101 S.Ct. 2142, 49 L.W. 4575 (1981).

The Supreme Court then found that, since the Christian schools in question were part of the ministry of the church, they were exempt from unemployment taxes. How this will affect other Christian schools which are not as closely tied to a church as in the *St. Martin* case, remains to be seen. But, because of the close relationship between the churches and their school ministries in this case, it was an ideal one to present to the Supreme Court as a test case, from the standpoint of the Christian schools.

St. Martin and the Northwestern Lutheran Academy had taken a two-pronged approach to the issue: (1) They argued that they were covered by the statute which exempted church employees; and (2) they argued that, even if they were not exempt within the meaning of the statute, then the statute violated the First Amendment. The Court did not rule on the second argument, as it was unnecessary to do so in light of its ruling on the first. But the Court noted a common principle of constitutional interpretation, that in a close case a court should construe or interpret a statute in such a way as to render it constitutional. In other words, instead of construing the statute so broadly as to cover church school employees, and then declare the statue unconstitutional, the Court gave it a narrow construction and assumed it was constitutional.

Being part of a church ministry has certain advantages. One is tax-exempt status. The zoning laws which exempt churches from certain restrictions may not apply to separately incorporated Christian schools. The same could be true of state and local tax laws which exempt churches.

The Christian school that wants to be considered a church ministry should be tied as closely as possible to the church in an organizational sense. For example, it might be unwise to incorporate the Christian school separately, if one wishes to claim that it is a ministry of the church. After all, the Sunday school is not incorporated separately, nor is the ladies' aid society, the youth fellowship, the senior citizens' fellowship, or the ministries of the church. Separate incorporation could suggest separate ministry.

If possible, for the purpose of tying the Christian school to the church, it is desirable to finance the school through the church instead of charging tuition. Granted, this may seem impractical or impossible, especially for Christian schools which attract a substantial number of students whose parents do not attend the church. But a number of schools do it, especially those of Lutheran Church, Wisconsin Evangelical Lutheran Synod. There could also be a tax advantage in this arrangement for the parent who contributes generously to the church.

Christian Education as a Parental Right

Some Christians, especially some within the Calvinist tradition, adhere to the doctrine of "sphere sovereignty." They believe there are three spheres of influence: the state, the church, and the home. They regard education as being within the sphere of the home, not the church and certainly not the state. And there is considerable scriptural support for their position: Deuteronomy 6:5-7;

Proverbs 4:1-2, 10-11, 5:1, 22:6; Matthew 18:6; Ephesians 6:4. Consequently, these Christians operate their Christian schools under the authority of the parents rather than that of the church. Their education is decidedly Christian, and their Christian school officials are likely to work closely with church authorities and perhaps even use church facilities, but the school is a separate legal entity from the church. For these Christians, the structure of their Christian school is as much a matter of religious conviction as those who make their school part of the church. Are their convictions less entitled to the protection of the First Amendment than those of other Christians? If the Department of Labor were to exempt church-related schools from paying unemployment tax, but not exempt other Christian schools, couldn't these Christians claim a denial of "equal protection" under the Fourteenth Amendment?

For purposes of zoning regulations or other statutory provisions which exempt churches on other than constitutional grounds, the church-related school may possibly have a legal advantage over the Christian school which is not directly related to the church. But for First Amendment and other constitutional purposes, the independent Christian school should stand on an equal footing with the church-related school. If it doesn't, it may have a valid "equal protection" argument.

The constitutional right to control the education of one's child is not limited to those who do so for religious reasons. Parental rights have been recognized as "fundamental" constitutional rights, even though the basis for that parent's education decision is not at all rooted in religious considerations.

The right is rooted in the right of privacy. In *Roe v. Wade*, 410 U.S. 113 (1973), the U.S. Supreme Court acknowledged that privacy is a "fundamental" right, and it includes activities relating to "child rearing and education."

At common law, a parent had the right to control his child's education. This right was eroded to some extent in the late 1800s and early 1900s, as the public school system became commonplace and as most states passed compulsory education statutes requiring parents to send children of certain ages to school.[19] But as the twentieth century progressed, an increasing number of court decisions have reasserted and expanded the parental right to control a child's education. One landmark decision took place in 1923. *Meyer v. State of Nebraska*, 262 U.S. 390 (1923) involved a Nebraska statute which prohibited the teaching of foreign languages in private schools. Striking down this requirement, the U.S. Supreme Court declared:

> The problem for our determination is whether the statute as construed and applied unreasonably infringes the liberty guaranteed to the plaintiff in error by the Fourteenth Amendment:

---

19. Mary-Michelle Upson Hirschoff, "Parents and the Public School Curriculum: Is There a Right to Have One's Child Excused from Objectionable Instruction?," *Southern California Law Review*, 50:871-959; see also Samuel L. Blemenfeld, *Is Public Education Necessary?* (The Devin-Adair Company: Old Greenwich, Connecticut, 1981).

"No state . . . shall deprive any person of life, liberty or property without due process of law."

While this court has not attempted to define with exactness the liberty thus guaranteed, the term has received much consideration and some of the included things have been definitely stated. Without doubt, it denotes not merely freedom from bodily restraint but also the right of the individual to contract, to engage in any of the common occupations of life, to acquire useful knowledge, to marry, to establish a home and bring up children, to worship God according to the dictates of his own conscience, and generally to enjoy those privileges long recognized at common law as essential to the orderly pursuit of happiness by free men. . . .

Plaintiff in error taught this language in school as part of his occupation. His right thus to teach and the right of the parents to engage him so to instruct their children, we think, are within the liberty of the amendment.

. . . the Legislature has attempted materially to interfere with the calling of modern language teachers, with the opportunities of pupils to acquire knowledge, and with the power of parents to control the education of their own.

Two years later, in another landmark case, the Supreme Court struck down as unconstitutional an Oregon law compelling all children of certain ages to attend public school. In *Pierce v. Society of the Sisters of the Holy Names of Jesus and Mary*, 268 U.S. 510 (1925), the Court declared:

Under the doctrine of *Meyer v. Nebraska*, 262 U.S. 390, 43 S.Ct. 625, 67 L.E.D. 1042, 29 A.L.R. 1146, we think it entirely plain that the Act of 1922 unreasonably interferes with the liberty of parents and guardians to direct the upbringing and education of children under their control. As often heretofore pointed out, rights guaranteed by the Constitution may not be abridged by legislation which has no reasonable relation to some purpose within the competency of the State. The fundamental theory of liberty upon which all governments in this Union repose excludes any general power of the state to standardize its children by forcing them to accept instruction from public teachers only. The child is not the mere creature of the state; those who nurture him and direct his destiny have the right, coupled with the high duty, to recognize and prepare him for additional obligations.

The "reasonable relationship" test is no longer applied by the courts in matters involving fundamental rights; rather, as previously said, the test used is "compelling state interest." Let us also note that neither *Meyer* nor *Pierce* involved the First Amendment free exercise of religion; rather, both involved the Fourteenth Amendment right to "liberty." Freedom of religion was not an issue in *Meyer*, and while in *Pierce* the Society of Sisters was operating a religious Catholic school, there was a companion case of *Pierce v. Hill Military Academy* which involved a purely secular private military school. These cases demonstrate that the right of parents to direct the education of their children exists independently of religious considerations, although religious considerations may give a new dimension to that right. Professor Leo Pfeffer has called the *Pierce* decision the "Magna Charta of the American Parochial system."[20]

Undoubtedly, the most significant case involving Christian schools and parental rights is *Wisconsin v. Yoder*, 406 U.S. 205 (1972). Jonas Yoder was a parent who held to the Amish faith. For religious reasons, he and other Amish parents believed it was wrong to send their children to the public schools because of the worldly influence that existed there. Instead, their children attended private schools run by the Amish themselves. These Amish schools were taught by Amish teachers who had less than a high school education, and the instruction concentrated on basic skills plus emphasis upon the beliefs and morals of the Amish community. For sending his children to this Amish school instead of a public school or state-approved private school, Yoder was found guilty of violating the compulsory-attendance law and was fined five dollars.

But the Supreme Court reversed his conviction, holding that Wisconsin's compulsory attendance law, while constitutional on its face, was unconstitutional as applied to Yoder because it violated his religious beliefs which were protected by the First Amendment, and because it violated his right as a parent to control the education of his children. The Court in effect exempted Yoder and his Amish brethren from the requirements of the compulsory-attendance statutes.

The state argued that it had a "compelling interest" which overrode Yoder's First Amendment rights. But the Court rejected that contention:

> There is no doubt as to the power of the state, having a high responsibility for education of its citizens, to impose reasonable regulations for the control and duration of basic education. . . . Providing public schools ranks at the very apex of the function of the state. Yet even this paramount responsibility was, in *Pierce*, made to yield to the right of parents to provide an equivalent education in the privately operated system. . . . thus, a State's interest in universal education, however highly we rank it, is not totally free from a balancing when it impinges on fundamental rights and interests, such as those specifically protected by the Free Exercise Clause of the First Amendment, and the traditional interest of parents with respect to the religious upbringing of their children so long as they, in the words of *Pierce*, "prepare (them) for additional obligations.". . .
>
> We turn, then to the State's broader contention that its interest in its system of compulsory education is so compelling that even established religious practices of the Amish must give way. Where fundamental claims of religious freedom are at stake, however, we cannot accept such a sweeping claim; despite its admitted validity in the generality of cases, we must searchingly examine the interests that the State seeks to promote by its requirement for compulsory education to age sixteen, and the impediment to those objectives that would flow from recognizing the claimed Amish exemption.

20. Leo Pfeffer, quoted by Lynn R. Buzzard and Samuel Ericsson, *The Battle for Religious Liberty* (Elgin, Illinois: David C. Cook Publishing Company, 1982) p. 143.

The Court identified the following functions of the compulsory education statute: to minimize the danger of child labor, to prepare children for meaningful occupations so they will not become a public charge, and to prepare children to exercise the responsibilities of citizenship. The Court then found even though the Amish schools did not comply with the technical requirements of the compulsory-education statute in that they did not have state-certified teachers, etc., they were, nevertheless, able to fulfill the purposes behind the statute:

> There is nothing in this record to suggest that the Amish qualities of realiability, self-reliance, and dedication to work would fail to find ready markets in today's society. Absent some contrary evidence supporting the State's position, we are unwilling to assume that persons possessing such valuable vocational skills and habits are doomed to become burdens on society should they determine to leave the Amish faith, nor is there any basis in the record to warrant a finding that an additional one or two years of formal school education beyond the eighth grade would serve to eliminate any such problem that might exist.

The Court then invoked the doctrine we have referred to earlier as "least restrictive means." That doctrine, we will recall, is that even if the state can demonstrate that it has a "compelling interest," it may not use that compelling interest to justify a violation of one's fundamental rights, unless the state is unable to fulfill its compelling interest by any "less restrictive means." Since the state's compelling interest could be fulfilled even if the Amish were granted an exemption from the compulsory education statute, the Court held that the doctrine of "least restrictive means" required that the Amish be exempted from the statute.

Recently, the principles of *Yoder* were applied in a Massachusetts case in which First Amendment religious liberty was not an issue. A similar conclusion was reached solely upon the basis of the parents' right to control the education of their child.[21]

The "least restrictive means" doctrine is of vital importance in cases of this nature, for the doctrine requires the state to tailor its regulations as precisely as possible to avoid infringement upon fundamental rights. As the Supreme Court said in *U.S. v. Robel*, 389 U.S. 258 (1967), "it has become axiomatic that precision of regulation must be the touchstone in areas like education which so closely touch our most precious freedoms."

Recent cases have established that the doctrine of "least restrictive means" is to be given broad application, so much so that the courts will not sustain a restrictive regulation merely because granting exemptions, etc., would involve administrative inconvenience. The Supreme Court said in *Stanley v. Illinois*, 405 U.S. 645 (1972):

> The establishment of prompt efficacious procedures to achieve legitimate state ends is a proper state interest worthy of cognizance in constitutional

---

21. *Perchemlides v. Frizzle*, Hamshire County Superior Court, Civil Action NO. 16641 (Massachusetts), November 13, 1978.

adjudication. But the Constitution recognizes higher values than speed and efficiency. Indeed, one might fairly say of the Bill of Rights in general, and the due process clause in particular, that they were designed to protect the fragile values of a vulnerable citizenry from the overbearing concern for efficiency and efficacy that may characterize praiseworthy government officials no less, and perhaps more, than mediocre ones.

Similar language is found in *Cleveland Board of Education v. La Fleur*, 414 U.S. 632 (1974): "Administrative convenience alone is insufficient to make valid what otherwise is a violation of due process of law." The state must, therefore, tailor its regulations very specifically to avoid infringing upon parental and religious freedoms.

State Regulation of Private Schools

The regulation of Christian schools is one of the most explosive issues of concern to Christians today. Declaring that "Caesar" has no right to license God, Christian pastors and parents have gone to jail rather than to submit to "Caesar's" regulation of their Christian schools.

Such regulations vary widely from state to state. Some states require all private schools be licensed by the state. Others require that private schools meet certain minimum standards, such as using only state-certified teachers. Others have tried to impose curriculum requirements or dictate what textbooks should be used. Others regulate the length and hours of the school day and the school year. Some require that private school children be subject to standardized testing to determine whether they are making adequate progress.

Many Christians strongly object to these requirements. Some contend that the standards imposed by the state require the Christian school do certain things that violate Christian principles. Others maintain that the regulations are unnecessary and wasteful for private schools. Others object on principle that the state has no right to regulate private schools. Some have refused to obtain licenses even though it was recognized by all parties that the school fully qualified for the license. In at least one instance, a teacher who was fully qualified to obtain state certification refused to do so on religious grounds. As a result the state of Michigan prosecuted her for teaching her children at home in violation of Michigan law that required certified teachers. But the court upheld her right to do so, noting her religious objection to certification, noting her educational qualifications, and noting that merely becoming certified would not make her a better teacher.[22] The court therefore dismissed the charges, but many Christian schools and Christian parents have not been so fortunate.

How can the Christian school and the Christian parent defend against such regulations?

The jurisdictional argument is worth considering. As discussed earlier, education is inextricably intertwined with religion. Since education is essentially a religious matter, it is outside the jurisdiction of the state. Government has only derivative powers, those granted by the state and federal constitutions. Nothing in the federal Constitution gives the federal government any jurisdiction

22. *Michigan v. Nobel*, 57th Dist. Ct. for the County of Allegan, Michigan (December 12, 1979).

whatsoever over religion. Consequently, religion is outside its authority. While this was the intent of the framers of the Constitution, it became especially clear with the adoption of the First Amendment.

Now, since the courts have ruled that the Fourteenth Amendment applies the First Amendment to the states, the jurisdictional limitation upon religion which formerly applied to the federal government now applies to the states as well. Consequently, the states have no jurisdiction over religion either. And if education is essentially a religious matter, the state has no jurisdiction to regulate education.

While this argument has considerable merit, it is novel in today's legal system, and courts often hesitate to accept such arguments. At this time, it would be advisedly used in addition to other applicable arguments.

William Ball, a leading First Amendment attorney, has argued successfully in several cases that government regulation of private schools violates the establishment clause of the First Amendment by constituting excessive entanglement of government with religion. In so doing he has meticulously demonstrated that government regulation puts the state in the business of telling the church or Christian school what it must do in a vital area of its ministry. He has demonstrated that the state makes value judgments concerning the philosophy that underlies teaching in Christian schools, and that all of this constitutes excessive entanglement. (See *Lemon v. Kurtzman*, supra.)

The strongest argument against state regulation, in my opinion, is two-pronged. It is based, first, on the free exercise clause of the First Amendment, and second, upon the privacy right of the parent to direct the upbringing and education of his child. Wherever possible, these two rights should be coupled together.

To stand up in court, Christians must demonstrate that state regulation violates sincere and deeply held religious convictions, and that these convictions are central to their faith. Mere preferences are not protected by the First Amendment.

Government intrusion on religious convictions must be precisely documented by client and attorney. In *Ohio v. Whisner*, 351 N.E. 2d 750 (1976), attorney William Ball demonstrated that a comprehensive set of regulations imposed by the state of Ohio upon private schools had the practical effect of limiting the extent to which these schools could teach Christian doctrine and forced them to become practically the same as the secular public schools. The Ohio Supreme Court decided the case in favor of the private school, striking down the state's regulatory scheme as unconstitutional.

Others have objected to state licensing requirements on the grounds that government has no authority to license God. The term "license" involves permission to operate, and when the state grants a license to a Christian school, the state in effect says that it (the state) has authority to tell the school whether or not it may operate. If the Christian school is the ministry of a church, this means a lesser entity (the state) has the power to license a greater entity (the church). This is like Caesar attempting to license God!

In the early centuries of Christianity, the problem between the church and Rome was that the church refused licensure from the state. Though the state granted other religions permission to operate and would have granted similar permission to Christians, they would grant licensure only if the Christians would acknowledge the sovereignty of the state. The Christians refused, since they believed in the sovereignty of God alone. Significantly, our Constitution does not use the term "sovereignty." At the Constitutional Convention, George Washington insisted that sovereignty belonged to no earthly government, but to God alone.[23] Many Christian schools have used this argument with mixed results. Two state supreme courts have rejected the argument, North Dakota in *N.D. v. Shaver & Steinwand*, 294 N.W. 2d 883 (1980) and *N.D. v. Rivinius*, 328 N.W. 2d 220 (1982); and Nebraska in *Neb. v. Faith Baptist Church of Louisville*, 301 N.W. 2d 571 (1981), appeal dismissed 454 U.S. 803 (1981). But the argument has been successful in some lower court decisions, and could ultimately prevail.

Others object to teacher certification on the grounds it usually requires training at state accredited institutions where humanistic indoctrination and objectionable methodology may be part of the curriculum. Such an objection could be successful if carefully documented and presented by expert witnesses.

Still others might argue that teacher certification requirements prevent their Christian school from operating in accordance with their Christian convictions. They might establish that certified teachers are not available to work at the low salary their school can afford to pay. In doing so, of course, they would have to prove reasonable effort to find certified teachers by advertising or other means. Or, they might argue that they have not been able to find any Christian certified teachers that share their religious convictions. Again, they will have to demonstrate reasonable effort.

Teacher certification requirements were upheld in the *Shaver*, *Rivinius*, and *Faith Baptist* cases previously mentioned. In those cases the courts ruled that teacher certification imposes only a minimal burden upon the defendant's religious convictions, if any at all. In effect, the courts have ruled that the objection to teacher certification was not "central" to the defendants' religion. A stronger showing of centrality might have produced a different result. In the *Shaver* case, the pastor of the Christian school testified that his requirement for a teacher was that the teacher be "born again", that he would not object to hiring a certified teacher so long as that teacher were "born again", that there may very well be certified teachers who are "born again", and that he had made no efforts to find any such teachers. The court therefore felt he had failed to prove the law infringed upon his religion. Again, different facts could have produced a different result.

Other courts have struck down state regulations. In the *Whisner* case mentioned above, the Ohio Supreme Court granted Whisner and his co-defendants an exemption from the Ohio minimum standards. The court stated:

---

23. R. J. Rushdoony, "Historic Role of the Church and Family in Education" lecture, Oral Roberts University, October 23, 1981.

Under the facts of this case, the right of appellants to direct the upbringing and education of their children in a manner in which they deem advisable, indeed essential, and which we cannot say is harmful, has been denied by application of the state's "minimum standards" as to them. The uncontroverted testimony establishes that appellants were aware that Tabernacle Christian School did not conform to all the "minimum standards", but that such was not considered necessary by them because the education afforded their children enrolled in the school fulfilled their educational and religious preferences.

In the opinion of a majority of this court, a "general education of a high quality" can be achieved by means other than the comprehensive regimentation of *all* academic centers in this state. In the words of Thoreau:

> If a man does not keep pace with his companions, perhaps
> it is because he hears a different drummer. Let him step to
> the music which he hears, however measured or far away.

Having demonstrated that application of the "minimum standards" to appellants violates their constitutional rights in two different ways, we turn, now, to the question of whether those standards may yet be sustained by the state. As in *Wisconsin v. Yoder, supra* (406 U.S. 205, 233), "when the interests of parenthood are combined with the free exercise claim of the nature revealed by this record, more than merely a 'reasonable relation to some purpose within the competency of the state' is required to sustain the validity of the state's requirement under the First Amendment." What is required is a finding that "there is a state interest of sufficient magnitude to override the interest claiming perfection under the free exercise clause." *Id* at page 214. Moreover, even if the state can establish the requisite degree of interest, it must yet demonstrate that such interests cannot otherwise be served in order to overbalance legitimate claims to the free exercise of religion. . . .

The state did not, either in this court or in the lower courts, attempt to justify its interest in enforcing the "minimum standards" as applied to a nonpublic religious school. In the face of the record before us, and in light of the expert testimony summarized in the statement of the case herein, it is difficult to imagine a "state interest of sufficient magnitude to override the interest claiming protection under the free exercise clause." *Wisconsin v. Yoder, supra*. at page 214. And, equally difficult to imagine, is a state interest sufficiently substantial to sanction abrogation of appellants' liberty to direct the education of their children. We will not, therefore, attempt to conjure up such an interest in order to sustain application of the "minimum standards" to these appellants.

Christian schools won another victory in Ohio in 1980, when the Ohio Supreme Court struck down an attempt by state officials to prevent Olin from sending his child to a nonconforming Amish school (*Ohio ex rel. Nagle v. Olin*, 415 N.E. 2d 279). The state argued that the exemption from state standards applied only to the Amish, and Olin was of a different faith. Olin considered himself a "born again" or "biblical Christian" but was "not affiliated with any organized religious denomination." But the Ohio Supreme Court ruled:

> The fact that his beliefs are not in total conformity with those of the Amish or any other organized religion does not make them any less religious, or his sincerity in them any less real. Olin's beliefs are rooted in the Bible and his interpretation of it; not in secular consideration. It was not contended Olin's profession of belief was a sham or a subterfuge adopted in order to avoid the obligation of sending Jennifer to a state-chartered school. Despite the delicacy of the question whether particular beliefs are "religious," the only finding justified on the record is that Olin's beliefs grow out of deep religious conviction, are truly held, and are entitled to the protection of the First and Fourteenth Amendments.

The court concluded, "We believe that such a set of less-restrictive standards could be adopted." Olin was therefore exempted from the state's requirements and permitted to send his child to the Amish school.

In a case directly related to teacher certification, *Kentucky State Board for Elementary and Secondary Education v. Rudasill*, 589 S.W. 2d 877 (1979), the Kentucky Supreme Court struck down an attempt by the state of Kentucky to regulate Christian schools in that state. The Court ruled:

> It cannot be said as an absolute that a teacher in a nonpublic school who is not certified under KRS 161030 (2) will be unable to instruct children to become intelligent citizens. Certainly, the receipt of "a bachelor's degree from a standard college or university" is an indicator of a level of achievement, but it is not a sine qua non the absence of which establishes that private and parochial schoolteachers are unable to teach their students to intelligently exercise the elective franchise.

The U.S. Supreme Court has thus far refused to address the issue, so the battle rages on!

Once it has been established that the state regulation violates one's religious convictions, the burden shifts to the state to demonstrate that its interest in education is so compelling as to justify overriding religious convictions, and that its compelling interest cannot be achieved by any less restrictive means. The *Wisconsin v. Yoder* case, supra, held that the state's interest in education consists of training children in the duties of citizenship so that they will be responsible members of the community, and training them for a productive occupation so that they will be able to support themselves and their families and not become public charges. The Court held, however, that the Amish were fulfilling that interest in their nonconforming schools. The Court therefore concluded that the state's interests could be accomplished by less restrictive means, and granted the Amish exemption from Wisconsin's compulsory attendance law.

To establish that the Amish were fulfilling the state's interest, attorney Ball employed some interesting tactics. He brought in educational experts to testify that the Amish possessed the basic skills necessary to function as citizens and secure gainful employment. He subpoenaed the local sheriff to testify that the Amish had an extremely low crime rate, and local welfare officials to testify that virtually none of the Amish were on welfare, experienced teenage pregnancies, etc. Similar testimony could be used concerning the graduates of Christian schools.

Despite the logic of these arguments, some judges feel that if Christian schools are exempted from state regulation, the result will be substandard education. Some legislators share these concerns.

To satisfy these concerns, the Christian schools should note the following arguments:

(1) *Christian Schools Provide Quality Education.* Traditionally, American governments have not sought to regulate that which there was no reason to regulate. Where, then, is the evidence that Christian schools are substandard in quality and in need of the state's ministrations? State education officials who attempt to justify such regulations generally speak in vague, abstract, and hypothetical terms, such as, "It is possible that, if Christian schools are exempt from regulation, some children at those schools might not receive a good education." But, again, is there evidence that this is actually happenening? Thorough studies have concluded that pupils in Christian schools are doing better than their public school peers. Alan N. Grover, Executive Director of Christian Schools of Ohio, points out Stanford Achievement Test scores of the children in Whisner's Tabernacle Christian School had made between one and two years' academic progress in eight months time.[24] Similar results could be documented for most Christian schools.

In April, 1981, sociologist James Coleman released a government-funded survey of 58,728 public and private high school seniors and sophomores, conducted by Coleman's National Opinion Research Center. According to the *Tulsa World*:

> The students were tested on a 1½-hour battery of achievement tests prepared by the Educational Testing Service. On 20 reading questions, the average public school senior got 10.8 correct, the average Catholic school senior 11.9 and other private school seniors 13. On 27 vocabulary questions, the public sector got 12.9, Catholics 15.1 and other private 15.9. On 32 math questions, the scores were 18.9, 21.1 and 22.4 respectively.[25]

Though this particular survey did not distinguish Christian schools from other private schools,[26] another study focuses specifically upon Christian schools. James Braley, Director of Curriculum Services for the Western Association of Christian Schools, has released a report on the recent Stanford Achievement Test scores for students in schools belonging to that association. Test scores revealed that students in Christian schools belonging to the Western

24. Alan N. Grover, *Ohio's Trojan Horse: A Warning to Christian Schools Everywhere* (Greenville, South Carolina: Bob Jones University Press, 1977), p. 6.

25. *Tulsa World*, April 4, 1981.

26. *The Alabama Alert* (Alabama Christian Education Association, Inc.), Vol. 6, No. 5 (May 1981), p. 2.

Association, grades 1-8, are achieving from 6-19 months ahead of the national norm.[27]

The National Education Association and others have sharply criticized the Coleman study, contending that the reason private schools perform better is that these children come from wealthier families and that private schools can be selective on admissions. This may be true of some elite, nonreligious private schools. But many evangelical churches are composed primarily of lower middle class, blue-collar people with average to slightly less than average incomes and perhaps considerably less than average educational backgrounds. Furthermore, Christian schools have only a fraction of the funds available to the public schools. They usually do not have the expensive facilities of the public schools and have a lower wage scale.

Why have the Christian schools been so successful? Several characteristics are worth noting: an emphasis on basic skills; teachers who view their work as a Christian calling and are therefore highly dedicated (I have never heard of a teachers' strike in a Christian school, even though salaries are much lower!); stricter discipline standards which create a better learning atmosphere; and parental interest in education. After all, parents who pay $1,000 per year per child for tuition are going to be very interested in getting their money's worth, and are likely to work more closely with their children to insure that they are learning.

The Coleman study also did not distinguish between accredited and non-accredited private schools, or schools using certified or noncertified teachers. Such a study could be very revealing and important for future litigation.

(2) *Freedom In Other States.* Public school officials sometimes argue that the high quality of Christian schools is the result of state regulation. If the regulations were removed, the quality would diminish. This is a fallacy since many states do not regulate Christian schools and their quality does not suffer. Oklahoma accredits private schools only on a voluntary basis. The vast majority of private schools in Oklahoma are not accredited and are not required to use certified teachers. Many states—among them Connecticut, Illinois, Indiana, Maryland, Missouri, New Jersey, New York, South Carolina, and Vermont—simply require that nonpublic instruction be essentially equivalent to public schools, with no specific requirements concerning teacher qualifications or certification. Others, such as Iowa, Kansas, and Virginia, have special exemption provisions in their laws for those who object to public education on religious grounds. North Carolina recently abolished all restrictions upon church-related private schools, as have Alabama, Arizona, and others. In fact, in most states private schools have almost unlimited freedom to operate as they see fit. And yet, there is no evidence whatsoever that private education in these states suffers in the least from the lack of government control. In a free society, the burden

---

27. Dr. Paul Kienel, Executive Director, Western Association of Christian Schools, "The Advantages of a Christian School Education," *Christian School Comment*, undated.

of proof should rest on those who seek to regulate, not on those who want to be free from regulation.

(3) *Private Schools are Largely Self-Policing.* At the present time, tuition alone at private schools averages above $1,000 per child. This does not include the cost of books, transportation, and many other expenses usually assumed by the parents. In addition, the parent who sends his children to a private school has already paid for a public education through his tax dollars. How many parents are going to forego a "free" public education, and spend at least $1,000 per year per child for private education, unless they are convinced the private school affords a better education? The private school that fails to provide quality education is not likely to stay in business very long, for it will not attract or keep many customers.

(4) *State Regulations are Counterproductive.* Teacher certification is not a *sine qua non* of a good teacher. Many incompetent teachers have obtained and retained certification, while many excellent teachers lack certification. Teacher certification requirements normally include a four-year degree, a major in education and many peripheral methodology courses. Under such requirements, in many states William Shakespeare could not teach literature, Leonardo da Vinci could not teach art, Leonard Bernstein could not teach music, George Washington could not teach government, Abraham Lincoln could not teach law, Galileo could not teach astronomy, and Albert Einstein could not teach science or mathematics. Nor could John Stuart Mill teach political science or Thomas Edison teach electricity, because they never went to school at all—they were educated by their parents at home.

Furthermore, a private school may require a different type of teacher than a public school. Most of the education courses that are necessary for certification are geared toward public school education. A teacher who is certified to teach in a public school and trained to utilize the curriculum materials commonly found in public schools, may be totally confused and lost when faced with the type of individualized curriculum used in, for example, Accelerated Christian Education. As Ralph West, Director of Evaluation for the Commission on Independent Secondary Schools of the New England Association of Schools and Colleges, stated in expert testimony in the *Whisner* case, "A teacher with all of the credentials in the world may be superb in one school situation, and terrible in another."[28]

(5) *State Regulations are Ineffective.* Historically, state regulations on education have utterly failed to improve the quality of instruction.

Education officials who call for upgraded standards and for regulation of private schools, do so on the ground that such upgraded standards are necessary to lift the American people out of the abyss of ignorance, a myth that began with Horace Mann and continued with John Dewey and is still recited today. They would have us believe that, prior to the advent of the public school system,

28. Ralph West; quoted in Grover, p. 10.

the American people were woefully ignorant. Since public schools have been with us for such a long period of time, few question these assertions.

What are the facts about education prior to the establishment of the public schools? Listen to Dupont de Nemours, who surveyed education and wrote around 1800 at the request of Thomas Jefferson:

> Most young Americans . . . can read, write and cipher. Not more than four in a thousand are unable to write legibly—even neatly; while in Spain, Portugal, Italy, only a sixth of the population can read; in Germany, even in France, not more than a third; in Poland, about two men in a hundred; and in Russia not one in two hundred. England, Holland, and the Protestant Cantons of Switzerland, more nearly approach the standard of the United States, because in those countries the Bible is read; it is considered a duty to read it to the children; and in that form of religion the sermons and liturgies in the language of the people tend to increase and formulate ideas of responsibility. Controversy, also, has developed argumentation and has thus given room for the exercise of logic.
>
> In America, a great number of people read the Bible, and all the people read a newspaper. The fathers read aloud to their children while breakfast is being prepared—a task which occupies the mothers for three-quarters of an hour every morning. And as the newspapers of the United States are filled with all sorts of narratives—comments on matters political, physical, philosophic; information on agriculture, the arts, travel, navigation; and also extracts from all the best books in America and Europe—they disseminate an enormous amount of information, some of which is helpful to the young people, especially when they arrive at an age when the father resigns his place as reader in favor of the child who can best succeed him.
>
> It is because of this kind of education that the Americans of the United States, without having more great men than other countries, have the great advantage of having a larger proportion of moderately well-informed men; although their education may seem less perfect, it is, nevertheless, better and more equally distributed. But this does not mean that the general education cannot be improved.[29]

Consider that! A literacy rate in 1800 of 99.6 percent! In contrast, *Chicago Tribune* writer Eric Zorn reports that "Today's estimates on the number of funtionally illiterate Americans—those who cannot read a want ad, bus schedule, or label on a medicine bottle—run as high as 25 million; another 34 million are just barely capable of simple reading tasks."[30] All this, despite generations of upgraded state standards!

DuPont de Nemours was not alone in his observations. Daniel Webster,

29. DuPont de Nemours, *National Education in the United States of America* (Newark, Delaware: University of Delaware Press, 1923), pp. 3-5; quoted in R. J. Rushdoony, *The Messianic Character of American Education*, pp. 329-330.

30. "Johnny Still Can't Read: A Horror Story of the Computer Age," *Tulsa World*, August 23, 1981, Sec. 1, p. 1.

speaking at Plymouth, Massachusetts in 1820, said of American education:

> We know that, at the present time, an attempt is making in the English
> Parliament to provide by law for the education of the poor, and that a
> gentleman of distinguished character has taken the lead in presenting a
> plan to government for carrying that purpose into effect. And yet, although
> the representatives of the three kingdoms listened to him with astonish-
> ment as well as delight, we hear no principles with which we ourselves have
> not been familiar from youth; we see nothing in the plan but an approach
> towards that system which has been established in New England for more
> than a century and a half. It is said that in England not more than *one
> child in fifteen* possesses the means of being taught to read and write; in Wales,
> *one in twenty*; in France, until lately, when some improvement was made,
> not more than *one in thirty-five*. Now, it is hardly too strong to say, that
> in New England *every child possesses* such means. It would be difficult to find
> an instance to the contrary, unless where it should be owing to the negligence
> of the parent; and in truth, the means are actually used and enjoyed by
> nearly every one. A youth of fifteen, of either sex, who cannot read and
> write, is very seldom to be found.[31] [Emphasis original.]

Alexis De Tocqueville, the French judge and political observer who traveled
the United States in 1831-1832, commented extensively on the advanced state
of learning in the America of his day. As he said in *Democracy in America*,

> The observer who is desirous of forming an opinion on the state of instruc-
> tion among the Anglo-Americans must consider the same object from two
> points of view. If he singles out only the learned, he will be astonished to
> find how few they are; but if he counts the ignorant, the American people
> will appear to be the most enlightened in the world. The whole popula-
> tion, as I observed in another place, is situated between these two extremes.
>   In New England every citizen receives the elementary notions of human
> knowledge; he is taught, moreover, the doctrines and the evidences of its
> Constitution. In the states of Connecticut and Massachusetts, it is extremely
> rare to find a man imperfectly acquainted with all these things, and a per-
> son wholly ignorant of them is a sort of phenomenon. . . . What I have
> said of New England must not, however, be applied to the whole Union
> without distinction; as we advanced towards the West or the South, the
> instruction of the people diminishes. In the states that border on the Gulf
> of Mexico a certain number of individuals may be found, as in France,
> who are devoid even of the rudiments of instruction. But there is not a
> single district in the United States sunk in complete ignorance. . . .[32]

De Tocqueville also said about American education:

31. Daniel Webster on Education. Discourse at Plymouth, December 22, 1820. *The Works of
Daniel Webster, Vols. I & II, Boston, 1851. Reprinted in Verna M. Hall, The Christian History of the American
Revolution: Consider and Ponder* (San Francisco: Foundation for American Christian Education, 1976),
p. 222.
  32. De Tocqueville, *Democracy in America*, 1:315-316.

The general principle in the matter of public education is that anyone is free to found a public school and to direct it as he pleases. It's an industry like other industries, the consumers being the judges and the state taking no hand whatever . . . You ask me if this unlimited liberty produces bad results. I believe that it produces only good . . . the effort made in this country to spread instruction is truly prodigious. The universal and sincere faith that they profess here in the efficaciousness of education seems to me one of the most remarkable features of America, the more so as I confess that for me the question is not yet entirely decided. But it is absolutely clear in the minds of the Americans, whatever their opinions political or religious. The Catholic himself in this matter gives his hand to the Unitarian and the Deist. Thence results one of those powerful efforts, quiet but irresistable, that nations sometimes make when they march toward a goal with a common and universal impulse.

There has never been under the sun a people as enlightened as the population of the north of the United States. Because of their education they are more strong, more skillful, more capable of governing themselves and understanding their liberty; that much is undeniable.[33]

De Tocqueville also noted the effect of education in producing good citizenship:

Another point demonstrated by America is that virtue is not, as it has long been pretended, the only thing which can preserve Republics, but that enlightenment more than anything else facilitates that social state. The Americans are hardly more virtuous than others, but they are infinitely better educated (I speak of the mass) than any other people of my acquaintance. . . . The mass of those possessing an understanding of public affairs, a knowledge of laws and precedents, a feeling for the best interests of the nation, and the faculty of understanding them, is greater in America than any place else in the world.[34]

Others have noted the quality of early American colleges. To be admitted as an undergraduate to William and Mary College, for example, in colonial days, the prospective student had to be able to not only read and write and converse, but also to debate, in Greek.[35] How many seminary professors could debate in Greek today?

Reflecting a degree of scholarship that is most uncommon today, John Adams wrote to Thomas Jefferson, saying:

I am very glad you have seriously read Plato, and still more rejoiced to find that your reflections upon him so fervently harmonize with mine. Some 30 years ago I took upon me the severe task of going through all his works. With the help of two Latin translations, and one English, and one French

---

33. De Tocqueville, quoted in George W. Pierson, *Tocqueville in America* (Garden City, New York: Anchor Books, 1959), pp. 293-294.

34. Ibid., p. 350.

35. Sheldon Emry, "God's Law on Property and Inheritance," Cassette lecture dated March 15, 1981 (*America's Promise*, Box 5334, Phoenix, Ariz. 85010).

translation, and comparing some of the most remarkable passages with the Greek, I labored through the tedious toil. My disappointment was very great, my astonishment was greater, my disgust shocking . . . His *Laws* and his *Republic* from which I expected most, disappointed me most.[36]

In contrast, after generations of minimum standards designed to improve quality education, we see the millions of illiterates and functional illiterates mentioned by Zorn. The standardized testing scores have continually declined over the past several decades even though the tests themselves have been revised several times to make them easier. And we are speaking only of academic achievement. It would be interesting to conduct another study, comparing public and private schools in such areas as moral standards, rate of drug use, number of juvenile court appearances, Bible knowledge, suicide rate, truancy rate, unemployment rate after graduation, crime rate after graduation, percentage going on to higher education, and mental problems.

Even as state education departments have upgraded their teacher certification standards, student's standardized test scores have followed a steady, two-decade decline in almost inverse proportion. In April 1983, the National Commission of Excellence in Education issued a blistering twenty-nine-page report decrying "a rising tide of mediocrity" in education and declaring that "if an unfriendly foreign power had attempted to impose on America the mediocre educational requirements that exist today, we might well have viewed it as an act of war."[37]

Can we truly say that the standards established by state departments of education have produced higher quality education in modern America? Can we truly say that the record of the public schools gives public school officials the mandate to impose their standards upon the private schools?

If public school officials are truly concerned with improving educational quality rather than expanding their control or eliminating competition, they would go to the private schools to learn how public education could be upgraded!

(6) *Less Restrictive Means Exist.* Even if some regulation is necessary, the doctrine of "least restrictive means" requires consideration of other means of regulation. One possibility is standardized testing. Standardized tests have commonly been used to measure learning achievement and by implication teacher competence in the public schools. Now that the public school tests scores are declining, the National Education Association has responded not by calling for better teachers, but by condemning standardized testing! One school system has even decided to offer courses in how to take the tests!

In *Wolman v. Walter*, 433 U.S. 229 (1977), the U.S. Supreme Court recognized that standardized testing is one means by which state authorities can measure the progress of students in private schools to make sure they are

---

36. John Adams to Thomas Jefferson, *Jefferson's Works*, Vol. 15, pg. 156; quoted by W. Cleon Skousen, "Miracle of America" (Salt Lake City, Utah: Freemen Institute, 1981), pp. 37-38.

37. "Mediocrity in Education Termed Threat to Nation," *Tulsa Tribune*, April 26, 1983, p. 1.

receiving a quality education. In the *Rudasill* case, supra, the Kentucky Supreme Court recognized the validity of standardized testing:

> If the legislature wishes to monitor the work of private and parochial schools in accomplishing the constitutional purpose of compulsory education, it may do so by an appropriate standardized testing program.

And the Massachusetts court in *Perchemlides*, supra, also recognized the propriety of standardized testing:

> As a method of insuring that at least minimal standards are being maintained, the superintendent and the committee may require that the child be periodically tested, although the method of testing must logically be related to the type of educational program that the parents have chosen to follow.
>
> If it turns out that a child does not test as well as might have been hoped, however, it makes sense to remember that we do not remove our children from public school when they fail tests. The testing process should be viewed, at least initially in any case, as an opportunity to remedy any shortcomings that may be uncovered, unless the shortcomings are so significant as to reflect serious defects in the methodology of the home education program and substantial failure on the part of the child to make reasonable educational progress.

Other court decisions, however, such as *Faith Baptist* in Nebraska and *Rivinius* in North Dakota, have questioned the value of standardized testing.

We have already discussed the *Faith Baptist* case of Nebraska, in which Pastor Everett Sileven and others have been jailed for refusing to submit to state licensing and state certification. The controversy has continued to simmer.

Late in the fall of 1983, warrants were issued for the arrest of seven fathers and mothers of children who attend Faith Christian School. The fathers were arrested, and the mothers and children left the state. The fathers remained in jail for contempt of court, for refusing to divulge to the court information about the school—information which, many believe, is privileged under the Fifth Amendment.

Due to the national storm created over the confrontation, on December 12, 1983, the Governor of Nebraska created a special Governor's Christian School Issue Panel to study the problem and make recommendations. On January 26, 1984, the Panel issued its thirty-nine-page report.

"Can this conflict be resolved?", the Report asked. "Yes, and without a lot of difficulty."[38] The Panel then proceeded to recommend that Nebraska Christian schools be exempt from state-imposed curriculum, teacher certification, and related requirements, provided their students take standardized tests and perform acceptable on them. The Panel noted the arguments for and against

---

38. The Report of the (Nebraska) Governor's Christian School Panel, January 26, 1984, pp. 1ff.

standardized testing but concluded that "the better evidence is that standardized tests can be of some help in determining academic achievement."[39] As this book goes to print, Nebraska's unicameral legislature is considering the implementation of these recommendations.

Standardized testing is not a perfect indicator of student progress. But Dr. Raymond Moore insists that it is the best indicator available, a more effective indicator than teacher certification.[40] Arizona imposes no regulations on private schools and simply requires home schools to give their students annual standardized tests. If this is sufficient to monitor educational progress in Arizona, it should be sufficient in other states as well.

(7) *Private Accreditation.* Another possibility, which I do not necessarily endorse but mention for further consideration, is to allow private agencies to accredit private schools. For example, the national headquarters for Accelerated Christian Education could accredit A.C.E. schools; or, since most states have a state association of Christian schools, the state could delegate the accreditation power to that association.

(8) *Lack of Uniformity.* One might also look at whether the state's regulations are applied uniformly to all schools, or whether certain Christian schools have been singled out for discriminatory enforcement as a means of closing them down. This might raise due process and equal protection arguments. In *Whisner*, the defense established that many of the state's public schools did not comply with the minimum standards which were being forced upon the private schools.

(9) *Vagueness.* The due process clause of the Fourteenth Amendment might be used to attack the procedures for enforcement, or even to attack the regulations generally on the ground of vagueness. The Supreme Court of Wisconsin recently struck down that state's compulsory attendance law on the ground of vagueness, *Wisconsin v. Popanz,* 332 N.W. 2d 750 (1983). The Georgia Supreme Court followed suit in *Roemhico v. Georgia,* 251 Ga., 308 SE 2d 154 (1983).

(10) *Lack of Authority.* One should also look to the state's own constitution and statutes, to see whether authority exists for the regulations in question. In some states, the state board of education was established by a provision of the state constitution, or by a comprehensive act of the legislature. Frequently, the constitutional provision or legislative act gives the state board of education the authority to regulate public schools in the state, but does not mention anything about authority to regulate private schools. If so, state regulations may not be valid or maybe an unconstitutional delegation of power. The legislative history of applicable state laws should be researched to determine if they were intended to apply to private schools, or whether private schools were to be exempted. In this area, state constitutions, statutes, and regulations

39. Ibid., pp. 26ff.
40. Dr. Raymond Moore, stipulated testimony, *Minnesota v. Budke*, Ottertail County, Minnesota, June 1982.

will vary sharply from one state to another. While constitutional principles apply throughout the country, it is important to study the constitution, enabling act, statutes, and regulations of each individual state.

Health and Safety Standards

Many fundamental Christians who strenuously object to government control over their curriculum, teacher qualifications, etc., are nevertheless willing to accept some government regulation of school health and safety standards. Since this concerns physical safety and physical needs, many regard it as legitimately within Caesar's domain. They insist, however, that such regulations be drafted and applied reasonably and fairly, keeping in mind the unique needs of a private school.

In 1980, I represented the teacher of a small, one-room private school with about a dozen students in the north woods country of rural Minnesota. She was charged with several safety violations, some of which were clearly applied unreasonably. For example, one regulation required a wall between the furnace and any area used for classrooms. Now, for a large public school that uses a boiler or other large furnace, that probably makes sense. But this one-room school used a wood-burning stove, as do many homes and businesses in northern Minnesota; and a wall separating the stove from the students would merely prevent the heat from circulating, and the students would freeze! Fortunately, those regulations provided for obtaining a variance from that regulation. The school complied with other reasonable regulations.

Others have noted disparities between regulations governing churches and regulations governing schools. This is especially true concerning maximum occupancy. It seems strange that a church building should legally be permitted to hold 600 persons for Sunday school on Sunday morning, but only 200 for school during the week, unless it is thought that Providence is more protective on Sunday mornings than at other times.

Certainly Christians, viewing man as created in the image of God and viewing children as a special gift of God, believe that Christian schools and day-care centers should be as safe as possible. But they have the right to insist that health and safety standards be tailored to fit the special needs of a small church school, and that the regulations be applied reasonably.

Christian Schools and the IRS

As if Christian schools didn't have enough problems with state and local education establishments, it appears they have another adversary: the Internal Revenue Service.

The recent case of *Bob Jones University v. Internal Revenue Service*, [103 S. Ct. 2017, 76 L. Ed. 157 (1983)], poses a grave danger to all Christian institutions. One is tempted to dismiss the case because of Bob Jones University's unpopular racial views. But the IRS selected this defendant to establish what could be the most dangerous precedent for Christian institutions yet decided by any court anywhere.

Believing that the Bible prohibits interracial marriage and that an integrated campus could lead to interracial marriage, Bob Jones University refused to enroll blacks until 1975. In that year the University relaxed its policy somewhat, and began admitting blacks but refused to allow interracial dating. The IRS determined that this was a racially discriminatory policy, and therefore revoked Bob Jones University's tax-exempt status. While this might seem reasonable on the surface, nothing in the Internal Revenue Code prohibits tax-exempt organizations from practicing discrimination, and Congress, in its various Civil Rights Acts, specifically exempts religious institutions!

But that didn't stop the IRS. They claimed that tax exemption is not a constitutional right; it is simply a matter of legislative grace. The government can exempt those whom it pleases, and tax the others. And the government should exempt only those organizations or institutions whose actions conform to "public policy".

But wait a minute! What is "public policy"? And who decides what constitutes this policy? Congress never said private Christian schools couldn't discriminate. The IRS, an unelected governmental body, reached that determination entirely on its own. And the Supreme Court agreed!

So not only is tax-exempt status limited to those institutions which follow "public policy"; the IRS can make its own determinations as to what public policy is. This sounds dangerously close to totalitarianism.

The implications are frightening. If the IRS can determine that schools which practice racial discrimination violate public policy, why can't they do the same for schools that practice sexual discrimination or religious discrimination? What about schools that refuse to admit women, or men, or homosexuals? What about schools that require a Christian (or Jewish, or Moslem) profession from their students and faculty?

While the *Bob Jones* decision was limited to educational institutions, it could easily be expanded to churches and charities. What prevents the IRS from determining that churches which refuse to ordain female clergy, or homosexuals, or atheists, are violating public policy and not entitled to tax-exempt status?

It has been argued that Bob Jones University remains free to exercise its religious beliefs; it simply loses its tax-exempt status by doing so. In a sense that is true; but as the United States Supreme Court recognized long ago in a landmark case, *McCulloch v. Maryland*, 17 U.S. (4 Wheat.) 316 (1819), " The power to tax involves the power to destroy." The decision does not prohibit Bob Jones University from operating, but it will certainly make its operation more difficult.

Suppose you wanted to give a gift of one million dollars to a Christian college. You thought about giving the gift to Bob Jones University, and you also thought about giving it to Liberty Baptist College. Then you discover that a gift to Liberty Baptist will be tax deductible; but no such deduction is allowed for a gift to Bob Jones University. Might this not influence your decision? The IRS action affects not only Bob Jones University but also the average citizen's right to freely exercise his religion.

IRS action is not limited to those schools which overtly practice discrimination. In 1978, the IRS issued a proposed ruling which, if it had gone into effect, would have required all church schools and other tax-exempt schools in the United States to either meet a racial quota or implement an elaborate affirmative action program to recruit minority students and faculty. Those schools that failed to do so would have their tax-exempt status revoked, and if the school was operated by a church, the church would also lose its tax exemption.

Using a devious technique, the IRS tried to slip the regulation into effect quietly by publishing the proposed ruling in the Federal Register without holding any hearings.

The proposed ruling would have been disastrous for many Christian schools, even though most of those Christian schools engaged in no racial discrimination. Many had low minority enrollments because of cultural or geographical factors over which they had no control. One example is Hillcrest Lutheran Academy in Fergus Falls, Minnesota. Hillcrest is a three-year high school, operated by the Church of the Lutheran Brethren of America, a low-church, evangelical Lutheran body composed of approximately 10,000 members, most of whom live in rural, upper midwestern or northwestern parts of the country. Lutherans in America generally come from the predominantly Lutheran countries of Europe, Scandinavia and Germany. When they arrived in America, they formed Lutheran synods which generally followed the ethnic lines of the old countries. The Lutheran Brethren were organized in 1900 as a union of several churches which separated from another Lutheran synod of Norwegian background. Since the Lutheran Brethren exist largely in areas poppulated by Scandinavian people in general and Norwegians in particular, they continue to reflect that background, although they impose no racial restrictions on membership and in fact actively evangelize people of all races and are working to establish congregations in other parts of the country such as the south and southwest. They engage in extensive missionary activity in Africa and Asia, and it is said that the Lutheran Brethren mission church in Africa has a larger membership than does the Church of the Lutheran Brethren in the United States.

Nevertheless, because of the ethnic background of the Church of the Lutheran Brethren in America, Hillcrest Lutheran Academy reflects that same background. The overwhelming majority of its students (but not all of them) are white, and most of these are Norwegian. The school itself is located in Otter Tail County, which has the second-highest percentage of Norwegian-Americans in its population of any county in the entire nation, and there are very few nonwhites in the entire county or, in fact, within a substantial distance. Clearly, a racial quota would be disastrous for Hillcrest Lutheran Academy, and an extensive affirmation action program would be extremely difficult to implement. Yet, the proposed IRS ruling gave no consideration to the unique needs of a school such as Hillcrest Lutheran Academy, or a school run by the Syrian Orthodox, or by an Orthodox Jewish School, or any other such body.

Fortunately, the word got out before the ruling went into effect. The IRS received over 300,000 letters protesting the proposed ruling, and when, under pressure from Congress, the IRS finally held hearings, over 200 people came to testify against the ruling and only one came to testify in favor of it. But the IRS gave no indication of rescinding its proposal. Consequently, Congressman John Ashbrook (R-Ohio) and Robert Dorman (R-Calif.) amended the 1979 treasury appropriation bill with a special provision which prohibited the Internal Revenue Service from expending any funds to revoke the tax-exempt status of private schools.

In 1980, IRS officials threatened to again try to impose the ruling after the 1979 treasury appropriations bill expired, but Congress stopped them again. However, in what appears to have been a "sweetheart" suit in which the IRS, while technically a defendant, actually cooperated with the plaintiffs, a Mississippi group called The Lawyers' Committee for Civil Rights Under Law brought an injunctive action against the Internal Revenue Service in the Federal District Court in the District of Columbia to require the IRS to pressure Christian schools in Mississippi in a manner similar to the 1978 proposal. The IRS did not vigorously oppose the suit, and when the order was granted, the IRS did not appeal it. The order presently affects only Mississippi, although there are now efforts under way to expand it in light of the *Bob Jones* decision. The court battle is far from over as other schools and churches fight to retain their tax-exempt status. Very recently, Congress has once again voted to deny the IRS any funding to carry out this order, but there are indications the IRS may interpret the bill contrary to the congressional intent.*

One school subject to IRS harassment is run by Grace Bible Church of Greenwood, Mississippi, a church with less than thirty members. Its school, Greenwood Christian School, has an enrollment of fewer than fifteen students. The school's first graduate was a National Merit Scholar, and standardized tests have indicated that the school provides good education. The school currently has no black students, but has enrolled black students in the past, has never turned away minority students, and expects to enroll minority students in the future. Yet, this school is subject to the order and to IRS harassment just as much as any other school. Even the church itself is affected by the order; the District of Columbia court order of June 2, 1980, requires Grace Bible Church and others to supply the IRS with an annual statement as to the racial composition of the church's board of elders.[41] The issue is still being litigated in the courts. Fortunately, the battle is far from over. If the IRS moves to revoke the church's tax-exempt status, the church should then be able to litigate the constitutional issues.

What motivates such harassment? Either a conscious and deliberate desire to make things difficult for private and/or Christian schools, or a belief that Christian schools are in fact thinly disguised "segregation academies"

* *See end of chapter.*
41. *The Advocate*, January 1981, pp. 14a-15a.

established to avoid racial integration. An investigation by University of Wisconsin scholars Virginia Davis Nordin and William Lloyd Turner dispels the notion of segregation. Their study, which may be found in the February, 1980 issues of *Phi Delta Kappan*, found that Christian schools are growing not only in the South but all across the country, and in areas like rural Wisconsin, where the desire to avoid integration could not possibly be a factor. The study further found that parents who send their children to Christian schools, regardless of their geographical area, give the same reasons for doing so: ''poor academic quality of public education, a perceived lack of discipline in the public schools, and the fact that public schools were believed to be promulgating a philosophy of secular humanism that these parents found inimical to their religious beliefs.''

The study further found that parents who enroll their children in Christian schools tend to come from churches of the sponsoring denomination or from churches holding similar doctrinal positions. The parents and students tend to be very active in their churches, indicating that religion and not racism is the motivating factor behind Christian schools.

The study further found that once a parent decided to enroll his child in a Christian school, he usually enrolled all his school-age children simultaneously and kept them in Christian school for the remainder of their school years. If the purpose was merely to avoid busing, one would think that the parents would have taken only the children affected by busing and enrolled them in private school, and would have returned them to public school once the busing threat ended.

One final fact should be noted. The study focused in on two fundamentalist schools in Louisville, Kentucky, which are frequently accused of being segregation academies established as one-year havens for parents who wish to avoid forced busing. It concluded that the percentage of the students in the two fundamentalist schools which would have been subject to busing during the current school year had they been enrolled in public school, was smaller than the percentage of such students in the general Louisville population![42]

The Accreditation Factor

On rare occasions, one is privileged to actually live history in the making. It was my privilege to serve as a visiting professor of law at Oral Roberts University's new O. W. Coburn School of Law, during the school's recent accreditation battle with the American Bar Association.

After much planning, the O. W. Coburn School of Law opened for its first freshman class in the fall of 1979. The school sought accreditation from the American Bar Association, because in order to practice law one must take and pass a state bar exam. In forty-three states and the District of Columbia one

---

42. Virginia Davis Nordin and William Lloyd Turner, *Phi Delta Kappan*, February 1980; cited and quoted in *Human Events*, vol. 40, no. 28 (July 12, 1980), pp. 1, 6.

is not allowed to take the state bar exam unless he has graduated from an ABA-accredited law school.

The law school was optimistic about accreditation, provided it could get a fair hearing. But the faculty was concerned about getting a fair hearing. For one thing, the school teaches a philosophy of law which is diametrically opposed to that of most law schools in the United States, in that it stresses traditional law as God-given absolutes instead of the legal positivism prevalent today. And second, the O. W. Coburn law students, like all students at Oral Roberts University, are required to express a Christian commitment. Every student is required to sign the Code of Honor Pledge, in which he recognizes that "our Lord and Savior, Jesus Christ, is the Whole Man," and express his aim to "follow in His footsteps and to develop in the same ways in which He did." The student promises that he will "endeavor to seek the will of God for my life and to exemplify a Christlike character, through my daily personal prayer life and study of the Word of God, and through faithful group worship on and off campus." He further promises to yield his personality to the "healing and maturing power of the Holy Spirit and earnestly strive to manifest God's love toward [my] fellowman by following Christ's example to 'do unto others as I would have them do unto me.' " Faculty members are required to make the same commitment. Students who refuse to make the commitment are not enrolled. While such a commitment is obviously essential to the integrity and preservation of any Christian institution, there had been intimations that the ABA might consider it to be in violation of ABA Standard 211, which then provided, "The law school shall maintain equality of opportunity without discrimination or segregation on the ground of race, color, religion, national origin, or sex."

In the fall of 1980, an ABA site team visited the university to evaluate the O. W. Coburn School of Law. Several months later, the team issued a 100-page report on O. W. Coburn School of Law. It contained a few minor suggestions for improvement, but on the whole was highly complimentary of the school, its library, facilities, faculty, students, and its overall spirit. After receiving and reading the report, the law school faculty thanked God and the site team that ABA accreditation seemed assured.

But by a letter dated May 3, 1981, the Accreditation Committee of the ABA denied accreditation. It gave four reasons for doing so: (1) The Code of Honor Pledge as applied to students violates Standards 211 (a) (ii); (2) The requirement of a Christian commitment for faculty members violates ABA Standard 211 (b); (3) The school's faculty salary structure was insufficient to attract and retain persons of high ability; and (4) Demand for admission for the second-year class had fallen below the school's estimates.

It was clear from the beginning that the issue boiled down to the Christian commitment of the university. Reasons three and four were clearly superfluous, and were later dropped even as a pretext for denying accreditation. Faculty salaries at the O. W. Coburn School of Law, while very slightly below the national average for law schools, were higher than those of several ABA-accredited law schools, and were comparable to the average law school faculty salaries for other law schools in the South and Southwest. The decline in enrollment of the 1980 freshman class compared to the 1979 freshman class was due to a lack of active recruiting and also to an overall decline in law school enrollments nationwide that year, and had nothing to do with whether ORU was providing quality legal education and producing good lawyers. Despite the accreditation battle, enrollment for the 1981-82 school year increased. After the battle was over, enrollment increased dramatically in 1982-83 and 1983-84.

Attempts to resolve the matter quickly proved fruitless. At one meeting, an Accreditation Committee member asked the ORU dean what he would do if one of his law professors married another person of the same sex. When the dean responded that such a person would be fired, the questioner seemed disturbed. Shortly thereafter, the law firm retained to represent ORU recommended that the university file suit in federal district court against the American Bar Association, alleging a denial of First and Fourteenth Amendment rights. The law school faculty unanimously voted to follow that recommendation.

The lawsuit was filed in June 1981. At a hearing in the United States District Court for the Northern District of Illinois, Eastern Division, July 15, presiding Judge James Moran stated, "I have very serious doubts about 211 as presently constituted." ORU law clerk Marc Powell described the hearing,

> The ABA had fifteen lawyers in the courtroom—we had three. When the judge instructed our attorneys to draft the order, they (ABA attorneys) stormed out. They didn't talk to anyone.[43]

On July 17, Judge Moran issued an order "That defendant American Bar Association is enjoined from denying provisional accreditation to ORU's Law School in whole or in part on the basis of ABA Standards 211's prohibiton against religious restrictions."

In obedience to this order, in August 1981, the American Bar Association granted ORU its provisional accreditation—the maximum accreditation any new law school can receive. The ABA also voted to amend Standard 211 to a less restrictive form.

In 1982 the ABA again amended Standard 211. The standard now exempts from the nondiscrimination requirement schools with a distinct religious purpose or affiliation, provided they make their discriminatory policies clear to all concerned, provided they do not unduly infringe upon academic freedom, and provided their policies do not preclude a diverse student body. At the time the amended version was adopted, those sponsoring the change assured the convention delegates that the amended standard should not preclude the Coburn School of Law from achieving full accreditation, provided its present policies are continued. The amendment passed without opposition; however, the phrases

43. *Tulsa Tribune*, 16 July 1981.

"diversity" and "academic freedom" are vague and nebulous and could become troublesome to Christian law schools if given a restrictive interpretation by a hostile accreditation committee.

The basic issue which had confronted the ABA actually transcended Oral Roberts University. It involved whether a Christian law school can exist in the United States of America today. In order for it to be Christian, it obviously must employ faculty members who share its Christian convictions. It must also admit students who are sympathetic to its Christian commitment, both in their world view and in their life-style. The ABA rule would require ORU to employ law professors who believe and teach directly contrary to its Christian philosophy. This would destroy the very things for which ORU and all other Christian schools stand.

The ABA's position was couched in terms of academic freedom and religious toleration. In actual result, it was the opposite. For they would make all law schools the same, since none could maintain a unique and distinct world view and life-style. R. J. Rushdoony said it well:

> Let us examine this idea of academic freedom a little more closely; in actuality, it is a totalitarian doctrine which is hostile to real academic freedom. Academic freedom means, if taken literally, freedom of the academy, that is, freedom of the school. It means or should mean, that anyone has the freedom to establish a school to propagate his ideas and to maintain that school without interference, as long as it does not violate the criminal and moral laws of society.
>
> If the idea of academic freedom stated by *Columbia Encyclopedia*, the American Association of University Professors, and others were applied to religious freedom, and it is being applied, the result would be anarchy. It would mean that in every church every kind of religious idea would have equal rights. This would make it impossible to maintain the integrity of any church.
>
> The same is true of colleges and universities. Let us assume that we, as a group of persons with a particular kind of religious faith, holding to a system of Christian theology, to a particular school of economics, a type of philosophy, and a very definite concept of education, established a college. The modern doctrine of academic freedom would *deny* us the right to have our kind of school; it would insist that we could have no standard of faith and character which we could require of all faculty members. The modern doctrine of academic freedom would rob us of the right of controlling our own school, because it would demand the total independence of all faculty members to be "without control or restraint." We would be obliged to support the school without any right of control, or else we would be called intolerant, fascistic, and many like names for withdrawing our support.
>
> The practical result of this doctrine of academic freedom is the destruction of freedom . It denies us the right to establish schools to propagate, develop, and establish a particular faith and philosophy. This concept of academic freedom is a superb totalitarian doctrine, an instrument for the

destruction of any and every educational institution. No institution can be free to maintain its faith and philosophy when the total right of subversion is insisted on by the doctrine of so-called academic freedom. *All the rights, all the power, are placed in the hands of subversives by this idea of academic freedom.* The right to hold to a particular faith and philosophy, and to maintain a college in loyalty to that position, is specifically denied. The doctrine is called academic freedom, but it is actually *academic totalitarianism.*[44] (Emphasis original.)

Academic freedom, then, means that Oral Roberts University has, or should have, the right to establish a law school to propagate a biblical philosophy of law. The student who wishes to learn that philosophy of law, and the teacher who wishes to teach that philosophy of law, may associate with the university in doing so. The teacher who wishes to teach a different philosophy of law is free to apply elsewhere or even establish his own law school.

That is what academic freedom is really all about. If a school wishes to expose its students to all viewpoints and inculcate no particular philosophy to its students, it is free to do that. If the purpose of the school is to promote a particular viewpoint, it should be free to do that also.

But the ABA would have denied Oral Roberts University the right to have a Christian law school. The ABA would have denied ORU students their right to study law from a Christian standpoint. And the ABA would have denied Christian citizens their right to employ an attorney with that type of training. Far from being religious liberty, this constitutes the establishment of secularism expressly prohibited in *Abingdon v. Schempp*, supra. The ABA Accreditation Committee operated under the guise of tolerance and liberty, but its actions actually promoted intolerance and bigotry.

Law schools are not the only schools having problems with accreditation. In many fields of study, schools are forced to compromise their standards and doctrinal positions in order to obtain accreditation. The result is not only the suppression of true academic freedom but also a weakening of the entire accreditation process. All too often, accreditation or lack thereof is no longer an indication of a school's academic standards.

One good example is Dallas Theological Seminary. No one questions the quality of instruction at Dallas. It is often called the "Harvard of the Evangelicals." Even Richard Quebedeaux, who would not be in agreement with the strong conservatism of Dallas Theological Seminary, nevertheless acknowledges in his book, *The Worldly Evangelicals* that the curriculum at Dallas "may well be the most traditional, highly structured, and academically demanding professional theological curriculum in the United States today."[45] Yet Dallas steadfastly refuses to seek accreditation from the Association of Theological Schools, because in order to do so it may have to compromise its

44. R. J. Rushdoony, *Law and Liberty*, pp. 51-52.
45. Richard Quebedeaux, *The Worldly Evangelicals* (San Francisco: Harper & Row, 1978), p. 31.

requirement of adherence to its doctrinal position, its stand on admitting women as Th. M. students or faculty members, its dress code, and other standards. Dallas has sought and obtained accreditation from the Southern Association of Colleges and Schools, because that association considers only academic standards and nothing more. But despite the high quality of instruction at Dallas, a few theological schools will not accept some transfer credits from Dallas Theological Seminary because it is not accredited by the Association of Theological Schools. Probably many smaller and less-known schools have suffered far more for their refusal to compromise their standards in order to obtain accreditation, than has a prestigious institution like Dallas.

It is argued that accreditation is, after all, nothing but a recommendation by a private accrediting associaton. Such an association ought to be free to accredit on whatever standards it chooses. That might be acceptable, so long as accreditation does not involve any "state action." However, in many fields of study, denial of accreditation can lead to denial of certain rights, privileges, or benefits, conferred or denied by the state. If a law school is denied accreditation by the American Bar Asociation, then for all practical purposes its graduates cannot practice law in forty-three states or the District of Columbia, because those states have implicitly recognized the American Bar Association as their official accrediting agency. Furthermore, graduates of an unaccredited law school cannot hold government positions with the Department of Health, Education and Welfare, or serve as judge advocates in the United States Armed Forces, since those institutions require that all their attorneys be graduates of ABA-accredited law schools. Thus, ABA accreditation becomes in effect "state action."

This is true in other areas as well. Education majors who graduate from unaccredited colleges might, in some jurisdictions, be denied teaching certificates. Graduates of an unaccredited medical school might be denied the right to practice medicine, and the list could go on and on. In a few instances, students at unaccredited schools have even been denied benefits by the Veterans' Administration. When the state decides whether to grant or deny certain rights, privileges or benefits based upon accreditation or the lack thereof, then said accreditation becomes in effect "state action" and the accrediting agency must therefore respect the constitutional rights of the individual person or institution.

In a few instances, the state itself seeks to act as an accrediting agency. The state of New Jersey, for example, required that no institution of higher education may offer degrees, conduct classes leading toward degrees, or even advertise its existence, unless it obtains a license from the state. Shelton College and the Bible Presbyterian Church which sponsors it brought suit against the state of New Jersey in federal district court, challenging whether the statue can be applied to genuinely religious institutions of higher learning. On behalf of Shelton College, Attorney William Ball argued that a genuinely religious college has the right, under the First Amendment, to teach, to solicit students, to advertise, and to issue degrees. Federal Dist. Ct. Judge Dickinson R.

Debevoise agreed, and issued an injunction prohibiting the state of New Jersey from interfering with Shelton College's right to teach and advertise. The state appealed, and the Third Circuit Court of Appeals affirmed the ruling of Judge Debevoise. However, Judge Debevoise refrained from ruling on the question of whether Shelton College could issue degrees without a license, as that issue was being litigated in the state courts of New Jersey.[46]

On August 9, 1982, the New Jersey Supreme Court ruled that the state could prohibit Shelton College from issuing degrees unless the school is licensed by the State Board of Higher Education. Shelton College then appealed to Federal Judge Debevoise, who determined the the New Jersey Supreme Court had exceeded its jurisdiction in deciding the constitutionality of the statue because the Federal District Court had reserved that issue to itself. The constitutionality of the New Jersey requirement is thus still being litigated in the federal courts.

Arguments can be made for and against accreditation. Defenders of accreditation argue that the practice is necessary to weed out "diploma mills" that issue worthless degrees. But this argument assumes, first, that the state and/or accrediting agencies have the right to regulate such matters; and second, that the state is capable of distinguishing between a diploma mill and a legitimate institution, whereas citizens and students are not.

Is the state capable of evaluating the quality of education at a pervasively religious institution? Can the state evaluate and accredit religious programs without becoming "excessively entangled" with religion? If the state can prohibit unlicensed religious institutions from issuing degrees in such fields as ministry and theology to students planning to enter the ministry or other Christian service, does this not constitute a substantial burden upon free exercise of religion? Isn't the state then dictating who can and cannot serve as a pastor?

One thing is clear. Whenever accreditation takes on the color of state action, the criteria to be considered by the accrediting agency should be strictly limited to matters that directly pertain to academic standards and which affect professional competence. Anything beyond that invades the constitutional rights of American citizens and becomes academic totalitarianism.

Government Aid to Private Schools

The courts have often struck down government aid to private schools as an unconstitutional establishment of religion: *Committee for Public Education and Religious Liberty (PEARL) v. Nyquist*, 413 U.S. 756 (1973); *Levitt v. Committee for Public Education and Religious Liberty*, 413 U.S. 472 (1973); *Meek v. Pittenger*, 421 U.S. 349 (1975).

The cases that have ruled otherwise have involved government aid in areas where religious doctrine was clearly not involved. For example, in *Wolman v.*

---

46. William Ball, "Federal Court Uphold Right of College to Teach and Advertise Without License from State Board of Education," *The Advocate*, April 1980, p. A-11; Kathryn O'Mally, attorney associated with William Ball, telephone interview, 3 September 1981.

Walter, 433 U.S. 229 (1977), the Supreme Court approved government aid in the form of loaning textbooks to parochial school students, state-financed academic testing of parochial school students using standardized tests, and providing therapeutic services such as guidance counseling, speech help, and remedial reading. The Court said these services were constitutional, so long as they were performed away from the "pervasively sectarian atmosphere of the church-related school." In *Cochran v. Louisiana State Board of Education*, 281 U.S. 370 (1930), a Louisiana statute providing for the purchase of secular textbooks for use by school children in both public and private schools was held to be constitutional, since the primary beneficiaries were not the parochial schools but the children, some of whom happened to be enrolled in parochial schools. For similar reasons, the Court upheld the state policy of providing school bus transportation for children to and from private schools. *Valencia and Lanzi v. The Blue Hen Conference, et al.*, 476 F. Supp. 809 (DC. Del. 1979) approved, at least in part, private school participation in public school athletic programs.

State-financed busing of students to private schools has generally been upheld as constitutional, *Everson v. Board of Education*, 330 U.S. 1 (1947). And on June 29, 1983, the Supreme Court upheld a Minnesota law providing tuition tax credits for parents who incur expenses sending their children to private or public schools, *Mueller v. Allen*, 77 L.Ed. 2d 721. It is possible that the rigid position taken by the courts a decade or so ago is being relaxed somewhat, and that other indirect forms of aid will be allowed.

The Court often seems to distinguish between direct and indirect forms of aid. The test seems to be: Does the government program benefit primarily the school, or the student and his parents? If it benefits the student or his parents, it is more likely to be considered indirect and therefore constitutional.

The Court also considers whether the aid furthers the clearly religious purposes of the school, or simply the more secular purposes. For example, if the government supplied secular textbooks, that might be permissible; if it supplied Bibles, that would be struck down.

Many proposals to aid private schools are being considered. Increasingly, people recognize that the parents of private school children are the victims of "double taxation" since they pay taxes to support the public schools and then pay tuition to private schools. Though it is partly a matter of choice, it is also a matter of religious necessity for many. Aid to private schools might be justified as an accommodation of religion, since it seeks to redress an imbalance that makes it difficult for Christians to exercise their religious beliefs. Many also argue that such aid would permit more minorities and lower-income persons to send their children to private schools. Others recognize that private schools save the taxpayers billions of dollars a year and the taxpayers' education bill would rise sharply if all private school students enrolled in public schools.

Tuition tax credits are being considered in many states as well as in Congress. The Supreme Court's latest ruling, coupled with the National

Commission's Report and rising dissatisfaction with public schools, should increase chances for passage.

Another proposal is the "voucher plan," whereby the state would issue to the parents of each school-age child a voucher or check which the parent can "cash in" to pay for his child's education at the public or private school of his choice. This proposal has an excellent chance of being upheld as constitutional because it aids parents rather than schools and because it allows the parent to utilize either public or private schools, and thus does not necessarily favor either.

Still another proposal is a tax "check-off," whereby taxpayers would be allowed to indicate on their tax forms that the share of their taxes designated for education be paid to a private school chosen by the taxpayer. All undesignated funds would be allocated to the public schools.

A similar proposal would allow taxpayers to declare a conscientious objection, based on religious training and belief, to supporting the public schools. Such persons would then be exempted from paying that portion of their taxes to support public schools, upon a showing that they have made a contribution equal or greater in amount to a private school. This proposal might gain constitutional support from the *Abood v. Detroit Board of Education* decision, 431 U.S. 209 (1977), in which the Supreme Court ruled that an employee may refuse to pay union dues provided he contributes a comparable amount to charity.

These proposals have generated great excitement and optimism and may be effective in the future.

However, private schools should be very cautious about seeking or accepting public assistance. Government aid leads to government control. Though there is less a danger with the voucher plan or tuition tax credits than with direct aid to private schools themselves, even there the danger is present, for the state might attempt to restrict the types of schools for which vouchers or tax credits would be acceptable.

Such control might begin with seemingly innocuous regulations that nearly everyone could support, such as prohibiting the use of vouchers or tax credits for schools that practice racial discrimination. But that regulation could lead to prohibiting vouchers or credits for schools that refuse to employ atheists, or homosexuals, or that use uncertified teachers, or that teach "too much religion." The prospect is dangerous. And once the private school becomes dependent upon government funds, it would have great difficulty turning them down when the regulations become onerous. The pressure to "knuckle under" would be hard to resist, and it would come not only from government officials but also from well-meaning parents and church members who don't want to be burdened with the extra costs that would result from losing government funds.

Another subtle danger may exist which Christians have probably never dreamt of. In chapter 11 we discussed lawsuits under Section 1983 of the Civil Acts Right of 1871. Private persons and institutions cannot be sued under this statute, only those persons who operate under color of state action. Recently the 10th Circuit U.S. Court of Appeals in *Williams v. Milonas* ruled that, because it received as much as a third of its funding from government sources and participated in state educational programs, a Utah private school can be sued under federal civil rights laws since, due to the government funding, its actions become "state action." Parents had claimed that the school's use of lie detector tests, mail censorship, excessive physical force, and isolation violated the First and Fourteenth Amendments.[47] Whether this will be accepted by other courts is uncertain, but it is another dangerous possibility.

Tom Anderson tells of a Georgia backwoodsman who captured a pack of wild hogs that everyone knew could not be captured. Asked how he did it, the backwoodsman drawled, "I started by setting out a few ears of corn for them. For weeks none of the hogs would touch the corn. Then a few would sneak up, grab an ear, and scamper off into the underbrush. Before long they were all eating the corn, each knowing that if he didn't, the others would. And they stopped hunting for food on their own. I started building a fence around the corn, and then a trap door. And as they were quietly eating, I sprung the trap. They really squealed when they found out I had 'em," the backwoodsman concluded, "but *I can trap any animal on the face of the earth if I can just get him to depend on me for a free handout!*"[48]

I have previously argued that if government aid to private schools violates the establishment clause, then to the same extent government control of private schools violates the free exercise clause. But the reverse is also true. Government aid may be a genuine attempt to help private schools and redress the imbalance of "double taxation," but it also may be merely "baiting the trap" in order to obtain government control over private schools.

If Christian schools become dependent upon government funds, they may find themselves having to make compromises to avoid losing those funds. In this way, Christian schools could rob themselves of the Christian character that is the very reason for their existence.

> Be not ye afraid of them. Remember the Lord, who is great and awe-inspiring, and fight for your brethren, your sons, and your daughters, your wives, and your houses. (Nehemiah 4:14b).
>
> For if thou altogether holdest thy peace at this time, then shall there enlargement and deliverance arise to the Jews from another place; but thou and thy father's house shall be destroyed: and who knoweth whether thou art come to the kingdom for such a time as this? (Esther 4:14).

47. "Government Funding Makes Private School Open to Suits, Say Federal Courts," *Church & State*, June 1983, p. 20.

48. Tom Anderson, "Bapartisan Treason," LPN Record.

* Currently IRS Form 5578, Annual Certification of Racial Nondiscrimination for a Private School Exempt from Federal Income Tax, makes special provision for religious schools at which at least 75 percent of the students come from the sponsoring denomination or which draw their students from certain areas of the country. See this form for further information.

Chapter 17

The Christian and Home Schools

In the fall of 1978, a Christian man came to my law office and asked me to represent his family on a legal matter. A delinquency petition had been filed in the juvenile court in his county, charging that his children were juvenile delinquents because they were habitually truant from school. My client and his wife had removed their children from the public schools and were teaching them in a school they had established in their own home.

This was my first exposure to home schooling.

But home schooling is far more commonplace than I had realized, and its ranks are swelling rapidly. I know of no accurate statistics as to exactly how many children are enrolled in home school. John Holt of Holt & Associates, a home-school advocate and author of a magazine entitled *Growing Without Schooling*, estimates the figure to be at least 10,000, though he stresses that is a very conservative estimate.[1] Dr. Raymond S. Moore, a developmental psychologist and former teacher, principal and city school superintendent, college dean and president, graduate programs officer for the U.S. Office of Education, and now Director of the Hewitt Research Center, has estimated that, including children who are excused from school for disability or for other reasons are enrolled in some form of home instruction program, the total number of children enrolled in home study may be as high as 250,000 to 500,000.[2] Precise figures are hard to establish because home schoolers are by nature independent people, and many do not wish to "go public" for fear of harassment by public school authorities.

Many parents who teach their children at home do so through the use of curricula supplied by various schools across the country. An old and well-known

1. Telephone interview with Donna Richoux, *Growing Without Schooling* editor, Boston, Massachusetts, 2 September 1981.
2. Telephone interview with Raymond S. Moore, Berrien Springs, Michigan, 2 September 1981.

school is Calvert School (105 Tuscany Road, Baltimore, Maryland 21210). Founded in 1897, Calvert School currently has approximately 5,000 students enrolled in its program 3,000 of whom are in the United States. Its students have included the children of former U.S. Ambassador George F. Kennan, and the children of business executives, missionaries, military personnel, and others stationed in remote areas where American schools are not readily available. Entertainers, evangelists, and other parents who constantly travel and want to keep their families with them, have often used Calvert School materials; these include the well-known children of the Osmond singing team, and the Lowell Lundstrom Gospel Team. Unlike some other home school curricula, Calvert's material is not organized around a narrowly Christian theme. However, it does stress strong academic standards, good morals, and wholesome materials. Prior to enrollment, Calvert normally requires parents to obtain permission from local school authorities or supply other evidence that they have a legal right to engage in home schooling.

One of the fastest-growing home school centers is Christian Liberty Academy (203 East McDonald Road, Prospect Heights, Illinois 60070). This school stresses traditional education, fundamentalist Christianity, patriotism, and a conservative political persuasion. "On-campus" students attend Christian Liberty Academy in a traditional Christian school setting in Prospect Heights, but the vast majority of its students are in "satellite schools" operated by their parents in homes across the nation. All graduates of Christian Liberty Academy receive a high school diploma which does not distinguish between its on-campus and off-campus graduates. Parents perform the actual face-to-face instruction in their homes, and tests, papers, book reports, etc., are sent in to Christian Liberty Academy to be graded and returned. Each student is tested at admission and furnished with a curriculum that reflects his or her level of achievement in each subject. For example, a ten-year-old child may be at a fourth grade level in Math, second grade in English, and sixth grade in geography.

Pensacola Christian Correspondence School (5409 Rawson Lane, Pensacola, Florida 32503) has a similar orientation and uses the A Beka series produced through Pensacola Christian College.

American Christian Academy (P.O. Box 335, Colleyville, Texas 76034) has devised a program of home schooling using materials similar to Accelerated Christian Education (ACE), which stress self-study and self-reliance.

The Hewitt-Moore Child Development Center (P.O. Box 9, Washougal, Washington 98671) has developed a Christ-centered curriculum based upon solid professional research in child development.

The Christian Life Academy distributes a home school curriculum called Alpha-Omega. It may be ordered through the Academy at P.O. Box 5858, Lynwood, Washington 98036.

The Home Study Institute (Washington, D.C. 20012) is operated by Seventh-Day Adventists but also serves people of other denominations and is highly recommended. Rod and Staff, a Mennonite publisher (Crockett, Kentucky

41413), publishes books for use in home achooling that are used by Christians of many denominations. Those desiring a Catholic education might turn to courses offered by Our Lady of Victory Catholic School (P.O. Box 5181, Mission Hills, California 91345). And those desiring a more open or liberal educational system might turn to Santa Fe Community School (P.O. Box 2241, Santa Fe, New Mexico 87501). Many parents, however, choose to design their own curricula.

Is a Home School Really a School?

In one home school case I represented, the county superintendent of schools refused to even look at the home school to see if it met his standards. Even after the judge dismissed the charges against the mother, the superintendent still stated to the press that he would not go out there because there was nothing to investigate; he investigated only schools, and a home by definition is not a school.

But unless the law of a particular state gives a unique definition of school, there is little to support that superintendent's position. The *American Heritage Dictionary of the English Language* defines "school" simply as "an institution for the instruction of children."[3] And *Black's Law Dictionary* defines "school" as "an institution or place for instruction or education."[4] Some courts have agreed with this definition. In 1950, the Supreme Court of Illinois, reversing the conviction of a home-school parent for an alleged violation of the state's compulsory education statute, stated:

> Appellants contend the State has failed to prove the child was not attend-
> ing a "private school" within the intention of the legislature. They argue
> that a school, in the ordinary meaning of the word, is a place where in-
> struction is imparted to the young, that the number of persons being taught
> does not determine whether the place is a school, and by receiving instruc-
> tion in her home in a manner shown by the evidence, the child was attend-
> ing a private school. We agree with this construction of the statute. Com-
> pulsory education laws are enacted to enforce the natural obligations of
> parents to provide an education for their young, an obligation which
> corresponds to the parent's right of control over the child. . . . The object
> is that all children shall be educated, not that they shall be educated in
> an particular manner or place. See *Commonwealth v. Roberts*, 159 Mass. 372,
> 34 N.E. 402. Here, the child is being taught third-grade subjects, has regular
> hours for study and recitation, and shows a proficiency comparable with
> average third-grade students. There is nothing in the record to indicate
> her education is in any way being neglected. We think that the term "private
> school," when read in the light of the manifest object to be attained, includes
> the place and nature of the instruction given to this child. The law is not
> made to punish those who provide their children with instruction equal

3. *American Heritage Dictionary of the English Language*, 1976 ed., s.v. "School".
4. *Black's Law Dictionary*, 4th ed. (1957), s.v. "School."

or superior to that obtainable in the public schools. It is made for the parent who fails or refuses to properly educate his child. [*People v. Levisen*, 90 N.E. 2d 213 (1950)].

And in a similar decision, the Appellate Court of Indiana stated:

> A school, in the ordinary acceptation of its meaning, is a place where instruction is imparted to the young. If a parent employs and brings into his residence a teacher for the purpose of instructing his child or children, and such instruction is given as the law contemplates, the meaning and spirit of the law have been fully complied with. This would be the school of the child or children so educated, and would be as much a private school as if advertised and conducted as such. We do not think that the number of persons, whether one or many, make a place where instruction is imparted any less or more a school. [*State v. Peterman*, 70 N.E. 550 (1904)].

So in the absence of any statutory definition of school in your state, a home school would probably be considered a school. Some states, however, have statutory provisions which define school in other ways. Pennsylvania Statute 24:2731, in a requirement of highly questionable constitutionality, defines a private school as " a school maintained, or classes conducted, for the purpose of offering instruction for a consideration, profit, or tuition, to five or more pupils at one and the same time. . . ." Under Pennsylvania law, home instruction is legal if approved by the local superintendent, but it does not constitute a school. Minnesota statute 120.10, the constitutionality of which is currently being litigated, defines school as one "in which all of the common branches are taught in the English language from textbooks written in the English language and taught by teachers whose qualifications are essentially equivalent to the minimum standards for public school teachers of the same grades or subjects. . . ." In Minnesota, unless the home school parent/teacher has "qualifications" "essentially equivalent" (whatever those terms mean) to public school teachers, the home instruction does not qualify as a school.

The statutes across the fifty states vary widely. As a general observation, if the statute simply says "public or private school" without further definition, the home school will probably qualify as a private school. However, if the statute contains language such as "public or private school or other means of instruction," the courts will probably conclude that the legislature did not intend home schools to be considered as private schools, but rather as "other means of instruction." See *T.A.F. and E.M.F., Juveniles v. Duval County*, 273 So. 2d 15 (1973).

Is a Home School Legal?

The only way to answer this is to look at the statutes of the state in which you live. The statutes vary, and some of them are ambiguous and confusing. For further clarification, it may be necessary to seek attorney opinions, state court decisions, or state department of education rulings.

The laws of some states expressly permit home schools. For example, New Jersey statute 18L14-14, provides that:

> Every parent, guardian or other person having custody and control of a child between the ages of six and sixteen years shall cause said child regularly to attend the public schools of the district or a day school in which there is given instruction equivalent to that provided in the public schools for children of similar grades, ages and attainments *or to receive equivalent instruction elsewhere than at school.* (Emphasis supplied.) (See *State v. Massa*, 231 A. 2d 252, 254 [1967]).

Massachusetts A.L.M.c 76§1 allows for home instruction for a child who is "being otherwise instructed in a manner approved in advance by the superintendent or the school committee." Since Oklahoma does not define "school" and does not require that private schools be accredited or use certified teachers, home schools have had little difficulty in that state. The same is true in many other states.

Utah Statute 53-24-1 (B)(2) expressly authorizes home schooling, as does Arizona Statute 15-802 (B)(1). Others implicitly allow home schooling by their silence. Some states, like New Jersey, simply require "equivalent instruction" elsewhere than at school.

Though no state expressly forbids home schooling, some make it very difficult. North Dakota Statute 15-34. 1-03 (1) requires that all parochial and private schools be approved by the County Superintendent of Schools and the Superintendent of Public Instruction, and that no such school shall be approved unless the teachers therein are legally certified in the state of North Dakota. Thus, home schools are not permitted in North Dakota unless the parent is a certified teacher or wealthy enough to hire one.

Home schools are gaining increased acceptance among professional educators. Ten years ago they were unheard of; five years ago they were scoffed at as an unworkable throwback to the nineteenth century. But as public school standards decline, more and more professional educators see merit in home schooling. The February 1983 issue of *Phi Delta Kappan*, the nation's most respected publication dealing with education, contained several articles highly favorable to home schooling.

One such educator is Dr. Raymond Moore. A developmental psychologist and former graduate programs officer for the U. S. Office of Education, Dr. Moore has been a public elementary teacher, principal, school superintendent, professor of education, and college dean and president. In 1964 Dr. Moore established the Hewitt Research Center, a national foundation to study and promote efficiency in education. As Dr. Moore studied the deficiencies of the American educational system, he became increasingly convinced, somewhat against his will at first, that home schools were achieving the desired learning results that public schools failed to achieve. He has since become an articulate advocate of home schools and has written many books, including *School Can Wait* (Washougal, Washington: Hewitt, 1979); *Home Grown Kids: A Practical*

Handbook for Teaching Your Children at Home (Waco, Texas: Word Books, 1981); *Home-Spun Schools: Teaching Children at Home — What parents are Doing and How They are Doing It* (Waco, Texas: Word Books, 1982); and *Better Late Than Early* (New York: Reader's Digest—Hewitt, 1976). He and his wife, also an educator, publish a monthly newsletter called the "Parent Educator and Family Report" which can be ordered through the Hewitt Research Foundation, Box 9, Washougal, Washington 98671.

Another home school advocate is John Holt. Author of such well known works as *How Children Fail* and *How Children Learn*, Holt has recently become a forceful advocate of home schools and discusses home schooling extensively in his book, *Teach Your Own: A Hopeful Path for Education* (New York: Delacorte Press, 1981). Holt publishes a monthly newsletter titled "Growing Without Schooling" which may be ordered through John Holt at 729 Boylston Street, Boston, Massachusetts 02166.

Still a third is Ed Nagel, headmaster of the Santa Fe Community School. He has formed the National Association for the Legal Support of Alternative Schools and publishes a newsletter entitled "Tidbits" which can be ordered through P.O. 2823, Santa Fe, New Mexico 87501. Like Holt, Nagel operates from a liberal perspective, rather than that of an orthodox Christian. Many Christians will disagree with some of Holt's and Nagel's ideas, but their materials can be most helpful nevertheless.

A fourth (and I could name many others) is John Marlett, a former public school teacher, principal, superintendent, and professor at Sheybogan County Teachers College. Frustrated by the permissivism, humanism, and poor quality of public schools, Marlett retired to his rural home in the north woods country of Minnesota and established a home school for his own eight children and several neighboring children of his denomination. He frequently testifies in home school cases and is developing a school curriculum based on the Bible.

Some states and school systems actively cooperate with home schoolers. John Holt describes instances in which home school children are allowed to participate in band, orchestra, athletics, or other public school programs. Such cooperation is possible with private and parochial schools also. [5]

But in a few states public school officials bitterly fight home schools. Several reasons account for this. The very idea of a home school runs contrary to what many public educators have believed all their lives—that children learn best in a group, institutionalized setting. And the educational establishment regards home schools as a personal threat, because as the movement continues to grow, it could threaten the livelihood of teachers and administrators. Furthermore, many school districts receive state aid based on the number of students enrolled in their schools. In some states, this aid amounts to more than $1000 per student which is lost to the local school district (and saved by the taxpayers) if the student is taught at home.

5. John Holt, "Schools and Home Schoolers: A Fruitful Partnership," Phi Belta Kappan, February 1983, pp. 391-394.

Is Home Schooling a Constitutional Right?

Home schools are legal in some states. Other state laws are ambiguous and require a ruling from the court. But if state law prohibits home schooling, another question must be asked: Is the law constitutional?

Many court decisions have touched upon this question, but few have addressed it directly. Generally, the courts have tried to construe statutes in certain ways so as to be constitutional or have decided the cases on other grounds that allow home schooling.

In the previous chapter we discussed at length the constitutional principles of free exercise of religion, compelling state interest, and least restrictive means which apply to the defense of Christian schools. Most of these principles apply almost identically to home schools. Thus the cases of *Wisconsin v. Yoder, Wisconsin v. Popanz, Ohio v. Whisner, Kentucky v. Rudasill,* and others are relevant for home schoolers as well—as are the cases decided against Christian schools such as *North Dakota v. Shaver, North Dakota v. Rivinius,* and *Nebraska v. Faith Baptist Church.*

Home schoolers suffered a loss in *West Virginia v. Riddle,* (No. 14910, W. Va. Dec. 11, 1981). Mr. and Mrs. Riddle had withdrawn their children from the public school for religious reasons and were teaching them at home. The court acknowledged that "by all accounts and the record below, the Riddles did an excellent job—possibly better than the public schools could do."

But the court noted that West Virginia law provided a remedy for those who objected to public education. Section 18-8-1 [1951] allows those who object to public education to request that the County Superintendent of Schools exempt them from the compulsory attendance law and approve instruction in the home. Yet the Riddles had never requested any such exemption. The court ruled that this exemption procedure provided a constitutionally sound, flexible vehicle for balancing the state's interest against the First Amendment rights of students and parents. The court therefore affirmed the conviction. If the Riddles had sought exemption, it might have been approved. Had the exemption been disapproved, and the Riddles had then gone to court, the result might have been different.

Nebraska home schoolers won a victory in *In Re Interest of Rice* (285 N. W. 2d 223 [1979]). Mr. and Mrs. Rice had taken their child out of the public schools and were teaching him at home through curricula supplied by Christian Liberty Academy. Instead of prosecuting the parents for not sending their child to school, the state took the matter to juvenile court, claiming the child was neglected. The Nebraska Supreme Court noted that the child was making adequate educational progress and concluded that the child was therefore not neglected. However, the court did not rule upon the constitutionality of the compulsory attendance law or whether the parents were technically in compliance with it.

To date, the case that has most directly addressed the question of the constitutionality of laws which prohibit home schooling is a lower-court decision in the State of Minnesota in 1980, *Minnesota v. Lundsten*.[6] Minnesota statute 120.10 requires that children attend school, and defines "school" as (1) a public school or (b) a private school in which all the common branches of learning are taught in the English language out of textbooks printed in the English language, and by teachers whose qualifications are essentially equivalent to the minimum standards for public-school teachers of the same grades and subjects. In this case, I represented a northern Minnesota family who had established a home school using correspondence courses from Christian Liberty Academy. They even gave their home school a name, Northwoods Academy. The mother did the teaching though she was not a certified teacher nor a college graduate. She had slightly over one semester of college, with an excellent grade-point average, had extensive secretarial experience, had taught Sunday school and served as a Sunday school superintendent for many years and was highly regarded in that capacity, and had even served on the school board. But she was not a certified teacher and was nowhere close to being certifiable. We used a two-pronged argument: (1) that the home school was in compliance with the statute, since the statute spoke of a "qualified" rather than a "certified" teacher, and "qualification" simply means "the possession by an individual of the qualities, property, or circumstances, natural or adventitious, which are inherently or legally necessary to render him eligible to fulfill an office or perform a public duty or function";[7] and (2) even if they were not in compliance with the statute, the statute was unconstitutional as it violated their right to the free exercise of religion and their right as parents to control the education of their children.

We attempted to establish compliance with the statute by presenting the testimony of two expert witnesses, professors of education, who had visited and evaluated this home school and testified favorably as to the curriculum and the mother's teaching ability; by pointing to her extensive teaching experience on the school board; and by arguing that the best proof of a qualified teacher is whether or not she can teach. We attempted to prove that she could teach by introducing as evidence the result of standardized testing which demonstrated that the students had made good progress during the school year, better than that which their public-school contemporaries would be expected to accomplish, and by showing samples of the school work they were doing in the home school compared with the sloppy work they had done in the public school. The state, however, argued that the statute required that a teacher be certified or very close to being certifiable. The jury agreed with the state, finding the parents guilty. Since there were no other issues concerning compliance with the statute other than the qualifications of the mother as a teacher, this was in effect, a finding that her qualifications were not essentially equivalent, and therefore the parents did not comply with the compulsory education statute.

---

6. Order, *Minnesota v. Lundsten*, Lake of the Woods County, Minnesota, May 20, 1980.
7. *Black's Law Dictionary*, 4th Ed. s.v. "Qualification".

We then argued to the judge that the statute was unconstitutional, for in accordance with the *Yoder* ruling cited earlier, the purposes of the compulsory education statute were being fulfilled by the home school. Therefore, even if the statute was not technically complied with, the state's compelling interest in education was being fulfilled. We then established by painstaking examination of the textbooks used in the public school, that the teaching in the public school conflicted with the parent's religious beliefs, and therefore violated their right to the exercise of free religion and their right as parents to control the education of their children. We argued that, since the state's compelling interest was being fulfilled without technical compliance with the statute, the state had no right to enforce the compulsory attendance statute against these parents in violation of their constitutional rights.

The court agreed ruling that the Minnesota compulsory attendance statute was constitutional on its face, but unconstitutional as applied to my clients. As Judge Shanahan wrote in his decision:

> The States' purpose in requiring that private school teachers possess certain qualifications, is merely to effectuate the compulsory education statute. As previously noted, the compulsory education is to prepare for the responsibilities of citizenship and to teach children to be self-sufficient and self-reliant. There has been no demonstration that these goals are not being fulfilled in this case, in fact, quite to the contrary. The testimony indicates that the children are in a structured well-run program that more than fulfills the requirements. Rev. Paul D. Lindstrom, who is headmaster of Christian Liberty Church, Prospect, Illinois, testified that the Northwood Academy (Lundsten School) [the name my clients had given to their home school] is affiliated with the Christian Liberty Church and that they pass on the progress of the child's education and that on the completion of the 12th grade, the child receives a certificate of completion or diploma. That there are higher educational institutions that recognize their students as qualified for entrance for higher education. The State made no attempt to discredit this testimony and the State failed to show that the Lundsten children are not being taught courses which will make them good citizens, self-supporting and self-reliant in the future. The State did not show that the children are idle or any abuse in child labor, but to the contrary agreed that they are attending school at home and being taught the common branches. The State has failed to demonstrate a compelling interest superior to the right of the defendants.

The judge therefore set aside the jury's verdict and granted an exemption from the compulsory-education statute. The county attorney, who was a very capable and honorable opponent throughout the trial, decided after consultation with state officials not to appeal the decision, which was probably a wise decision based on the excellent record established to sustain the judge's ruling.

Because the decision was not appealed, it remains only a county court decision, and therefore, its national or even statewide effect is limited. But basically the decision upholds the right of parents to educate their children in home schools, provided (1) they can demonstrate that public schooling violates their religious convictions and/or parental rights; and (2) they are capable of providing their children with an education of sufficient quality to fulfill the state's compelling interest in education. A definitive ruling by the Supreme Court could be in accord with these principles.

Three more home school cases have taken place in Minnesota since the *Lundsten* decision, though none of them have addressed the issues as thoroughly. In 1983 in Houston County, home schoolers won a victory on constitutional grounds in *Minnesota v. Tollefsrud*. They suffered losses in Itasca County (*Minnesota v. Newstrom*) and in Otter Tail County (*Minnesota v. Budke*), but the *Budke* conviction was unanimously reversed by a three-judge district court panel which granted the Budke family exemption from the statute on grounds similar to *Yoder*. The State has appealed the *Budke* ruling and the Defense has appealed the *Newstrom* ruling, so both cases are currently before the Minnesota Supreme Court.

Still another case has attracted considerable publicity and deserves careful attention: *Duro v. North Carolina*, 712 F2d 96 (1983). North Carolina generally does not regulate private schools, but does require that all children attend school (North Carolina General Statute § 115C-378). State officials contend that home schools do not qualify as schools under their statute—a questionable contention. Duro petitioned the Federal District Court to enjoin the State of North Carolina from prosecuting him for his home school, claiming that any requirement that his children attend school violates his First Amendment right to free exercise of religion. The District Court agreed, but the 4th Circuit Court of Appeals reversed holding that the state's interest in education outweighed Duro's right to free exercise of religion. The Supreme Court denied certiorari and refused to hear the case.

This decision has been publicized as a defeat for home schools, but in reality it can easily be distinguished from most other cases: (1) Duro made no argument that his home instruction would prepare his children for the obligations of citizenship or to be able to support themselves. The Court expressly noted his failure to do so and thereby provided home school attorneys with the "handle" by which to distinguish the *Duro* case from their own. Most home schoolers do make this argument, and quite successfully. (2) Duro made no argument that his home school constituted a school within the meaning of the statute; instead, he argued his case solely on constitutional grounds. (3) The Court based its decision not only on the state's interest in education as articulated in *Yoder*, but also on Article 1, § 15 of the North Carolina Constitution which guarantees children the right to an education. That provision obviously has no application outside North Carolina; in fact, the U.S. Supreme Court has ruled in *San Antonio Independent School District v. Rodriguez*, 411 U.S. 1 (1973), that education is not a fundamental right under the U.S. Constitution.

Is Home Schooling a Good Idea?

While home schooling may not be right for everyone, on the whole it is a positive development. In general, a system which includes a diversity of educational opportunities available to parents makes for a better and freer society than one in which everyone is educated the same way and by the same institutions. The former leads to freedom and diversity; the latter leads to regimentation, brainwashing, and totalitarianism.

Academically, we have noted that students in private schools tend to do better than students in public schools. Dr. Raymond S. Moore, whose impressive qualifications were noted earlier, claims direct or indirect contact with over 10,000 home-school children, and he has yet to see one who is not performing significantly better than national norms. He further states that all national studies on home schools to date show home school children to be significantly higher in academic achievement than the national norms. Based upon his own studies, Dr. Moore believes they rank higher in behavior and sociability as well.[8]

Some might question how this is possible in a home-school setting where the only teachers are parents who in all probability are not certified and perhaps not even college graduates. There are several answers. First, what parents may lack in academic preparation, they may more than make up for in their personal knowledge of their children and rapport with them. Second, in a home-school setting they are able to give their children much more individualized attention. According to Dr. Reed A. Benson, studies have shown that the average public school student receives an amazingly small amount of direct person-to-person contact with his teacher. Also, in private/home school, instruction can be individualized so that the student can work at his own level. He is not held back by students who are slower or less motivated, nor is he forced to work beyond his level to keep up with students who are ahead. He does not have to move on until he fully understands the material.

In the *Lundsten* case mentioned above, one expert witness who testified for the defense was Dr. Charles Nielson, former Professor of Elementary Education at the University of North Dakota and present Director of the Learning Laboratory at Itasca Community College of Grand Rapids, Minnesota. Dr. Nielson testified that the personal relationship a parent/teacher has with his child/pupil is vitally important for learning. He further testified that the best teacher may not be able to provide good education in the wrong circumstances. Some teachers may be well-qualified to handle a formal, structured classroom, but be utterly incapable of teaching their own children because the necessary rapport just isn't present. Other parents may be academically or otherwise unprepared to handle a large classroom situation, but might be very effective at teaching their own children. Some might be good at both, and some might be good at neither. Dr. Nielson further testified that in a very

---

8. Dr. Raymond Moore, Stipulation of Expected Testimony, *Minnesota v. Budke*, (Otter Tail County, Minnesota, June 25, 1982); Telephone conversation between Dr. Moore and John Eidsmoe, February 1, 1984.

real sense everyone is a teacher and everyone is a student every day of his life, and that all teaching and learning experiences—sitting in classrooms observing teachers, reading about teacher instruction, teaching Sunday school, teaching ordinary household chores to one's children, etc.—serve to make one a better teacher.[9]

Dr. Raymond Moore has evaluated thousands of home schools. At some of these home schools, he says, one or both parents is a certified teacher; in most cases they are not. Sometimes they are college graduates, sometimes only high school graduates, and sometimes less than high school graduates. Dr. Moore states that in all of these evaluations he has not been able to detect any correlation whatsoever between the academic progress of the home school children and the educational background or teaching credentials of the parent/teacher! He says the home school children of high school graduate parent/teachers average just as well as the children of college-educated parent/teachers and certified parent/teachers. On the surface this sounds surprising, for it contradicts everything we've been told. Dr. Moore insists that it makes sense, because the basic qualities of an effective teacher, especially at the lower grade levels—warmth, responsiveness, and rapport—cannot be learned in a classroom.[10]

But what about socialization? Is the child who is a product of a home school going to grow up isolated from others, and unable to relate to others in a social environment?

This is a valid question, but it is not within the jurisdiction of the court to decide. As District Court Judge Lindsay Arthur ruled in a recent Minnesota case,

> Socialization is a much proclaimed need, but in a free society it fortunately cannot be required, to the contrary even monasticism cannot be denied if it be freely chosen. And socialization is not ever and always beneficial; Associating with detrimental individuals is usually detrimental, particularly in the young and malleable.[11]

And in the Massachusetts *Perchemlides* case, the court ruled:

> The question here is of course not whether the socialization provided in a school is beneficial to a child, but rather, who should make that decision for any particular child. Under our system, the parents must be allowed to decide whether public school education, including its socialization aspects, is desirable for their children.[12]

---

9. Dr. Charles Nielson, trial testimony, *Minnesota v. Lundsten*, Bemidji, Minnesota, February 22, 1980.

10. Dr. Raymond S. Moore, Stipulation of Expected Testimony, *Minnesota v. Budke*, Otter Tail County, Minnesota, June 24-25, 1982.

11. *In the Matter of the Welfare of (Names of juveniles not released)*, file no. 89134, Judge Lindsay Arthur, Dist. Ct., 4th Juvenile Dist., Hennepin Co., Minnesota (1978).

12. *Perchemlides v. Frizzle*, Hampshire County Superior Court civil action no. 16641 (Massachusetts), November 13, 1978, Judge John H. Greaney.

Both of these rulings perhaps reflect the U.S. Supreme Court's ruling in *Yoder* 92 S. Ct. at 1537:

> We must not forget that in the Middle Ages important values of the Western World were preserved by members of religious orders who isolated themselves from all worldly influences against great obstacles. There can be no assumption that today's majority is "right" and the Amish and others like them "wrong." A way of life that is odd or erratic but interferes with no rights or interests of others is not to be condemned because it is different.

But most of the home-school people are not eccentrics who isolate themselves from the mainstream of society. Most are social people, well-liked by others in the community, and in some cases have served on school boards or held other responsible positions of public trust. They have never been in conflict with the law; most have never even had a traffic ticket. They differ from others only in that they have strong convictions and are willing to act upon them.

Furthermore, their children have generally been well adjusted according to the conclusion of psychologists. The children generally have many friends, associate regularly with their public-school friends after school, and have an additional advantage: they relate to people of all ages, rather than merely those of their own grade level.

Other ways exist to provide socialization: church, Sunday school, Boy and Girl Scouts, 4-H Clubs, and the old institution we call the neighborhood. In some communities, home school families frequently get together to provide added socialization for their children. This has a decided advantage over the socialization of the public schools. This way, parents can guide the socialization of their children, foster the development of good social manners and habits, and build important character qualities. Exposure to drugs, obscene language and other undesirable influences can be avoided.

Social maladjustment probably results more from inadequate family relationships than from inadequate interaction with one's peers. A close home life fostered by the home school could help a child develop a strong sense of security and self-worth which would better enable him to socialize with his peers as he matures. Actually, much fear of the home school idea probably stems from the fact that "we've never done it that way before," and much of our attachment to a formalized school setting is based upon the old idea, "this is the way we've always done it."

Nevertheless, a home school may not be for everyone. In some families both parents work, thus making home school difficult (but not impossible, because some families do it). In others, the necessary rapport may be lacking. In still others, the family may feel that it simply does not have the ability to ensure adequate socialization outside the school setting. Those who decide full-time home schooling is not for them may still consider home instruction as a supplement to regular schooling.

For those who decide on home schooling, the following suggestions may be helpful:

(1) Before making a firm decision, obtain competent legal advice regarding the legality of home schooling in your jurisdiction. If the laws of your state make home schooling illegal, you may have to establish their unconstitutionality through an appeal to the state supreme court or even to the federal courts. If public school education violates your religious convictions and you can provide quality education for your children at home, you should ultimately be successful in a constitutional battle. There are, however, no guarantees and a court battle is expensive. It is important to remember that a court case poorly prepared and lost sets an unfavorable precedent that will hurt other home schoolers.

(2) To establish that you are serious about home schooling and that you are not merely using home schooling as a subterfuge for truancy, draw up a formal structure for your home school. Incorporation is not necessary unless required by local law. Draw up a formal constitution setting forth the name and purposes of your school, its officers, procedures, etc. Have this notarized, so the date on which your school was founded is established lest someone say it was drawn up as an afterthought.

Maintain regular days and hours of classroom instruction. Though this may be somewhat flexible in a home-school setting, it should not appear that classes are conducted haphazardly.

(3) Make sure your children have adequate educational resources available. These may include items such as desks, books, encyclopedias, globes, etc. Used sets of encyclopedias and good books can often be picked up at Salvation Army or Goodwill stores for reasonable prices. Also, take advantage of frequent field trips to educational places such as zoos, libraries, museums, concerts, etc. The growing home computer market has tremendous possibilities for home schooling in terms of information, computer programs, and other resources.

(4) Make sure that music, art, and physical education are not neglected. Singing can be done around the piano or with a guitar. Calisthenics or individualized sports such as jogging, cross-country skiing, skating, or swimming could be stressed or team sports encouraged at the local YMCA or YWCA, church league, or Little League organization. Some have even found private or public schools willing to accept their children in school activities.

(5) Assistance from other home schooling groups is available. Often in larger communities home schoolers have associations to support one another and give their children the opportunity to socialize. Several organizations which assist home schoolers include the Hewitt Research Center, P.O. Box 9, Washougal, Washington 98671; Holt & Associates, 729 Boylston St., Boston, Massachusetts 02116; and the National Council of Parent Educators, 6508 65th St., Columbus, Nebraska 68601. One of the most active state organizations is the Texas Assn. for Home Educators, P.O. Box 835105, Richardson, Texas 75083. This organization provides many helpful services, including information on curricula and teaching aids, legal information and a lawyer referral service, an exchange service to help home school families get in touch with other home school families

in the area, information on how to start a home school, and a newsletter.

Two groups provide legal support for home school families prosecuted by the state. The Home School Legal Defense Association, P.O. Box 26280, Fort Worth, Texas 76121 serves primarily Christians, while the National Association for the Legal Support of Alternative Schools, P.O. Box 2823, Santa Fe, New Mexico 87501, serves others as well. To obtain financial support from these organizations, it is generally necessary to join before you are prosecuted.

Home schoolers have different reasons for objecting to the public schools. Some are religious and political conservatives who feel the public schools are liberal, socialistic, humanistic, or immoral. Others are "free spirits" who think the public schools are repressive and conformist. While each group has different motivations and premises, they come to remarkably similar conclusions. On one point they are firmly united: Parents have the right to direct the education of their children and they can usually do it better than the state.

(6) Consider utilizing a structured curriculum furnished by some of the institutions listed earlier in this chapter. Schools such as Christian Liberty Academy and Pennsacola Christian Correspondence School offer curricula compatible with the beliefs of conservative Christians. Calvert School offers a curriculum of academic excellence. Ed Nagel's Santa Fe Community School offers assistance in establishing a more liberal curricula. A structured curricula can be helpful, especially for inexperienced home school teachers. Some home school parents start with an organized program, then devise their own after a few years of experience.

(7) Always be courteous with public-school authorities or other government officials. Do not necessarily assume they are your enemies. Remember that according to Romans 13:4 they are God's servants, and accordingly, deserve respect. It is even possible that "with well-doing ye may put to silence the ignorance of foolish men" (I Peter 3:15). But be careful about relying upon them for assistance; remember they may be under great pressure from peers or superiors.

(8) Do not start home education unless you have the time and dedication to do a good job. If you enter into it haphazardly or halfheartedly, you will do your children a disservice and give home schooling a bad name for everyone else.

The struggle of private schools and home schools to be free from state control, and the struggle of state authorities to control them, is being waged fiercely by both sides—and for good reason. Christian education presents the clearest modern challenge to the authority and jurisdiction of the Omnipotent State. Others protest state regulation of various aspects of their lives; but none have articulated their challenge in clear philosophical, ideological, and jurisdictional terms.

When Christian parents and Christian educators proclaim "Jesus is Lord!", they declare by implication that Caesar is *not* Lord—that Caesar has no jurisdictional authority over the education of their children. For God has given that authority to parents, and He has coupled that authority with the command that children be raised in the nurture and admonition of the Lord.

> Hear, O Israel: the Lord our God is one Lord:
> And thou shalt love the Lord thy God with all thy heart,
>   and with all thy soul, and with all thy might.
> And these words, which I command thee this day, shall be
>   in thine heart;
> And thou shalt teach them diligently unto thy children, and
>   shalt talk of them when thou sittest in thine house, and
>   when thou walkest by the way, and when thou liest down,
>   and when thou risest up.
> (Deuteronomy 6:4-7)

Chapter 18

The Christian and the Cults

> But there were false prophets also among the people, even as there shall be false teachers among you, who secretly shall bring in destrictive heresies, even denying the Lord that bought them, and bring upon themselves swift destruction. And many shall follow their prenicious ways, by reason of whom the way of truth shall be evil spoken of. And through covetousness shall they, with feigned words, make merchandise of you; whose judgment now for a long time lingereth not, and their destruction slumbereth not. (II Peter 2:1-3)

Thus spoke Peter, writing approximately A.D. 66. Cults are not a modern phenomenon; they have been with us for thousands of years. The Gnostics, the Pelagains, the Donatists, the Montanists, the Arians, the Socinians, and many others have reared their heads throughout history, and it is amazing to note the similarities between the modern cults and those of ancient times. As Solomon said, there is nothing new under the sun (Ecclesiastes 1:9). Upon close examination the doctrines of the modern cults are usually just new combinations of the older heresies, cast in new trimmings.

But Paul warned Timothy that "The time will come when they will not endure sound doctrine but, after their own lusts, shall they heap to themselves teachers, having itching ears; and they shall turn away their ears from the truth, and shall be turned into fables," (II Timothy 4:3-4). In I Timothy 4:1 Paul indicates that this rise in apostasy shall be a sign of the last days before Christ's return.

Whether or not we are living in the last days, no one but the Father knows for certain (Mark 13:32). But one sign that we may be living in the last days is the unmistakable evidence that cults are rapidly growing in modern society. University of Chicago anthropologist Irving Zaretsky estimates that the number of Americans involved in "fringe religious cults" may be as high as twenty million or even more.[1] Though many think this figure is exaggerated, all agree that cults are growing dramatically.

What is a Cult?

The dictionary definition, "a system or community of religious worship and ritual, especially one focusing upon a single diety or spirit"[2] could include almost any religious group. But what are the distinguishing marks of a cult? On what basis may we claim that the Jehovah's Witnesses are a cult, but the Presbyterians are not?

Dr. Anthony A. Hoekema, professor of systematic theology at Calvin Theological Seminary, offers the following explanation of the distinguishing traits that differentiate a cult from a church or denomination: (1) The cult makes an abrupt break with historic Christianity and its confessions. (Note, however, that many cults do not have origins in Christianity at all; many have their origins in the East.) (2) They have a tendency to major in minors—that is, they take minor points of Scripture, and build major doctrines around them. (3) They exhibit a tendency toward perfectionism, a feeling of superior holiness. (4) They attach great significance to an extrascriptural source of authority, such as Mary Baker Eddy's *Science and Health*, or the Jehovah's Witnesses' *Watchtower*. (5) They venerate a person besides the Lord Jesus Christ as equal to Him or nearly equal to Him, or even superior to Him. Such a person could be Jim Jones, Hare Krishna, Swedenborg, Mary Baker Eddy, or Sun Myung Moon. (6) They devalue the person of the Lord Jesus Christ. Often they call Him the Son of God, but redefine the term in such a way as to mean that He is not equal to God, certainly not the Second Person of the Godhead as traditional Christians believe. (7) They deny justification by grace alone. Again, they often redefine their terminology. Many cultists claim to believe in grace, but frequently rely upon works for salvation or an admixture of grace and works. (8) They regard their group as the exclusive community of the saved; all others outside the group are headed for a lost eternity. (9) They believe their group will have a central role in eschatology, that is, in the last days.[3]

Van Baalen notes that the cultist also displays a strong hostility and suspicion of everyone outside his group.[4]

The church generally has identified as the mark of a heretic or a cult, their rejection of the Trinitarian nature of the God head and their rejection of the hypostatic union (union of the fully divine and fully human natures) of Jesus Christ.

---

1. Irving Zaretsky, cited by James C. Hefley, *The Youthnappers* (Wheaton, Illinois: Victor Books, 1977), p. 9.

2. *The American Heritage Dictionary of the English Language*, s.v. "Cult."

3. Anthony A. Hoekema, *The Four Major Cults*, (Grand Rapids, Michigan: Eerdmans, 1963, 1965), pp. 373-388.

4. Jan Karel Van Baalen, *The Chaos of Cults: A Study in Present-Day Isms* (Grand Rapids, Michigan: Eerdmans, 1938, 1965), pp. 359-360.

We must use these criteria carefully in evaluating religious organizations. Nearly all religious organizations exhibit at least one of these traits to a greater or lesser degree. Certainly some of them are somewhat characteristic of evangelical Christianity. Though the line between a cult and traditional religion is fine and sometimes difficult to distinguish, it can be drawn with the counsel of Scripture and the guidelines suggested above.

Why are the Cults growing?

James C. Hefley suggests several reasons for the recent growth of cults. First, he believes the lack of strong family ties creates insecurity among young persons, and the cults become the "family" many young persons desire. Dr. Herbert Hendin, a Columbia University psychoanalyst who studies youth movements for the Center for Policy Research, says, "I've never seen one of these young people who didn't have some kind of serious failure in family life."[5]

Second, Hefley mentions the superficiality of other relationships, particularly romantic relationships, as a reason why young people today turn to cults. They are looking for someone to whom they can belong, and the cults offer them that sense of security. Third, Hefley suggests that modern American education, by undermining belief in absolute values, leaves youth with nothing to cling to. In the search for certainty, they turn to the cults.

And fourth, Hefley blames the church. Many of today's churches teach a watered-down, liberalized version of Christianity which involves no absolute truths and leaves people searching for answers. Other churches may involve a dead orthodoxy, where there is no spiritual life. The cults promise young people the certainty and vitality that they often have not found in the church.[6]

Are Cults Dangerous?

I believe they are. First, they teach false doctrine. That alone has disastrous consequences and can even mean eternal damnation for adherents.

Second, some cults seem to involve an allegiance to foreign powers which could compromise the security of the United States. Third, many cults tend to break up the American family unit. It is true that Jesus said, "For I am come to set a man at variance against his father, and a daughter against her mother, and the daughter-in-law against her mother-in-law" (Matthew 10:35). But taken in context, that is the exception rather than the rule. We are told in Exodus 20:12 that we are to honor our parents, and obedience to parents is further stressed in Ephesians 6:1-4 and Colossians 3:20-21. The ideal situation is a family united in the Christian faith. But the cults, by their special emphasis upon the young and impressionable, often ignore older persons and set children against their parents.

---

5. Herbert Hinden, quoted in *U.S. News and World Report*, June 14, 1976: quoted in Hefley, p. 198.
6. Hefley, pp. 197-205.

The tactics used by many cults are especially dangerous. Christians are certainly commanded to evangelize and to try to persuade others to accept the Christian faith. Certainly persuasion is a legitimate tool in a free society. But the tactics used by the cults often go beyond mere persuasion. They include many tactics comparable to the brainwashing used by the Communists on American prisoners of war in Korea and Vietnam.

The Unification Church of Sun Myung Moon is a good example. The "Moonies" recruitment campaigns concentrate on college campuses and other places where large numbers of young people congregate. They seem to single out those who appear lonely, and offer them friendship. Generally they begin with bland statements about Bible study and love of God and country that are compatible with orthodox Christianity (Moon, to his credit, is an avowed anticommunist).

Shortly thereafter, the proselyte is invited to attend a weekend retreat. There, all the subtle techniques of brainwashing are brought to play. It is well known that people are more susceptible to psychological suggestion when they are fatigued, so every effort is made to keep the newcomers fatigued: little sleep at night, food low in lasting energy, etc. The indoctrination at these retreats is strong, and most of all, the newcomer is given little or no opportunity to be alone, because solitude enables one to think, and thinking produces questions. Most of all, he is made to feel he belongs, that this is the family and friendship that he has been searching for. After a weekend retreat such as this, often followed by week-long retreats, the newcomer frequently emerges a complete zealot, willing to give all for the Unification Church.

Though not characteristic of all cults, the tendency of some such as People's Temple toward violence is frightening. The satanic cults in particular have at times engaged in both animal and human sacrifice, both historically and in the present.[7]

Finally, by their excesses, cults tend to give all religions including traditional Christianity a bad name. The recent effort by the Internal Revenue Service to restrict the activities of tax-exempt religious organizations poses a threat to all churches, but is motivated in part by concern over abuses by the cults.

Are Cults Protected by the First Amendment?

Cults are protected by many constitutional guarantees, such as freedom of speech, freedom of press, freedom of assembly and association, and the right to privacy. Those rights apply to everyone, religious or otherwise. And the free speech guarantee applies to everyone including cultists, so long as it does not involve solicitation of crime, subversion, violent revolution, obscenity, or a threat to public safety.

But what about the First Amendment guarantees of religious freedom? Do

7. Dick Donovan, "Deadly Horror of the Devil Cults," *Weekly World News* 3:2 (October 20, 1981), p. 37.

these include protection of the cults? Obviously, this depends upon whether or not the cults are regarded as religions in the constitutional sense of the term.

In chapters 8, 9, and 10, we analyzed the background, framing and meaning of the First Amendment. We saw that there probably was no precise consensus as to the meaning of the term "religion" in that day. Some, like Madison and Jefferson, and also some of the Baptist leaders, probably understood the term to apply to all religious groups including what we today would call cults. Jefferson, you will recall, said the amendment provided freedom to those who do believe and to those who do not believe; and a leading Baptist explained that the amendment freed persons to believe in one god, two gods, twenty gods, or no god at all.

While this was probably the view of many who were influential in that day, it probably was not the view of the majority of American citizens, or that of the majority of congressmen and senators who passed the First Amendment, or that of the majority of state legislators who ratified it. They understood the First Amendment, as Justice Story understood it later, as referring to the various sects or denominations within a general Christian framework. As we noted in the *Beason, Reynolds,* and *Latter Day Saints* cases, the Supreme Court in the nineteenth century also leaned to that viewpoint.

But the courts today regard the First Amendment in a much broader sense. In *West Virginia Board of Education v. Barnette*, 319 U.S. 624 (1943), the Supreme Court struck down legislation requiring all public school children to salute the American flag, on the ground that this violates the right of the Jehovah's Witnesses to the free exercise of their religion, which prohibits saluting the flag.

United States v. Ballard, 322 U.S. 78 (1944) involved a cult known as the "I Am" movement. Ballard and his wife claimed supernatural forces empowered them to heal diseases and injuries and enabled them to communicate special teachings to others. They used the mails to solicit funds and memberships in the "I Am" movement. The government charged them with mail fraud, claiming that these representations were false and that the Ballards knew them to be false. The court ruled that the issue of the truth or falsity of the defendant's beliefs could not be submitted to a jury, because it was not the province of the state by means of a jury or any other government agency to make a determination as to truth or falsity of religious belief: "The law knows no heresy, and is committed to the support of no dogma, the establishment of no sect." (*Watson v. Jones*) The court further said:

> Men may believe what they cannot prove. They may not be put to the proof of their religious doctrines or beliefs. Religious experiences which are as real as life to some may be incomprehensible to others. Yet the fact that they may be beyond the ken of mortals does not mean that they can be made suspect before the law. Many take their gospel from the New Testament. But it would hardly be supposed that they could be tried before a jury charged with the duty of determining whether those teachings contained false representations. The miracles of the New Testament, the

Divinity of Christ, life after death, the power of prayer are deep in the religious convictions of many. If one could be sent to jail because a jury in a hostile environment found those teachings false, little indeed would be left of religious freedom. The fathers of the Constitution were not unaware of the varied and extreme views of religious sects, of the violence of disagreement among them, and of the lack of any one religious creed on which all men would agree. They fashioned a charter of government which envisaged the widest possible toleration of conflicting views. Man's relation to his God was made no concern of the state. He was granted the right to worship as he pleased and to answer to no man for the verity of his religious views. The religious views espoused by respondents might seem incredible, if not preposterous, to most people. But if those doctrines are subject to trial before a jury charged with finding their truth or falsity, then the same can be done with the religious beliefs of any sect. When the triers of fact undertake that task, they enter a forbidden domain. The First Amendment does not select any one group or any one type of religion for preferred treatment. It puts them all in that position.

In *Founding Church of Scientology v. United States*, 409 F. 2d 1146 (D.C. Cir. 1969), the Court in effect recognized that the First Amendment covers Scientology, holding that the Court could not inquire into the sincerity of the Scientologists' religious beliefs.

We have previously noted *Torcaso v. Watkins*, in which the Supreme Court identified secular humanism and other nontheistic belief systems as religions. The court expressed its broad definition of religion in *United States v. Seeger*, 380 U.S. 163 (1965), saying, "Local boards and courts in this sense are not free to reject beliefs because they consider them 'incomprehensible.' Their task is to decide whether the beliefs professed by a registrant are sincerely held and whether they are, in his own scheme of things, religious."

Recently the Georgia Supreme Court ruled that a building used by those of the Wiccan cult (the so-called "white witches") must be exempted from property taxes because it is "a place of religious worship," *Ravenwood Church of Wicca v. Roberts*, 292 S.E. 2d 657 (1982).

Other courts have reached different conclusions concerning cults, but their opinions generally do not address the First Amendment; rather, they are based on statutory considerations. For example, the U.S. Internal Revenue Service has recently begun a "crackdown" on tax-exempt religious organizations, defining with specificity what organizations are and are not religious. The Church of Scientology of California has battled the IRS in the federal courts, and has lost thus far. But the issue there is not whether the Church of Scientology is a religion covered by the First Amendment, but whether it is a religion as defined by the Internal Revenue Code and the regulations of the IRS. Similarly, the Unification Church has recently been denied property-tax exemption in New York City after a five-member panel of the appellate division of the Supreme Court ruled three to two that its primary purpose is not religious and four to one that the local tax commission was right in refusing to exempt three

Unification Church properties.[8] But again, this and other cases involve statutory and regulatory definitions, not the First Amendment.

How then do we answer this question? While the framers of the First Amendment might not have agreed, it is clear that the present-day courts have defined "religion" to include the cults. This may not mean that every activity of the cults is protected, but their basic right to worship, believe, pray, and proselytize is protected.

Deprogramming

During the 1960s and 1970s, as the cults proliferated, parents and relatives of cult members became very concerned. They formed organizations such as FREECOG (Free Our Children from the Children of God), Citizens Freedom Foundation, International Foundation for Individual Freedom, Citizens Organized for Public Awareness of Cults (COPAC), Citizens Engaged in Reuniting Families (CERF), and other groups. Also at this time a California official named Ted Patrick almost lost a nephew to a cult and became alarmed about the brainwashing activities of the cults and their efforts toward "mind-control." Patrick and others then began a practice which has been called "deprogramming."

Deprogramming involved two steps. First, the cult member was removed from the cult. Since the cultists were often suspicious of such activity and attempted to hold their members incommunicado, this was often difficult. Sometimes the cultist was deceived by false pretenses, such as telling him that a relative was dying; sometimes the removal involved some degree of force.

Once the individual was isolated from the cult, a "counterbrainwashing" session took place, sometimes lasting a week or more. William O. West, formerly a member of the Divine Light Mission, was succesfully deprogrammed and now represents the International Foundation for Individual Freedom (IFIF). West defends and explains the deprogramming process as follows:

> Deprogramming aims at breaking the chains of fear, guilt, and repetitive thought, and at forcing objective evaluation of the unexamined beliefs that were injected into the victim's unresisting mind by the cult leaders after the behavioral chains were originally established. The examination of what the person already believes is the deprogrammer's goal, rather than trying to force him to adopt a new belief. Deprogramming neutralizes the mind. . . . [Deprogramming] must of necessity include a dramatic, and hopefully shocking, presentation of alternative interpretations of specific phenomena. If a deprogrammer can induce his subject to attempt to defend his cult against charges for which he does not have previously memorized answers, the subject will be forced to think and, eventually, to recognize that he has accepted on blind faith, certain ideas which are contrary to

8. Case No. 1885, 5 May 1981; cited in *A Newsletter on Taxation and Religion* [National Conference of Christians and Jews], vol. 1, no. 1 (July/Aug. 1981), p. 7.

biblical teachings, and certainly open to question. At this point it is customary to encourage the subject to read aloud Matthew 24 and to consider the possibility that the leader of his particular cult is not the Messiah, a reincarnated prophet, or the "handmaiden of the Lord," as the self-appointed demagogues invariably claim.[9]

Beth Spring, writing in *Christianity Today*, says deprogramming is becoming more sophisticated and uses more individualized techniques.[10] Galen Kelly, a deprogrammer and criminal justice specialist, says that deprogramming "has worked with prison gangs, terrorists, and teenage prostitutes. Deprogramming has been generally successful, but it has to be brought into the open, professionalized, and clarified in order to survive."[11]

Spring quotes a woman formerly involved with The Way International as saying, "There was no way I would have been able to extricate myself, except by deprogramming. . . ."[12]

Flo Conway and Jim Siegelman, writing in the January 1982 issue of *Science Digest*, plead for wider acceptance of deprogramming. They contend that former cultists suffer from nightmares, amnesia, hallucinations, violent outbursts, and suicidal tendencies. They call deprogramming a "life saving intervention" and claim former deprogrammed cultists recover faster than former members who were not deprogrammed.[13]

Others are more skeptical of deprogramming. They are concerned that deprogrammers violate the religious convictions of adult young people who are entitled to believe what they choose, and who are entitled to be brainwashed if that is their desire. Bill Squires, head of the Berkely Christian Coalition, says of deprogramming,

> It seems to dismantle a person's whole ideological structure, which can be seriously damaging to the personality. I know personally some deprogrammed people who, when approached with the Gospel, respond "Well, it sounds very good, but how do I know you're not just trying to program me again?" so they are extremely cynical and very, very cautious. They feel that they have been ripped off once by something they considered to be an ultimate spiritual reality and they are not going to be taken again. So it kind of cripples them in response to a real redemption.[14]

Others share that concern. Dr. James Gordon, a psychiatrist formerly with the National Institute of Mental Health, says coercive deprogramming is not

9. William O. West, "I Know Deprogramming Works," *Eternity*, September 1976, pp. 75-76; quoted in Hefley, pp. 190-191.

10. Beth Spring, "Better Ways to Combat Cults Are Being Developed," *Christianity Today*, November 26, 1982, pp. 44-46.

11. Galen Kelly, quoted by Beth Spring, ibid.

12. Sharon Bell, quoted by Beth Spring. ibid.

13. Flo Conway and Jim Siegelman, *Science Digest*, January 1982, cited in "A Plea for More Deprogramming," *Christianity Today*, March 5, 1982, pp. 48, 69.

14. Bill Squires, quoted in ibid., p. 192.

the way to proceed and should never receive legal or medical sanction. All too often, he says, psychiatrists lack religious understanding themselves. They "tend to see religion through pathological lenses. That has to be rectified; religion has to be seen as a legitimate expression of the human spirit. Only then can we see how it is manipulated."[15]

Others question the effectiveness of deprogramming. Steve Hassan is the founder of Ex-Moon, an organization for people who have left the Unification Church. He estimates there are only 4,000 active "Moonies" in the U.S. and 25,000 former Moonies. Yet, he says, only a few hundred Moonies have been successfully deprogrammed. The vast majority have left on their own.[16] Hassan advocates "exit counseling." Possibly exit counseling could be called voluntary deprogramming, since it involves exposing the cult member to outside information about his group and his leader, but only so long as he is willing to listen.[17]

I believe forcible deprogramming is dangerous. While I have the greatest sympathy for parents whose children are involved in cults, I am convinced the dangers of deprogramming outweigh any possible advantages.

First, adult cult members are citizens with constitutional rights. The First Amendment protects their right to choose their own religion. That right must be reserved inviolate.

Second, deprogramming is a threat to Christians. The law makes no distinction between traditional Christian denominations and the cults. If deprogramming can be used against cultists, why not against Christians as well?

As we have seen, many mental health professionals regard all religion as a pathological symptom of mental illness. To many such persons, evangelical Christianity is just another cult.

Ted Patrick tries to distinguish between cults and "the real thing." He once refused a Jewish family's request that he "rescue" their daughter out of a Baptist Church because "that church was the real thing." But he did attempt, unsuccessfully, to deprogram a member of a charismatic Episcopal Church in Houston, Texas. And he recently declared in a *Penthouse* article, "Falwell has more people under mind control than Moon. He leads the biggest cult in the nation."[18] Do we really want Ted Patrick to have authority to decide what is the "real thing" and what is not?

At the beginning of this chapter, we discussed several valid criteria for distinguishing between cults and traditional religions. But a secular humanist deprogrammer is likely to disregard these distinctions and treat Christianity as just another cult. The enemies of religious liberty often begin their attack

---

15. James Gordon, quoted by Beth Spring, p. 46.

16. Steve Hassan, cited by Beth Spring, p. 44. Note that the Unification Church does not accept Hassan's figures; they claim nearly 40,000 U.S. adherents.

17. Ibid.

18. Beth Spring, "Who Decides What is a Cult and What is Not?", *Christianity Today*, November 26, 1982, pp. 46-48.

by striking at an unpopular group in order to set a precedent which can be used against all religions. When the California attorney general tried to impound the funds of Armstrong's Worldwide Church of God, many Christians refused to get involved. Many even said that Armstrong was getting what he deserved! Only belatedly did they realize that the attorney general's action constituted a threat to all religions, for it tried to establish that all church contributions constitute a charitable trust for the benefit of the public, to be overseen by the government. *People exrel. Deukmejian v. Worldwide Church of God, Inc.*, 127 Cal. App. 3d 547, 178 Cal. Rptr 913 (1981).

A threat to one religion is a threat to all religions. I therefore believe we need to look at other alternatives besides deprogramming.

What Can Be Done About Cults?

The Jonestown tragedy brought a widespread call for a government crackdown on cults. If cults are allowed to exist unfettered, it was said, similar tragedies will occur. But let us remember that Jones had been a city housing official, his facilities were licensed, and People's Temple had been closely involved with government all the way.[19] I remain skeptical of the use of government to prevent cult abuses. But many things can be done.

Minors

Much depends upon the age of the child. If the child is a minor and has not been emancipated by marriage, military service, or other means, the child's freedom of self-direction is much more limited, and the parent has considerable authority. He may remove the child from the cult by force, so long as he is able to do so without creating a breach of the peace. However, since this possibility can never be totally eliminated, the parent is strongly advised to obtain the assistance of law enforcement personnel and/or the courts before taking any action. The concerned parent might begin by contacting the police or sheriff, explain that his child is being held by a cult (whether the child has gone to the cult voluntarily, and whether he is capable of making such a decision, is unknown), and asking the assistance of the sheriff to pick up the child and bring him home. If the law enforcement officials refuse to become involved, the parent might then retain an attorney and file a petition with the court, requesting a preliminary injunction directing the sheriff to pick up the child and return the child to the home, and also a temporary restraining order prohibiting the cult from having any further contact with his child. If the problem continues, the parent can then seek to have the injunction and order made permanent.

Guardianship

If the cult member is an adult, the parent's options are far more limited.

19. R.J. Rushdoony, "Standards," *Chalcedon Position Paper No. 7* (P.O. Box 158, Vallecito, California 95251), 1979.

As an adult, whether he is eighteen (if that is the age of majority in that particular state) or fifty, he is held to be responsible and free to make his own decisions. In other words, the parent has no more right to force him to adhere to the parent's religious beliefs than the cultist has to force the parent to adhere to his.

But there are things a parent can do. First, if the parent has reason to believe that the adult son or daughter is being held against his will, or that his child has been so brainwashed as to be unable to make decisions on his own, he could file a petition in court asking that the court declare the child mentally incompetent, and establish the parent as his legal guardian. Once this is done, the parent/guardian has approximately the same legal authority to remove the child/ward from the cult, as he would have if the child were a minor. Hefley says that some parents have been successful in getting orders of this nature, and mentions a specific case in North Carolina.[20] However, other parents have attempted to get such orders and failed. In *Schuppin v. Unification Church*, 435 F. Supp. 603 (D.C.Vt. 1977), the Schuppins brought an action in federal district court alleging that the Unification Church had alienated and estranged their daughter from her family and friends. The suit alleged that the young lady (who was past the age of majority) was being held in involuntary servitude in violation of 18 U.S.C. 1581; had been enticed into compulsory service in violation of 18 U.S.C. 1583; had been mentally restrained from terminating her employment with the cult in violation of the Thirteenth Amendment; had been forced to work long hours without compensation in violation of 29 U.S.C. 206-207; had been denied FICA benefits in violation of 26 U.S.C. 3101 and 42 U.S.C. 409-410; had not been furnished W-2 forms in violation of 26 U.S.C. 3401, 3402, and 6501; and been seduced into unfit habitations, and had her relationship with her family destroyed.

A psychiatrist testified that Tamara Schuppin was not mentally competent, but he based this only upon what he had been told, since he had never seen or examined her. The parents sought to remove Tamara from the cult and compel her to undergo a psychiatric study to determine her level of competence. Tamara, on behalf of the cult, personnally appeared in court and objected to her parents' action, claiming that she was not being held involuntarily. The court dismissed the parents' action, holding that the parents could intervene only if Tamara Schuppin was mentally incompetent. As to the psychiatrist's testimony, the court ruled that "whatever pertinence his conclusion might have is so attenuated by the remoteness of his inquiry from its subject that it cannot be deemed to authorize this court to intrude on Tamara's privacy to compel her to undergo psychiatric study with a view toward including her against her will as a plaintiff in this matter."

In the *Schuppin* case, the parents were in a difficult situation. Without a psychiatric study, they couldn't prove her incompetent; and without some

20. Ibid., pp. 187-188.

evidence of incompetence, they couldn't get a court-ordered psychiatric study. The decision may seem unfair in many ways, and yet there is a reason for it: Tamara's right to privacy. The court can't order a psychiatric study any time someone requests it. Rather, there must be some substantial evidence of incompetence before the court can order someone to undergo such a study against his will.

While the Schuppins were unsuccessful, other parents might be successful. Psychiatric testimony would be most helpful, even though speculative and based upon heresay information. If the child has previously been evaluated by psychiatrists or psychologists or social workers, even if years ago, their observations could have a greater evidentiary basis than did those of the psychiatrist in the Schuppin case. Also, if the psychiatrist's testimony were coupled with the testimony of expert witnesses who know about that particular cult and its mind-control practices, the parents' case could be strengthened even further. Evidence of drug use, either by the individual cult member before or during his involvement with the cult, or by members of that particular cult generally, might also be helpful in convincing a court that further psychiatric study is necessary.

Of course, guardianship proceedings can pose a danger to Christian liberty. In the Soviet Union and other Communist countries, Christians and other "enemies of the people" are routinely confined to insane asylums since religiosity is a sign of mental illness and anti-social attitudes.

This has happened even in the United States. Eighteen-year-old Robin Polin, the daughter of Jewish parents in Tulsa, Oklahoma, is of above-average intelligence but since birth has been unable to hear or speak. In 1982 another deaf person, using sign language, told her about Jesus Christ. She wanted to know more, and the other person referred her to a Baptist minister, who led her to accept Jesus Christ as her Lord and Savior.

Outraged by this, her parents tried to dissuade her from Christianity and her father finally told her she must either live by his rules which include the virtual disassociation with her Christian friends and ceasing to worship Jesus in the home, or leave home. She sorrowfully chose the latter.

Her parents then filed a petition with the District Court of Tulsa County asking that Robin be declared incompetent and that they be made guardians over her.

In a five-day trial, the court heard testimony from both sides. A school psychologist who was a friend of Robin's parents testified that Robin functioned socially and interpersonally as a nine-year-old child, according to a test she administered. However, this psychologist had not interviewed Robin for over a year, did not know sign language, and therefore could not communicate with Robin except by pantomine or in writing. Other qualified professionals who had experience working with deaf and mute persons testified that Robin was competent. Testimony established that Robin could drive, had above-average intelligence, had been allowed to travel out of state, was planning to go to a Christian college in the fall, and prior to her conversion had contemplated an unaccompanied tour of Israel with her parents' approval.

Nevertheless Judge Robert D. Frank, a Unitarian, ruled in favor of Robin's parents. In a decision that many believe displays strong bias against fundamental Christianity, Judge Frank ruled Robin incompetent and placed her under the guardianship of a non-Christian sister, despite Robin's vehement and tearful protests. The order provided that she be allowed freedom to practice Christianity if she so desired, but her guardians have sometimes refused to allow her to attend church services.[21] To gain her freedom, Robin had to appeal to the Oklahoma Supreme Court, which on November 29, 1983, ruled in her favor. Chief Justice Donald Barnes reversed Judge Frank's decision, calling it a "chilling infringement" on Robin's religious freedom. So Robin is now free, but the traumatic court battle disrupted over six months of her life. (In the Matter of the Guardianship of Robin Andrea Polin, No. 60342. Supreme Court, Ok. Nov. 29, 1983; *Oklahoma Bar Journal*, Vol. 54, No. 46, p. 3085.)

Guardianship proceedings have an appropriate place in the legal system. But both the mental health profession and the legal system are so subjective today that they can easily be misused. Where issues of religious freedom are involved, guardianship proceedings should be used only with great caution.

Neutral Zones

Still another possibility might be to enact laws allowing law enforcement officers to take the cult member to a neutral place for questioning apart from the influence of other cult members, for the sole purpose of determining whether or not he is in fact being held against his will. Perhaps such a law should provide that this may be done only upon order of a court, after a petition is presented to the court by a parent, county attorney, or other interested person and upon probable cause. Possibly the questioning should be conducted by someone other than the police officers.

Hefley relates that New York City police have "designated a special meeting place for Moon youth members of the Unification Church and their parents at the Midtown South Precinct, a block from the Moonies' Hotel New Yorker. The police guarantee the Moonies they will not be kidnapped. And if one decides to return home, the police will not permit interference from other Moonies."[22]

Voluntary Deprogramming

Voluntary deprogramming has been successful in some cases. Sometimes former cultists experience guilt and other mental problems after having left

---

21. In the matter of the guardianship of Robin Andrea Polin, Tulsa County District Court, Oklahoma, PG 83-76, May 12, 1983; information based upon examination of court order and pleadings and interviews with John M. Young, attorney for Robin Polin.

22. Ibid., pp. 189-190.

the cult, and they volunteer for treatment. One such group is Return to Personal Choice of Newton, Massachusetts. It is composed of mental health professionals, lawyers, and clergy, and affiliated groups are in Texas, Minnesota, Pennsylvania, and New York.[23] Voluntary deprogramming is sometimes called exit counseling. Many who leave cults realize that they have emotional scars and that they need help in overcoming them.

Combating Error with Truth

In some instances, cassettes and literature that point out the errors of the cult may be helpful. Two groups providing such literature are the Spiritual Counterfeits Project (P.O. Box 4308, Berkeley, California 94794), and the Christian Research Institute (San Juan Capistrano, California).

Criminal Violations

One should not overlook the possibility that the cult could be prosecuted criminally for outright violations of the law. Such violations could include assault, abuse, kidnapping, false imprisonment, soliciting funds under false pretenses, or criminal fraud. The authorities should be asked to deal with these offenses as with any other violations.

Establishment Clause

Since the courts have determined that cults are religions under the First Amendment, they are covered by the establishment clause as well as the free exercise clause. Sometimes cult or cult-related organizations establish programs for charity, counseling, job training, education, or prevention of crime and drug abuse—often with good results. Such programs may be admitted into the public schools or even given governmental funding by authorities who either do not know of or are not concerned about their cult connotations. Christians should carefully scrutinize such programs and disestablish them where necessary. One case in which this was done successfully was *Malnak v. Maharishi Mahesh Yogi*, 440 F. Supp. 1284 (1977); affirmed 592 F. 2d 197 (1979). The court held that Transcendental Meditation (T.M.) is sufficiently religious in character that the establishment clause forbids it from being taught in public schools.

Do's and Don't's

Hefley summarizes a list of helpful "do's and don't's" prepared by Citizens Freedom Foundation:

> *Do* record all names, addresses, phone numbers of persons known to be associated in any way with your child's activities.
> *Do* establish and continue an association with an organized group of parents with similar problems.

23. Ibid., p. 193.

Do maintain a written chronology of events associated with your child's activities relating to the group.

Do answer all communications from your child in sincere, firm, but unrecriminating language.

Do collect related items from newspapers, magazines, and other sources.

Do keep your "cool," avoid threats, be firm but open for communication at all times.

Do not feel guilty or alone. This is a common problem faced by thousands of parents all over this nation. It affects families of all religious, economic, and family backgrounds.

Do not send money to your child or to the group; without economic support the group cannot survive.

Do not give original documents to ANY party (unless required by law); provide copies ONLY.

Do not be persuaded by "professionals" to spend large amounts of money for "treatments" or legal action, until you have verified their credentials and qualifications for handling YOUR problem.

Do not give up; remember your child is a product of your love, training, heredity, and home environment. These influences can never be permanently eliminated by any techniques.[24] (Emphasis original.)

Remember that God is not limited by the chains of the cults. He can break through any isolation or brainwashing to reach someone for His Kingdom. As Steve Hassan noted earlier, there are 25,000 former Moonies in the U.S. and only 4,000 active members. If his figures are correct, many more have left that cult than have remained within it.

And the Christian should never forget or neglect the two most potent weapons of all against cults: prayer, and the Word of God.

24. Citizens Freedom Foundation, cited by ibid., pp. 182-183.

Chapter 19

The Christian and the Media

The term *media* has a bad connotation to many Christians. They believe the media have been hostile toward Christians, have filled the home with anti-Christian and antifamily values, and promoted indecency and violence.

Though there is a great deal of truth to these allegations, the media is actually a "neutral force" which can be used for good or evil. It is important that Christians know how to use the media for good, and how to combat those who would use it for evil.

Use of the Media

One might think that the use of the electronic media involves the same application of First Amendment rights as the use of newspapers, lecture halls, and other facilities. But there is a difference, for the media uses the airwaves. I have a wide freedom to publish whatever I wish, so long as I can afford to do so. The fact that ten other newspapers are in town does not prevent me from publishing an eleventh, and to sell it to everyone who is willing to buy.

But I do not have the same freedom to establish my own television or radio station. A radio station requires a frequency, and only a limited number of frequencies are available. Consequently, the right to use the airwaves is not as unlimited as the right to publish or lecture. As the Supreme Court ruled in *Red Lion Broadcasting Co. v. FCC*, 395 U.S. 367 (1969), nothing in the First Amendment allows one to "monopolize a radio frequency to the exclusion of his fellow citizens." It is, the Court said, "idle to posit an unabridgeable First Amendment right to broadcast comparable to the right of every individual to speak, write or publish." Since the airwaves belong to the public, "the interests of the listening public are paramount to the interests of the individual application."[1]

1. In the Matter of Young People's Association for the Propagation of the Gospel, 6 F.C.C. 178 (1938).

For this reason, the Federal Communications Commission (FCC) was established to regulate the broadcasting industry. The FCC takes the position that the broadcasters are to serve the needs of the general public, and must provide programming that meets those needs. The public has a right to know "all sides of important public questions, fairly, objectively, and without bias."[2] To ensure that broadcasters fulfill that duty and at the same time safeguard the broadcaster's own First Amendment rights, the FCC has formulated the "Fairness Doctrine."

The Fairness Doctrine holds that (1) broadcasters have to devote a reasonable amount of broadcasting time to the presentation of controversial issues of public importance, and (2) their coverage of controversial issues must adequately present conflicting viewpoints, although the broadcaster may also indicate which viewpoint he prefers.[3]

The Fairness Doctrine has four basic aspects: (1) political candidates are entitled to equal opportunities (often called the "equal time" rule); (2) individuals have the right to respond to personal attacks (the "personal attack" rule); (3) the broadcaster must serve the public by considering the needs of the community; and (4) the broadcaster must present conflicting views on controversial issues of public importance.[4] Also, the "political editorial" rule directs that a broadcaster who endorses a candidate must inform all of the candidate's opponents of the endorsement within twenty-four hours and provide time for rebuttal.

The FCC has frequently received complaints that broadcasters have failed to adhere to the Fairness Doctrine. For example, during the 1980 election, candidates Reagan and Anderson demanded equal time to respond to a Carter press conference. However, the FCC ruled that the fairness doctrine does not apply to live coverage of a news event like a presidential news conference.[5]

In evaluating these complaints, the FCC has generally given broadcasters a great deal of leeway in determining whether or not an issue is in fact controversial as the FCC uses the term, and whether or not the broadcaster gave conflicting views adequate consideration. On determining what constitutes a controversial issue, the FCC has held that such subjects as atheism, evolution, birth control, and even abortion are non-controversial, even though the average person might think those issues are highly controversial.[6] Likewise, the broadcasting of public worship services or religious programs that teach the traditional religious tenets of the Christian faith are not considered by the FCC to be controversial, even though many people might strongly disagree with

2. Mayflower Broadcasting Company, 8 F.C.C. 333, 340, (1940).

3. Robert Whitlow, "The FCC's Fairness Doctrine and the First Amendment", *The Christian Lawyer* Vo. VIII No. 1 (Spring 1979, pp. 21-22.) Throughout this chapter, I am indebted to the fine work of Mr. Whitlow.

4. Whitlow, p. 22-23.

5. *Tulsa World*, Sept. 20, 1981, J-2 (AP).

6. Whitlow, pp. 33-36.

those tenets.[7] Also, the FCC considers only the major point of the broadcast. Minor subpoints which the speaker may touch upon are not considered controversial issues for purposes of the Fairness Doctrine.[8] Furthermore, in determining whether the broadcaster has given adequate coverage to conflicting views, the FFC looks at the broadcaster's total programming. Though one program may reflect only one viewpoint, consideration to other viewpoints on other programs may be sufficient.[9]

The religious broadcaster who wishes to obtain and keep an FCC license will stand a better chance of doing so if he demonstrates to the FCC that his programming meets the needs of the general public, or at least the general religious community rather than the needs of one particular church or denomination. His chances will be further enhanced if he includes considerable news coverage and programs on controversial issues. Such programs of special interest to Christians are available nationwide or could be produced locally.

The FCC seems to give considerable discretion to religious broadcasters and is less likely to consider an issue controversial if presented from a religious standpoint. If a particular radio speaker addresses a controversial political issue such as abortion by explaining pertinent Scriptures, there is less danger of violating the Fairness Doctrine. Many secular-minded persons do not realize that the Scriptures speak extensively on such issues as government, war and peace, crime and punishment, economics, labor-management relations, psychology, freedom and slavery, international relations, and many other current controversial topics. Motivated by biblical convictions, it is the Christians' responsibility to address these issues. At the same time, it may be helpful to mention and explain other possible positions on the issue in an objective and educational way. Not only is this more likely to satisfy the Fairness Doctrine; it is often more effective.

In September 1981 the new Republican chairman of the FCC recommended that Congress repeal the Fairness Doctrine. He argued that the marketplace, not the government, should determine what is shown on the media.

Both sides have strong arguments. Wayne Godsey, president of the Radio-Television News Directors Association, argues for repeal, claiming that the Fairness Doctrine has intimidated the media from taking controversial stands and endorsing candidates. Vince Wasilewski of the National Association of Broadcasters agrees; he says that because of the Fairness Doctrine, newscasting has become an "inhibiting, self-conscious, often confusing minuet."

But Andrew Jay Schwartzman, Director of the Media Access Project, counters that the rights of the listeners take precedence over those of the broadcasters. And Samuel Simon of the National Citizens Committee for Broadcasting calls the attempted repeal "an unbelievable power grab by the networks to control the electoral process. I'll tell you what could happen. For the

7. Whitlow, pp. 38.
8. Whitlow, p. 45.
9. Whitlow, p. 35.

first time we could have a three-party system—the ABC, CBS and NBC parties. This is it. These guys are going for the jugular.''[10]

The potential broadcaster might also consider the advantages of the newly-developing "low-power television." Low-power TV reaches a smaller audience, but its cost at present is less than one-tenth that of the more conventional channels. And since there is less competition for frequencies and permits, the FCC has indicated that it will regulate low-power TV in a more lenient manner than other forms of broadcasting, at least for the present.[11]

Defamation, Slander and Libel

The person who speaks out on controversial issues must always be careful to avoid defamatory, slanderous, or libelous remarks. As we have already noted, defamatory speech, like obscene speech, is not covered by the First Amendment.

What is defamation? According to *Black's Law Dictionary* defamation consists of injuring a person's character, fame, reputation or business by false and malicious statements. Defamation may be divided into two categories, slander and libel. Slander is defamation by means of the spoken word, while libel is defamation in writing.[12]

Not only individuals can be defamed; corporations or business or associations can also sue for defamation. However, there can be no lawsuit for defamation of a dead person. Were you to defame Joseph Stalin, his heirs could not sue you.

To sue for defamation, one must prove several things. Usually one must prove that this statement is false, but there are exceptions. In a few jurisdictions one may be sued for defamation even though the statement was true, if the statement was not made with good motives and justifiable ends. For example, if a radio broadcaster were to repeatedly and maliciously accuse someone of a sexual impropriety which took place years ago, and continually bring it up for no apparent reason other than to ruin the person's reputation, he might be sued for defamation even though the statement was true. In a few other jurisdictions, as at common law, defamatory statements are presumed to be false, and the person who made the statement must prove that the statement is true. In most cases, however, the burden is on the plaintiff to prove that the claimed defamatory statement is false.[13]

Second, the plaintiff must prove that the statement is malicious. An innocent error of fact will normally not be considered defamatory. How "malicious" the statement must be depends upon who is being defamed. If the victim of defamation is a "public person", he must prove not only that the statement

10. The quotes from Godsey, Wasilewski, Schwartzman and Simon are all from the *Tulsa World*, September 20, 1981, J-2 (AP).

11. *Religious Broadcasting*, January 1981, pp. 51-58.

12. *Black's Law Dictionary, Fourth Edition*, s.v. Defamation, Slander, Libel

13. William L. Prosser, John W. Wade, and Victor E. Schwartz, *Torts: Cases and Materials*, 6th Ed. (Mineola, New York: Foundation Press, 1976), p. 973.

was false, but also that the person who made the statement did so knowing it was false or with reckless disregard for the truth. If he is a "private person", he need only show that the statement was false and that the person who made it did so negligently.[14]

Who is a "public person"? In *New York Times Co. v. Sullivan*, 376 U.S. 254 (1964), the Supreme Court established the "public official doctrine", holding that those who hold public offices are fair subjects for commentary by the media and others, and therefore imposed a higher standard upon them: they cannot sue for slander or libel unless they can prove both falsity and that the slanderer knew the statement was false or acted in reckless disregard of the truth. Sullivan, a county commissioner, was held to be a public official. But not all government employees are public officials under this doctrine, only those whose "position in government has such apparent importance that the public has an independent interest in the qualifications and performance of the person who holds it, beyond the general public interest in the qualifications and performance of all government employees."[15] The courts have also recognized that many individuals of public prominence who do not hold government positions. Thus the "public official" doctrine was expanded to become the "public figure" doctrine in two companion cases, *Curtis Publishing Co. v. Butts* and *Associated Press v. Walker*, 388 U.S. 130 (1967). The doctrine has been still further expanded to matters of general or public interest, as in *Rosenbloom v. Metromedia, Inc.*, 403 U.S. 29 (1971). As to who is a private person, I suppose the best definition would be, anyone who is not a public person!

Third, in some instances the person must prove that he has been damaged by the defamatory remark. He might show that the statement hurt his business, that it caused him to lose an election, that he had lost friends because of it, or that his reputation in the community was damaged. The rule used to be that for libelous remarks (those in writing) one need not show damages, but for slanderous (oral) remarks it was necessary. This distinction, however, has been somewhat eroded in recent years. There are four categories of oral remarks that are intrinsically slander and for which one need not prove damages: imputations of major crime, allegations of a loathsome disease such as venereal disease, remarks likely to affect the individual's business or profession, and allegations of serious sexual misconduct. The reason for the original libel/slander disinction was that written or printed words were more likely than mere spoken words to have wide circulation and thereby cause damages. However, with the development of radio and television, the spoken word might have greater circulation and greater impact than written words, and this distinction might be reconsidered in regard to broadcasting.

Finally, the plaintiff must prove that the person who libeled or slandered him, in some way communicated the remark to a third person. Not only is

---

14. Ibid.
15. *Rosenblatt v. Baer*, 383 U.S. 75 (1966).

the maker of the remark potentially liable; the person who helps him by publishing the remark may also be liable for damages. The courts distinguish between "primary publishers" (book publishers, etc.) who are liable, and "secondary publishers" (booksellers, etc.) who are not. What about the radio or TV station which obtains a taped broadcast containing slander, and broadcasts the tape without any knowledge of the defamation? Is the station a primary publisher or a secondary publisher? The courts are not agreed on that question; there are decisions on both sides.[16]

One thing else should be noted: certain privileged communications are not actionable even though they may be defamatory in all other respects. These include statements made in court under oath, and statements made before legislative bodies of government.

The Christian broadcaster should therefore be cautious, but not intimidated, about what he says. He can take precautions to avoid being sued for libel. First, he should check his facts carefully: remember that truth is almost always a defense. And it is advisable to keep and use documentation for facts.

Second, when one discusses controversial issues, it is best to attack ideas rather than persons. If it is necessary to talk about persons, it is sometimes better to do so without naming them personally. This is not an absolute defense to defamation suits; you can be sued for defamation by innuendo or by implication if you describe a situation that so clearly relates to a particular person that the public is likely to relate the remarks to that person. But you are still less likely to run into difficulty addressing ideas.

Also, it is best to keep malice out of your remarks. Whatever needs to be said, can be expressed in a dispassionate manner. Distinguish between fact and opinion. Rather than stating "That rat Jones is a Commie!", it would be wiser to say, "I believe Jones is a Communist because of the following evidence. . . ."

If it is clearly shown that your statement or a statement you have helped publish, is false, the best thing to do is issue a prompt and prominent retraction. This can help to minimize damages, and may soothe the anger of the defamed person. Before doing so, you may wish to consult an attorney and obtain an agreement in writing, by which he agrees to release you from any possible damages for defamation.

Finally, if all else fails, the National Association of Broadcasters offers libel/First Amendment insurance.[17] This might be a prudent investment for the broadcaster who stands at risk in this area.

---

16. Prosser, 1001-1003. See *Sorenson v. Wood*, 243 N.W. 82 (1932); *Miles v. Louis Wasmer, Inc.*, 20 P.2d 847 (1933); *Kelly v. Hoffman*, 61 A.2d 143 (1948); *Summit Hotel Co. v. National Broadcasting Co.* 8 A.2d 302 (1939).

17. *Religious Broadcaster*, January 1981, p. 62.

Pornography and other Objectionable Uses of the Media

There are very few subjects on which the courts have wavered more than the regulation of pornography.

The issue is not whether pornography is protected by the First Amendment. Since *Roth v. Goldman*, 172 F. 2d 788 (2d Cir. 1949) cert. den. 337 U.S. 938, the courts have agreed that that which is truly obscene is outside the protection of the First Amendment. The issue is, what is obscene? Are topless photos obscene? Are topless photos permissable, but bottomless photos obscene? Is a literary masterpiece obscene because it contains sexual overtones?

During the 1950s and 1960s, the courts took a narrow view of what constituted pornography. In *Memoirs v. Massachusetts*, 383 U.S. 413 (1966), Justice Brennan wrote that in order for a work to be considered obscene, three elements must coalesce:

> (a) the dominant theme of the material taken as a whole appeals to a prurient interest in sex; (b) the material is patently offensive because it affronts community standards relating to the description or representation of sexual matters; and (c) the material is utterly without redeeming social value.

This definition was expanded in *Miller v. California*, 413 U.S. 15 (1973). The Miller test is as follows:

> (a) whether "the average person, applying contemporary community standards" would find that the work, taken as a whole, appeals to the prurient interest. . . . (b) whether the work depicts or describes, in a patently offensive way, sexual conduct specifically defined by the applicable state law; and (c) whether the work, taken as a whole, lacks serious artistic, political, or scientific value.

That *Miller* test, which has been the courts' rule for eight years, is a three-part test that bears comment. First, it involves "contemporary community standards." In other words, standards of obscenity may vary in various parts of the country. What is obscene in Orange City, Iowa, might not be obscene in Atlanta, Georgia; and what is obscene in Atlanta might not be obscene in New York.

Second, the illegal conduct must be clearly documented in the statute. The would-be pornographer has a right to know with a reasonable degree of certainty, what is and is not permitted. The statute may not be so broad as to cover things not constitutionally obscene, or it might be struck down for vagueness.

Third, in determining whether the work has artistic, political, or scientific value, the work must be considered in its entirety, not as an isolated part. Unlike the *Memoirs* case mentioned above, the test is not whether it is "utterly without redeeming social value," but whether the work, "*taken as a whole*, lacks *serious* artistic, political, or scientific value.*" (emphasis supplied). This broadens the definition of obscenity considerably. As the Court said in *Kois v. Wisconsin*, 408 U.S. 229,231 (1972), "a quotation from Voltaire in the flyleaf of a book [does not] constitutionally redeem an otherwise obscene publication."

Admittedly, this definition leaves a lot of unanswered questions. But it does provide some guidance for the Christian lawmaker who wants to fight pornography but wants to do so within the limits of the Constitution. Certainly, based on this definition, almost any community could regulate "hardcore" pornography. Some communities could regulate more than others.

Neil Gallagher, in his excellent book *How to Stop the Porno Plague*,[18] suggests a model ordinance for the general regulation of pornography that appears to meet the standards of the *Miller* test. He also suggests certain other areas that the state or community can regulate.

One is the public display of pornographic literature in a manner that makes it easily accessible to children. The courts will allow the state to go considerably further in regulating pornography for the protection of children than for the protection of adults. Laws that prohibit the public display of such magazines in places where children are likely to see them would be held constitutional so long as they are properly drawn. Gallagher notes an interesting side effect of such legislation. When people have to ask for pornographic literature instead of seeing it openly displayed, sales of pornographic literature to adults drops 75 to 95 percent.[19]

The showing of offensive films where they are easily observed by an unwilling public, such as drive-in movies whose screens are visible from the highway, is an area of legitimate public regulation. Even R-rated films that might not be considered obscene under the *Miller* test can be regulated if visible to unwilling viewers. Such ordinances must be drawn carefully, however. In *Erznoznik v. Jacksonville*, 422 U.S. 205 (1975), the Supreme Court struck down as unconstitutional an ordinance that prohibited drive-in theaters from showing films containing nudity when visible from a public street or public place. The court said the prohibition against nudity was much too broad and could include any type of nudity however "innocent" or "educational." An ordinance that more carefully described the types of nudity that were prohibited might have been upheld.

Recognizing that "a State has absolute power under the Twenty-First Amendment to prohibit totally the sale of liquor within its boundaries," and has "broad power" to "regulate the times, places and circumstances under which liquor may be sold," the Supreme Court upheld a New York Statute prohibiting topless dancing on premises which sell liquor, *New York State Liquor Authority v. Bellanca*, 452 U.S. 714 (1981). In *Young v. American Mini Theaters, Inc.*, 427 U.S. 50 (1976), the court upheld two Detroit zoning ordinances which prohibited adult theaters within 500 feet of a residential area or within 1,000

---

18. Neil Gallagher, *How to Stop the Porno Plague*, (Minneapolis: Bethany Fellowship, 1977).
19. Gallagher, p. 122, 131-132.

feet of other regulated establishments. Other types of obscenity subject to legitimate regulation are indecent exposure, live sex acts on stage, and indecent massage parlors.

United States v. Reidel, 402 U.S. 351 (1971), upheld the constitutionality of Section 1461 of Title 18 of the United States Code which prohibits the knowing use of the mails for delivery of obscene matter.

The state has a stronger interest in regulating obscenity as it relates to minors than as it relates to adults. In *Ginsberg v. New York*, 390 U.S. 629 (1968), the Supreme Court upheld the constitutionality of a state law prohibiting the distribution to minors of sexually explicit materials, even though those materials might not be considered obscene as related to adults. The *Ginsberg* rationale would seem to allow laws prohibiting the sale of *Playboy* to minors even though *Playboy* is probably not obscene under the *Miller* test.

Recently a father was driving in a car with his young son. He turned on the radio and caught the end of a twelve minute monologue entitled "Filthy Words" from an album of "comedy routines." Upset about the indecent language, he complained to the FCC. The FCC agreed with him and, while it did not place an absolute prohibition on that type of broadcast, it directed the radio station to restrict such broadcasts to times of day when children are not likely to be listening. The Supreme Court affirmed the FCC's action in *FCC v. Pacifica Foundation*, 438 U.S. 726 (1978). Similar offensive broadcasts could be reported to the FCC for action.

Probably no type of pornography is more disgusting or dangerous than "kiddie porn," the use of children in pornography. Kiddie porn exploits children, causes lifelong emotional scars, appeals only to perverts, and could trigger violent sexual attacks on children. The production, promotion, distribution, and display of kiddie porn should be a felony crime and should be strictly enforced. Holding that "the States are entitled to greater leeway in the regulation of pornographic depictions of children" than of adults, the Court upheld such a law in *New York v. Ferber*, 102 S. Ct. 3348 (1982).

In *Stanley v. Georgia* 394 U.S. 557 (1969), the Supreme Court held that the possession and viewing of obscene materials in the privacy of one's own home is protected by the privacy right guaranteed in the First and Fourteenth Amendments. The Court said,

> If the First Amendment means anything, it means that a State has no business telling a man, sitting alone in his own house, what books he may read or what films he may watch. Our whole constitutional heritage rebels at the thought of giving government the power to control men's minds.

But this decision applied only to private possession and use, not to purchase, sale or distribution. And if *Stanley* had invited others to come into his home to view the film, whether for a fee or otherwise, the result might have been different.

One problem in the movie industry is "block bidding." Under this system a motion picture theater owner is required to bid for a number of movies as a whole to show in his theater. He often cannot pick only the movies he wants; either he buys all of them or he gets none at all from that company. Thus he is practically forced to buy some R-rated or X-rated movies along with the PG and G movies. Some theater owners claim that they would like to show only wholesome entertainment, but because of block bidding cannot. A few states have passed legislation prohibiting block bidding, and such legislation could be of considerable value in cleaning up the movie industry. Beyond that, it might help to improve the overall quality of the theater, since without block bidding theater owners could not be forced to buy and show mediocre films. Such legislation, if actively pushed, should have a good chance for passage. Church and community groups should strongly support it; and some theater owners might even support it. The only active opposition is likely to be the motion picture industry, which doesn't have too much influence with the legislatures of most states.

Strong laws against pornography are not likely to have much effect unless they are actively enforced. It is possible that an overworked police department or an indifferent prosecutor might not consider pornography important, unless the public brings it to his attention. Charles H. Keating, Jr., Director of Citizens for Decency through Law, Inc., notes that a recent survey commissioned by Connecticut Mutual Life Insurance Co. found a wide and dramatic gap between the views of the American public and those of its leaders, on religious and moral issues. (This may be why the evangelical church does not get very thorough, accurate or favorable coverage by the national media; the media are out of touch with the general public.) About 1,600 people were asked, among other questions, "Are pornographic movies morally wrong or is this not a moral issue?" Result: 68 percent of the American public considered pornographic movies morally wrong; only 32 percent said they are not a moral issue. But of America's leaders, only 56 percent said porno films are morally wrong; 44 percent disagreed. And among American leaders in law and justice (those charged with enforcing anti-pornograph statutes), only 41 percent thought such films are morally wrong: 59 percent said such films are not a moral issue. Look at the gap:

	Morally wrong	Not a moral issue
General Public	68	32
Leaders	56	44
Education	50	50
Government	47	53
News Media	46	54
Law & Justice	41	59[20]

20. "The Connecticut Mutual Life Report on American Values in the 80's. The Impact of belief;" cited by Charles H. Keating, Jr., *National Decency Reporter*, Vol. 28, No. 4, July-August 1981, p. 3.

No wonder pornography laws are not enforced; a majority of the nation's leaders in law and justice do not believe in them! Certainly not all prosecutors and policemen reflect this attitude. Some enforce these laws vigorously; many others would do so if encouraged by the public. This is where the Christian citizen can be of help by working for good laws and cooperating with police and prosecutors to enforce them.

Sometimes a complaint to the manager of the store that sells pornography is all that is necessary to bring action. Obviously that's not likely at an "adult" bookstore. But Gallagher says that many drugstore owners pay little attention to the kind of magazines carried on their shelves as they are stocked by a wholesaler. He suggests that the reader take the magazines to the counter, bring them to the attention of the owner, and ask if he was aware that such magazines were on his shelves. In a surprising number of cases, Gallagher says, the owner professes his ignorance and expresses dismay at the magazines. Whether his reactions are genuine or not may be debatable, but at any rate the magazines are frequently removed.

Unlike the movie industry, store owners are free to reject magazines they don't want to sell. Wholesalers may exert pressure to take all magazines or none, because they make a greater markup on pornography than on other publications. Some even offer a cash bonus for displaying pornography in a prominent place. But if the store owner steadfastly refuses, Gallagher says, his wishes will nearly always be respected and he will be allowed to select the magazines he wants to sell.

If a valid ordinance prohibits pornography but the store owner refuses obey it, it may be necessary to take more drastic action. You may have to buy the magazine, take it to the police or prosecutor (it is helpful to know which persons in those offices are most supportive of your position), for evidence. If the case goes to court, you may have to testify as to where you purchased the magazine—an unpleasant task, but necessary to enforce the law.[21]

The recent spread of cable television has brought a distasteful side-effect: X-rated or R-rated movies right in the American home. Some argue that this is an invasion of privacy. Others counter that watching it is voluntary. But what about children?—one can't police older children all the time.

As we have seen, the Courts have said that the First Amendment does not give one the exclusive right to use the airwaves. They are the property of the public, and exist for the benefit of the public, and therefore the public has considerable voice as to what is shown on television. In most areas, a cable television company must obtain a franchise from the local government. Public hearings are usually scheduled to determine whether the franchise should be granted to a company. That is the opportune time to bring attention to the moral quality of the programming. At that time the cable television company is eager to "sell" itself to the community. It wants to avoid controversy at

21. See Gallagher generally.

all costs, and is probably willing to compromise. That is the time to get the company to agree, as part of its contract or franchise with the locality, that certain types of films will not be shown under any circumstances. Once the company is established, it is much less likely to heed complaints. And since many cable television stations do not use commercial advertising, there may be no sponsor to bring pressure at a later date.

As for the national media, letters to the networks, the local stations, and perhaps the local newspapers may be of some help. Ultimately, their goal is to make money by selling program time to sponsors. These sponsors pay handsomely for the privilege of advertising their products on television. They will do so only if they are convinced that such sponsorship and advertising will sell products and make more money.

Rev. Don Wildmon was concerned that television was permeated with programming which, while probably not obscene under the *Miller* test, nevertheless presented sex and violence in such a way as to subvert traditional Christian morality. He therefore organized the Coalition for Better Television, a coalition of smaller groups that rated television programs and took steps to implement a nationwide boycott of products sold by companies who sponsor objectionable programs.

The media reacted predictably. Many of the public never did understand the Coalition's proposed boycott, because their information came from the media. Among other charges, the media accused the Coaliton of advocating censorship, returning to the Dark Ages, repealing the First Amendment, and a thousand other such things. Television producer Norman Lear began a campaign to counter the "intolerant messages and antidemocratic actions of moral majoritarians."[22]

But Lear's remarks reveal that he understands neither tolerance, democracy, nor the Moral Majority. First, because of the limited number of frequencies available, the First Amendment does not give Norman Lear nor anyone else the unqualified right to use the media to broadcast anything he chooses. The airwaves belong to the public, and while the broadcaster has some freedom of expression on the airwaves, the needs and desires of the public must be considered as well.

Secondly, the Moral Majority and The Coalition for Better Television never advocated censorship. Censorship is an act of government. If the government were to ban the program "Dallas," that would be censorship. But Rev. Wildmon and his supporters never advocated that. They never advocated that government interfere with television at all. All they said was that they, as a group, would not buy the products of the companies that sponsored the objectionable programs. That isn't undemocratic. That's democracy in action, letting the law of supply and demand determine what will and will not be shown on television.

22. Norman Lear, quoted in *Moody Monthly*, September 1981, p. 123.

Once again we see the chronic tendency of liberals to assume they have a monopoly on the First Amendment. The same First Amendment that gives Norman Lear the right to write whatever he wants, gives Rev. Wildmon the right to say he doesn't like what Norman Lear writes. And the First Amendment also gives him the right to freely associate with others to advance his beliefs. Boycotts are a legitimate First Amendment weapon.

Chapter 20

The Christian and Abortion*

In my hometown of Sioux City, Iowa, a liberal Protestant clergyman once appeared on a radio talk show to argue for the "Pro-Choice" position. When asked about the Bible, he declared flatly, "The Bible doesn't say anything about abortion."

I disagree. True, you will not find a passage that specifically says, "Thou shalt not have an abortion." But many passages of Scripture do touch on abortion or contain clear implications concerning it. When these passages are taken together, they clearly establish that abortion is contrary to the Word of God.

The basic passage is the commandment of Exodus 20:13: "Thou shalt not kill." Using that translation and taking Exodus 20:13 as a literal, absolute, sweeping command, we can understand the commandment to prohibit not only abortion, but also military service, animal sacrifice, and even swatting flies! However, the word for kill in Exodus 20:13 is *ratsach*, and this almost always means an intentional and unjustified killing of a human being—in other words, murder. All murder involves killing, but not all killing is murder. For other types of killing such as accidental deaths, killing in war, killing in self-defense, or the execution of criminals, different Hebrew words are used, such as *katal* and *harag*.

So we must carefully consider whether "thou shalt not kill" applies to abortion. As we have seen, the commandment prohibits the unjustified killing of a human being. Clearly, the act of abortion is intentional. But let us ask ourselves: (1) Does it involve the killing of a human being and (2) is it justified?

Is the Unborn Child a Human Being?
I believe the various passages of Scripture which touch upon this question,

*This chapter appears, in similar form, as an entry in *Bioethics and Law: An Ecumenical Reader* (Ann Arbor, Michigan: Servant, 1983-84).

when taken as a whole, compel an affirmative answer. Let us look at what the Scripture has to say [1]

(1) *The languages used in the Bible make no distinction between the unborn child and children who are already born.*

Let us consider the various words which are used in the Bible for the unborn child.

(a) *Brephos* - *Brephos* is a Greek word used for "baby." The term is used for "babe" in Luke 1:44, where Elizabeth says of her unborn child, John the Baptist, "the *babe* in my womb leaped for joy." In the next chapter, the angel says to the shepherds, "ye shall find the *babe* wrapped in swaddling clothes, lying in a manger" (Luke 2:12). Again, the word is *brephos*.

Paul uses the same word in I Timothy 3:15, when he says of Timothy, "From a *child* thou hast known the holy scriptures. . . ." Note, now, that the authors of Scripture make no distinction in the use of the word *brephos*. It is used for an unborn child in Luke 1 and for a child already born in Luke 2, and used again for a young child in I Timothy.

(b) *Huios* - *Huios* is commonly used for "son" in the New Testament. In Luke 1:36, the angel tells Mary, "Thy cousin, Elizabeth, hath also conceived a *son*," using *huios*. Five verses earlier in Luke 1:31, the angel told Mary, "thou shalt conceive in thy womb, and bring forth a son," again using *huios* for the child conceived and a child brought forth. And two chapters later, God the Father says to the Lord Jesus Christ, "Thou art my beloved *Son*" (Luke 3:22). And at this time, Jesus was a young adult. Again, the New Testament makes no distinction between an unborn child and a child already born in the use of the word *huios*.

(c) *Ben* - *Ben* is the Old Testament Hebrew word, commonly translated as son or child. It appears hundreds of times in Scripture, normally for a child already born, but not always. In Genesis 25:21-24, we read of Jacob and Esau in the womb of their mother, Rebekah: "And the *children* struggled within her. . . ." And the word used for children is *ben*. We see the word ben used for Ishmael when he was 13 years old (Genesis 17:25) and for Noah's adult sons (Genesis 9:19).

(d) *Gehver* - Job 3:3, "Let the day perish wherein I was born, and the night in which it was said, There is a *manchild* conceived." The word is gehver. It is used approximately sixty-five times in Scripture, usually for a man or men.

(e) *Gohlahl* - In his agony, Job lamented the fact that he was born. In Job 3:16, he expressed the wish that he could have been miscarried, "as infants which never saw light." Clearly, in that context, infants are unborn children—

1. I am indebted to Rev. Bruce Einspahr of Columbia Bible Church, Pasco, Washington, whose taped message dated November 1981 was of great help to me in exegeting these passages.

children who never were born, but who were miscarried. But the word used is *gohlahl*. We find this word on twenty occasions in Scripture, and in each other instance it is used for a child already born. For example, in Lamentations 4:4 we read, "The young children ask bread," and again, the word is *gohlahl*.

These linguistic factors are significant. The authors of Scripture, writing under divine inspiration, do not refer to the unborn child as a fetus, or as tissue, or in some other "subhuman" capacity. They use the same terminology for the unborn child as for the child already in being. That indicates that they regarded him as a human being.

(2) *The Biblical authors identify themselves with the unborn child.*

In Psalm 139:13-16, David says, "Thou hast covered *me* in my mother's womb." He does not say thou has covered the fetus that became me, or thou hast covered by the embryo. Rather, he identifies himself with the unborn child in the womb: Thou has covered *me*.

We see a similar reference in Isaiah 49:1: "The Lord hath called *me* from the womb."

Note also Jeremiah 1:5: "before *thou* camest forth out of the womb, I sanctified *thee* and I ordained *thee* a prophet unto the nations." God, the speaker in the above passage, sanctified and ordained Jeremiah while he was still in the womb! And Jeremiah identifies himself with that unborn child in the womb.

(3) *The Bible speaks of the death of the unborn child.*

Job says in 10:18-19, "Wherefore then hast thou brought me forth out of the womb? Oh that I had given up the ghost, and no eye had seen me! I should have been as though as I had not been; I should have been carried from the womb to the grave."

Jeremiah expresses a similar desire in chapter 20:15-18, "Cursed be the man who brought tidings to my father, saying, A manchild is born unto thee; making him very glad . . . Because he slew me not from the womb; or that my mother might have been my grave, and her womb to be always great with me. Wherefore came I forth out of the womb to see labour and sorrow, that my days should be consumed with same?"

The authors of Scripture speak of the unborn child as dying. How can one die if one is not alive?

(4) *The Bible affords legal protection to the unborn child.*

Exodus 21:22-25 is probably the passage of Scripture which speaks most directly to the question of abortion. However, many shy away from the use of this passage because in many English translations, it seems ambiguous. After a thorough study of the passage, however, I am convinced that the passage affords legal protection to the unborn child.

In the King James translation, the passage reads as follows: "If men strive, and hurt a woman with child, so that her fruit depart from her, and yet no mischief follow: he shall be surely punished, according as the woman's husband will lay upon him; and he shall pay as the judges determine. And if any mischief follow, then thou shall give life for life, eye for eye, tooth for tooth, and hand for hand, foot for foot, burning for burning, wound for wound, stripe for stripe."[2]

The key phrase is in verse 22: "her fruit depart from her." Some translations, including the New American Standard, render this passage as "miscarriage." But an analysis of the words used clearly demonstrates this translation to be in error. The word for fruit is *yehled*. It is found eighty-nine times in the Old Testament. In every other place, it is translated as a human being—a child, children, a boy, or a young man. In no other passage is it used for fruit or for fetus (or anything less than "human").

Second, the word for depart is *yatsah*. In every other passage where this verb appears in connection with childbirth, except possibly Numbers 12:12, which may refer to a stillborn child, it is used for a live birth: Ecclesiastes 5:14-15; Jeremiah 20:18; Genesis 25:23-26, Genesis 38:28-30. If Moses had wanted to speak about a miscarriage, there are at least two distinctive Hebrew words which mean miscarriage and which he could have used. He could have used the word *shakol*, a word which he used for miscarriage just two chapters later in Exodus 23:26, and which also appears in Hosea 9:14. Or he could have used *nephel*, a word which is used for miscarriage in Job 3:16, Psalm 58:8, and Ecclesiastes 6:3. But Moses chose not to use those words. Instead, he used the word *yatsah*, which normally means live birth. I am convinced that Moses, writing under the inspiration of the Holy Spirit, knew what he was saying and meant exactly what he said: "her fruit (children) depart from her"—a premature but live birth.

The word used later in the passage for "mischief" is *ahsohn*. The term simply means mischief or harm and could refer to anything from death to a sore finger. Some have understood the mischief of this passage to refer only to harm to the mother; but as we have seen, since the passage contemplates a live birth, there is no reason to think that the mischief cannot pertain both to the mother and to the child.

When properly translated, the meaning of the passage is clear. If men are involved in a fight and hurt a pregnant woman so that she delivers her child prematurely, but there is no injury to the mother or child, the husband is to be compensated only for his time, expenses, inconvenience, etc., and perhaps pain and suffering as well. But if the mother or child is injured, as a result, or if either die as a result, the *lex talonis*, or law of like punishment applies: eye for eye, tooth for tooth, life for life.

The clear meaning of this passage is that the unborn child is a human being

2. An excellent analysis of this passage is found in "Miscarriage or Premature Birth: Additional Thoughts on Exodus 21:22-25," by H. Wayne House, *Westerminster Theological Journal* 41:105-123, Fall 1978. See also C.F.Keil and F. Delitzsch, *Commentary on the Old Testament* (Grand Rapids: Eerdmans, Reprint 1975), translated by James Martin, 1:134-135.

whose right to life is protected just like anyone else's right to life. The criminal penalty for causing the death of the unborn child is death!

(5) *The Bible ascribes sin to the unborn child.*

In Psalm 515, David says, "Behold, I was shapen in iniquity; and in sin did my mother conceive me."

David does not mean that the act of conceiving him was sinful; there is no suggestion that David was illegitimate. Rather, he means that the child has a sin nature from the point of conception.

This naturally raises the question, does the sin nature reside in the human body, or in the soul or spirit?[3]

Ezekiel 18:4 and 18:20 state, the "soul that sinneth, it shall die." This indicates that the sin nature probably resides in the soul/spirit, not in the body. If the sin nature resides in the soul/spirit and the child has a sin nature from conception, the child must have a soul/spirit from conception. In any event, the fact that a sin nature is attributed to the unborn child clearly establishes that the unborn child is a person, not a mass of tissue.[4]

---

3. For purposes on this discussion I shall use the terms soul and spirit interchangeably. I lead strongly toward the trichotomous view of man as having a body, soul, and spirit. But the question of whether the soul and spirit are the same, different, or two different aspects of the same is not essential to this discussion and need not be determined here.

4. We need not revive at this point the longstanding debate between creationism and traducianism. Creationism in this context refers not to the creation of the world or of human life, but to the doctrine that whenever a new human life is formed, God creates afresh a new human soul/spirit, whether at the point of conception or at some time thereafter. The traducian view, on the other hand, holds that the soul/spirit is passed down hereditarily from parents to their children in a manner somewhat similar to the passage of physical characteristics. If one accepts the traducian view, the personhood of the unborn child is virtually settled, for the traducian view necessarily requires that the child has a soul/spirit from the point of conception, since he inherited that soul/spirit from his parents. However, the creationist view does not require a different conclusion as to personhood, for one may very well conclude that God creates a new soul/spirit for each person at the point of conception.

I lean strongly to the traducian view. As we have seen, Psalm 51:5 establishes that the child has a sin nature from the point of conception, and Ezekiel 18 indicates that the sin nature resides in the soul/spirit. If, as the creationists maintain, God creates a fresh soul for each new child, then according to Psalm 51:5, he must create a sinful soul. This cannot be, for God cannot be the author of sin.

There are several passages used to support creationism. Isaiah 57:16 refers to "the souls which I made." Zachariah 12:1 declares that "the Lord. . . . formeth the spirit of man within him." It may be significant, however, that the word for "make" in Isaiah 57:16 is *asah*, meaning to make or accomplish, and the word "formeth" in Zachariah 12:1 is *yatsar*, meaning to form or get into a mold. If the authors of Scripture had meant a new creation of the soul/spirit, they would probably have used the word *barah*, which normally means a new or ex nihilo creation. Finally, Ecclesiates 12:7 reads, "Then shall the dust return to the earth as it was, and the spirit shall return to God who gave it." But the word for "gave" is *nahthan*, which usually means "give," but can also mean make, appoint, put, hang up, yield, or deliver. These passages are, therefore, not conclusive evidence for creationism, and in fact, the choice of words might indicate traducianism.

(6) *The unborn child shows signs of personhood.*

In Luke 1:44, Elizabeth says, "the babe in my womb leaped for joy" when she (Elizabeth) came into the presence of Mary, who was carrying Jesus in her womb. Elizabeth's child, John the Baptist, leaped for joy in the womb! A mere glob of tissue cannot leap for joy. This is an expression of emotion, and therefore a sign of personhood.

In Genesis 25:22, we read about Esau and Jacob within the womb of Rebecca, "And the children struggled together within her." This again, is a sign of personhood.

(7) *The medical evidence supports this viewpoint.*

For the Christian who regards the Bible as the authoritative Word of God, the medical evidence is secondary. When the Word of God speaks clearly, the Word of God controls. But it is reassuring to know that the medical evidence largely supports the view that human life begins at conception.

Consider the medical facts. From the moment the sperm and egg come together to form a fertilized zygote, from that moment on the newly formed child has a genetic makeup unique from that of his mother and father, a genetic makeup that is uniquely his and will remain fixed throughout his life. If we could analyze that genetic makeup, we would know from conception the child's sex, future hair color, bone structure, skin color, and many other traits. From that time on, the genes, chromosomes, DNA and RNA are fixed and do not change. It is appropriate to say that, from that time on, the unborn child is not a "potential human being," but rather a human being with potential.

Many people are amazed to learn how quickly the unborn child develops. Two weeks after conception, the child already has a blood supply and blood type. His blood and his mother's blood come into contact through a membrane, but they do not mingle. By the end of the third week, the heart is beating and a body rhythm has been established that will last all the child's life. By the fourth week, the brain, arms, legs, kidneys, liver, and digestive tract have begun to take shape. At the end of four weeks, the embryo is already ten thousand times larger than it was at conception. By the end of the second month, the child is still less than one thumb's length in size, but everything—hands, feet, head, organs, brain—is in place. The child even has fingerprints!

During the third month of pregnancy, the palms of the hands become sensitive as do the soles of the feet. The child will grasp an object placed in his hand and can make a fist. He swallows, his lips part, his brow furrows, and he is capable of moving to avoid light or pressure. His eyelids even squint. By the end of the third month, the baby has fingernails, sucks his thumb, and recoils from pain. After the third month, the development of the unborn child consists largely of growth and strengthening. All of the vital organs are already present.[5]

5. The above information is generally accepted medical fact. Specific sources include: Gary Bergel and C. Everett Koop,"When You Were Formed in Secret"(Elyria, Ohio: Intercessors for America,

Dr. Paul E. Rockwell gives an amazing account of his contact with an unborn child:

> Years ago, while giving an anesthetic for a ruptured tubal pregnancy (at two months), I was handed what I believed to be the smallest human being ever seen. The embryo sac was intact and transparent. Within the sac was a tiny, 1/3-inch human male swimming extremely vigorously in the amniotic fluid, while attached to the wall by the umbilical cord. This tiny human was perfectly developed with long, tapering fingers, feet and toes. It was almost transparent, in regards to the skin, and the delicate arteries and veins were prominent to the ends of the fingers. The baby was extremely alive and did not look at all like the photos and drawings of 'embryos' which I have seen. When the sac was opened, the tiny human immediately lost its life and took on the appearance of what is accepted as the appearance of an embryo at this stage, blunt extremities, etc.[6]

Not only does the unborn child have the physical characteristics of a human being; scientific evidence indicates that he has personality characteristics as well. He is able to react to pain; if the womb is touched with a sharp instrument, the fetus will draw away from the instrument. He is able to move, and some move more than others, indicating different personality traits among individual unborn children. At times, he even tries to make sounds as early as the third month.[7]

In 1981 a fascinating book was published, *The Secret Life of the Unborn Child*, by Thomas Verny, M.D., and John Kelly. The purpose of the book is not to argue for or against abortion, or for or against humanity of the fetus; rather it is to establish that psychological influences upon the unborn child affect his entire life. The information in this book is astounding. For example, the authors have established that if a child has been used to hearing his father's voice while in the womb, he is able to pick out his father's voice in a room even in the

1980, p.6); C. Everett Koop, "The Right to Live," *The Human Life Review* (New York: The Human Life Foundation, Inc., 1975) Fall I, No. 4, pp. 65-87; N.J. Varrill, "The Person in the Womb" (New York, Dodd, Mead, 1968), pp.42-44; Allan C. Barnes, *Intrauterine Development* (Philadelphia: Lee Febiqer, 1968), p. 455; W.J. Hamilton and H.W. Mossman, *Human Embryology,* (Baltimore, Williams and Wilkins, 1970), p. 188; A.W. Liley, as quoted by Senator James L. Buckley, "A Human Life Amendment," *The Human Life Review I*, Winter 1975 (The Human Life Foundation, Inc.,1975), pp.7-20; Trypena Humphrey, "The Development of Human Fetal Activity in its Relation to Postnatal Behavior," *Advances in Child Development and Behavior,* Hayne W. Reese and Lewis P. Lipsitt, editors, (New York: 1975), pp.12 & 19; L.B. Arey, *Developmental Anatomy: A Textbook and Laboratory Manual of Embryology,* 7th Edition, (Philadelphia: W.B. Saunders, 1965), pp.85-105; P.S. Timiras, *Developmental Physiology and Aging,* (New York and London, MacMillan, 1972); David Granfeld, *The Abortion Decision,* (Garden City, N.Y.: AA 1969, 1971), p. 15-28; *Christian Action Council Resource Manual,* pp. sm-19-21.

6. Paul E. Rockwell, M.D., quoted by Gary Burgel and C. Everett Koop, *When You Were Formed In Secret,* (Elyria, Ohio: Intercessors for America, 1980), p.6.

7. Burgel and Koop, op cit., pp.1-17; Granfeld, op cit., pp. 15-28.

first hour or two after birth, and the child responds to his father's voice emotionally.[8]

The authors describe the account of a young American mother who had lived in Toronto, Canada during her pregnancy and sometime thereafter moved to Oklahoma City. One day, when her child was two years old, she was surprised to find the child sitting on the living froom floor chanting, "Breathe in, breathe out, breathe in, breathe out"—the words of the Lamaze exercise for childbirth. The possibility that the child had picked up these words from a source such as television was dismissed as impossible, for those words are used only in the Canadian version, not the American version. There was only one possible explanation: "the child had memorized the words while she was still in the womb."[9]

The authors quote Boris Brott, conductor of the Hamilton (Ontario) Philharmonic Symphony:

> . . . as a young man, I was mystified by this unusual ability I have—to play certain pieces sight unseen. I'd be conducting a score for the first time and, suddenly the cello line would jump out at me; I'd know the flow of the piece even before I turned the page of the score. One day, I mentioned this to my mother, who is a professional cellist. I thought she would be intrigued because it was always the cello line that was so distinct in my mind. She was; but when she heard what the pieces were, the mystery quickly solved itself. All the scores I knew sight unseen, were ones she had played while she was pregnant with me.[10]

Verny and Kelly say of the unborn child:

> By almost any measure, he is a fascinating human being at this point (from the sixth month in utero onward). He can already remember, hear, even learn. The unborn child is, in fact, a very quick study, as a group of investigators demonstrated in what has come to be regarded as a classic report.
>
> "They taught 16 unborn babies to respond to a vibrating sensation by kicking. Normally, an unborn child won't react that way to such a gentle sensation. He will ignore it, in fact. But in this case, the investigators were able to create what behavioral psychologists call the conditioned or learned response in their young subjects by first exposing them several times to something that would make then kick naturally—a loud noise (it was made a few feet from each mother and her child's reaction was monitored by sensors strapped on her abdomen). Then the investigators introduced the vibration. Each child was exposed to it immediately after the noise was made near his mother. The researchers' assumption was that after enough exposures, eventually the association between vibration and kicking would

---

8. Thomas Verny and John Kelly, *The Secret Life of the Unborn Child,* (New York), Summit Books, 1981, p. 31.

9. Ibid., p. 23.

10. Boris Brott quoted by Verny and Kelly, Ibid., pp.22-23.

become so automatic in the babies' minds, that they would kick even when the vibration was used without noise. And it proved correct. The vibration became their cue and the kicking in response to it the learned behavior.[11]

One more study out of this book is particularly fascinating:

Dr. Michael Lieberman showed that an unborn child grows emotionally agitated, measured by the quickening of his hearbeat, each time his mother thinks of having a cigarette. She doesn't even have to put it to her lips or light a match; just her idea of having a cigarette is enough to upset him. Naturally, the fetus has no way of knowing his mother is smoking, or thinking about it, but he is intellectually sophisticated enough to associate the experience of her smoking with the unpleasant sensation it produces in him. This is caused by the drop of his oxygen supply (smoking lowers the oxygen content of the internal blood passing the placenta), which is physiologically harmful to him, but possibly even more harmful are the psychological effects of maternal smoking. It thrusts him into a chronic state of uncertainty and fear. He never knows when that unpleasant physical sensation will recur or how painful it will be when it does, only that it will recur. And that's the kind of situation which does predispose toward a deep-seated condition of anxiety.[12]

All of this evidence is significant, for it is scientific confirmation of exactly what the Bible is saying, that the unborn child has all of the attributes and characteristics of a human being.

(8) *Alternative positions as to the beginning of life are wholly unsatisfactory.*

There are basically four alternative positions as to the beginning of life. The first is that human life begins at birth; the second is that human life begins at viability; the third is that human life begins at quickening; and the fourth is that human life begins at implantation. Let us analyze each of these in the light of Scripture and logic.

Birth

The primary (and usually the only) Bible passage cited in support of this position is Genesis 2:7: "And the Lord God formed man of the dust of the ground, and breathed into his nostrils the breath of life; and man became a living soul." From this passage it is sometimes argued that one is not completely human until he begins breathing, that is, at birth. However, an analysis of this verse does not support that position.

First, this is a unique, one-time event. The formation of Adam does not answer the question of whether human life begins in the womb, because Adam was never in a womb. He was the first man, and he was formed out of the dust as a adult, mature human being. Obviously, God had to give him a

11. Ibid., pp. 19-20.
12. Ibid., pp. 20-21.

soul/spirit, because there was no other way he could get one. Never has anyone else been formed out of dust, not even Eve! Nowhere are we told that God breathed into Eve the breath of life. The probable reason is that Eve was formed out of living, organic matter, Adam's rib. Before God had breathed into Adam the breath of life, Adam was still dust, inorganic matter—perhaps something like a clay statue! This had been true of no one since that time.

Second, even if we concede that in order to be human one must breathe air, the fact still remains that the unborn child uses oxygen. He simply takes in oxygen in a different manner before birth—through his placenta. There are certain medical procedures by which air is inserted into the womb, and occasionally the unborn child will take a gulp of air during that procedure. Does that make him human?

In the final analysis, birth is simply a change of environment in which one acquires the ability to breathe for himself. This by no means makes him any more or any less human than he was before.

Viability

Viability means the ability of the child to sustain life outside the womb. Many argue that the unborn child becomes human at the point of viability.

First, let us note that this position has no scriptural support whatsoever.

Second, viability varies with time. A generation or so ago, viability was generally thought to be about the sixth month after conception. But because of modern medical procedures, the child born prematurely much younger than the sixth month is often capable of surviving—at the fifth month, or possibly even younger. Does this mean that children become "human" sooner today than they did a generation ago? As medical science advances, will children become "human" even sooner still?

Furthermore, this is a very subjective test. In many cases there is no way of knowing whether a child, given adequate medical treatment, could have survived outside the womb. It is left to the subjective opinion of the doctor.

Finally, what does viability have to do with being human? The child who is already born can survive for, at most, a few hours or a few days without someone to care for him. Does this mean he is not human?

In short, viability is no basis for determining whether or not the unborn child is human. The viability test simply cannot stand up in the light of Scripture or common sense.

Quickening

Some argue that the unborn child becomes human at the point of quickening. Quickening is sometimes used interchangeably with viability, but it actually has a different meaning. It refers to the point at which the mother first feels the unborn child move within her womb.

First we should note that, like viability, the idea that a child becomes a human at the point of quickening has no scriptural support whatsoever.

Second, quickening is a very subjective test because it depends upon the mother's feeling rather than actual movement. A baby may move long before he is large enough or strong enough for his mother to feel that movement. In fact, there is cellular activity from the point of conception.

Third, quickening varies with individual babies. Some begin moving more quickly than others. And throughout pregnancy some are more active than others. But this does not mean that some babies become "human" sooner than others.

Like the test of birth and the test of viability, the test of quickening lacks scriptural support and has no basis of logic or common sense. It must therefore be rejected as a test of "humanness."

Implantation

A fourth position is that human life begins at implantation—the point at which the fertilized egg implants in the uterus. The main reason for this position is that, prior to implantation, twinning can take place, whereas no twinning can take place thereafter. It is argued that this fertilized egg cannot be a human being if it is capable of dividing into twins.

Again, the position lacks scriptural support. From a scientific standpoint, the fertilized egg is not substantially different after implantation.

One explanation is that when God intends twinning to take place, he places two human lives in the same fertilized egg at conception, and separates them at twinning.

Perhaps a better explanation is that at conception a human life comes into being. If twinning takes place, a second human life comes into being at that point.

At any rate, implantation usually takes place before the mother is even aware of the pregnancy. The question of whether life begins at conception or .viability therefore has little impact on the decision to have or not have an abortion.

We may summarize as follows:
(1) The authors of Scripture make no linguistic distinction between unborn and born children.
(2) The Biblical authors identify themselves with the unborn child.
(3) The Bible speaks of the death of the unborn child.
(4) The Bible affords legal protection to the unborn child.
(5) The Bible ascribes sin to the unborn child.
(6) The Bible shows the personality of the unborn child.
(7) The medical evidence supports the above analysis of Scripture.
(8) Other positions—birth, viability, quickening and implantation—lack support in Scripture, evidence, and logic.
(9) Therefore, human life begins at conception.
(10) Therefore, the unborn child is a living human being.

Is Killing the Unborn Child Justifiable?

We have established that the unborn child is a human being, and therefore killing him constitutes the killing of a human being. But to establish that abortion violates Exodus 20:13, we must also inquire whether or not the killing of that unborn child is justifiable. Let us, therefore, examine some of the commonly advanced justifications for abortion.

(1) *Should a mother have control over her own body and the right to choose whether or not to bear a child?*

For the most part, I agree that a woman should have control over her own body. But as the above evidence has demonstrated, the unborn child is not part of her body; he or she is a separate and distinct human being.

A primary function of government—some libertarians would say, the only legitimate function of government—is the protection of human rights. Most basic of these human rights is the right to life, because without that right no other right can be exercised or enjoyed. Government, then, has a fundamental duty to protect human life.

But at what point should that protection begin? If government is going to protect human life, it must make a determination at what point to begin and end that protection. The most logical point at which to begin the protection of the right to life, is the point at which life begins. And as scriptural and medical evidence demonstrates, human life begins at conception.

It follows, therefore, that government has a duty to protect human life from the point of conception. Since that right is more basic and fundamental than the right to choose, when the two come into conflict, the right to life should take precedence.

As a practical matter, however, the woman may exercise her right to choose in other ways: through birth control, through adoption, or through abstinence.

(2) *Should abortion be allowed for cases of rape or incest?*

First, let us place this problem in its proper perspective. While pregnancy resulting from rape is extremely serious for the persons involved, it happens far less frequently than is commonly supposed. A study reported in the *Illinois Medical Journal* found that there were no pregnancies resulting from rape in a nine-year-period in Chicago.[13]

Other reports show no pregnancies resulting from rape in over thirty years in Buffalo, New York,[14] none in over ten years in St. Paul, Minnesota,[15] and none in Philadelphia in a decade.[16] One reason is that more than one-third

13. E.F. Diamond, "ISMS Symposium on Medical Implications under the Current Abortion Law in Illinois,"*Illinois Medical Journal*, May 1967, p. 677.

14. M.Simms, " A District Attorney Looks at Abortion,"*Child and Family,* Vol. 8, Spring, 1969, pp. 176-180.

15. Dennis Horan, editor, *Abortion and Social Justice,* (N.Y.: Sheed and Ward, 1972), p. 48.

16.Judge Armand, Della Porta, Letter to Senator Richard Schweiker, July 12, 1977; cited in Christian Action Council Resource Manual, p.sm-110.

of rapists are either impotent or have premature or retarded ejaculation.[17] Pregnancies resulting from incest are similarly rare, and those pregnancies which result from incest and which are subsequently aborted are even more rare.[18]

Since they are very rare, pregnancies resulting from rape and incest should not be used to justify abortion on demand. If abortion is to be allowed for rape and incest, statutes should be narrowly drawn to limit abortion to those circumstances only, and such laws should have adequate safeguards to insure that the pregnancy has indeed resulted from genuine rape or incest and that this charge is not being used simply as an excuse to obtain an abortion solely for reasons of convenience.

However, I would oppose a law allowing abortion even for rape or incest. For one thing, the unborn child still has the right to life. It is wrong to punish an innocent child for the sin of his father (Deuteronomy 24:16).

Furthermore, abortion does not undo the harm of rape or incest. While having to bear an unwanted child can certainly be traumatic, abortion can be equally traumatic, if not more so. And the woman has a further option— she can give up the child for adoption.

Finally, most pregnancies resulting from rape can be prevented if reported and treated properly. If the rape is reported promptly, the patient can be given estrogen for several days, or a medical curettage, or diethylstilbesterol, all of which can prevent fertilization from taking place.[19]

By no means do I wish to minimize the traumatic effect of rape or incest. I only suggest: (1) that it is far less common than many people suppose, (2) that abortion does not solve the problem, and (3) that it is wrong to kill the child for the sin of his parents.

(3) *Should abortion be allowed for sake of the mental health of the mother?*

Again, I answer no. There is little evidence that abortion enhances mental health. In fact, a study done at the University of British Columbia's Department of Psychiatry, as reported in the March 3, 1978, issue of *Psychiatric News,* demonstrated that abortion often increases a woman's psychological stress.[20] The abortion may be more detrimental to a woman's mental health than bearing the child and putting him up for adoption.

There are numerous accounts of mothers who have gone through abortions,

17. A. Nicholas, Groth and Anne Wolbert Burgess, "Sexual Dysfunction During Rape," *The New England Journal of Medicine,* Oct.6, 1977, pp. 764-766.

18. Otto Pollack and Alfred S. Frideman, eds.,*Family Dynamics and Female Sexual Delinquency,* (Palo Alto, California; Sad Science and Behavior, 1969), p.62.

19. L. Kuchera, "Post Quital Contraception with Diethylstilbesterol, (DES)"*Journal of the American Medical Association,* October 25, 1971; Ada D. Ryan, M.D., Letter to Congressman Daryl Flood, Sept.13, 1977; cited in *Christian Action Council Resource Manual,* p.SM-110. These, of course, would constitute abortion if done after conception, but not if done before conception.

20. *Christian Action Council Resource Manual,* SM-18, SM-1M.

only to report they are haunted by psychological trauma, guilt, and regret thereafter.

Even if we were to concede that abortion could heal the mental health of the mother, we would then be faced with a conflict of rights: the mother's right to mental health versus the child's right to life. I would argue that the child's right to life is paramount.

(4) *Should abortion be allowed to prevent child abuse and unwanted children?*

First, note that we do not "mercifully" kill unwanted and abused children that are already born. Why should society do so before these children are born?

Second, there is no evidence that unplanned or unwanted pregnancies result in a higher proportion of unwanted or abused children. In fact, as abortion statistics have skyrocketed over the past decade, instances of reported child abuse have similarly increased! Edward Lenoski, Professor of Pediatrics at the University of Southern California has conducted an extensive study of over 1,300 battered children. He discovered that 91 percent of these children were the result of planned pregnancies, 90 percent were legitimate, and 24 percent were named after their parents as compared to only 4 percent of a control group.[21]

This seems strange until we realize two important factors: (1) Parents often change their minds about wanting a child during or after pregnancy. An unplanned or unwanted pregnancy does not necessarily result in an unwanted or unloved child, or vice-versa. (2) Parents who abuse their children usually love their children. The abuse stems not from lack of love, but from deep-seated psychological problems or lack of parenting skills.

Clearly, there is little reason to believe that abortion will solve the problem of unwanted or abused children.

(5) *Should abortion be allowed for birth defects?*

Before answering this question, let us consider an alternate proposal. Why not wait until the child is born, and can be observed more clearly to determine the nature and extent of his defects, and then put the child to death if he is severely defective? Or better yet, why not wait until the child is several years old and then put him to death if his defects are serious and uncorrectable?

"That's barbaric!" you say. And I agree. But if you accept the premise that the unborn child is a human being, what is the difference between killing him before birth and killing him after birth? Any argument for abortion based upon birth defects can be made with equal or greater force—and is in fact being made today—for infanticide!

The plain fact is, in most instances we cannot predict with any reasonable medical certainty whether a child will be defective or the extent of his defects. Retardation, for example, may be extreme, slight, or nonexistent. Furthermore,

---

21. *Christian Action Council Resource Manual*, pp. EPSM 1-129-130.

many persons with birth defects, such as Helen Keller, have lived happy and meaningful lives and have made valuable contributions to society.[22]

Finally, useful or not, wanted or not, "normal" or not, even the defective child has the right to life.

(6) *Should abortion be allowed to save the life of the mother?*

This may be the only legitimate exception in which it should be allowed.

Here we are faced with a serious dilemma: the child's right to life versus the mother's right to life. As a practical matter, the choice is usually one death or two, for in most instances where the mother is likely to die in pregnancy, the child is likely to die also. For this reason, and since the law does not require one person to give up his life for another, I believe the law should allow abortion to save the life of the mother, and for that reason only. (An additional but extremely rare exception might be a case involving twins, where the abortion of one twin might be necessary to prevent two deaths.)

This does not mean that all persons faced with this dilemma will opt for abortion. Some may believe that a deliberate act of killing is wrong under any circumstances, and such persons may choose to go through with the pregnancy and leave the consequences to God. While this is a viable option, it should not be required by law.

(7) *Should abortion be allowed because the majority wants it?*

No! First, human rights must not depend upon majority support for their protection. The primary reason our Constitution protects human rights is that majorities may deny those rights to unpopular or unwanted minorities. The unborn child's right to life is a God-given right and it deserves legal and constitutional protection whether the majority agrees or not.

Second, a majority does *not* favor abortion. The majority's views are difficult to determine because many people are undecided and because poll results vary according to how the questions are asked. For example, in 1980 the New York Times/CBS Poll asked respondents, " Do you think there should be an amendment to the Constitution prohibiting abortions, or shouldn't there be such an amendment? Twenty-nine percent favored this amendment; sixty-seven percent opposed it. But when the same poll asked the same exact persons, "Do you believe there should be an amendment to the Constitution protecting the life of the unborn child, or shouldn't there be such an amendment?" Fifty percent said they favored this amendment, and only thirty-nine percent opposed it. Yet the meaning of the two questions was practically the same![23]

Poll results may vary in other ways. Ask whether the decision to terminate

22. An excellent book which illustrates the special place a "defective" child may have in God's plan is *The Christmas Duck* by Ken Gire Jr. (Milford, Michigan) Mott Media, 1983.

23. New York Times/CBS Poll, The New York Times, August 18, 1980, p.1; cited by Dr. Raymond J. Adamek, "Abortion and Public Opinion in the United States," *National Right to Life News,* April 22, 1982, insert p.2.

pregnancy should rest solely with a woman and her doctor, and a majority will likely answer yes. Ask whether society should allow abortion on demand, and a majority will answer no. Throw in an added complication—should a married woman be allowed to abort a child without her husband's consent?—and the response will be more negative. Ask it in a very emotional way—"Do you favor the wanton murder of innocent unborn children?"—and the response will be overwhelmingly no!

Still another problem arises in the way technical exceptions are worded. The blanket question, "Do you favor or oppose abortion?" is not really fair because many will give different responses under different circumstances. How would you answer that question if you favor abortion only to save the life of the mother, or only in cases of rape or incest? And what of the frequently asked question, "Should abortion be legal in (a) all circumstances; (b) some circumstances; or (c) no circumstances?" Many staunch right-to-life advocates find themselves reluctantly circling (b) on that question, because they believe abortion should be legal to save the life of the mother.

Over the years I have seen countless polls on the subject of abortion. Despite the confusion in wording, I detect the following general conclusions about public sentiment:

(1) The issue of abortion is clouded with confusion and uncertainty.
(2) A majority believes human life begins at conception—or at least, that position has far more adherents than any of the alternative positions.
(3) A substantial majority is opposed to abortion.
(4) A majority opposes abortion on demand.
(5) A strong majority believes abortion should be legal to save the life of the mother.
(6) No clear consensus exists on whether abortion should be legal for other reasons such as mental health, rape or incest, or financial necessity.
(7) A majority opposes public funding of abortions, except perhaps in special cases.
(8) No clear consensus exists on the issue of a constitutional amendment.
(9) Abortion is not a "women's issue"; men are just as likely to favor liberalized abortion as women, and perhaps slightly more so.

The polls indicate that pro-life forces have more work to do in educating the public. But they also establish that the public is *not* pro-abortion.

(8) *What do we conclude from this?*

I conclude the following:

(1) Human life begins at conception.
(2) Abortion constitutes the taking of human life.
(3) This taking of human life is not justified, except possibly to save the life of the mother.
(4) With that single possible exception, abortion violates the commandment of Exodus 20:17: "Thou shalt not kill."

What is the Present State of the Law?

Based upon the foregoing analysis, one might think that abortion would be illegal in the United States except to save the life of the mother. And this was the law in nearly all states until 1973.

But in 1973, a landmark U.S. Supreme Court decision, *Roe v. Wade,* 410 U.S., 113, effectively struck down all anti-abortion statutes as unconstitutional. The court reasoned that the "life, liberty and property" clause in the Fourteenth Amendment guaranteed to a pregnant woman the privacy right to determine for herself whether or not to terminate a pregnancy.

In that case, the state of Texas argued that the Fourteenth Amendment guarantee that no state shall deprive any person of life, liberty or property without due process of law, also protects the unborn child's right to life. Unfortunately, the Supreme Court ruled that the term "person" as used in the Fourteenth Amendment was not intended by its authors to include unborn children.

The court conceded that the state may have some legitimate interest in regulating abortion after the first trimester of pregnancy for health and safety reasons; however, such restrictions could only be for the purpose of health and safety, such as requiring that abortions take place in hospitals, under sterile conditions, by licensed physicians. The court also ruled that after the second trimester—that is, after the sixth month of pregnancy—the states may have a legitimate interest in protecting "potential life", and may therefore restrict abortions in the third trimester of pregnancy except where abortion is necessary to preserve the life or health of the mother. However, since many pro-abortion doctors will readily certify any patient as needing an abortion for the sake of her mental health, the practical effect of *Roe v. Wade* is to allow abortion on demand.

The Supreme Court was wrong in *Roe v. Wade*—tragically wrong. First, the Court's conclusion that the authors of the Fourteenth Amendment did not mean to include unborn children in the term "person" ignores the fact that this amendment was passed and ratified during the same period of time (1868) when most of the nation's anti-abortion statutes were passed. And the "pro-choice" argument that these statutes were passed primarily to protect the mother from dangerous surgery is utterly wrong. All surgery in that day and that time was dangerous, yet there were no laws preventing appendectomies. Furthermore, the term used in the Iowa statute, and probably others as well, for abortion was "foeticide," the Latin term for killing ("cedo") and unborn child ("fetus").

Second, even if we acccept the Court's conclusion that "person" in the Fourteenth Amendment does not include unborn children, that does not mean the state has no compelling interest in protecting their right to life. Animals are not persons under the Fourteenth Amendment, yet we have laws preventing cruelty to animals. Strangely enough, livestock have more protection under the law today than unborn children!

There is an interesting parallel between *Roe v. Wade* and the *Dred Scott* decision of 1857 (60 U.S. 393, 19 Howard 393) and the *Antelope* decision of 1825 (10 Wheaton 66). These latter cases concluded that blacks were not "persons" as defined by the Fifth Amendment. Even still, this did not mean that blacks could be legally killed, and a person who killed a black could be tried for murder. In other words, legal "personhood" is not to be equated with the right to life.

Since *Roe v. Wade* there have been an estimated fifteen million abortions in the United States, and further court decisions have expanded the right to abortion. In *Planned Parenthood in Central Missouri v. Danforth*, 428 U.S. 52 (1976), the Court struck down a Missouri law requiring that a married woman have the written consent of her spouse for an abortion, that a minor have the written consent of her parents for an abortion, and that a physician use due care and skill to preserve the life and health of the fetus insofar as it is possible.

In *Bellotti v. Baird*, 443 U.S. 622 (1979), the Court again struck down as unconstitutional a state statute—this time from Massachusetts—requiring parental consent for an abortion on an unmarried minor. But two years later, in *H. L. v. Matheson*, 450 U.S. 398 (1981), the Court upheld as constitutional a Utah statute which required a physician to "notify, if possible" the parents or guardian of a minor upon whom an abortion is to be performed, and in *Harris v. McRae*, 448 U.S. 297 (1980), the Supreme Court upheld as constitutional the Hyde Amendment which prohibited most federal funding for abortions. However, several state supreme courts have struck down laws prohibiting state funding of abortions on the ground that such prohibitions violate the equal rights amendment provisions of the respective state constitutions.

While the "pro-choice" argument is that abortion should be a private and voluntary matter, the fact is that government coercion is still involved. Despite *Harris v. McRae*, government funding of abortion remains a reality in many areas, and taxpayers who oppose abortion are thereby required to subsidize an operation which they regard as murder. There have even been several instances in which courts have even considered ordering minors to undergo abortions "in their best interest" against their will![24] To my knowledge, however, no such involuntary abortion has been carried out to date.

Many are forced to subsidize abortion through group insurance policies that include abortion coverage. In a few recent cases, doctors have been held liable for the expenses and inconvenience of raising a child in "wrongful life" actions in which a plaintiff has alleged that she is saddled with an unwanted child because her doctor failed to counsel her to obtain an abortion.

While the legal and political battles rage on, the national holocaust continues—over one million abortions per year, fifteen million since 1973.

What Can Be Done?

Those who fight for the life of the unborn child often become discouraged. Ten years have passed since *Roe v. Wade*, yet it often seems that little progress has been made.

However, more people are coming to realize that the unborn child is in fact

---

24. Frankie Schaeffer, *A Time For Anger,* (Westchester, Illinois: Crossway Books, 1982), pp. 72-74.

a human being, and that his right to life deserves protection. Let us remember that the battle to abolish slavery took over sixty years, and the battle for full racial equality is still being waged a century later. But few would deny that progress has been made and victories have been won.

I believe there is much that can be done to restore legal protection to the unborn child. Let me suggest several steps:

(1) The most basic necessity is for a "human life amendment" which would declare that life begins at conception and which would thereby extend the right of life to the unborn. The practical effect of this amendment would be to over-rule *Roe v. Wade* and make abortion illegal again.

(2) So far, efforts to pass a human life amendment have not been successful. For this reason, many have seen hope in the "Hatch Compromise" offered by Senator Orin Hatch of Utah, which is basically a states' rights position. The Hatch amendment would not totally prohibit abortion, but would reserve to each individual state the right to do so.

(3) While *Roe v. Wade* remains the law of the land, the options of abortion opponents are severely limited. It is possible, however, that *Roe v. Wade* could be overruled, or at least sharply limited. Justices Rehnquist and White still seem firm in their dissent from *Roe v. Wade*. Justice O'Connor shows signs of agreeing with Rehnquist and White, and it is even possible that Chief Justice Burger could be persuaded to join them. Those four, coupled with the appoint-ment of several new conservative justices over the next four years, could alter the balance of power on the Court.

Still, the Court is reluctant to expressly overrule previous decisions. To achieve a different result, it is often necessary to establish new facts or legal principles that distinguish a new case from the former one.

One way of doing this might be the human life bill. This bill, currently in Congress, would constitute a congressional declaration that human life begins at conception. The majority in *Roe v. Wade* had ruled that there was no con-sensus as to when human life begins. This congressional declaration might pro-vide that necessary consensus, especially if backed by expert medical and legal testimony.

Another possibility is a human life bill at the state level. Such a declaration that human life beings at conception, backed by expert testimony, might establish the compelling state interest needed to justify this alleged interference with the woman's right to privacy.

Still another possibility, almost completely unexplored thus far, is the use of the term "Posterity" in the Constitution. The Preamble states that one of the purposes of the Constitution is to "secure the Blessings of Liberty to ourselves and our Posterity." The word "liberty" in the "life, liberty or pro-perty" clause of the Fifth Amendment, adopted two years after the Constitu-tion, would appear to have the same meaning as in the Preamble; there is no reason to distinguish it. And the "life, liberty or property" clause of the Four-teenth Amendment—upon which the right to an abortion is based—has virtually the same wording as the same phrase in the Fifth Amendment.

The point is this: by relating the life and liberty interests protected in the Fifth and Fourteenth Amendments to the liberty interest of the Preamble, we can establish that the framers were concerned, not only about themselves, but about future generations (''Posterity'') as well. This could supply a constitutional basis for applying the protection of the Fourteenth Amendment guarantee of life to the unborn child. I suggest this possibility be explored further.

(4) Other steps can be taken short of outright prohibition of abortion. A statute which required parental notification before an abortion was upheld in *Matheson*, and similar statutes should be upheld in other states. Some believe that a parental consent requirement might be upheld despite *Danforth* and *Belotti*, if it were drawn to require consent either by a parent or a judge.

(5) Laws providing that employers who provide health coverage for their employees need not include abortion coverage in those policies should also be upheld by the courts, and Christians should work for such laws in their respective states. One form of such legislation would provide that no insurance policy shall include abortion coverage unless such coverage is added as a special rider. This protects the general public from having to underwrite the cost of abortions through their insurance premiums.

(6) Despite *Harris v. McRae*, public funding of abortion continues in many localities. In most jurisdictions such funding could be eliminated by simple legislation, and this by itself would eliminate many abortions.

(7) Laws providing that hospitals may refuse to allow abortions and laws protecting medical personnel from liability for refusing to perform abortions or advise abortions are sorely needed in many localities.

(8) We should also explore the possibility of legislation to protect the unborn child from pain. Abortion works in various ways. The dilatation and curettage and suction methods sometimes cut the baby into pieces or suck him into a jar. Saline injection (salt poisoning) slowly burns and poisons the baby to death. The prostaglandin chemical abortion induces premature labor. This causes the uterus to contract intensely, sometimes killing or decapitating the baby. Other times, the baby survives the violent birth to be killed or die of neglect.[25] During these procedures the mother is given an anesthetic for pain. The baby is given none.

Isn't it strange that our society has laws providing for the humane slaughter of livestock, but none whatsoever for unborn children?

Expert medical testimony can readily establish that the unborn child is capable of experiencing pain. This should provide an adequate basis for legislation outlawing the inhumane infliction of pain upon the unborn child. Certain types of abortions should be prohibited or at least require that an anesthetic be given to the child as well as to the mother. Such a proposal would place

---

25. John Lippis, *The Challenge to be Pro-Life*, (Washington, D.C.: National Right to Life Educational Trust Fund), pp. 5-7.

the courts and the pro-abortion forces in a difficult dilemma. They would either oppose the legislation, thereby taking the embarrassing position that the unborn child has less right to be free from pain than does an animal; or they would support the legislation, thereby conceding that the unborn child does have certain rights. Perhaps an expectant mother might think twice about having an abortion, knowing that the baby in her womb is human enough to experience pain and require an anesthetic.

(9) Abortion has frequently resulted in the delivery of live babies. A few have even survived and gone on to be adopted and live normal lives. (One might ask the abortionist whether such a child is human. If so, when and how did he become human; if not, what is he?) Laws which would require a physician to use medical care to save the life of any aborted baby delivered alive, regardless of whether in the opinion of the doctor the baby is "viable," are desperately needed. Immediate legislation should be enacted to terminate the practice of experimenting on live fetuses. Such legislation was passed in the House of Representatives in the fall of 1982, but has not yet been passed by the Senate. That such barbarity can go on in a supposedly civilized society is absolutely incredible.

(10) Stronger legislation and more vigorous enforcement of existing legislation to prevent infanticide are desperately needed. As noted earlier, infanticide is a logical outgrowth of abortion. Ten to fifteen years ago, abortion opponents were ridiculed for arguing that abortion would lead to infanticide, but today their prophecy has become a grim reality.

Many were shocked out of complacency by the "Infant Doe" tragedy of April 1982. Born on Good Friday (April 8) in Indiana, Infant Doe was afflicted with Down's Syndrome and also needed corrective surgery so his stomach could properly receive food. Doctors believed the chances for successful surgery were good to excellent, and there was no way of knowing with certainty what degree of retardation, if any, would result from the Down's Syndrome. But the parents opted to refuse corrective surgery, intravenous feeding, or other life support—in other words, they chose to starve their baby to death.

The hospital contacted the local courts, and two local courts refused to intervene, since the parents had made their decision after consultation with medical personnel. The Monroe County Prosecutor's Office and the legal guardian for Infant Doe then appealed to the Indiana Supreme Court, asking that the child be temporarily removed from the custody of his parents so that medical treatment could be performed. On Wednesday, April 14, the Indiana Supreme Court voted 3-1 to refuse the request.

The Prosecutor and guardian then appealed to the U.S. Supreme Court, joined by a couple who sought to adopt the baby. But six days after birth; before the Supreme Court acted, Infant Doe died of starvation and related complications.[26]

26. Joseph Rebone with Dave Andrusko, " A Chronology of Infanticide: The Life and Death of Infant Doe,"*National Right to Life News,* May 10, 1982, pp. 1, 11, 13.

The unique feature of the Infant Doe tragedy is that it received nation-wide attention. Many doctors claim that what happened to Infant Doe is nothing but business-as-usual in countless hospitals across the country. This is nothing short of murder and must be stopped.

(11) While we must protect the life of the unborn child, we must also be concerned about the expectant mother. Her trauma, financial pressure, and other problems are very real. We must do more than just prohibit abortion— we must provide the expectant and troubled mother with the emotional, psychological, educational, financial and spiritual support she needs to carry her child through pregnancy and deliver the child successfully.

Fortunately, there are several organizations which do exactly that. One is Birthright, loosely affiliated with the National Right to Life Committee, Inc. Another is the Save-A-Baby program recently established by the Old-Time Gospel Hour of Dr. Jerry Falwell—often branded by pro-abortionists as an enemy of pregnant mothers. Our government's double standard is reflected in the strange fact that these organizations receive no government funds while the pro-abortion Planned Parenthood agencies receive millions from the public treasury. Save-A-Baby and Birthright both deserve our support.

(12) We can work as individuals or we can work as organized groups. The National Right to Life Committee, Inc., is a well-organized group, which works for the rights of unborn children. Those wishing to work against abortion could probably increase their effectiveness by uniting with National Right to Life. Its address is: Suite 402, 419 7th Street, N.W., Washington, DC 20004, telephone (202 638-4560). We need to work, not only on the legislative front, but also as individuals, one-on-one, to educate our fellow citizens as to the right to life. If one pregnant mother can be persuaded not to have an abortion, that is a human life saved.

> "And the King shall answer and say unto them,
> Verily I say unto you,
> Inasmuch as ye have done unto one of the least of these my brethren,
> Ye have done it unto me." Matthew 25:40.

Chapter 21

The Christian and Other Issues

When George Washington became President in 1789, the Federal Government had a grand total of 350 civilian employees. These 350 persons served a total population of three million without such "helps" as telephones, typewriters, computers, copy machines, or efficient transportation.

Let's think about that for a minute. That's approximately one civil servant for every 8,500 citizens. Now our population is 218 million. If we had kept the same ratio, we would now have 25,000 civilian federal employees.

But, it is argued, changing times have made our society much more complicated than in 1789. I question whether it is the changing times or the bureaucrats themselves that have made our society more complicated, but let's grant that point. Let's say society today is ten times more complicated than in 1789, so we need ten times more government. That would be 250,000 civilian employees.

But in fact, in 1981 the Federal Government has three *million* civilian employees—each one exercising some kind of control over the lives of our citizens. That's 8,571 times more than in 1789, and the ratio has changed from 1/8,500 in 1789 to 1/70 in 1981.[1] And our taxes have increased accordingly.

The point is this. Religion is and always has been part of American life. But government is a part of our lives now, too, more so than the founders of our country ever dreamt. And since religion and government are both today so much involved in our lives, religion and government interact and conflict in ways our forefathers never imagined. This interaction and conflict regularly produce new and unprecedented constitutional questions. This book could never cover every constitutional issue of importance to Christians. But in this chapter we will discuss several that are very important.

1. W. Cleon Skousen op. cit, p. 103.

Zoning, Churches, and Home Bible Studies

What could possibly be wrong with zoning ordinances?

Plenty, if they are misused! While the initial purpose of such ordinances may have been benevolent, zoning can be used to encroach upon fundamental American freedoms. City and state officials may use zoning ordinances to prohibit, restrict, or discourage that which they cannot constitutionally prohibit by means of traditional criminal statutes.

Suppose your city passed an ordinance making it a criminal misdemeanor for anyone to attend church. Obviously, that ordinance would violate the First Amendment.

But suppose, instead, the city passed a zoning ordinance prohibiting church buildings within the city limits. By so doing they accomplish that which they could not accomplish through the normal criminal process.

Would such a law be constitutional? Almost certainly not, as the courts have ruled in *North Shore Unitarian Soc. Inc. v. Village of Orchard Lake*, 200 Misc. 524, 109 N.Y.S. 2d 803 (1951); and *Mooney v. Village of Orchard Lake*, 333 Mich. 389, 53 N.W. 2d 308 (1952).

But what if the city, instead of completely prohibiting churches, passed a zoning ordinance restricting churches to one limited, remote, and perhaps undesirable part of town? Or what if the city tried to prohibit churches from locating in residential neighborhoods and restricted them to business or industrial districts instead? The majority view seems to be that such zoning laws have a chilling effect upon the free exercise of religion and therefore must be struck down, *Community Synagogue v. Bates*, 1 N.Y. 2d 445, 136 N.E. 2d 488 (1956); *American Friends v. Schwab*, 417 N.Y.S. 2d 991 (1979); *Church of Christ v. Metropolitan Board of Zoning*, 371 N.E. 2d 1331 (Ind. Ct. App. 1978).

But the California courts have upheld zoning ordinances which exclude churches from residential districts, *Church of Jesus Christ of Latter-Day Saints v. City of Porterville*, 203 P. 2d 823 (1949); *City of Chula Vista v. Pagard*, 159 Cal. Rptr. 29 (1979). Still others allow churches to be excluded from residential zones when competent evidence is presented that the neighborhood will be adversely affected, *West Hartford Methodist Church v. Zoning Board of Appeals*, 121 A. 2d 640 (Conn. 1956); *Arch Diocese of Portland v. County of Washington*, 458 P. 2d 682 (Oregon 1969). In considering adverse affect, the court might consider traffic problems, detriment to property values, and loss of tax base.[2]

---

2. For traffic congestion, see *Board of Zoning v. Decatur Ind. Co. of Jehovah's Witnesses*, 117 N.E. 2d 115 (Ind. 1954); *State Ex rel Tampa v. City of Tampa, Florida*, 48 So. 2d 78 (1950); Application of Covenant Community Church, Inc., 444 N.Y.S. 2d 415 (1981); *Mikvah of South Shore v. Granito*, 432 N.Y.S. 2d 638 (1980). In all of these cases traffic congestion was deemed insufficient reason to prohibit churches. As for diminution of property values, see Anderson, *American Law of Zoning*, Vol.1, p. 453: "The high purpose and moral values of a religious use outweigh mere piqueneary loss to a few individuals." In *Jacobi v. Zoning Board of Adjustment*, 196 A. 2d 742 (1964), the Supreme Court of Pennsylvania ruled that local zoning boards may not consider loss of tax revenue by allowing church use of property.

Others, instead of prohibiting or restricting the location of churches, restrict the way church property can be used. A zoning ordinance that restricts a certain part of town to private residences only may contain an exception for churches, but zoning officials may narrowly define the exception so as to allow worship services, but prohibit such activities as Christian schools. Christian schools, they reason, are not a normal use of a church.

Is the Christian school a normal use of a church? In chapter 16 we examined the facts. Several courts have held that it is: *Diocese of Rochester v. Planning Board,* 136 N.E. 2d 827 (N.Y. 1956); *St. John's Roman Catholic Church v. Town of Darien,* 184 A. 2d 42 (Conn. 1962); *City of Concord v. New Testament Baptist Church,* 382 A. 2d 377 (N.H. 1978). But other courts have issued opposite ruling, *Damascus Community Church v. Clackamas County,* 610 P. 2d 273 (Ore. Ct. App. 1980). As we discussed in chapter 16, to establish that a Christian school is a ministry of the church, everything possible should be done to tie it to the church structure, such as including it in the same corporation.

Often zoning ordinances do not absolutely prohibit Christian schools from operating in churches; they merely require a special use permit or variance. Some Christians refuse to obtain such permits, claiming that the requirement itself violates the First Amendment. They fear that if they submit to the state's authority once, they will be prohibited from challenging that authority later. For example, if a conditional use permit was obtained in 1984, and then objected to on religious grounds in 1985, the court may question the sincerity of the objection because the permit was sought a year earlier. One way of resolving this dilemma might be to apply for the permit and attach a statement to the application to the following effect:

> We believe on religious and constitutional grounds that the state has no jurisdiction over religion and no authority to require a permit of this type. In the spirit of Romans 12 which requires that we attempt to ''live peaceably with all men'' and Romans 13 which requires that we obey the civil authorities (but see Acts 5:29), we do hereby apply for this permit. By so doing, however, we make no affirmation that we will apply for such permits in the future, and we in no way waive our right to object to such requirements in the future on religious and constitutional grounds. It is hereby agreed by us in submitting this application and by the state in accepting it, that this action establishes no precedent whatsoever and it may not be used in court in the event we object to obtaining such permits in the future.

There is no guarantee that this will fully protect a constitutional case, but it may help.

Other courts have defined the scope of church functions to include indoor and outdoor youth activity as well as religious social clubs, *Community Synagogue v. Bates,* 136 N.E. 2d 488 (N.Y. 1956); a lighted recreation field, *Corporation of Presiding Bishop v. Ashton,* 448 P. 2d 185 (Idaho 1968); a church activities building, *Board of Zoning v. New Testament Bible Church,* 411 N.E. 2d 681 (1980);

a parsonage and "sisters' home," *Board of Zoning Appeals v. Schulte*, 172 N.E. 2d 39 (Ind. 1961); adult Sunday school classes, Sunday morning activities, Wednesday church meetings, study groups, and ladies fellowships, *Twin-City Bible Church v. Zoning Board of Appeals of Urbana*, 365 N.E. 2d 1381 (Ill. 1977); and coffee houses, day care centers, drug rehabilitation centers, and dormitories, 62 A.L.R. 3d 197. On the other hand, a retreat center, day camp and youth center in a residential zone were held not to be normal church use in *Christian Retreat Center v. Board of City Commission*, 560 P. 2d 1100 (Ore. 1977).

Edward Bassett, the father of modern zoning concepts, wrote:

> When in 1916 the framers of the greater New York building zone regula-
> tion were discussing what buildings and uses should be excluded from
> residential districts, it did not occur to them that there was the remotest
> possibility that churches, schools, and hospitals could properly be excluded
> from any districts. They considered that these concomitants of civilized
> residential life had a proper place in the best and most open localities.[3]

Unfortunately, today zoning is sometimes used in ways our forefathers would not have condoned.

The most shocking news is yet to come! Not only have zoning officials tried to restrict churches and their uses; they have even invaded the privacy of the home and prohibited certain religious observances in private homes. Zoning ordinances that prohibit churches in residential neighborhoods have often given such broad definitions to "church" as "any place where people meet to worship God or study the Bible."

Samuel E. Ericsson, Director of the Center for Law and Religious Freedom, writes:

> In 1980, Mayor Tom Bradley of Los Angeles stated that, "a Bible study
> would not be a permissible use in a single-family residential area . . . since
> this would be considered a church activity." In a town near Boston, the
> building commissioner notified a clergyman that inviting more than four
> people to his home for a Bible study was a violation of the "Home
> Occupation" ordinance. In Atlanta, a zoning official stated that any kind
> of regular home Bible study which includes nonresidents is illegal without
> a special use permit. Home owners in Los Angeles were warned that if
> even one nonresident entered their home for a religious service, a cease
> and desist order could issue. Two Maryland residents were issued a cita-
> tion for using their home for worship services without a use and occupancy
> permit. In Canton, Michigan, a local pastor was told by a zoning official
> that any regular Bible study in a home was a violation of the zoning

---

3. "Zoning and the Church: Toward a Concept of Reasonableness," 12 *Conn Law Rev.* 571-574 (1980); quoted by Mike Schmidt, "Religious Freedom and the Zoning Laws," paper submitted for Constitutional Law II, O. W. Coburn School of Law, Tulsa, Oklahoma, Spring 1983.

ordinance and the code for Canton makes no provision for a special use permit.[4]

Ericsson hastens to add that, after Christian Legal Society officials met with Mayor Bradley and explained their First Amendment concerns to him, the Mayor backed away from this position and home Bible studies are now allowed in Los Angeles. However, the problem crops up in an increasing number of localities across the nation.[5]

In Atlanta, Georgia officials notified Mrs. Luci Johnson that a regular home Bible study which included nonresidents was illegal without a special use permit which would cost $200. According to the Director of the Bureau of Buildings, before the permit could be issued an application would have to be filed, the property advertised, and a public hearing conducted.[6]

Several such cases have gone to court. Maranatha Ministries International filed suit against the city of Seattle asking for declaratory and injunctive relief prohibiting the city from enforcing a notice of violation served upon Marantha Ministries directing them to "discontinue use of property for Bible study classes or obtain a permit to establish such use" and advising that a "criminal complaint and you will be summoned to appear in municipal court" if such use is not discontinued. The case was settled out of court with a consent decree signed by both parties in which the city agreed that the daily Bible studies and weekly Christian fellowship meetings held by Maranatha Ministries do not violate the Seattle zoning ordinances and that the city would not prosecute Maranatha Ministries for those activities.[7]

In another part of the country, Rabbi Naftali Grosz and others sought similar relief against the city of Miami Beach because of their threat to prosecute Rabbi Grosz for holding daily worship services in his home. The Federal District Court held that the ordinance imposed a burden upon the free exercise of the Rabbi's religion, and entered a preliminary injunction restraining the city of Miami Beach from prosecuting Rabbi Grosz.[8]

Now, one might conceivably argue that zoning ordinances are necessary to prevent parking problems, traffic congestion, noisy disturbances, etc.—although

4. Samuel E. Ericsson, "Your Home is Not Always Your Castle," *The Advocate*, Summer 1981, p. 4.

5. Samuel E. Ericsson, personal conversation with John Eidsmoe, Tulsa, Oklahoma, February 1983.

6. 76 *Northwestern Law Review*, 786 (1981), cited by Schmidt, p. 9. See also 38 *The Presbyterian Journal*, 3 (1980), cited in fn. 2, "Zoning Ordinances, Religious Uses of Land, and the Free Exercise of Religion," Paige Cunningham and Samuel E. Ericsson, available through Christian Legal Society.

7. *Maranatha Ministries International v. City of Seattle*, No. 81-2-13220-1 (Wash. Super. Ct., King Co., March 9, 1982); cited in *Religious Freedom Reporter*, Vol. 1, No. 11, p. 289-290, Vol. 2, No. 5, May 1982, p. 136.

8. *Grosz v. City of Miami Beach*, No. 81-608-CIV-JE (S. D. Fla. April 8, 1982); cited in *Religious Freedom Reporter*, Vol. 2, No. 6, June 1982, p. 169-170.

no one has alleged that this was a problem in any of the cases cited. But that could apply to any type of private gathering, not just Bible studies. These zoning ordinances do not prohibit inviting people in your home to drink beer, watch a football game, or study Shakespeare. But if you invite people into your home to study the Bible, watch out, because then you're a "church." If such zoning ordinances were truly intended to protect the public against traffic congestion, noise, etc., they would apply equally to all home gatherings, not just to churches.

As applied, such ordinances clearly violate the First Amendment guarantees of free exercise of religion, freedom of speech, and freedom of association. They also violate the "liberty" concept of the Fifth and Fourteenth Amendments, the "privacy" guarantee of the Ninth and other amendments, and the "equal protection" clause of the Fourteenth Amendment.

One might argue that a home Bible Study is not a church, because many define "church" as a gathering where, among other things, the sacraments are performed.[9] But why should it matter if a home Bible study is a church? After all, the Christians of the first century met in homes (Romans 16:5, I Cor. 16:19; Colossians 4:15; Philemon 2), as did many churches in the early history of America, such as those of John Wesley and the Methodists.[10]

The Christian at Work

Most people spend a substantial portion of their waking hours at work. They do not and cannot set their Christianity aside during those hours. Every Christian is in full time Christian service, whether he wants to be or not; the only issue is the quality of that service. The Christian therefore needs to know how to conduct himself at work, and he needs to know his legal rights and obligations concerning his employment.

The Civil Rights Act of 1964, 42 U.S.C. 2000e, prohibits employers from discriminating on the basis of race, color, religion, sex, or national origin, in hiring or firing employees or in compensation, terms, conditions, or privileges of employment. The effect of this law is that an employer may not refuse to hire a person or deny a raise in pay, promotion, vacation, or other conditions relating to employment, solely because of Christian beliefs.

The act also applies to employment agencies and labor unions, but it does not apply to employers with fewer than fifteen employees. Nor does it apply to private clubs or religious corporations. Christian schools, for example, need not hire non-Christian teachers. The courts are less clear on whether it applies

---

9. Francis Pieper, *Christian Dogmatics* (St. Louis: Concordia, 1953), 4 vols., III:420. This is part of the basic Lutheran definition of church or congregation. Under this definition such groups as Youth for Christ, or Young Life, while they perform a valuable function for Christianity, are not, technically speaking churches, nor do they generally claim to be.

10. Paige Cunningham and Samuel E. Ericsson, "Zoning Ordinances, Religious Uses of Land, and the Free Exercise of Religion," (Available through the Christian Legal Society, 820 Ontario, Oak Park, Illinois 60302) p.10.

to such arguably religious corporations as Christian publishing companies, radio stations, etc.

In *Kern v. Dynalectron Corp.* (U.S.D.C., N. Dist. Texas, Fort Worth Division, Civil Action No. 4-79-346-K), a Southern Baptist helicopter pilot was fired from his job because he refused to convert to Islam. The Virginia-based company insisted that he convert in order to work on a project at the Sacred Mosque in Mecca, Saudi Arabia, since Saudi law prohibits non-Muslims from entering the holy area at Mecca under penalty of beheading. When he refused to convert, he was discharged. On October 19, 1983, the district court ruled against Kern's claim. The court placed great emphasis upon the company's claim that Kern knew of the requirement to convert prior to accepting employment with Dynalectron. Unfortunately, Kern died before the case went to trial, and this undoubtedly hindered his attorney's ability to refute the company's claim.

One provision of the Civil Rights Act of 1964, 42 U.S.C. 2000e (j), gives strong protection to religious workers:

> The term "religion" includes all aspects of religious observance and practice, as well as belief, unless an employer demonstrates that he is unable to reasonably accommodate to an employee's or prospective employee's religious observance or practice without undue hardship on the conduct of the employer's business.

The effect of this statute is that an employer must accommodate the religious beliefs and observances of the employee, unless he is unable to do so without causing undue hardship on his business. If the employer refuses to do so and fires or refuses to hire the employee because of these religious beliefs or practices, his action constitutes religious discrimination under the law.

Let us suppose, for example, that a Jew or Seventh Day Adventist is asked to work on Saturdays, but refuses to do so on religious grounds. His employer says, "Work Saturdays or be fired." He refuses, and loses his job. Religious discrimination? That depends upon whether or not the employer can show that accommodation of the employee's religious beliefs (letting him off without pay on Saturdays, and possibly letting him work Sundays or extra hours on other days) would cause undue hardship on the employer's business. In *Riley v. Bendix Corp.* 464 F.2d 1113 (C.A. Fla. 1972), that court held that this would not be an undue hardship, and consequently the employer was guilty of religious discrimination. Similar results were reached in *Jackson v. Veri Fresh Poultry, Inc.*, 304 F. Supp. 1276 (D.C. La. 1969) and *Dewey v. Reynolds Metals Co.*, 304 F. Supp. 1116 (D.C. Mich. 1969). But in *Kettell v. Johnson and Johnson*, 337 F. Supp. 892 (D.C. Ark. 1972) the employer had tried to accommodate the employee's schedule by relieving him of most Saturday work but the employee refused to work at all on Saturdays, and the court found that reasonable accommodation had been made and the employer was not guilty of religious discrimination. In *U.S. v. City of Albuquerque*, 545 F.2d 110, (C.A.N.M. 1976), cert. den. 433 U.S. 909, the city showed that accommodating a Seventh Day

Adventist would have required other firemen to work as long as thirty-eight consecutive hours. The court held that accommodation would cause an undue hardship, and therefore ruled this was not discrimination. However, mere involuntary reassignment of work schedules is not enough to cause "undue hardship" *Reid v. Memphis Pub. Co.*, 369 F. Supp. 684, (D.C. Tenn. 1973), aff. 521 F.2d 512, cert. den. 429 U.S. 964. The trend is toward requiring employers to accommodate religion in arranging work schedules.

Some religious beliefs obviously cannot be accommodated. If a winetaster at a brewery gets "saved" and will no longer touch liquor, the brewery clearly cannot accommodate him by giving him only nonalcoholic beverages to taste. But if the company can reassign him to another position in which he would not have to taste wine, it probably can be required to so in order to accommodate his religion. See *Gavin v. People's Natural Gas Co.*, 613 F. 2d 482 (C.A. Pa. 1980).

Religious beliefs that require the employee to adopt a certain dress or hairstyle would be subject to the same test: Would accommodation cause undue hardship to the employer's business? On April 8, 1981 the Equal Employment Opportunity Commission decided in favor of a woman whose Pentecostal religion required that she wear a skirt. The employer refused to hire her to work as a bus driver because the dress code for bus operators required pants. The EEOC decided there was no legitimate reason the employer could not accommodate the woman's religious beliefs, and therefore upheld her claim.[11]

If the employee's religion required that he wear a turban and a robe, the employer could probably accommodate him without undue hardship, unless he worked with customers who would be offended by this or unless he worked in a "hardhat" area where his turban would be a safety hazard. The courts have held that the mere fact that accommodation would cause some fellow workers to be unhappy was not sufficient to establish undue hardship to the employer's business. *Burn v. Southern Pacific Transportation Company*, 589 F. 2d 403 (C.A. Ariz. 1978), cer. den. 439 U.S. 1072. However, the employee must cooperate with the employer in trying to work out a reasonable accommodation, *Chrysler Corp. v. Mann*, 561 F.2d 1282 (C.A. Mo. 1977), cert. den. 434 U.S. 1039.

In recent years the constitutionality of the religious accommodation clause has been challenged several times. It involves the classic confrontation between the establishment clause and the free exercise clause. Some claim it is necessary to ensure that employees can freely exercise their religious beliefs; others claim it constitutes an establishment of religion by preferring religious employees over others. In *Nottelson v. A.O. Smith Corp.*, 489 F. Supp. 94 (D.C. Wis. 1980) the clause was upheld as constitutional, though the company has appealed. But in *Yott v. North American Rockwell*, 602 F. 2d 904, cert. den. 445 U.S. 928

---

11. Decision of Equal Employment Opportunity Commission, No. 81-20 [1979], cited in *Religious Freedom Reporter*, vol. 2, No. 10, October 1981, pp. 252-253.

(C.A. Cal. 1979) it was struck down by the district court as unconstitutional (the circuit court decided the issue on other grounds and did not decide the constitutional question). More recently the Ninth Circuit held the clause constitutional in *Anderson v. General Dynamics*, 648 F.2d 1247 (C.A. Cal. 1978), and the U.S. Supreme Court denied certiorari.

One of the most controversial accommodation questions concerns the employee who has religious objections to labor union membership. Though the courts have not allowed employees to be entirely free of obligations to labor unions, they have granted them some right of accommodation. The courts have said that the employee can be required to do nothing more for the union than tender an initiation fee and pay periodic dues (*NLRB v. General Motors Corporation*, 373 U.S. 734, 742 [1963]). Further than that, the court ruled the only fee that the union can extract from one who doesn't want to be associated with the union is one which covers the employee's share of negotiating and administering the collective bargaining (*Abood v. Detroit Board of Education*, 431 U.S. 209, 1977). See also *Tooley v. Martin-Marietta Corp. & United Steelworkers of America, Local 8141*, 648 F.2d 1239 (9th Cir. 1981). And in *McDaniel v. Essex*, 571 F.2d 338 (C.A. Mich. 1978) the court held that an employee who has religious convictions against union membership may elect to pay the equivalent of dues to a charity instead of to the union.

These rulings, of course, were based upon the accommodation clause of the Civil Rights Act of 1964. On December 24, 1980, this specific protection was enacted into federal law through H.R. 4774, Section 19 of which provides that:

> Any employee who is a member of and adheres to established and traditional tenets or teachings of a bona fide religion, body, or sect which has historically held conscientious objections to joining or financially supporting labor organizations shall not be required to join or financially support any labor organization as a condition of employment; except that such employee may be required in a contract between such employees' employer and a labor organization in lieu of periodic dues and initiation fees, to pay sums equal to such dues and initiation fees to a nonreligious, nonlabor-organization charitable fund exempt from taxation under section 501 (c) (3) of title 26 of the Internal Revenue Code, chosen by such employee from a list of at least three such funds designated in such contract, or if the contract fails to designate such funds, then to any fund chosen by the employee. If such employee who holds conscientious objections pursuant to this section requests the labor organization to use the grievance-arbitration procedure on the employee's behalf, the labor organization is authorized to charge the employee for the reasonable cost of using such procedure.

So far there has been no challenge to the constitutionality of this statute, but it could be challenged in the future.

Of course, this is not an issue in those states that have adopted right-to-work laws that prohibit anyone from being compelled to join a union as a condition of employment. Currently, those states are Alabama, Arizona, Arkansas,

Florida, Georgia, Iowa, Kansas, Louisiana, Mississippi, Nebraska, Nevada, North Carolina, North Dakota, South Carolina, South Dakota, Tennessee, Texas, Utah, Virginia, and Wyoming.

What about witnessing on the job? In *Flynn v. Maine Employment Security Commission* (Me. 448 A. 2d 905, 1982), the court ruled that a security guard at a Catholic hospital who was fired for violating a prohibition against discussing religion with hospital patients, was fired for misconduct and therefore not entitled to unemployment benefits.[12] And in *Collins v. Virginia Employment Commission*, No. 68142 (Circuit Court, Fairfax County, Virginia, August 22, 1980), an employee alleged that she was terminated from her position as Citizen Advocacy Coordinator with the Northern Virginia Association for Retarded Citizens for refusing to sign an agreement to abide by a policy prohibiting references to a deity or prayer in written communications with clients. The case is still pending in the courts. (No. 3, March 1981, pp. 49-50.) It seems likely that the guarantee of free speech would protect a person's right to witness, especially if others are allowed to express opinions derogatory to religion. A key question in this type of case is whether the witnessing has an adverse effect on the employer's business.

An interesting case that was recently filed in Federal District Court in Tulsa, Oklahoma, involves John Blackwell. An over-the-road truck driver for a nationwide firm, Blackwell frequently was on the road for as long as a month at a time. Often he was assigned a partner, and the two would ride together for as long as several weeks, utilizing a sleeping compartment behind the driver's seat of the cab or sharing a motel room if they had to stop overnight.

In the fall of 1982, as Blackwell approached a terminal in Maryland, the dispatcher advised him that he would be assigned a female co-driver to accompany him back to Tulsa. Blackwell refused, saying that riding with a woman for that length of time would place a strain on his marriage, which he considered to be a sacrament in his Catholic faith. For his refusal, he was promptly terminated.

Blackwell claims that 42 U.S.C. 2000e (j) requires the company to accommodate his religious beliefs. The case raises interesting issues of religious discrimination, sexual discrimination, and sexual preference, and could set an interesting precedent.[13]

What should a Christian do if he feels an employer has discriminated against him? Before filing suit in Federal District Court, he must first file a complaint with the Equal Employment Opportunity Commission. The EEOC examines the case and determines whether there is reasonable cause to believe discrimination took place. If reasonable cause is found to exist, the EEOC can bring suit against the employer or attempt a settlement. If it does not or cannot do either,

---

12. *Religious Freedom Reporter*, Vol. 2, No. 9, September 1982, p. 255.

13. John Blackwell, personal conversations with John Eidsmoe, Tulsa, Oklahoma, 1982 and 1983.

the EEOC must issue a letter to the complaintant granting him the right to sue. After the ''right to sue'' letter has been issued, the employee/complaintant may file suit against the employer in Federal District Court within ninety days.

What about the rights of the Christian employer? Can he legally hire an all-Christian staff? Probably not, unless his company qualifies as a private club or religious association, or unless he has fewer than fifteen employees. He may certainly consider the general moral character of his prospective employees, and a Christian testimony might be evidence of good moral character. He might also attract Christian applicants by advertising only in Christian periodicals or on Christian radio stations.

Does this mean that the Christian employer has less religious liberty on his own premises than do his non-Christian employees? That certainly isn't the true meaning of the law, although sometimes the administrative agencies that enforce these laws are staffed by persons who harbor a distinct bias against business, property rights, and the entire American free enterprise system. It is probably legal for an employer to witness to his employees or customers, set reasonable standards for the moral conduct of his employees while on the premises, and use Christian decor, Christian posters, or Christian background music. But he should not do so in such a manner as to make the non-Christian uncomfortable while working for him. And if the place of business is to have a distinctively Christian atmosphere, it might be advisable to make sure the prospective employee is aware of this before he accepts the position.

Federal violations are investigated, upon complaint, by the U.S. Civil Rights Commission, and complaints must be made to the commission within 180 days after the alleged discrimination took place. Complaints of discriminatory acts done under color of state law may be grounds for private lawsuits in federal district court under 42 U.S.C. 1983, in addition to the various state remedies available.

So far our discussion has been limited to federal law. State or local antidiscrimination laws also affect individuals, and state and local agencies for the enforcement and administration of these laws may possibly impose stricter rules than federal authorities.

The Christian employee should keep two additional admonitions in mind. First, nondiscrimination legislation is a two-edged sword. The same law that prevents the non-Christian employer from firing a Christian employee also keeps the Christian employer from having an all-Christian shop. Such legislation has positive and negative effects.

Second, the Christian needs to use caution in witnessing at work. While the right to read the Bible and pass out tracts may be constitutionally protected (especially if others are allowed to read *Playboy* and football schedules), it may not be a good witness at all. Remember an employee is hired, not to witness, but to *work*. Witnessing on company time is the same as stealing, if it interferes with the work responsibilities of the day. Opportunities to witness at work will arise, but the best witness of all is a job well done as unto the Lord.

Witnessing in Public

Does the Christian have the right to use public facilities to witness to others? In most cases the answer is yes. This is especially true if the place is a "First Amendment forum," that is, an area in which people commonly exchange views and talk about issues of importance. And if the state or municipality makes a practice of allowing some types of free-speech activity to take place in that facility, it cannot bar others. (*Police Department of Chicago v. Mosley*, 408 U.S. 92, [1972]).

But the government may require that those wishing to hold organized meetings, parades, protests, etc., obey reasonable restrictions as to time, place, size, etc., to meet the state's compelling interest in public safety, avoidance of traffic congestion, crowd control, etc. The state may also require the religious organization to pay for the use of public facilities, if other organizations are similarly required to pay. Whether the state may single out religious organizations and make them pay for the use of public facilities, while private nonreligious organizations are allowed to use them free of charge, is still an open question.

Individual acts such as handing out tracts, one-on-one witnessing, etc., are probably permissible on public streets and other such facilities. But recently the Supreme Court decided that Minnesota State Fair officials had a compelling interest in requiring Hare Krishna devotees to observe certain limitations in soliciting funds at the state fair (*Heffron v. International Society for Krishna Consciousness*, 452 U.S. 640, 69 L.Ed. 2d 298 [1981]). It may be significant that the court made an apparent distinction between Krishna witnessing and Krishna fund raising; the latter was more subject to restriction than the former.

What about witnessing on private property? For the most part, the owner of private property has the right to direct who will and will not set foot on his property. No one has the right to use another's home or front yard for a demonstration!

Stores and other places of business are public accommodations, and therefore an owner cannot refuse service to anyone on the grounds of race, creed, or color. However, he could restrict access to those who have come to do business. He could exclude those who have come to demonstrate, witness, hand out literature, or the like.

A shopping center may be a different situation. Due to the multiplicity of stores and persons on the premises for other reasons, a shopping center may become a "First Amendment forum" in which the right of free speech and expression fully applies. The Supreme Court in *Lloyd v. Tanner*, 407 U.S. 551 (1972), held that a shopping center may enforce a rule prohibiting the distribution of handbills on its property. However, in *Pruneyard Shopping Center v. Robins*, 447 U.S. 74 (1980), the Court said that if state law requires shopping centers to make their facilities open to the distribution of literature, the courts will enforce that law. In short, the Court seems to be saying that if state law says you can witness or disseminate literature in shopping centers, you have the right to do so; if not, the shopping center has the right to prohibit such activity, at least so long as it prohibits all groups and ideas and not just some.

The Christian and the State: Six Models

As we close this study of the Christian and the Constitution, a final word is in order.

We live in an age of renewed evangelical interest in government. This is far from unique in the history of the church; but it differs from the "hands off" posture of many Christians of the past several generations. I welcome this renewed interest. God's Word has a great deal to say about government, and the church that fails to preach what God says about government is not preaching the whole counsel of God.

But many evangelicals do not know which direction to take in relation to government. Do we want a "Christian state"? A nation of religious liberty? Something in between? A little of both?

Christians shout loudly about religious liberty when they fight against government regulation of Christian schools and IRS attempts to tax religious organizations. But when they work for prayer in the public schools, the posting of the Ten Commandments, and religious observances in public life, they proclaim our nation's Christian heritage. Are these twin postures compatible?

Let me suggest six possible models of church-state relationships.

The Christian State

In this model, the Christian religion, or maybe a particular Christian denomination, is officially established as the state church. The nation is avowedly Christian, and its institutions proclaim and propagate Christian doctrine. Church membership and attendance may or may not be required, but both are definitely encouraged. Those who dissent are for the most part allowed to believe as they choose and practice their beliefs, but they nevertheless have to pay taxes to support Christian activities of the state.

The God-Fearing State

The God-fearing state is not avowedly Christian, but its institutions presuppose a Divine Being. Its coins might be engraved with the phrase "In God We Trust" and similar phrases might be found throughout public institutions. The public schools would not teach an official creed of religious doctrine, but in general terms give assent to a nearly universal belief in God. Children in public schools may voluntarily engage in prayer and Bible reading. The state recognizes that the liberties of its citizens are derived from God, and those liberties cannot be secure if the conviction that they are God-given is removed.

While the state publicly acknowledges God, it does not force that belief upon those who do not. Atheists, agnostics, and other dissenters are free to form their own religious societies, operate their own private schools, and express their opinions as they see fit.

W. Cleon Skousen has identified five beliefs which he considers to be the basic religion adhered to universally by the founders of our country and by the general public at that time: (1) The Creator is the Supreme Power in the universe; (2) The Creator has revealed a moral code for happy living which clearly distinguishes right from wrong; (3) The Creator holds mankind responsible for the way men treat one another; (4) There is a future life; and (5) There will be a day of judgment in the next life for what was done in this life. He cites Benjamin Franklin, Samuel Adams, John Adams, and Thomas Jefferson as men who articulated this basic "religion of America."[14] Traditional Christians may wonder whether this basic "religion of America" was truly universal, particularly in the works-righteousness which is implied therein, and whether it is too watered down to constitute true Christianity. But a basic belief in God is a belief that nearly all Americans have agreed on, then and now.

The Accommodating State

The accommodating state conscientiously endeavors to follow the policy of accommodating neutrality as announced in *Zorach* and elsewhere. The state does not officially acknowledge God in any of its public pronouncements, but it makes every effort to accommodate the beliefs and exercises of those who do acknowledge God and wish to worship Him. Churches are given tax-exempt status; the public schools practice released time by which children may be released for a certain period of time each week for religious instruction at their respective churches. While the state does not officially compose prayers, it does allow students to use public facilities for religious meetings and it might allow a period of silence during which those who wish to pray may do so.

The state officially recognizes human rights including the right of religious liberty, but it does not recognize God as the source of those rights. It is silent as to the source of human rights. To avoid establishing a religion of secular humanism, the state is careful to accommodate Christians by teaching a two-model approach to origins. In short, while the state officially takes no position on the worship of God or even on His existence, it is very accommodating to those who do.

The "Hands Off" State

The "hands off" state takes no position on the existence of God or the source of human rights, and it scrupulously avoids any and all contact with religion. Private schools, for example, receive no aid whatsoever from the government; neither does the government seek to regulate them in any way. Public schools, if they exist at all, avoid teaching any topics that could be associated with religious or moral values. They teach nothing at all about origins or sex education or values clarification, and in other areas stick strictly to bare facts and

14. W. Cleon Skousen, *Miracle of America: Study Guide* (Salt Lake City, Utah: Freeman Institute, 1981), pp. 33-34.

nothing more. Recognizing that origins is a sensitive issue, state-sponsored museums avoid any and all displays or exhibits that have implications on the subject, as do national parks, historical markers, etc. In short, the state tries to stay out of people's lives in any area in which religion could be a factor.

The Secular State

The secular state does not recognize God at all, and religious citizens may not use public facilities for any religious activities. The public schools teach the humanist view of origins (evolution) and teach morals and values clarification from a humanistic or man-centered standpoint. Those who object to this view have limited freedom to establish private schools, entirely at their own expense.

The secular state tolerates churches so long as they do not operate contrary to public policy. But religious citizens may not use public facilities for meetings, prayers, worship, or any other religious purposes, although humanists and secularists are free to use public facilities for their purposes. While it may not be officially declared, the secular state adopts the religion of secular humanism as its established state religion.

The Anti-Christian State

The anti-Christian state officially rejects Christianity and perhaps theism in general. Christian churches have no unalienable rights; they are tolerated, if at all, only because their continued existence serves the state's purposes. The state's official policy is anti-Christian and it uses all its facilities to advance that policy. Public school attendance is probably made compulsory, and the schools indoctrinate children in the state's world view.

Many of those who came to America as colonists sought to establish Christian states in a new "promised land." By the time of the American War for Independence they had moved closer to the God-fearing state. Today America still has a few vestiges of the God-fearing state, many attributes of the accommodating state, and a few of the "hands off" state. But the model that is rapidly emerging in this country, and which many are striving actively to promote, is the secular state, the state that has secular humanism as its established religion and accords Christians only a limited freedom to dissent.

In which direction should America be moving? In which direction should Christians try to guide America? The anti-Christian state and secular state are obviously unacceptable. And no Christian that I know of wants a Christian State, for that is contrary to the basic idea of limited government as set forth in Scripture. The "hands off" state has many acceptable features, but it may be impractical.

At times government officials must take a stand on the nature and existence of God. I recall in my work with juvenile court, an instance when the Social Services sought to have a young girl committed for psychiatric treatment. Among the evidence presented by the Social Services was her claim that angels visited her.

Now, if you don't believe angels exist, the problem is settled—the girl is suffering psychotic delusions and is in need of treatment. But if angels do exist, there are several possibilities. She might still be having psychotic delusions; but on the other hand she may truly communicate with angels, and she may be blessed. What would the Social Services have done with Mary, or Daniel, or Jacob, or Abraham? What would the juvenile authorities have done with young Samuel, who heard the voice of God calling him at night?

What if the girl claimed to visit with the Devil? Again, it depends upon your religious viewpoint. A humanist would say she's insane, since the Devil doesn't really exist. A Satanist might say she is specially blessed, while a conservative Christian might conclude that she's demon possessed. How can a judge or state official lay his religious beliefs aside while deciding questions of this nature?

The model I believe Christians should envision for their country is somewhere between the God-fearing state and the accommodating state, with some features of the "hands off" state. There are some areas in which the state should not get involved because of the religious sensitivities of the population as a whole. And the state should carefully accommodate all religions, making it possible for all, including athiests, to enjoy the maximum blessings of a free society. But we must never forget that our nation owes its many blessings to God, and to its Christian heritage. For that reason I believe our nation should publicly acknowledge God. For God is the only firm basis for any kind of religious liberty at all. As Thomas Jefferson said, "The God who gave us life, gave us liberty at the same time."[15] And he added, "Can the liberties of a nation be thought secure, when we have removed their only firm basis, a conviction in the minds of the people that these liberties are the gifts of God?"[16]

15. Thomas Jefferson; The Writings of Thomas Jefferson (1892, 1899), comp. Paul Leicester Ford, Vol. 1, p. 447; cited by *Freemen Digest: Thomas Jefferson* (Freemen Institute, Salt Lake City, Utah, 1981), p. 92.

16. Thomas Jefferson; quoted by B. F. Morris, *Christian Life and Character of the Civil Institutions of the United States* (Philadelphia: G. W. Childs, 1864) p. 35; quoted by Anson Phelps Stokes and Leo Pfeffer, *Church and State in the United States* (Evanston: Harper & Row, 1950, 1964), p. 55.

Part 3

The Christian
and
Man's Law

Chapter 22

Reconciling Disputes
Among Christians

In part one we examined the relation of biblical law to human society. In part two we studied the U.S. Constitution. In part three we shall consider the practical issues that confront the Christian. In these chapters we will discuss such problems as how to incorporate a church and obtain tax-exempt status, how to resolve church-property disputes, privileged communications, and clergy malpractice. We will also discuss how to find and work with a lawyer, and how to handle yourself in court. But first we need to consider a more basic question: Should the Christian go to court at all?

First Corinthians 6:1-8 sheds some light on the problem. Paul, writing to what is often described as the most carnal church in the New Testament, warns them about many sins in their midst: allowing an apparently incestuous relationship, dishonoring the Lord's Supper, factionalism, dissension between rich and poor, and immodest dress. But another evil which Paul condemns in this passage is Christians suing other Christians in court. Let's look at the passage:

(1) Dare any of you, having a matter against another, go to law before the unjust, and not before the saints?
(2) Do ye not know that the saints shall judge the world? And if the world shall be judged by you, are ye unworthy to judge the smallest matters?
(3) Know ye not that we shall judge angels? How much more things that pertain to this life?
(4) If, then, ye have judgments of things pertaining to this life, do ye set them to judge who are least esteemed in the church?
(5) I speak to your shame. Is it so, that there is not a wise man among you? No, not one that shall be able to judge between his brethren?
(6) But brother goeth to law with brother, and that before the unbelievers.

(7) Now, therefore, there is utterly a fault among you, because ye go to law one with another. Why do ye not rather take wrong? Why do ye not rather allow yourselves to be defrauded?

(8) Nay, ye do wrong, and defraud, and that your brethren.

Paul simply warns that Christians should not sue one another in the civil courts. One reason is that public airing of disputes between Christians is "bad publicity" for the church. It weakens our testimony as believers and leads the world to conclude that Christians can't get along with one another. It also tends to factionalize the church, because a dispute usually becomes much more bitter when it goes to court.

Another reason is that believers are capable of judging their own members and do not need the outside world to judge. Rather than submitting our disputes to the worldly courts, we should submit them to a "wise man" in the church who is able to "judge between his brethren" (v. 5). Paul argues, *a fortiori*, that when Christ comes we will live and reign with Him, and at that time we shall judge the world and even judge angels. If we can judge difficult matters like these, how much more are we capable of judging petty disputes among Christians? Even those who are "least esteemed in the church" (v. 4) are better able to judge disputes between Christians than are the secular courts.

Calvin suggests a final reason: In Corinth and many other pagan societies, the pagan secular courts used oaths to heathen deities and other practices that compromised the convictions of God-fearing people.[1] Consequently, the Jews had their own court system since their rabbis interpreted Exodus 21:1 as prohibiting them from taking a case before idolatrous judges.[2] Paul, who had a background as a Pharisee, urged Christians to follow a similar practice.

Of course, the Bible recognizes that disputes among Christians will occasionally take place. Paul's condemnation addressed, not so much to the fact that disputes exist, but to the problem of believers taking each other to court. What should be done about disputes today? Jesus explained a practical system for resolving disputes between believers in Matthew 18:15-17:

(15) Moreover, if thy brother shall trespass against thee, go and tell him his fault between thee and him alone: if he shall hear thee, thou hast gained thy brother.

(16) But if he will not hear thee, then take with thee one or two more, that in the mouth of two or three witnesses every word may be established.

(17) And if he shall neglect to hear them, tell it unto the church: but if he neglect to hear the church, let him be unto thee as an heathen man and a publican. (cf. Deuteronomy 17:6, 19:15; John 8:17; II Corinthians 13:1; Hebrews 10:28)

When two Corinthian Christians had a dispute, this admonition was easy

---

1. John Calvin, quoted by John Peter Lange, *Lange's Commentary on the Holy Scriptures*, Vol. 10, p. 121.

2. *Interpreters' Bible*, Vol. 10, p. 69.

to implement. First, the believer who believed he had been wronged was to approach the other believer himself so that they could reconcile the dispute together. If that didn't work, he was to take two or three witnesses with him, probably elders from the church. If that didn't work, he brought the matter to the attention of the church. If the erring believer still refused to listen to the advice of the church body, he was to be disciplined by the church.

How can this be applied today? Instead of one church in each community, we have many—not only many churches, but many denominations. Let us suppose a dispute takes place between a Baptist and a Nazarene. The Baptist says, "You can't sue me; we're both Christians. Haven't you ever read I Corinthians 6?"

Nazarene: "What do we do, then?"

Baptist: "Matthew 18 says we should take the dispute to the church and let them resolve it."

Nazarene: "Fine; come on over to my church. My pastor will tell you who's right."

Baptist: "Nothing doing; we're going to my pastor." And so on.

How do we apply I Corinthians 6 to our society of many churches and demoninations? Does the passage apply only to members of the same church?

Another problem is that many people today claim to be Christians even though they disbelieve the Bible and have never experienced God's salvation. Being a Christian, at least until recently, was thought to be part of being an American. We're Americans; America is a Christian nation; therefore, we're Christians. In Paul's day the lines were much more clearly drawn. Though there were false professors and heretics even in that day, one seldom called himself a Christian unless he was truly committed to Christ. Today, it is much more difficult to determine who is a Christian and who is not. Should we apply I Corinthians 6 to any dispute in which both parties are members of the same church? Or only to disputes between evangelicals? Or only to those who clearly recognize one another as Christians? Or to everyone who calls himself a Christian?

A third difference is the great complexity of legal cases today. In Paul's day law was much more complex than many of us imagine, especially commercial law. But it did not involve the extensive use of expert testimony and other complexities of today. The elders of a local church may be quite capable of resolving a disputed bill over the sale of some grain. But are they capable of deciding a complex wrongful injury suit involving expert medical testimony as to extent and duration of injuries, issues of contributory or comparative negligence, or strict liability?

Still another complication is the widespread use of insurance. Most people, Christians included, are insured against most types of liability. In many states automobile insurance is mandatory, and many banks require homeowner's insurance which usually contains a comprehensive personal liability provision. If A and B have an automobile accident in which B is injured and A is at fault,

B submits his medical bills, claim for lost time, etc., to A's insurance company. That company evaluates the claim and pays what it considers the claim to be worth. If the company denies liability, B has to sue. But in most jurisdictions he cannot sue his insurance company; he has to sue A. A then turns the lawsuit over to the insurance company, which is responsible to defend him and to pay B if the court decides A is liable.

On the surface B is suing A; in fact, in most jurisdictions the jury is not even allowed to know whether or not A has insurance. But that is a mere formality. In reality B is suing the insurance company, and A is just a figurehead who receives the papers. A may even believe B has a valid claim that the insurance company should pay, but the insurance company handles the case and A is bound by his insurance contract to cooperate with the company in the defense of the case.

Is B wrong to submit a claim to the insurance company? If the insurance company refuses to pay and B feels the company is wrong, may B sue A to collect from A's insurance company? Good question. More about that later.

Clearly the application of I Corinthians 6 to modern society presents difficulties. I am sure many Christian lawyers have at times secretly wished Paul hadn't written those words! But he did, and they are the inspired Word of God, "profitable for doctrine, for reproof, for correction, for instruction in righteousness." So how do we apply them today?

First, the passage should be understood as an admonition to both sides to settle their differences out of court. That includes the defendant as well as the plaintiff. The Christian who negligently injures another, refuses to make it right, and then self-righteously says, "You can't sue me; I'm a Christian; read I Corinthians 6,"is just as out of line as the other party, if not more so.

Second, the passage applies only to disputes between Christians. Paul does not mean that a Christian cannot or should not go to court to obtain justice against a non-Christian, although there are certainly circumstances in which turning the other cheek is appropriate also. The principle might apply more literally to disputes between Christians in the same church, since the potential for division and injuring the church's testimony is greater then and the mechanism for resolving the dispute is present within the local church. But the passage certainly has at least a secondary application toward other Christians as well. In general, Christians should try to resolve disputes with others, even non-Christians (Rom. 12:19).

Third, I see no reason why a Christian may not file an insurance claim against the insurer of another Christian. After all, the other Christian has contracted with that insurance company and paid premiums to that company to handle such matters. But the problem arises, what if the insurance company refuses to pay, and I still think I have a valid claim? May I sue? And there's a further complication: Many insurance lawyers say that insurance companies are much more likely to offer a better settlement if they are served with a formal lawsuit than if the injured party has only filed a claim against the company. Under such circumstances, I believe the Christian is justified in filing suit if in his lawyer's judgement it is in the interest of his claim to do so. He is trying to collect from the insurance company—not from his fellow Christian. But he should act without malice in his heart, and the defendant should accept the suit in that light. Plaintiff and defendant alike should contemplate the possible divisive effect their action may have upon the church.

Fourth, except in insurance cases, the Christian should "go through channels" rather than go to court. He should first try to settle directly with his Christian brother. If that fails, he should try to get some other Christians to arbitrate or mediate the dispute. If even that fails, he might invoke the help of the whole church, at least if both parties belong to the same church.

But what if that fails? Christ says in Matthew 18:17, "let him be unto thee as an heathen and a publican." Now, the Christian can sue a heathen or a publican. Once he's gone through channels, should he sue his backslidden Christian brother? If it is necessary to put a stop to a continuing injustice, either to himself or to others, possibly he can. In fact, if the backsliding Christian has a continuing practice of defrauding others, the Christian may have a duty to sue him, both to teach him a lesson and to protect others.

Careful examination of I Corinthians 6:1-8 reveals that in no place does Paul specifically command believers not to sue one another. Rather, he asks the rhetorical questions: "Dare any of you . . . go to law before the unjust?" "Why do ye not rather take wrong?" Paul asks rhetorical questions because he wants us to consider these alternatives. Circumstances may exist in which a lawsuit is necessary, but it should be utilized only after all other means of resolution have failed. We should not be so set upon gaining recovery for ourselves that we fail to consider what course of action will do most to advance the glory of God. As the *Interpreters' Bible* says,

> There may be matters which concern the church in which the law of the land is involved. Instances will readily recur to all students of church history. There was the case of the disposal of church property, for example, at the time of the disruption of the Presbyterian Church of Scotland. In such cases there is every legitimate reason for taking adequate legal measures.[3]

Donald S. Metz says in the *Beacon Bible Commentary*, "A Christian need not be a pawn, nor should he permit himself to be misused. But, in Paul's thinking, it was better to endure an injustice or to sustain a financial loss than to suffer spiritual damage."[4] Even in an insurance matter, the Christian should consider the effect of his claim upon the unity of the church and weigh the benefits to be gained against the potential for division.

What about Christian lawyers? Can a Christian lawyer sue another Christian? I believe he can. First of all, he is not suing in his own behalf; he is acting

---

3. Ibid., p. 71.

4. Donald E. Metz, *Beacon Bible Commentary* (Kansas City, Missouri: Beacon Hill Press, 1968), Vol. VIII, p. 362.

on behalf of his client. Certainly there is nothing wrong with a Christian attorney going to court against another Christian attorney. The passage applies primarily to clients, not to their attorneys. But it also has a secondary application to attorneys, for it impresses upon them the obligation to do everything possible to achieve a satisfactory settlement out of court, and to go to court only as a last resort. That may be especially true and especially possible with Christian clients, but the Christian attorney should make the effort with all clients. One reason the courts do not give prompt justice is that their dockets are backlogged with litigants who refuse to settle their claims.

Should Christians of different churches resolve their claims? Should two Christians within the same church resolve their dispute if it involves issues so complex that the church authorities are unable to make a decision? Sometimes the attorneys can arbitrate or mediate the case themselves. Arbitration is binding while mediation is not. In arbitration the parties usually agree in writing that they will be bound by the arbitrator's decision. In mediation each party has the legal right to reject the mediator's solution and pursue justice by other means.

To facilitate and encourage arbitration and mediation among Christians, the Christian Legal Society recently organized the Christian Conciliation Service (CCS). Local CCS services have been established in several communities and they will reach out to other cities in coming years. The local CCS committees try to identify persons within the Christian community whose spiritual gifts and temperament enable them to function effectively as peacemakers between disputants, and arrange for such persons to be available to arbitrate or mediate disputes when called upon. Christians might find CCS to be advantageous for the following reasons: (1) Their disputes will be resolved by committed Christians in a Christian atmosphere; (2) CCS is not affiliated with any denomination and is therefore able to maintain neutrality among Christians; (3) CCS avoids publicity which could be damaging to the testimony of Christians and their churches; and (4) CCS does everything possible to minimize costs. Those needing the Christian Conciliation Service may contact the Christian Legal Society at P.O. Box 2069, Oak Park, Illinois 60303.

A century ago, some mainline denominations excommunicated their members for suing fellow believers. Today that is not done. It is time for churches to assume their responsibility in this matter—not just to discipline those who file suit, but to use the pulpit to educate their members as to their responsibility to reconcile disputes according to I Corinthians 6:1-8 and Matthew 18:15-17. Not only that, but churches should make their offices available for the reconciliation of disputes. Along with committees on stewardship, youth, education, missions, the aged, and the relief of need, churches should have a special committee on reconciliation. We must work to make the reconciliation we have experienced in Christ a practical reality among believers.

> And all things are of God, who hath reconciled us to Himself by Jesus Christ, and hath given to us the ministry of reconciliation;
> To wit, that God was in Christ reconciling the world to Himself, not

imputing their trespasses unto them, and hath committed unto us the word of reconciliation. (II Corinthians 5:18-19)

If it is possible as much as lieth in you, live peaceably with all men. (Romans 12:19)

Agree with thine adversary quickly, while thou art in the way with him; lest at any time the adversary deliver thee to the judge, and the judge deliver thee to the officer, and thou be cast into prison. (Matthew 5:25)

Blessed are the peacemakers, for they shall be called the children of God. (Matthew 5:9)

Chapter 23

You and Your Lawyer

Lawyers can be intimidating. They dress in fancy suits, carry big briefcases, have razor-sharp minds, and like nothing better than to crucify a witness on the stand, close in for the kill, stab him in the jugular vein, twist the knife to increase the pain, and then stand back to watch him bleed.

The legal profession, in fact, is not highly respected by the general public, in comparison to other professions. Lawyers are thought to be money hungry, underhanded, and willing to twist the truth to win at any cost.

Part of this negative image is justified, for many lawyers are unethical. This disintegration of legal ethics is directly related to the secular humanism, moral relativism, and legal positivism being taught in most law schools today. Part of it, however, is due to the adversarial nature of the legal system.

An unfortunate aspect of the practice of law is that in order for a lawyer to help someone, he often has to hurt someone else. The prosecutor who seeks justice for the state and for the victim of a crime must do so by inflicting harm upon the criminal defendant. Perhaps the harm is deserved, but it is harm nevertheless. The lawyer who represents an accident victim suing the driver of the car must make the other side lose in order to make his side win. Ideally, the winning side is that which deserves to win and the losing side is that which deserves to lose—but usually both sides believe they deserve to win or they would have settled out of court.

Let us suppose that when you went to the hospital there was one doctor for you and one against you. One tried to make you well and one tried to make you sick. That is the way it often is when you go to court—one lawyer is for you and one lawyer is against you. Naturally, you don't think too much of the lawyer who is against you. You tend to regard him as your enemy, and since in your eyes you are a "good guy," the opposing lawyer must be a "bad guy." And the profession as a whole seems to be lumped with the "bad guys."

As a result, polls indicate that people rate the legal profession as a whole much lower than they rate their own personal attorneys. Ask the man on the street what he thinks of the legal profession, and he may respond, "They're a bunch of crooks." Ask him what he thinks of his own personal lawyer, and he will probably say, "Oh, he's just fine, but all the others are crooks."

Whether or not you like or trust lawyers, the day may come when you need one. The purpose of this chapter is to help you choose a lawyer wisely and work with him effectively, so that your experience with the legal system will be pleasant, satisfying, and successful.

Choosing a Lawyer

The telephone directory lists the lawyers available in each community. But this sometimes awesome list reveals nothing about the quality of the lawyers, nor does it generally tell which lawyers are most effective for specific types of problems. The fact that you may recognize a name or two from the local news or newspaper doesn't help much, because the lawyers who get the most publicity are not necessarily the best. Obviously further investigation is necessary.

If you have lived in the area for some time, possibly there is a lawyer who has represented other members of your family. He might therefore be more familiar with you and your affairs than would a total stranger. If you are new in the community or your family has never needed a lawyer, you might ask some of your acquaintances at work, at church, or in your social circle to recommend a lawyer. Businessmen in your church who are familiar with the reputations of various lawyers in the community may be able to suggest someone.

Sometimes county and state bar associations have lawyer referral services which will arrange for you to see a lawyer who is qualified to handle your problem. Sometimes the county attorney's office, or the local legal aid society, will suggest a lawyer who can help you, although more often they will refuse to do so in order to avoid showing favoritism among attorneys.

Several lists of attorneys are published nationwide. Sometimes these are careful to list only highly qualified attorneys; others list any lawyer who is willing to pay for the listing. The most popular lawyers' directory is the *Martindale-Hubbell Law Directory*, consisting of eight enormous volumes and published annually by Martindale-Hubbell, Inc., of Summit, New Jersey. With few exceptions, all lawyers are listed without charge in the front of each volume, according to state and city. The remainder and majority of the volume contains extended background information about certain firms and individual lawyers: where they were born, attended law school, other degrees, membership in professional associations, published works, types of cases handled, representative clients, etc. However, the fact that an attorney or firm is given an entended listing in *Martindale-Hubbell* says little about the quality of the firm. It only means that firm has paid for that extended listing.

Lawyers in *Martindale-Hubbell* are given two ratings. These ratings are based on confidential evaluations by judges and other attorneys in the community, and are, therefore, somewhat subjective. The legal ability of the lawyer is rated as "a" (very high), "b" (high), or "c" (fair). They are also rated on adherence to ethical standards; a "v" indicates faithful adherence. However, no attorney can receive an "a" rating unless he has practiced for ten years, and none can receive a "b" unless he has practiced for five years. Also, many attorneys are not rated at all, either at their own request or because the publisher does not have adequate information. These ratings may be of some value, and *Martindale-Hubbell* performs a fine service by letting attorneys know of other attorneys in other communities to whom they can refer cases; but they are clearly not conclusive as to lawyer quality.

The Christian Legal Society also publishes a membership directory, which is helpful for those who want to find a Christian lawyer in another jurisdiction. The Christian Yellow Pages of the community may also list lawyers. Some Christian organizations list lawyers who can help with estate-planning problems. Some companies or unions have prepaid legal services plans which have lists of approved attorneys. If you have such a plan and want your insurance to cover your legal costs, check first to make sure the attorney you choose is on the approved list.

Persons who are unable to afford legal counsel are often entitled to court-appointed attorneys or public defenders in criminal cases, or legal aid in civil cases. Usually, to qualify for this type of assistance one has to meet fairly stringent standards. Income must be below a certain level which varies according to the size of the family. There is a limit to how much property one can own, and sometimes special consideration is given to financial obligations, extenuating circumstances, etc.

Legal aid is sometimes handled by the bar association on a pro bono or gratuitous basis. Every attorney is expected to devote a reasonable amount of his practice to representing those who cannot afford counsel. Despite lawyers' negative public image, they probably do more gratuitous work than do many other professions. Most cities have a legal aid society, staffed by full time or part-time legal aid attorneys, who represent indigent clients. In cities where a law school is located, the school frequently runs a legal clinic staffed by senior law students under the supervision of a law professor.

In rural and small-town areas a new concept of legal aid has developed: Judicare. In these areas it would be impractical to maintain a full time office staffed by legal-aid attorneys. If there were only one central office in an area like northern Minnesota, clients would have to travel too far to visit the office, and the staff attorneys would have to travel too far to attend court hearings in the various counties. On the other hand, if offices were located in each county or town, the cost would be prohibitive. So the Judicare concept was developed under which a person applies for legal services (usually at the Department of Social Services), is found to be eligible according to income standards, and is then issued a card authorizing him to receive legal services at Judicare expense. The client then takes the card to the private lawyer or law firm of his choice. The Judicare office pays the private lawyer for legal services rendered at a considerably lower rate than normally charged to clients. Generally, clients have rated the Judicare program more satisfactory than in other legal-aid programs.[1]

If a case which involves First Amendment issues, other sources of help are available. The Christian Legal Society occasionally takes an active role in such cases, and has a wealth of briefs, books, and other materials available to assist the attorney in the defense of such a case. Another organization, the Christian Law Association, specializes in the defense of Christian schools, day-care centers, and churches on constitutional issues. Operated by the law firm of David Gibbs and Charles Craze (P.O. Box 30290, Cleveland, Ohio 44130), CLA consists of many churches, schools, and individuals who pay yearly dues for membership. If any CLA member is harassed by a governmental agency on an issue of religious freedom, Gibbs & Craze will defend them without charge provided the case meets certain qualifications. The practice is similar to prepaid legal services. The National Association for the Legal Support of Alternative Schools (Box 2241, Santa Fe, New Mexico 87501) can refer private schools and home schools to attorneys with experience in those areas. The N.A.L.S.A.S. has proposed a similar program of prepaid insurance for legal costs in such instances.

John W. Whitehead has established the Rutherford Institute, P.O. Box 510, Manassas, Virginia 22110, to defend Christian causes such as private schools, the right to life, and Christians in Communist countries. Another helpful organization is the Catholic League for Religious and Civil Rights, 1100 West Wells Street, Milwaukee, Wisconsin 53233.

In some cases, one might turn to Americans United for the Separation of Church and State, 8120 Fenton Street, Silver Springs, Maryland, 20910. This organization takes a strong separatist stance and is therefore at odds with Christian organizations at times. For example, AU has strongly opposed the teaching of creation in public schools, and has opposed any type of government aid to church schools. On the other hand, it has supported churches in their efforts to resist government harassment.

Still another organization is the American Civil Liberties Union. The ACLU takes an even more radical separationist stance than Americans United. It has a distinctively Leftist bias, though it may officially deny that charge, and individuals in the ACLU are often hostile to Christianity. The ACLU employs a double standard in that it strongly opposes any attempt to "establish" Christianity but is blind to the establishment of secular humanism.

The first time I defended a home school case, I sought assistance from the Minnesota Chapter of the ACLU. They refused my request because of a possible conflict between the rights of the parents and those of the children, even though the children were in total agreement with their parents in this instance.[2]

1. Murray L. Schwartz, *Lawyers and the Legal Profession: Cases and Materials* (Indianapolis: Bobbs-Merrill Company, Inc., 1979), p. 763.

2. Minnesota Civil Liberties Union, Letter to John Eidsmoe, February 13, 1979.

But in the highly-publicized Polovchak case which involved a Russian immigrant couple who wanted to forcefully take their son back to the Soviet Union, (he refused to go partly for religious reasons) the ACLU jumped to the defense of the parents, even though good reason exists to believe the boy could suffer political persecution if returned to the Soviet Union against his will.[3] How strange that the ACLU was willing to defend the right of a parent to force his child to live in the Soviet Union, but not the right to give his child a Christian education at home!

Nevertheless, in a First Amendment case the ACLU might be persuaded to offer assistance, and its help could be valuable. It could indicate a cross-section of support for a position from both sides of the political spectrum.

What qualities should you look for in a lawyer? Besides his general reputation in the community, it is important that you choose an attorney you like, especially if your relationship with him will continue over a period of time. If you are uncomfortable working with your attorney, chances are he is equally uncomfortable with you, and it might be wise to consider switching.

Another important factor is experience—not just experience in the general practice of law, but experience with your specific type of problem. A lawyer who is proficient in workers' compensation law may know virtually nothing about estate planning or juvenile law or the defense of Christian schools. Experience is something that is gained with time. Obviously, every attorney has to start somewhere and an attorney who has never handled a certain type of case before may do an excellent job.

Another consideration in choosing an attorney is cost. It is important not to pick an attorney just because he is the cheapest, or because he is the most expensive. Neither the cheapest nor the most expensive lawyer is necessarily the best for a particular problem. One attorney may charge $50 per hour, another may charge $75. But if the more expensive attorney has handled your type of case before, he may be able to prepare it in less than half the time, and in the end may cost you less and do a better job.

An attorney should appraise your case honestly and realistically. That may mean a far different assessment than you hoped for. The easiest thing in the world for an attorney to do is tell his client that he has an airtight case and will win a million-dollar verdict in court. The client may think that attorney is great—until he loses the case. Most attorneys would prefer to err slightly on the pessimistic side so as not to raise false expectations. After all, if an attorney tells his client he is going to win and then loses, the client is likely to think the lawyer misled him or did a poor job. But if the attorney tells the client he is likely to lose and then wins, the client is ecstatic and thinks his lawyer has just accomplished the impossible!

During your interview, your lawyer may seem too objective. It may bother you that he does not become emotionally involved in your case. Bear in mind

3. Ludmilla Thorne, "The Littlest Defector," *National Review*, March 18, 1983, pp. 314-320, 341.

that detachment enables him to view your problem from all perspectives and advise you accordingly. As you tell your story, he may play "devil's advocate," raising questions and arguments his opponent is likely to raise in court, to see how you answer them or whether they can be answered at all. Don't resent this; he is just trying to evaluate all the facts to properly apply the law. Of course, if he seems totally unsympathetic to you and your position, you may want to get a second opinion.

If the problem is a local one, it is usually best to retain a local attorney. He knows the community and the court system better than an outside attorney and is thus better able to gauge the court's reactions. Long-distance calls as well as travel expenses are usually added to your bill.

Likewise, if your problem is in another jurisdiction, it is probably best to retain counsel in that jurisdiction—not where you live. For example, if you live in New Jersey and are involved in a child custody battle in Arizona, it is probably best to retain an Arizona lawyer. Before taking legal action you might wish to consult a New Jersey lawyer in case the case could be transferred to your home state. Normally, it is advantageous to fight on your own home ground.

But there are situations best handled by outside counsel. On a highly controversial matter, local lawyers might not be too zealous about taking on the local establishment. Though that shouldn't be true, it sometimes is in a smaller town where the lawyers and community leaders all know one another. In that situation, an attorney from another county might provide better representation.

How important is it that your attorney be a Christian? Important but not controlling in most cases. Many non-Christian attorneys are impeccably honest and reputable, and highly capable of representing Christians. A non-Christian lawyer can draw a will that is just as valid and effective as a will drawn by a Christian. Of course, if you want to make certain bequests to charitable institutions, or if you want to name a lawyer as a trustee for that purpose, a Christian lawyer might be more sympathetic to your desires and better able to execute them. In a case involving religious freedom, a Christian attorney might better understand your religious convictions and be better able to frame them in such a way as to make a successful First Amendment case.

Working with a Lawyer

It is important to establish a good working relationship with your lawyer based on mutual trust and respect. The following suggestions will help build that relationship.

First, expect to pay your attorney and make clear that you expect to pay. Many try to take advantage of a lawyer's services without paying, and, sadly, Christians are among the worst offenders. Though it should not be true, many Christians expect free counsel from a Christian lawyer.

This attitude is wrong. Most of these people would not dream of asking a Christian grocer for free groceries, or a Christian retailer for free clothing. They forget that Lincoln said, "A lawyer's time and advice are his only stock in trade." The lawyer has gone through four years of college and three years of law school to acquire his knowledge of the law, and he spends much time and money expanding and updating his knowledge. The lawyer sells his time, advice and services, just like the grocer sells groceries.

Much of the objection to paying lawyers stems from a widespread opinion that lawyers' fees are exorbitant, which may be true in some cases. On the other hand, most clients don't realize the tremendous cost of doing business. They often assume that the lawyer who charges $100 per hour takes home $100 per hour, and after an eight hour day pockets $800. But that money is not the lawyer's salary. First, he can't charge for all the hours he works. Much of his time in the office is spent reading legal publications to update his knowledge, supervising employees, organizing his office, filling out forms, and the other administrative details that necessarily consume time. Generally, an attorney is doing well to bill six hours out of an eight hour day. From that money he must pay office rent, secretary's salary, janitorial fees, paralegal expenses, and other salaries. He has to pay for his heat and air conditioning, his electricity, his parking fees, bar association dues, subscriptions to legal journals, and many other expenses. He also has to purchase or rent office equipment such a typewriter, dictaphone, copy machine, desks, chairs, and furniture for his waiting room. Office supplies such as paper, pens, pencils, typewriter ribbons, carbon paper, xerox paper, etc. must be continually replenished.

Another vital expense is the lawyer's library. In the practice of law, books are tools. Legal volumes average over twenty dollars each. Many cost much more. Some series must be updated yearly.

Furthermore, a lawyer must purchase malpractice insurance. In 1980 this cost as much as $4,000 per year in the state of California, but less elsewhere. Of course there are countless miscellaneous expenditures. A lawyer's profit margin varies greatly depending upon his business arrangement. Law firms that employ special investigators, paralegals, office managers or accountants, have greater efficiency but higher overhead. Most lawyers must take in an average of $25-$30 per hour just to meet office expenses. Only after that can they begin to think of profit.

Lawyers charge for their services in three basic ways: by the hour, by the job, or by the contingent fee. Most lawyers use all three types of fee arrangements. Most routine office work and research is billed by the hour. The drafting of a will is sometimes based on a flat fee schedule, as are divorces, bankruptcies, deeds, abstract opinions, and the like. "Fee-generating" cases—liability cases where one is suing for damages, as in a motor vehicle accident—are usually handled on a contingent fee basis. Under this arrangement, the lawyer gets a certain percentage of whatever the client wins in the case. If the client loses, the lawyer gets nothing but out-of-pocket expenses. The exact percentage rate varies according to the amount in controversy, the complexity of the case, and the likelihood of recovery.

Contingent fees have come under attack in recent years as contributing to the lawyer's greed. Certainly they can be misused; but without the contingent fee many middle and lower-middle class clients could never afford the cost of a lawsuit. The contingent fee also provides an incentive for the lawyer to do an excellent job, for the more his client wins, the more he earns.

Lawyers usually insist upon some type of retainer fee. This is, in effect, a "down payment" on the lawyer's services. It secures the lawyer's representation and prevents him from representing any adverse parties in the action. It is also some assurance that the attorney will be paid. A lawyer may request additional payments as his services continue.

It is important, for your satisfaction as well as your lawyer's, that you make sure the costs are clearly understood at your first meeting. At that time your lawyer will probably be unable to give an exact figure as to what the case will cost, because it's difficult to accurately estimate tha amount of work involved. He doesn't know whether the case will be settled out of court, or go to trial, or how long the trial will last, or whether an appeal will be necessary. Unexpected problems may cause delays or unexpected complications may make the case cost less or more (unfortunately, usually the latter) than the lawyer originally calculates. But at that first meeting you and your lawyer should reach a clear understanding as to how you are to be billed (if an hourly rate, what that hourly rate is), at what times you are expected to pay, and his best estimate of the number of hours involved. If a retainer is required, you should clarify how that retainer is to be handled. Clarify if the fee is refundable if the case is settled quickly.

Second, always make an appointment to see your lawyer. Unless it is extremely urgent or your lawyer has made it clear he doesn't mind walk-ins, don't go down to the office without an appointment. Also, unless he specifically says otherwise, avoid calling your lawyer at home unless absolutely necessary. Most attorneys put in far more than an eight hour day. It is wrong to presume on a lawyer's home or family. Some clients assume they shouldn't have to pay for legal services because they called or visited their lawyer at home instead of at the office!

Third, when you see an attorney about a legal problem, have all the relevant documents with you: contracts, insurance policies, bills, canceled checks, receipts, correspondence, etc. If in doubt, bring it; that which might not seem relevant to you might be very relevant to your lawyer. Failure to bring appropriate paperwork could result in an extra trip, an extra appointment, extra expense, or possibly even inaccurate legal advice.

Fourth, give your attorney all the facts he needs to advise you properly. If you have difficulty keeping the information straight, it might be helpful to write a narrative account of the entire incident. Refer to it as you consult with your lawyer, or give him a copy if he requests it. As he asks you details about the situation give concise and accurate answers. Some facts which may seem irrelevant or insignificant to you may be very important for a legal reason of which you are not aware. Never try to dress up the facts or conceal some of them to make your case look better to your lawyer. Your lawyer can advise you only if he knows all the facts, good and bad. In court, any fabrications will probably be uncovered anyway, and then both you and your lawyer will suffer.

Communications between client and lawyer are privileged. He is not allowed to disclose anything you tell him to anyone outside his office. If he did, he could be disbarred and sued for malpractice. There has to be an attorney-client relationship for the privilege to apply, however; if your golfing buddy happens to be a lawyer, things you tell him out on the golf course might not be privileged. And a few types of communications are not privileged. If you tell your lawyer that you have committed perjury in court, or that you plan in the future to commit a crime or fraudulent act, he not only may, but is probably required by the Code of Professional Responsibility to advise the proper authorities.

Don't be unwilling to talk to the paralegals or secretaries in your lawyer's office about your problem. Communications with them are privileged, too, so long as they are made in the course of their work. And if, when you call for your attorney, the secretary answers the phone and asks about the nature of your problem, don't be offended or conclude that she's prying. By finding out who you are and what your case concerns, she can pull the relevant files and have them on the attorney's desk so he can refer to them while talking to you. The result is better service. In some offices attorneys have trained their secretaries, legal assistants, and paralegals to do some preliminary work for them. Frequently, routine wills, tax returns, guardianship reports, estate inventories, and the like are prepared by experienced secretaries, subject to review by the attorney. Since this saves the attorney time, the result is a cost savings for you.

Fifth, once you have retained a lawyer, don't badger him constantly about your case. Some things in law take time. If he hasn't communicated with you about your auto accident, it may be because he hasn't heard back from the insurance company's lawyer yet. Of course, if trial dates or filing deadlines are rapidly approaching and you have no indication that progress has been made, then a polite reminder is in order, and if that doesn't produce results, perhaps something stronger is needed. But remember that a lawyer has to charge for his time; and if he doesn't write or call you every day, it may be that he is trying to save you money.

If you have given your attorney a fair chance and are dissatisfied with his service, it may be that you should change lawyers. But it may also be that you and your lawyer haven't communicated properly, and you don't understand what he is doing for you or why he is doing it. Before changing attorneys, it would be advisable to make an appointment, state your concern frankly but tactfully, and give him an opportunity to explain. After the meeting, you may understand each other better, or you may both agree you should change attorneys. He may be a very good attorney, but not the right one for you.

If you believe your attorney has handled your case in an incompetent, unprofessional, or unethical manner, you might wish to complain to the grievance committee. Various bar associations have established committees to police the legal profession, and they are becoming more and more stringent in their requirement of ethics and professionalism. Violators are handled with increasing severity, and the bar does a good job of policing its members. Sometimes these committees are formed at the county level, sometimes at the district or state level. Sometimes nonlawyers serve on these committees, sometimes their hearings are public, sometimes they are closed. In most jurisdictions, either the lawyer or the client has the right to appeal the committee's decision to the courts. Among the sanctions the committee can impose are restitution or extra service to the client, reprimand, a requirement that the lawyer go through extra legal education to overcome his deficiencies, and finally temporary or permanent suspension or revocation of his right to practice law. Because of the severe repercussions of a grievance complaint upon the lawyer's practice and reputation, give your lawyer every opportunity to explain or correct his mistake before filing a formal grievance.

One final, self-serving suggestion: Your lawyer might appreciate a copy of this book.

Chapter 24

Your Conduct in the Courtroom

Many people are afraid to go to court, especially if they have to testify. They are afraid to crumble on the witness stand. But I have questioned thousands of witnesses in court, many of whom had never even been inside a courtroom before. Not one has ever panicked. Though some were a little nervous at first, they generally relaxed and warmed up as the testimony proceeded. Nearly all have said afterward that the experience was not nearly as bad as they had expected. Some even enjoyed it.

If subpoenaed as a witness, you are legally required to appear in court. Failure to do so can result in a fine or imprisonment for contempt of court. Also, if subpoenaed, you are generally entitled to a nominal witness and mileage fee. If there are pressing reasons why you cannot attend, you should advise the attorney who subpoenaed you, assuming he is friendly to your position, or the other attorney, if he is not. It may be that the schedule can be rearranged, or the attorneys can take your deposition (sworn testimony before a court reporter other than in a courtroom; it is typed in transcript form and presented to the court in your absence), or take an affidavit, or stipulate your expected testimony. But if that cannot be done, you *must* honor the subpoena.

If you are uncertain what to say in court, consult the attorney who subpoenaed you, or the attorney who supports your position. Find out what information he wants from you, and think over your answers in advance. Ask if you will be allowed to refer to written notes to refresh your memory. Also, check over the subpoena to see whether it requires you to bring any documents or evidence to court. Sometimes it is helpful to watch a few court proceedings, as they are almost always open to the public. This is especially helpful if you can watch the attorneys who will be questioning you, to learn something of their style.

In order to present the best possible image, you might ask your lawyer how he thinks you should dress. The appropriate dress might vary according to the locality or to the image you wish to project. In general, it is best to dress conservatively, and to appear respectable but not extravagant.

There is no one right way to testify. Everybody's style must fit his own personality. Generally, it is best to appear assured but not arrogant. Think over the questions carefully before answering, and don't let an attorney bully you into saying something you don't mean. Be as specific as possible in your answers, but don't claim to be sure of something if you are not. If you believe you saw something but are not certain, express yourself accordingly. It is generally best to confine yourself to short, simple answers to the questions. Don't go off on tangents or volunteer additional information, especially when questioned by an attorney who is hostile to your position.

The attorney who calls you as a witness will question you first; that is called direct examination. Then the opposing attorney has the opportunity to question you; that is cross-examination. After that, the first attorney can ask additional questions on redirect, then recross. How long this can go on depends on the particular court. Remember that attorneys are allowed to ask leading questions on cross-examination, but cannot ask leading questions on direct. Thus, the cross-examining attorney may try to put words in your mouth; don't let him. An attorney may stand right next to you, address you in an angry or sarcastic tone of voice, or take other steps designed to rile you to anger.[1] The best way to defeat him is not to return anger for anger, but to resolve from the beginning to maintain your equilibrium and do it no matter what.

A court hearing is serious business. At times humor is appropriate in court; most of the time it isn't. Do not use humor unless you are certain it will be well received.

It is always best to confine your testimony to the facts you have observed and relate them calmly and dispassionately. You may lose some credibility if you appear too biased toward either side. Even harmless actions can effect your credibility as a witness. Sitting with the defendant's parents or friends might affect the judge's perception of your objectivity. Consult the attorney favorable to your position as to whether he wants you to remain in the courtroom after your testimony or whether it would be better to leave. Of course, if the court holds you subject to possible recall, you have to stay.

Be careful of your conduct outside the courtroom. Judges and juries may react negatively if they hear you using profanity in the hall or see you smoking in the restroom. These perceptions can affect them considerably.

Above all else: Tell the truth, the whole truth, and nothing but the truth! So help you God!

Being your own Lawyer

The conventional wisdom is that he who is his own lawyer has a fool for a client.

---

1. Some judges will not allow this, but unfortunately, many do.

Not only is the layman usually unfamiliar with legal principles and procedures; he is also so emotionally involved in his case that he is unable to look at it objectively. Because of this, even lawyers are reluctant to represent themselves and often hire other lawyers to represent them.

But at the risk of being labeled a heretic, there are times when it may be best for you to represent yourself. On minor matters it may not pay to be represented by a lawyer. It is hardly worth the cost to pay a lawyer $500 to represent you on a $75 insurance claim or a $15 traffic ticket, and you can probably handle a simple matter like that almost as well as a lawyer can. Most jurisdictions now have small claims courts or conciliation courts in which people commonly represent themselves. In some of them, lawyers are not even allowed.

Furthermore, sometimes the court bends over backwards to be fair to the person representing himself, letting him introduce hearsay evidence, present motions in improper form, etc. Some laymen have "gotten away" with things in court that no judge would ever let a lawyer get away with!

Some judges are very receptive to the client who wishes to represent himself and will afford him every courtesy. Others are hostile to the idea and will obstruct it whenever possible. The U.S. Supreme Court has ruled that the Sixth Amendment implies that one has a right to forego counsel and represent oneself, if he is mentally competent and able to handle the case without causing undue obstruction to the administration of justice.[2] This does not mean, however, that the nonlawyer has the right to represent someone other than himself. Anyone who attempts to do so could be charged with unauthorized practice of law.

The nonlawyer who wants to represent himself should study the laws pertinent to his case. Some statute books are available at the public library, or at the law library of a local law school. Also, there is usually a law library in the city, county, or federal courthouse. A number of good books written in laymen's terms summarize legal principles. However, no such books (including this one) should be relied upon to the exclusion of studying the statutes and cases themselves.

If you are going to represent yourself, it is wise to maintain good relations with the courthouse personnel—the clerks, bailiffs, deputies, reporters, etc. They can do much to make things easier for you, or more difficult for you, depending upon how they are disposed. And judges and juries can be unconsciously influenced by their nonverbal reactions; a scowl or snicker from the clerk or bailiff while you are testifying might lead the jurors to dislike or disbelieve you; a smile or nod of approval might have the opposite effect, intended or unintended.

Even if you plan to represent yourself, you may wish to consult an attorney. After you have prepared your case, make an appointment to discuss it with an attorney so that he can point out weaknesses you may have overlooked.

---

2. *Faretta v. California*, 422 U.S. 806 (1975)

Though some attorneys may refuse to advise you on that basis, others will. The fee for that consultation will be much cheaper than hiring an attorney for the full trial.

Though there are a few legal matters a layman can handle, no one should write his own will. In some states self-written wills are not acceptable. In other states they are accepted if they conform to certain standards, but even then it is not advisable. Wills are highly technical documents designed to legally protect property and heirs. A provision that seems clear to you may be ambiguous to the court. And for obvious reasons, when your will is probated you will not be available to explain or correct it! Furthermore, complicated procedures for witnessing a will vary from state to state and must generally be followed to the letter for the will to be valid.

Legal Citations

Especially when working on First Amendment cases, my clients frequently read about related cases and bring them to my attention. Newspapers and news magazines often report them, and some religious magazines discuss cases of special interest to Christians. Sometimes clients have given me books or pamphlets which mention legal precedents that could be helpful.

I appreciate these suggestions. I can learn much from laymen and lay publications. But the omission of one fine detail causes much frustration. It would be so helpful if laymen, writers and reporters could include the legal citations that tell lawyers where to find further information on the case.

Hundreds of cases have been mentioned in the book. Most of these cases are cited with some numbers and letters after them. Chances are you have wondered what that legal code is all about!

Those seemingly insignificant numerals are the key to locating more information about those cases and citing them as precedents. A lawyer's office usually contains row after row, stack after stack of books. Some of these are legal encyclopedias; some are statute books; some are special treatises on particular areas of law. But the majority of them, those endless numbered volumes of gray or brown books, are compilations of court decisions.

Court decisions are listed in various books, according to the court that made the decision. U.S. Supreme Court decisions are printed in a set of volumes called the United States Reporter, abbreviated simply "U.S." Several volumes of the U.S. Reporter are printed each year, and numbered consecutively. The Amish school case, *Wisconsin v. Yoder*, was decided by the United States Supreme Court in 1972. It is printed in the 406th volume of the United States reporter, starting on page 205 (it is 44 pages long). It is therefore cited as 406 U.S. 205. If quoting a particular sentence out of the judge's decision, and that sentence is found on page 213, both the page on which the case started and the page where the quote is found should be listed: 406 U.S. 205, at 213. The year is usually placed in parentheses after the citation (1972). That indicates the year the Supreme Court issued its decision, not the year the case was originally tried in the lower court.

Below the Supreme Court are eleven circuit courts of appeals, each covering several states. The decisions of the circuit courts are recorded in the Federal Reporter. The Federal Reporter began publication around 1880, and by 1924 it had printed 300 volumes. So in 1924 they started numbering over again, and the new volumes were called 1 Federal Reporter Second Series, cited simply 1 F.2d, and so on. So the case of *Jeu Jo Wan v. Nagle* would be cited 9 F.2d 309, and to indicate what circuit court decided the case we add (C.C.A. Cal.), meaning Circuit Court of Appeals for California would be added.

The lowest court in the Federal system is the federal district court. One district is in each state and the larger states have several. Not all federal district court decisions are reduced to writing, but those that are, get printed in a series called the Federal Supplement. The case of *Davis v. Page* took place in Federal District Court for New Hampshire in 1974, so it is cited 385 F. Supp. 395 (D.C.N.H. 1974).

There are volumes for each region of the country which print the various state supreme court decisions. The Pacific Reporter (P.) prints the decisions of the supreme courts of Alaska, Arizona, California, Colorado, Hawaii, Idaho, Kansas, Montana, Nevada, New Mexico, Oklahoma, Oregon, Utah, Washington, and Wyoming. The Northwest Reporter (N.W.) covers Iowa, Michigan, Minnesota, Wisconsin, Nebraska, North Dakota and South Dakota. The Southwest Reporter (S.W.) handles Arkansas, Kentucky, Missouri, Tennessee, and Texas. The Southern Reporter (So.) takes care of Alabama, Louisiana, Florida, and Mississippi; and the Southeastern Reporter consists of decisions from Georgia, North Carolina, South Carolina, Virginia, and West Virginia. The Northeastern Reporter (N.E.) is for Illinois, Indiana, Massachusetts, New York, and Ohio; and the remainder are in the Atlantic Reporter (A.): Connecticut, Delaware, District of Columbia, Maine, Maryland, New Hampshire, New Jersey, Pennsylvania, Rhode Island, and Vermont. Most of these states also print their own reporters for their state supreme court decisions, but these duplicate the area reporters and are seldom cited. Many have discontinued publication for that reason.

Thus, the Ohio Christian School case, *State v. Whisner*, can be found at 351 N.E. 2d 750 (1976), while another battle out west, *Santa Fe Community School v. New Mexico State Board of Education*, can be found at 518 P. 2d 272 (1974).

All U.S. Supreme Court decisions are printed in three sources, the U.S. Reporter (U.S.) the Supreme Court Reporter (S.Ct.) and the Lawyers' Edition (L.Ed.). A full citation for *Wisconsin v. Yoder* would, therefore, be 406 U.S. 205, 92 S.Ct. 1526, 32 L.Ed.2d 15 (1972). But most lawyers simply cite the U.S. Reporter. Sometimes the Supreme Court will simply refuse to hear a case. Then it is listed with the Circuit Court citation and the Supreme Court's denial of certiori, as in *Meyer v. Oklahoma City*, 496 P. 2d 789 (1972).

Thus it is imperative that these citations be used to report on a case. With them, the lawyer or librarian can find any case in a matter of seconds. Without them, finding a case is like looking for a needle in a haystack.

One final matter, both for Christians and for lawyers who represent them: be careful about using distinctively ''Christian'' terminology in the court room. Consider the mindset of the judges and juries and select appropriate terminology.

This does not mean you have to compromise your convictions. Rather, state them in terms a worldly person can understand. Instead of saying, ''He is a wonderful, Spirit-filled brother in the Lord,'' say, ''He is a fine Christian man.'' Instead of saying, ''We really get blessed fellowshipping around the Word,'' say, ''We find Christian fellowship and Bible study an enjoyable and enriching experience.'' To be successful in court, Christian convictions must be expressed clearly and firmly, and in terms the world can understand.

Chapter 25

Incorporation
and Tax-Exempt Status

We often associate corporations with big business: General Motors, U.S. Steel, IBM, and the like.

In fact, many corporations are small entities. Sometimes a person in business all by himself will choose to incorporate; and recent years have seen a tendency for rural families to incorporate their family farming operations, for current tax and liability advantages, to save on inheritance taxes, and keep the farm in the family for succeeding generations.

What is a corporation? According to *Black's Law Dictionary* it is an "artificial person or legal entity created by law, consisting of one or more individuals who have associated together and whose association is recognized by law as having a distinct personality and legal existence distinct from that of its individual members."[1] A corporation, like an individual, can enter into binding contracts, sue and be sued, and even be prosecuted criminally under the law.

The story is told of a businessman who placed a sign in his corporate office, "This is a nonprofit corporation. It wasn't intended that way, but it is." But a nonprofit corporation is more than just a corporation that isn't making a profit. Rather, a nonprofit corporation is established in such a way that its articles of incorporation clearly provide that the profits (if any) of the corporation shall not inure to the benefit of any private individual.

There are several reasons for incorporating. One is limited liability. If a group of persons organizes to form a church and does not incorporate (or is not under the corporate umbrella of a parent denomination), it is simply a private association, and each member can be personally held liable for the debts of that

---

1. *Black's Law Dictionary, Fourth Edition,* s.v. Corporation.

association. For example, if an unincorporated church sponsors a hayride, and a child falls off the haywagon and is badly injured, he and his parents can sue the association; and if the court awards them more than the association has in assets, the individual members of the church/association can be required to make up the difference out of their own pockets. If the church is incorporated, the church can still be sued, but the plaintiff can collect only the assets or income of the church itself. The individual members or officers are not liable for the debts of the corporation over and above what they have personally invested in the corporation, unless they themselves have committed fraud or gross negligence.

Another reason is tax-exempt status. Contrary to popular opinion, forming a nonprofit corporation is not the same as gaining tax-exempt status. Some nonprofit corporations, such as the Republican or Democratic Party, are nonprofit but not tax-exempt. And it is possible to gain tax-exempt status for an unincorporated association, although it is sometimes more difficult.

A third reason, in some localities, may be exemption from local property taxes. Some jurisdictions may exempt nonprofit corporations from local property tax, but that depends on the locality. And in some states private associations cannot own real estate; real estate has to be owned by one or more of the individual members. Incorporation may make ownership of real estate much easier.

A final reason to incorporate is that in some states corporations enjoy certain advantages over unincorporated associations in payroll deductions and other matters. If you are contemplating incorporation, you should discuss the relative advantages and disadvantages with your attorney, in light of your own specific needs and the laws of your state. Disadvantages of incorporation may include extra paper work, including possibly the need to register as a foreign corporation if you are doing business in other states.

Incorporation is a state matter. Each state grants nonprofit corporation status according to its own laws. These laws vary considerably. Some, like those of Minnesota, are very complex and specific in their requirements. They regulate the functions and titles of the officers of the corporation, the number of trustees, the system of notice of meetings and frequency thereof, means of transferring property, and many other minute aspects of the corporate existence. In Minnesota, incorporating a nonprofit corporation is as complex as incorporating a business. In many other states, nonprofit corporation laws are much simpler. You will need to check the laws of your state.

In all states you will have to file articles of incorporation. This is the corporate document that establishes the purpose and powers of your organization and defines what your corporation is. Again, the requirements vary from state to state, but generally the articles must include at least the name and purpose of the corporation, the names and addresses of the initial members of the board of directors and registered agent (the person who is authorized by law to accept notice of any pending lawsuits against the corporation), and the incorporators (those who sign the articles and commence the corporation). These articles of incorporation are filed with a state or county agency (generally, the secretary of state at the state capitol), where an official examines them and, if they conform to all state requirements, approves them and grants corporate status.

Some corporations have members; some do not. Churches generally have members, the members of the church and the members of the corporation being the same; other nonprofit corporations generally do not. William H. Ellis and Joel Paget, two experienced attorneys who represent Christian organizations, claim that most states place greater requirements on corporations with members as to annual meetings, votes to change the articles, and other procedural matters, than corporations without members.[2] There is probably little advantage for a non-church to have members, unless extending memberships helps the organization gain financial supporters.

Articles of incorporation usually cover only the important matters, such as the name and purpose of the corporation, its statement of faith, powers of the corporation, its officers and their duties, annual meetings and other meetings, type of notice required, means by which property may be transferred, procedure for amendment of articles, parliamentary authority, authority for exacting bylaws, prohibitions on racial discrimination and substantial political activity, prohibition against profits inured to the benefit of private individuals, means of compensation, and effect of dissolution of the corporation. More specific matters are usually reserved for the bylaws since these can be amended more easily and one need not file a notice of change in bylaws with the secretary of state (at least, in most states). To change the articles of incorporation, the change must be filed with the secretary of state, usually accompanied by a fee.

Many churches and religious organizations have a constitution as well as articles of incorporation and bylaws. Unless unique provisions in the laws of a state make a constitution desirable, it is usually better to have articles of incorporation and bylaws. A constitution is unnecessary duplication, and can present difficulties if it contains provisions that conflict with the articles. Several years ago I represented a church in a legal transaction concerning the sale of church property. The sale had to be approved by the congregation, so the congregation had to hold a meeting. But how were the members to be notified? The articles specified one means of notification (reading the notice from the pulpit at four successive Sunday worship services), and the constitution specified a different means (mailed notice to all members)—and neither provision quite agreed with the state law, which had been revised since the articles had been filed! In most cases, well-drafted articles of incorporation make a constitution unnecessary. Your articles *are* your constitution.

Once incorporated, you enjoy the advantages I have mentioned (except tax-exempt status, which will be discussed shortly), but you also incur certain

2. William H. Ellis and Joel Paget, *Legal Guidelines for Christian Organizations* (Oak Park, Illinois: Christian Legal Society, 1977), p.8.

obligations. In some states you are required to file an annual report, indicating any changes in your officers or directors, summarizing your activities, etc. This report usually goes to the secretary of state, accompanied by a small fee, and is generally quite simple and routine.

Finally, some argue that incorporation places one under the control of the state, since a corporate charter implies permission from the state to operate. Since the state has chartered the corporation, the state can control it. Some therefore argue that churches should avoid incorporation to remain free of government control. It is too soon to predict how the courts will handle these arguments.

If your corporation does business in other states, it may be necessary to register as a foreign corporation in those states. If yours is a small corporation such as a husband-wife singing team that travels across the country presenting concerts, literal compliance with these laws may be quite an administrative burden and may be reason to reconsider whether incorporation is really a good idea in your case.

If your church is a part of a denomination which is incorporated and had exempt status, it *may* be that you can function as part of that corporation and need not incorporate separately, especially if the church is new or is a "home mission" project. Your denomination's chief legal counsel can probably best advise you there, but you may wish the advice of your own local attorney.

If a church operates several types of ministries such as a Christian school, a retirement home, or a day-care center, it will have to determine whether to structure those ministries as part of the church itself or incorporate them separately. From the standpoint of financial liability, it might be advantageous to incorporate them separately. If a child is injured in the day-care center, he or his parents might sue the day-care center. If the center is under the corporate structure of the church, then the assets of both the church and the day-care center could be in jeopardy. On the other hand, if the day-care center is incorporated separately, then only the day-care center's assets can be subject to the lawsuit—unless the day-care center operates on church property, in which case they could be jointly liable.

On the other hand, the Christian school or day-care center which is incorporated separately from the church, might not enjoy all the First Amendment constitutional protections of a church. In some states, church-related schools are specifically exempted from requirements such as teacher certification; possibly this exemption might not apply to a separately incorporated Christian school.

It is important to weigh the constitutional protections of being associated with the church against the liability advantages of incorporating separately. In most situations, it is advisable to keep all church ministries under the same structure.

Tax-exempt Status

Many assume that nonprofit corporations are automatically tax-exempt. But that's a separate matter. Nonprofit corporate status is granted by the state; tax-exempt status is granted by the Internal Revenue Service. And except for churches, unless you have applied to the IRS and been approved, you are *not* tax-exempt.

Since the U.S. Internal Revenue Code automatically exempts churches from income taxes, they are not required to apply for tax-exempt status, although they may choose to do so. Even though tax-exempt without applying, there may be advantages to applying for tax-exempt status. Once the IRS has issued a determination letter declaring the church to be tax-exempt, the church's status as tax-exempt is more secure. Someday the IRS regulation granting automatic tax-exempt status to churches might be changed. In the future it might be more difficult to obtain tax-exempt status. In many areas, regulations are already becoming stricter. Also, the church which has applied for and been granted tax-exempt status by the IRS, may have less difficulty obtaining exemption from state income, property, and sales taxes than the church which has not gone through that procedure. In some states, all that is necessary to obtain exemption from state and local taxes is to present a copy of the IRS determination letter to the state or local officials. Without that document, local exemption may be much more difficult or even impossible.

Others argue that by applying for tax-exempt status, you make the IRS aware of your existence and are subject to IRS monitoring. They also point out that if tax-exempt status is later denied, the IRS will not interfere with the deductions taken by contributors if they believed in good faith that their contributions were tax-exempt. There are strong arguments on both sides.

Tax-exempt status has three advantages. First, those who contribute to your ministry may deduct contributions from their taxes. Second, the tax-exempt organization does not have to pay taxes on its earnings, although frequently a nonprofit corporation will not have any taxable earnings. Third, while it is not legally intended that way, tax-exempt status connotes respectability and responsibility.

The provision of the U.S. Internal Revenue Code which covers tax-exempt status is 26 U.S. 501 (c). Under the various subsections of 501 (c), some of the organizations entitled to tax-exempt status are:

(1) Corporations organized by Act of Congress.
(2) Corporations organized for exclusive purpose of holding title to property and collecting income therefrom for organizations which are tax-exempt under the other subsections of 501(1).
(3) Organizations operated exclusively for religious, charitable, scientific, testing for public safety, literary, or educational purposes, to foster national or international sports competition so long as it does not provide athletic facilities or equipment, or to prevent cruelty to children or animals.
(4) Civic leagues or organizations operated exclusively for the promotion of social welfare, or local associations of employees for charitable, educational, or recreational purposes.

(5) Labor, agricultural, or horticultural organizations.

(6) Business leagues, chambers of commerce, real estate boards, boards of trade, or professional football leagues.

(7) Clubs organized for pleasure, recreation, and other non-profitable purposes.

(8) Certain fraternal beneficiary societies.

(9) Certain voluntary employees' beneficiary associations.

The most significant for our purposes is 501(c)(3), religious, charitable, scientific, safety, literary, or educational organizations.

To apply for tax-exempt status under 501(c)(3), you must complete and file with the IRS an application for recognition of exemption, commonly referred to as package 1023. These forms, which should be readily available from the IRS, are about the size of a small comic book. Among other things, the applicant is required to list the name and address of the organization and its employer ID (obtainable through the local Internal Revenue office), source of the organization's finances, types of activities, officers, directors, trustees, any relationships with public officials or other organizations, the types of services your organization expects to provide to the community, and a summary of your organization's assets, revenue, and expenses. You must also attach a current copy of your articles of incorporation (or other document such as a constitution if your organization is not a corporation) bearing the signature of the directors of the corporation and the endorsement of your secretary of state, and a signed copy of the bylaws if you have them, (If you don't have bylaws, that should be specifically stated so your application is not denied for that reason). The application must be signed by an elected officer, director, trustee, or person authorized by power of attorney.

The IRS then examines the application and approves or disapproves it. If not approved, the determination letter by the IRS usually explains the reasons for disapproval. If it is not clear, it is a good idea to talk with the IRS agent who made the determination. Perhaps it is a minor technical problem with the way your articles are drafted, or an omission on your application that can easily be corrected and resubmitted. You have the right to appeal to higher officials in the IRS, or ultimately to the federal courts, if you are still not satisfied with their decision.

To meet with IRS approval, the corporate articles or organizational constitution must contain a clause providing that no part of the net earnings of the corporation go to the benefit of any private shareholder or individual and that no substantial part of the organization's activites consist of attempts to influence legislation or intervention in any political campaign on behalf of any candidate for public office. If you plan to apply for tax-exempt status, it is wise to make sure these items are included in your articles of incorporation when first organized.

Some tax-exempt organizations are required to file an informational return to the IRS each year, called Form 990. This form asks the organization to analyze its revenue, expenses, and fund balances, list its assets, describe its activities, etc., for the past year. However, many organizations are not required to fill out this form. Churches do not have to file 990, nor do Christian schools below college level, mission societies, or religious orders. Also, any 501(c) tax-exempt organization is free from any requirement to file 990 if its gross receipts are normally less than $10,000 annually. Gross receipts include the total contributions, dues, interest, dividends, rental income, royalties, gain from sale of assets, net sales, and other sources of revenue. Here is another advantage to keeping all ministries under the church's corporate umbrella rather than incorporating them separately.

Political Activity

We have previously noted the requirement that tax-exempt organizations not spend a substantial amount of their activities influencing legislation or intervening in political campaigns for public office. This clause has caused some problems for Christian organizations.

For one thing, the code does not prohibit all political activity; it only requires that political activity not constitute a "substantial" portion of the organization's activities. But what is "substantial"? Is ten percent? Twenty-five percent? Five percent? One percent?

How does one determine how "substantial" an organization's political activites are? Does one look to the percentage of total organizational time spent on political activity? Or the percentage of funds which go to politics? Or the amount of space in the organization's literature or facilities devoted to politics?

To interpret vague terms like these and to amplify the Internal Revenue Code, the IRS has prepared a comprehensive (and highly confusing) set of regulations. These regulations do not have the force of law, in that they have not been approved by Congress, and if they are found to conflict with the Internal Revenue Code or other provisions of federal law, they will be invalidated by the courts. But they do exist, and the IRS uses them to interpret the tax laws. The regulations are vague, for section: 1.501(c)(3)(1)(c)simply says:

> (1) . . . An organization will be regarded as "operated exclusively for one or more exempt purposes only if it engages primarily in activities which accomplish one or more of such exempt purposes specified in section 501(c)(3). An organization will not be so regarded if more than an insubstantial part of its activities is not in furtherance of an exempt purpose.
>
> (3)(iv) . . . In determining whether an organization has such characteristics, all the surrounding facts and circumstances, including the articles and all activities of the organization, are to be considered.

Thus "substantial" means "more than an insubstantial part," and in determining what is substantial, all of the organization's activities and documents are considered.

Another problem is the distinction between the sacred and the secular. The code seems to assume that that which is political cannot, by definition, be religious. One is secular; the other is sacred. But the code and the IRS do not distinguish between the organization which is involved in politics for purely secular reasons, and those who enter the political arena because their religious convictions compel them to do so. There are many who believe God's Word takes a strong stand against abortion, pornography, homosexuality, and other evils, and that it is their Christian duty to speak out on these matters. They would, in their minds, be unfaithful to God if they did not speak out on these issues, try to influence legislation on these issues, and try to elect candidates who share their beliefs. Many Christians believe there can be no distinction between the sacred and the secular; I am of that view myself.

A case in point is *Christian Echoes National Ministry, Inc. v. U.S.*, 470 F. 2d 849 (C.A. Okla. 1972), cert. den. 414 U.S. 864. Christian Echoes, better known as Christian Crusade, had been a tax-exempt organization for many years, but around 1970 the IRS revoked its status because a substantial portion of its activity was political. Christian Crusade went to court, and the Federal District Court ruled in its favor. The court noted that Christian Crusade considered communism, socialism, and liberalism to be contrary to the Christian faith, and that the political activites of Christian Crusade were motivated by religious convictions. The court held that the First Amendment prohibited the court from determining what is religious and what is political.

But the Circuit Court of Appeals reversed, holding that if that were the case, then Congress could not restrict the tax-exempt status of religious organizations at all. The circuit court said,

> The political activites of an organization must be balanced in the context of the objectives and circumstances of the organization to determine whether a substantial part of its activites was to influence or attempt to influence legislation. A percentage test to determine whether the activities were substantial obscures the complexity of balancing the organization's activities in relation to its objectives and circumstances.

The circuit court therefore held that many of Christian Crusade's activities were political, that these political activities were substantial, and therefore reversed the district court and upheld the IRS in revoking tax-exempt status. The Supreme Court refused to hear the case, denying certiorari. In another case, *Haswell v. U.S.*, 500 F.2d 1133 1974, cert. den. 419 U.S. 1107, the court also rejected the idea of a percentage test and denied tax-exemption. The court noted that approximately twenty percent of the organization's activities were political, but rejected the idea of a percentage test and denied tax-exemption.

The court in *Christian Echoes* noted that "tax exemption is a privilege, a matter of grace rather than right," and that the only infringement upon Christian Crusade's religious freedom was the denial of tax-exempt status. Christian Crusade remained free to conduct its activities as before; the only difference was that its supporters could not deduct their contributions from their taxes.

However, it may be argued that tax-exempt status *is* a matter of constitutional right. In *McCulloch v. Maryland*, 17 U.S. (Wheat. 4) 316, 431 (1819), the U.S. Supreme Court declared that "the power to tax involves the power to destroy." And in *U.S. v. Butler*, 297 U.S. 1 (1936), the Court noted that the "power to confer or withhold unlimited benefits is the power to coerce or destroy." Many organizations could not survive without their tax-exempt status; their contributors would give to other causes instead.

At the very least, the IRS cannot be arbitrary and discriminatory in the way it enforces the provisions of 501(c)(3) concerning political activity. Many believe the IRS has shown political bias in that it has focused regulation on conservative organizations such as Christian Crusade but ignored the equally extensive political activities of liberal organizations such as the National Council of Churches. This may well be a denial of equal protection of the laws as guaranteed by the Fourteenth Amendment, although the court in *Christian Echoes* said there was no evidence on the record of selective or arbitrary enforcement.

Recently the IRS has attempted to define a "church." The IRS claims this is motivated by the attempts of many individuals or organizations to masquerade as churches when they actually have no religious purpose at all. A businessman might get ordained through a "diploma mill," incorporate his family or business as a nonprofit corporation, and claim to be a religious organization. To prevent such persons from taking advantage of the taxpayers, the IRS has adopted a fourteen-point checklist by which IRS officials determine whether or not the organization is in fact a "church" based on the following church characteristics:

> (1) a distinct legal existence; (2) a recognized form of worship; (3) a definite ecclesiastical government; (4) a formal doctrine; (5) a distinct religious history; (6) a membership not associated with any other church; (7) an organization of ordained ministers; (8) ministers ordained after completing a course of study; (9) a literature of its own; (10) established places of worship; (11) regular congregations; (12) regular religious services; (13) Sunday and religious schools; and (14) seminaries.[3]

What's a passing score on this checklist? To be defined as a church, must one meet all fourteen criteria? Or is ten enough? or six? Or two? The guidelines don't say. Much is left to the subjective discretion of the IRS official who reviews the church.

These criteria could definitely work against some groups of Christians. A substantial body of believers, whose numbers are estimated at about 70,000 are commonly known as Plymouth Brethren. They usually don't formally claim that name for themselves. They believe that denominational titles are contrary to Scripture as they tend to divide Christians. Thus, they prefer to be known simply as Christians, saints, or brethren. Generally their local places of meeting are called chapels or halls rather than churches, because they believe the word

---

3. *Tax-Exempt Organizations, Foundations, Churches, Hospitals, Trade Associations, and other Organizations.* (Englewood Cliffs, New Jersey: Prentice-Hall, 1981).

"church" connotes the body of believers, not the building. So they usually name their local place of assembly something like Tulsa Chapel, Watertown Gospel Hall, etc. They began in England in the 1800s under the influence of men like John Nelson Darby and others. At that time they were known simply as brethren, and the brethren in various areas were known as the London Brethren, Liverpool, etc. But the largest assembly was located in Plymouth, and consequently the name "Plymouth Brethren" was attached to the entire group.

Few church bodies are as dedicated to the Word of God as are the Plymouth Brethren. Few study the Word as faithfully, send as many missionaries per capita, or endeavor as zealously to practice the principles of New Testament Christianity.

But how would the Plymouth Brethren fare under this IRS checklist? (1) A distinct legal existence. As a denomination they have no formal organization, believing that such denominational structures are unscriptural and divisive. Locally some are incorporated, some are not.

(2) A recognized form of worship. They do have a distinctive way of conducting worship services, but they oppose formalism in worship and have no liturgy.

(3) A definite ecclesiastical government. They are governed locally by elders, and even this form of government is often informal.

(4) A formal doctrine. While they accept the Word of God as the rule of doctrine, they oppose manmade creeds as being human additions to the Word of God. Many other evangelicals share this view.

(5) A distinct religious history. Due to the informal nature of the Plymouth Brethren, their religious history is indistinct.

(6) Membership not associated with any other church. Most persons associated with Plymouth Brethren consider the Plymouth Brethren their "church" and belong to no other. But they do not practice formal church membership, because they believe church membership has no basis in Scripture, divides Christians from one another and can be a crutch which leads to a false sense of salvation.

(7) An organization of ordained ministers. There are no ordained ministers and consequently no organization. The Plymouth Brethren believe in the Reformation doctrine of the priesthood of all believers. Consequently they believe the distinction between clergy and laity practiced by many churches is unscriptural. They are governed locally by elders, but even these are not formally ordained.

(8) Ministers ordained after completing a course of study. Those who preach in Plymouth Brethren assemblies are generally well-versed in the Word of God, but usually they have had no formal seminary training.

(9) A literature of its own. There is some literature by the Plymouth Brethren, but not to the extent of other bodies due to the size and informal structure of the movement.

(10) Established places of worship. Most Plymouth Brethren assemblies have buildings for worship, but many meet in homes.

(11) Regular congregations. Again, there is no church membership, but otherwise the Plymouth Brethren could probably meet this qualification.

(12) Regular religious services. Most Plymouth Brethren assemblies would qualify under this test.

(13) Sunday and religious schools. Again, most would meet this test.

(14) Seminaries. Persons associated with the Plymouth Brethren operate a Bible college (Emmaus Bible Institute, Oak Park, Illinois), but they have no seminary.

Through this analysis it may readily be seen that the IRS checklist favors established, formal churches and makes it difficult for informal, low-church, unconventional religious bodies to qualify. Indeed, one might wonder whether the church of the New Testament would be accepted by the IRS. The churches at Philippi, Corinth, and Thessalonica might well have difficulty under parts 1, 2, 3, 4, 5, 6, 7, 8, 10, 11, and 14 of the test! Yet there is no suggestion in the Constitution or in Scripture that this type of body is any less a church than a highly structured, formal denomination.

Christians themselves do not agree on the definition of a church. Lutherans generally believe that a body in which the Word is not preached and the Sacraments are not administered, is not a church. Yet other "churches" do not preach from the Bible and a few do not use the Sacraments. Nor do Christians agree on when the church began. Dispensationalists generally believe the Church began at Pentecost, whereas many others believe the church existed in the Old Testament.

That being the case, it is dangerous for the IRS—or for any other government body—to define a church. Such attempts should be regarded with concern and vigilance.[4]

---

4. Another matter for concern is the recent attempt by the IRS to regulate the racial policies of Christian schools—a precedent which could lead to regulation of religion. This was discussed in Chapter 16.

Chapter 26

Estate Planning
and Charitable Giving

This is supposed to be a Christian book; why spoil it by talking about money? After all, doesn't the Bible say that money is the root of all evil?

No, the Bible doesn't say that. Rather, the Bible says "the *love* of money is the root of all evil" (I Timothy 6:10). And literally that should read "a root," not "the root." Money is not evil; but our attitude toward money can be wrong.

The Bible has a lot to say about money. Old Testament passages decry the debasing of the currency, passages which modern economists should read (Isaiah 1:22). More to the point, the Old and New Testaments both speak extensively of taking up collections for the benefit of the church and the needy, and the parable of the talents establishes that we are to use our resources—material as well as spiritual—wisely in Christ's service (Matthew 25:14-30).

The purpose of this chapter is to advise the Christian to can be a wise steward of the worldly goods God has entrusted to him, and how he can take maximum advantage of tax savings available when giving to the Lord's work.

One word of caution: Tax saving is not the same as tax evading. Romans 13:6 and Matthew 22:21 both establish that we are to pay whatever taxes we legally owe. God has given authority to civil government, and it takes money to run a government. Consequently, He has given government certain powers of taxation.

But there is a difference between tax evasion and tax avoidance. Suppose there is a toll bridge across a river. The person who tries to sneak past the ticket booth and get across without paying is guilty of evasion and this is clearly wrong. But the person who swims across the river so he won't have to pay the toll for the bridge has not *evaded* payment. He has *avoided* payment by a legitimate means.[1]

The Christian should willingly and promptly pay whatever taxes he legally owes. But he should also take whatever steps are legally available to arrange his estate and financial transactions so as to minimize his tax liability. The more he saves in taxes, the more is available for the Lord's work. And the government has designed the tax laws to encourage contributions to churches and charities.

Estate Planning

The word "estate" brings a picture to most people's minds. Most of us see a large acreage with a beautiful house, outbuildings, servants' quarters, etc.

That is an estate, but the word means more than that. Even the poorest pauper has an estate. Your estate consists of everything you own. If all you own is the shirt on your back, then that shirt is your estate.

Estate planning is accumulating, arranging, and designating all of your property, real or personal, so that when you die it will pass to the right persons with as little expense and inconvenience as possible.

All too often, people start thinking about estate planning on their deathbeds. Many never get that opportunity, for death is sudden and unexpected. But estate planning should begin long before retirement or the onset of illness. Estate planning should begin NOW.

Estate and Inheritance Taxes

Estate and inheritance taxes are different. Estate taxes are imposed by the federal government upon the estate while it is being probated, before its assets are distributed to the beneficiaries. Inheritance taxes are imposed by the various state governments, though a few states impose estate taxes instead, after the beneficiaries have received their inheritance.

Inheritance taxes vary greatly from state to state and therefore cannot be discussed at length here. Normally, they are minor compared to federal estate taxes and do not figure too prominently in estate planning.

Federal estate taxes were modified substantially by the Economic Recovery Act of 1981. The basic exemption, formerly $125,000, has been increased to $176,000 in 1981, $225,000 in 1982, and gradually up to $600,000 in 1987. Also, the marital deduction has been increased from 50 percent to 100 percent of the estate. Formerly, in addition to the basic exemption, you could will either

---

1. For this illustration and other information in this chapter, I am indebted to Robert F. Sharpe, *Before You Give Another Dime* (Nashville: Thomas Nelson, 1979). Other valuable works in this area include Robert F. Sharpe's *The Planned Idea Giving Book: Creative Ways to Increase the Income of Your Institution* (Nashville: Thomas Nelson, 1978); Conrad Teitell, *Counsellor's Guide to Charitable Contributions* (Casselton, North Dakota: North Dakota Community Foundation, 1977); John D. Cunnion, *How Trusts Can Save You Income, Estate and Gift Taxes* (Larchmont, New York: Business Reports, Inc., 1966); and Arthur Young, *Economic Recovery Act of 1981: An Analysis of the New Legislation* (Arthur Young & Co., 1981).

an additional $125,000 or 50 percent of your estate to your spouse, whichever is greater, tax free. As of 1981, any and all amounts you will to your spouse are tax free. When the property passes on to your children, there may be taxes, if the size of your estate exceeds the basic exemption at that time.

Gift-tax laws have also been amended. Until recently, one could give up to $3,000 per year to each donee, without paying gift tax. But that rule has been eliminated in favor of a lifetime exclusion. The gift tax exclusion and the standard estate tax deduction have been combined, and this combination is reflected in the increased standard deduction of the Economic Recovery Act of 1981.

These changes are a positive step. Estate taxes had been widely criticized because they increased the suffering of the bereaved, because they taxed wealth that had already been taxed when earned as income, and because they sometimes required families to sell all or part of the family farm or business just to pay the taxes, rather than keep the property in the family.

Nevertheless, estate taxes are still a factor for some estates. The remainder of this chapter will help you plan intelligently with estate taxes in mind.

Last Will and Testament

A basic tool of estate planning is the will. A will is a document that directs the disposition of your estate at the time of your death.

It has been said that the state has already written a will for you, and that will is going to govern the disposition of your estate if you die without writing one yourself. That is basically correct. If you die without a will, you are said to have died *intestate*. This simply means you died without a will. Every state has laws of intestacy that govern the distribution of the estate of an intestate person. Some states provide that one-third of the estate goes to the spouse and the remaining two-thirds to any children. Others give half to the spouse and half to the children; while still others provide that a certain minimum amount (say the first $15,000) goes to the spouse with the rest divided between the spouse and children, etc. Many resent such laws, but they are necessary because the vast majority of people die without leaving wills. If you don't want the law of intestacy to apply to your estate, have a will written NOW!

Many writers and lawyers passionately believe everyone should have a will. It is wise first to consult the laws of intestacy in your state. If they are to your liking, there may be no need for you to have a will.

If you are a single person and have no children, then the laws of intestacy in most states provide that your entire estate (minus taxes and probate costs) will go to your parents. If that is what you want, and if your estate is sufficiently small so that there is no real problem with estate or inheritance taxes, then you may not need a will at this time. If you are married without children, the laws of intestacy in most states provide that if either of you should die, the deceased person's entire estate will pass to his spouse. But if you are married and have children, you will probably need a will. And if you want to leave some of your property to a church or charity, or wish to make any specific bequests which are not in accordance with the laws of intestacy, you need a will. Perhaps you desire that a certain piece of jewelry go to a grandchild, or that your son have the option to buy the farm, or that you want your old homestead to be sold and the proceeds go to the church. If so, you need a will.

Many false conceptions about wills persist. Contrary to rumor, a will does not eliminate the need for probating your estate. You can reduce or eliminate the need for probate by other means, such as joint tenancy, but a will does not mean your estate will escape probate. Nor does a will eliminate the need for taxes. In a complex or large estate, a properly drawn will might reduce taxes; but the mere fact that you have a will does not by itself eliminate taxes.

Another mistaken concept is that only the husband needs a will. If one spouse needs a will, chances are the other spouse needs one also. We cannot know with certainty which spouse will live longer, and in most families property is held jointly or in common or is in the wife's name. In most cases both husband and wife should have a will or sign a joint will. Since the wife's will is likely to be virtually identical to the husband's, most lawyers don't charge much for drawing up two wills or drawing up a joint will.

I strongly recommend against writing you own will. In some states holographic (handwritten) wills are not even acceptable. In some they are acceptable only if they conform to certain legal procedures. Passing property by inheritance is a complicated matter and may involve technicalities you have not considered. You might write a will that says, ''I leave my property in equal shares to my children, Tom and Bill, and if they die before me, then to my grandchildren.'' that sounds clear enough. But if at the time of your death Tom is living but Bill is not, does Tom get Bill's share or does Bill's share go to the grandchildren?—and which grandchildren, those by Bill or those by Tom as well? Or suppose Tom has one child and Bill has two: If Tom and Bill have both died before you, how is your estate to be divided among the grandchildren—does Tom's child get half and Bill's children each get one-fourth (the per stirpes method, which is used in most states if you can't specify otherwise), or does each child get one-third (the per capita method)?

Or suppose your will says, ''I give my son Tom my house, and the remainder of my estate to my son Bill.'' But what if the house has been sold before you die? Does Tom then get nothing and Bill get everything? Or should the remainder of the estate be divided equally between them? Or should Tom get a portion of the estate equal to the value of the house? Countless other complications may arise that you could not possibly realize. The questions probably won't arise until after your death, and at that time, for obvious reasons, you won't be able to explain your intentions! A lawyer is trained to recognize these problems and to draft your will so that its meaning is clear and precise.

Before seeing a lawyer about a will, it is advisable to think carefully about what you want done with your estate after your death. Advance thought and consideration will help both you and your attorney. Here are some things to think about before seeing a lawyer about a will:

(1) Whom do I want to receive my property upon my death? And in what shares? It is usually best to divide your estate into percentages instead of specific amounts. If you give $10,000 to Tom, and the remainder to Bill, you don't know whether Bill will inherit $100,000 or be left with nothing. It is generally better to say, "half to Tom, half to Bill."

(2) Who should be the alternative beneficiary if my intended beneficiary dies before me? Commonly, a husband and wife will leave everything to each other, with the further provision that if the other dies first, then the property passes in equal shares to the children. It is a good idea to include still another clause providing an alternate beneficiary in the event neither the children nor any grandchildren survive the testator. Often this will be a parent, friend, church or charity. A common alternate beneficiary clause for young married couples is to say that one-half goes to the husband's parents or their heirs, and one-half goes to the wife's parents or their heirs. That way both sides of the family are included regardless of who dies first.

(3) Are there any specific items of property you want to leave to a specific person? It is important to be detailed in this part of the will, but not too specific. If a client wanted to leave "all the tools in the garage" to a certain person, what if some of the tools were lying outside when he died? If too specific, the client would have to change his will every time he bought a new pair of socks!

(4) Whom do you wish to name as the executor of your estate? The executor (sometimes called a personal representative) will handle the paperwork involved with the probate of your estate. Among other things, he will have to make an inventory of your estate, pay your debts out of the estate, collect debts owed to your estate, supervise the distribution of your estate, etc. A lawyer will assist him in doing this. Nevertheless, your executor should be a responsible person who is somewhat familiar with your estate. He should be young enough that he is likely to be living and competent at the time of your death. Also, some states require that the executor be a resident of your state. It is wise to name an alternate executor in case the executor is for any reason unwilling or unable to so serve. Husbands and wives commonly name each other as primary executor, and then name a parent or sibling as the alternate. If you have no relatives or close friends to whom you would entrust this responsibility, many banks and lawyers are willing to serve as executors for a fee.

(5) If you have minor children, do you wish to name a guardian for them in your will? Such a designation is not 100 percent binding upon the court. Children cannot be willed like property, and the court must consider whether the person you have designated is competent to serve as guardian. Nevertheless, if you have designated a reasonably competent person, the court will follow your designation nearly all of the time. Raising someone else's children is a big responsibility; not everyone cares to assume. Before naming a guardian in your will, it is wise to first discuss it with that person. This is probably the

most important decision included in your will. Pick someone who is not only stable and responsible, but who loves your children and who will give them the spiritual training you desire them to have. Sometimes two families will reach an understanding with each other—if you should die, we'll take care of your children, and vice versa. It is often wise to name your guardian as an alternate executor for your estate.

(6) Do you wish to designate any portions of your estate to church or charity? If so, what, or what percentage? Sometimes a person will designate a church or charity as an alternate beneficiary. Perhaps you want your wife and children to have all of your estate if you die before them, but if they die before you, you'd rather the money go to your church than to distant relatives.

(7) Before seeing your lawyer, prepare a brief inventory of your estate, listing all real property and major items of personal property, their locations and approximate valuations (minus any balances owed on them). Also prepare a list of names and addresses of all persons and institutions you wish to name in your will (with correct spellings).

What do you do with a will after it has been prepared? There is no legal reason why you can't share it with your family members, although many do not care to do so. Whether you divulge the contents of your will to your family members or not, inform them in writing that you have prepared a will and designate where it may be found. In many instances a will is not discovered until months or years after the testator's death, and who knows how many times a person's will has never been found at all?

Where should your will be kept? In some states there is a will registry at the county courthouse. There you can place your will for safekeeping, where it will be kept in confidence until your death. Most lawyers are happy to keep the original of your will in a safe in their office. The will is then readily available should that attorney handle the probate of your estate. If another lawyer probates your estate, the first attorney is required to give the will to him. You might also wish to keep your will in a fireproof box or safe in your home.

There are some problems with keeping a will in a safety deposit box at a bank. Some banks promptly seal your safety deposit box as soon as they learn of your death, and will not open it until ordered to do so by a court. This could be months after your death and may add much confusion to the probate of your estate. By this time, for example, another person besides the one you have named may have been designated by the court as the executor of your estate or temporary guardian of your children. If you want to leave your will in a safety deposit box, make sure you have a clear understanding with the bank as to their policies in this regard.

It is wise to review your will about once a year to see whether your intentions are still the same. Maybe you have changed your mind about willing half your estate to your brother; or maybe you want a different executor or guardian. Also, every few years it is wise to have an attorney review your will to see whether new laws require that it be revised. This can be done either by preparing a codicil (amendment) to it, or by drawing up an entirely new will.

Trusts

A trust is a legal instrument by which property is placed under the care of one person for the benefit of another. For example, your minor children may not be mature enough to handle an estate of many thousands of dollars. To make sure they do not spend it all on candy and gum, the courts will often presume a trust or conservatorship for the children until they are of age. The person designated to handle the property for them is called the "trustee," meaning that he has been entrusted with the property for their benefit. This trustee can be a spouse, a relative, a friend, an attorney, or a corporation with legal authority to manage trusts, such as a bank.

Trusts also have certain tax advantages. If you will your property outright to someone else, part of it may be taxable under federal estate tax laws. Trusts can avoid or reduce that tax liability. Let us suppose you will all of your property to your wife, and she wills it to the children, and they will it to their children (your grandchildren). There may be federal estate taxes and state inheritance taxes upon the property when you die, then again when your wife dies, and still a third time when your children die. This can reduce the size of the estate greatly. If your estate consists of a home, a farm, or a business, part or all of it may have to be sold just to pay the taxes.

As an alternative, you could establish a trust for the benefit of your wife and children during their lifetimes, with the remainder to go to your grandchildren when your children or wife die, whichever occurs last. Under such a trust, the property would be taxed only once, when it actually passes to your grandchildren. Of course, there is also a disadvantage. While your wife and children would enjoy the income from the trust throughout their lifetime, they probably would not be able to use the principal of the trust. For example, if the trust consisted of a farm, they probably could not sell the farm even if it were advantageous for them to do so. (Though there are ways a trust could be established to allow for this possibility.)

A trust is often prepared as part of a will, but not necessarily so. A trust can be a separate document. And while most trusts are testamentary in that they take effect upon the death of the grantor, some trusts can take effect during your lifetime; these are called living trusts or *inter vivos trusts*. Living trusts can be revocable or irrevocable, as you direct. An obvious advantage to making a trust revocable is that you retain control of it, though you may lose some of the tax advantages.

Trusts are highly complicated matters, far more so than wills. The layman should not attempt to engineer one without the help of an attorney.

Joint Tenancy

Two or more persons can own property by at least two means: joint tenancy and tenancy in common. Let us suppose, for example, that we are talking about a forty-acre tract of land which we shall call Greenacre. Tenancy in common means that each tenant owns an undivided one-half interest in Greenacre. Each, that is, owns only half of Greenacre, not the whole forty acres. But because it is an undivided half, neither can point to any particular twenty acres as his half. Either could sell his one-half interest with or without the consent of the other, but neither could sell or give away the other tenant's half.

But joint tenancy is different. Strange as it may seem, each joint tenant owns the whole property, along with the others. Under the laws of some states, any joint tenant can sell or give away the entire property without the knowledge or consent of the others. Other states provide that all joint tenants must agree to the sale or there is no sale at all.

Joint tenancy is not limited to real estate. Automobiles, bank accounts, and other property interests can be held in joint tenancy. If a bank account is in joint tenancy, either party may be able to withdraw some or all of the money from the account without the knowledge or consent of the other. This, however, may depend upon how the account is established. In some states, it is not considered to be a joint account, and property is not considered to be joint property, unless it is listed as being in the names of Mr. and/or Mrs. John Smith. If it is simply Mr. and Mrs. John Smith, it is presumed to be tenancy in common and both must consent to any sale or withdrawal. In one state the presumption against joint tenancy is so strong that the court will presume the property was intended to be held as tenancy in common, unless the deed clearly states, "Mr. and/or Mrs. John Smith, as joint tenants and not as tenants in common." Others require the phrase, "with the right of survivorship."

In estate planning, joint tenancy has both a distinct advantage and a distinct disadvantage. The advantage is that property owned in joint tenancy need not be probated. The very instant a joint tenant dies, the property becomes 100 percent the property of the remaining party. It avoids conflicts with probate, and probate costs. The savings and convenience are very significant.

But the disadvantage lies in taxes. You will recall that each joint tenant is considered at law to be an owner of 100 percent of the joint property. Consequently, when he dies, the tax authorities presume that the joint property belonged entirely to him, and they figure his estate taxes accordingly. Let us suppose that our forty acre tract, Greenacre, is worth $2,500 per acre, for a total value of $100,000. If Smith and Jones owned Greenacre as tenants in common, then Mr. Smith would be presumed by the tax authorities to own half of it and at his death his estate would have to pay taxes on $50,000. But if Smith and Jones owned Greenacre as joint tenants, the IRS would presume that Mr. Smith owned all of it, and would assess his taxes based on the $100,000 figure. Of course, that is a rebuttable presumption. If Jones can contest the presumption by showing that he had worked and contributed half the cash to pay for Greenacre, Mr. Smith's tax liability might be reduced considerably.

This principle used to apply to joint tenants who were married couples as well. But section 2040 of The U.S. Internal Revenue Code provides that property held in joint tenancy by persons dying after 1982 is deemed to be owned half by the descedent and half by the survivor, provided spouses are the only joint tenants.

As previously indicated, recent changes in the laws of estate taxation have so greatly increased the exemptions, that the majority of estates are not taxed at all. Unless the estate is substantial, the probate and convenience advantages of joint tenancy probably outweigh the possible tax disadvantages.

Insurance

Life insurance has been described as a way of building a quick estate. By paying annual or monthly premiums, your loved ones are protected so that if you should die at an early age, they will receive substantial insurance proceeds to provide for their needs.

There are several types of life insurance. "Whole life" builds up a cash value, so that each month your insurance policy is worth more. If you die young, your family will be provided for by insurance proceeds. On the other hand, if you live to a certain age, such as sixty-five, you will receive a large lump sum payment, annuities or monthly payments. Many policies also include such extra benefits as the privilege of borrowing against the cash surrender value of the policy, waiver of premium in case you are disabled, etc. Such a policy is more than protection. It is an investment.

There are also "term life" policies. Term insurance is protection, nothing more. If you die young, your loved ones receive substantial insurance proceeds. But if you live past a certain age, such as sixty-five, or if at any time you discontinue the policy, you get nothing at all.

Term policies are divided into two types, level term and declining term. Level term pays the same amount regardless of how old you are when you die; if you die at forty-five your family gets the same as if you had died at twenty-five. But the annual premium increases as you get older and your risk of death increases. Declining term, on the other hand, starts with a high payment if you die at an early age, and gradually decreases as you get older. But the premium remains the same, year after year. For example, I have declining term insurance for which I pay $108.00 per year. Had I died before age 30, it would have paid my family $70,000; from age 30-35, $50,000; from 36-39, $40,000; from 40-44, $30,000; from 45-49, $20,000; from 50-54, $10,000; beyond that, nothing.

If I should live beyond fifty-five, then all the money I paid into this policy will have been wasted except for the peace of mind it has given me. I will have built up no estate for myself or my family with that money. But on the other hand, term insurance is far, far cheaper than whole life insurance.

Many believe it is financially advantageous to buy term insurance instead of more costly whole life, and put the difference into real estate, a savings plan, or other investment. Others argue that many do not have the discipline to save on their own, and that whole life insurance is a means of forced savings.

Regardless of which insurance plan you choose, insurance policies are an important tool in estate planning. Insurance proceeds normally do not pass with your estate through probate. They are paid directly from the insurance company to the beneficiary named on your policy. It is therefore important to make sure your policy correctly reflects your intended beneficiary. If you say in your will that all your insurance proceeds should go to your Aunt Mary, but say on your insurance policy that they go to Uncle Harry, they will go to Uncle Harry. The only time a will has anything to say about insurance proceeds is if neither your beneficiary nor alternate beneficiary is living. Then the insurance proceeds are paid into your estate and probated along with the rest of your estate.

While insurance proceeds are normally not probated with your estate, they are taxed with your estate. If your estate consists of $100,000, but you also have insurance proceeds of $50,000, then your estate is taxed as $150,000. The only way to avoid this is to transfer the ownership of your policy to another person; but if that person dies before you, the cash surrender value of the policy could be taxed with that person's estate.

The insurance industry is continually devising new forms of insurance to meet consumer needs. It would be wise to check with your insurance agent to see what new plans might be available for you.

Record-Keeping

One important aspect of estate planning is keeping accurate records. Every person should have a safe place for keeping records. With the qualifications mentioned earlier about wills, this could be a safety deposit box at a bank, or better yet, a locked, fireproof safe or box at home. There you should have all cancelled checks and important receipts for at least the past three years, your tax returns, warranties, birth certificates, marriage certificates, baptismal certificates, Social Security cards, insurance policies, titles to property, stocks, bonds, certificates of deposit, passbooks, military discharges, and other important records. It is also wise to keep and periodically update an inventory of everything you own and some type of ledger of your income and expenses.

Charitable Giving

"God loveth a cheerful giver." (II Corinthians 9:7).

Let us, therefore, examine some of the means by which we can manage our resources so as to maximize our giving to Christ and His church.

Outright Gifts of Cash

In the past, if you have chosen to itemize deductions, you have been able to deduct your church and charitable contributions on Schedule A of your income tax return. This is true of any cash contribution for which you have a cancelled check, receipt, or other written evidence, provided it is made to a tax-exempt organization—and you will recall from the last chapter that churches are automatically exempt under 501 (c) (3) of the Internal Revenue Code. In any given year, the charitable deduction cannot exceed 50 percent of your income, but you can carry over excess contributions and deduct them from your income in any of five successive years thereafter.

For example, let us suppose your annual income is $100,000. In 1981, you give $75,000 to your church. You can deduct only $50,000 on Schedule A for that year; you must pay tax on the remaining $50,000. But you can carry the remaining $25,000 contribution forward for five years and deduct it in any year you contribute less than 50 percent. If in 1985 your income remains $100,000 but you only give $25,000 in that year, you can deduct the remainder of your 1981 contribution at that time.

Cash contributions for which you don't have receipts or cancelled checks, such as the coins your children put in the Sunday school plate or the dollar you gave to the lady who rang your doorbell for the March of Dimes, must be itemized on Schedule A, listing the donee and amount. So long as the amounts claimed are reasonable and credible, most IRS examiners will take your word for it.

You cannot deduct the value of your services to the church, such as the time you spent raking the church lawn. But you can deduct expenses you have incurred on behalf of the church. If, for example, as church treasurer you made some long distance phone calls to the denominational headquarters at your expense, those are deductible. If you were called upon to preach or speak at a function at a church fifty miles away, your unreimbursed travel expenses should be deductible provided you have kept good records. The rate of reimbursement for mileage would probably be the same as for employee business expenses.

The Economic Recovery Act of 1981 leaves these provisions intact, but it adds a new provision for those who take the standard deduction. Starting in 1982, persons who take the standard deduction can, in addition, deduct 25 percent of the first $100 of their charitable contributions. The deduction will remain the same in 1983; in 1984 it will increase to 25 percent of the first $300. In 1985, 50 percent of all charitable contributions will be deductible, and 100 percent of all charitable contributions will be deductible in 1986. At that time the charitable deduction provision for those who take the standard deduction will terminate, unless Congress decides to extend it further.

Gifts of Tangible Property

Let us suppose that your church needs a piano. Years ago, you bought a piano for your daughter when she was taking music lessons; but now that she is married and living elsewhere, the piano merely occupies space. You can give the piano to the church, and deduct on Schedule A the present fair market value of the piano from your taxes. "Fair market value" is an estimate of what the piano would sell for today, given its present used condition.

Perhaps the property you give to the church is an antique that has appreciated in value over the years, such as a painting. Perhaps you bought an antique painting fifty years ago for $1,000, and now it is worth $10,000. If you give that painting to the church, what can you deduct—$1,000 or $10,000?

The answer again is that you deduct the present fair market value, which is $10,000. But must you subtract the appreciation ($9,000) from the amount you report? The answer depends upon whether or not the item you gave is related to the ministry of the church. If it is (such a religious painting which the church will place in its foyer), you do not have to deduct the appreciation at all; you can simply take the whole $10,000 as a deduction. But if it is not related to the ministry of the church, you have to reduce the deduction by 50 percent of the appreciation ($10,000 fair market value minus $1,000 original cost equals $9,000 appreciation; 50 percent of $9,000 appreciation equals $4,500; $10,000 minus $4,500 equals $5,500, the amount you can deduct on Schedule A).

The IRS advises churches and charities to issue receipts for tangible property simply naming and describing the items received without indicating the value of those items.

Gifts of tangible property are deducted at the current fair market value. True with one exception: property given by a business that was part of its equipment or inventory. The business may deduct that gift based on its cost of acquisition, plus one-half of its appreciation.

Giving Stocks

Perhaps you purchased 100 shares of stock in a major corporation many years ago. You are now financially comfortable and do not need the stock, you would like to give it to a Bible college. But, you wonder, should I give the stock to the college outright, or should I sell the stock and give the money to the college instead?

The answer depends upon whether the stock has appreciated or depreciated in value. You incur a capital gain or capital loss if you sell the stock first. For tax purposes, you want the capital loss, but you do not want the capital gain.

Let us say the stock was purchased in 1960 for $1,000 per share, and it is now worth $2,000 per share. If you sold the stock before giving it to the Bible college, you would incur a $1,000 capital gain on each share, for a total of $100,000, 40 percent of which would be reportable as income. But if you gave it to the Bible college, none of that capital gain would have to be reported. The Bible college could then sell it for $200,000 and not have to pay tax on any of it, because the Bible college is a tax-exempt institution. And you can claim the entire $200,000, the current fair market value, as a deduction, even though you bought it for only $100,000.

But let us suppose you bought the stock in 1960 for $1,000 per share, and it is now worth only $500 per share. There is a $500 per share capital loss, total of $50,000, 40 percent of which is deductible. In that case, it makes more sense to sell the stock, take your capital loss deduction, and give the proceeds of the sale to the Bible college. Since the stock is currently worth only $50,000, the current fair market value, you could deduct only $50,000 if you gave the stock to your church. But if you sold it on the market and gave the proceeds to the church, you could deduct both the $50,000 cash gift and 40 percent of the $50,000 capital loss. The principle is: If the value has *increased*, give it outright. If the value has *decreased*, sell it, give the proceeds, and deduct the capital loss.

Giving Real Estate

In Acts 4:36-37 we read that Joseph (Barnabas) sold his land and brought the money and laid it at the apostles' feet, a gift to the new church.

But the Romans, for all their ingenuity, had not thought of capital gains taxes. If Barnabas were living today, he would have had to consider whether the real estate had appreciated or depreciated in value.

The principle is the same as with stocks. If the real estate has increased in value, the best plan is to give the real estate to the church and deduct the current fair market value as a charitable contribution—using a written appraisal from a respected local appraiser to establish that value. But if the land has depreciated in value, then you should sell the land, give the proceeds to the church, and deduct both the proceeds and the capital loss.

Giving Life Insurance

Sometimes life insurance policies are a convenient way of giving.

Let us say you are fifty years old and financially secure. As a young man, knowing the uncertainties of the future, you purchased substantial life insurance to protect your family. Now you do not need that protection. Your children are grown and married, and you have plenty of assets to take care of yourself and your wife for the rest of your lives. So if you want to give a substantial gift to the church, the most practical way to do it might be to give that life insurance policy.

You can benefit your church or charity through a gift of life insurance in many ways. You could name the church as an alternate beneficiary—the insurance proceeds go to your wife if she survives you, but if she does not, they go to the church. Or, you could list the church as a co-beneficiary; half goes to your wife, half to the church.

A third possibility is to assign the annuities from your policy (if your policy has annuities) to your church, or make the church a residual beneficiary if you die before the guaranteed annuities or benefits are used up.

A fourth possibility is to assign the dividends from your policy to your church, if yours is a mutual company that issues dividends. Even though such a dividend is regarded by the IRS as a partial premium refund and, therefore, not reportable as income, the gift to the church may still be deducted on Schedule A as a charitable contribuiton.

Or, fifth, you could simply assign the rights of ownership to the charity.

After doing so, if you continue to pay premiums on the policy, those premiums are deductable.

Some churches rely heavily upon pledges from their members for future financial planning. Perhaps you have made a substantial pledge to your church, and the church has relied upon that and other pledges in its building program. Were you to die and be unable to fulfill your pledge, that could upset the church's plans considerably. One possibility might be to purchase a declining term policy to cover your pledge, naming the church as beneficiary. That way, if you were to die before your pledge was fulfilled, the insurance proceeds would fulfill the pledge for you.

Deferred Giving

Under some circumstances you may wish to give some property to your church but want to retain an interest in it for a while.

For example, you may want the church to have your farm, but you need a place to live. Or perhaps you would like to give your shares of IBM to the church, but you are worried that you might need the income from that stock in your old age. Yet you realize that the church could benefit from that gift now, rather than waiting until your death.

There are ways of solving those problems.

One way might be to give the farm to the church, reserving the right to live in the farmhouse for the remainder of your life. Additionally, you may also wish to reserve the income from the farm (or a portion of it) for the rest of your life.

There are advantages to giving this way. It enables you to complete the transaction now, and avoid uncertainties or will contests after you are dead. Also, by completing the transaction now, you gain a tax deduction for you can deduct the full current fair market value of the farm from your income tax, and if that value exceeds your income for that year, you have a carryover for the next five years.

The tax deduction, however, applies only if you make the gift irrevocable—that is, a gift that you cannot get back if you change your mind or even if your financial circumstances change and you need the property again. Revocable gifts—those you can take back—also have a place in estate planning, but do not provide tax deductions. You can deduct the gift only if it is irrevocable. Some Christian organizations may tell you orally that, even though your gift is irrevocable on paper, they will voluntarily give it back to you if you change your mind. Such organizations may very well be honorable and keep their promises, but you should bear in mind that legally they cannot be forced to return real estate, unless they put the promise in writing—and then the gift becomes revocable and loses its tax advantages.

Another option is to give the farm to the charity with the provision that the charity will pay you an annuity for the rest of your life. This way, the church gets the farm now and can use it as it sees fit, but you get a lifetime guaranteed income that suits your needs. This guaranteed annual annuity is the church's legal responsibility to pay to you, even in years of crop failure or business recession. It may give the church the capital it needs to expand and give you the security you need for the future.

The tax aspects of giving in return for annuities vary with many factors, including your age. If the charity cannot provide this information, it may be necessary to see a lawyer or tax specialist to determine this matter.

Giving through Retirement Plans

Pension and retirement plans often provide valuable options for charitable giving. It may be that you have earned a substantial pension, but because you have been successful and frugal, you do not need it. There are ways those retirement benefits can be assigned to charity.

Retirement plans work in different ways, and sometimes your retirement plan will give several options. It may provide a guaranteed pension or annuity for life, and those rights could simply be assigned to your church. That way, every year you live, your church would receive a substantial check from your retirement company.

Others may offer an annual payment for the rest of your life, but guaranteed for a certain number of years (let's say twenty). At age sixty-five you begin receiving payments. In the event you die at seventy-five, that leaves ten years of guaranteed payments which could be assigned to your church.

Still a third plan offers you an annual payment for a certain number of years—again, let's say twenty. As before, you could assign the payments to a church or charity in case you should die before the twenty years are up. The problem with this plan is that if you live beyond the specified time, you receive nothing further from the plan. But this plan would probably offer substantially larger annual payments than the second plan mentioned above.

Giving through Living Trusts

As explained earlier, a living trust is a document that places property in the custody of one person for the benefit of another. A living trust differs from a testamentary trust in that a living trust takes effect during your lifetime, whereas a testamentary trust does not take effect until you die.

Living trusts can be revocable or irrevocable. A revocable trust can be revoked by the donor (you) at any time you desire, whereas an irrevocable trust is final and cannot be changed. But the irrevocable trust enables you to deduct the fair market value of the property as a charitable contribution, whereas the revocable trust involves no tax deductions until it becomes final upon your death.

Revocable living trusts do have advantages. They provide the donor with the option to revoke the bequest at any time if he needs the property or if the church or charity isn't living up to his expectations. They give the church the immediate benefit of the property, instead of waiting until your death. They save expenses since property in the living trust normally does not pass through probate (although it is counted with your estate for tax purposes, subject to charitable deductions). It relieves you of the responsibility of managing that portion of your estate. And it involves privacy, since the trust instrument is not a matter of public record.

Living trusts, revocable or irrevocable, are flexible instruments that can be tailored to meet your unique needs. Here are several common arrangements: (1) The charitable remainder annuity trust, much like the gift annuity plan in that in return for your gift the church provides you with a guaranteed fixed annuity for life. (2) The charitable remainder unitrust, which differs from the annuity trust in that instead of a fixed monetary amount, the church guarantees the donor an annuity based on a fixed percentage of the value of the property given in trust. For example, if you place a farm worth $100,000 in a living trust, the unitrust might guarantee you an annuity of 6 percent of the value of the farm. This year that would be $6,000. Ten years from now the value of the farm may have doubled, making your annuity $12,000; or it may have fallen by 50 percent, reducing your annuity to $3,000. (3) The pooled-income investment is similar to the charitable remainder unitrust, except that the annuity is based upon the donor's pro rata share of the charity's investment fund, not the value of the gift itself.

Obviously, these plans are seldom used by local churches, though most of them could be with little difficulty. But denominations, missionary organizations, and Christian colleges often have such plans and will be happy to explain them to you more fully. Some will even prepare the trust, but for your protection have it reviewed by your attorney.

Giving through Testamentary Trusts

A testamentary trust does not take effect until your death. Often it is prepared in conjunction with your will, though it can be a separate document.

Such a trust can be arranged in several ways. Perhaps you own a substantial estate and want it to benefit several charitable organizations. Rather than having your executor sell all of your property and divide the proceeds among those organizations, you may prefer that your estate be kept intact.

You might then establish a trust whereby your estate is managed by a trustee, who divides the income from your estate each year among the organizations you have designated and according to the percentages you have specified. Or, you might want to give your trustee the authority to name the organizations to be benefited and the amounts that should go to each.

Still another possibility is that you want your children to benefit from your estate but want some to go to charity as well. You might have your estate placed in trust, with the provision that twenty-five percent of the annual income from the trust goes to each of your three children, and the remaining twenty-five percent to a church or charity. You might provide that the trust continue until the last of your children have died, at which time it shall be liquidated and the proceeds divided among your grandchildren and/or charities as you specify in the trust instrument. The possibilities are endless.

Giving Through Your Will

Finally, you can include churches and charities in your will. You might will a particular piece of property to your church, or you might direct that the church receive a fixed percentage of the total value of your estate.

Or perhaps you want your wife and children to inherit your estate, but do not particularly care whether more distant relatives receive anything from your estate. Your will might then provide something to this effect: "I give, devise, and bequeath all of my property, real, personal or mixed, to my wife, or if she does not survive me, then to my children or their issue in equal shares per stirpes. But if neither my wife nor any of my children or their issue survive me, then and in that event I bequeath my estate to the Faith Lutheran Church of Viking Valley, Minnesota."

A few states limit the amount you can give to charity in your will. Iowa Code §633.266, for example, provides that a charitable bequest may not exceed one-fourth of the total estate if there is a spouse, child, grandchild or parent of the deceased who challenges the will. In the event such an excessive bequest is challenged, the court will reduce it to one-fourth of the estate and give the remainder to the heirs.

If you wish to give more of your estate to charity than the law of your state allows, several options are available. You might make some lifetime gifts to the charity, divesting yourself of part of your estate before your death. Or you could make the charity a joint tenant of your property with you, so that upon your death the property automatically becomes the property of the charity without passing through probate with your estate. Or you might take out a substantial life insurance policy, naming the charity as your beneficiary, so that upon your death the insurance proceeds go directly to the charity instead of passing through your estate. Still another possibility is a living trust.

Doubling Your Contribution

If you are an employee of a major company, you may be able to double your giving. Quite a few companies have programs whereby they will match your gift to an educational institution on a one-to-one basis. If you give $100 to the college of your choice, your company will match the gift by giving an additional $100. This is generally limited to gifts to educational institutions, but some companies include churches or charities. It is worthwhile to check whether your employer has such a plan and whether your intended beneficiary is included or could be included.

Securities Law

Securities include most stocks and bonds, but the term is broader than that. A security is a written evidence of indebtedness, based upon an investment of money or other property with an expectation of profit or appreciation by the efforts of a third person. Church bonds for building projects, among other things, could be classed as securities.

There are both federal and state laws and regulations concerning securities. The federal laws are administered and enforced by the Securities and Exchange Commission (SEC). These securities laws can include a requirement that securities be registered with a government agency, a requirement that all relevant information about the securities be disclosed to prospective customers, or a prohibition against fraud. Registration is often required before making a public offer of securities, and in a few states private offers may also be covered. In some jurisdictions, churches, charities, and educational institutions may be exempt from state securities laws; in others they are not.

Securities violations by a church or organization can be expensive and damaging to a ministry. The law is so vague, that an innocent person with good intentions can find himself in serious trouble. Rev. Jerry Falwell had an extensive legal battle with the government over alleged sale of securities. He won, but at enormous legal expense.

Before offering anything that could possibly be defined as a security, it is wise to obtain competent legal advice. Rather than relying on the word of a representative of a bonding company or securities company, obtain your own legal counsel.[2]

A Closing Word

Man's laws change rapidly. Probably no chapter of this book is more subject to change than this one on estate planning and charitable giving. Some of the information in this chapter could be superceded by new laws and regulations in coming weeks, months, and years.

Also, the wisdom of estate planning depends upon state statutes, and these vary considerably in different areas. This chapter was prepared to alert you to problem areas and to suggest possibilities for solving them. But before you take any final action in estate planning, it is important to consult a lawyer or other professional.

I cannot close this chapter without considering the widow and her two mites (Mark 12; Luke 21). No one suggested that she consider gift annuities, life estates, pooled-income investment funds, or living trusts. She simply gave what she had, and no corporate donor matched her gift. But Christ valued her gift above all others, because she gave out of love for God.

This was a shock to those who thought they could impress God by the size of their gifts. But God doesn't really need our gifts. He simply chooses to work with them and through them. And if one gives a million dollars with a proud heart, seeking to be justified thereby, God despises that gift.

It has been said that it is not what you give, but what you have left over

2. Wendell R. Bird, Lecture, Bob Jones University, Greenville, South Carolina, October 12, 1981.

that counts. That is closer to the truth, but even that comes short of the mark. "God loveth a cheerful giver"! What really counts is neither how much you give nor how much you have left over. What really counts is your mental attitude while giving.

Many seem to believe that a gift to God isn't really a gift at all unless we suffer somehow by giving it. God may indeed call us to sacrificial giving, but the mere fact that we suffer because of a gift does not mean our gift merits special approval from God. It is possible that a pauper could give his last dollar to the church. But if he did so with a proud or bitter spirit, that gift would be as meaningless as the gift of the self-justifying millionaire!

It is not wrong to plan our giving to make the most efficient use of our resources. If we love God, we will make wise use of the resources He has given us. And the gift that truly pleases God is the gift that is given out of love for Him and by the power of His Spirit. "Every man according as he purposeth in his heart, so let him give; not grudgingly, or of necessity: for God loveth a cheerful giver." (II Corinthians 9:7).

Chapter 27

Tax Planning for Pastors
and Religious Workers

We often assume that if we're getting paid $1000 per month, we take home
$1000 per month. But what really counts financially is not what our monthly
pay is, but what is left of it after deductions.

Fortunately, a pastor and his church board have some control over these
deductions and can arrange them to effect tax savings- and tax savings result
in extra money for the pastor and his church. Instead of paying a pastor $1500
per month, a church could expend $1400 per month, but by designating
substantial portions of that $1400 as fringe benefits, the pastor could actually
be taking home more money than with a straight salary of $1500 per month.

Let's take a look at our tax laws and see how this could be done.[1]

What Must Be Reported As Income?

To begin with, the pastor's base salary must be reported, just as any other
citizen must report his salary. Also, special honoria which he receives for
preaching in other churches or for performing weddings or funerals or other
special services are reportable income. If he does part-time work at another
occupation, that also is reportable income. If he has published a book or written
a magazine article and received royalties for writings, those royalties are income.

Of course, other types of income such as capital gains, interest, dividends
over $200, and farm income, if any, must be reported just as anyone else would
have to report them.

---

1. For general information in this area of law, see Kenneth G. Hungerford, II and William
C. Slack, *Federal Income Tax Handbook for 1978 Returns* (Grand Rapids, Michigan: Baker Book House,
1979); Worth, *Income Tax Handbook for Ministers and Religious Workers* (Grand Rapids, Michigan:
Baker Book House, 1980, 1981); Price Waterhouse, *Abington Clergy Income Tax Guide, 1984 Edition
for 1983 Returns*, Revised and updated (Nashville: Abington, 1983).

Gifts are a difficult subject. In many churches, the pastor's income is regularly supplemented by gifts from the parishioners over and above his regular salary. Though gifts need not be reported as income, the question is whether these are really gifts or remunerations for services. To determine this, the IRS would consider several questions: Is it provided in your call or employment agreement that such an offering will be taken? Does the offering take place periodically rather than spontaneously and sporadically? (For example, many churches have a custom of taking up a Christmas offering for the pastor.) Does the gift or offering bear any relation to any particular service the pastor has performed? A "yes" answer to any of the previous questions would indicate that the gift offering is taxable income; a"no" answer would indicate that it is not. But no one "yes" or "no" answer will by itself determine if the gift is taxable, it must be viewed as a whole.

What Need Not Reported As Income?

Four terms are often confused with one another: exclusion, deduction, exemption, and credit. Each has a slightly different meaning.

When we call something an *exclusion*, we mean that it does not need to be reported as income at all; the IRS doesn't even have to hear about it. Most gifts come into this category.

A *deduction* is an expense we can subtract from our income. Charitable contributions, professional expenses (if you have paid them yourself), etc. are deductions. We report a certain amount of income on our tax forms, and then deduct those expenses to arrive at our taxable income.

An *exemption* is a certain kind of deduction. The most common exemption is that which is provided for persons dependent upon your income, such as your spouse and children.

Finally, a *credit* is an item you can subtract from the tax you pay, rather than from the income figure on which you compute your tax liability. For example, you are entitled to claim as a credit one-half of your contributions to candidates for public office, to a maximum of $50.00 or $100.00 for a married couple filing jointly. If your income tax is figured at $950 for this year, and you have given $100 in political contributions, you can claim one-half of that amount ($50) as a credit and subtract it from your tax. You then owe the IRS $900 instead of $950.

Exclusions

Items that need not be reported as income at all are called exclusions.

The most obvious and substantial exclusion is the parsonage. Many churches own a house that is set aside for the pastor, and is provided for him without charge as a condition of his employment. The pastor need not report the value of this parsonage as income, nor need he report the church's payment of the utilities, furnishings, improvements, repairs, etc.

But what about the pastor whose church does not own a parsonage? The church may then designate a portion of the pastor's salary as a "housing allowance" and that portion need not be reported as income, provided (1) the pastor is a licensed, ordained, or commissioned clergyman in accordance with the usage of the denomination; (2) the pastor is performing the services of a minister of the Gospel; (3) the allowance is designated by the church as a "housing allowance"; and (4) the allowance is entirely used by the pastor for housing expenses—including house payments or rent, furnishings, utilities, improvements, repairs, etc.

Note that the allowance must be so designated by the employer, the church. Merely having it so designated by the denomination, or by the pastor himself, is not enough to satisfy the IRS. Note, also, that the housing allowance must be used entirely for housing. If the church designates $600 as a monthly housing allowance, but the pastor purchases a home with mortgage payments of only $350 plus other housing expenses of $100, his total housing cost is only $450. The remaining $150 is reportable as income. To save taxes, the pastor might wish to apply the difference on the principal of his loan. Better yet, he may wish to structure his home mortgage so the total costs will approximate his housing allowance.

The housing allowance can be a real benefit to the pastor who wants to acquire a home of his own. Home ownership is one of the best hedges against inflation and one of the best means of building an estate. It does, however, have problems. For example, if the pastor owned a house while serving one church, and then accepted a call to another church which owned a parsonage, he would then probably want to sell his house at the first church. Since he would not be buying another personal residence at the new location, he would have to pay capital gains tax on 40 percent of the appreciation of the old house. In other words, if he bought the house for $40,000 and sold it for $50,000, he would have a $10,000 profit. He would then have to pay tax on $4,000 of that capital gain. That tax could be delayed by purchasing a new residence within two years of the sale of the old, but that is difficult to do if the new church has a parsonage.

The problem can be handled in several ways. The pastor could keep his old house and rent it out for income, possibly to the new pastor. Or, he could purchase a new house at his new location and have the church sell or rent out his parsonage.

Gifts

Most gifts need not be reported as income, provided they are not part of the pastor's original call agreement, are not given on a regular or expected basis, and are not given in return for particular services performed by the pastor. Parishioners can help their pastors by means of gifts. Sometimes a farmer will give a side of beef to his pastor. Normally, the gift would not have to be reported by the pastor as income, and the farmer could deduct it, using the cost of acquisition plus cost of feed, etc. One pastor tells me that he was given an all-expense-paid trip to the Holy Land by one of his parishioners, believing the pastor would be enriched by the experience and be a more effective preacher if he had visited the places he was preaching about. Often a parishioner who owns a lake cabin can save his pastor a lot of money by making that cabin available to the pastor for a vacation. The gift possibilities are endless.

Job-Related Expenses

As in many other occupations, the pastor necessarily incurs expenses while carrying out his duties. He occasionally has to make long-distance telephone calls; he has to buy books and magazines to keep up to date on religious news and developments; he has to drive to hospitals, or visit parishioners, and other places; he may have to go to denominational meetings. All of these expenses are deductible—including the cost of this book!

A pastor and his church might choose to handle these expenses in any of three ways. First, he might (with the consent of the church) simply charge all of these items to a church expense account rather than purchasing gas, books, etc., himself, or pay for them himself and submit receipts to the church for reimbursement.

Second, the church could pay a slightly higher salary, recognizing that the pastor will be paying these expenses himself. He could then deduct these expenses from his income tax, using Schedule C (Professional Expenses) if he is considered self-employed, as most pastors are, or if not, Form 2106 (Employee Business Expense). He would then have to keep careful records of his expenses, saving receipts and cancelled checks.

Or third, the church could pay him a specific allowance for books, another allowance for gasoline, etc. He would not have to report this allowance as income, provided he uses all of it for the purpose designated. For example, the church might pay the pastor, in addition to his salary and other benefits, a $200 annual book allowance. If he spends only $150 on books, he has to report the remaining $50 as income. If he spends $250 on books, he may deduct the extra $50 as a professional expense or employee business expense.

Of all these possibilities, the first is usually the best choice. That way, since the expense account is kept by the church and churches are automatically tax-exempt, the account is not normally subject to review and examination by the IRS. Also, the pastor is not restricted to precise figures for specific needs.

Insurance

In chapter 26 we discussed life insurance—whole life and term. If the church provides a term policy for the pastor, the premiums for the first $50,000 of that term policy need not be reported as income for the pastor. If the church is the beneficiary of the policy, none of it need be reported as income.

If the church provides a whole life policy and pays the premiums, those premium payments need not be reported as income for the pastor, if: (1) He forfeits all benefits under the policy if and when he leaves the employ of the church; *or* (2) the church is the beneficiary under the policy.

Health and accident-insurance policies paid by the church also need not be reported as income by the pastor. It therefore makes sense in most cases for the church to provide such policies, rather than the church paying extra salary to the pastor to purchase his own life insurance.

Scholarships

Scholarships that enable the pastor to earn a higher degree which is related to his pastoral duties need not be reported as income. Other types of scholarships are excludable only if given by a governmental unit or a tax-exempt educational institution, and then are excludable up to $300 per month.

Retirement Pay

Pensions and retirement income are generally taxable as ordinary income when received by the retired pastor, However, there may be exceptions. If a church should vote to give a pastor a special retirement honorarium and the IRS is satisfied that it was awarded as a gift rather than formal compensation for services rendered, it may be excludable as a gift. Language would have to be clear in the church minutes that the intent was to provide a gift, and it would probably have to be arranged to coincide with the pastor's actual retirement so it will not appear to be a condition of employment.

Pastors are generally classed as self-employed persons, and tax laws in the past have discriminated against self-employed persons in regard to retirement benefits.

But in 1975 the tax laws were changed to allow Individual Retirement Accounts (IRA's). An IRA is like a private retirement fund. It enables the self-employed person to establish a fund for his retirement and contribute up to 15 percent of his income each year to that fund. The fund then pays an annuity each year after retirement. All of the money contributed to the IRA is excludable from income. If a person with a salary of $20,000 per year contributes 15 percent ($3,000) to an IRA, he need only report $17,000 as income. He then pays tax on the annuities as he receives them after retirement.

Well, what is the benefit of that, you ask? What difference does it make whether I pay taxes now or pay taxes when I receive it in my old age? Why not just put it in a savings account now and draw it out as needed?

The advantage is that you are probably making substantially more income now than you will be after retirement. Consequently you are probably in a higher tax bracket now than you will be then. By deferring the payment of taxes until you are in a lower bracket, you are saving money.

The Economic Recovery Act of 1981 provides that as of January 1, 1982, regular wage earners may establish IRAs the same as self-employed persons.

Deductions

Deductions are expenses which can be subtracted or deducted from income.

The most common deductions include job-related expenses, charitable contributions, medical expenses, interest, some taxes, and casualty losses. We shall examine only those deductions that are of special concern to pastors.

Job-Related Expenses

Job-related expenses are deductible on Schedule C (Professional Expenses) or on Schedule 2105 (Employee Business Expense) if you are not self-employed. They include mileage expended on the job, supplies purchased, books and magazines related to work, postage, membership in professional associations, attendance at church or ministerial conventions (usually restricted to inside the continental U.S.), and other such things. All of these, however, are deductible only if paid by the pastor and he has not been reimbursed for them. We earlier discussed the possibility of expense accounts or expense allowances, either of which is excludable from income. It cannot be both ways, though; one cannot charge it to the church, get reimbursed and also claim a deduction. Nor can book expenses be deducted if they were covered by a book allowance which has been excluded from income.

The cost of installing a telephone in the pastor's home, and the flat monthly rate the telephone company charges for telephone service, are fully deductible if paid by the pastor. This is true whether the residence is a parsonage or owned by the pastor. But the cost of long distance calls must be apportioned; those made for church or business purposes are deductible, while those placed for personal purposes are not. It is important to keep telephone bills as records for this deduction.

Interest

Interest payments are tax deductible, including late-payment penalties.

Until July 1, 1983, pastors were in an advantageous situation. The pastor could be given a housing allowance, which need not be reported as income. Additionally, if he bought a house, the interest payments on the mortgage were deductible.

This meant the pastor had, in effect, a "double deduction." Suppose his salary was $1,500 per month, and in addition he was given a housing allowance of $500 per month. That $500 need not be reported as income. Let's further suppose he bought a house with a monthly mortgage payment of $400. When one first takes out a mortgage, nearly all of the mortgage payment is interest; perhaps the first year an average of $375 of that $400 would be interest. While he actually earned $2,000 per month, his housing allowance reduced his taxable income to $1,500 per month and the interest deduction reduced it still further to $1,125 per month.

But that has been changed. In January 1983 the Internal Revenue Service issued revenue ruling 83-3. This ruling went into effect July 1, 1983, for those ministers who did not occupy or had not purchased a new residence prior to January 3, 1983. To avoid an undue hardship upon those who had purchased a residence expecting to receive the double deduction, the ruling will not go into effect until July 1, 1985 for those ministers who have occupied or purchased a residence prior to January 3, 1983. The new ruling prohibits clergymen from deducting those taxes and interest paid on their residences if they have also received a tax-exempt housing allowance. The "double deduction" is thereby eliminated.

The ruling applies only to taxes and interest paid upon the pastor's residence. If the pastor were to move out of his house, occupy rental housing, and rent his house to someone else, he could presumably still get the double deduction. If he were to do this, however, he might lose the deferred capital gain benefit that applies to sale or exchange of personal residence, should he ever decide to sell his house in the future.

This change is not a new law passed by Congress, or even a new regulation of the IRS. It is simply an IRS ruling, interpreting existing laws and regulations—and it stands in opposition to previous rulings. Various Christian groups may challenge the ruling in court. Also, Rep. Stan Parris (R-VA) has introduced a bill in Congress (H.R. 1905) that would overturn this ruling. If the bill passes, the "double deduction" could be restored.

Moving Expenses

When a pastor accepts a call to a new church, moving expenses are deductible to the extent they are paid by the pastor and not reimbursed by the church. To be eligible for this deduction, the pastor must work full-time at the new pastorate for at least seventy-eight weeks of the following two years; at least thirty-nine of which must be in the first twelve months. Also, there is a distance requirement: the new church must be more than thirty-five miles from the old residence.

Deductible moving expenses include the cost of travel, the cost of moving household goods, househunting trips, temporary living quarters at the new location for up to thirty days after arrival at the new location, the cost of selling the old residence and purchasing a new residence (including the cost of realtor fees, advertising, lawyer fees, etc., not including price of new residence).

As a related item, job hunting trips are also deductible. Travel expenses to the new church to "candidate," to preach, or to be interviewed by the church board are deductible to the extent these were not reimbursed. Also, if the pastor's wife traveled to the new location to find a job for herself, her travel expenses are also deductible.

Education Expenses

A pastor's unreimbursed educational expenses are also deductible, provided they (1) do not qualify him for a new trade or profession, and (2) are reasonably necessary to maintain or improve skills in his present trade or profession. Tuition and other educational expenses are then deductible provided they are not reimbursed by the church. Clearly this would apply if studying for an advanced degree in theology, or in guidance or counseling, or some related field. But what if a pastor decides to study for a master's degree in business administration on the theory that such training would better enable him to administer a large church? That would be a borderline question for the IRS or the courts to resolve.

Whenever a deduction or exclusion is reasonable but questionable, it might be wise to explain the situation in a typewritten statement attached to the return. In the situation of the pastor studying for a degree in business administration, he might set forth the administrative responsibilities and financial problems of the church and the need for sound business management. The IRS may or may not allow the deduction, but almost certainly will not conclude that the pastor is evading tax responsibilities and charge penalties. In the event the deduction is denied, the pastor would have to pay the remaining tax plus interest.

Withholding Tax and Estimated Tax

Taxes are paid in one of two ways: Either our employer withholds the tax from our income and we file a return by April 15 and pay the difference or receive a refund; or we file an estimated tax declaration and make quarterly payments to the IRS. Most employees have their tax withheld. Most self-employed persons file the estimated tax declaration and make quarterly payments.

A clergyman serving a church is considered to be self-employed and thus not covered by withholding tax. He must therefore file an estimated return, using Form 1040-ES. On this form he estimates the tax owed for that year and pays a quarterly estimated tax. The estimated tax can be computed by one of the following methods: (1) last year's tax liability; (2) last year's income, figured at this year's tax rates and personal exemptions; (3) estimating this year's income based upon all available facts such as guaranteed salary, estimated number of weddings to be performed, etc. Two additional methods, annualization of income and actual tax, are quite complicated and will not be discussed here.

Estimates are filed on Form 1040-ES. This is a four-part form, and one part is due each quarter: April 15, June 15, September 15, and January 15. Each of these estimated tax forms should include a payment that will represent roughly one-fourth of the tax liability for that year.

If it turns out at the end of the year that income and tax liability has been overestimated, a refund can be obtained. If, on the other hand, it turns out that tax liability has been underestimated, you must make up the difference. Furthermore, if you have not paid at least 80 percent of your tax liability by January 15 of the following year (note that the January 15, 1983 form completes the 1040-ES payments for 1982), or in the alternative file a complete return by February 1, you may be subject to a penalty of 7 percent of the unpaid tax.

This requirement of filing estimated tax returns applies to self-employed persons generally, and ministers who are serving churches are usually considered to be self-employed. But what about an ordained minister who is not serving a church? He may still be exempt from withholding taxes if he is (1) employed by his religious body; *or* (2) employed by someone else in "service in the exercise of his ministry." And what is service in the exercise of a ministry? That's a difficult question for the courts or the IRS to decide. If, for example, a pastor teaches religion courses at a university, or serves as a hospital chaplain, he probably is serving in the exercise of his ministry. But if he is teaching courses such as mathematics that do not directly relate to ministry, and if he is teaching at a university that is not operated by his denomination, then he is probably not serving in the exercise of his ministry and therefore covered by withholding taxes. Many situations could pose problems, and must be decided on a case-by-case basis.

Social Security

Before 1968, clergymen were not covered by Social Security unless they elected to be covered. Since 1968, however, clergymen are covered unless they elect not to be covered.

If you are opposed to Social Security on the grounds of religion or conscience, you may elect noncoverage. However, you must make that election on or before the due date of your tax return for the second year in which you have had at least $400 in earnings from the ministry.

For example, if you graduate from seminary in June 1984 and begin serving a church in September, you will (we hope) make more than $400 in earnings from the ministry in 1984. Assuming you again make more than $400 through the ministry in 1985, you must file your election of noncoverage on or before the due date of your 1985 return, that is, by April 15, 1986.

Note also that the objection must be based on grounds of religion or conscience. A mere belief that the Social Security system is unsound and that private pension plans pay a better return is insufficient for this purpose. A belief that Social Security is unscriptural because it involves reliance upon a worldly system instead of on God and His church, would be adequate. And a belief that Social Security is socialistic and that socialism is not Christian should also be sufficient. Note, however, that the precise reasons or the nature of the objection need not be specified. You simply make the election on IRS Form 4361 (Application for Exemption from Self-Employment Tax for Use by Ministers, Members of Religious Orders and Christian Science Practitioners). If you choose to be covered, there is presently no way you can revoke that decision after the two-year period prescribed above has passed. However, if you elect to be exempt, you can revoke that election by filing Form 1040X (Amended Individual Income Tax Return) and attach Form 4361-A.

Prior to January 1, 1984, churches and other religious organizations elected to be covered by filing Form SS-15, (Certificate Waiving Exemption From Taxes Under the Federal Insurance Contributions Act). If such a certificate was filed, each nonclergy employee who wanted to be covered was required to file (or have attached to the organization's SS-15) a Form SS-15a, containing the employee's signature, address, and Social Security number and stating that he elected to be covered. Those who did not so state were assumed to be "nonconcurring employees" and were not covered.

However, new legislation changes this effective January 1, 1984. From that date forward, all religious organizations and religious workers (except ordained ministers who elect noncoverage) are covered by Social Security, and such coverage is compulsory. This could impose a substantial burden upon churches and religious organizations, and could also infringe upon the convictions of many religious workers. The purpose of the new legislation appears to be to try to save a nearly-bankrupt Social Security system by bringing as many workers as possible under its umbrella—a remedy similar to trying to save a sinking ship by bringing more people on board. Efforts are currently under way to prevent or delay this change, both in Congress and in the courts.

This chapter has not covered every area of personal income tax. Rather, it has been directed to clergymen and religious workers. Since tax laws change regularly, this information should be checked with current sources.

Chapter 28

Church Property

Church buildings hold fond memories for many people. Baptisms, weddings, testimonies, fellowship, Bible studies—and for many, salvation itself. It is hard to imagine a more peaceful and inspiring sight than a country church, its spire pointing heavenward on a hilltop or amid the trees.

But even a church building involves legal details. Let us look at church property transfers and church property disputes.

Church Property Transfers

A well-known attorney once commented that few transactions are more subject to error than church property transfers. Perhaps this happens because church officials are often volunteers, acting without compensation. Possibly church officials, believing theirs is a spiritual calling, don't want to get involved in the mundane details of real estate technicalities.

But I must caution against carelessness in this area. Church business is God's business, and it should be conducted accordingly, for God is not the author of confusion (I Corinthians 14:33). And sloppiness in church-property transactions may cause problems in later years, even generations later. I have sometimes wondered, tongue-in-cheek, whether the biblical admonition, "visiting the iniquity of the fathers upon the children, unto the third and fourth generation" (Num. 14:18), refers to church property transfers! If there is one word of caution to be noted concerning church property transfers, it is this: **DO IT RIGHT!** Take the extra time, prepare the extra papers, spend the extra money if necessary, but do it right! In the end, it will save time, paperwork and money.

First, if your church is considering the purchase or sale of land, find out who in the church must sign the paperwork for the sale or purchase and who must approve his actions. To determine this, check the articles of incorporation or bylaws—and your consititution if it is separate from your articles of incorporation. Also check the statutes to determine whether your church's documents agree with current state law concerning transfers of church property.

Perhaps your articles of incorporation provide that the trustees sign for any transfer of church real estate, but that they can do so only if the transfer is approved by the congregation. How does the congregation give its approval? Check your articles again for many contain specific provisions as to the type of notice required for such a meeting. Sometimes the required notice is different if the meeting is to decide whether to buy or sell real estate. They may provide that the notice is to be mailed to all members, or that it is to be read at church worship services on two or three successive Sundays, or some other arrangement. Make sure your notice complies with the requirement!

Notices should be specific as to the time and place of the meeting, who is eligible to attend, the subject of the meeting, the property proposed to be transferred, the proposed seller or buyer, the reason for the transfer, and the proposed price. It is best to give both a legal description of the property and a description people will understand:

> All members of the congregation of Faith Lutheran Church are hereby notified of and asked to attend a business meeting of said congregation to be held at 7:30 p.m. Monday, December 14, 1981, for the purpose of determining whether or not to approve the proposed purchase of the real estate legally described as Lot 6, Block 4, Johnson's Addition to the Town of Viking Valley, Valkyrie County, Minnesota, located at 1465 Battleax Boulevard, at a price of $10,000, for the purpose of erecting a parsonage thereon.

The church secretary should keep careful records of the notice given (keeping its precise wording) and the dates upon which it was read, and of the proceedings of the business meeting.

All of the legal documents concerning the transfer of property should be prepared by an attorney to ensure that they are done properly. These will include an earnest money agreement by which the purchaser deposits a certain amount of money to hold the property, a purchase agreement which sets forth the exact terms of the sale, and a warranty deed which actually transfers the title of the property when the transaction is complete, or a contract for deed by which the purchaser agrees to make periodic payments and the seller holds the deed until the contract for deed is paid in full. In some areas the earnest money agreement, purchase agreement, and/or contract for deed may be combined into a single document. Local laws or customs may require different or additional documents or procedures, accentuating the need for an attorney.

Unless you live in an area where title insurance is used, a purchaser should always have an abstract updated and approved. An abstract of title is a bundle of papers, bound together, which summarize the history of the real estate in question. If properly done, it will include summaries of every legal transaction which has ever affected the property, including every sale, mortgage, lien, tax payment, assessment, will bequest, every platting or subdivision, easement, and every zoning ordinance. Often the abstract contains interesting historical information about the property.

The seller is normally responsible to have the abstract brought up to date. He does this by taking it to an abstract company where it is compared to the current courthouse records and adds any new developments which have not been noted on the abstract. The seller then gives the abstract to the buyer, who has an attorney review and approve it. The attorney may conclude that a defect in the title needs to be corrected. He may point out that in 1955 a lien or mortgage was never satisfied. Or he may object that taxes for 1962 were never paid. Or he may discover that a pipeline easement across the land of which the buyer was totally unaware. Or he may be concerned that the property was owned by a Mr. Smith, but Mr. Smith died in 1930 leaving the property to his four daughters Mary, Joy, Louise and Flossie. Before the executor of Smith's estate sold the property to Jones, he obtained quitclaim deeds from Mary, Joy, and Louise, but Flossie was already dead and he never obtained quitclaim deeds from Flossie's children. This is a title defect that needs to be cleared up. Otherwise, Flossie's children may continue to own a one-fourth interest in the property, and a bank would probably not approve a loan for building purposes under such circumstances. The lawyer may clear this up by obtaining the necessary deeds from Flossie's children, or he may have to remedy the problem by a court procedure called an action to quiet title.

Once the sale is complete, the deed, and possibly certain other legal documents as well depending upon the local requirements, should be recorded at the courthouse. That way the property cannot be sold to anyone else—a possibility in some jurisdictions.

One additional consideration is the need for a survey of the property. If the property has never before been surveyed or platted, this should certainly be done. Even if it has been platted into this particular parcel of land, it is still a good idea if there is any question about the boundaries of the land. There have been cases in which buildings have been constructed, only to find out later that they were built partially on or too close to the neighbors' land.

And finally, before ever entering into such a transaction, check local zoning ordinances to make sure the intended use of the property is permitted under local law or that zoning variances will be granted. Get the variance or a firm promise before purchasing the land, or include in your purchase agreement a right to rescind if the variance is not granted. It would be tragic to purchase a plot of land for the purpose of operating a day-care center, only to find that day-care centers are not permitted in that part of town.

Again, the watchword: Do it right! Be meticulous! And see an attorney!

Church Property Disputes

God's people don't always see eye to eye on everything. Over the years many splits have occured within local churches and between local churches and their respective denominations. When a church splits, or when a local church withdraws from its denomination, the question often arises, who gets the ownership and control of the church property? The majority or the minority? The local church or the denomination?

The issue has often arisen in the context of the fundamentalist-modernist controversy of the past century. Probably this controversy has nowhere been more evident than in the Presbyterian Church of the United States (PCUS). The PCUS national leadership has been liberal, but at the local level there are many fervent and articulate conservatives. As a result, many of the cases which have come to the courts concerning church property disputes have involved Presbyterians.

One of the earliest such cases was *Watson v. Jones*, 80 U.S. 679 (1871). The Walnut Street Presbyterian Church of Louisville, Kentucky had organized in 1842, purchased its property in 1853 and incorporated in 1854. While neither the deed nor the charter mentioned affiliation with the Presbyterian Church of the United States, (PCUS), it was agreed that this was the intent.

The governing body of a local Presbyterian church is called a session, and is composed of elders and the pastor. In 1863 a majority of the session wanted a certain pastor, but a majority of the congregation did not. The dispute went to the presbytery (district offices), who called for a new election. But the session officials blocked the church door and refused to allow entrance, so the majority of the congregation held a meeting on the sidewalk and elected new session members. The majority of the old session refused to recognize the election of these new members, so the new session members asked the Chancery Court of Louisville to recognize the election as valid. The court did so.

But the governing body of the district also suffered a split, due in part to the passions of the Civil War. The majority faction of the Walnut Street Church recognized one faction in the district presbytery: the other faction recognized the other. The General Assembly, the national governing body of the Presbyterian Church, recognized the same district presbytery that the majority of Walnut Street Church had recognized.

After much legal maneuvering, with various courts holding for both sides, the issue finally came before the U.S. Supreme Court. The Court recognized that church trustees hold church property solely as fiduciaries for the church and that they can exercise power not in their own individual capacity but on behalf of the church and as a session body. The court recognized that it was possible for one to dedicate property to a church by way of trust, assuming that it will be used for the promotion of specific doctrine, and that the court has a responsibility to see that the property is not diverted from its intended purpose. But unless such a trust is expressly stated, the court will not assume it exists. And on matters of faith, eccesiastical rule, custom, or church law, once the highest church tribunal has decided these questions, the courts must not interfere with its discretion. Since the highest body of the Presbyterian

Church had recognized the majority faction at Walnut Street, the Court went along with its decision.

Another such case is *The Presbyterian Church of the United States v. Mary Elizabeth Blue Hull Memorial Presbyterian Church*, 393 U.S. 440 (1969). Mary Elizabeth Blue Hull Memorial Presbyterian Church (Hull Church), a local Presbyterian church in Georgia, withdrew from the Presbyterian Church of the United States (PCUS), claiming that PCUS had departed from the faith by adopting liberal or neo-orthodox attitudes, including statements opposing American involvement in Vietnam, support of Supreme Court decisions prohibiting prayer and Bible reading in public schools, dissemination of statements denying the Trinity, subverting parental authority, and advocating civil disobedience.

The Georgia courts followed a rule of law that local church property is held by the local church in trust for the parent denomination, with the sole condition that the parent denomination must not depart from the faith it held at the time of affiliation. The court then put the question to the jury: Had PCUS departed from the faith it had held when Hull Church joined PCUS? The jury ruled that PCUS had departed from the faith, and consequently the trust was broken and the property rightfully belonged to Hull Church.

Later PCUS appealed to the U.S. Supreme Court, and the Supreme Court reversed. The Supreme Court held that the courts should not decide questions of doctrine. The issue of who has held to the faith and who has erred may seem clear in some cases, but in others it may be highly complex. It is not the prerogative of judges and juries to decide such religious questions. Were the court to do so, it would excessively entangle itself in religious matters.

The case was therefore remanded to the Georgia Supreme Court, which held that the implied trust theory had been adopted with the condition that a parent denomination not be allowed to depart from the faith. Since that condition had been invalidated by the U.S. Supreme Court, the Georgia Supreme Court held that the whole theory of implied trust (that local churches hold property in trust for the parent denomination) must fall, and thus invalidated the whole idea. The Georgia Supreme Court then held that, since legal title was vested in Hull Church, the Hull Church owned the property and was entitled to keep it.

Another interesting case is *Maryland and Virginia Eldership of the Church of God v. Church of God at Sharpsburg*, 396 U.S. 367 (1970). In this dispute between the parent denomination and two secessionist congregations, the issue again was ownership of the church property. The court had decided in favor of the local churches because of state law regarding the holding of property by religious corporations, language in the deeds conveying property to the local church corporations, the terms of the charters, and the constitution of the parent denomination. Based upon all of these, the court held that the property belonged to the local churches. The U.S. Supreme Court affirmed, ruling that these were ''neutral principles of law'' and the lower courts could employ such principles in resolving this type of dispute.

The most recent U.S. Supreme Court decision on the subject is *Jones v. Wolf*,

443 U.S. 595 (1979). The majority of the congregation (164 members including the pastor) of Vineville Presbyterian Church of Macon, Georgia voted to separate from PCUS and join a conservative denomination, Presbyterian Church in America; a minority of ninety-four members voted to remain with PCUS.

The district presbytery investigated and declared that the minority was the true church, and ruled that the church property belonged to the minority. Armed with this decision, the minority went to the Georgia courts to enforce it. But the Georgia courts ruled for the majority in the local church. By a narrow 5-4 vote, the U.S. Supreme Court affirmed the Georgia court ruling. The Supreme Court held that absent some indication to the contrary, the courts may assume that the majority acts for the church. The four dissenting judges argued that the First Amendment requires that the courts give "compulsory deference" to the decision of ecclesiastical tribunals in such matters, and that if the highest body of Presbyterian Church of the United States ruled for the minority, that ruling was binding on the courts. But the majority of the Supreme Court disagreed, saying that courts were not bound to give "compulsory deference" to church tribunals but could decide such matters according to "neutral principles of law".

Two recent state court decisions are of further interest. In *Trinity Presbyterian Church v. Tankersley*, 374 So. 2d 861 (1979), the majority of Trinity Church decided to withdraw from PCUS, and the East Alabama Presbytery assented in their decision. But the General Assembly of PCUS declared the East Alabama Presbytery's assent to be null and void and revoked it. The lower court ruled in favor of the PCUS and the minority faction of Trinity Church, holding that it was precluded from deciding ecclesiastical questions the church tribunal had already declared. But the Supreme Court of Alabama reversed, saying that the decision of an ecclesiastical tribunal is binding on ecclesiastical questions only. The court then held that since this was a property question, not an ecclesiastical question, the PCUS decision was not binding. The Alabama Supreme Court ruled for the majority of Trinity Church, allowing them to withdraw from PCUS and keep their property.

Mills v. Baldwin, 362 So. 2d 2 (1978), is another Presbyterian Church case. Here the lower court ruled that there was no implied trust in favor of the parent denomination, because there had been no money from PCUS to the local church and there was no evidence that the property was ever intended to benefit anyone but the local church. But the Florida Supreme Court reversed. The real issue, the court said, was not who owned the church building; Madison Presbyterian Church owned the building. The real issue was, who represented Madison Presbyterian Church? Since the district presbytery had recognized the minority faction as representing Madison Church, the courts were bound by that decision.

It will readily be seen that these disputes have produced varying results. Several principles, however, emerge from the courts' decisions:

(1) The courts will not decide matters of doctrine. Even if the church articles state that in the event of a dispute the party adhering to the inerrancy of Scripture and the historic doctrines of the faith shall have title to the property, the courts will not enforce that article because that would inject the courts into the resolution of doctrinal questions that are outside the courts' jurisdiction or competence. But Justice Harlan, in his concurring decision in the *Hull* case, did say that in some clear matters the courts could get involved. For example, if someone left property to a church in a will on the express condition that the church never ordain women in the ministry, the courts might look to the factual question of whether or not the church had ordained women, and act accordingly.

(2) If a church is hierarchical in nature, the courts will give considerable but not absolute deference to the decision of the highest tribunal of the denomination. At the same time, the court may consider other principles of law, and the court may examine whether or not the church tribunal has followed its own rules in reaching a decision. As the court said in *Gonzales v. Roman Catholic Archbishop*, 280 U.S. 1 (1929),

> In the absence of fraud, collusion, or arbitrariness, the decision of the proper church tribunals on matters purely ecclesiastical although affecting civil rights, are accepted in litigation before the secular courts as conclusive, because the parties in interest made them so by contract or otherwise.

And in the *Trinity Church* case mentioned above, the Alabama Supreme Court noted that the minority had not followed proper church procedures in pressing its complaint.

(3) The courts decide nonecclesiastical matters, questions which do not directly concern doctrine or theology, according to "neutral principles of law".

These may vary from court to court and state to state, but one should consider the following questions.

In whose name is the deed to the property? Is it in the name of the local church only, or jointly with the parent denomination, or in trust for the parent denomination ?

What do the local church's articles of incorporation or constitution or bylaws say about property ownership? Does it mention anything about property being in trust for the parent denomination, or reverting to the parent denomination in the event of a property dispute or secession?

What does the parent body's constitution, rules, or other governing document say about local church property? If it says that such property is held in trust for the parent denomination or reverts to the parent denomination, is there anything in the local church's articles, constitution, bylaws, or other records indicating that the local church has assented to the authority of that rule or document? For example, if the *Methodist Discipline* (the handbook of the United Methodist Church) says that property is held in trust for the parent denomination[1], is there anything in the local Methodist church's documents

---

1. *The Book of Discipline of the United Methodist Church 1980* (Nashville: United Methodist Publishing House, 1980), Section 2530, p. 598.

which establishes that that local church has accepted the *Methodist Discipline* as authoritative?

Is there any state law that affects the disposition or ownership of church property, or is there any previous case law in the state on the subject? Bear in mind that older case law may be superceded by the U.S. Supreme Court decisions in *Hull, Church of God*, and *Jones v. Wolf.*

What is the commonly accepted practice in that denomination?

Is that congregation's form of government primarily hierarchial or primarily congregational? The more congregational it is, the stronger the chances of the local church to retain ownership of the church property.

Has the local church received any financial help from the parent denomination and has any of that money gone toward the purchase or maintenance of the church property in question?

Often a dispute arises as to who speaks for the local church, the majority or the minority. In a contested election the issue might be, which side is the majority? In a hierarchical church the courts give considerable weight to the decision of the highest ecclesiastical tribunal as to which faction to recognize as speaking for the local church. In an independent or congregational church, the court would give considerable weight to rules of parliamentary procedure. If the church articles specify a particular set of rules (such as *Robert's*) as parliamentary authority, the court would probably adopt them as binding. If not, the court would consider commonly accepted principles of parliamentary procedure, except where inconsistent with the church's articles or bylaws. In church disputes, the case is much stronger if parliamentary rules have been followed.

The Christian Legal Society's Christian Conciliation Service (CCS) is willing to assist in the resolution of disputes of this nature and may be reached at P.O. Box 2069, Oak Park, Illinois 60303, phone (312) 848-7735.

Finally, all prospective litigants in church property disputes are referred to chapter 22 and reminded of I Corinthians 6:1-8.

Chapter 29

The Christian
and Copyright Laws

Copy machines are standard equipment in most offices, churches and many homes. Though they are useful inventions, extreme caution should be exercised as to why copies are made, how they are distributed and how they are used. Many innocently violate the Copyright Act of 1976.[1] Penalties could include a fine of $10,000 and/or one year in prison, more for certain types of copyright offenses and repeat offenses. The copyright owner could sue for an injunction prohibiting further copyright violations, an order impounding and disposing of the copies already made, costs and attorney's fees, plus actual damages, or statutory damages.[2]

Once you are aware of the law, your actions could be described as "willful." Section 504(c) (2) of the Copyright Act of 1976 provides that if the copyright infringement was committed "willfully," the court may increase the award of statutory damages to $50,000!

The "Why" of Copyright Laws

Writers, artists, composers, performers, and publishers make their living by producing works of art. They need to profit from the work they produce. While a handful make it big and get rich, the vast majority make a meager living. Many have to support themselves with second jobs. Copyright laws are a means of preserving the profit from a work of art for its author or creator. The founders of our country recognized the need for such protection, and consequently provided in Article I, Subsection 8 of the Constitution that "The Congress shall have power . . . To Promote the Progress of Science and useful Arts, by securing for limited Times to Authors and Inventors the exclusive Right to their respective Writings and Discoveries."

1. Copyright Act of 1976, Public Law 94-553, 94th Congress, 90 Stat. 2541.
2. Ibid., Section 501-510.

Creativity would be greatly stifled if there were no copyright protections. Why should anyone write a book, if someone else could just copy it and sell the copies at a lower price? Why should anyone write a song, or a play, or a motion picture script, if anyone can copy and use it without charge? Copyright laws are a means of insuring the biblical ideal that each man shall enjoy the fruit of his own labor (Isaiah 65:21-22).

Harsh though it may seem, copyright infringement is STEALING! It is profiting from the fruit of another man's labor. And sad to say, Christians are among the worst offenders. Christians who wouldn't think of stealing groceries from a grocer or clothes from a department store or money from a bank, all too often think nothing of stealing works of art from a writer. And very often they steal from fellow Christians.

Copyright laws provide that the maker or publisher of an original and tangible work may register the work with the United States Copyright Office. He then has the exclusive right to reproduce the copyrighted work, produce derivative works based upon it, distribute copies of it, perform it publicly, or display it publicly.[3] Under the old copyright laws, a copyright lasted for twenty-eight years and could be renewed for an additional twenty-eight years. Under the 1976 law, copyrights last for the lifetime of the author and fifty years thereafter (if there is more that one author, fifty years after the last of the authors dies).[4] Works copyrighted before the 1976 law went into effect may be renewed when their twenty-eight years expire, but the renewal is for forty-seven years instead of twenty-eight years.[5] A copyright is a property interest and may be willed just as any other property, subject to the fifty-year term specified in the statute.

Acceptable Uses of Copyrighted Material

Not every use or reproduction of copyrighted material infringes upon copyright laws. There are exceptions.

Someone else's idea may be restated in your own words, and not violate the copyright. It is often said that one cannot copyright ideas, only copyright the expression of ideas.[6] The question then arises: Are the organization and wording of a work sufficiently different from those of the original so as to constitute a new item rather than a plagiarization of the old? That is for the judge or jury to decide. Merely changing a word here and there will not be sufficient to avoid copyright laws. The courts look at the overall organization, wording, and content, and also consider whether the copier had access to or was aware of the original work.

3. Ibid., Section 106.

4. Ibid., Section 302.

5. Willis Wager, *A Musician's Guide to Copyright and Publishing* (Brighton, Massachusetts: Carousel Publishing Corp., 1975, 1978), p.22.

6. Judge Learned Hand, *Nichols v. Universal Pictures Corporation*, 45 F. 2d 119 (2 C.C.A. 1930).

It is not a copyright infringement to use or reproduce a work after its copyright has expired. After the expiration, a copyrighted work is said to become part of the public domain, meaning anyone is free to use it. However, one might copyright a new arrangement of a song that is part of the public domain.

Also, unless one has reason to believe a work is copyrighted, he is usually justified in copying a work that does not bear a copyright notice. The copyright notice normally appears on the title page or page thereafter of a book, or a corner of a recording or work of art. It usually includes a copyright symbol, which is normally a "c" inside a small circle, plus the name of the copyright holder and the date the work was copyrighted.

To aid in interpreting the copyright laws, the courts apply the doctrine of "fair use". Section 107 of the Copyright Act of 1976 provides, as had court decisions before 1976, that

> the fair use of a copyrighted work, including such use by reproduction in copies . . . , for purposes such as criticism, comment, news reporting, teaching (including multiple copies for classroom use), scholarship, or research, is not an infringement of copyright.

In other words, if you use the copyrighted material for one of these purposes, and your use is "fair," it is legal.

But what is "fair"? Section 107 does not define that, but it does give some guidelines for determining fairness:

> In determining whether the use made of a work in any particular case is a fair use, the factors to be considered shall include—
>
> (1) the purpose and character of the use, including whether such use is of a commercial nature or is for non-profit educational purposes;
>
> (2) the nature of the copyrighted work;
>
> (3) the amount and sustantiality of the portion used in relation to the copyrighted work as a whole; and
>
> (4) the effect of the use upon the potential market for or value of the copyrighted work.

More exceptions to the copyright law are in section 110. This section declares that the following are not infringements:

(1) Performance or display of a work by instructors or pupils in the course of face-to-face teaching activities of a nonprofit educational institution, in a classroom or similar place devoted to instruction, provided no unlawful copies are used and provided all copies display the copyright label.

(2) Performance of a nondramatic literary or musical work or display of a work, if done by a governmental body or educational institution for the purpose of teaching or training students, disabled persons, or government employees.

(3) Performance of a nondramatic literary or musical work or a dramatic-musical work of a religious nature, or display of a work, in the course

of services at a place of worship or other religious assembly.

(4) Performance of a nondramatic literary or musical work otherwise than in a transmission to the public, without charging admission and for the purpose of raising money for educational, religious, or charitable purposes, provided the copyright owner has not objected to the performance.

(5) Performances to be aired in private homes. In light of a currently pending case, the exact effect of this section is open to question.

(6) Performance of a nondramatic musical work by a governmental body or nonprofit agricultural or horticultural organization in the course of a fair or exposition.

(7) Performance of a nondramatic musical work by a sales establishment without charging admission and for the sole purpose of selling copies of the work (thus promoting the aims and profits of the copyrighted author).

(8 & 9) Special performances of nondramatic work for the handicapped, not intended for commercial advantage and done through facilities of a government body, a non-commercial educational broadcast station, a radio sub-carrier, or a cable system.

Because of the vagueness of Sections 107 and 110, several organizations have drafted guidelines for their clarification. The Ad Hoc Committee of Educational Institutions and Organizations on Copyright Law Revision, the Authors League of America, and the Association of American Publishers have agreed on guidelines for teacher photocopying. These guidelines do not have the force of law, but since the U.S. House of Representatives called it a "reasonable interpretation of the minimum standards of fair use,"[7] it is likely that a court would give these considerable weight in determining the intent and meaning of the law.

The guidelines provide that a teacher may make a single copy from a book, an article from a periodical or newspaper, a short story, short essay, or short poem, or a chart, graph, diagram, drawing, cartoon, or picture from a book, periodical, or newspaper, for his own scholarly research or for his use in teaching or preparing for class. The teacher may also make and distribute one copy to each student in his class, provided he does so for only one course, takes no more than one item or two excerpts from the same author nor three from the same volume during the class term, and does not make multiple copies more than nine times during any particular course. "Short" poems are defined as having fewer than 250 words and 1 or 2 pages; excerpts of longer poems should meet the same limits. Short prose is 2,500 words or fewer, and excerpts should be confined to 1,000 words or 10 percent of the entire work, whichever is fewer. The copying should be at the instance and inspiration of the individual teacher and not directed by higher authority. There shall be no copying of consumable

---

7. House Report 72, p.70; quoted by Melville B. Nimmer, *Copyright and Other Aspects of Law Pertaining to Literary, Musical and Artistic Works Illustrated, 2 ed.* (St. Paul; West, 1971, 1979), p.402.

works such as workbooks, standardized tests, and test booklets—works that are used up by the students and cannot be reused. Copying shall not be a substitute for purchasing textbooks, and shall not be repeated from term to term. There shall be no charge to the student beyond the actual cost of photocopying.[8]

Obviously, these guidelines must be applied with common sense. They are intended to make sure the copyrighted author receives the rightful fruit of his labor.

Neither the statute nor the guidelines define a teacher. Certainly, a strong argument could be made that a pastor, or a Sunday school teacher is a teacher. The term pastor and teacher appear to be used together in Scripture (Ephesians 4:11), and one qualification of elders is that they are "apt to teach" (I Timothy 3:2).

Under these guidelines, and under the fair use doctrine in general, there is no reason why a pastor or teacher cannot make use of a direct quote from a copyrighted author (giving due credit or blame, of course) for the purpose of teaching, criticizing, commenting, studying, or advancing scholarship.[9] William S. Strong suggests that such quotations should in most cases be limited to two or three paragraphs at a time. If you intend to use the material in a publication it is wise and courteous to obtain permission, if possible, which permission is usually quite freely granted.[10]

A special area of concern involves the photocopying of sheet music. Similar guidelines were worked out by the Music Publishers Association of the United States, Inc., the National Music Publishers Association, Inc., the Music Teachers National Association, the Music Educators National Conference, the National Association of Schools of Music, and the Ad Hoc Committee on Copyright Law Revision. These guidelines allow emergency copying to replace purchased copies which are lost or otherwise unavailable and which are needed for an imminent performance, provided purchased replacements are substituted in due course. The teacher may make multiple copies, one for each student, but may not copy an entire work or a performable unit of the work, and must limit the photocopying to ten percent of the work. If the entire work is out of print or available only in a larger volume, the teacher may make a single copy of the entire work. The teacher may edit or simplify the musical work so long as he does not alter the fundamental character of the work or its lyrics. The teacher or his educational institution may make and retain a single recording of the performance for evaluation or rehearsal purposes. The teacher may not copy from consumable works such as exercises, workbooks, tests and

---

8. "Teacher Photocopying Guidelines", quoted by Nimmer, op. cit., pp.402-404.

9. *Rosemont Enterprises, Inc.,v. Random House, Inc.*, 366 F. 2d 303 (2 C.C.A. 1966).

10. William S. Strong, *The Copyright Book* (Cambridge, Massachusetts:MIT Press, 1981), pp.112-113.

answer sheets, and all copying must include the copyright notice that appears on the printed copy.[11]

A church does not need permission to perform a nondramatic literary work, a musical work, or a dramatic-musical work of a religious nature in the course of religious services or at a religious assembly. The church or Christian school choir could present a concert for the public, take up an offering, and probably even charge admission, without violating copyright laws.[12] But the guidelines summarized above would prohibit the choir director or teacher from making multiple copies of the entire concert work for the choir members.[13] And while the teacher may make and retain a tape of the concert, selling tapes or cassettes of the concerts would appear to violate the guidelines unless the copyrighted author gave his permission. Bear in mind again that these guidelines are not law, but the courts might give them considerable weight in making a decision.

Libraries also face copyright problems, and this could include church or Christian school libraries. Section 108 of the Copyright Act of 1976 provides that libraries may copy materials under certain conditions: (1) if the work is unpublished and a copy is necessary for preservation and security; (2) if the work is unpublished and another library requests a copy for its own collection; (3) if the work is published, a copy is needed to replace one that is lost, stolen, damaged or deteriorating, and the library is unable, despite reasonable efforts, to obtain an unused replacement at a fair price; or (4) if a copy has been requested by a user of the library or by another library on behalf of one of its users.[14] Again, the copyright should be clearly displayed.

Securing Permission to Use Copyrighted Materials

Most authors and publishers are cooperative about giving permission to use their materials, so long as they are used in a manner that will not adversely affect sales of their materials. The more widely a book is quoted in reviews and commentaries, the more it is likely to sell.

To obtain permission, first determine who owns the copyright. That should be stated on the title page or the page thereafter; or if it isn't, it may be found in *Audiovisual Marketplace* or *Literary Marketplace*, publications of R.R. Bowker Company, or in the indexes of the National Information Center for Educational Media. These publications may be found in most libraries.[15] You might also contact the U.S. Copyright Office.[16] You should write to the copyright

---

11. Ibid., pp. 124-126.

12. Copyright Act of 1976, Section 110(3) and (4). Note that subsection 4(A) prohibits admission charges only if the proceeds are not used exclusively for educational, religious, or charitable purposes.

13. Angel Tucciarone and Nicholas P. Cafardi, *Copyright and the Church Musician* (Diocese of Pittsburgh, 1977), pp. 8-9.

14. Strong, pp. 128-129.

15. Association for Educational Communications and Technology and Association of Media Producers, *Copyright and Educational Media* (Washington, D.C., 1977), p. 18.

16. Strong, p.123.

holder and obtain his written permission, advising him of the correct title of the material you wish to reproduce, a description of the portions you wish to reproduce, the type of reproduction, number of copies, intended use, distribution, and whether the material will be sold or whether there will be a charge for viewing it.[17]

It is generally necessary to obtain the copyright holder's written permission to use the material; his mere silence or failure to respond is not enough. However, if you have made diligent efforts to locate the publisher and are unable to do so, you might be justified in going ahead and reproducing the material.

Obtaining Copyrights For Your Own Works

A completed manuscript or work of art, has a "common-law copyright" called the "Right of First Publication." "Publication" in that sense means making the work available to the public. Merely xeroxing a few copies for use in a classroom would not be publication; but printing the book and making it available for sale would be. It might be advisable to place on the copies language to this effect: "Copied for limited use. Not for publication. Common Law Copyright reserved."[18]

It is sometimes suggested that an author send himself a copy of the manuscript by registered or certified mail. That does nothing to establish the copyright, but the date on the postmark of the sealed envelope may help establish that the work was completed on a specific date.

To obtain a formal copyright, write "Copyright _____(symbol)_____ . ___(Date)___ by _____(your name)_____ . All Rights Reserved." Then write to the Register of Copyright, Library of Congress, Washington, D.C. 20559 and ask for the necessary copyright form. When you receive the form, fill it out, attach a copy of what you have written and a check for ten dollars and send it to the same address. The Register of Copyright will then send you a certificate with a copyright number on it. Once you publish your work, you may wish to assign your copyright to the publisher,[19] or you may simply rely upon your common law copyright and let the publisher make the formal copyright arrangements. Further information and forms on copyrighting material can be found in the book *Copyright It Yourself* by E.G. Hirsch.[20]

A Closing Word

Copyright laws are necessary to protect the property rights of writers and artists. Infringing upon copyrighted material is stealing someone else's property. It is sinful. And it can be dangerous.

17. Copyright and Educational Media, pp. 19-20.
18. John C. Hogan and Saul Cohen, *An Author's Guide to Scholarly Publishing and the Law* (Englewood Cliffs, New Jersey: Prentice-Hall, Inc., 1965), pp. 25-29.
19. Wager, op.cit., pp.5-6.
20. E.G. Hirsch, editor, *Copyright It Yourself* (Wheeling, Illinois: Whitehall Company, 1979).

Chapter 30

An Overview of
Domestic Relations Law

Counseling is a major responsibility of most pastors. Next to preaching and teaching, many pastors spend more time counseling than in any other aspect of ministerial activity. And domestic relations problems—marital difficulties—are one of the most frequent subjects of counseling.

In domestic relations, law and ministry overlap. The pastor or counselor must be aware that divorce is a legal problem. Often a parishioner counsels with his pastor and his lawyer simultaneously as well as with social workers or psychologists as well. It is important that pastors, counselors, and laymen understand the legal aspects of divorce and domestic relations just as lawyers must understand the spiritual and emotional aspects of divorce.

The Bible Speaks on Divorce

While the Bible allows divorce (Deuteronomy 24:1-4), it was never the direct and perfect will of God. Rather, God allowed divorce because of the hardness of men's hearts (Matthew 19:8, Mark 10:5). At best, divorce is an accommodation of divine institutions to the sin nature of man.

For the Christian, divorce is never the will of God, except possibly when one spouse has committed adultery or fornication. Even that exception is questionable. Neither Mark nor Luke mentions the fornication exception. In Mark, Jesus simply says,

> Whosoever shall put away his wife, and marry another, committeth adultery against her.
> And if a woman shall put away her husband, and be married to another, she committeth adultery. (Mark 10:11-12).

And in Luke, He says likewise,

> Whosoever putteth away his wife, and marrieth another, committeth adultery: and whosoever marrieth her that is put away from her husband committeth adultery. (Luke 16:18).

Let us turn, then, to the Book of Matthew, where the fornication exception does appear. In Matthew 19:9, Christ says in the King James translation, "And I say unto you, Whosoever shall put away his wife, except it be for fornication, and shall marry another, committeth adultery: and whoso marrieth her which is put away doth commit adultery." This is an accurate translation of the *Textus Receptus*, the Greek manuscripts from which the King James Version was translated. But there are variant readings, and many believe the phrase "except it be for fornication" was not in the original manuscript at all. Some even question whether the phrase was originally in the Matthew 5:32 passage, but based on present manuscript evidence, it appears it was original.

Let us consider the term fornication. The Greek word used in Matthew 5:32 and 19:9 is *porneia*, from which we get our English word pornography. It literally means fornication, and most agree that it can refer to either premarital or extramarital sex, and may include any unnatural or improper sex. But Christ said that anyone who divorces (except possibly for fornication) and remarries, commits adultery. For "adultery" He used an entirely different Greek word, *moichatai*, which refers strictly to adultery.

Why did He use two different words? Obviously, a married person cannot engage in premarital sex; he can only engage in extramarital sex. Why didn't Jesus use the term *moichatai* throughout the passage?

One suggestion is that the fornication exception applies not to adultery but the discovery that one's spouse was sexually involved prior to the marriage. This could be the "uncleanness" referred to in Deuteronomy 24:1. The person with whom he or she was previously involved is, then, the true spouse, as implied by I Corinthians 6:16. Divorce is then justified because there was no true marriage.

A better interpretation is that *porneia* refers to certain types of void marriages, such as incestuous marriages, bigamous marriages, or homosexual marriages. If a man had two wives, or if a father had married his daughter, or if two men were married to each other, we certainly would not say to them, "What God hath joined together, let no man put asunder." This type of marriage is not only sinful; it is also void, and should be dissolved immediately. I personally believe this is the only exception Christ mentions in these passages and the rarity of this exception may be the reason Mark and Luke chose not to mention it.

What, then, is the effect of divorce upon remarriage? With this possible exception of fornication, the Bible prohibits remarriage. In fact, the Bible goes so far as to say that remarriage (except to each other) after divorce is adultery, apparently because one is still married to his first spouse in the eyes of God.

Some have argued that this adultery upon remarriage is a one-time thing, but thereafter a new marriage is contracted which is just as binding as the first. But an examination of the Greek text does not bear this out.

Among the various tenses in Greek are the present, which denotes continuing action, and the aorist, which often denotes point of time action. For example, let us take a sentence about shooting a gun. Using the aorist tense, I might say, "I shot the gun," and you would think of a single shot at a certain point of time. But if I were to say, "I am shooting the gun," I would use the present tense and you would think of an afternoon of target practice. These distinctions are helpful even if imprecise.

In that light, let us look at the sentence in Mark 10:11: "Whosoever shall put away his wife, and marry another, committeth adultery against her." Now, if "committeeth adultery" were meant as a one-time act, it would probably be an aorist. But it isn't; it is a present middle indicative, indicating continuing action. In fact, the use of the present for "committeth adultery" is in marked contrast with the use of the aorist elsewhere in the verse: "Whosoever shall put away (aorist, perhaps indicating point of time) his wife, and marry (aorist, again, point of time) another, committeth adultery (present, indicting continuous action, like 'keeps on committing adultery') against her."

The same tense distinction may be found in Matthew 19:9. It seems to be in Matthew 5:32 as well, although "committeth adultery" is used twice in that verse (in the second use, it is present tense; in the first usage, the texts vary, some using the present and some using the aorist). In the Luke 16:18 passage all of the verbs are present tense.

But wherever the distinction is clear, the message appears to be that one who divorces his spouse and marries another is engaged in a continuing adulterous relationship with his new spouse. Except for the possible ground of fornication, one who divorces his spouse seems to be permanently prohibited from marrying anyone else.[1]

Christians may differ on the interpretation of these passages. But one thing is clear: According to God's Word, divorce is a serious matter. God intended marriage as a lifelong relationship, and in I Corinthians 7, He even uses marriage as a picture of the relationship between Christ and His Church. Divorce, for whatever reason, is always a departure from the plan of God.

The Traditional View of Divorce

The legal system's view of divorce was once much closer to the biblical view than it is today. Traditionally, marriage was viewed as a lifetime contract between two parties. Therefore, a party who wanted a divorce had to prove

---

1. It does not necessarily follow that one who has been divorced and remarried should terminate his new marriage and go back to his first spouse, or remain celibate. One might argue that the new (albeit adulterous) marriage involves new duties and responsibilities, and dissolving this new marriage would be a greater evil than continuing it—especially if there are children by this new marriage.

that the marriage contract had been breached, much as he would prove breach of contract in other types of civil cases. The law spelled out specific means by which one might breach the marriage contract, and these were called grounds for divorce. They varied from state to state, but generally included adultery, desertion, imprisonment, alcoholism, drug addiction, chronic insanity, non-support, cruel and inhuman treatment, and in a few states impotence, sexual perversion, bigamy, or child abuse. Generally, only an innocent party could sue for divorce, and in many states one could defend against a divorce action by proving that the plaintiff had also breached the marriage contract. This was called recrimination. If a wife sued her husband for divorce and alleged cruel and inhuman treatment as a ground, the husband might defend against the divorce by proving that the wife had committed adultery.

The defense of forgiveness also applied in many states. If a husband sued his wife for divorce, using adultery as his ground, the wife could defend by proving that after the husband found out about the adultery he "forgave" her by continuing to live with her as husband and wife.

One ground listed above, cruel and inhuman treatment, has different meanings in different states. In some states, the term is interpreted rather strictly and one must prove physical injury or something very similar. In others, the term is a catchall for anyone who wants a divorce but can't point to specific grounds.

No-fault Divorce (Dissolution of Marriage)

As our nation departed from its biblical heritage and divorce became increasingly common, a movement arose to dispel traditional notions about divorce, make it easier and less painful, and remove the stigma. In the late 1960s and during the first half of the 1970s, many states adopted what is called "no-fault divorce."

Under no-fault divorce, it is no longer necessary to prove that one party or the other breached the marriage contract, or that the other party is innocent. To obtain a divorce one need only prove that the parties are incompatible. Statutes in no-fault states commonly require one to allege in his divorce petition that "there has been an irretrievable breakdown in the marriage relationship," or that "the legitimate objects of matrimony have broken down and there is no reasonable likelihood that they will be restored." The party at fault could sue the other party for divorce and win! In fact, even the term "divorce" was often changed in the statute and the legal papers, and the innocuous term "dissolution of marriage" substituted instead.

As of 1980, sixteen states plus the District of Columbia and the Virgin Islands had abolished traditional divorce and adopted no-fault dissolution of marriage: Arizona, California, Colorado, Connecticut, Florida, Hawaii, Iowa, Kentucky, Michigan, Minnesota, Missouri, Montana, Nebraska, Oregon, Washington, and Wisconsin.

Fifteen states plus Puerto Rico have retained the traditional concept of divorce: Arkansas, Illinois, Louisiana, Maryland, New Jersey, New York, North Carolina, Ohio, Oklahoma, Pennsylvania, South Carolina, South Dakota, Utah, Vermont, and Virginia.

Additionally, nineteen states have retained traditional grounds for divorce but have added "incompatibility" or "irreconcilable differences" as additional grounds, thus in effect adopting no-fault divorce: Alabama, Alaska, Delaware, Georgia, Idaho, Indiana, Kansas, Maine, Massachusetts, Mississippi, Nevada, New Hampshire, New Mexico, North Dakota, Rhode Island, Tennessee, Texas, West Virginia, Wyoming. Of these, five states (Alaska, Maine, Massachusetts, Mississippi, and West Virginia) provide that incompatibility can be used as a ground only if both spouses agree to it.[2]

Advocates of no-fault divorce contended that the new system would eliminate collusion and fraud in divorce proceedings. Formerly, when both parties wanted a divorce, couples sometimes had to manufacture grounds. No-fault divorce probably has eliminated most of this, since such grounds for divorce are no longer needed.

It was also argued that no-fault divorce would remove the bitterness from divorce proceedings. My own observation based upon practicing law and counseling divorce clients in four no-fault states, is that the bitterness is as deep as ever, especially where children or property are involved.

Another argument was that no-fault divorce procedures would make divorce cheaper. Again, the effect upon legal fees has been negligible. Divorce costs are generally higher in Minnesota, which has no-fault divorce, then in Oklahoma which does not.

It was also hoped (by some) that no-fault concept would eliminate the stigma of divorce. This has happened, for divorce has become commonplace and socially acceptable. It seems that fewer and fewer couples work to preserve their marriages.

There are several negative factors in no-fault divorce. First, it reflects and contributes to a retreat from the traditional view that a person is responsible for his actions. Formerly, it was thought that if a marriage didn't work, it was because one or both parties refused to make it work. Under the no-fault view, the failure of the marriage is nobody's fault—it was the circumstances; things just "didn't work out"; they were "incompatible."

Second, innocent persons have been injured by no-fault divorce concepts. All too often, a partner wants a divorce simply because he or she is tired of being married or is interested in someone else. The other partner may have been a good spouse. The result can be that the spouse who wanted nothing but a good marriage and family, can lose the home, children, estate, and many life goals, simply because of the other's selfish desires. For this reason, I strongly believe that if no-fault concepts are to be applied at all in civil society, they should apply only if both spouses agree to proceed under no-fault provisions.

In the early 1970s it appeared that no-fault divorce would sweep the country. But by the mid-1970s, the momentum for no-fault divorce had slowed down, until it now appears to be at a standstill. About one-third of the states operate under no-fault, a third under traditional concepts, and the remaining third under some type of hybrid system. Criticism of no-fault divorce seems to be on the rise with a new desire to return to traditional concepts, though to date no state has repealed its no-fault divorce laws.

The Mechanics of Divorce

The precise legal procedure and terminology varies from state to state, but generally the process of divorce includes certain steps.

The party who wants a divorce sees an attorney, who usually insists on a retainer fee. The attorney than files a petition with the court, a copy of which is served on the defending spouse, asking that the court grant the plaintiff a divorce or (in no-fault states) that the marriage be dissolved. Usually the petition also asks that the plaintiff be awarded certain property from the marriage. (Often, at the lawyer's suggestion, the plaintiff will ask for more than he really wants, expecting to compromise later.) If there are children, the petition may ask for custody of the children, plus child support.

Since it will probably take several months at least before the divorce is finalized, the court makes some temporary arrangements for custody of the children, alimony, property division, etc. Consequently, the divorce papers initially served upon the defendant will probably include an order from the judge granting temporary custody of the children to the plaintiff and possibly granting use of the house as well. This does not mean the judge has made a final decision about children or property. It is simply a temporary provision until the judge can hear the evidence. If there is a potential for violence, the papers may include an injunction or restraining order prohibiting the defendant from harassing or molesting the plaintiff or the children or trespassing on the property until further order of the court. Some lawyers and judges automatically include such orders; others do so only when necessary.

The next step is the initial hearing, which usually takes place about a week after the papers are served. At this time the court will hear some limited evidence to determine who should have custody of the children, who should have possession of what property, what alimony or support should be paid, and other matters, until the divorce is final. In some jurisdictions the judge may at this time require the parties to undergo marital counseling.

Between the temporary and final hearings, many divorces are resolved, either by the parties' reconciliation, or by the parties and their attorneys agreeing on the issues of child custody, support, property, etc. If the parties do agree, then the final hearing is called an uncontested divorce. Usually the defendant does not attend this hearing, and the plaintiff simply testifies as to the grounds for divorce and the agreement as to child support, alimony, property division, etc. Usually these matters are placed in a written agreement or stipulation, signed by both parties and their lawyers, and this stipulation is presented to the court as an exhibit. The judge then grants the divorce according to the terms of the stipulation, and issues a divorce decree.

If, on the other hand, the parties cannot agree on these matters, the case comes before the court as a contested divorce. If the issue is child custody, each party presents evidence that he is more fit to have custody than the other. This can include testimony of psychologists and caseworkers, friends, ministers, neighbors, medical records, and many other things. If the issue is property, each might provide evidence of his debts and needs, and establish what property he brought into the marriage. Frequently, these hearings are bitter events. The judge then has the difficult task of sorting out all the evidence and rendering a just decision.

In some states, the judge may restore the wife's maiden name to her, if she requests it. She should not forget to make this request, if that is her wish.

When the court awards child custody to one party, he normally grants visitation rights to the other. If the parties are reasonable and communicate rationally, it is ususally best to state in the divorce decree that the noncustodial parent has "reasonable visitation rights." If they cannot be cooperative, it may be necessary to order the specific times, days, and holiday visitation rights.

Child Support, Alimony, and Taxes

Let us assume the wife has custody of the children, and that the husband is paying child support to the wife. Child support is then not tax deductible to the husband, and the wife does not have to report it as income since it is paid for the benefit of the children rather than personal income. The fact that the wife remarries does not by itself affect the husband's obligation to pay child support. He must continue to pay child support until the child reaches the age of majority or is otherwise emancipated, dies, or is adopted.

Alimony is just the opposite. It is income to the wife, and must be reported by her as income, and the husband may deduct it from his income tax. Alimony normally ends when the wife remarries.

After a divorce, which parent claims the children as tax exemptions? Usually the court will rule on that question in the divorce decree; the judge may provide that the husband gets the exemption for one child and the wife can claim the other. Lawyers often make this one of many negotiating points. On the whole, it is advantageous to both parties if the spouse in the higher income tax bracket can claim the exemptions.

If the divorce decree does not mention tax exemptions, then the Internal Revenue Code provides that the parent who contributes over half the child's support can claim that child as an exemption. If the husband has paid more than $1200 per year per child, the IRS presumes that he has contributed the majority of support, and it is up to the wife to prove otherwise. If the husband has paid less than $1200 per year per child, then he is presumed to have contributed less than half the child's support unless he can prove otherwise. Total support includes the reasonable cost of the child's sleeping quarters, meals, clothing, medical costs, and other normal expenses of daily living.

Modification of Divorce Decrees

Even "final" divorce decrees are not final as to child custody, visitation, support and alimony. If there is a change in circumstances, either party can file a motion asking the court to amend or modify its order.

For example, at the time of divorce a husband may be earning $50,000 per year. Consequently, the court determines he is able to pay child support of $1,000 per month and alimony of $1,000 per month. Two years later, the company he works for goes bankrupt, he loses his job, and he has to take a job for $20,000 per year. Under such circumstances he should not simply stop paying support and alimony, for he could be cited for contempt of court. Rather, he should have his attorney file a motion with the court which issued the decree, asking them to modify the support and alimony provisions, reducing them to a reasonable figure he can afford.

Or perhaps at the time of the divorce the court determined from the available evidence that the wife was more fit to have custody of the children. But three years later, she has a live-in boyfriend and has become an alcoholic. The husband, meanwhile, has remarried, established a stable home, and has a responsible job. Under these new circumstances, the court might well determine that the best interest of the children would be served by transferring them to the custody of their father.

Some states have limited the frequency with which modifications of divorce decrees may be sought. A state law might provide that a spouse may not seek a modification more than once a year, since it is obviously unfair that the other spouse should be subjected to the harassment of a lawsuit every few months.

Some states prohibit divorced persons from marrying anyone except each other for a certain time period after the divorce. In other states a divorce decree is temporary or interlocutory; it does not become final for several months.

"Let the Healing Waters Flow . . ."

Too many law offices are "divorce mills." Rather than trying to resolve marital conflicts and bring families together, too many lawyers simply rush their clients through the divorce process and then wash their hands of the matter. The lawyer should be a healer. He should do his utmost to resolve conflict, not acerbate it. The pastor and social worker can be of tremendous help to the lawyer in this regard. Neither should forget that the subject of their effort is not merely a client, a parishioner, or a patient; but a person. And a marriage in trouble is not just a contract or a legal relationship; it is a family, a divinely ordained institution of God. We should work to preserve the family. And we should enlist God's help in prayer.

Chapter 31

An Overview of Criminal Law

Do Christians ever commit crimes? After thirteen years of practicing law, I am convinced the answer is yes.

Christians still have their old sin natures. They still have some measure of freewill and Satan is trying harder than ever to lead them astray. That's quite a combination for disaster!

Sometimes a Christian will have trouble with an unjust law, such as government regulation of Christian education. Sometimes a Christian may be falsely accused. Sometimes a professing Christian may be involved in crime. And sometimes the Christian himself may backslide and let the old sin nature take over. I have defended evangelical Christians who have been prosecuted for political reasons: violating compulsory school attendance laws, and fighting federal control of agriculture. I have also represented professing Christians on speeding violations, bad checks, fraud, forgery, theft, disorderly conduct, assault, and bribing an officer of the law. Whether guilty or innocent, sincere or insincere, these people need the help and understanding of family, friends, their pastor and church.

Crime

A crime is defined in *American Jurisprudence* 2d as an act committed in violation of a public law forbidding it, or omitted in violation of a public law commanding it.[1] Unlike civil law which involves one party suing another, criminal actions are brought by the state and are captioned *State vs. Smith*.

Rights of the Accused

Because of the immense power of the state and the relative helplessness of the individual, our legal system affords certain rights, or protections, to the

---

1. *American Jurisprudence 2d* (Criminal Law §1)

individual citizen accused of a crime. Most of these have their roots in the Bible. Many can be traced through the English system of common law, and some are expressly protected by the Constitution and Bill of Rights.

One of the foremost rights of the American citizen who is accused of a crime is the presumption of innocence. It is not the citizen's responsibility to prove himself innocent, as is the case in many countries. Rather, it is the government's burden to prove him guilty. If neither side can produce any proof, the presumption of innocence stands and he must be acquitted. And the burden of proof is not a mere preponderance of evidence, or clear and convincing evidence, as is the case in civil lawsuits. Rather, the government must prove the defendant guilty by proof beyond a reasonable doubt. That is a very substantial burden of proof. It is difficult to define "proof beyond a reasonable doubt." One might say that preponderance of evidence means one must be 51 percent certain; clear and convincing evidence means one must be 70 percent certain; and proof beyond a reasonable doubt means one must be 95 percent certain. But percentages are misleading, because proof beyond a reasonable doubt is not a mathematical formula. One court has said that proof beyond a reasonable doubt is easy to understand but difficult to define, and that attempts to define it usually do nothing but create confusion.[2] One of the best definitions is that which is often used in jury instructions in military courts: that a reasonable doubt is one that is not forced or fanciful but which arises naturally in the mind.

The Sixth Amendment guarantees to the defendant a fair and impartial trial by a jury of his peers. He is entitled to a speedy and public trial, and to be present at the trial. He has the right to confront his accusers and hear them testify against him, and to cross-examine them on their testimony. He has the right under the Fifth Amendment to testify or not testify as he sees fit, and the court is not to assume he is guilty simply because he refuses to testify (though sometimes juries do conciously or subconciously hold this against the defendant). He has the right under the Sixth Amendment to present witnesses in his defense, and require the presence of such witnesses by means of subpoena. He has the right to obtain from the prosecution information favorable to his case. And he is entitled to the assistance of an attorney.

The Fourth Amendment protects the privacy of the American citizen against unreasonable searches and seizures. It provides that law enforcement officials may not search a person or his property except (1) incident to a lawful arrest, (2) with his consent or the consent of a person authorized to give consent, (3) in a bona fide emergency, or (4) with a search warrant based upon a sworn statement establishing probable cause to believe the search will turn up contraband or evidence of criminal activity.

Most of us are thankful for this guarantee of privacy. Most of us appreciate our privacy and do not want government officials searching our property, even though we have nothing to hide. But the protection against unreasonable search

2. *State v. Morrison*, 67 Kansas 144, 72 P. 554 (1903).

and seizure has produced a controversial consequence: the exclusionary rule.

Here is how the exclusionary rule works. Suppose the police break into "A" 's house without a warrant, consent, emergency, or lawful arrest, and find stolen property therein. "A" is then charged with possession of stolen property, or possibly with theft.

Clearly, "A" 's constitutional rights were violated by the search. But what can be done about it at that point? That's where the exclusionary rule comes in. The courts have held that evidence seized in violation of the Fourth Amendment cannot (with a few exceptions) be used in evidence against the defendant.[3] The reason is that without such a rule there is no incentive for police officers to respect the citizen's constitutional rights. The unfortunate result is that a police error or violation may often allow an obviously guilty defendant to go free.

The same principle also applies to the Fifth Amendment protection against self-incrimination. Believing that police frequently extracted involuntary confessions from suspects, and considering a confession given in ignorance of one's rights to be the same as involuntary, the U.S. Supreme Court ruled in *Miranda v. Arizona*, 384 U.S. 436 (1966), that confessions given during custodial interrogation by one suspected of a criminal offense may not be used in court against him unless the police have first advised him that (1) he has a right to remain silent, (2) anything he says can be used against him in court, (3) he has a right to an attorney, and (4) the state will provide an attorney for him if he cannot afford one. The effect, again, is that in some cases guilty defendants go free because the police fail to read them their rights, and at times the police are deprived of valuable information because after reading the rights the suspect refuses to say anything.[4]

The dilemma is serious: How can society prevent guilty defendants from escaping justice, while at the same time safeguard the Fourth and Fifth Amendment rights of all citizens? The exclusionary rule has the unfortunate effect of allowing guilty persons to avoid conviction even in the face of overwhelming evidence. But without the exclusionary rule, there would be no reason for police officers to respect anyone's right to privacy or silence.

There are signs the courts may be retreating slightly from the exclusionary rule and construing it more narrowly, but it is highly unlikely that the courts will eliminate the rule entirely in the foreseeable future.

Defenses

One defense to a criminal charge is obvious: innocence. But there are also affirmative defenses, most of which the defendant must prove by preponderance of evidence.

---

3. *Mapp v. Ohio*, 367 U.S. 643 (1961).

4. See "The Effect of *Miranda v. Arizona* Upon Law Enforcement in the State of Iowa", independent study paper by John A. Eidsmoe, University of Iowa College of Law, Iowa City, Iowa, 1970.

Affirmative defenses often involve intent. Under our legal system one normally cannot be convicted of a crime unless he had the intent to commit the crime. Under an affirmative defense, the defendant in effect confesses to the act, but cites extenuating circumstances as a basis not to be punished for the crime.

Insanity is one such defense, for it involves proving that one could not, because of his insane condition, form the requisite mental intent to commit a crime. The definition of insanity varies from state to state. Some states follow the M'Naughten rule that one is insane only if he did not know the nature and quality of his act, or if he did know it, he did not know it was wrong. Others add an additional ground for insanity, called the "irresistable impulse rule," by which one is insane if his diseased state of mind rendered him incapable of exercising the normal governing power of the will so as to control his actions under the compulsion of an insane impulse to act. Still others follow the Durham rule, which asks whether there is a substantial causal connection between the mental disease and the crime. And others look to the proposed rule of the American Law Institute, which asks whether, as a result of the defendant's mental disease, the defendant lacks substantial capacity either to appreciate the criminality of his conduct or to conform his conduct to the requirements of the law. Normally, a defendant is presumed to be sane, and it is his burden to prove that he is insane—usually by preponderance of evidence.

There seems to be widespread dissatisfaction with the use of the insanity defense, and some are calling for its abolition. Alternatives are being explored. Minnesota allows a special verdict. "Not Guilty by Reason of Insanity," after which the defendant is committed for treatment. Illinois has a special verdict, "Guilty but Insane," by which the defendant does not escape moral responsibility for his actions but his mental state is considered in determining the sentence.

Another defense involving intent is accident: I killed him, but I didn't mean to; the gun went off accidentally. That is a defense to murder, but not necessarily to manslaughter.

Another affirmative defense is entrapment: I did it, but the only reason I did it was that the police officer talked me into it. Entrapment is a defense because it is felt that our police have better things to do than tempt innocent persons to commit crimes. But the mere fact that an officer offers to buy marijuana from a defendant does not by itself constitute entrapment, if the defendant was already predisposed to sell marijuana and the officer just gave him the opportunity. The issue in an entrapment defense is, did the criminal intent first arise in the mind of the officer and transfer from him to the defendant, or was it in the mind of the defendant already? That can be a difficult question for the court to decide.

A grant of immunity by the prosecution is a defense. So is double jeopardy, or the statute of limitations. Ignorance of fact can also be a defense; for example, if I am charged with receiving stolen property, the fact that I honestly and reasonably believed it was not stolen is usually a valid defense. Ignorance of the law is usually not a defense, but it can be in a confusing area of the law where one has relied upon the advice of an attorney or on a decision of a court.

Necessity can also be a defense, as when someone lost in a blizzard unlawfully enters a building to avoid freezing to death. Self-defense is a form of necessity, if one can prove that his actions were reasonably necessary to protect himself from the danger of death or injury.

Trial Procedure

Usually a criminal case begins when a complaint is filed with the police or prosecutor. In less serious cases the prosecutor may personally file a criminal charge; in others he may refer the matter to a grand jury which hears the evidence and decides whether to indict.

When the charge is filed in a serious case, the defendant is usually arrested. He may have to post bail to be released, or he may be released on his own recognizance. In very serious cases he may be held without bail.

The first hearing is usually the arraignment, where the charges are read and rights explained. Preliminary matters such as the appointment of an attorney are usually handled at this hearing also.

At the next stage of the proceeding (sometimes combined with the first in a single hearing), the defendant pleads guilty or not guilty and files any appropriate motions. After these are decided, the case is set for trial, either before the judge alone or before a jury.

The prosecution begins with an opening statement (sometimes waived). The defense attorney sometimes makes his opening statement immediately afterward, sometimes not until after the prosecutor rests his case. The prosecutor and the defense attorney each presents his case. Usually both sides are given an opportunity for rebuttal evidence. Then there are closing arguments, the jury is instructed, and then deliberations occur. If the trial is before the judge alone, he may announce his decision immediately or he may deliberate a while and then issue his decision in writing.

A verdict of acquittal ends the case. If the defendant is found guilty, there is still the sentencing portion of the trial. Classically, there are four reasons for punishing criminals: (1) to avenge justice (Romans 13:4); (2) to restrain criminals (while a criminal is in jail he cannot commit crimes); (3) to deter other potential offenders (Deuteronomy 13:11; 17:33; 21:22); and (4) to rehabilitate the offender, either teaching him that crime does not pay or showing him a better way to live. To these we might add a fifth reason: to prevent private individuals from taking the law into their own hands and taking personal vengeance on their own.

In more serious cases there is usually a presentence investigation, often conducted by a probation officer or other court official. This officer will consider, among other things, the offender's past record, his employment, his state of mind, and his potential for rehabilitation. At this time the pastor and Christian friends can be of immense help and support by working with the officer as character witnesses. Presentence investigation reports are very important. Judges consider them seriously, and many judges follow them almost automatically.

A criminal trial is a time of immense emotional and spiritual turmoil, not only for the defendant but also for his family. Friends and clergy can be an important source of strength and comfort. And as in all times of turmoil, many defendants are drawn to the Lord through this difficult time and many make commitments to Christ.

Chapter 32

An Overview of Juvenile Law

We have talked about civil law. We have talked about criminal law. Now let us look at a unique hybrid: the juvenile court.

It is tragic that juvenile justice occupies a rather lowly place in today's judicial system. In a typical law firm, juvenile cases are often referred to the youngest and least experienced attorney. And often the least experienced prosecutor and the judge with the least seniority in the district get "stuck" with juvenile court. The others work in the adult criminal system or in civil cases involving large sums of money.

But juvenile court is a very important branch of the American judicial system. It involves not money but human lives. And it involves not the lives of hardened adult criminals, but those of impressionable young children. A juvenile court proceeding probably has a far greater impact on the life of the child than criminal or civil trials have on adults.

Juvenile courts developed in the late 1800s. Before that, under common law, children under the age of seven were considered incapable of committing criminal offenses. Between seven and fourteen there was a rebuttable presumption that the child was incapable of committing a crime. Over the age of fourteen, the child was presumed to be responsible for his actions and was tried in court as an adult. The result was that many juveniles were convicted of adult crimes and imprisoned with adults. To avoid that unfortunate consequence, many more who had obviously committed crimes were acquitted by juries and returned to the streets to go on committing crimes.[1]

The reform movement developed in the early 1800s and, with some setbacks, gradually gained momentum as the century progressed. Much of its thinking was based upon principles of legal positivism which were at variance with

---

1. Sanford J. Fox, "Juvenile Justice Reform: an Historical Perspective," 22 Stanford Law Review 1187 (1970), reprinted in Sanford J. Fox, *Modern Juvenile Justice: Cases and Materials* (St. Paul: West Publishing Company, 1981), pp. 86-87.

classical views of criminology. The differences between those views could be summarized as follows:

Classical	Reform/Positivism
Legal principles are absolute and God-given.	Legal principles are relative, man-made, and utilitarian.
Sin and human volition cause crime.	Environment causes crime.
Punishment prevents crime.	Rehabilitation and changed environment prevent crime.
The legal system should study laws, not men.	The legal system should study men, not laws.
Punishment should be based on the crime, not the criminal.	Punishment should be based on the criminal, not the crime.

The basic concept of juvenile court is the Latin term *parens patriae*, the state acting, or in the place of the parents. Let us remember that according to reform/positivist thinking, environment is the root cause of crime. If a child has problems with the law, the problem is his enviornment, and his environment consists largely of his home and his parents. Thus, juvenile crime reflects parental failure. And since the parents have failed, the state must step in to act in place of the parents through the juvenile court.

The juvenile court acts under the guiding principle of the "best interest of the child." The court's purpose is not to punish the child, but to rehabilitate and help him to become a well-adjusted member of society. After all, the child is not fully responsible for his actions. He has done what he did because his environment caused him to do so. And the way to change the child is to change the child's enviornment—through foster homes, group homes, reform school, and the like.

Now, since the court is acting in place of the parent, and since the court is acting in the best interest of the child to help him rather than to punish him, juvenile courts dropped the formalities of criminal trials. Even the terminology is changed from the criminal-court jargon. Juvenile court does not use "charges," "indictments," or "complaints"; rather, a "petition" is filed against the juvenile—in fact, not *against* the juvenile but "*in his interest*"— alleging him to be delinquent and stating the reasons for that allegation. Bringing him to the police station is not called "booking," it is called "intake," The "verdict" is called an "adjudication," and it does not find the child "guilty" or "not guilty"; it simply finds whether he did or did not do the act in question and whether he is or is not delinquent. And the "sentence" subsequently determined is not a sentence at all, but a "disposition." He is not "jailed," he is "detained" or "institutionalized." In fact, the child himself is not called the "defendant"; he is the "respondent," the "client," the "ward," or the "patient." And the juvenile court proceeding is not a "trial"— it is a "hearing."

Many of the procedural safeguards that protect criminals in adult trials were likewise dropped. After all, a father wouldn't advise his son, "David, you are suspected of the offense of talking back to your mother. I hereby advise you that you have a right to remain silent. Anything you say can be used against you. You have a right to an attorney, etc." And since the court acted in place of the parent, the court didn't have to employ these safeguards, either. The ideal was a relaxed informal setting in which the judge, the juvenile, his parents, and the social worker sat down around a conference table and reflected upon the child's problem and what could be done to help him.

Unfortunately, juvenile court did not always work that way in practice. All too often, overworked judges did not have time to devote proper attention to cases, and simply ordered into effect the predetermined recommendations of social workers. These social workers were ususally well-intentioned, but often they had no concept of or respect for the constitutional rights and safeguards of the judicial system. As a result, many innocent juveniles were railroaded into delinquency adjudications and reform institutions, there to mix and with hard-core delinquents and learn the fundamentals of crime for an adult career. As Dean Roscoe Pound of Harvard Law School said in 1937, "The powers of the Star Chamber were a trifle in comparison with those of our juvenile courts. . . ."[2] And, as the Supreme Court said in *Kent v. U.S.*, 383 U.S. 541 (1966), ". . . there may be grounds for concern that the child receives the worst of both worlds: that he gets neither the protections accorded to adults nor the solicitous care and regenerative treatment postulated for children."

In Re Gault

Juvenile justice took a dramatic turn when, in 1967, the U.S. Supreme Court decided *In Re Gault* (387 U.S. 1). The case involved a fifteen-year-old boy named Gerald Gault, who was alleged to have made an obscene phone call. The woman who accused young Gerald claimed she recognized his voice over the telephone. Gerald was picked up by the police and taken to juvenile detention. His parents were not notified of the arrest and did not know where Gerald was until they called the police late in the day. No criminal complaint or juvenile petition was served upon the parents, and they did not even see the petition until after the hearing. Even then, the petition did not refer to any factual basis for the charge. No pre-trial hearing took place to determine whether Gerald needed to be in detention, and the authorities never offered an explanation as to why pre-trial detention was necessary.

At the adjudication, Gerald did not have an attorney and was not advised of his right to one. No attorney was appointed for him. The complaining witness was not present, and she had not even made a sworn or written statement; the police officer simply testified as to what she had told him over the phone. Nevertheless, the juvenile court judge determined that Gerald had made the obscene phone call, and he committed Gerald to the State Industrial School

2. Roscoe Pound, quoted in *In Re Gault*, 387 U.S. 1 (1967).

until age twenty-one. The statute provided no right of appeal, so Gerald and his family pursued the matter through a writ of habeas corpus. There was no transcript of the juvenile-court procedure, so the higher courts had to rely upon the lower court personnel's memory as to what happened, and their memory and that of Gerald's parents conflicted on several points.

If Gerald Gault had been an adult, he would have been entitled to a full criminal trial; court-appointed counsel, the right to subpeona witnessess; the right to testify or remain silent; the right to confront and cross-examine government witnesses; the right to be presumed innocent; and all the other rights our legal system provides. And if he had been found guilty and the verdict was affirmed on appeal, he could have been fined up to fifty dollars and jailed up to ninety days. But because Gerald Gault was a juvenile, all of these rights were denied him, and he was sentenced to what was, in effect, a prison term of six years—all in his "best interest"!

The Supreme Court of the United States struck down this action as unconstitutional. The Court recognized that the goal of juvenile courts is the best interest of the child, but also recognized that in practice that does not always work out. State reform schools, the Court recognized, have many of the characteristics of prisons, and at the very least constitute a deprivation of liberty. The Supreme Court therefore ruled that in any juvenile proceeding in which the juvenile could be removed from his home and placed in a restricted environment, the juvenile is entitled to certain procedural rights. These include the right to notice of the charges against him, said notice to be furnished to him sufficiently in advance so he has time to prepare a defense, and said notice to describe his alleged misconduct with sufficient detail so he knows what he must defend against. He has the right to an attorney and this includes the right to state-appointed counsel if he is indigent. He is entitled to the privilege against self-incrimination, as this guarantees the reliability of confessions, and the right to confront and cross-examine the witnesses against him. And he has the right to a transcript of the court proceedings and the right to appeal the juvenile court's decision to a higher court.

This does not mean that the juvenile has all the same rights an adult has in a criminal trial. Rather, the juvenile is entitled to all the rights of the Constitution and the American legal system which can be afforded without disrupting the basic purpose of the juvenile court, which remains the best interest of the child. Subsequent cases have held that the juvenile has the right to protection against double jeopardy,[3] the right to a speedy trial,[4] and the right to be presumed innocent until proven guilty beyond a reasonable doubt.[5] But other cases have held that the juvenile is not entitled by the Constitution to a jury trial or a public trial, as this would disrupt the juvenile

3. *Tolliver v. Judges of Family Court*, 59 Misc. 2d 104, 298 N.Y.S. 2d 237 (1969).
4. *Piland v. Clark County Juvenile Court*, 85 Nev. 489, 457 P. 2d 523, (1969).
5. *In re Winship*, 397 U.S. 358 (1970).

court concept of confidential hearings conducted for the best interest of the child.[6]

Types of Juvenile Cases

Some think that every child who comes before the juvenile court is a delinquent. In fact, the jurisdiction of juvenile court is much broader than that. Juvenile courts commonly handle delinquency cases, dependency cases, child-custody matters, and many others.

The laws of most states distinguish the types of juveniles brought before the court. The definitions vary somewhat from state to state, but generally, a "delinquent" child is one who has committed some type of act which, if done by an adult, would be a crime. Typical delinquency cases involve drugs, theft, assault, and disorderly conduct.

Another type of juvenile who is often classed as "delinquent" is the "status offender." A status offender is one who commits an act that would not be illegal if he were an adult. Truancy from school is a status offense, since adults are not legally required to go to school. Some alcohol-related offenses are status offenses. Curfew violations are status offenses, since there is usually no curfew for adults. Other status offenses include incorrigibility and running away from home. While these are usually classed as delinquent, a few states give status offenders a special classification of "unruly."

Then there are "dependent," "deprived," or "neglected" children. These are children in need of the court's help, not because they have done anything wrong, but because they are not receiving adequate care. Possibly they are orphans; possibly they are victims of child neglect or child abuse. Possibly the parents have mental problems or drug problems and are therefore unable to be effective parents. The distinctions between "abuse," "neglect," and "dependency" are difficult to define. Roughly speaking, abuse is willful mistreatment, neglect is willful failure to provide proper care, and dependency results from the parent's inability to provide proper care. Frequently, juvenile court personnel use the all-inclusive term CHINS (Children In Need of Supervision), or CINS or PINS, to describe all such children.

In the early days of the juvenile-court movement, there was little, if any, distinction between CHINS and delinquent children.[7] After all, they were the products of their respective environments, and all needed a change of environment to solve their problems! But in recent years both the courts and the legislatures have recognized a difference between the two, and they have accorded the alleged delinquent greater due process rights and constitutional protections.[8]

---

6. *McKeiver v. Pennsylvania*, 403 U.S. 528 (1971).

7. Fox, op. cit., pp. 85-86.

8. *State Ex Rel. Harris v. Calendine*, 233 S.E.2d 318 (W. Va. 1977); *Matter of Spaulding*, 373 Md. 690, 332 A.2d 246 (1975); *Matter of Walker*, 282 N.C. 28, 191 S.E.2d 702 (1972); *District of Columbia v. B.J.R.*, 322 A.2d 58 (1975), cert. den. 421 U.S. 1016 (D.C. 1975).

The Delinquency Proceeding

Since the goal of the juvenile court is to serve the best interest of the child, it tries to avoid most of the trappings of a criminal court. Sometimes juvenile court is conducted around a conference table; in some jurisdictions an actual courtroom is used. Sometimes the juvenile court judge wears a robe; sometimes he does not. Sometimes a juvenile court referee is appointed who conducts hearings. He is a judge in every respect except that the judge has to approve his final rulings.

A juvenile court hearing is bifurcated; that is, it is divided into two stages. The first stage, the adjudication phase, corresponds roughly to the trial portion of a criminal case in which guilt or innocence is determined. At this stage evidence is presented by the state to establish that the child did commit the alleged delinquent act, and the defense attorney cross-examines the state's witnesses and then presents his own case much as he would in a criminal trial. The judge then finds that the child did or did not do the act in question and that the child is or is not delinquent.

A finding that the child did not do the act is like a verdict of acquittal. It ends the proceeding. If the judge finds otherwise, it is necessary to move on to the disposition hearing stage, which roughly corresponds to sentencing. During this stage the rules of evidence are somewhat relaxed, and the judge may consider social workers' reports, psychological profiles, school records, and other such documents. He may also hear recommendations from probation officers and others as to what should be done. The defense may present evidence as to what he believes the disposition should be; this could include other expert testimony, or it could include the testimony of the parents and the child. The judge may talk directly and informally with the parents and child, to understand their perspectives on the problem.

The juvenile court judge has a wide variety of options at his disposal. He can give the child a lecture and a reprimand, or he can place the child on a supervised or unsupervised probation. He might, as a condition of probation, require that the child submit to regular counseling. If the case involves theft, vandalism, or some other form of monetary damage, the judge might require as a condition of probation that the child make restitution. Sometimes, as a condition of probation, the child must perform a certain number of hours per week of service to a church or charity to be selected by the child and his probation officer. This gives the child something to do with his time, helps his self-image by making him feel he is contributing to society, and occasionally opens up a whole new field of interest.

If the judge believes the child needs a more structured setting, he may order that the child be placed in the custody of the Social Services or placed in a foster or group home. He might, if needed, direct that the child be committed to a mental institution or drug rehabilitation unit. The most drastic action he can take is to commit the child to the state reform school. Sometimes, to give the child an incentive to straighten up, a judge commits the child to the state reform school and then stays the commitment pending the child's good behavior, placing the child on a strict probation in the meantime (similar to a suspended sentence).

Pastors and youth workers can be of great help during the disposition portion of the hearing. The judge normally does not want to remove the child from his home, unless he is convinced the child cannot get the guidance and support he needs at home. The willingness of church leaders to assist the child and his family through counseling and other means, plus the opportunity for the child to find wholesome friends through the church youth group or Sunday school, could make the difference as to whether the child is allowed to remain at home.

If the child is in need of outside help, there are many creative possibilities which the pastor and lawyer should explore. Find out whether grandparents or other relatives might be willing to take the child briefly. That will save the state money, parental contact can be preserved, and the removal of the children from the home and their subsequent return to the home will be much less traumatic. Christian psychologists and guidance counselors are available, as are Christian institutions for troubled or delinquent youths.

The Dependency Proceeding

In a dependency proceeding, the state alleges the parent has not provided proper care for his child. The threat that the child could be removed from the home is often present. As a result, the state is in conflict with the parent, the state is in conflict with the child, and the parent and child are often in conflict with each other.

The hearing usually begins with evidence from the state that the child is in need of supervision. A caseworker may testify that she has visited the house on several occasions and found it messy. A teacher may testify that the child often seems hungry in school and shows up with bruises or burns. Neighbors may testify that the child is loud and unruly, not properly dressed for winter, and/or the parents frequently scream or swear at the child or beat him unmercifully. (In many states the law requires the reporting of information about suspected child abuse.) Psychologists may testify that the child is emotionally disturbed, socially and mentally slow, and in need of additional care or stimulation.

The defense then presents evidence. The parents may explain the allegations. The reason the house seems messy to the caseworker is that she always comes on Monday while the mother is doing laundry. The child always has a good breakfast in the morning and simply says he is hungry because he is bored in school. The child received the bruises in a fight on the school playground, which the teacher should have been supervising, and the burn occurred when the child accidentally touched the kitchen stove. The neighbors are old and think all kids are loud and unruly, and they think the parents beat them unmercifully because they don't believe in spanking at all. And the child seems emotionally disturbed because he is upset at being taken out of the home and interviewed by the psychologist; and he is not socially or mentally slow, just a "late bloomer." The defense may produce neighbors, friends, relatives or experts to support their position. In closing argument, the defense attorney may point out that there is no such thing as a perfect parent, and that if the authorities closely observe any family in the state they will always be able to find a few instances which, when taken out of context and placed together, sound like child neglect.

That argument has a ring of truth. No child receives perfect treatment. But there is a point at which a child crosses the fine line between "normal" and "neglected." It is the duty of the judge to determine whether the child has crossed that line.

If the judge finds that the children are not neglected or dependent, the case is ended—though he may give the parents some suggestions on how to improve their effectiveness so as to avoid future difficulties with the law. If he finds they are in need of supervision, he has many options. He can order the parents and/or children to undergo counseling. He can place the children in the legal custody of the Social Services but let them continue to live with their parents provided the parents do certain things, like obtain counseling, keep the house clean, etc. He might direct that the Social Services send a homemaker into the home once a day or once a week, to cook the children a hot meal, help keep the house, and try to teach the mother some homemaking skills. He might have the children placed in foster homes. An extreme case might result in termination of parental rights, after which the children are placed for adoption. However, this is a separate proceeding which would require special notice. Seldom is this done unless every other option has been tried and proven unsuccessful.

As in a delinquency proceeding, the church can be of great help to the family in a dependency hearing. With the parents' permission, the pastor might testify that, based upon his many years of association with that family, he knows them to be stable people who love their children deeply. He might meet with the Social Services or the county attorney and share with them his perspectives on the family, and may convince them that the family isn't all bad after all. If he is convinced the family needs assistance, he can try to persuade the family to accept counseling or other help from the Social Services and cooperate with them instead of fighting them. If the family has had problems in the past, he might convince the Social Services that the family is aware of the problems and is working on them. The very fact that he is interested and willing to help might persuade the Social Services or the court that there is hope for this family after all.

Juvenile Court in Biblical Perspective

Recent years have seen increasing disillusionment with the results of juvenile court. Liberals often believe juvenile courts ride roughshod over the constitutional rights of juveniles. Conservatives believe juvenile courts are ineffective, lacking any enforcement power over juvenile crime.

Most Americans agree that a crackdown on juvenile crime is long overdue. As a result, more and more juveniles are being transferred into adult court and tried as adult criminals. A few even favor abolishing juvenile court and returning to common law principles of juvenile responsibility, or handling juvenile offenses in criminal court, convicting them of adult offenses but granting some leniency in sentencing due to their age. While there is much merit in their arguments, a better solution in my judgment would be to give juvenile court more "power." As a juvenile court referee, I had the power to commit a child to the State Industrial School of North Dakota for two years, and then extend that commitment, because that was "in his best interest." But I couldn't fine him a penny, and I couldn't put him in jail even overnight (except while awaiting a hearing), because that was punishment.

Juvenile court works in the child's best interest. That is a noble goal. But the reformers overlooked the fact that sometimes the child's best interest may be served by appropriate punishment (Proverbs 13:24; 22:15; 23:13-14). Instead of transferring juveniles to adult court, the juvenile court could be given the power to fine a juvenile or place him in confinement for a brief period of time—provided, of course, that he is segregated from adult offenders.

Few will deny that a child is influenced by his environment. But Christians most emphatically deny that the child is controlled by his environment, or that merely changing the environment will change the child. The problem of sin is much deeper than that. We do not learn sin from our environment: it is part of our human nature and has been since the Fall. As David says in Psalm 51:5, "Behold, I was shapen in iniquity; and in sin did my mother conceive me." And in Psalm 58:3, "The wicked are estranged from the womb: they go astray as soon as they be born, speaking lies." Sin, then, is inherent in us. We are not sinners because we sin; we sin because we are sinners. The fact that a child commits acts of delinquency does not necessarily mean his parents have failed to raise him properly. Even in the best of environments, a child may still choose the wrong path.

The juvenile-court concept of *parens patriae* has little support in Scripture. Children belong to God (Psalm 127:3-5), not to the state. And God has entrusted parents with the responsibility of providing for them, training them, and making decisions for them (I Timothy 5:8; Ephesians 6:1-4; Colossians 3:20-21; Exodus 20:12; Deuteronomy 6:5-7; Proverbs 4:1-2, 10-11; 5:1; 13:24; Matthew 18:6).

According to the Bible, then, what role does government have in the care and control of children? Based upon Exodus 22:21-25 and 23:1-3, it might be argued that government is responsible for orphans. Possibly the term orphans could be extended to include those whose parents are still living but who, due to insanity, retardation, alcoholism, or other reasons, are either unable or unwilling to give them the care they need.

But what if there is a functioning family unit with a delinquent child? Look at Deuteronomy 21:18-21:

> If a man have a stubborn and rebellious son, who will not obey the voice of his father, or the voice of his mothers, and that, when they have chastened him, will not hearken unto them:
>
> Then shall his father and his mother lay hold on him, and bring him out unto the elders of his city, and unto the gate of his place;
>
> And they shall say unto the elders of his city, This our son is stubborn and rebellious, he will not obey our voice; he is a glutton, and a drunkard.
>
> And all the men of his city shall stone him with stones, that he die: So shalt thou put evil away from among you; and all Israel shall hear, and fear.

Several things should be noted about this passage. We are not told the age of the youth, and the Hebrew word for son ("ben") is of no help to us here; but the description of him as a glutton and a drunkard would indicate that this is not a small child. Both parents had to unite and stand together in the complaint. "When they have chastened him" means that the parents must have done their part to discipline the youth, so that his misconduct is not due to parental failure. The Jewish Talmud, expanding upon the Torah, provided that for a first offense the unruly son was formally warned and flogged by a local tribunal of three. If he presisted in his unruliness, he was tried before a court of twenty-three, and in his trial he was afforded the exacting protections of the Jewish criminal code. Ludwig believes that capital punishment was not imposed upon a son before he reached the age of majority.[9] That might be open to question, and one might argue as to how literally this passage should apply today. But one thing is clear: The role of the state is to support and buttress parental authority, not undermine it. And this is the *only* passage in Scripture which in any way justifies government interference with a functioning family unit.

This does not mean parents have the right to do whatever they choose to their children. Children are not property; they are human beings. Child abuse is condemned by God's Word (Ephesians 6:4; Colossians 3:21), and the willful child abuser can be tried like any other criminal. But God has entrusted the child to the parents' care, and the parents should be given wide latitude in determining how that child should be raised.

What may seem like child abuse or neglect to one may be merely a different philosophy or method of raising children. A social worker who believes children should never be spanked is likely to think that a parent who spanks his children is barbaric and abusive. That parent may think the social worker is overly permissive. Verses such as Proverbs 13:24, 22:15, and 23:13-14 give clues as to who is right, but each parent should be free within reasonable limits to determine what method of parenting works best. I have seen child abuse allegations

---

9. Frederick J. Ludwig, "History of Significance of Immaturity for Responsibility", *Youth and the Law* (1955), pp. 12-19); reprinted in Fox, supra, pp. 429-30.

brought over such issues as feeding schedules and amounts, even though there were experts supporting both the parents' opinion and the social worker's viewpoint.

Those who favor more government intervention with the family assume that once the child is placed in the benevolent hands of the state, his problems will cease. Nothing could be further from the truth. The state's record in caring for children is far from enviable. Dr. Vincent DeFrancis, Director of the Children's Division of the American Humane Asociation, claims countless children are shifted from one foster home to another for many of the formative years of their lives, simply because it is easier to obtain government funds for foster care programs than to try to salvage home situations. He believes that a good caseworker could salvage a minimum of twenty-five homes per year without placing the children outside the home, and the cost of doing so would be far less than foster care. Even though the child's home situation may be less than desirable, Dr. DeFrancis says, the effect of taking him out of that home and placing him in a strange foster home is traumatic and damaging. Even the most abused child, he says, does not want to be separated from the only home he has ever known. Even though most foster parents are undoubtedly loving and dedicated to the welfare of children, foster care can in many cases do more harm than good.[10]

And when the state places children in institutions, its record is no better. As the West Virginia Supreme Court of Appeals recently noted, "It is generally recognized that the greatest colleges for crime are prisons and reform schools."[11] And Martin Guggenheim writes in *Children's Rights Report*:

> The juvenile justice system appears to be little more than an excuse to circumvent basic rights of Americans. . . .
>
> In 1973, for example, a Texas federal court revealed that a juvenile court judge had found delinquent and ordered the incarceration of seventy-five children who had never even appeared in court. Additionally, hundreds of children were found confined in the juvenile prison system who had never been represented by counsel.
>
> Bear in mind that this is many years after Gault. . . .
>
> The State as an Abuser of Children
>
> Regardless of the facts, people in the juvenile justice system cannot overcome the myth that state intervention is good for children. This is true despite the fact that the reality of the system has been graphically exposed time and again. Consider what the state of Texas had done to its children in the 1970's.
>
> When new children (known as "fresh fish") were admitted to the Mountain View State School for Boys, they were regularly beaten by other

10. Dr. Vincent DeFrancis, Lecture, National College of Juvenile Justice, University of Nevada, Reno, Nevada, March 1, 1977.

11. *State Ex Rel. Harris V. Calendine*, 233 S.E. 2d 318 (1977).

boys at the facility as an initiation rite, under the supervision of the guards. Guards also employed a system of "racking": Boys were lined up against a wall with their hands in their pockets while a correctional officer punched each one in the stomach. Documented reports from Mountain View include the case of one boy who was hit and kicked by a guard until knocked unconcious and another boy who was knocked down and had tear gas sprayed in his face for not answering questions about why he had attempted suicide. Another boy struck by a guard ended up "with a hole going straight through" his eardrum.

Some of the less shocking included work details established by the institution. In one work detail, known as "picking," boys were forced to line up foot to foot with their heads down and were required to strike the ground with heavy picks swung overhead as the line moved forward. They did this for five hours at a time with three fifteen-minute breaks. During the breaks, all were required to sit with their head between their legs looking down without talking. In a second detail, aptly called "grass pulling," boys were required to bend from the waist with their knees straight and pull grass out of the ground without talking or looking at one another for six hours a day. If they bent their knees they were "racked" or otherwise beaten. It is perhaps unnecessary to add that nothing was ever planted in these fields. The work was ordered solely for discipline. . . .

. . . the Texas abuses can in no way be considered isolated, and they do condemn the entire system.

In New York State, for example, at least until three years ago, children who were confined to the training schools were subjected to solitary confinement, lasting occasionally up to seven days, hog-tied (the binding together of hands and feet behind their backs) and the indiscriminate injection of thorazine to control excited behavior. Moreover, more than half of the children subjected to these conditions never committed a crime. (The same was true in Texas.)

Far from being isolated, state abuse of children is the most rampant problem we face. The state is by far, the greater abuser of children in this country. And the abuse is imposed, it is to be remembered, not as punishment, but for the children's "own good."

Instead of citing examples of abuse at Mountain View in Texas, I could have chosen to illustrate the conditions found to exist in New York's Willowbrook School for the Retarded. There children have been allowed to choke to death because of an insufficient number of staff to supervise and assist children when eating meals. An additional example of state abuse of children involves New York's foster care system. The New York City Comptroller's office reported this year that some 11,000 children had been kept in foster care status "an average of 5 and ½ years longer than necessary" and that the foster care agencies regularly move children from foster home to foster home, often causing permanent damage, preventing them from becoming happy, loving and trusting adults.[12]

12. Martin Guggenheim, "A Call to Abolish the Juvenile Justice System," *II Children's Rights Report No. 9*, June 1978; reprinted in Fox, supra, pp. 50-53.

One might well protest that these are the exceptions, not the rule. Certainly there are many institutions where such conditions do not exist. But likewise, parental abuse of children is the exception rather than the rule. Most parents love their children dearly and raise them well. On the whole, parents do a far better job of raising children than does the state.

This should not be surprising. God has placed children in the care of their parents, and He has created in parents a natural love for their children that far surpasses any love the state can provide.

State intervention is sometimes necessary, but it should be the exception rather than the rule, and it should be allowed only after all else has failed. And the goal of state intervention, is at all possible, should be to restore the family, not tear it apart.

The family is God's order for the human race.

Let us disturb it only with the greatest hesitation.

And when we must disturb the family, let us do so as little as possible, and as briefly as possible.

Chapter 33

The Priest-Penitent Privilege

In nineteenth-century France, a Catholic priest was charged with murder. A widow had been found murdered, and circumstantial evidence pointed to Father Pierre. The priest could have cleared himself, for he knew who really committed the crime. The true murderer had revealed his deed to Father Pierre in the confessional, but a Catholic priest takes a vow to keep such matters confidential. So Father Pierre allowed himself to be convicted of murder and sentenced to life imprisonment rather than reveal a privileged communication. Not until he had served more than twenty years of his sentence—much of it on Devil's Island—did the truth come out as the murderer confessed on his deathbed.[1]

The issue of privileged communications again raised its head in Collin County, Texas, during the summer of 1981. In that case a Presbyterian pastor refused to answer questions about a woman he had counseled. A Texas District Court Judge found him in contempt of court and sentenced him to three days in jail and a $600 fine, in apparent defiance of a Texas statute that allows pastors to refuse to testify on matters told to them in counseling or confession. The sentence was reversed on appeal to the Texas Court of Criminal Appeals.[2]

A "privileged communication" is a statement made in confidence to one of certain classes of persons, which is kept confidential and cannot be used in court. The law recognizes that it is in the best interest of society that full communication be allowed certain types of relationships, and that such full communication can be preserved only if participants can be assured that their communications will be kept confidential.

1. Tom Dowling, "The Unfrocked One", *Liberty*, May/June 1981, p.23. God's plan is working even through such misfortunes as this. Father Pierre spent his life ministering to his fellow prisoners, and even after he was cleared of the crime, he refused to leave the prison.

2. *Church and State*, November 1981, p. 22; *Tulsa World*, July 16, 1981.

For example, communications between a lawyer and his client are privileged. A lawyer could not prepare a proper defense for his client if he does not know all of the facts, so it is essential that a client tell a lawyer everything. A client could not do that if the lawyer could be subpoenaed to testify in court. There are a few exceptions to the attorney-client privilege, such as threats to commit a crime in the future or acknowledgements of fraud perpetrated upon the courts; but in general comments made between an attorney and his client are privileged.

Another example is the doctor-patient privilege. To treat a patient properly, a doctor needs to know the facts. So he asks, "How did you get this leg wound?" And the patient answers, "Jones stabbed me with a butcher knife while I was robbing him." If doctors could be required to testify in court as to what patients tell them, patients will not tell doctors the truth, and this could hinder proper medical treatment. In most jurisdictions the same privilege applies to communications between a patient and his psychotherapist.

Communications between husband and wife have generally been considered confidential, though there are exceptions such as when the husband has beaten the wife and one is suing the other. The family is important as the basic unit of society, and the family is best preserved when its members are free to communicate with one another without the fear that one will be called upon to testify against the other. It is also based in part on the biblical view that a husband and wife are "one flesh" and one cannot be required to incriminate the other anymore than one can be required to incriminate himself. Unfortunately, the attack on the family in contemporary society has been accompanied by an erosion of the husband-wife privilege. The privilege applies only to communications between husbands and wives, not children and parents, except in New York where parent-child communications are privileged as well. The present movement to extend this protection to parent-child communications elsewhere in the nation should be encouraged.

A privileged communication that has gained much attention in recent years is the newsman-informant privilege. Many journalists believe they should not be required to reveal the sources of information given to them in confidence, as this would erode confidential news tips. This privilege did not exist at common law, but it is protected by the laws of several states.

Some privileged communications are discretionary, others are mandatory. In Arkansas, a pastor may not be compelled to testify against his parishioner on matters told to him in confidence, but he may testify if he chooses. It is the pastor's choice. In Michigan and New York, however, the choice is the parishioner's. Even if the pastor wants to testify, he may not if the parishioner objects. Only the parishioner can waive the privilege,[3] and usually only the parishioner can invoke it.

3. David W. Louisell, John Kaplan, and Jon R. Waltz, *Principles of Evidence and Proof*, (Mineola, New York: Foundation Press, 1977), pp. 621-22.

Background of the Clergyman-Parishioner Privilege

Research into the historical origins of this privilege reveals some very divergent claims. Klein, for example, says, "It is well recognized that there was no common law privilege in the case of confidential communications or confessions made to a clergyman."[4] The protection, he says, is purely a matter of state statute, though most states have passed laws protecting the privilege.[5] But Underhill says that "By the early common law, following the rule of the modern Roman and canon law, statements made to a priest in a confession were privileged, except, perhaps, in case of high treason."[6]

Klein's statement that there was no priest-penitent privilege at common law seems to be a faith assumption of many courts and commentators. However, I believe it can be demonstrated that there is a basis for this privilege, at least in the early (pre-Restoration, 1660 A.D.) common law.

Greenleaf agrees with Underhill that the privilege did exist in Roman law: "The Roman law adopted this principle in its fullest extent; not only excepting such confessions from the general rules of evidence, as we have already intimated, but punishing the priest, who revealed them."[7] (By Roman law is apparently meant not the early pre-Christian law of Rome but the later, Christianized Justinian Code.)

The privilege seems to have been recognized in early England. Wigmore cites a 1606 case in which the Superior of the Jesuits refused to answer certain questions because he was "bound to keep the secrets of Confession." When the Earl of Nottingham asked him whether, if one confessed to him today that he planned to kill the king tomorrow, he would reveal it, the Superior replied that he would conceal it. No attempt was made to compel the Superior to answer questions dealing with confidential confessions.[8] In 1945, Justice Duffy, an Irish judge, upheld the privilege, saying, "I have no doubt that the seal of the confessional was respected in the courts of England before the Reformation . . . and its recognition before the Norman Conquestion in 1066 seems to be proved."[9]

Since the Protestant Reformation (others say, since the Restoration of the monarchy in England in 1660), the privilege has been much more limited. Unlike a private person, a priest or pastor need not report a crime to the authorities if he learned of it in confidence, but he could be required to testify

---

4. Irving J. Klein, *Law of Evidence for Police* (St. Paul: West Publishing Co., 1978), p. 151.

5. Ibid.

6. H. C. Underhill, *A Treatise on the Law of Criminal Evidence, 4th Ed.*, Revised and Edited by John L. Niblack (Indianapolis: Bobbs-Merrill Publishing Co.), 1898, 1935), §340, pp. 653-55.

7. Simon Greenleaf, *A Treatise on the Law of Evidence*, Vol. I (New York: Arno Press, 1842, 1972), §247, pp. 279-81.

8. *Garnett's Trial*, 2 How. St. Tr. 218, 255 (1606); cited by John Henry Wigmore, *Evidence in Trails at Common Law*, Revised by John T. McNaughton (Boston: Little, Brown & Co., 1961), Vol. VIII, §2394, p. 869.

9. *Cook v. Carroll*, Ir. R. 515, 517 (High Ct., 1945), cited by Wigmore, Vol. VIII, §2394, p. 871.

about it if subpoenaed.[10] The reasons for this limitation are not well articulated anywhere. Perhaps the underlying reason was the rising anti-Catholic sentiment during the Reformation and the Protestant desire to displace the priesthood from its elevated and privileged position. But before the Reformation there is good reason to believe the privilege did exist and was widely respected.

Regardless of its common law status, the privilege is well recognized by statute. More than two-thirds of the states of the United States have enacted statutes to protect it; these include Alaska, Arizona, Arkansas, California, Colorado, Florida, Georgia, Hawaii, Idaho, Indiana, Iowa, Kansas, Kentucky, Louisiana, Maryland, Minnesota, Missouri, Montana, Nebraska, Nevada, New Jersey, New Mexico, New York, North Dakota, Ohio, Oklahoma, Oregon, Puerto Rico, South Dakota, Utah, Vermont, Washington, West Virginia, Wisconsin, and Wyoming. In addition, Pennsylvania has recognized the privilege by a court decision.[11] Even in states that do not expressly recognize the privilege, prosecutors and judges are usually reluctant to intrude upon the confidentiality of the priest-penitent relationship.

The priest-penitent privilege (often called the clergyman-parishioner privilege, since it obviously applies to Protestants as well as Catholics) is based in part on the utilitarian principle that the interest of society is best served if parishioners are allowed to make full disclosure to their pastors without having to fear that their confessions will be used against them in court. Partly it is to protect the minister or priest from being placed in a very difficult situation, since in many cases their denominations require they swear not to disclose such confidences. Partly it is to protect the religious liberty of the parishioner. In many denominations, confession to a pastor or a priest is either a sacrament or at least a rite of great religious significance. Denying the right to confess in confidence could have a chilling effect upon the free exercise of religion.

At least one court has recognized that the priest-penitent privilege is protected by the First Amendment. In 1855 a man was tried for allegedly having killed his wife, and the Very Reverend John Teeling was summoned to testify as to what the wife had told him in her dying confession. He refused to testify, saying, "Any statement made in her sacramental confession, whether inculpatory or exculpatory of the prisoner, I am not at liberty to reveal." The lower court ordered him to reveal the wife's statement (perhaps disclosing who had killed her); but the presiding judge of the circuit court reversed, saying:

> I regard any infringement upon the tenets of any denomination as a viola-
> tion of the fundamental law, which guarantees perfect freedom to all classes
> in the exercise of their religion. To encroach upon the confessional, which
> is well understood to be a fundamental tenet in the Catholic Church, would
> be to ignore the Bill of Rights, so far as it is applicable to that Church.

10. Greenleaf, Vol. I, §247, p. 283.
11. Wigmore, Vol. VIII, §2395, pp. 873-76.

In view of these circumstances, as well as of other considerations connected with the subject, I feel no hesitation in ruling that a priest enjoys a privilege of exemption from revealing what is communicated to him in the confessional.[12]

The Application of the Privilege Today

As we have noted, the vast majority of states have statutes protecting the priest-penitent privilege. These statutes vary somewhat, and consequently the precise application of the privilege in any particular state depends upon the precise wording of the statute and how the courts of that state interpret the statute. Nevertheless, some general principles apply in most cases.

Who is Covered?

The privilege applies to communications made to a clergyman or similar church official. The precise wording varies from state to state. Arizona speaks of a "clergyman or priest." Arkansas protects a "minister of the gospel or priest of any denomination." California establishes the privilege for a "clergyman, priest or religious practitioner of an established church." Florida provides that "no minister of the gospel, no priest of the Catholic church, no rector of the Episcopal Church, no ordained rabbi, no practitioner of Christian Science, and no regular minister of religion or any religious organization or denomination usually referred to as a church" shall be required to testify. South Dakota simply protects one who acts as a "spiritual advisor." These are typical of the wording of most state statutes.

It would seem clear that anyone who serves as a regular minister of an established church would be protected under most statutes. A "regular minister" would probably be one who performs the functions normally performed by a minister in most churches. If he is ordained and licensed, and paid a salary, that might help establish his credentials to a court, but it should not be necessary. If he regularly preaches and counsels parishioners on spiritual matters, and if no other person in the church more closely fits the definition of a "minister," he would probably qualify.

What about other church officials, such as elders, deacons, Sunday school teachers, and the like? The law is unsettled. In *Reutkemeier v. Nolte*, 179 Iowa 342, 161 N.W. 290 (1917), the Iowa Supreme Court recognized a Presbyterian elder as a "minister of the Gospel" within the meaning of the Iowa statute, and consequently a communication to those elders was ruled to be privileged. Even though the elders did not occupy full time, salaried positions in the church, the court noted the lifelong call of Presbyterian elders and the high respect accorded to them in the church. But an Indiana court ruled in *Knight v. Lee*, 80 Ind. 201 (1881), that an elder and deacon of the Christian Church was not a clergyman within the meaning of the statute.

---

12. Louisell, Kaplan and Waltz, p. 622. The authors note that the records of the case were lost in the Civil War, so little more is known about it.

The law is also unsettled as to parachurch employees, such as staff members of Campus Crusade for Christ or Young Life, who frequently counsel young persons. A recent federal case, *In Re Verplank*, 329 F. Supp. 433 (1971), held that the privilege applied to draft counselors, some of whom were not ordained clergymen, but who were workers under the direction of a clergyman. *In Re Murtha*, 115 N.J. Super 380, 279 A2d 889 (1971), held that communications to a Catholic nun were not privileged since she served as a school teacher and did not exercise any priestly functions, but there were specific facts in that case that made it unique. A similar ruling denied the privilege of a communication to an apparently unordained employee of the Catholic Welfare Association of Minneapolis (*State v. Lender*, 124 NW2d 355, Minn. 1963).

What if a church secretary overhears a counseling session? In all probability the privilege applies to her as well.[13] If the secretary or other church person is considered an agent of the church or pastor and is present to assist the pastor in his counseling work, there should be no problem. But the general rule is that communications made in the presence of third parties are not privileged because there is no confidentiality.

The privilege seems to apply to anyone who comes to a pastor for counseling; it is not limited to members of the pastor's church.[14]

What Situations are Covered?

The parishioner must have come to the pastor for counseling. A mere casual conversation on the golf course normally will not be sufficient to invoke the privilege. There could, of course, be circumstances in which a pastor might counsel someone on the golf course, and the privilege would apply. But it would be more difficult to convince a court that it was an actual counseling session in the course of pastoral duties, than if the session took place in the pastor's office. In one case a person met a priest on the train and confessed a crime to him, and that was held to be nonprivileged.[15]

In other than an office situation, to make sure the privilege applies it would be advisable to state in clear language at the beginning of the counseling session that pastor and parishioner both understand this to be a counseling session in which the priest-penitent privilege of confidentiality does apply. Though that won't necessarily guarantee that it applies, it may help to convince a court of the intentions of the counseling session.

What Types of Statements are Covered?

Verbal statements are obviously covered, though some cases have held that these are limited to confessional or penitential statements—those admitting some

---

13. *Cimijotti V. Paulsen*, 219 F.Supp. 621 (1963), appeal dismissed 323 F.2d 716 (D.C. Iowa 1963); cf *People v. Brown* 368 N.Y.S.2d 645, 82 Misc.2d 115 (1974).

14. *Matter of Swenson*, 183 Minn 602, 237 N.W. 589 (1931).

15. *State v. Brown*, 95 Iowa 381, 64 N.W. 277 (1895).

type of wrongdoing.[16] Letters and other written communications are also likely to be held privileged so long as they are written directly to the pastor, in confidence, and as part of counseling or confession; but evidence turned over to a pastor or priest, such as a stolen watch, is not. A statement made to a pastor with the intent that the pastor communicate it to a third party ("Tell my wife I said this. . . .") is not privileged.[17]

The courts disagree as to whether the pastor's personal observations about the parishioner's demeanor, actions, etc., during counseling are privileged. An Iowa court has held that such observations are privileged; a Missouri court has held that they are not.[18]

In most situations the privileged status of a confession or counseling session should be clear. In the difficult or borderline cases it may be necessary to seek advice from a competent attorney.[19]

16. *In the Matter of Swenson*, 237 N.W. 589, 183 Minn. 602 (1931).

17. *Gilhooley v. State*, 58 Ind. 182; *Milburn v. Haworth*, 47 Colo. 593, 108 P 155 (1910).

18. *Boyles v. Cora*, 232 Iowa 822, 6 N.W.2d 401; *State v. Kurtz*, 564 S.W.2d 856 (Missouri 1978).

19. Since writing this chapter, an excellent book has come to my attention: *The Right to Silence*, William Harold Tiemann and John C. Bush (Nashville: Abington Press, 1983). Tiemann & Bush cover privileged communications in great detail and thoroughly refute the notion that the privilege did not exist in pre-Reformation common law. Their appendix which contains the statutes of the various states is most helpful.

Chapter 34

Clergy Malpractice

Malpractice!

The very word sends shivers up the spines of doctors and lawyers. In the state of California, medical malpractice can cost a doctor as much as $20,000 a year, and a lawyer as much as $4,000 a year. Elsewhere costs are less extreme, but still high and rising. A pastor might well ask, "Could this happen to me?"

It has happened. In the fall of 1979 a story surfaced about a pastor who had counseled a woman and suggested a trial separation from her husband. Incensed over this, the husband shot and wounded her. Claiming that the pastor had given her bad advice and that this advice had led to the shooting, the woman brought a malpractice action against the pastor. An article in the March-April 1980 issue of *Liberty Magazine* suggested that this story was purely fiction, a "plant" by an insurance company to sell malpractice insurance.[1] But in a later *Liberty Magazine* article, the attorney for Church Mutual Insurance Company claimed that the incident did take place, as he handled it personally, but that the plaintiff subsequently dropped the case.[2]

Another widely publicized case occurred in Burbank, California. In 1979 an emotionally disturbed seminary student, twenty-four years old, committed suicide. In March, 1980, his parents sued Grace Community Church of the Valley, its pastor and staff, asking an unspecified amount of damages, and alleging liability on three counts. First, they claimed that the pastor and staff had discouraged and thus effectively prevented their son from seeing psychiatrists or other professional help outside the church, and had instead simply counseled him to read the Bible, pray, listen to taped sermons, and counsel with church counselors. This, they said, was clergy malpractice, especially since the church officials knew that the young man was depressed and had suicidal tendencies. Second, they claimed the church was negligent

---

1. Maury M. Breecher, "Ministerial Malpractice", *Liberty Magazine*, March-April 1980.
2. John F. Cleary, "To Insure or Not to Insure?", *Liberty Magazine*, July-August 1980, pp. 14-15.

in its selection and training of lay spiritual counselors and that these counselors were negligently unavailable to the young man when he needed and requested them. Third, the parents (who were Catholic) alleged that the church and its staff engaged in "outrageous conduct" by ridiculing and disparaging the Catholic faith.

The church filed a demurrer, arguing that any actions taken or recommendations made by Grace Community Church and its staff were protected by the First Amendment and therefore not within the jurisdiction of the California Superior Court. The court overruled the demurrer, ruling that the parents' charges, if true, constituted a cause of action.

The church then filed an answer to the parents' claim. Contrary to the parents allegations, the church claimed the young man was seen by at least eight physicians, psychologists, and psychiatrists in the few months before he committed suicide. According to the church, the staff had made appointments for him and repeatedly encouraged him to keep them, and had recommended that the young man undergo psychiatric hospitalization, which he refused.[3]

The court then granted a summary judgment dismissing the parents' claim,[4] and ministers all across the country breathed a sigh of relief.

For those unduly anxious over clergy malpractice, remember that very few such cases have ever been filed. So far as I can determine, not a single such case has ever been won by a plaintiff anywhere in America.

But I also warn against undue apathy. The *Nally v. Grace Community Church of the Valley* dismissal has been appealed. And regardless of the result on appeal, the court did not hold that a clergyman could never be sued for malpractice, only that there was insufficient proof of malpractice in that case. Another case could be different.

Suing a pastor for malpractice might seem incredible today, but a few decades ago no one ever thought of suing a doctor or a lawyer. Now such suits are commonplace, and becoming more so. There are many activities in which a clergyman could possibly be sued for malpractice. Here are a few: (1) Giving advice that turns out to be wrong and causes unfortunate results. (2) Allegedly causing trauma or psychological damage to impressionable persons (especially young children) by preaching about hellfire or developing guilt feelings about sin. (3) Defaming the character of a person in a sermon or other communication (see chapter 19 dealing with defamation). (4) Assuming a role for which one is unqualified, such as a pastor acting as a psychiatrist when he has had little or no psychiatric training. (5) Refusing or failing to refer a counselee to a physician, psychiatrist, or other professional when such a professional is needed. (6) Causing alienation of affection by urging a husband or wife to divorce

---

3. Samuel E. Ericsson, "*Clergy Malpractice: Constitutional and Political Issues*" (Oak Park, Illinois: Center for Law and Religious Freedom, May 1981), pp. 2-4.

4. "Clergy Malpractice Suit", *Church and State*, November 1981, pp. 21-22.

his or her spouse. (7) Making improper sexual advances, a charge which is difficult to refute even when totally false.

What is Malpractice?

Professor William L. Prosser is widely recognized as the nation's foremost authority on tort law, the law of negligence. He identifies four elements that have to be proven in order to establish negligence and liability.

First, Prosser says, there must be a *legal duty to conform to a certain standard.* Everyone is required to obey the rules of the road while driving so as not to endanger the safety of other persons. In the absence of a clearly defined rule or standard, conduct is judged by the standard of a "reasonable man": Would a reasonably prudent man have acted similarly under similar circumstances?

A professional person is judged by a different standard. In the absence of rules of his profession, he is judged by the standard of a reasonable practitioner of his profession. The doctor who performs an appendectomy has a duty to his patient to use the skill and learning commonly possessed by members of his profession in good standing, and a specialist will be judged by the standard of specialists. The fact that he has followed the customary procedure in his community is evidence of freedom from negligence, but it is not conclusive. If a clergyman were to advise a wife to leave her husband, and a jury were to find that a reasonably prudent clergyman would not have done so, that might be a basis for malpractice. Likewise, if a clergyman were to advise a parishioner that he should not see a psychiatrist, and a jury were to find that a reasonably prudent clergyman would have advised that parishioner to see a psychiatrist, that again might be the basis for a malpractice action.

Second, there must be a *failure to conform to the required standard.* The ordinary person, in other words, must have failed to obey the rules of the road or conduct himself as a reasonably prudent man. The doctor who performed the appendectomy must have failed to use the commonly accepted surgical procedures or must have failed to conduct himself as a reasonably prudent doctor. Similarly, the clergyman must have breached his duty to exercise due care toward his parishioners.

Third, there must be a *reasonably close causal connection between the negligent conduct and the resulting injury.* This is commonly called "proximate cause" or "legal cause." The defendant's negligent failure to obey the rules of the road (i.e., driving in the left lane, or failing to signal) must have been the cause of the accident. The doctor's failure to use reasonable care (such as not using the proper anesthetic) must have caused the patient's death or injury. The clergyman's negligent advice or conduct must have caused the harm to the parishioner. For example, if the *Nally* case had gone to court, a causal connection might have been established by having psychiatrists testify to a strong likelihood that the young man's suicide could have been prevented if he had been hospitalized or given psychiatric help. It would then be up to the jury to decide whether to believe that testimony.

Fourth, there must be *actual loss or damage.*[5] In the *Nally* case the loss was the death of the son. Loss or damage in other cases could include psychological disturbance, mental anguish, physical injury, or financial loss.

Unique Problems of Clergy Malpractice

Medical malpractice and legal malpractice are difficult areas of law, but clergy malpractice promises to be even more so. The third and fourth elements mentioned above for tort liability—proximate cause and actual loss—are very difficult to evaluate, especially in a clergy malpractice case. Who really can measure "damage" or "loss" when the clergyman's mission is primarily spiritual? How do we measure emotional trauma which may result from hearing about hell, against the spiritual reward which results from deliverance from sin? When the clergyman counsels "faith" and "repentance," how does anyone know for sure whether the counselee truly followed the clergyman's advice? And who can say with any degree of certainty what would have happened if the pastor had not counseled the woman to separate from her husband, or if he had referred the young man to a psychiatrist? These are highly speculative in any case, and especially so with clergy malpractice.

But the greatest problems rest with the first two elements: duty to conform to a certain standard, and failure to do so. But when does a pastor have a "duty" to conform to a standard? Does such a duty exist whenever he counsels, or only to those who pay for his services, or only to his church members? And by what standard is a pastor to be judged?—Indeed, by what standard *can* a pastor be judged?

One might ask, what about the standard of a reasonably prudent clergyman? But who sets the standard for clergymen? The pastor deals primarily with spiritual matters beyond the jurisdiction or competence of the courts.[6] The Bible-believing pastor looks to the Word of God as his rule or standard of conduct. Is the court then to judge whether the Bible is a valid standard, or how it is to be interpreted?

In marital counseling, the Bible-believing pastor will explain to his counselees the biblical view of marriage and divorce. Perhaps he interprets God's Word as prohibiting divorce, and therefore counsels against it, and a few weeks later one of the spouses is killed in a family quarrel. What court has a right to say that God's Word is wrong, or that the pastor misapplied God's Word?

Let us examine the possible liability for failing to refer a counselee to a psychiatrist. One might argue to a jury that a psychiatrist could have done the counselee a world of good, and that a reasonably prudent clergyman would have recognized that and would have referred him to a psychiatrist. But what if the only psychiatrists in the area are humanists whose views and methods

---

5. William L. Prosser, *Handbook of the Law of Torts* (West Publishing Co., St. Paul Minn. 1971) §30, p. 143.

6. *U.S. v. Ballard*, supra.

are different from or hostile to those of Christians? (This is true of a large segment of the psychiatric profession!) The pastor may with good reason believe that his parishioner would suffer great spiritual damage if he were placed under the care of a non-Christian psychiatrist. He may well believe that he has a Christian duty to protect his parishioner from that type of influence. Denying the pastor his right to counsel his parishioners in that manner might violate the free exercise clause of the First Amendment.

If the court recognizes the methods of modern psychiatry and requires pastors to substantially conform to those standards, this might also constitute an establishment of religion. The pastor believes in good faith that his methods, and not those of the psychiatrist, are the best means of treating his parishioner's problems. It is impossible to separate the religious realm from the psychiatric realm. The psychiatrist and his methods are influenced just as much by his religious world view as the pastor and his methods are influenced by his world view. As Samuel Ericsson, special counsel for the Center for Law and Religious Freedom and attorney for Grace Community Church in the *Nally* case, has said, ". . . it is impossible to separate the 'cure of minds' from the 'cure of souls'. . . . For nearly 2,000 years pastors, priests, rabbis and other spiritual counselors in churches have been providing the balm for those suffering from depression, guilt and anxiety."[7]

If the minister is involved in the practice of psychology, the psychologist is just as involved in the practice of religion. Sigmund Freud strongly believed that psychoanalysis was not a specialized branch of medicine; rather, he described it as within the realm of religion:

> (T)he words, "secular pastoral worker," might well serve as a general formula for describing the function (of) the analyst . . . We do not seek to bring (the patient) relief by receiving him into the catholic, protestant or socialist community. We seek rather to enrich him from his own internal sources. . . . Such activity as this is pastoral work in the best sense of the words.[8]

Carl Jung, whose renown in psychiatry is second only to that of Freud, has said that

> . . . most cases the sufferer consults the doctor in the first place, because he supposes himself to be physically ill . . . that is why patients force the psycho-therapist into the role of a priest, and expect and demand of him that he shall free them from their distress. That is why we psycho-therapists must occupy ourselves with problems which, strictly speaking, belong to the theologian.[9]

7. Ericsson, p. 6.

8. Sigmund Freud, quoted by Thomas S. Szasz, *The Theology of Therapy: The Breach of the First Amendment Through the Medicalization of Morals, New York University Review of Law and Social Change,* Vol. V., No. 2(1975), 127, 133-135; quoted by Ericsson, pp. 6-8.

9. Carl Jung, quoted by Szasz, quoted by Ericsson, ibid.

If a person is a homosexual, what is best—that he accept and act out his homosexuality, as some psychiatrists would advise; or that he confess his sin of homosexuality to God and seek deliverance from it through God's power? Does a court have a right to decide that?

Or what if a person is suffering from guilt? Should he rationalize his guilt, as many psychiatrists would suggest; or should he recognize that his guilt feelings are due to the fact of sin, and that he needs to trust Christ's atoning death on the Cross as his salvation from sin? Is this a proper subject for a court to decide?

Prosser has noted in other areas of negligence law that

> The courts have been compelled to recognize that there are areas in which even experts will disagree. Where there are different schools of medical thought, it is held that the dispute cannot be settled by the law, and the doctor is entitled to be judged according to the tenets of the school he professes to follow. This does not mean, however, that any quack, charlatan or crackpot can set himself up as a "school," and so apply his individual ideas without liability. A "school" must be a recognized one with definite principles, and it must be the line of thought of at least a respectable minority of the profession.[10]

So by what school of thought do we judge the clergyman? Should pastors have a separate standard of conduct from psychiatrists and other professionals? What about schools of thought within the clergy? Should Catholics be judged differently from Protestants? Within Protestantism, should Methodists be judged differently from Baptists? Should Southern Baptists have a different standard from General Conference Baptists? And what about independent churches—are their pastors to be regarded as "quacks, charlatans, or crackpots"? There are as many schools of thought within psychology as within organized religion. Even Christian psychologists hold a wide divergence of viewpoints—Dr. Jay Adams and Dr. Clyde Narramore are both committed Christians, yet their viewpoints and methods differ considerably.

Let us remember the three-prong test of *Lemon v. Kurtzman* for determining whether government activity constitutes an establishment of religion: (1) Does it have a secular purpose? (2) Does it either advance or inhibit religion? (3) Does it involve excessive entanglement with religion? If the court were to adopt the standards of the modern psychiatric profession (which themselves are highly subjective and disputed among psychiatrists) and require clergymen to conform to them in their counseling, would the court not be advancing the humanistic religions held by many psychiatrists and inhibiting the fundamentalist religion of many pastors? And by determining which branch of pastoring is the norm and using it as the standard of conduct to which all reasonably prudent pastors must conform, is the court not engaged in "excessive entanglement" with religion?

10. Prosser, §32, p. 163.

For constitutional and policy reasons, clergy malpractice is one area of law that the courts would be well advised to leave alone. The courts have neither the competence nor the authority to decide such matters.

Suggestions for Avoiding Clergy Malpractice Suits

No one can guarantee that the courts will not get involved in clergy malpractice suits in the future. The courts have handed down some astonishing decisions in recent years. The following suggestions may help the clergyman who wants to minimize the risk of malpractice suits. If any of them conflict with your calling or your duties, feel free to disregard them—at your own risk

(1) Avoid trying to run other people's lives. Share the Word of God and its precepts with them, and lay the possible options before them, but let them choose what action to take.

(2) Make clear to your counselees that they are seeing you voluntarily. Do not pressure them to come to you or to accept your counsel.

(3) It might help your case in court if you had your counselees sign releases, prior to your counseling them, something to this effect:

I hereby state that I have some to Pastor _____ voluntarily to seek his counseling. I hereby release Pastor _____ and _____ Church from any and all liability for the results of this counseling.

You will have to decide for yourself whether obtaining such releases would hinder your ministry.

(4) Do not promise results. Do not guarantee that you will repair their marriages, restore their emotional balance, or make them popular with their friends. Promise only that you will do your best, and hope that with God's help, that will be enough.

(5) Keep records of your counseling sessions, as there could be disagreement later as to what you told them. Ideally, it would be wise to tape record counseling sessions. But if you advise the counselee that you are taping the session, he might not talk freely with you, and doing it secretly raises serious ethical problems and may be illegal in some states. It probably makes more sense to make notes after each counseling session—but by all means, keep those notes confidential! And don't talk about your counselees, even to your spouse—and especially not in sermon illustrations, whether the counselee is named or not!

(6) Recognize your limits. If you are not qualified to do certain types of counseling, don't do it until you are qualified. It is unwise to forbid the counselee to seek psychiatric help. If emotional problems appear, you might do well to recommend such help. (Similar principles might apply to the faith healer and his relationship to the medical profession.) A few such professionals may be in your area who are Christian or whose views are at least compatible with the Christian view, and you can cultivate a working relationship with them.

(7) If possible, it is best to avoid being alone while counseling someone of the opposite sex. Emotionally troubled persons, especially those with

marital problems, can easily form romantic attachments, and whether real or fantasized, allegations of sexual misconduct can ruin your ministry and marriage and possibly be a basis for a malpractice suit or even criminal charges. Whenever possible, it is wise to have your secretary, your wife, or a church member present while you do such counseling—or if that is not possible, at least leave the door ajar.

(8) The possiblity that someone might claim psychological trauma or damage due to your preaching about hellfire always exists. It is difficult to guard against this possibility without compromising the Word of God. Probably the best protection is to preach the whole counsel of God, the Gospel as well as the Law. While preaching hellfire, also preach deliverance through Christ.

(9) The best way to avoid malpractice suits is—Don't malpractice! Always remember that you are not playing games, you are dealing with people's lives—now and eternally. This should cause you to practice a higher standard than the humanistic psychiatrist. Remember, also, that you have a source of help that the non-Christian counselor does not have—prayer and the Word of God.

Malpractice Insurance—Yes or No?

Several companies, such as Church Mutual Insurance Company of Wisconsin, have recently begun to offer malpractice insurance to clergymen, similar to that offered to doctors and lawyers. Many have criticized this type of insurance as a big money-making scheme by insurance companies, playing upon unfounded fears over a few isolated lawsuits.[11]

However, clergy malpractice insurance should not be lightly dismissed. We do not know what the future holds, and the widespread publicity over the *Nally* case could encourage others to file malpractice claims. Such a claim, if successful, could destroy an unprotected ministry.

Most pastors could not afford the legal costs of a malpractice suit. Most—if not all—clergy malpractice policies, like other types of malpractice insurance and liability insurance in general, should pay the cost of defense in a lawsuit as well as any liability. This protection could be valuable.

Malpractice and liability policies generally provide that the client cooperate with the insurance company in defending against such a lawsuit. This means a full disclosure of all facts relevant to the case. Refusal to divulge such information to the insurance company, could cancel coverage. While it has not yet been decided, a court could maintain that the information is not privileged in a clergy malpractice suit, since the counselee has effectively waived the privilege by bringing the lawsuit. Make sure the policy spells out what happens under those circumstances.

At the present time, the risk of being sued for malpractice is very low. Most clergy malpractice insurance premiums are very low, at least at present. The church could provide the coverage or the pastor could pay the premiums. They're tax deductible as a professional or business expense.

11. Breecher, op cit.

Church Liability Insurance

Could your church be sued?

Prior to 1942, churches and charitable organizations were immune from lawsuits in most states. It was thought that the money contriubuted to charities was held in trust for charitable purposes and should not be diverted to pay for liability claims. It was also believed that the "good Samaritan" who devoted himself to charitable causes should not be punished for an honest mistake, as this was not only unfair but would also discourage people from working for charity. It has been argued that a person benefitting from a charity should not be allowed to sue that charity.

In 1942, that viewpoint began to change. A famous decision by Justice Rutledge[12] started the ball rolling, and today in most states churches and charities can be sued just like any other person or business. As Prosser says,

> The present state of the law is one of rapid overthrow of the immunity of charities, not yet fully accomplished. In its complete form, it still exists only in Maine, New Mexico and South Carolina. In seven other states by statute [Arkansas, Maryland, Louisiana] or without it [Colorado, Georgia, Nebraska, Tennessee], liability is imposed where it is apparent that the assets of the charity will not be depleted by the plaintiff's recovery, as where this is liability insurance—although in most jurisdictions the fact that the defendant is insured usually has been held to make no difference. Seven other courts [Alabama, Connecticut, Louisiana, New Jersey, North Carolina, Rhode Island, Texas, and Virginia], with more of an emphasis on the "waiver" theory, deny liability to recipients of the benefits of the charity, such as hospital patients or students, but allow recovery by others, such as employees, invitees and strangers. Three more [New Jersey, North Carolina, Ohio] have abolished the immunity as to charitable hospitals, but left it as to religious institutions and other charities.[13]

As Prosser says, this is a rapidly changing field. Prosser wrote in 1971, and the circumstances in many states have changed in recent years. Do not rely upon charitable immunity without obtaining competent local legal advice.

In states that retain charitable immunity, either fully or as to recipients of charity, the protection would in all probability apply to clergy malpractice cases. In others, charitable immunity does not protect the pastor, nor does it protect the church against lawsuits. Such lawsuits could arise from quite a number of events: a church-sponsored ski trip during which a child breaks a leg, a youth fellowship hayride during which someone falls off the hayrack and is injured, an accident while a church official is driving on church business, a fall on slippery church steps, an injury in the nursery, and many others.

For this reason, unless clearly exempted by state law, it is advisable for every

---

12. *President and Director of Georgetown College v. Hughes.* 76 U.S. App. D.C. 123, 130 F.2d 810 (1942).

13. Prosser, §133, pp. 994-95.

church and religious organization to have liability insurance. Not only can it preserve the ministry from financial disaster; it can also provide compensation for a truly injured person.

The Christian Lawyer

"The law of the Lord is perfect, converting the soul. . . ." (Psalm 19:7)

Perhaps some of my readers will be lawyers, law students, or prospective students of the law. To such readers I pose the question: What is a Christian lawyer?

My law school days were frustrating. Those were the Vietnam war years (1967-70), the days of student protests, and the University of Iowa was aflame with talk of radical reform and even revolution. As a young conservative, I rebelled against the school's leftist bias. I expected that sort of thing from undergraduate professors, but for some reason thought law professors should have more sense. I was an immature Christian, not particularly well-versed in the Scriptures. I wanted to serve God through law practice but was confused as to how that could be done.

For many years I was not a Christian lawyer; I was a lawyer who happened to be a Christian. I was active in an evangelical church, studied the Word of God faithfully, witnessed whenever possible, and frequently preached at church and in rescue missions. But it troubled me that my law practive seemed to bear little relation to my Christian life. I wanted to glorify God through my law practice. But the only way I could do so, so far as I could tell, was to practice the highest ethical standards, display a Bible verse on my wall, and occasionally witness to a client or fellow attorney. I did all of these things, but something seemed to be missing. My years as an assistant county attorney, an Air Force judge advocate, a juvenile-court referee, and in private practice were interesting, exciting, and for the most part enjoyable. But I never felt completely fulfilled.

In 1977-80 I was a full-time seminary student, practicing law part time to pay expenses. During this time I began to study the Scriptures and integrate them with my legal philosophy. Partly through cases the Lord sent my way and through my own reading, I became aware of the constitutional issues of religious liberty facing American Christians. I threw myself into the study of these issues—and this book is the result.

What is a Christian lawyer? Let me suggest twelve answers.

First, he is a Christian. That is, he knows that he is redeemed, not by any works that he had done, but by the Finished Work of Jesus Christ on Calvary's Cross (Eph. 2:8-9). He knows that he is a sinner by nature and by choice, condemned to eternal death (Ezk. 18:4; Romans 3:10,23; 6:23). And he knows that he would have no chance of salvation but for the fact that Jesus Christ took on human flesh and died on the cross as his substitute (Romans 5:8-9). He comes to Christ in simple faith and trust, clinging to Him only for his salvation in this life and the next (John 3:16,18).

Second, he is a lawyer. He is not content to just meet the bare minimum standards. Rather, he views his trade as a profession and as an art, and he strives for excellence in all that he does. He takes the Scripture imperative, "whatsoever ye do, do it heartily, as to the Lord" (Colossians 3:23) and applies it to the practice of law.

Third, the Christian lawyer integrates the Scriptures with his philosophy of law. He knows that God's Word has much to say about law, and he strives to bring every thought into captivity to Christ, exercising dominion in His Name. He knows that man's law is not the highest authority. There is a higher law—God's law as revealed in Scripture and conscience—that he proclaims God's law to tyrants and anarchists alike.[1]

Fourth, he understands the legal principles the Founding Fathers wrote into the Constitution of the United States. He knows the American Constitution is based upon biblical principles and a sound view of human nature, and he defends the Constitution against those who would circumvent it and render it impotent by legislation or judicial fiat. He knows that ours is a system of limited government based on delegated powers only, and that the preservation of that concept is essential to the preservation of liberty.

Fifth, he appreciates the Scriptural and constitutional basis of religious liberty. He vigorously defends the right of Christians to worship God, study the Word of God, proclaim the Gospel, practice its teachings, and raise their children in the Christian faith. And he does not spend the bulk of his time criticizing other Christians. Even though he may disagree with the philosophy or strategy of some Christians, he recognizes that all Christians are in a battle against a common enemy, and he does not waste time and energy discrediting them.

Sixth, the Christian lawyer is a spokesman for the Christian community, a bridge between Christians and the world. He goes before Caesar and articulates the concerns of Christians in language Caesar can understand and appreciate.

---

1. In recent years two law schools have been established that teach an integrated view of law and theology and that stress the existence and relevance of God's higher law: O. W. Coburn School of Law, associated with Oral Roberts University, 7777 S. Lewis, Tulsa, Oklahoma 74171; and Simon Greenleaf School of Law, 1530 Shadow Ridge Lane, Orange, California 9266 , founded by Dr. John Warwick Montgomery. Several other Christian groups are contemplating the formation of law schools. The aspiring lawyer might consider attending one of these institutions.

Seventh, he is also the Christians' gladiator, defending the rights of Christians against Caesar's lions in the great arenas, the courts and legislatures of our land.

Eight, he bears witness for Christ through his law practice—to his clients, his fellow attorneys, and others with whom he comes in contact. He bears witness not only by word but also by deed, practicing the highest ethical standards so that others may see Christ in him. He views the canons of ethics as a good starting point for Christian legal conduct, but he does not stop there. He recognizes that the ethical obligations of the Christian lawyer may go beyond the canons of ethics.

Ninth, he knows that he has authority as an officer of the court, and he recognizes God as the source of his authority. Consequently, he uses that authority wisely and humbly in the service of God.

Tenth, he is a servant. Romans 13 describes rulers as "ministers of God," and the word for minister is *diakonos*, meaning servant. He knows that he is a servant both of God and of his fellowman, and he sees his law practice as an opportunity to serve others. He performs immense services for his fellowmen through his law practice. He solves problems, organizes estates, and obtains justice in the courts.

Eleventh, he is a healer. He tries, when possible, to live peaceably with all men, and urges his clients to do likewise. He knows that a lawsuit is a traumatic and costly ordeal for all concerned, plaintiffs, and defendants, winners and losers alike. While he can be a worthy opponent in battle, he tries not to create but to resolve conflict. He tries to bring husbands and wives together, not pull them apart; he tries to bring plaintiffs and defendants to the conference table to resolve their differences.

And twelfth, the Christian lawyer looks to God, through prayer and the Word, as his source of help in the practice of law as in all other things. He knows that God is in sovereign control of history, and that God uses our failures to His glory in His infinitely wise plan. He knows that God controls the judicial system, whether or not the judicial system recognizes that fact: "The king's heart is in the hand of the Lord, as the rivers of water: he turneth it withersoever he will." (Proverbs 21:1). He looks to God's strength for help in battle. He trusts God's plan for comfort and apparent defeat. And he gives God's sovereignty the glory in victory.

This is the Christian lawyer.

Would there were more like him!

Could this be your calling?

"O how love I thy law! it is my meditation all the day."

(Psalm 119:97).

BIBLIOGRAPHY

Adamek, Raymond J. "Abortion and Public Opinion in the United States," *National Right to Life News*, April 22, 1982, insert p. 2.

Adams, Jay. *Competent to Counsel*. Grand Rapids, Mich.: Baker Book House, 1970.

Alabama Alert, Alabama Christian Education Association, Inc. Vol. 6, No. 5, (May 1981), p. 2.

Allem, Warren. "Backgrounds of the Scopes Trial at Dayton, Tennessee," Master's thesis University of Tennessee.

"An Open Forum: Federal Judge Upholds Voluntary Prayer Groups at High School," *Church and State*, June 1983, p. 3.

Anderson, Robert M. *American Law of Zoning*. 5 Volumes, Vol. 1. Rochester, New York: The Lawyers Co-Operative Pub. Co., 1976, p. 453.

Anderson, Tom. "Straight Talk," Lectures at Bob Jones University, Greenville, South Carolina, Oct. 14, 1981.

Antieau, Downey and Roberts. *Freedom from Federal Establishment: Formation and Early History of the First Amendment Religion Clauses*. Milwaukee: Bruce, 1964.

Applegate, James (Ed.). *Adventures in World Literature*. New York: Harcourt, Brace, Jovanovich, 1970.

Arey, L. B. *Developmental Anatomy: A Textbook and Laboratory Manual of Embryology*, 7th Edition. Philadelphia: W. B. Saunders, 1965.

Armand and Porta. Letter to Senator Richard Schweiker, July 12, 1977. *Christian Action Council Resource Manuel*. Washington D.C.: Christian Action Council, nd.

Armour, Rodney. "Values for a Humanistic Society," *Religious Humanism*, Vol. 13, No. 4 (Autumn 1979), p. 168-173.

"Attorney General Opinion, State of California No. 79-524," *The Advocate*. April 1980, p. A-7.

Baalen, Jan Karel Van. *The Chaos of Cults: A Study in Present-Day Isms*. Grand Rapids, Michigan: Eerdmans, 1938, 1965.

Bainton, Roland. *Christian Attitudes Toward War and Peace*. Nashville: Abingdon Press, 1950.

Ball, William. "Federal Court Upholds Right of College to Teach and Advertise Without License from State Board of Education." *The Advocate*, April 1980, p. A-11.

Barnes, Allan C. *Intrauterine Development.* Philadelphia: Lea & Febiger, 1968.

Barry, Alfred. *Smith's Dictionary of the Bible.* ("Law," Vol. 2, p. 1600.) Grand Rapids, Michigan: Baker Book House, 1869, 1971.

Bartz, Paul A. "Luther on Evolution." Master's thesis, Concordia Theological Seminary, Fort Wayne, Indiana, 1977.

Bates, Searle M. *Religious Liberty: An Inquiry.* New York: International Missionary Council, 1945.

Beer, Sir Gaven de. "Evolution," *Encyclopedia Brittanica: Macropedia: Knowledge in Depth.* 30 Volumes. Vol. 10, p. 723. Chicago: Encyclopedia Britannica, 1978.

Bergel, Gary and Koop, C. Everett. "When You Were Formed in Secret." Elyria, Ohio: Intercessors for America, 1980.

Berman, Harold J. *The Interaction of Law and Religion.* Nashville, Tennessee: Parthenon Press, 1974.

Bernard, L. L. and Bernard, Jessie. *Origins of American Sociology.* New York: Russell & Russell, Inc., 1943, 1965.

Beth, Loren P. *The American Theory of Church and State.* Gainesville, Fla.: University of Florida Press, 1958.

Bible-Science Newsletter, Vol. 19, No. 8 (August 1981), p. 8.

Bird, Wendell R. "Freedom of Religion and Science Instruction in Public Schools," *Yale Law Journal.* Vol. 87, No. 3 (January 1978), p. 561.

_____. "Lecture," Bob Jones University, Greenville, South Carolina, October 12, 1981.

Blackstone, Sir William. *Commentaries on the Laws of England.* (orig. pp. 40-43, reprinted as pp. 39-42.) New York: Augustus M. Kelley, 1765, 1803, 1969.

Blau, Joseph L. (Ed.). *Cornerstones of Religious Freedom in America.* Evanston, Ill.: Harper & Row, 1949.

Bliss, Richard B. "Evolutionary Indoctrination and Decision Making in the Schools," *Impact.* June 1983, p. 4.

Blumenfeld, Samuel L. *Is Public Education Necessary.* Old Greenwich, Connecticut: The Devin-Adair Company, 1981.

The Book of Discipline of the United Methodist Church 1980. Nashville: United Methodist Publishing House, 1980.

Botterweck, G. Johannes and Ringgren, Helmer. *Theological Dictionary of the Old Testament.* Translated by John T. Willis. ("Berith," Vol. II, p. 253.) Grand Rapids, Michigan: Eerdmans, 1975.

Breecher, Maury M. "Ministerial Malpractice," *Liberty Magazine*, March-April, 1980.

Buckley, James L. "A Human Life Amendment," *The Human Life Review*, I, New York: The Human Life Foundation, Inc., Winter, 1975, pp. 7-20.

Bullinger, E. W. *The Witness of the Stars*. Grand Rapids, Mich.: Kregel, 1893, 1970.

Burns, Edward McNall. *The American Idea of Mission: Concepts of National Purpose and Destiny*. New Brunswick, New Jersey: Rutgers University Press, 1957.

Burny, Thomas and Kelly, John. *The Secret Life of the Unborn Child*. New York: Summit Books, 1981.

Buzzard, Lynn and Ericsson, Samuel. *The Battle for Religious Liberty*. Elgin, Ill.: David C. Cook, 1982.

Cairns, Huntington. *Law and the Social Sciences*. New York: Augustus M. Kelly, 1935, 1969.

Calvin, John. *Institutes of the Christian Religion, Book IV*. (Vol. 2, p. 1505) Philadelphia: Westminster Press, 1973.

"Case No. 1885, 5 May 1981," *A Newsletter on Taxation and Religion*, Vol. 1, No. 1, (July/August 1981), p. 7.

Cavendish, Richard (Ed.). *Man, Myth and Magic: An Illustrated Encyclopedia of the Supernatural*. New York: Marshall Cavendish Corporation, 1970.

Chafer, Lewis Sperry. *Systemic Theology*. (Vol. 7, pp. 225-226.) Dallas, Texas: Dallas Seminary Press, 1948, 1962.

"Challenge to the Schools," *Tulsa Tribune*, April 14, 1982, p. 1-F.

Chambers, Whittaker. *Witness*. New York: Random House, 1952.

Clark, Robert T. and Bales, James D. *Why Scientists Accept Evolution*. Grand Rapids, Mich.: Baker Book House, 1966.

Clarke, Adam. *Clarke's Commentaries*. Nashville, Tenn.: Abingdon Press.

Cleary, John F. "To Insure or Not to Insure?" *Liberty Magazine*, July-August 1980, pp. 14-15.

"Clergy Malpractice Suit," *Church and State*, November 1981, pp. 21-22.

Cole, R. A. *Zondervan Pictorial Encyclopedia of the Bible*. ("Law and the Old Testament," Vol. 3, p. 884.) Grand Rapids, Michigan: Zondervan, 1975.

"Congress Will Set Doctrine on What Makes TV Fair, Equal," *Tulsa World*, Sept. 20, 1981, p. J-2.

Conway, Flo and Siegelman, Jim. *Science Digest*, January, 1982.

Cooke, Jacob F. (Ed.). *The Federalist*. Middletown, Conn.: Wesleyan University Press, 1961.

"Copyright Act of 1976," 94th Congress, 90 Stat. 2541.

Copyright and Educational Media, Washington: Association for Educational Communications and Technology, 1977.

Cord, Robert L. *Separation of Church and State: Historical Fact and Current Fiction*. New York: Lambeth Press, 1982.

"Corinthians," *Interpreters' Bible*. 12 Volumes. Vol. 10, Nashville: Abingdon Press, 1953.

Cornelius, R. M. "Their Stage Drew All the World: A New Look at the Scopes Trial," *Tennessee Historical Quarterly*, XL:2, Summer 1981.

"Corporation," *Black's Law Dictionary.* 4th Edition. St. Paul, Minn.: West Publishing Co., 1968.

"Criminal Law," *American Jurisprudence 2d.* Vol. 21A, Rochester, New York: The Lawyer's Co-Operative Publishing Co., 1981.

"Cult," *American Heritage Dictionary of the English Language.* William Morris, Editor. New York: American Heritage Publishing Co., 1971.

Culver, Robert Duncan. *Toward A Biblical View of Civil Government.* Chicago: Moody Press, 1974.

Cunnion, John D. *How Trusts Can Save Your Income, Estate and Gift Taxes.* Larchmont, New York: Business Reports, Inc., 1966.

Curti, Merle. *The Growth of American Thought.* Evanston, Ill.: Harper & Row, 1964.

Dale, Lloyd. Oral presentation republished in, *Bible-Science Newsletter.* April 1981.

"Darwin, Charles," *Encyclopedia Brittanica: Macropaedia: Knowledge in Depth.* Sir Gavin DeBeer (15th Ed., Vol. 5) 30 Volumes. Chicago: Encyclopedia Britannica, 1978.

Darwin, Francis (Ed.). *The Life and Letters of Charles Darwin.* New York: D. Appleton & Co., 1898.

_____. *The Autobiography of Charles Darwin and Selected Letters.* New York: Dover Publications, 1958.

"Defamation," *Black's Law Dictionary.* Fourth Edition. St. Paul, Minn.: West Publishing Co., 1968.

DeFrancis, Vincent. Lecture, National College of Juvenile Justice, University of Nevada, Reno, Nevada, March 1, 1977.

"Democracy." *Webster's Third New International Dictionary.* Springfield, Mass.: G. & C. Merriam Co., 1976.

Denton, Jeremiah A. *When Hell Was In Session.* Clover, S. C.: Commission Press, 1976.

Diamond, E. F. "ISMS Symposium on Medical Implications Under the Current Abortion Law in Illinois," *Illinois Medical Journal,* May 1967, p. 677.

Donovan, Dick. "Deadly Horror of the Devil Cults," *Weekly World News,* Vol. 3, October 20, 1981, p. 37.

Dowling, Tom. "The Unfrocked One," *Liberty,* (May/June, 1981), p. 23.

Dufwa, Thamar E. *The Viking Laws and the Magna Carta: A Study of the Northmen's Cultural Influence on England and France.* New York: Exposition Press, 1963.

Edwards, Paul and Pap, Arthur. *A Modern Introduction to Philosophy.* New York: Free Press, 1957, 1963.

Eidsmoe, John A. *God and Caesar: Biblical Faith and Political Action.* Westchester, Ill.: Crossway Books, 1984.

_____. "The Effect of *Miranda v. Arizona* Upon Law Enforcement in the State of Iowa," Independent study paper, University of Iowa College of Law, Iowa City, Iowa, 1970.

Ellis, William H. and Paget, Joel. *Legal Guidelines for Christian Organizations.* Oak Park, Illinois: Christian Legal Society, 1977.

Ellul, Jacques. *The Theological Foundation of Law.* Translated by Marguerite Wieser. New York: Seabury Press, 1969.

Emry, Sheldon, "God's Law on Property and Inheritance," Cassette Lecture, *America's Promise*, Phoenix, Ariz., March 15, 1981.

Ericsson, Samuel E. "Your Home is Not Always Your Castle," *The Advocate*, Summer 1981, p. 4.

_____. "Clergy Malpractice: Constitutional and Political Issues," Oak Park, Ill.: Center for Law and Religious Freedom, May 1981.

Fairbairn, Patrick. *The Revelation of Law and Scripture.* Winona Lake, Ind.: Alpha Publications, 1979.

Fine, William F. *Progressive Evolution and American Sociology.* Ann Arbor, Mich.: UMI Research Press, 1979.

Fox, Sanford J. *Modern Juvenile Justice: Cases and Materials.* St. Paul: West Publishing Co., 1981.

Frank, Jerome. *Law and the Modern Mind.* New York: Coward-McAnn, Inc., 1935.

Freeman Digest: Thomas Jefferson. Salt Lake City, Utah: Freeman Institute, 1981.

Frommer, Arthur. *The Bible in the Public Schools.* New York: Liberal Press, 1963.

Gaebelein, Frank E. *The Pattern of God's Truth: Problems of Integration in Christian Education.* New York: Oxford University Press, 1954.

Gallagher, Neil. *How to Stop the Porno Plague.* Minneapolis: Bethany Fellowship, 1977.

Gardner, Martin. "Two Astrophysicists Insist Creation Can Be Proven Mathematically: Ex-Disbelievers Make Analogy Concerning Rubik's Cube," *Tulsa World.* April 1, 1982.

Gatti, Richard D. and Gatti, Daniel J. (Ed.). *Encyclopedic Dictionary of School of Law.* West Nyack, New York: Parker Publishing Co., 1975.

Geisler, Norman L. *The Creator in the Courtroom: 'Scopes II'.* Milford, Michigan: Mott Media, 1982.

Gish, Duane. *Evolution: The Fossils Say No!* San Diego: Creation-Life Publishers, 1972, 1977.

Gjerness, Omar. *Knowing Good from Evil.* Fergus Falls, Minn.: To be published.

"Government Funding Makes Private School Open to Suits, Say Federal Courts," *Church & State*, June, 1983, p. 20.

"Government Regulations: Zoning," *Religious Freedom Reporter*, Vol. 1, No. 11, Vol. 2, No. 5, No. 6, 1982.

Granfeld, David. *The Abortion Decision.* Garden City, New York: AA 1969, 1971.

Grazia, Alfred de. *The Velikovsky Affair.* New Hyde Park, New York; University Books, 1966.

Greathouse, William M. "Romans," *Beacon Bible Commentary* (Vol. 8). Kansas City, Mo.: Beacon Hill Press, 1968.

Greenleaf, Simon. *A Treatise on the Law of Evidence.* Vol. I, Sec. 247. New York: Arno Press, 1842, 1972.

Grimes, Allen P. *Democracy and the Amendments to the Constitution.* Lexington, Mass.: Lexington Books, 1978.

Groth, A. Nicholas and Burgess, A. W. "Sexual Dysfunction During Rape," *The New England Journal of Medicine*, October 6, 1977, pp. 764-766.

Grover, Alan N. *Ohio's Trojan Horse: A Warning to Christian Schools Everywhere.* Greenville, South Carolina: Bob Jones University Press, 1977.

Hahn, Herbert F. *The Old Testament in Modern Research.* Philadelphia: Fortress Press, 1954, 1966.

Hall, Verna M. *The Christian History of the Constitution of the United States of America.* San Francisco: Foundation for American Christian Education, 1966, 1978.

Hallowell, John H. *Main Currents in Modern Political Thought.* New York: Holt, Rinehart & Winston, 1950, 1960.

Hamilton, W. J. and Mossman, H. W. *Human Embryology.* Baltimore: Williams and Wilkins, 1970.

Hansen, Joel F. "Jefferson and the Church-State Wall: A Historical Examination of the Man and the Metaphor," *Brigham Young University Law Review,* 1978, p. 647.

Harrison, Everett F. *Introduction to the New Testament.* Grand Rapids, Michigan: Eerdmans, 1977.

Hefley, James C. *The Youthnappers.* Wheaton, Illinois: Victor Books, 1977.

Henderson, Earnest F. *Select Historical Documents of the Middle Ages.* New York: Biblo & Tannen, 1965.

Herrick, Genevieve F. and Herrick, John. *The Life of William Jennings Bryan.* Boston, 1925.

Herron, Ima Honaker. *The Small Town in American Drama.* Dallas: Southern Methodist University Press, 1969.

Hibbs, Albert R. and Eiss, Albert F. *Earth-Sciences: Investigating Man's Environment.* River Forest, Ill.: Laidlaw Brothers, 1971.

Hirsch, E. G. (Ed.). *Copyright It Yourself.* Wheeling, Illinois: Whitehall Company, 1979.

Hirschoff, Mary-Michelle Upson. "Parents and the Public School Curriculum: Is There a Right to Have One's Child Excused from Objectionable Instruction?," *Southern California Law Review*, Vol. 50 (1977), p. 871-959.

Hodge, Charles. *Systematic Theology.* New York: Charles Scribner's Sons, 1895.

Hoekema, Anthony A. *The Four Major Cults.* Grand Rapids, Michigan: Eerdmans, 1963, 1965.

Hofstadter, Richard. *Social Darwinism in American Thought.* New York: George Braziller, Inc., 1944, 1955.

Hogan, John C. and Cohen, Saul. *An Author's Guide to Scholarly Publishing and the Law.* Englewood Cliffs, New Jersey: Prentice-Hall, Inc., 1965.

Holt, John. "Schools and Home Schoolers: A Fruitful Partnership," *Phi Delta Kappan*, February 1983, pp. 391-394.

Hopkins, Charles Howard. *The Rise of the Social Gospel in American Protestantism.* New Haven, Conn.: Yale University Press, 1940.

Horan, Dennis (Ed.). *Abortion and Social Justice.* New York: Sheed and Ward, 1972.

House, H. Wayne. "Miscarriage or Premature Birth: Additional Thoughts on Exodus 21:22-25," *Westminster Theological Journal*, Vol. 41 (Fall 1978), pp. 105-123.

"Humanism," *The American Heritage Dictionary of the English Language.* William Morris, Ed. New York: American Heritage Publishing Co., 1976.

Humanist Manifestos I and II. Buffalo, New York: Prometheus Books, 1973, 1978.

Humphrey, Trypena. "The Development of Human Fetal Activity in its Relation to Postnatal Behavior," *Advances in Child Development and Behavior*, H. W. Reese and L. P. Lipsitt, Editors. New York: 1975.

Hungerford, Kenneth G. and Slack, William C. *Federal Income Tax Handbook for 1978 Returns.* Grand Rapids, Michigan: Baker Book House, 1979.

Hunt, Alan. *The Sociological Movement in Law.* London: Macmillan Press, 1978.

Huxley, Julian. *The Humanist Frame.* New York: Harper & Brothers, 1961.

_____. *Evolution: The Modern Synthesis.* New York: Harper & Brothers, 1943.

_____. and Kettlewell, H. B. D. *Darwin and His World.* New York: Viking Press, 1965.

Inbau, Thompson and Moenssens. *Criminal Law Cases and Comments.* (2nd Ed.) Mineola, New York: The Foundation Press, 1979.

"Individual Rights/Responsibilities: Religious Discrimination/Employment Practices," *Religious Freedom Reporter*, Vol. 2, No. 9, September 9, 1982, p. 255.

"Johnny Still Can't Read: A Horror Story of the Computer Age," *Tulsa World*, August 23, 1981, Sec. 1, p. 1.

Johnson, Robert L. *Humanism and Beyond.* Philadelphia: United Church Press, 1973.

Johnson, William J. *George Washington the Christian.* Nashville, Tenn.: Abingdon Press, 1919.

Keating, Charles H. *National Decency Reporter*, Volume 28, No. 4 (July/August 1981), p. 3.

Keith, Bill. *Scopes II: The Great Debate.* Shreveport, Louisiana: Huntington House 1982.

Kerkut, G. A. *Implications of Evolution.* London: Pergamon Press, 1960, 1965.

Kienel, Paul. "The Advantages of a Christian School Education," *Christian School Comment*, undated.

King, Margaret J. "Religion, Humanism, Popular Culture," *Religious Humanism*, Vol. 13, No. 4 (Summer 1979), pp. 126-131.

Kinnane, Charles H. *A First Book on Anglo-American Law.* Indianapolis: Bobbs-Merrill Co., Inc., 1932, 1952.

Klein, Irving J. *Law of Evidence for Police.* St. Paul: West Publishing Co., 1978.

Kline, Meredith G. *Treaty of the Great King — The Covenant Structure of Deuteronomy: Studies and Commentary.* Grand Rapids, Michigan: 1963.

Koenig, Louis W. *Bryan: A Political Biography of William Jennings Bryan.* New York: Putnam, 1971.

Koop, C. Everett. "The Right to Live," *The Human Life Review*, Fall I, No. 4, New York: The Human Life Foundation, Inc., 1975, pp. 65-87.

Kuchera, L. "Post Quital Contraception With Diethylstilbesterol, (DES)," *Journal of the American Medical Association*, October 25, 1971.

LaHaye, Tim F. *The Battle for the Mind.* Old Tappan, N.J.: Revell, 1980.

Lamont, Corliss. *The Philosophy Of Humanism.* New York: Frederick Unger Publishing Co., 1977.

Lamplighter, The, Vol. 27 (March, 1981) p. 3.

Lange, John Peter. *Lange's Commentary on the Holy Scriptures.* Translated by Phillip Schaff. Grand Rapids, Mich.: Zondervan, 1960.

Langford, J. J. "Galilei, Galileo," *New Catholic Encyclopedia.* Vol. 6, pp. 250-255.

"Law," *Black's Law Dictionary* (4th ed.) St. Paul Minn.: West Publishing Co., 1968.

Lawrence, Jerome and Lee, Robert E. *Inherit the Wind.* New York: Bantam, 1955.

"Lawsuit Prospects Dim in Arkansas, Bright in Louisiana," *Students for Origins Research Newsletter.* Vol. 4, p. 2 (1981).

Levine, Larence W. *Defender of the Faith: William Jennings Bryan: The Last Decade.* New York: Oxford University Press, 1965.

Lewis, C. S. *God in the Dock.* Grand Rapids, Mich.: Eerdmans, 1970.

Lewis, Thomas. "Humanistic Eudaemonism," *Religious Humanism.* Vol. 13, No. 2 (Spring 1979) pp. 64-73.

Lippis, John. *The Challenge to be Pro-Life*, Washington, D.C.: National Right to Life Educational Trust Fund, nd, pp. 5-7.

Louisell, Kaplan, and Waltz. *Principles of Evidence and Proof.* Mineola, New York: Foundation Press, 1977.

Lutheran Cyclopedia. St. Louis: Concordia Press, 1975.

Madison, James. *The Federalist Papers.* New York: New American Library, 1961.

Malbin, Michael J. *Religion and Politics: The Intentions of the Authors of the First Amendment.* Washington, D.C.: American Enterprise Institute for Public Policy Research, 1978.

Manning, Leonard F. *The Law of Church-State Relations in a Nutshell.* St. Paul: West Publishing Co., 1981.

Marnell, William H. *The History of Religious Freedom in America.* Garden City, New York: Doubleday, 1964.

Marshall, Peter and Manuel, David. *The Light and the Glory.* Old Tappan, N.J.: Fleming H. Revell Co., 1977.

Marx, Karl and Engels, Friedrich. *The Communist Manifesto.* New York: Washington Square Press, 1965.

"Maternal Concerns," *Christian Action Council Resource Manual*, Washington, D.C.: Christian Action Council, nd, SM-22.

Mead, Sidney. *The Lively Experiment, the Shaping of Christianity in America.* New York: Harper & Row, 1963.

"Mediocrity in Education Termed Threat to Nation," *Tulsa Tribune*, April 26, 1983, p. 1.

Meldau, Fred John. *Witness Against Evolution.* Denver Christian Victory Publishing Co., 1953.

Metz, Donald E. *Romans; I & II Corinthians: Beacon Bible Commentary*, 10 Volumes (Vol. VIII), Kansas City, Missouri: Beacon Hill Press, 1968.

Minnesota Civil Liberties Union, Letter to Author, February 13, 1979.

Mitchell, Basil. *Law, Morality and Religion in a Secular Society.* New York: Oxford University Press, 1967, 1978.

Montgomery, John Warwick. *The Law Above the Law.* Minneapolis: Bethany Fellowship, 1975.

Moore, Raymond S. Telephone Interview. Barrien Springs, Michigan. Sept. 2, 1981.

Morain, Lloyd L. *The Humanist.* Sept.-Oct. 1980, p. 4.

Morris, B. F. *Christian Life and Character of the Civil Institutions of the United States.* Philadelphia: G.W. Childs, 1864.

Morris, Henry M. "Goliath Crieth," *Good News Broadcaster.* May 1982, p. 17.

Murren, Debbie and Wood, Patricia. "Public School or Christian School," *Virtue*, (July/August 1981), pp. 24-27.

"Natural Law," *Encyclopedia of the Lutheran Church.* (Vol.3) Minneapolis: Augsburg Press, 1965.

"News: Producer Counters Television Boycott Threat," *Moody Monthly*, September 1981, p. 123.

Nimmer, Melville B. *Copyright and Other Aspects of Law Pertaining to Literary, Musical and Artistic Works Illustrated*, 2nd Ed. St. Paul, Minn.: West Publishing Co., 1979.

Nordin, Virginia Davis and Turner, William Lloyd. "More Than Segregation Academics: The Growing Protestant Fundamentalist Schools," *Phi Delta Kappan*, Vol. 61, No.6, (February 1980) p. 391.

"Obscenity," *American Heritage Dictionary of the English Language*. William Morris (Editor). New York: American Heritage Publishing Co., 1982.

O'Malley, J. Steven. "Theology and Jonathan Edwards." Lectures at Oral Roberts University, Autumn, 1982.

Otto, James H. and Towle, Albert. *Modern Biology*. New York: Holt, Rinehart & Winston, 1963, 1977.

Padover, Samuel K. *The Complete Jefferson*. New York: Duell, Sloan and Pearce, Inc., 1943.

Parkes, Henry. *Gods and Men: The Origins of Western Culture*. New York: Knopf, 1964.

Parrington, Vernon. *Main Currents in American Thought*. New York: Harcourt, 1930.

Patterson, Bennett B. *The Forgotten Ninth Amendment*. Indianapolis: Bobbs-Merrill, 1955.

Pentecost, J. Dwight. *Things to Come*. Grand Rapids, Mich.: Zondervan, 1958, 1978.

Perry, Ralph Barton. *Puritanism and Democracy*. New York: Vanguard Press, 1944.

Pfeffer, Leo. *Church, State and Freedom*. Boston: Beacon Press, 1953.

Pieper, Francis. *Christian Dogmatics*. 4 Volumes (III:420). St. Louis: Concordia, 1953.

Pierson, George W. *Tocqueville in America*. Garden City, New York: Anchor Books, 1959.

Plass, Ewald M. (Comp.). *What Luther Says*. 3 Volumes. Saint Louis: Concordia Publishing House, 1959.

Pollack, Otto and Frideman, A. S. *Family Dynamics and Female Sexual Delinquency*. Palo Alto, Calif.: Sad Science and Behavior, 1969.

Price, Waterhouse. *Abingdon Clergy Income Tax Guide, 1984 Edition for 1983 Returns*. Nashville: Abingdon Press, 1983.

Pritchet, Herman C. *The American Constitution*. St. Louis: McGraw-Hill, 1977.

Prosser, William L. *Handbook of the Law of Torts*. St. Paul, Minn.: West Publishing Co., 1971.

Prosser, Wade and Schwartz. *Torts: Cases and Materials*. 6th Edition. Mineola, New York: Foundation Press, 1976.

"Qualification," *Black's Law Dictionary*. 4th Edition. St. Paul, Minn.: West Publishing Co., 1968.

Quebedeaux, Richard. *The Worldly Evangelicals*. San Francisco: Harper & Row, 1978.

Randall, John Herman. *The Making of the Modern Mind*. Chicago: Houghton Mifflin Company, 1940.

Reagan, Ronald. "The Problems We Face in America," (Speech on cassette tape) Salt Lake City, Utah: The Freeman Institute, 1981.

Rebone, Joseph and Andrusko, Dave. "A Chronology of Infanticide: The Life and Death of Infant Doe," *National Right to Life News*, May 10, 1982, pp. 1, 11, 13.

Rian, Edward H. "The Need: A World View," *Toward a Christian Philosophy of Education*. Comp. John Paul von Grueningen, Philadelphia: Westminster Press, 1957.

Rice, Charles E. *The Supreme Court and Public Prayer: The Need for Restraint*. New York: Fordham University Press, 1964.

Richoux, Donna (Ed.). *Growing Without Schooling*. Boston, Massachusetts. Telephone Interview, September 2, 1981.

Roberts, Oral. "Five Great Healings are Coming to the Body of Christ," *Abundant Life*, July 1983, p. 7.

Ross, Herbert H. *A Synthesis of Evolutionary Theory*. Englewood Cliffs, N. J.: Prentice-Hall, Inc., 1962, 1964.

Rowley, Donald. "Liberal Religion and Humanism," *Religious Humanism*, Vol. 13, No. 4 (Autumn 1979) p. 158-167.

Rushdoony, R.J. "Human Nature and the Abuse of Power," *The Chalcedon Report* No. 187 (March, 1981), p. 1.

––––––––––– . *The Institutes of Biblical Law*. Nutley, N.J.: Craig Press, 1973.

––––––––––– . *This Independent Republic*. Fairfax, Virginia: Obern Press, 1978.

––––––––––– . *Freud*. Nutley, N.J.: Presbyterian and Reformed Publishing Company, 1977.

––––––––––– . *The Biblical Philosophy of History*. Phillipsburg, N.J.: Presbyterian and Reformed Publishing Company, 1979.

––––––––––– . *The Messianic Character of American Education*. Nutley, N. J.: Prague Press, 1963.

––––––––––– . *The Mythology of Science*. Nutley, N. J.: The Craig Press, 1967.

––––––––––– . *The Nature of the American System*. Fairfax, Virginia: Thoburn Press, 1978.

––––––––––– . *Law and Liberty*. Fairfax, Virginia: Thoburn Press, 1971.

––––––––––– . "Historic Role of the Church and Family in Education," Lecture at Oral Roberts University, Tulsa, Okla., October 23, 1981.

––––––––––– . "Standards," *Chalcedon Position Paper No. 7*. P. O. Box 158, Vallecito, California, 95251, 1979.

Ryan, Ada D., M.D. Letter to Congressman Daryl Flood, September 13, 1977. *Christian Action Council Resource Manual*. Washington, D.C.: Christian Action Council, nd, p. SM-110.

Sauvigny, G. DeBertier de. "Charlemagne," *New Catholic Encyclopedia*. Vol. 3, p. 498. St. Louis: McGraw-Hill, 1967.

Schaeffer, Frankie. *A Time for Anger*. Westchester, Illinois: Crossway Books, 1982.

"School," *American Heritage Dictionary of the English Language*. William Morris, Editor. New York: American Heritage Publishing Co., 1971.

"School," *American Jurisprudence 2d*. Vol. 68, Sec. 155. Rochester, New York: The Lawyers Co-Operative Publishing Co., 1973.

"School," *Black's Law Dictionary*, 4th Edition. St. Paul, Minn.: West Publishing Co., 1968.

Schwartz, Murray L. *Lawyers and the Legal Profession: Cases and Materials*. Indianapolis: Bobbs-Merrill Company, 1979.

Scopes, John T. and Presley, James. *Center of the Storm, Memoirs of John T. Scopes*. Chicago: Holt, Rinehart & Winston, 1967.

Sharpe, Robert F. *Before You Give Another Dime*. Nashville: Thomas Nelson, 1978.

_____ . *The Planned Idea Giving Book: Creative Ways to Increase the Income of Your Institution*. Nashville: Thomas Nelson, 1978.

Shute, Evan. *Flaws in the Theory of Evolution*. London, Canada: The Temside Press, 1961; Nutley, N.J.: The Craig Press, 1966.

Silving, Helen. *Sources of Law*. Buffalo, New York: William S. Hein Co., 1968.

Simms, B. M. "A District Attorney Looks at Abortion," *Child and Family*, Vol. 8, Spring, 1969, pp. 176-180.

Simon, Sidney B. and Howe, Leland W. *Values Clarification: A Handbook of Practical Strategies for Teachers and Students*. New York: Hart Publishing Co., 1972.

Skousen, W. Cleon. *Miracle of America Study Guide*. Salt Lake City, Utah: Freemen Institute, 1981.

Smith, William and Wale, Henry. *A Dictionary of Christian Biography*. New York: AMS Press, 1967.

Smudski, Robert. "Evolution: The Way of Growth," *Religious Humanism*. Vol. 13, No. 2 (Spring 1979) pp. 79-86.

Spring, Beth. "Better Ways to Combat Cults Are Being Developed," *Christianity Today*, November 26, 1982, pp. 44-46.

_____ . "Who Decides What is a Cult and What is Not?," *Christianity Today*, November 26, 1982, pp. 46-48.

Stewart, Potter. "Or of the Press," *Hastings Law Journal*. Vol. 26, 1975.

Stokes, Anson and Pfeffer, Leo. *Church and State in the United States*. Evanston: Harper & Row, 1959, 1964.

Stone, Irving. *Clarence Darrow for the Defense*. Garden City, New York: Doubleday & Company, 1941.

Strauss, Leo. *Natural Right and History*. Chicago: University of Chicago Press, 1953, 1963.

Strong, William S. *The Copyright Book*. Cambridge, Mass.: MIT Press, 1981.

Sunderland, Luther D. "Evolution of Evolution and the Creation of New Tactics," *Bible-Science Newsletter*, Vol. 19, No. 8 (July 1981) p. 8.

Tax-Exempt Organizations, Foundations, Churches, Hospitals, Trade Associations and Other Organizations. Englewood Cliffs, New Jersey: Prentice-Hall, 1981.

Taylor, E. L. Hebden. *The Christian Philosophy of Law, Politics and the State*. Nutley, New Jersey: Craig Press, 1966.

Teitell, Conrad. *Counsellor's Guide to Charitable Contributions*. Casselton, North Dakota: North Dakota Community Foundation, 1977.

Thieme, R. B., Jr. *Daniel Chapter 6*. Houston, Texas: Berachah Tapes and Publications, 1975.

Thorne, Ludmilla. "The Littlest Defector," *National Review*, March 18, 1983, pp. 314-320, 341.

Timiras, P. S. *Developmental Physiology and Aging*. New York: MacMillan Publishing Co., 1972.

Titus, Herbert W. "Education, Caesar's or God's: A Constitutional Question of Jurisdiction," *Journal of Christian Jurisprudence*. Oklahoma City, Oklahoma: IED Press, 1982.

Tocqueville, Alexis de. *On Democracy, Revolution and Society: Selected Writings*. John Stone and Stephen Mennell, Eds. Chicago: University of Chicago Press, 1980.

Tribe, Lawrence H. *American Constitutional Law*. Mineola, New York: Foundation Press, 1978.

Tucciarone, Angel and Cafardi, Nicholas P. *Copyright and the Church Musician*. Pittsburgh: Diocese of Pittsburgh, 1977.

Ullman, W. "Donation of Constantine," *New Catholic Encyclopedia*. New York: McGraw-Hill, 1967.

Underhill, H. C. *A Treatise on the Law of Criminal Evidence*. 4th Edition. John L. Niblack (Ed.). Indianapolis: Bobbs-Merrill Publishing Co., 1898, 1935.

Varrill, N. J. "The Person in the Womb," New York: Dodd, Mead, 1968, pp. 42-44.

Wager, Willis. *A Musician's Guide to Copyright and Publishing*. Brighton, Mass.: Carousel Publishing Corp., 1975, 1978.

Walther, C. F. W. *The Proper Distinction Between Law and Gospel*. St. Louis, Missouri: Concordia Publishing House, 1884.

Waring, Luther Hess. *The Political Theories of Martin Luther*. Port Washington, New York: Kennikat Press, Inc., 1910, 1968.

Warshofsky, Fred. "When the Sky Rained Fire: the Velikovsky Phenomenon," *Reader's Digest*, December 1975.

Weinberg, Arthur. *Attorney for the Damned*. New York: Simon & Schuster, 1957.

West, William O. "I Know Deprogramming Works," *Eternity*, September 1976, pp. 75-76.

Whitehead, John W. *The Separation Illusion: A Lawyer Examines the First Amendment*. Milford, Mich.: Mott Media, 1977.

_____ . and Conlan, John. "The Establishment of the Religion of Secular Humanism and its First Amendment Implications," *Texas Tech Law Review*, Vol. 10, 1978.

Whitlow, Robert. "The FCC's Fairness Doctrine and the First Amendment," *The Christian Lawyer*, Vol. VIII, No. 1, Spring 1979, pp. 21-22.

Wiggin, Eric E. "Should Your Grade Schooler Receive Accelerated Christian Education?," *Christian Life*, August 1981, p. 41.

_____ . *The Christian Teacher and Law Supplement 1978*. Oak Park, Ill.: Christian Legal Society, 1978.

Wigmore, John Henry. *Evidence in Trials at Common Law*. Revised by John T. McNaughton. Vol. VIII, Sec. 2394. Boston: Little, Brown and Co., 1961.

Wine, Sherwin. "If Humanism is a Religion," *Religious Humanism*, Vol. 13, No. 3 (Summer 1979) pp. 107-114.

Worth, *Income Tax Handbook for Ministers and Religious Workers*. Grand Rapids, Mich.: Baker Book House, 1980, 1981.

Wright, Howard E. "The Mythology of the Evolutionists," *Bible-Science Newsletter*, May 1981.

Young, Arthur. *Economic Recovery Act of 1981: An Analysis of the New Legislation*. Arthur Young & Company, 1981.

Zondervan's Pictorial Encyclopedia of the Bible. ("Covenant [In the Old Testament]", J. Barton Payne, Vol. 1, P. 1000). Grand Rapids, Mich.: Zondervan Publishing House, 1975.

"Zoning and the Church: Toward a Concept of Reasonableness," *Conn. Law Review*, Vol. 12, 1980, p. 571-574.

"Zoning Ordinances, Private Religious Conduct and the Free Exercise of Religion," *Northwestern Law Review*, Vol. 76, 1981.

INDEX

Schuppin, Tamara, 335-336
Schuppin v. Unification Church [435 F. Supp.
603 (D.C. Vt. 1977)], 335
Schwartz, Sheila, 196
Schwartzman, Andrew Jay, 343
Science, 58
creationism and, 236-237, 255
of earth, 214
religion of, 217
study of, 271
Science 81, 223
Science and Health, 326
Scientology, 330
Swedenborg, Emanuel, 326
Scientific method, 75
humanism and, 182, 186, 188, 193,
195
positivism and, 83
Scientific Origins Bill, 226, 244
Scientology, 330
Scopes, John, 201-213
Scopes Trial, 231, 241
transcript compared to play, 201-212,
212n
two-model approach and, 239
Search warrant, 486-487
The Secret Life of the Unborn Child, 361
Secular humanism,
as religion, 191, 221, 230
establishment of, 230, 391, 406
evolution and, 229
God's law and, 93
law and, 403
promotion of, 198
public schools and, 273, 298
See also humanism
Secularism, 146
establishment of, 302
in courts, 115
in legislatures, 115
in schools, 259
Securities and Exchange Commission
(SEC), 448
Securities Law, 447-448
Segraves v. California [No. 278978, Dept.
15], 231, 239
Segraves, Kelly, 231, 233, 240
Selective service, 151
Self-defense, 489
Self-incrimination, 104, 494

Senate, 101-102
Senate Journal, 131
Senators, election of, 103
Sentencing, 489, 496
Separation of church and state,
Anabaptists and, 113
Calvinists and, 113
colonies and, 123, 126, 142, 161
education and, 268
fallacy of, 104
First Amendment and, 144
Israel and, 55, 110
Lutherans and, 114
Old Testament and, 111-112
two-model approach, 241
Separation of power,
Constitution and, 102
Puritans and, 119
Separatists, 117
*Serbian Eastern Orthodox Diocese v.
Milivojevich*, [426 U.S. 696, (1976)],
133n
Sermon on the Mount, 54
Seventeenth Amendment, 103
Seventh Day Adventists, 229, 310, 383-
384
Sex,
education, 195, 255, 261, 390
extramarital, 478
humanism and, 185
perversion of, 480
premarital, 478
Shakespeare, William, 287
Shamgar, 110
Shanahan, Judge, 317
Shapiro v. Thompson [394 U.S. 618 (1969)],
175
Shelton College, 303-304
Shem, 52
Sherbert v. Verner [374 U.S. 398 (1963)],
158, 175
Sherman, Roger, 132, 136
Sheybogan County Teachers College, 314
Sidney, Algernon, 42
Siegelman, Jim, 332
Sileven, Everett, 292
Silving, Helen, 28-29
Simmons, Menno, 113
Simon Greenleaf School of Law, 524n
Simon, Samuel, 343